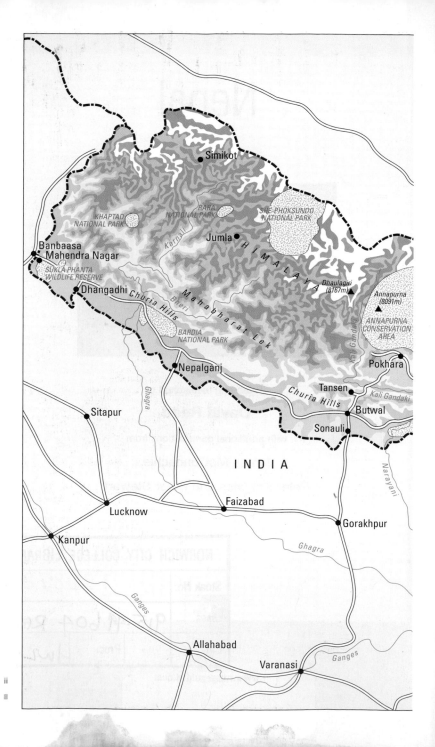

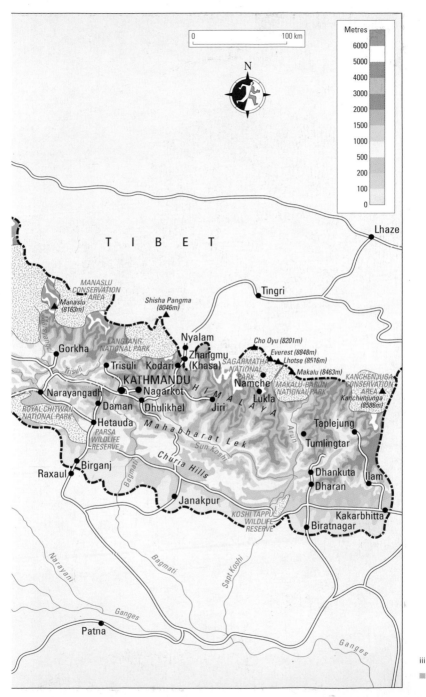

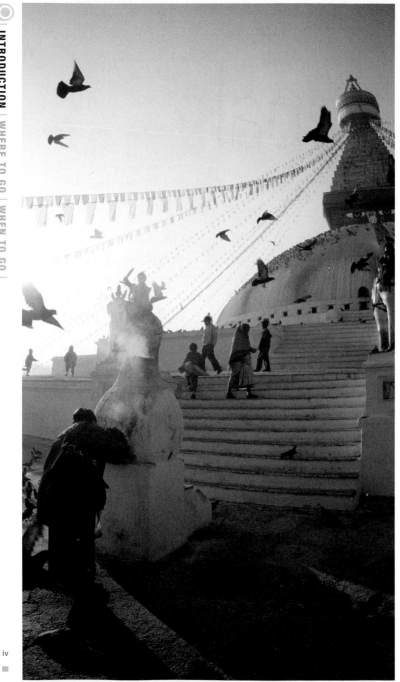

Introduction to

Nepal

Nepal forms the very watershed of Asia. Landlocked between India and Tibet, it spans terrain from subtropical jungle to the icy Himalaya, and contains or shares eight of the world's ten highest mountains. Its cultural landscape is every bit as diverse: a dozen major ethnic groups, speaking as many as fifty languages and dialects, coexist in this narrow, jumbled buffer state, while two of the world's great religions, Hinduism and Buddhism, overlap and mingle with older tribal practices.

Yet it's a testimony to Nepali tolerance and good humour that there's no tradition of ethnic or religious strife. Unlike India, Nepal was never colonized, a fact which comes through in fierce national pride and other, more idiosyncratic ways. Founded on trans-Himalayan trade, the dense, medieval cities display unique pagoda-style architecture, not to mention an astounding flair for festivals and pageantry. Above all, though, Nepal is a nation of unaffected villages and terraced countryside – more than eighty percent of the population lives off the land – and whether you're trekking, biking or bouncing around in packed buses, sampling this simple lifestyle is perhaps the greatest pleasure of all.

But it would be misleading to portray Nepal as a fabled Shangri-la. One of the world's poorest countries, it suffers from many of the pangs and uncertainties of the developing world; **development** is coming in fits and starts, and not all of it is being shared equitably. Heavily reliant on its big-brother neighbours, Nepal was, until 1990, run by one of the last remaining absolute monarchies, a regime that combined China's repressiveness and India's bureaucracy in equal measure. It's now a **democracy**, but a

Fact file

- With a **land area** of 147,000 square kilometres, Nepal is about the size of England and Wales. Its **population** of 24 million is expected to double in thirty years.

- Prior to 1951, only a few hundred outsiders had visited Nepal. Today, the country receives about 300,000 tourists annually, most of them from neighbouring India.

- Nepal is the world's only **Hindu kingdom**. Officially, nearly ninety percent of the population is Hindu, with **Buddhists** making up most of the rest – though many Nepalis combine Hindu, Buddhist, shamanistic and animistic practices.

- A popular revolution in 1990 ushered in a parliamentary **democracy** within the framework of a constitutional **monarchy**, based largely on the British model. However, Nepali politics is highly volatile: ten successive governments held power during the democracy's first twelve years.

- With a per-capita annual **income** of US$220, Nepal ranked 77th out of 90 developing countries in the UN's 2001 Human Poverty Index. **Life expectancy** is just 58 years, and more than ten percent of children die before they reach their fifth birthday. **Literacy** is 66 percent for males, 38 percent for females. Only fifteen percent of Nepalis have access to **electricity**.

very precarious one. Political freedom has done little to improve the lot of the average family, while corruption and frequent changes of government have led to widespread disillusion and spawned an intractable **Maoist insurgency**.

Travel within Nepal isn't straightforward or predictable. Certain tourist areas are highly developed, even overdeveloped, but facilities elsewhere are rudimentary; **getting around** is time-consuming and often uncomfortable. Nepalis are well used to shrugging off such inconveniences with the all-purpose phrase, *Ke garne?* (What to do?). Nepal is also a more fragile country than most – culturally as well as environmentally – so it's necessary to be especially sensitive as a traveller.

Where to go

G iven the country's primitive transport network, most travellers stick to a well-worn circuit, with the result that certain sights and trekking routes have become rather commercialized. However, the

beaten track is remarkably thin and easy to escape in Nepal – and this guide is intended, first and foremost, to give you the confidence to do just that.

Everyone touches down in **Kathmandu** at some point, but for all its exotic bustle, the capital is rather rough-going these days – logistically it makes a good base, but you won't want to spend lots of time here. Hindu temples, Buddhist stupas, rolling countryside and huddled brick villages provide incentives for touring the prosperous **Kathmandu Valley**, as do the his-

> **The beaten track is remarkably thin and easy to escape in Nepal**

torically independent city-states of **Patan** and **Bhaktapur**. The surrounding central hills are surprisingly undeveloped, apart from a couple of mountain view points, but a few lesser routes, such as the road to the **Tibet border** and especially the **Tribhuwan Rajpath**, make for adventurous travel – particularly by mountain bike or motorcycle.

The views get more dramatic, or at least more accessible, in the **western hills**. **Pokhara**, set beside a lake and under a looming wall of peaks, is the closest you'll find to a resort in Nepal. Other hill towns – notably **Gorkha** with its impressive fortress, **Manakamana** with its wish-fulfilling temple, and laid-back **Tansen** – offer scenery with history or culture to boot.

Nepal's diversity really becomes apparent in the ethnic villages and teeming jungle of the **Tarai**. Most travellers venture no further than **Chitwan National Park**, where endangered Asian one-horned rhinos are easily viewable, but **Bardia**

The pace of change

Visitors to Nepal sometimes feel as if they've stepped into the past. The Kathmandu Valley's towns certainly feel medieval, but it's when you trek in the roadless foothills of the Himalaya that you really enter another age. In Nepal, development comes with a new road, but it's easy to step off that magic asphalt carpet – there's still less than 5000km of blacktopped highway. Beyond the tarmac, people live largely on what they can grow, nothing is bought or sold that can't be carried on a porter's back, and, in remoter areas, children or old people may ask you how many days it takes to hike to your country. But change, when it comes, is fast. The first road connecting Kathmandu with the outside world was completed in 1956, and traffic jams and pollution are part of daily life today.

National Park and two other rarely visited wildlife reserves are out there for the more adventurous. **Lumbini**, Buddha's birthplace in the western Tarai, is a world-class pilgrimage site, as is **Janakpur**, a Hindu holy city in the east. Rolling tea plantations, weekly markets and a rich cultural mix figure prominently in the spectacular and little-visited **eastern hills**, most easily reached from the Tarai.

And of course Nepal is probably the most famous destination in the world for a growing range of outdoor activities. **Trekking** from village to village through

The Maoist threat

Since 1996, Nepal has been in the throes of a violent **Maoist insurgency** (see p.498), which by 2002 had driven the country to the brink of civil war and made many parts unsafe for travel.

As this book went to press, the fighting was confined mainly to remote rural areas where tourists don't go. Most travellers were sticking to the more popular destinations, where the risk of encountering Maoist activity was low, and were experiencing only relatively minor inconveniences: rescheduled travel arrangements, highway security checks, night-time curfews, occasional general strikes (*bandhs*), and the unnerving – or, depending on your point of view, reassuring – sight of armed security personnel.

But while the revolutionaries insist they have no intention of targeting tourists, travel in Nepal now unquestionably entails some extra **risk**. If the situation continues to deteriorate, much of the country could become a virtual no-go zone, effectively ruling out activities like trekking and rafting. Even if it doesn't, there is a small chance of travellers inadvertently getting caught up in the hostilities.

It's essential to get the **latest information** before you travel – try the websites listed on p.21.

the hills and up into high Himalayan valleys is an unmissable experience. The scenery varies from cultivated terraces or lush rhododendron forests to glacier-capped peaks, but the cultural interactions are often, in retrospect, the most rewarding part of a trek. Nepal's rivers, meanwhile, are the liquid counterparts to its mountains, and **rafting** offers not only adventure but also a different perspective on the countryside and wildlife. Yet another alternative means of locomotion, **mountain-biking** brings you in contact with the land and its people at your own pace.

Trekking from village to village through the hills and up into high Himalayan valleys is an unmissable experience

When to go

I t's hard to generalize about the climate of a country ranging in elevation from near sea level to the 8850m peak of Mount Everest. About the only thing that can be said is that all but a few parts of Nepal are governed by the same **monsoonal pattern**, with temperatures varying according to **elevation**.

Five **seasons** prevail in Nepal, but whenever you choose to go, you'll have to weigh other factors: most visitors want good mountain visibility, but don't forget about festivals and wildlife – or crowds and disease.

Around half of all tourists visit Nepal in the **autumn** (late September to late November), and for good reasons. The weather is clear and dry, and temperatures aren't too cold in the high country, nor too hot in the Tarai.

The lay of the land

Nepal divides into three altitude zones, running roughly west to east. The northernmost is the **Himalayan chain**, broken into a series of *himal* (permanently snow-covered mountain ranges) and alpine valleys. The largest part of the country consists of a wide belt of middle-elevation **foothills** and steep-sided valleys; Nepal's traditional heartland, this zone includes two ranges (the Mahabharat Lek and the lower, southernmost Churia hills) as well as the miraculous bowl of the Kathmandu Valley. Finally, the **Tarai**, a strip of flat, low-elevation jungle and farmland along the southern border, is (topographically speaking) an extension of the Gangetic Plain of northern India.

With the pollution and dust washed away by the monsoon rains, the mountains are at their most visible, making this the most popular time for trekking. Two major festivals, Dasain and Tihaar, also fall during this season. The downside, however, is that the tourist quarters are heaving, prices are higher and it may be hard to find a decent room.

Winter (December and January) weather is mostly part clear and stable. It isn't especially cold at lower elevations – it never snows in Kathmandu, and afternoon temperatures are balmy – but the "mists of Indra" can make mornings dank and chilly (especially in unheated budget lodgings). Most travellers head down into India, leaving the tourist areas fairly quiet – too quiet, sometimes, especially in trekking areas. This is an excellent time to visit the Tarai, where temperatures are relatively mild.

Spring (February to mid-April) brings steadily warmer weather and longer days, plus weddings and more festivals. Rhododendrons are in bloom in the hills towards the end of this period, and as the Tarai's long grasses have been cut, spring is the best time for viewing wildlife despite the increasing heat. All these pluses bring another tourist influx, albeit not as heavy as in the autumn. The one factor that keeps people away is a disappointing haze that obscures the mountains from lower elevations, though it's usually possible to trek above it. Alongside the pre-monsoon, spring is also the season when you're more likely to pick up a stomach bug.

The monsoon

A seasonal wind driven by extreme temperature fluctuations in Central Asia, the Asian monsoon is one of the world's great weather phenomena. As air over the Asian landmass warms in late spring and early summer, it rises, sucking in more air from the ocean periphery to take its place. The air drawn

from the south, passing over the Indian Ocean, is laden with moisture; as soon as it's forced aloft and cooled (whether by updrafts over hot land, or by a barrier such as Nepal's hills and mountains), it reaches its saturation point and releases its moisture. With the approach of autumn, the flow reverses: cooling throughout the continent blows dry air outwards, bringing clear, stable conditions. In Nepal, the monsoon generally advances from east to west, and overall drops more precipitation in the east than in the west. Local terrain can affect rainfall considerably: areas lying in the "rain shadow" north of the Himalaya see very little monsoon moisture, while south-facing slopes may receive precipitation long before the plains to the south do. The latter effect is most dramatic where monsoon winds slam into high ranges with few intervening foothills, as they do around Pokhara.

During the **pre-monsoon** (mid-April to early June) the heat grows progressively more stifling at lower elevations. Afternoon clouds and increasingly frequent showers help moderate temperatures a bit after mid- or late May, but this is offset by rising humidity. People get a little edgy with the heat; the pre-monsoon is known as the time for popular unrest, but also for the Kathmandu Valley's great rainmaking festival. Trek high, where the temperatures are more tolerable.

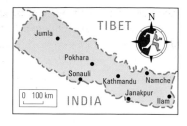

Nepalis welcome the **monsoon**, the timing of which may vary by a few weeks every year, but typically lasts from mid-June to mid-September. The rains break the enervating monotony of the previous months, and make

Average temperatures and rainfall

	Feb	Apr	June	Aug	Oct	Dec
Ilam (1200m)						
°C Min	10	16	18	19	16	8
°C Max	18	25	25	25	25	18
Rain (cm)	0	6	32	28	8	0
Janakpur (70m)						
°C Min	9	16	24	25	20	10
°C Max	24	35	36	34	29	24
Rain (cm)	1	4	23	24	5	0
Jumla (2420m)						
°C Min	-3	3	13	15	6	-5
°C Max	13	22	24	24	24	15
Rain (cm)	4	3	7	17	4	0
Kathmandu (1300m)						
°C Min	4	12	19	20	13	3
°C Max	19	28	29	28	27	19
Rain (cm)	4	6	25	35	4	0
Namche (3450m)						
°C Min	-6	1	6	8	2	-6
°C Max	6	12	15	16	12	7
Rain (cm)	2	3	14	24	8	4
Pokhara (800m)						
°C Min	8	15	20	21	17	7
°C Max	21	30	29	29	26	20
Rain (cm)	3	9	57	71	22	0
Sonauli (90m)						
°C Min	10	18	24	26	21	10
°C Max	26	37	38	35	30	25
Rain (cm)	1	6	28	41	8	0

the fields come alive with rushing water and green shoots. This can be a fascinating time to visit, when Nepal is at its most Nepali: the air is clean, flowers are in bloom everywhere, and fresh fruit and vegetables are particularly abundant. But there are also drawbacks: mountain views are rare, leeches come out in force along the mid-elevation trekking routes, roads may be blocked by landslides, and flights may be cancelled.

things not to miss

It's not possible to see everything that Nepal has to offer in one trip – and we don't suggest you try. What follows is a selective and subjective taste of the country's highlights: outstanding national parks, spectacular wildlife, adventure sports, history and beautiful architecture. They're arranged in five colour-coded categories to help you find the very best things to see, do and experience. All entries have a page reference to take you straight into the guide, where you can find out more.

01 The Himalaya Page **446** • The dramatic Khumbu peaks rear above Gokyo Lake in the Everest region.

02 **Old Kathmandu** Page **106** • An intensely urban quarter of narrow alleys, bustling markets and countless temples and shrines.

03 **Daal bhaat** Page **45** • Nepal's national dish, *daal bhaat* (rice and lentils) comes in countless variations.

04 **Bungy jump** Page **257** • This suspension footbridge 160m above the steep Bhote Koshi gorge offers a thrilling jump.

05 **Swayambhu** Page **127** ● A sacred Buddhist temple complex, magnificently set atop a conical hill overlooking Kathmandu.

06 **Thangka** Page **70** ● Tibetan Buddhist beliefs are colourfully expressed in traditional thangka paintings.

07 **Mani Rimdu** Page **527** ● Masked dancers commemorate Buddhism's victory over the ancient Bon religion at Tengboche Monastery in the Everest region.

08 **Indra Jaatra** Page **112** ● A wild week in old Kathmandu, featuring chariot processions, masked dancers and effigies of the god Indra.

09 **Metalware** Page **66** • Shopping for Buddhas? Patan's artisans have excelled in casting metal statues for centuries.

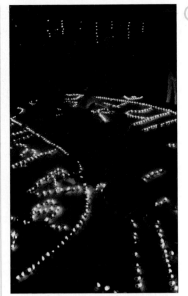

10 **Tihaar** Page **57** • Five days of festivities – including the lighting of oil lamps – in honour of Lakshmi, the Hindu goddess of wealth.

11 **Wildlife viewing** Page **343 & 371** • Elephant rides get you close to the action in the national parks of the Tarai.

12 Yoga and meditation
Page **72** • The Kathmandu Valley is a veritable spiritual supermarket for Westerners seeking teachers in either Hindu or Buddhist traditions.

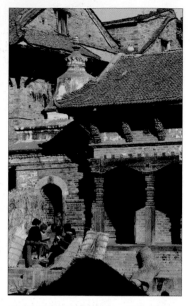

13 Bhaktapur Page **222** • The almost medieval Kathmandu Valley town of Bhaktapur is entirely built in dark carved wood and glowing pink brick.

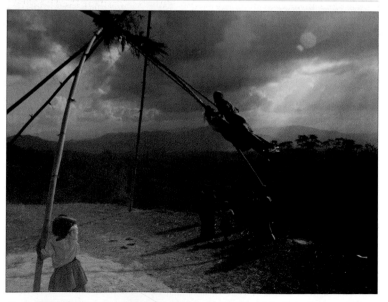

14 Dasain Page **57** • Dasain is the high point of the Nepali festival calendar – children celebrate by playing on bamboo swings.

15 **The Tarai** Page **323 & 379** • Few travellers explore the flat, steamy southernmost strip of Nepal, along the Indian border.

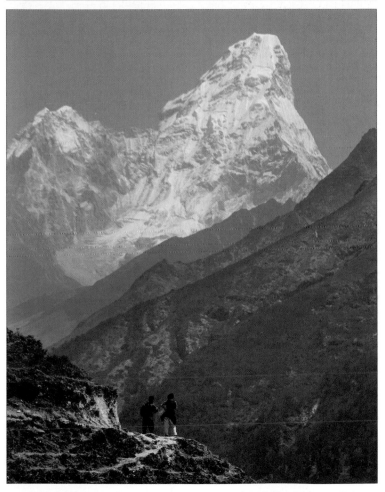

16 **Trekking** Page **411** • The ultimate Thing Not To Miss in Nepal: an unequalled scenic and cultural experience.

17 The Middle Hills Page **401** • Contoured by terraced fields and marked by countless footpaths, the rolling Himalayan foothills are Nepal's heartland.

18 Momo Page **47** • These steamed meat or vegetable dumplings, resembling plump ravioli, are a vastly popular snack.

19 Weddings Page **54** • Processions led by uniformed brass bands are a common sight on astrologically auspicious days (usually in spring).

20 Shivaraatri Page **56** • This winter festival brings tens of thousands of Shiva devotees to Pashupatinath.

21 **Patan Durbar Square** Page **108** • The most aesthetically refined of the Kathmandu Valley's three royal squares – not to mention a romantic spot for dinner.

22 **Rafting** Page **455** • A wonderful way to experience rural Nepal: running rapids, floating past jungle and villages, and camping on sandy beaches.

23 **Phewa Tal** Page **306** • From the World Peace Pagoda, the view stretches across Pokhara's lake to the Annapurna range beyond.

24 **Chiya** Page **49** • Porters, like everyone else, take regular breaks for *chiya*: hot, sweet, milky, spiced tea.

25 **Patan Museum** Page **141** • Nepal's classiest museum, housed in a tastefully restored seventeenth-century palace.

26 **Pashmina** Page **69** • Pashmina shawls, in every colour, shade and degree of fineness, are sold in Kathmandu's Thamel district.

27 **Janaki Mandir** Page **390** •
Worshippers come to Janakpur's
Mughal-style Janaki Mandir in the name of
the legendary lovers, Ram and Sita.

28 **Raato Machhendranath**
Jaatra Page **147** • The image of a
rain-bringing deity is pulled through the
streets of Patan in a swaying, sixty-foot-high
chariot – absurdly good fun.

29 **Mountain-biking** Page **469** • The terrain is steep and the trails gnarly, but
there's plenty of scope for mellow cultural rides, too.

30 Pashupatinath Page **190** • The Pashupati Mandir, at the edge of Kathmandu, is the holy of holies for followers of Shiva.

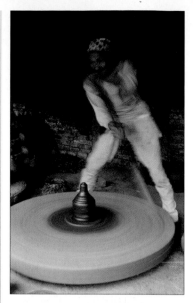

31 Pottery Page **230** • Clay pots are made by traditional methods in Bhaktapur's Potter's Square.

32 Wildlife Page **550** • The endangered one-horned black rhinoceros hides among tall grasses in Chitwan National Park.

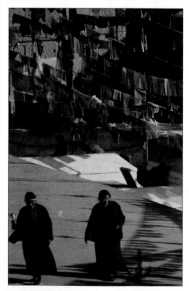

33 Boudha Page **196** • A thriving Tibetan Buddhist community around the great stupa of Boudha, just outside Kathmandu.

us'
Rou

We've tried to make t
is divided into five m
you want in one of

colour s

The front colo
tour of Nepal
to give you
suggestions
tell you w
include
our aud
aspect
miss

conten

1

...ng the
...gh Guide

...is Rough Guide a good read and easy to use. The book
...ain sections, and you should be able to find whatever
...hem.

...ection

...r section offers a quick
...The **introduction** aims
...feel for the place, with
...on where to go. We also
...hat the weather is like and
...basic country fact file. Next,
...hors round up their favourite
...s of Nepal in the **things not to**
...section – whether it's great food,
...zing sights or a special hotel.
...ght after this comes a full **contents**
...st.

basics

The Basics section covers all the **pre-departure** nitty-gritty to help you
plan your trip. This is where to find
out which airlines fly to your
destination, what paperwork you'll
need, what to do about money and
insurance, about internet access, food,
security, public transport, car rental –
in fact just about every piece of
general practical information you
might need.

guide

This is the heart of the Rough Guide,
divided into user-friendly chapters,
each of which covers a specific region.
Every chapter starts with a list of
highlights and an **introduction** that
helps you to decide where to go,
depending on your time and budget.
Likewise, introductions to the various
towns and smaller regions within each
chapter should help you plan your

itinerary. We start most town accounts
with information on arrival and
accommodation, followed by a tour of
the sights, and finally reviews of places
to eat and drink, and details of
nightlife. Longer accounts also have a
directory of practical listings. Each
chapter concludes with **public
transport** details for that region.

contexts

Read Contexts to get a deeper
understanding of what makes Nepal
tick. We include a brief history, articles
about religion and development
dilemmas, and a detailed further
reading section that reviews dozens of
books relating to the country.

language

The **language** section gives useful
guidance for speaking Nepali and pulls
together all the vocabulary you might
need on your trip, including a
comprehensive menu reader. Here
you'll also find a glossary of words and
terms peculiar to the country.

index + small print

Apart from a **full index**, which
includes maps as well as places, this
section covers publishing information,
credits and acknowledgements, and
also has our contact details in case you
want to send in updates and
corrections to the book – or
suggestions as to how we might
improve it.

Map and chapter list

contents

colour section i–xxiv

basics   9–84

guide   85–484

contexts 485–568

language 569–584

Index 585–597

map symbols

maps are listed in the full index using coloured text

⊣⊢	Railway	⌐⌐	Pass/bridge
▬▬	Highway	☗	Viewpoint
══	Main road	◠	Cave
──	Minor road	♦	Point of interest
──	Dirt track	◉	Accommodation
──	Ferry crossing	▣	Restaurant
■-■-■	International boundary	⚠	Campsite
─ ─ ─	Chapter division boundary	ⓘ	Tourist office
xxxxxxx	Steps	⊠	Post office
◄──	One-way street	♉	Museum
------	Path	⊞	Hospital
──	River	★	Bus stop
▬▬	Ridge line	⊙	Statue
✈	International airport	⊠—⊠	Gate/arch
✔	Domestic airport	■	Building
⋏⋏	Mountain range	▦	Park
▲	Mountain peak	▧	Beach

basics

basics

Getting there

In the autumn and spring tourist high seasons (late Sep to mid-Nov, and late Feb to late March), flights to Kathmandu – Nepal's only international airport – fill up months ahead, so book well in advance if you plan to travel at these times. As relatively few airlines serve Kathmandu, you may well find yourself making several hops with two or even three different carriers. Most people book tickets through to Kathmandu, but you can also make your own way to a major regional air hub such as Delhi or Bangkok, and take a separate onward flight from there. These alternative gateways are popular mostly with travellers on longer trips, and those entering Nepal overland from neighbouring countries.

Airfares depend on the time of year, but timings of the high, low and shoulder seasons are calculated differently by each airline, and may not always coincide with Nepal's tourist seasons. More important is where you're flying from; details are given in the relevant sections below. Price ranges quoted below assume midweek travel, though flying at weekends may not add much (or anything) to the fare, particularly if an airline only operates a couple of flights to Kathmandu each week, as is often the case.

You can usually cut costs by going through a **specialist flight agent** – either a consolidator, which buys up blocks of tickets from the airlines and sells them at a discount, or a **discount agent**, which in addition to dealing with discounted flights may also offer special student and youth fares and a range of other travel-related services. At the time of writing, charter flights to Nepal were operating only out of the Netherlands and Germany.

You might want to consider buying a **Round-the-World** (RTW) ticket, but as cheaper off-the-peg tickets don't allow you to fly both into and out of Kathmandu; you'll have to make your way overland in at least one direction, book a separate connecting flight, or pay for a specialist, tailor-made RTW ticket. Figure on a minimum of £1200/US$1500 for a RTW ticket that includes Nepal, though you could spend as little as £700/US$1000 if you make your own way from Delhi or Bangkok.

Many airlines and discount travel websites offer you the opportunity to **book tickets online**, cutting out the costs of agents and middlemen. Good deals can often be found through discount or auction sites, as well as through the airlines' own websites.

Online travel and booking agents

Ⓦ **www.cheaptickets.com** US-based discount flight site.

Ⓦ **www.cheapflights.com** Flight deals from the UK and Ireland, as well as travel agent details and links to other travel sites.

Ⓦ **www.etn.nl/discount.htm** A hub of consolidator and discount agent Web links, maintained by the nonprofit European Travel Network.

Ⓦ **www.expedia.com** Discount airfares, all-airline search engine and daily deals.

Ⓦ **www.hotwire.com** Bookings from the US only. Last-minute savings of up to forty percent on regular published fares. Travellers must be at least eighteen and there are no refunds, transfers or changes allowed. Log-in required.

Ⓦ **www.priceline.com** Bookings from the US only. Name-your-own-price website that has deals at around forty percent off standard fares. You cannot specify flight times (although you do specify dates) and the tickets are non-refundable, non-transferable and non-changeable.

Ⓦ **www.skyauction.com** Bookings from the US only. Auctions tickets and travel packages using a "second bid" scheme. The best strategy is to bid the maximum you're willing to pay, since if you win you'll pay just enough to beat the runner-up regardless of your maximum bid.

Ⓦ **www.travelocity.com** Destination guides, hot web fares and deals on car hire and accommodation. Provides access to the travel agent system SABRE, the most comprehensive central reservations system in the US.

ⓦ www.travelshop.com.au Australian website offering discounted flights, packages, insurance, online bookings.
ⓦ www.uniquetravel.com.au Good range of packages and good-value flights from Australia.

Flights from the UK and Ireland

There are no nonstop **flights** from London to Kathmandu, and the half-dozen airlines that operate direct routes all make at least one stop en route, which means around twelve hours' total travel time. **Fares** to Kathmandu are seasonal, with airlines generally charging full whack (£550–650) for departures from late September to late November, and from early March to mid-April, as well as during the Christmas period. It's often possible, however, to find discounted fares (£500 or less), especially on less convenient routes, and prices drop steeply and suddenly in low season to £350–450.

From London, Gulf Air, Lauda (Austrian Airlines), Pakistan International Airways (PIA) and Qatar airways offer the most direct routings. Be warned, however, that in 2002 PIA had to temporarily suspend its Kathmandu flights due to political quarrels that prevented the Pakistani carrier flying over India. The Nepalese national carrier, Royal Nepal Airlines Corporation (RNAC), has also suspended all flights to and from Europe, and there was little sign of them restarting at the time of writing, but it's worth checking.

Seats with the above airlines get booked early; there are alternatives, but they take longer. Biman Bangladesh's flights via Dhaka are worth considering for their prices, especially in Nepal's high season, but it's a long flight and you'll have to wait some time in Dhaka for the connection to Kathmandu. Transavia flights from Amsterdam to Kathmandu can be booked through from London on KLM, but it means touching down twice, in Amsterdam and Sharjah.

Many other airlines (see p.13) fly **from London to Delhi**, from where you can travel overland or catch a separate connecting flight to Kathmandu (see p.19). Flying to Delhi expands your options for getting a seat on the day of your choice, but it won't get you there any faster, and this routing often turns out to be more expensive.

Flights on Thai and Singapore aren't really worth considering from Europe because you'll have to double back from Bangkok or Singapore, and fares are similar or slightly higher than the more direct-routed flights.

From the British regions, it usually works out quickest and cheapest to make your way to London and fly from there. PIA, however, normally flies from Manchester to Kathmandu via Karachi, and the fare is the same as from London (but note that reliability may be a problem. Air France, British Airways and KLM's Transavia wing fly to Delhi from numerous regional British airports via Paris, London or Amsterdam respectively.

There are no direct flights to Kathmandu from Ireland, so you'll have to fly via London. A fallback option, however, is to fly to India via another European hub, making a separate connection from Delhi to Kathmandu (see p.19). Fares to Delhi cost around €760–1015 in the winter high season, or roughly €510–760 in low season. Air France, British Airways, KLM and Swissair all fly from Dublin to Delhi via their respective capital cities. Royal Jordanian sometimes offers good deals to Delhi out of Shannon.

Airlines serving Nepal

Biman Bangladesh Airlines ☎ 020/7629 0252, ⓦ www.bimanair.com. Three to four flights weekly from London to Kathmandu, but it's a long route, stopping in either Rome or Frankfurt, and then Dhaka. Offers good deals, however, especially in the Nepalese tourist season.
Gulf Air ☎ 0870/777 1717, ⓦ www.gulfairco.com. Reliable service to Kathmandu via Abu Dhabi or Bahrain (and sometimes Dubai), with up to five flights per week (though usually just three weekly in the tourist season). Occasional good deals. On the final leg, flights get booked up by Nepalese migrant workers.
KLM/Transavia ☎ 0870/507 4074, in Northern Ireland ☎ 0990/074074, in Republic of Ireland ☎ 0345/445588, ⓦ www.klmuk.com, ⓦ www.transavia.nl. Fast, reliable Amsterdam to Kathmandu flight, twice a week in high season, with good timings; connections can be booked through from London on KLM, Transavia's parent, but it's cheaper to go through an agent, or call Transavia in the Netherlands (☎ 00312/0406 0406).
Lauda Air ☎ 0845/601 0934, ⓦ www.laudaair.co .uk. Some good deals, and the fastest way to Kathmandu at the time of writing, from London via

B

Vienna. Two flights per week in high season. Offers some good deals. Part of the Austrian Airlines group.

Pakistan International Airlines (PIA) ☎020/ 7499 5500, ⊛www.piac.com.pk. Two weekly flights to Kathmandu via Karachi (sometimes with an overnight at the PIA hotel), and sometimes a third via Islamabad. Not the best reputation for reliability, but occasionally offers cheap deals.

Qatar Airways ☎020/7896 3636, ⊛www.qatarairways.com. Fairly reliable and relatively quick daily flights from London to Kathmandu, via Doha.

Singapore Airlines ☎0870/608 8886, in Republic of Ireland ☎01/671 0722, ⊛www.singaporeair.com. Flights from London to Kathmandu via Bangkok – a very long way round.

Thai International ☎0870/606 0911, ⊛www.thaiair.com. Long but reliable flights from London to Kathmandu via Bangkok.

Other useful airlines

Air France ☎0845/084 5111, in Republic of Ireland ☎01/605 0383, ⊛www.airfrance.co.uk. Flights to Delhi via Paris, from numerous British airports and from Dublin.

Air India ☎020/8560 9996, ⊛www.airindia.com. Direct flights from London to Delhi; can also book Indian Airlines flights on to Kathmandu.

British Airways ☎0845/773 3377, in Republic of Ireland ☎0141/222 2345, ⊛www.britishairways.com. Daily direct flights to Delhi, not always at the most competitive prices.

Royal Jordanian ☎020/7878 6341, ⊛www.rja.com.jo. Cheap flights to Delhi (via Jordan) from London and Shannon.

Swissair ☎0845/601 0956, in Republic of Ireland ☎01/677 8173, ⊛www.swissair.com. Flights from London and Dublin to Delhi via Zurich.

Flight and travel agents

Bridge the World ☎020/7911 0900, ⊛www.bridgetheworld.com. Specializing in RTW tickets, with good deals aimed at the backpacker market. Discounted rates on RNAC flights between Nepal and India.

CIE Tours International Dublin ☎01/703 1888, ⊛www.cietours.ie. General flight and tour agent.

E-bookers ☎020/7757 2444, ⊛www.ebookers.com. Low fares on an extensive selection of scheduled flights.

Joe Walsh Tours Dublin ☎01/872 2555 or 676 3053, Cork ☎021/277959, ⊛www.joewalshtours.ie. General budget fares agent.

The London Flight Centre ☎020/7244 6411, ⊛www.topdecktravel.co.uk. Long-established agent dealing in discount flights.

North South Travel ☎01245/608291, ⊛www.northsouthtravel.co.uk. Friendly, competitive travel agency, offering discounted fares worldwide – profits are used to support projects in the developing world, especially the promotion of sustainable tourism.

Premier Travel Derry ☎028/7126 3333, ⊛www.premiertravel.uk.com. Discount flight specialists.

Rosetta Travel Belfast ☎028/9064 4996, ⊛www.rosettatravel.com. Flight and holiday agent.

STA Travel ☎0870/160 6070, ⊛www.statravel.co.uk. Worldwide specialists in low-cost flights and tours for students and under-26s, though other customers are welcome.

Trailfinders ☎020/7628 7628, in Republic of Ireland ☎01/677 7888, ⊛www.trailfinders.com. One of the best-informed and most efficient agents for independent travellers; produce a very useful quarterly magazine worth scrutinizing for RTW routes.

Travel Cuts ☎020/7255 2082, ⊛www.travelcuts.co.uk. Canadian-owned company specializing in budget, student and youth travel and RTW tickets.

Specialist agents and tour operators

Classic Journeys ☎01773/873497, ⊛www.classicjourneys.co.uk. Long-time Nepal specialists, offering the usual range of treks and trekking peaks, plus wildlife expeditions. Most tours include a couple of days' sightseeing in Kathmandu.

Dragoman ☎01728/861133, ⊛www.dragoman.co.uk. Extended overland journeys in purpose-built expedition vehicles.

Exodus ☎020/8675 5550, ⊛www.exodus.co.uk. Massive adventure tour operator, taking small groups for specialist programmes including walking, biking, overland, adventure and cultural trips.

Explore Worldwide ☎01252/76000, ⊛www.explore.co.uk. Big range of small-group treks and tours that include a few undemanding day-hikes, plus trips to Mustang in summer, and a combined Nepal/Bhutan cultural tour. Few supplements for single travellers.

Footprint Adventures ☎01522/804929, ⊛www.footprint-adventures.com. Established firm (with its own guidebooks) specializing in wildlife and birdwatching tours, plus trekking and rafting trips.

High Places ☎0114/275 7500, ⊛www.highplaces.co.uk. For the more serious trekker, specializing in high-altitude trekking and trekking peaks.

Himalayan Kingdoms ☎01453/844400, ⊛www.himalayankingdoms.com. Huge UK-based company offering group treks in Nepal and right across the Himalayas.

Jagged Globe ☎0114/276 3322, ⊛www
.jagged-globe.co.uk. Trekking peaks and serious
expeditions.

Muir's Tours ☎0118/950 2281, ⊛www.nkf-mt
.org.uk. Renowned ethical tourism operator running
small-group treks led by local guides, as well as
cultural trips such as Buddhist study tours.

Naturetrek ☎01962/733051, ⊛www.naturetrek
.co.uk. Leading specialist in birdwatching and
botanical tours, including treks.

Nepalese Trails ☎01691/648851,
⊛www.nepalesetrails.com. Small, committed UK
company offering cultural tours and treks, with good
ethical and environmental credentials.

Roama Travel ☎01258/860298,
⊛www.roama.com. Small family company with
Kathmandu connections, offering tailor-made tours
and treks to Nepal.

Sherpa Expeditions ☎020/8577 2717,
⊛www.sherpaexpeditions.com. Runs treks on both
well-trodden and less established routes, as well as
to trekking peaks.

Terra Firma ☎01691/870321, ⊛www
.terrafirmatravel.com. A wide range of treks,
trekking peak expeditions and wildlife/cultural tours,
plus rafting and mountain-biking expeditions and
tailor-made tours. Also organizes trips to Tibet, with
some options combining Tibet and Nepal.

Wildlife Worldwide ☎020/8667 9158,
⊛www.wildlifeworldwide.com. Trips for wildlife
enthusiasts, especially over-fifties, focusing on the
Western Tarai parks.

World Expeditions ☎020/8870 2600,
⊛www.worldexpeditions.co.uk. Australian-owned
adventure company offering treks in Nepal and Tibet
for anyone from beginners to amateur mountaineers.

Flights from the USA and Canada

Nepal is basically on the other side of the
planet from the US and Canada. If you live
on the east coast it's somewhat shorter to
go via Europe, and from the west coast it's
shorter via the Far East; either way, it's a
long haul involving one or more intermediate
stops. Several airlines fly to Kathmandu from
the US and Canada, but only Thai operates
a daily service (out of LA). When seat availability is tight ask about alternative routings:
plenty of other carriers fly to Delhi, Bangkok,
Hong Kong and other Asian cities, from
where you can catch a connecting flight to
Kathmandu (see p.19).

Seasonal considerations may help determine your route; these seasons don't neces-

sarily coincide with Nepal's autumn and
spring tourist seasons. Most airlines **flying
east** (over the Atlantic) consider high season
to be summer and the period right around
Christmas; low season is winter (excluding
Christmas), while spring and autumn may be
considered low or shoulder season, depending on route. **Flying west** (over the Pacific),
high season is generally June to July and
December to January, with everything else
being low season. **Prices** quoted below
assume midweek travel in low season, and
exclude taxes. High season fares are
$100–300 higher, and flying on weekends
may add another $100 or so. Taxes and
other surcharges can add $100 or more to
the fare.

From east and central USA

Flying eastwards, there are many route
options, depending on where you want – or
don't want – to stop over. Figure on spending at least twenty hours in planes.

The best consolidator fares are invariably
out of **New York**, and fall in the $1200–1500
range in low season. Singapore Airlines usually comes in near the top of that range, but
has excellent connections and the route
avoids political hotspots. Somewhat cheaper
tickets may be had on Gulf, Kuwait, Air
India, Austrian Airlines or various others
listed below; these often have you crossing
the Atlantic with one airline and then switch-
ing to another. Qatar Airways, which flies to
Kathmandu from London (and is slated
to start flying out of New York as well) is well
worth trying to connect with. The cheapest
deals going tend to be on less appealing airlines like PIA or Biman Bangladesh; you
might also be able to save a few dollars by
flying via Delhi with Aeroflot or Royal
Jordanian, and connecting to Kathmandu
from there (see p.19).

The story is similar from other eastern and
midwestern cities, but fares are $150–300
higher. In many cases the cheapest option
will be to go via New York to take advantage
of the rock-bottom consolidated fares from
there. From the midwest, **flying west** via
Los Angeles (see below) may not cost any
more, in case you've got a Far Eastern
stopover in mind.

From West Coast USA

From the West Coast, it takes about the same time to fly eastwards or westwards – a minimum of 24-hours' flying time – but **westbound** routes are generally cheaper and more peaceful. It's necessary to overnight somewhere either on the outbound or return flight (or both), usually in Bangkok or Singapore. Low season consolidator **fares** are usually in the $1100–1300 range. Thai and Singapore fly direct to Kathmandu via their respective capitals; Thai has daily flights and better service, but Singapore has the advantage of flying out of San Francisco as well as LA. Many other airlines (such as Cathay Pacific, Korean, China Air Lines, United and Northwest) can take you as far as Hong Kong or Bangkok, where you'll switch to Thai or Royal Nepal (though the latter is extremely unreliable).

From Canada

The cheapest discounted deals tend to be **from Toronto**, flying eastwards, and cost Can$1900–2200, depending on the season. Consolidators can route you on any number of airlines through London (see p.12) or Frankfurt (to pick up the Singapore Airlines connection), or use various European carriers to fly via their respective capitals to Delhi, and then hopping from there to Kathmandu. Westbound flights via southeast Asia on Thai or Singapore should cost only $100–200 more.

From Vancouver, flying west is the clear choice. Singapore has a direct service to Kathmandu (via Singapore), while China Air Lines, Air Canada and a few others fly to Bangkok, from where you can pick up Thai or Royal Nepal (Thai is vastly preferable). Those routes should come in at around Can$1800 low season. Other options are to fly via Seattle (served by Northwest) or Los Angeles (Thai's US gateway).

From other central and eastern cities, you can go via Toronto, Vancouver or possibly New York or Los Angeles. The latter two are worth considering because of the extremely cheap consolidator flights from there (see above). Most connecting flights to Toronto or Vancouver will add $200–300 to the above fares.

Airlines serving Nepal

Austrian Airlines ☎1-800/843-0002, ⓦwww .austrianair.com. New York to Kathmandu via Vienna, twice a week in season.

Biman Bangladesh ☎212/808-4477, ⓦwww.bimanair.com. Three flights a week from New York to Kathmandu via Brussels and Dhaka.

Gulf Air ☎888/359-4853, ⓦwww.gulfairco.com. Twice-weekly from New York to Kathmandu via London and Bahrain.

Pakistan International Airlines (PIA) ☎1-800/221-2552, ⓦwww.piac.com.pk. Four flights weekly from New York to Kathmandu via Manchester and Karachi or Lahore, plus connections to Delhi and Mumbai, and twice-weekly flights from Toronto to Kathmandu.

Royal Nepal Airlines Corporation (RNAC) ☎1-800/266-3725, ⓦwww.royalnepal.com. RNAC flies from Hong Kong to Kathmandu three times a week. Through-tickets from various US and Canadian cities can be booked with RNAC, however, as the airline has co-operative agreements with other carriers for the North America to Hong Kong leg.

Singapore Airlines ☎1-800/742-3333, ⓦwww .singaporeair.com. Los Angeles, San Francisco and Vancouver to Kathmandu via Singapore; New York, Newark or Chicago to Kathmandu via Frankfurt and Singapore; all routes fly three times a week.

Thai International ☎1-800/426-5204, ⓦwww .thaiair.com. Daily from Los Angeles to Kathmandu via Bangkok; also connections to Delhi and Calcutta.

Other useful airlines

Aeroflot ☎1-888/340-6400, ⓦwww.aeroflot.com. Various US cities and Montréal to Delhi via Moscow.

Air Canada ☎1-800/263-0882, ⓦwww.aircanada .ca. Toronto to Delhi via London; Vancouver to Bangkok.

Air India ☎1-800/223-2250, ⓦwww.airindia.com. New York and Toronto to Delhi and Calcutta via London.

British Airways ☎1-800/247-9297, ⓦwww .british-airways.com. Various US and Canadian cities to Delhi via London.

Cathay Pacific Airways ☎1-800/233-2742, ⓦwww.cathay-usa.com. Los Angeles and Vancouver to Hong Kong.

China Air Lines ☎1-800/227-5118, ⓦwww .china-airlines.com. Los Angeles, San Francisco and Vancouver to Bangkok and Delhi via Taipei.

KLM/Northwest ☎1-800/374-7747 in US ☎1-800/361-5073 in Canada, ⓦwww.nwa.com. Major US and Canadian cities to Delhi and Calcutta via Amsterdam; Los Angeles and Seattle to Hong Kong, Bangkok and Singapore via Tokyo.

Korean Air ☎1-800/438-5000, ⓦwww.koreanair
.com. Several US and Canadian cities to Bangkok via
Seoul.

Kuwait Airways ☎1-800/458-9248, ⓦwww
.kuwait-airways.com. New York and Chicago to
Delhi via London.

Lufthansa ☎1-800/645-3880, ⓦwww.lufthansa
.com. Many US and Canadian cities to Delhi via
Frankfurt and Karachi.

Royal Jordanian Airlines ☎1-800/223-0470,
ⓦwww.rja.com.jo. New York to Delhi via London
and Amman.

United Airlines ☎1-800/538-2929,
ⓦwww.ual.com. Los Angeles and San Francisco to
Bangkok via Tokyo or Taipei.

Flight and travel agents

Air Brokers International ☎1-800/883-3273,
ⓦwww.airbrokers.com. San Francisco-based
consolidator and specialist in RTW and Circle Pacific
tickets.

Council Travel ☎1-800/226-8624,
ⓦwww.counciltravel.com. Student/youth discount
travel agency with branches in many US cities.

Fly Time ☎212/760-3737. New York consolidator.

Hari World Travel ☎212/997-3300. New York
consolidator.

High Adventure Travel ☎1-800/350-0612 or
415/912-5600, ⓦwww.airtreks.com. Round-the-
World and Circle Pacific tickets; also Asian overland
connections. The website features an interactive
database that lets you build and price your own RTW
itinerary.

Himalayan Treasures & Travels ☎1-800/223-
1813. California consolidator.

Jaya Travels ☎1-877/359-5292, ⓦwww
.jayatravel.com. Chicago-based consolidator with
offices in several other cities.

Mount Everest Travel ☎303/620-9306. Denver-
based consolidator.

STA Travel ☎1-800/781-4040, ⓦwww.sta-travel
.com. Worldwide discount travel firm specializing in
student/youth fares and travel services with branches
in many US cities.

Super Travel ☎1-800/878-7371. New York-based
consolidator.

Third Eye Travel ☎1-800/456-3393,
ⓦwww.thirdeyetravel.com. California travel agent
specializing in Nepal.

Ticket Planet ☎1-800/799-8888, ⓦwww
.ticketplanet.com. Specialist in RTW fares.

Travel CUTS ☎1-800/667-2887, ⓦwww
.travelcuts.com. Organization specializing in student
fares, IDs and other travel services, with branches all
over Canada.

Specialist agents and tour operators

Above the Clouds Trekking ☎1-800/233-4499,
ⓦwww.aboveclouds.com. Family-run operator
offering some unusual treks such as routes in the
Solu and the Gorkha areas; also specializes in family
treks.

Adventure Center ☎1-800/227-8747, ⓦwww
.adventurecenter.com. Large company offering
affordable trekking trips in Nepal, with a wide variety
of routes, plus trekking peaks, overland tours and
rafting or wildlife expeditions.

Canadian Himalayan Expeditions ☎1-800/
563-8735, ⓦwww.himalayanexpeditions.com.
Reasonably priced small-group treks (from moderate
to strenuous) with rafting and wildlife extensions, as
well as trekking peak expeditions.

Friends in High Places ☎1-800/OK-NEPAL,
ⓦwww.fihp.com. Kathmandu-based company
offering mostly customized itineraries, especially
treks.

Himalayan Travel ☎1-800/225-2380,
ⓦwww.himalayantravelinc.com. Offers a wide
variety of affordable trekking routes, from standard to
off-the-beaten track, plus trekking peaks, rafting and
wildlife tours.

Journeys International ☎1-800/255-8735,
ⓦwww.journeys-intl.com. Worldwide trekking
agency specializing in eastern Nepal, with mostly
moderate-difficulty treks on standard routes, plus a
few off-the-beaten track options; family treks also
arranged.

Mountain Travel-Sobek ☎1-888/687-6235,
ⓦwww.mtsobek.com. High-end trekking and rafting
company, with easy to strenuous routes, plus wildlife
trips.

Peter Owens' Asian Treks ☎1-800/223-1813
or 415/835-3131, ⓦwww.InstantWeb.com/p
/peterowens. Affordable treks led by an engaging
retired professor.

Trek Holidays ☎1-800/661-7265, ⓦwww
.trekholidays.com. Canada-based representative of
several British adventure travel companies, offering a
large selection of overland, trekking, trekking peaks,
rafting and wildlife trips.

Worldwide Adventures ☎1-800/387-1483,
ⓦwww.worldwidequest.com. Easy to strenuous
treks, including some unusual and demanding routes
as well as family trekking, trekking peaks, rafting and
wildlife expeditions.

Flights from Australia and New Zealand

Flying to Nepal **from Australia** almost invariably means Thai Airways via Bangkok or

Singapore Airlines via Singapore, with a stopover on the way on both routes. Flying **from New Zealand** generally means travelling via Sydney. Singapore Airlines, however, flies direct daily from Auckland to Singapore, from where you can pick up the Sydney flight to Kathmandu.

A cheaper option might be to fly to Bangkok and pick up an onward ticket to Nepal (around US$200) from there, although obviously this option lacks the certainty of a through ticket. Fares to Delhi are about the same as to Kathmandu, so another possibility – although not the most economical one – is to fly into India and fly or travel overland into Nepal from there (see p.18). A final option is to fly via Hong Kong, from where connecting flights with Kathmandu periodically start up for a time (ask one of the travel agents listed below).

As ever, **airfares** depend on the time of year (which doesn't always correspond to the autumn and spring tourist seasons in Nepal). Generally, low season runs from mid-January to late February, and from early October to the end of November; high season is from around mid-May to August, and early December to mid-January; shoulder season comprises the rest of the year. Low season prices to Kathmandu via Singapore or Bangkok start at about A$1500 from Australia, or NZ$2000 from New Zealand, and may rise by $200–500 (either currency) in high season. Fares out of Perth may be cheaper by A$100 or so, since the flying time is shorter.

Round-the-World tickets start at around A$2200/NZ$2600, though as usual you'll usually have to make your own way to or from Kathmandu, in at least one direction. For all tickets, the best prices are usually found through the travel agents listed below.

Airlines

Singapore Airlines Australia ☎13 1011 or 02/9350 0262, New Zealand ☎09/303 2129 or 0800/808 909, ⊛www.singaporeair.com. Three or four flights a week from Singapore to Kathmandu, and numerous connecting flights from cities in Australia and New Zealand.
Thai Airways Australia ☎1300/651 960, New Zealand ☎09/377 3886, ⊛www.thaiair.com. Daily

flights to Kathmandu from Sydney, Auckland and Perth, with a one-night stopover in Bangkok required.

Flight and travel agents

Flight Centres Australia ☎02/9235 3522 or for nearest branch ☎13 3133, New Zealand ☎09/358 4310, ⊛www.flightcentre.com.au. Large Australian-owned discount flight agent, with branches all over Australia.
STA Travel Australia ☎13 1776 or 1300/360 960, New Zealand ☎09/309 0458 or 09/366 6673, ⊛www.statravel.com.au. Worldwide discount travel firm specializing in student/youth fares and travel services, with branches in many Australian cities.
Trailfinders Australia ☎02/9247 7666, ⊛www.trailfinders.com.au. Australian wing of the reliable ticketing and travel advice company.

Specialist agents and tour operators

Abercrombie and Kent Australia ☎03/9699 9766 or 1800/331 429, New Zealand ☎09/579 3369, ⊛www.abercrombiekent.com. Upmarket tours of India and Nepal.
India Nepal Travel Centre Australia ☎02/9223 6000, ⊛www.indianepaltravelcentre.com. Long-established company offering the standard treks in Nepal.
Intrepid Adventure Travel Australia ☎1300/360 667 or 03/9473 2626, ⊛www.intrepidtravel.com.au. Small-group tours, mostly treks but also wildilfe and rafting trips, with an ethical emphasis. No single supplements.
Peregrine Adventures Australia ☎03/9662 2700 or 1300/655 433, ⊛www.peregrine.net.au. Introductory-level tours of Nepal, some combining visits to India or Tibet.
Ultimate Descents International ☎03/543 2301; ⊛www.ultimatedescents.com. Leading rafting operator.

Getting there from neighbouring countries

Many travellers combine Nepal with a trip to India, even if they're just making the connection with a budget flight to or from Delhi. There are numerous **border crossings** between the two countries, and overland routes can easily be planned to take in many of northern India's most renowned sights. Even flying between Delhi and Kathmandu can reward you (with Himalayan views), and it also opens up a wider choice of international flights. Travel from Tibet is possible as long as you have the correct permit for travel in the country; entering Tibet from Nepal, however, is limited to group tours.

The classic **Asia overland** trip is just about alive and kicking, despite periodic political reroutings; leaving Europe behind at Istanbul, the usual approach from the west traverses Turkey, angles down through Iran, crosses Pakistan and enters India at Amritsar. Several expedition operators (see lists of tour operators on pp.13 and 16 run six- to eighteen-week trips in specially designed vehicles all the way through to Kathmandu. Expect to pay between £900 and £2500 for the one-way trip from Europe (usually London), depending on duration and level of luxury.

Overland from India

Transport connections between **India** and Nepal are well developed, with travel agents in Delhi, Darjeeling and other major train junctions in the north selling bus packages to Kathmandu. However, these are often rip-offs, and in any case it's an easy matter to ride to the border and make your own way from there – you'll almost certainly end up on the same Nepali bus anyway.

Three **border crossings** see the vast majority of travellers: Sonauli/Belahiya, the most popular entry point, reachable from Delhi, Varanasi and most of North India (via Gorakhpur); Raxaul/Birganj, accessible from Bodh Gaya and Calcutta via Patna; and Kakarbhitta, serving Darjeeling and Calcutta via Siliguri. A fourth, Banbaasa/Mahendra Nagar, is handy for the Uttar Pradesh hill stations and, thanks to a new road, is now the quickest way from Delhi to Kathmandu; it's still a long way from Mahendra Nagar to Kathmandu, but it would be quite possible to plan a trip to Nepal based solely around the western national parks and Pokhara. All these border crossings are described in the Guide.

Two **other border points** (near Nepalganj and Dhangadhi) are also open to tourists, but they're rarely used and are not easy to get to. Other crossings near Janakpur, Biratnagar and Ilam rarely admit foreigners, though they may eventually become official entry points. But since you can't be sure ahead of time that you'll be allowed through, you should probably enter the country via one of the official crossings to avoid a wasted journey; then, if you're up for adventure on the way out, check with Central Immigration in Kathmandu before setting off to find out what else is open.

By private vehicle

Needless to say, bringing a **private vehicle** into Nepal is a big commitment, and requires nerves of steel to cope with local driving conditions (see p.39 for tips). The trade-off is that you don't have to deal with Nepali buses, and you get to go at your own pace, bring lots more gear and have your own personal space. You can enter Nepal – slowly – via any official border crossing.

If you're driving all the way from your home country, the best strategy is to obtain a **carnet de passage**, a document intended to ensure you don't illegally sell the vehicle while out of the country. A *carnet* is available from the AA or similar motoring organizations. It may also be possible to get one in India if the vehicle (most likely a motorcycle) was purchased there. If you can't manage to obtain a *carnet*, you'll have to pay a per-diem duty rate on the vehicle when you enter Nepal; it works out to about $1 a day for a motorcycle or $3 a day for a car, and must be paid in advance for however many days you think you'll be in Nepal. You'd also do well to come equipped with an **international driving licence**.

By bicycle

Entering Nepal by **bicycle** involves no special paperwork, and the main routes are summarized below. Cycling from India is best done in December and January, when the weather is coolest. If entering via one of the far-western or far-eastern crossings, be prepared to spend one or more nights in really basic accommodation (like the floor of a teashop).

Birganj–Kathmandu A spectacular but extremely strenuous ride up and over the Tribhuwan Rajpath – the climb is so tough from the south that this is probably a better route for leaving Nepal than entering it. Unfortunately, Birganj is the least pleasant of

Nepal's border crossings. Distance 185km, elevations ranging from 90m above sea level to 2490m.

Kakarbhitta–Kathmandu An adventurous route from Darjeeling through little-visited plains country, though it requires a fair bit of hammering down long stretches of highway. The final leg can be along the Rajpath or an easier way via Chitwan. Distance 540km, elevations 80m–2490m. (Yet a third variation, Janakpur to Kathmandu via Dhulikhel, may soon be possible.)

Sonauli–Pokhara An excellent introduction to Nepal, this is a scenic, reasonably cycle-friendly route offering side trips to Lumbini and Tansen. The road may deteriorate over short stretches. Distance 185km, elevations 90–1500m.

Mahendranagar–Pokhara The most rural way from Delhi, with some long, straight, dull stretches across the plains. Passes two great wildlife parks and then joins the Sonauli–Pokhara route. Distance 750km, elevations 80–1500m.

Kodari–Kathmandu The only route from Tibet (see below). The mostly downhill Nepal stretch will seem tame compared to the ride from Lhasa to the border, though it's exciting enough coming up it. Distance 230m, elevations 630m–1640m.

From Tibet

Any advice concerning travelling in **Tibet** is liable to be out of date by the time it's printed, so seek current information before going there in anticipation of being able to cross into Nepal. At the time of writing, China was allowing individuals with the proper paperwork for Tibet travel to exit the country at Zhangmu (Kodari on the Nepal side) on the Lhasa–Kathmandu highway, but only groups were being permitted to enter Tibet there. **Landcruisers** ply a standard three- or four-day quasi-sightseeing route from Lhasa via Shigatze, Gyantse and Tingri to the border, from where you'll have to walk a bit (or, if the road is washed out, a lot) and then continue for almost another full day to Kathmandu by **bus**. See p.x for more information on seasonal considerations.

If you've managed to **cycle** all the way to Lhasa, you ought to be fit and acclimatized enough to make it the rest of the way to Nepal – but needless to say, this is an extremely arduous journey along a mostly unpaved road, crossing two passes of at least 5000m, and should only be attempted in good weather.

Asian connections by plane

Booking a separate flight between Kathmandu and any of the main **Asian air hubs** opens up a host of alternative international routes. You're unlikely to save much money by flying indirectly, particularly via India, but there may be a better choice of dates. Flying to Delhi and then on to Kathmandu is a fairly popular route, particularly from Europe, and it opens up the possibility of seeing something of India, even if you can't stomach going overland. Coming from Australia, New Zealand or the western side of the US or Canada, it's easy to break your journey in Southeast Asia, and there's a fair chance of saving money by picking up a separate ticket once you're there.

Kathmandu is also served by flights from major Indian cities, while services to smaller destinations in northern India come and go; the one private Nepalese airline to begin regional flights (Necon, from Kathmandu to Patna and Varanasi) had suspended these routes at the time of writing. It's worth checking what's available locally, however, as this sector of the market has long been earmarked for expansion.

One-way **airfares** between most Asian cities and Kathmandu don't usually vary much, though it's still always worth shopping around for a discounted ticket, particularly if you're booking from within Asia. For Delhi–Kathmandu flights, you may have trouble finding an agent that deals with RNAC or Druk Air, but Air India handles Indian Airlines' international bookings competently, and prices are usually comparable. Note that Royal Nepal Airlines Corporation (RNAC) and Indian Airlines (IA) give a 25 percent discount to under-thirties on the Calcutta, Delhi and Varanasi flights.

The following approximate single fares between Asian cities and Kathmandu are likely to cost slightly more when booked from outside Asia; returns, simply enough, cost double. Airlines serving the routes are given in brackets.

Asian connections

Bangalore (RNAC) – $250
Bangkok (Thai, RNAC) – $220
Calcutta (IA, RNAC) – $100
Delhi (IA, RNAC, Druk Air) – $150

Dhaka (Biman Bangladesh) – $90
Hong Kong (RNAC, Dragon) –$310
Karachi (PIA) – $220
Lhasa (China Southwest) – $275
Mumbai (IA, RNAC) – $250
Shanghai (RNAC) – $310)
Singapore (RNAC, Singapore) – $310–365
Varanasi (IA) – $75

Red tape and visas

All foreign nationals except Indians need a visa to enter Nepal. Tourist visas are issued on arrival with a minimum of fuss at the Kathmandu airport and at official overland entry points. Have a passport-size photo at the ready, and if possible bring exact change for the visa fee. At the airport, you're required to pay in Nepalese rupees and will have to change money at the counter next to the visa desk. At overland entry points, on the other hand, officials accept US dollars only, though there have been reports of Indian rupees being accepted for a small "fee".

The current **fee structure** seems fairly stable: visas currently cost $30 for a minimum of sixty days. If you plan on border hopping between Nepal and India (or Tibet), the double-entry ($55) or multiple-entry ($90) option may save some time and money, but it's not essential as you can get a re-entry stamp at any official border crossing, for the same price as a visa. Fees may change without warning, however, and at the time of writing there were rumours of special discounts aimed at attracting tourists, so double check at ⓦwww.immi.gov.np. Getting a visa from an overseas Nepalese embassy or consulate is really only worth doing if you happen to be in the neighbourhood.

Tourist visas can be **extended**, for thirty days at a time only, for a maximum of 150 days in a calendar year. Extensions are granted only at the Kathmandu or Pokhara Department of Immigration offices – a somewhat tedious procedure, especially in high season, when queues can run to two hours or more. The cost is $50 for thirty days ($75 double entry, $110 multiple entry). Submit your passport and one passport-size photo with your application. Instant photos are available from studios near Central

Immigration offices, but note that the office accepts only rupees (as opposed to all the entry points, which only accept US dollars).

If you **overstay**, you'll end up paying double the amount it would have cost to properly extend your visa, with the possibility of a further fine on top. Don't overstay more than a couple of days, and for heaven's sake *don't* tamper with your visa – tourists have been jailed for these seemingly minor infractions.

It is no longer necessary to have a **trekking permit** to visit the most popular trekking regions. You'll have to pay **national park entry fees**, however, which cover the most popular Annapurna, Everest and Langtang areas. A handful of very remote regions, such as Upper Dolpo and Mustang, are still restricted, and require permits to enter. For more detailed discussion, see Chapter Seven p.413.

Selected Nepalese embassies and consulates

A complete list of Nepalese embassies and consulates abroad can be found at ⓦwww .immi.gov.np or at ⓦwww.undp.org/missions /nepal/embassy.htm.

Australia Level 13, Pitt St, Sydney, NSW 2000
☏ 02/9223 6144.
India Barakhamba Rd, New Delhi 110001 ☏ 011/
332 7361, ⊕ 332 6857.
Netherlands Kezersgracht 463, 1017 DK,
Amsterdam ☏ 020/6241 530, ⊕ 6246 173.

New Zealand 278 A Remuera Rd, Auckland 5
☏ 09/520 3169, ⊕ 520 7847.
UK 12a Kensington Palace Gardens, London W8
4QU ☏ 020/7229 1594, ⊕ 7792 9861.
USA 2131 Leroy Place NW, Washington, DC 20008
☏ 202/667-4550, ⊕ 667-5534.

ℹ Information, websites and maps

The Nepal Tourism Board doesn't operate outside the country, and its few offices in Nepal don't exactly go out of their way for tourists. Staff can sometimes help with information on festival dates, local bus schedules and the like, and supply a growing range of printed materials if they're not out of stock. But for the most part, you're left to find your own way through a confusing thicket of advertising and signboards.

You'll always get the most useful information from other travellers. Check the informal **notice boards** in restaurants around the tourist quarters for news of upcoming events or to find travelling or trekking companions. In Kathmandu, the offices of the **Kathmandu Environmental Education Project** (see p.96) and the **Himalayan Rescue Association** (see p.96) can help out with information on trekking routes and conditions. Despite their shameless advertiser bias, *Nepal Traveller* and *Travellers' Nepal*, free monthly magazines distributed to the big hotels and travel agencies, are the best of several sources of what's-on information.

Nepal is very well served on the **internet**, though some sites are pretty self-serving, and some frankly bizarre – recent bright ideas have included e-goat sacrifice and videoconferenced e-funerals, both aimed at expat Nepalis. You only have to find one Nepal site to find the rest, since they're well linked. Trekking websites are recommended in the trekking chapter, while other specific sites are listed throughout the main guide text. If you're into **newsgroups**, try rec.travel.asia, which is unmoderated but has a small portion of postings devoted to Nepal matters, and can be excellent for getting answers to specific questions; or soc.culture.nepal, used more by academics and expat Nepalis. Bear in mind that both groups

are unmoderated, and that firsthand information isn't necessarily accurate or up-to-date.

Useful websites

ⓦ **www.catmando.com** Comprehensive lists of Nepal-based businesses, including hotels, travel and trekking agencies.

ⓦ **www.dfat.gov.au** Advice and reports on unstable countries and regions from the Australian Department of Foreign Affairs; not bad on Nepal.

ⓦ **www.fco.gov.uk/travel** This British Foreign and Commonwealth Office site is usually the most detailed government advisory service on travel to Nepal.

ⓦ **www.hec.org** A resource for trekkers and other travellers run by the Himalayan Explorers Connection. Trip reports, a newsletter, information on volunteer opportunities and other useful stuff.

ⓦ **www.nepal.com** Beautiful photos, but weak on information.

ⓦ **www.nepalhomepage.com** The premier Nepal gateway, including extensive FAQs on travel in Nepal, local yellow pages, directories of trekking agencies and embassies, photos and a festival calendar.

ⓦ **www.nepalnews.com** Superb news service with links to just about every Nepali media outlet, including English-language newspapers and magazines. Start with the Kathmandu Post or Nepali Times.

ⓦ **www.pilgrimsbooks.com** The online branch of Kathmandu's largest bookstore, with hundreds of Nepal-related titles available.

ⓦ **http://travel.state.gov/travel_warnings.html** The US State Department Travel Advisories' "Consular information sheets" detail the dangers of travelling in most countries of the world.

ⓦ www.visitnepal.com An impressively encyclopedic site with information on tourist sites, culture and activities, plus listings and links to many businesses catering to tourists.

ⓦ www.welcomenepal.com It's early days for the official site of the Nepal Tourism Board, but it may yet develop into an excellent resource.

Guides

Hiring a **guide** is a great way to get under the skin of Nepal. You'll have instant introductions everywhere you go, and will probably be invited home to meet the family, which will give a perspective on local lives that you couldn't possibly gain on your own. You'll also learn all sorts of things you won't get from a book (teaching Nepali swear words, for instance, is a guides' favourite).

Most people only think of hiring a guide for a **trek** (more on this in Chapter Seven), but a guide is even more essential when **tracking wildlife** in the Tarai parks. A growing number of travellers are discovering that they can escape the crowds of Chitwan by hiring a guide there and then moving on to remoter parks, which are otherwise accessible only on an expensive package.

Would-be guides often position themselves strategically at temples and palaces, but these "pay me what you will" characters often end up squeezing you for more than they're worth. Better to find one through an innkeeper, travel agent or someone you've already done business with.

An inexperienced guide hired informally will usually charge about Rs300 a day; someone with better English will command upwards of Rs700 a day, and an agency will charge even more for a licensed guide. Generally, you get what you pay for.

Maps

While **maps** published in Nepal have their quirks and errors, they're generally slightly better, not to mention cheaper, than those published overseas. Maps of particular areas, notably trekking and wildlife parks, are recommended in the relevant sections of the Guide. Most **country maps**, however, are hopelessly out of date in terms of roads, and inaccurate anywhere off them. New maps are published and new roads built all the

time, so it's even worth taking a look at a few and picking out the one with the most roads. Shangri-La Maps 1:1,000,000 *Nepal* is reasonably accurate, and Himalaya Map House's 1:900,000 *Nepal* includes useful insets of trekking areas and national parks. Cheaper maps are published by Mandala and the Nepal Tourist Board.

Free **city maps** of Kathmandu, available at the airport and through tourist offices, are adequate for most purposes. Bookshops and street vendors sell somewhat better maps of Kathmandu and Pokhara and their valleys: Nepa's pocket-size map of *Thamel, Kathmandu and the Valley* is accurate and handy. Mapple/Karto Atelier does a very useful and extremely readable series covering the main tourist areas, including the Kathmandu Valley, the Pokhara Valley, Chitwan and "Around Annapurna".

For **trekking**, **mountain-biking** and any other off-road travel, the most detailed are the 1:25,000 and 1:50,000 series' published by Finnish aid agency FINNIDA and the Nepalese government. They now cover almost the entire country and are comparable in quality to those published by the British Ordnance Survey and the USGS (United States Geological Survey). They're easier to find abroad than in Kathmandu, though the full range is available in the Maps of Nepal shop (see p.166) in Naya Baneswar, Kathmandu. A useful companion would be the inexpensive Helvetas Nepal 1:125,000 series (a separate Swiss/Nepalese co-operation) which doesn't give quite such detailed topographical information but is excellent for trails, bridges and villages.

Specialist map outlets

US and Canada

GORP Adventure Library online only ☎ 1-800/754-8229, ⓦ www.gorp.com.
Map Link Inc 30 S La Patera Lane, Unit 5, Santa Barbara, CA 93117 ☎ 805/692-6777, ⓦ www.maplink.com.

UK and Ireland

The Map Shop 30a Belvoir St, Leicester LE1 6QH ☎ 0116/247 1400.
Newcastle Map Centre 55 Grey St, Newcastle-

Nepali place names

Even though Devanaagari (the script of Nepali and Hindi) spellings are phonetic, transliterating them into the Roman alphabet is a disputed science. Some places will never shake off the erroneous spellings bestowed on them by early British colonialists – Kathmandu, for instance, looks more like *Kaathmaadau* when properly transliterated. Where place names are Sanskrit- or Hindi-based, the Nepali pronunciation sometimes differs from the accepted spelling – the names Vishnu (a Hindu god) and Vajra (a tantric symbol) sound like "Bishnu" and "Bajra" in Nepali. This book follows local pronunciations as consistently as possible, except in cases where this would be out of step with every map in print. Having said that, it's often hard to get a consensus on pronunciation – some people say Hetauda, others Itaura; some say Trisuli, others Tirsuli – so keep an open mind while map-reading.

upon-Tyne, NE1 6EF ☏ 0191/261 5622.
Stanfords 12–14 Long Acre, London WC2E 9LP
☏ 020/7836 1321, ⓦ www.stanfords.co.uk; maps by mail or phone order are available on this number and via ⓔ sales@stanfords.co.uk

Australia and New Zealand

The Map Shop 6 Peel St, Adelaide ☏ 08/8231 2033, ⓦ www.mapshop.net.au.

Mapworld 173 Gloucester St, Christchurch ☏ 03/374 5399, ⓕ 374 5633, ⓦ www.mapworld .co.nz.
Mapland 372 Little Bourke St, Melbourne ☏ 03/9670 4383, ⓦ www.mapland.com.au.
Perth Map Centre 1/884 Hay St, Perth ☏ 08/9322 5733, ⓦ www.perthmap.com.au.
Specialty Maps 46 Albert St, Auckland ☏ 09/307 2217.

Insurance

You'd do well to take out insurance before travelling, to cover against theft, loss and illness or injury. Before paying for a new policy, however, it's worth checking whether you're already covered: some all-risks home insurance policies may cover your possessions when overseas, and many medical schemes include cover when abroad.

After exhausting the possibilities above, you might want to contact a **specialist travel insurance** company, or consider the travel insurance deal we offer (see box on p.24). A typical travel insurance policy usually provides cover for the loss of baggage, tickets and – up to a certain limit – cash or cheques, as well as cancellation or curtailment of your journey. Most of them exclude so-called dangerous sports unless an extra premium is paid: in Nepal this can mean whitewater rafting, trekking and climbing, though probably not kayaking or jeep safaris. Many policies can be chopped and changed to exclude coverage you don't need – for example, sickness and accident benefits can often be excluded or included at will. If you do take medical coverage, ascertain whether benefits will be paid as treatment proceeds or only after return home, and whether there is a 24-hour medical emergency number. When securing baggage cover, make sure that the per-article limit – typically under £500 – will cover your most valuable possession. If you need to make a claim, you should keep **receipts** for medicines and medical treatment, and in the event you have anything stolen, you must obtain an official statement from the police.

Rough Guide travel insurance

Rough Guides offers its own travel insurance, customized for our readers by a leading UK broker and backed by a Lloyds underwriter. It's available for anyone, of any nationality, travelling anywhere in the world.

There are two main plans: **Essential**, for basic, no-frills cover; and **Premier** – with more generous and extensive benefits. Alternatively, you can take out **annual multitrip insurance**, which covers you for any number of trips throughout the year (with a maximum of sixty days for any one trip). Unlike many policies, the Rough Guides schemes are calculated by the day, so if you're travelling for 27 days rather than a month, that's all you pay for. If you intend to be away for the whole year, the Adventurer policy will cover you for 365 days. Each plan can be supplemented with a "Hazardous Activities Premium" if you plan to indulge in sports considered dangerous, such as skiing, scuba-diving or trekking. Rough Guides also does good deals for older travellers, and will insure you up to any age, at prices comparable to SAGA's.

For a policy quote, call the Rough Guide Insurance Line on UK freefone ☎0800/ 015 0906; US toll-free ☎1-866/220-5588, or, if you're calling from elsewhere ☎+44 1243/621046. Alternatively, get an online quote at ⊛www.roughguides.com/insurance.

Health

Hygiene is not one of Nepal's strong points. Sanitation is poor, and a lot of bugs make the rounds, especially during the spring and monsoon months. But don't panic – by coming prepared and looking after yourself while you're in the country, you're unlikely to come down with anything worse than a cold or the local version of "Delhi belly".

This section deals with health matters mainly in the context of Western-style medicine. Traditional ayurvedic and Tibetan practices are discussed later in the "Spiritual pursuits and alternative therapies" section (p.72 onwards). For more detailed health advice, refer to the books recommended on p.565, or visit the websites listed.

Before you go

No **inoculations** are required for Nepal, but hepatitis A, typhoid and meningitis jabs are recommended, and it's worth ensuring that you're up to date with tetanus, polio, mumps and measles boosters. For a few travellers, malaria tablets and injections for meningitis, Japanese B encephalitis and rabies may also be in order. All of these can be obtained in Kathmandu, often more cheaply than at home, but obviously it's bet-

ter to get nasty things like injections out of the way before starting your trip, especially as it takes some weeks for certain inoculations to take effect.

If you have any medical conditions or concerns about your health, don't set off to Nepal without first seeing a **doctor**. Medicines are sold over the counter everywhere, but obviously bring any prescribed medications. Also, consider having a dental check-up before you go. If you wear glasses, bring an extra pair; if you wear contacts, bring a backup pair of glasses as a precaution against dust and pollution.

Recommended inoculations

Most travellers decide to inoculate themselves against the following diseases which are, on the whole, fairly ghastly but not fatal.

Deciding which to protect yourself against is a matter of risk management.

Hepatitis A is an infection or inflammation of the liver that causes mild fever, nausea/vomiting, loss of appetite and jaundice. It's fairly common in Nepal, and while it won't kill you, it'll put a swift end to your travels and lay you up for several months after your return. It's transmitted through contaminated food and water, so sensible hygiene will reduce your risk of catching it, but you can't count on fastidiousness alone. The Havrix or Vaqta vaccines afford the best protection; this lasts for a year, or ten years if followed up by a booster within six to twelve months. Note that children under the age of about ten don't need to be vaccinated against hepatitis A, because the disease is very mild in childhood and getting it confers lifelong immunity.

Typhoid and paratyphoid are endemic in Nepal, and, like hepatitis A, they're spread through contaminated food and water, and are almost as common. These nearly identical diseases produce a persistent high fever, headaches, abdominal pains and diarrhoea, but are treatable with antibiotics and are rarely fatal. Paratyphoid usually occurs in epidemics and is less severe. The best inoculation is the capsular polysaccharide vaccine (Typhim Vi), which doesn't protect against paratyphoid, but is more effective against typhoid and relatively free from side effects; what's more, it's a single injection. Boosters are needed every three years. The Whole Cell Killed Typhoid Vaccine is slightly less effective against typhoid, and causes slight fever, but it does offer protection against paratyphoid. Least effective against either, but least unpleasant, is a series of tablets taken orally.

You should have a **tetanus** booster every ten years, whether you travel or not – and within five years of the last one if you've acquired a dirty wound. Assuming you were vaccinated for **polio** in childhood, only one booster is necessary during your adult life. Immunizations against **mumps** and **measles** are recommended for anyone who wasn't vaccinated as a child and hasn't already had these diseases.

Flu is no more prevalent in Nepal than elsewhere, but you might consider getting a flu shot before you leave just to reduce the risk of spending several days sick during your time in Nepal. A new flu vaccine is formulated each year and is usually available starting in mid- or late October.

Optional inoculations

The following diseases are all rare, but potentially fatal. They're discussed in descending order of how much you should be concerned about them.

Meningicoccal meningitis, spread by airborne bacteria (through coughs and sneezes, for example), is a very serious disease that attacks the lining of the brain, and can cause death in as little as a day. However, while localized cases are occasionally reported in Nepal, and there was an epidemic in the Kathmandu Valley in 1983–84, the chances of catching meningitis are remote. That said, the injection is very effective, causes few side effects, and lasts for three to five years.

Although **rabies** is a problem in Nepal, the best advice is just to give dogs and monkeys a wide berth. True, rabies is a scary disease, but it can be cured by an after-the-fact ("post-exposure") series of five injections, administered over a month, that are essentially 100 percent effective if given in reasonable time. The post-exposure series is available in Kathmandu, although it costs upwards of $600. The pre-exposure vaccine involves a series of three injections over a four-week period, which produces a protective antibody level for three years; if you get bitten, you'll still have to get two more boosters. It's probably not worth it except for children, who may not report every contact with animals to their parents. See p.29 for advice on dealing with animal bites.

Japanese B encephalitis, though potentially fatal, is mostly confined to the more jungly portions of the Tarai during (and shortly before and after) the monsoon, though a handful of cases have been diagnosed in Kathmandu. While there are no known cases of foreigners catching the disease in Nepal, visitors to Kathmandu and the Tarai who are staying for a long period between April and October should certainly consider vaccinating against it. Rural areas where

For advice on altitude sickness and other **trekking hazards**, plus a first-aid checklist, see p.427.

pigs are kept are most risky, notably Tharu communities in the western Tarai. The inoculation is in the form of three injections given over a three- to four-week period.

Hepatitis B is a more serious version of Hepatitis A, but (like AIDS) is passed on through blood and sexual contact. Therefore the vaccine is only recommended for those working in a medical environment or planning on engaging in unsafe sex. Long-term travellers are sometimes vaccinated on the grounds that they might have an accident and need to receive blood. The Twinrix vaccine combines Hepatitis A and B protection.

Don't bother with the **cholera inoculation** – few authorities now believe it's worthwhile, and the risk of catching cholera in Nepal is minimal.

Malaria prophylaxis

Most visitors to Nepal won't need to take **malaria** tablets. The disease hasn't been eradicated in Nepal, as is sometimes claimed, but it is unknown above 1000m, and rare outside the monsoon months. The risk to short-term travellers is very low indeed – there have been less than twenty cases since the mid-1980s. Even if the malaria risk is small, it's well worth taking the anti-mosquito measures described under "Precautions" (below), especially during the monsoon.

Prophylaxis (regular doses of tablets) *is* worth considering if you plan to visit the Tarai (which includes Chitwan and Bardia national parks) between June and September. Longer-term visitors and anyone visiting India should also seek expert advice, and rafters should note that malaria can also be present in valleys in the hills that are lower than 1000m. The new anti-malarial drug Malarone is, by all reports, a good option; note that tablets are much cheaper in Kathmandu than at home.

Precautions

The lack of **sanitation** in Nepal is sometimes overhyped – it's not worth getting too uptight about it or you'll never enjoy anything, and you'll run the risk of rebuffing Nepalese hospitality. The best advice is to follow the guidelines below when you can, and enjoy your meal.

Given that most travellers are careful about drinking dirty water, **food** is thought to be the worst culprit, and it's usually tourist restaurants and "Western" dishes that bring the most grief: more people get sick in Kathmandu than anywhere else in Nepal. Be particularly wary of prepared dishes that have to be reheated, and any food that's been sitting out where flies can land on it. Nepali food is usually fine and you can probably trust anything that's been boiled or fried in your presence, although meat can sometimes be dodgy, particularly lightly fried snack dishes. Raw, unpeeled fruit and vegetables – including pickles – should always be viewed with suspicion, as should tourist restaurants' claims to have soaked their salads in an iodine solution. Fruit juices and lassis contain a double danger, as they may be made with water or ice.

Kathmandu's **polluted air** gives many people respiratory infections within a few days of arrival; asthmatics and others with breathing problems are particularly affected. Minimize your exposure by staying off the main boulevards, wearing a face mask if necessary, and avoiding people who are hacking and wheezing tubercularly. You can also help your immune system by keeping warm, dry and well rested (especially if jet-lagged). Most importantly, get out of the valley to where the air is fresh as quickly as possible.

You need to be particularly vigilant about **personal hygiene** while travelling in Nepal. That means, above all, washing your hands often – waterless antibacterial soap comes in handy. Keep any cuts clean, and treat them with iodine to prevent infection. If you're staying in cheap guesthouses, bring a sleeping sheet to keep fleas and lice at bay. Scabies and hookworm can be picked up through bare feet, so it's best to wear shoes at all times, but flip-flops (also referred to as thongs or sandals, or *chappal* in Nepali) can be bought anywhere in Nepal, and provide reasonable protection.

When travelling in the Tarai, deprive **mos-**

quitoes of the opportunity to bite you. They're hungriest from dusk to dawn: during these times, wear repellent and/or long-sleeved clothes (watch out especially for ankles), and sleep under netting or use mosquito "mats" (small tablets that release a mosquito-repelling scent when heated in an electric device) or old-fashioned coils. Remember, though, that very few mosquitoes carry malaria, so you don't need to worry over every bite. If you do get bites or itches, try not to scratch them as infection may result. Tiger balm and even dry soap may relieve the itching.

Travellers in rural areas of the eastern Tarai need to protect against **sandfly** bites in the same way. Sandflies can transmit the disease Visceral Leishmaniasis (VL), also called Kala-Azar, which causes fever and potentially fatal enlargement of the spleen – but it hasn't affected any tourists to date.

Take the usual precautions to avoid **sunburn** and **dehydration**. Obviously, susceptibility to sunburn varies by individual, but during the sunny times of year you'll probably want at least medium protection, and high protection will be necessary while trekking. Sunscreen is available in tourist areas.

Water

Untreated **water** should be avoided where at all possible – and you may not always notice the risk. Clean or dirty, water is regarded as a purifying agent in Nepal, and plates, glasses and cutlery are customarily rinsed just before use: if you're handed wet utensils it's a good idea to give them a discreet wipe. Use pure water when brushing your teeth, and keep your mouth closed in the shower (no singing). Thamel restaurants are now pretty savvy about using purified water in **ice**, and drinking a cocktail or a fresh fruit juice isn't the game of Russian roulette it once was, but it's probably still worth steering clear. Similarly, many guesthouses provide water in drip-filter units, but you can't always be sure the water was boiled first, or that the filters are clean. Tea and bottled drinks are generally safe.

Mineral water is now widely available in Nepal, but to avoid leaving behind a trail of plastic garbage, you may prefer to purify your own. Boiling and filtering isn't an option for most travellers; adding iodine, however, is easy. **Iodine tablets** can be bought in outdoor-sports shops or, more cheaply, in tourist areas of Kathmandu. Simply add one tablet to a litre of untreated water. Cheaper still is **Lugol's Solution**, an aqueous solution of iodine sold by pharmacies all over Nepal with a free plastic dropper. Use four drops per litre (more if the water's cloudy), wait twenty minutes (thirty if it's cold), and drink freely. The faint medicinal taste can be removed by adding a small amount of vitamin C powder (available in any Nepalese pharmacy), but only do this *after* the water is purified.

To store your purified water, you can recycle an old mineral water bottle, slotting it into one of the natty string carry-bags sold by some handicrafts shops in Kathmandu. Sturdier bottles are sold in all trekking equipment stores, and double up nicely as hot-water bottles when it gets cold.

Alternatively, outdoors stores in Europe and the US stock a bewildering range of portable water-treatment devices, and you can sometimes find water bottles with in-built filters.

AIDS

Nepal's isolation gave it a decade's grace period from the **AIDS** epidemic, but the disease is now becoming a significant health problem – and the government is in denial. Official figures claim 2080 people infected with HIV, while the World Health Organization put the figure at around 65,000. Almost ninety percent of transmissions in Nepal are thought to be through heterosexual contact, especially in the context of prostitution. Indian brothels, where many Nepali women work (see p.542), are full of HIV-positive sex workers, and the disease is quickly spread from there to Nepal by businessmen and long-distance drivers.

Carry **condoms** with you (preferably brought from home, though the Nepali ones are getting more reliable) and insist on using them. (Condoms also protect you from other sexually transmitted diseases such as hepatitis B.) Trekking guides can be considered a relatively high-risk group, so sexual relationships should probably be treated with appropriate caution.

If you get a shave from a barber, make sure he uses a clean blade, and don't submit to processes such as ear-piercing, acupuncture or tattooing unless you're satisfied the equipment is sterile. Should you need an injection, make sure that new, sterile equipment is used. If you need a blood transfusion, bear in mind that the Nepalese blood supply isn't adequately screened; any blood you receive should be from voluntary rather than commercial donor banks.

Self-diagnosis

Chances are that at some point during your travels in Nepal you'll feel ill. In the vast majority of cases, it won't be something you need to see a doctor about, and sod's law says it will happen somewhere remote and inconvenient anyway. The following information should help with **self-diagnosis**, although it is *not* presented as a substitute for professional medical advice. However, if you're unable to get to a clinic – a strong possibility when trekking – you might choose to **self-medicate**, and dosages are given below.

Antibiotics definitely shouldn't be taken lightly: they pre-empt the body's ability to develop its own immunity to the disease, and can increase susceptibility to other problems by killing off "good" as well as "bad" organisms in the digestive system (yogurt or curd can replenish them to some extent, as can acidophilus tablets – which are also good for thrush and fungal infections). Some may cause allergic reactions or other unpleasant side effects, and the more a particular antibiotic is used, the sooner organisms build up a resistance to it. It's not a bad idea to travel with a course of one or more of the drugs mentioned here, but make sure you have the dosage explained to you. In the case of serious or persistent intestinal problems, you're strongly urged to have a **stool test** done at a clinic (see p.30), where the doctor can make an authoritative diagnosis and prescription.

Some of the illnesses and parasites you can pick up in Nepal may not show themselves immediately. If you become ill within a year of returning home, tell the physician who treats you where you've been.

Intestinal troubles

Diarrhoea is the most common bane of travellers. If it's mild and not accompanied by other major symptoms, it probably won't require any treatment and should pass of its own accord within a few days. In the meantime, however, it's essential to replace the fluids and salts you're losing – Jeevan Jal, sold in packets everywhere, is a cheap and effective oral rehydration formula. Bananas and cola drinks are also supposed to be good for replacing electrolytes. "Starving the bug to death" is an old wives' tale, though you're unlikely to have much of an appetite in any case. Diarrhoea tablets such as Lomotil and Immodium will plug you up if you have to travel, but they undermine the body's efforts to rid itself of the infection.

If the diarrhoea comes on suddenly and is accompanied by bad cramps and vomiting, there's a good chance it's **food poisoning**, which is brought on by toxins secreted by foreign bacteria. There's nothing you can do for food poisoning other than keep replacing fluids, but it should run its course within 24 to 48 hours. If you're feverish, have severe diarrhoea that lasts more than three days or if you see blood or mucus in your stools, seek treatment.

Bacterial diarrhoea, the cause in 85 percent of identifiable cases, is recognizable by its sudden onset, accompanied by nausea and vomiting, stomach cramps and sometimes fever. The treatment is one 400mg tablet of the antibiotic Norfloxacin/Norbactin every twelve hours for five days, or one 500mg tablet of ciprofloxacin every twelve hours for three days.

Giardiasis (**giardia**) produces three or four loose stools a day, and is often recognizable by copious, foul-smelling belches and farts. It occurs in about one in twenty cases of diarrhoea in Nepal, and is more commonly contracted while trekking. The cure is a single dose of 2g of tinidazole (four 500mg tablets of locally available "tiniba"), which can make you tired and nauseous for 24 hours, and absolutely shouldn't be mixed with alcohol in that time.

Amoebic dysentery is relatively rare. Setting in gradually, it manifests itself in frequent, small, watery bowel movements, often accompanied by fever. To self-medicate, take one 500mg tablet of Tinidazole four times a day for three days. This must be followed by taking one 500mg Diloxaride Furoate (Furamide) tablet every eight hours for ten days, in order to kill amoebic cysts that can infect the liver.

If the diarrhoea is associated with fatigue and appetite loss over many days, and occurs between April and November, it may be the result of **cyclospora** (sometimes called blue-green algae). Another waterborne condition, it's treated with the antibiotic trimethoprimsulfamethoxazole (Bactrim or Septra). Again, be sure to keep rehydrating. Iodine and chlorine do not kill cyclospora, so drink boiled water if you can during the peak months of June and July.

Finally, bear in mind that oral drugs, such as malaria pills or the contraceptive pill, are rendered less effective or completely ineffective if taken while suffering from diarrhoea.

Flu and fever

Flu-like symptoms – fever, headache, runny nose, fatigue, aching muscles – may mean nothing more serious than the latest virus floating around on Kathmandu's bad air. Rest and aspirin or other painkillers should do the trick. However, strep throat or a bronchial or sinus infection will require an antibiotic course such as erythromycin or amoxycillin. Flu symptoms and **jaundice** (yellowing of the eyes) point to hepatitis, which is best treated with rest and a plane ticket home.

A **serious fever** or delirium is cause for real concern. Diagnosis is tricky, but it's safe to say the sufferer needs to be taken to a doctor as quickly as possible. To begin with, try bringing the fever down with aspirin or paracetamol. If the fever rises and falls dramatically every few hours, it may be malaria, which, in the absence of medical help, can be zapped with three tablets of pyralfin (Fansidar). If the fever is consistently high for four or more days, it may be typhoid – again, only if no doctor is available, treat with ciprofloxacin/norfloxacin or chloramphenicol.

Minor symptoms

Minor **muscle cramps**, experienced after heavy exercise or sweating, may indicate you're low on sodium – a teaspoon of salt will bring rapid relief. Likewise, a simple **headache** may just mean you're dehydrated. (However, a severe headache, accompanied by eye pain, neck stiffness and a temperature, could mean meningitis – in which case get to a doctor pronto.)

Itchy skin is often traced to insect bites – not only obvious ones like mosquitoes, but also fleas, lice or scabies picked up from dirty bedclothes. The latter, a burrowing mite, generally goes for the spaces between fingers and toes. Shampoos and lotions are available locally. Air out your bedding and wash your clothes thoroughly.

Worms may enter your body through the skin (especially the soles of the feet), or through food. An itchy anus is a common symptom, and you may even see them in your stools. They are easy to treat with worming tablets, available from any pharmacy.

Animal bites and leeches

For **animal bites** or scratches, *immediately* wash the wound with soap and water for at least five minutes (some recommend half an hour), then rinse with Providone iodine (locally available as "Piodin"), or, if this isn't available, with 40–70 percent alcohol – local *raksi* will just about do the trick. This should kill any rabies virus on the spot; however, anyone bitten by an animal should hightail it to a Kathmandu clinic for expensive postexposure rabies shots, which are given three days apart within ten days of the bite. The disease's incubation period is between ten and ninety days – ideally, you're supposed to capture the animal alive for observation.

Thickly vegetated country, such as the Tarai national parks or low-lying trekking areas, can come alive with **leeches** during and immediately after the monsoon. Protect yourself by wearing insect repellent and long clothing – though the little tykes can work their way through most cloth, and even through the eyelets of your boots. There's probably little harm in letting them have their fill and dropping off, but there is a small risk of infection, particularly if you pick them off by hand and the mouth parts get left behind in the wound. Salt or, less conveniently, iodine, can be applied to make them drop off.

Getting medical help

In a non emergency situation, make for one of the traveller-oriented **clinics** in Kathmandu. Run to Western standards, these can diagnose most common ailments, write prescriptions, and also give inoculations. In other cities and towns, local clinics (often attached to pharmacies) can usually provide adequate care. A veritable cornucopia of Indian-manufactured medicines is available without prescription from **pharmas** (pharmacies) in all major towns, but always check the sell-by date.

In the event of serious injury or illness, contact your embassy for a list of recommended **doctors** in Kathmandu, which is where virtually all qualified GPs and specialists are based. Most speak English. It's a good idea to register with your embassy or consulate on arrival in Nepal; if you get into medical trouble, being registered will expedite assistance, and it's especially important if you go trekking or rafting to ensure prompt evacuation if necessary. There's a list of embassy and consulate contacts in Kathmandu on p.174.

Hospitals are listed in the Kathmandu and Pokhara sections of the guide; other hospitals are located in Dhulikhel, Tansen and the bigger Tarai cities. Most are poorly equipped and the standard of care is variable. Should you be unlucky enough to have to spend time in a Nepali hospital, note that nursing staff do not perform many of what we would consider to be routine functions: relatives are expected to feed patients, change bedpans, monitor IVs and so on.

Online medical resources for travellers

Ⓦ**www.cdc.gov** The Centers for Disease Control publish outbreak warnings, suggested inoculations, precautions and other background information for travellers.

Ⓦ**www.ciwec-clinic.com** The Kathmandu-based CIWEC Clinic is the most authoritative source of information on Nepal-related travel medicine, and its website contains excellent articles on inoculations, diarrhoea, rabies and other health matters.

Ⓦ**http://health.yahoo.com** Information on specific diseases and conditions, drugs and herbal remedies, as well as advice from health experts.

Ⓦ**www.sentex.net/~iamat** The International Association for Medical Assistance to Travellers is a non-profit organization which can provide a list of English-speaking doctors in Nepal and information on various diseases and inoculations.

Ⓦ**www.travmed.com** First-aid kits, mosquito netting, water filters, reference books and other health-related travel products for sale online. Hosts the annually updated *Travel Health Guide*, too.

Ⓦ**www.tripprep.com** Travel Health Online provides a comprehensive online database of necessary vaccinations for most countries, as well as destination and medical service provider information.

Travel clinics

Ⓦ**www.astmh.org** Listings of travel health centres in the US from the American Society of Tropical Medicine and Hygiene.

Ⓦ**www.britishairways.com** British Airways runs 28 regional clinics in the UK, offering vaccinations, tailored advice from an online database and a complete range of travel healthcare products.

Ⓦ**www.csih.org** Extensive list of travel health centres in Canada, published by the Canadian Society for International Health.

Ⓦ**www.istm.org** The website of the International Society for Travel Medicine, with a full list of clinics specializing in international travel health.

Ⓦ**www.tmvc.com.au** Details of all the travellers' medical and vaccination centres in Australia, New Zealand and Southeast Asia, plus general information on travel health.

Ⓦ**www.trailfinders.com** Knowledgeable, professional, no-appointment travel clinics in London, and in Australia at Ⓦwww.trailfinders.com.au.

Costs, money and banks

Your money goes a long way in Nepal. Off the tourist routes, it can actually be hard to spend US$5/£3.50 a day, including food, transport and accommodation. On the other hand, Kathmandu and some of the other tourist traps can burn a hole in your pocket rather faster than you might expect. Even so, it's still possible for a budget traveller to keep to US$8/£5.50 a day in the capital, but the figure can effortlessly balloon to $20 or more simply by choosing slightly nicer hotels and restaurants. If you like to travel in greater luxury, you should expect to spend $40 or more per day, depending mainly on standard of accommodation.

You'll inevitably pay over the odds for things at first, and it may even feel as if people are charging you as much as they think they can get away with, but that's hardly a market principle exclusive to Nepal. Some travellers make a wild show of pinching pennies, which some Nepalis find frankly embarrassing – they know how much an air ticket to Kathmandu costs. Others throw money around, which can be patronizing. Bargain where appropriate, but don't begrudge a few rupees to someone who's worked hard for them and who, all too often, needs them very badly. Youth/student ID cards are of practically no use.

A **value-added tax** (VAT) of ten percent is built into the prices of most goods and services, but many hotels and restaurants (particularly the more expensive ones) quote their prices exclusive of it (note that price codes given in this book are always inclusive of tax). An additional two percent "tourism service fee" is applicable to charges in tourist hotels and restaurants, but the cheaper places roll it into their prices.

No matter how tight your budget, it would be foolish not to splurge now and then on some of the things that make Nepal unique: trekking on your own costs almost nothing, but you might prefer to hire a porter or guide for $5–10 a day; or even pay upwards of $20 a day for a fully catered trek. Rafting, biking and wildlife trips also work out to be relatively expensive, but are well worth it. And few visitors will be able to resist buying at least something from Nepal's rich range of handicrafts.

One expense that you might not expect is having to pay a **fee** to enter some of the major monumental zones in the Kathmandu Valley. There have always been hefty fees to trek or view wildlife in the national parks and conservation areas, and of course you expect to pay to visit museums and certain buildings, but tourists are now charged admission to enter entire historic districts. And where Nepalis must pay a fee to enter, foreigners inevitably pay a much higher one. To some extent, these fees have been prompted by international pressure on Nepal to protect and clean up its UNESCO-designated World Heritage Sites. Local officials argue that users of the sites should fund their upkeep, and they don't see anything wrong with putting the main burden on foreigners – they cause impacts that locals don't, and it's their governments that are making a stink about cleaning up the sites.

Cash

Nepal's unit of currency is the **rupee** (*rupiya*), which is divided into 100 *paisa*. At the time of writing, the **exchange rate** was around Rs75 to the US dollar, Rs110 to £1 and Rs70 to the euro. Almost all Nepali money is paper (you'll rarely see **coins**). **Notes** come in denominations of Rs1, 2, 5, 10, 20, 25, 50, 100, 250, 500 and 1000.

More upmarket tourist businesses, or anyone charging more than Rs500–1000 for goods or services, will usually quote prices in US dollars, and may even expect payment in that currency. This Guide reflects the situation on the ground: the dollar price is listed if that's what the business quotes. A fistful of rupees will rarely be refused, but if you're planning to stay in classy hotels, or book flights or rafting trips, it's worth bringing some US currency. A selection of denominations is useful; make sure the bills are relatively new, too.

One minor annoyance of travelling in Nepal is **getting change**. Even in tourist areas, business people will hum and haw about breaking a large note. Trying to pass even a Rs100 note to a trekking lodge owner or a riksha driver is sure to invite delays, since few Nepalis can afford to keep much spare change lying around. It gets to be a game of bluff between buyer and seller, both hoarding a wad of small notes for occasions when exact change is vital. It pays to carry a range of smaller bills.

Travellers' cheques

Travellers' cheques are of course more secure than cash, and in Nepal they bring a slightly higher official exchange rate, just about offsetting the one percent commission you pay when buying them. Any major brand will do. **US dollar** cheques are widely accepted in tourist areas, and cheques denominated in other major currencies are usually accepted as well. If you're travelling off the beaten track it's wiser to stick to cash.

Be sure to keep the purchase agreement and a record of cheque serial numbers safe and separate from the cheques themselves. In the event that cheques are lost or stolen, the issuing company will expect you to report the loss immediately, using the emergency number given with the cheques. Most companies claim to replace lost or stolen cheques within 24 hours.

Credit and debit cards

Travel agents, luxury hotels and some of the midrange guesthouses accept major **credit cards**, but budget outfits don't, and while an increasing number of retailers take plastic, they typically add a three to five percent processing fee onto the amount, which you may be able to get waived during the bargaining process. Manual transactions (ie those not submitted by an electronic swipe device) may take months to appear on your bill. All but a very few traders are honest, but be

wary if a proprietor insists on taking your card out of sight for processing.

If you run low on funds in Nepal, by far the best way to replenish them is with a **credit card cash advance**. Some private banks issue cash advances against Visa/ MasterCard, and they typically charge no commission if you take the money in rupees. You'll still end up paying interest on the advance to your credit card company, unless you put extra into your account before you leave. American Express cardholders can similarly draw money at the Amex office in Kathmandu (see p.174).

A few banks, notably Standard Chartered, operate **ATMs** in Kathmandu and Pokhara (more are likely to follow in the big Tarai cities). These dispense round-the-clock rupee advances against credit cards (as well as against funds in your account if you have Visa, Maestro or Electron on your bank card), usually with a Rs250 commission. Queues are rare, but there have been reports of finding machines out of order.

Banks and moneychangers

Using **banks** in Nepal is, by south Asian standards, surprisingly hassle-free. Numerous private banks and the quasi-government Nepal Bank vie for tourist business, as do a horde of government-registered **moneychangers**. The government banks give slightly better rates and/or charge less commission than the private ones, while the private banks and moneychangers offer very similar rates once you've factored in commissions, which vary considerably.

Moneychangers can be found wherever there are significant numbers of tourists. Private bank branches are located mainly in larger cities, with government banks typically providing the only service in smaller, untouristed places. **Hours** for foreign exchange vary: at least one Kathmandu airport moneychanger operates around the clock, Nepal Bank's central Kathmandu (New Road) branch stays open seven days a week, and some private banks keep extended hours, but lesser branches generally change money only Sunday to Thursday 10am–2pm and Friday 10am–noon. Specific timings are given in the guide where they're notable. Moneychangers keep generous hours – usually 8am–8pm, seven days a week.

Hold onto all exchange receipts, as you'll need them for **changing money back** when you leave. Some private banks in Kathmandu will buy rupees back, as will banks at the Kathmandu airport and at official border crossings. However, they may have trouble giving the exact change equivalent in foreign currency, and they may be able to give it only in US dollars. If you're entering India, changing Nepalese currency into Indian currency is no problem.

The only reason to change money on the **black market** would be if all official outlets were closed. If you do it, haggle hard (make sure you know the official rate) and be on your guard for sleight-of-hand tricks.

Wiring money

Having money wired from home is never cheap or convenient, and should be considered a last resort. Visit the major companies' websites for more details (see below), or just ask at any large travel agency. The most convenient collection points are Sita World Travel and Annapurna Travels and Tours, both on Tridevi Marg in Kathmandu (for Western Union), and Bank of Kathmandu, at Kamalpokhari and in Thamel (for Moneygram).

Money-wiring websites

American Express Moneygram
Ⓦ www.moneygram.com.
Thomas Cook Ⓦ www.us.thomascook.com.
Western Union Ⓦ www.westernunion.com.

Getting around

Getting around is one of the biggest challenges of travelling in Nepal. Distances aren't great, but the roads are poor and extremely slow, and public buses are uncomfortable. Tourist buses make the best of the most travelled routes, however, and you can always hire a motorcycle, or club together with two or three others to charter a taxi or jeep on a daily rate. And don't rule out flying, even if only one way, which can enable itineraries that would otherwise seem out of the question, and reward you with stunning mountain views.

Nepal has one of the least-developed **road** networks in the world. Of the few highways that are paved, only one is wide enough for two buses to pass without having to slow down or go over onto the shoulders. Highways are irregularly maintained, and each monsoon takes a toll on road surfaces, so in the space of one year a stretch of road can go from wonderful to hellish (or vice versa). Whenever and wherever you travel, the route will probably be new in parts, disintegrated in parts, and under construction in parts. And as long as Maoist alarms continue, army checkpoints at temporary barriers will further increase journey times, as soldiers require passengers to disembark and walk to the other side of the checkpoint while the bus (and often a few local passengers) are searched. All this has an unfortunate effect on tourism: most travellers just aren't willing to endure the long, bumpy, cramped journeys it takes to get far afield in Nepal, so they stick to a circuit of a few easily accessible destinations in the middle of the country.

The **cost** of transport is trifling. Even the longest journeys on public buses will come to no more than Rs300, and the six-hour tourist bus to Pokhara costs less than Rs250. If you have enough people to fill it, a hired taxi or jeep works out at good value, costing under US$8 a head per day. Flights, of course, are much more expensive, with one-way fares in the region of US$60–110.

By bus

Public **buses** ply every paved road in Nepal, as well as quite a few of the unpaved ones. The bus network is completely and chaotically private – there seem to be as many bus companies as there are buses – but all fares are fixed for public services (not for tourist ones). **Fares** depend less on distance than on the state of the road and the time it takes to make the journey; for express buses it works out to about Rs20 per hour (night services cost a little more). Few travellers are ever quite prepared for the sheer **slowness** of bus travel in Nepal. Allowing for bad roads, overloaded buses, tea stops, meal stops, police checks, constant picking up and letting off of passengers, and the occasional flat tyre or worse, the average speed in the hills is barely 25km per hour, and on remote, unpaved roads it can be as little as 10kph. Along the Mahendra Highway, in the Tarai, it's more like 50kph in an express bus.

Bus frequencies and approximate journey times are given throughout the guide. Inevitably, these figures should be taken with a pinch of salt: the bus network seems to grow every year, but political troubles or festivals can dramatically reduce the number of buses, and some gravel or dirt roads are closed altogether during the monsoon. Journey times are more variable than you might imagine, too.

Open-air **bus stations** (*bas park* or *bas istand* in Nepali, and referred to as "bus parks" throughout the guide) are typically located in the smelliest, dustiest and muddiest parts of town. Some cities have more than one bus park to handle services along different routes. **Tickets** are sold either from a small booth or through the barred window of the *ticket ophis*, usually found in a busy corner of the bus park; often enough, all night-bus tickets are sold from one window or booth, all day-buses from another. Destinations may not be written in English, but people are usually happy to help you out if you ask.

In Kathmandu and Pokhara you may find it easier to make arrangements through a **ticket agent** (but heed the warnings given below), while in cities with inconveniently located bus stations you can ask your hotel to send someone to buy a ticket for you.

Ticket agents

With their funfair signs advertising "Bus and Train to India" and "Exciting Jungle Safari", **ticket agents** are the used-car salesmen of Nepal, preying on travellers' faith in the apparently limitless possibilities of the Orient. Though they make themselves out to be budget travel agencies, they're not registered with the government and they offer very limited services. Many are inept, and some are downright dishonest. Even the honest ones often make promises they're in no position to fulfil. Naturally, they all mark up the price of the tickets they sell.

For a seat on a public bus, a ticket agent can save you the trouble of making an extra trip to the bus station, and his commission will be money well spent. For tourist bus services, whose offices are often located just down the street, an agent doesn't provide much value for his fee, although in Nepal it's so hard to tell agents from actual service providers that you'll probably end up booking through an agent anyway. Ticket agents are also useful for hiring vehicles, but shop around.

Be wary when ticket agents try to sell you anything more complicated than the above. *Don't* book a trek or river trip through an agent – deal directly with the tour operator, who can give you straight information and will be accountable if anything goes wrong. Wildlife packages (see p.328) and tickets to India (see p.179) booked through an agent have additional drawbacks. Finally, go to a recommended travel agent to arrange air tickets or anything involving computerized bookings.

Tourist buses

Regularly scheduled **tourist buses** connect Kathmandu with Pokhara, Chitwan National Park, Lumbini and Nagarkot, and Pokhara with Chitwan and Sonauli. Additional services may start up in time.

The vehicles are usually in good condition, making for a much safer ride than in a public bus. They aren't supposed to take any more passengers than there are seats (though they may pick up a few anyway), so the journey should also be more comfortable and somewhat faster, too. There should be just two **seats** on either side of the aisle ("2x2"), making for a roomier ride than on public "2x3" buses, and the seats should be reasonably well padded. A couple of companies operate more expensive buses with intermittent air-conditioning, but you don't get much for paying roughly triple the cost. Services billed as minibuses are somewhat faster than full-sized buses. **Luggage** is kept safely stowed under a tarpaulin on the roof or in a cargo compartment, but put a lock on your bag just to be sure, and keep valuables with you inside.

Tickets are widely touted in Kathmandu and Pokhara. Buses depart from the tourist quarters of those cities, which saves you the trouble of hoofing it down to the bus station (or the expense of taking a taxi). Book seats at least one or two days in advance. Since tourist bus **fares** aren't regulated, and ticket agents often add an undisclosed commission onto the price, it's worth shopping around.

Public express buses

Long-distance public bus services generally operate on an **express** basis. Not that they don't make any stops: besides calling at all major towns en route, an "express" bus will stop as often as necessary on the way out of town until it's full, and will also let passengers off all over the place as it approaches its final destination. Still, express services are a lot faster and more comfortable than a local bus.

Express buses fall into two categories. **Day buses** usually cover the medium-distance routes (approximately 6–12 hours) and set off in the morning to arrive at their destination before nightfall or not long after. That means if a given journey takes, say, eight hours, you can be pretty sure that the last bus will depart no later than midday. Day buses may be 2x2s or 2x3s and can vary a lot in comfort level – some are fiendishly short on legroom.

Night buses, which operate on the longest routes (ten- to twenty-plus hours), depart in the afternoon or early evening to arrive the following morning. On these you're assured of 2x2 reclining seats with padding

and adequate legroom, although a few hours in the seat will reveal the extent of the padding, and the legroom may be taken up by other people's luggage. Between all the lurching, honking, tea stops and blaring music you won't get much sleep (bring earplugs and something to cover your eyes). Note that night journeys are also more dangerous, since it's not uncommon for drivers to fall asleep at the wheel. The main advantage of travelling by night is that it frees up time during the day and saves on the cost of accommodation (a prime consideration for Nepali passengers).

Like tourist buses, and unlike local buses, express buses allow you to **reserve seats** in advance. Do this, or you could end up in one of the ejector seats along the back bench. Numbering begins from the front of the bus: the prized seats #1A and #2A, on the left by the front door, often have the most legroom. Check the seating chart to see what's available – there will always be one for night buses, though not necessarily for day buses. Fortunately Nepalis don't tend to plan very far ahead, so you can usually get away with buying a ticket just a few hours beforehand; the exception is during the big autumn festivals, when buses are packed with people heading back to their villages and seats get booked up several days in advance. The ticket should indicate the vehicle number, which is useful for verifying that you're on the right bus. Normally seats can be reserved only at the bus's point of origin; getting on at a major junction along the route may be possible, but you'll probably have to stand.

Every public bus has at least one **conductor**, often a young boy. Most know enough English to at least understand where you want to go, and are remarkably diligent in letting you know when you've got there. If a conductor seems to disappear with your five-hundred-rupee note, it'll be because he's waiting until he's collected enough tickets to give you the change – which almost always will be exactly the right amount.

Most express buses give you the choice of stowing your **baggage** on the roof or in a locked hold in the back, and you may be able to persuade the conductor to let you take luggage on your lap, or stow it in the gangway. Having all your things with you is of course the best insurance policy against theft, but it's inconvenient. Putting bags in the hold is usually the next-safest option, especially on night buses; you may need to pay a small fee at the bus's point of origin. Baggage stowed on the roof is probably okay during the day, but you can never be completely sure – if possible, lock your bag to the roof rack, and keep an eye out during stops; you don't need to pay to store bags on the roof, but a small tip to the conductor may encourage him to keep his eyes open.

Local buses

Serving mainly shorter routes or slow, remote roads, **local buses** are ancient, battered contraptions with seats designed for midgets. The idea is to cram as many passengers in as possible – indeed, a bus isn't making money until it's nearly full to bursting, and it can get awfully suffocating inside. This can lead to infuriating false starts, as the driver inches forward and the conductor runs around trying to round up customers, since no local bus will leave the station with empty seats. Once on the road, the bus will stop any time it's flagged down.

Local buses often depart from a separate bus park or just a widening in the road, and tickets are bought on board. Since seats often can't be reserved, the only way to be sure of getting one is to board the bus early and wait. If you're just picking up a bus along the way you're likely to join the crush standing in the aisle, and low ceilings add to the discomfort.

Unless your **bag** is small, it will have to go on the roof; during daylight hours it should be safe there as long as it's locked, but again, keep all valuables on your person. **Riding on the roof** can actually be quite pleasant in good weather, but it's dangerous, illegal and you'll only be allowed to do it in remote areas between checkposts (except during big holidays, when the rules are relaxed). Even if you've got a seat, **safety** is a concern: these buses are often overworked, overloaded and poorly maintained. The newspapers are full of stories about buses in remote districts plunging into rivers or off precipices. On main roads, however,

it's comforting to remind yourself that at least you're travelling slowly.

By jeep and truck

Almost every roadhead in the country is being extended, often on local initiative, by way of a dirt track making its painful way deeper into the countryside. And where the bus comes to the end of the road, you can rely on finding a **jeep** to take you further. In some parts of the country you'll find old Land Rovers, in other parts Indian Marutis or even Nepalese Sherpas, but they're almost always fairly battered, often with some ingenious modifications to allow them to take more passengers. Where the road is well-used, jeeps of this sort leave as soon as they're full. In more remote areas, there may be just one vehicle making a single, daily return trip. Roads of this sort are prone to being closed by landslides, fallen trees and other natural shocks, particularly in the monsoon.

If no buses or jeeps are going your way, you may be able to get there by **truck**. Most trucks in Nepal are ungainly Indian-built Tatas ferrying fuel to Kathmandu or building materials to hill boomtowns, or "Public Carriers" – gaily decorated hauliers-for-hire operating on both sides of the Indian border. Many do a sideline in hauling passengers, and charge set fares comparable to what you'd pay on a bus. Fully laden, they go even slower than buses. The ride is comfortable enough if you get a seat in the cab, and certainly scenic if you have to sit or stand in the back – either way, the trip is bound to be eventful.

However, trucks aren't licensed as passenger vehicles, and so take little interest in passenger **safety** and are unaccountable for losses: watch your luggage. Women journeying by truck will probably prefer to join up with a companion.

If you're really stuck, you could try **hitching**. There aren't many private vehicles in Nepal, though, and anyone you manage to flag down will expect money.

By plane and helicopter

There may be times when $80 spent on an **internal flight** seems a small price to pay to avoid 24 hours on a bus or a week retracing your steps along a trail – and, of course, the views are thrown in free: an hour-long scenic loop out of Kathmandu, the so-called **"mountain flight"** is very popular among tourists who want to get an armchair view of Everest – for more on these, see p.176. Internal flights are generally reliable and reasonably priced (usually between $50 and $100, depending on the length), though try to steer clear of the government-owned Royal Nepal Airlines Corporation (RNAC), which has a deservedly poor reputation.

Given Nepal's mountainous terrain, aircraft play a vital role in the country's transport network, especially in the west, where planes are often used to carry in food during the winter. Of the thirty or so cities and towns with **airstrips** (see map below) almost half are two or more days' walk from a road. Most flights begin or end in Kathmandu, but two other **airports** in the Tarai – Nepalganj in the west, Biratnagar in the east – serve as secondary hubs. Popular destinations, such as Lukla in the Everest region, or a major Tarai city like Nepalganj, get up to ten flights a day. Obscure airstrips, however, particularly those in the remoter hill areas, may receive only one flight a week in certain seasons – or, indeed, none at all, if services are disrupted by Maoist activity. What's more, these less profitable routes tend to be served exclusively by RNAC, which was facing possible shutdown at the time of writing, though it may yet survive as a partially privatized concern (check with travel agents in Nepal). For

frequencies and flight times, see the "Travel Details" section at the end of each chapter; and double check locally.

Numerous **private airlines** compete fairly efficiently on the main domestic inter-city and tourist trekking routes. Their prices are around ten percent higher than RNAC, but are well worth it for increased reliability and flexibility; for more on booking tickets with them, see Chapter 1, p.178. Bear in mind, though, that many companies are going through a process of mergers, name changes and bankruptcies.

Three makes of propeller **planes** designed for mountain flying are principally used in Nepal: 44-seat Avros, 18-seat Dornier 228s and 17-seat Twin Otters. Flying in one of these small craft is a splendid way to get clear views of the Himalaya and the incredible maze of Nepal's middle hills. Thermals can make the ride bumpy, and landings on mountain airstrips are always memorable: many runways double as pastures, and a klaxon is sounded a few minutes before the arrival of aircraft to warn locals to get their livestock out of the way.

Domestic airlines and routes

Buddha Air Hattisar ☎01/542494, ⓦwww.buddhaair.com. Bhadrapur, Bhairawa, Biratnagar, Nepalganj, Pokhara.
Cosmic Air Kamaladi ☎01/246882, ⓦwww.cosmicair.com. Bharatpur, Bhairawa, Biratnagar, Nepalganj, Pokhara, Tumlingtar.

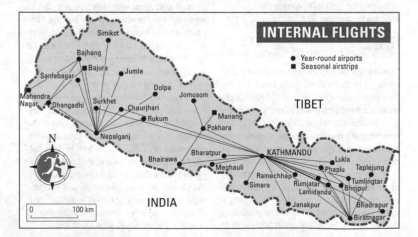

INTERNAL FLIGHTS

● Year-round airports
■ Seasonal airstrips

Gorkha Airlines Hattisar ☎ 01/436576, ⒲ www.yomari.com/gorkha. Bharatpur, Pokhara, Simara, Tumlingtar.

Mountain Air Hattisar ☎ 01/489065. Bhadrapur, Bhairawa, Biratnagar, Nepalganj, Pokhara.

Necon Air Sinamangal ☎ 01/480565, ⒲ www.neconair.com. Bhadrapur, Bhairawa, Biratnagar, Janakpur, Nepalganj, Pokhara, Simara.

Royal Nepal Airlines (RNAC) corner of New Road and Kantipath ☎ 01/220757. Tourist sales office handles flights to Bharatpur, Lukla and Pokhara. The domestic sales office, in the same building, handles all other internal flights: Bhojpur, Biratnagar, Chaurjhari, Dhangadhi, Lamidanda, Nepalganj, Ramechhap, Rumjatar, Surkhet, Tumlingtar.

Shangri-la Air Kamalpokhari ☎ 01/410026. Bhadrapur, Bharatpur, Bhairawa, Lukla, Nepalganj, Pokhara, Phaplu, Simara, Rumjatar.

Skyline Airways Hattisar ☎ 01/488657, ⒲ www.skyair.com.np. Bharatpur, Lamidanda, Lukla, Phaplu, Pokhara, Simara.

Yeti Airlines Lazimpath ☎ 01/421215. Lamidanda, Lukla, Meghauli, Phaplu, Rumjatar, Simara.

Sample domestic airfares

The following are one-way fares on **RNAC** at the time of writing, including a $2 insurance surcharge. Though quoted fares on private airlines are around ten percent more expensive, discounts can sometimes be found on busy routes.

Kathmandu to: Bhairawa ($74); Bharatpur ($50); Biratnagar ($79); Janakpur ($57); Lukla ($85); Nepalganj ($11); Pokhara ($63); Tumlingtar ($59).

Nepalganj to: Jumla ($46); Simikot ($90).

Pokhara to: Jomosom ($57).

Tickets

Tickets can be bought in hard currency only, usually US dollars. You can **book** tickets through a travel agent, who will have a handle on who's flying where and when, and may be able to offer a small discount off the quoted fare. At the time of writing, all domestic airlines were levying a $2 insurance surcharge on top of the prices quoted in the guide.

At off-peak times or away from the trekking routes – in the Tarai, for instance – you shouldn't have any trouble getting a **seat**. However, during the trekking season, flights out of airstrips along the popular trails may be booked up months in advance by trekking agencies. If you're finding you can't get a seat, all is not lost. Agencies often overbook, releasing their unused tickets on the day of departure, so you may be able to buy a returned ticket from the airline on the morning you want to travel. Otherwise, adjust your schedule and go a week or two later, by which time the agency peak should have tapered off.

Check in early for popular flights, which are often overbooked by the airlines. Getting there early will also improve your chances of getting a seat on the side of the plane with the best mountain views.

Safety and delays

Government scrutiny of the airline industry is minimal, and while it's true that most of the aircraft are leased from overseas companies that set maintenance and pilot performance requirements, the fact is that there are **crashes** every year. Terrain is the main problem; baggage overloading is another. Radar was installed at Kathmandu airport after the Airbus crashes of 1992, but for the most part you are relying on pilot skill and experience. It's a close call whether flying is more, or less, dangerous than travelling by bus, but all of this is perhaps a moot point because your whole attitude toward risk will change about five minutes into your first taxi ride in Nepal.

Another problem with flying in Nepal is **delays and cancellations**, usually due to weather. Few airstrips have even the simplest landing beacons, and many of them are surrounded by hills, so there must be good visibility to land – if there's fog or the cloud ceiling is too low, the plane won't fly – hence the old Nepali pilots' adage: "We don't fly when it's cloudy because the clouds have rocks in them". When planes are grounded, delays multiply throughout the system. Since clouds usually increase as the day wears on, delays often turn into cancellations. If your flight is cancelled, you may be placed at the bottom of a waiting list, rather than being given space on the next available flight; in busy times or during extended periods of bad weather, the wait can be several days. Pad your schedule accordingly.

Helicopters

A half-dozen companies offer charter **helicopter** services in Nepal. What they'd like to sell you is a three- or four-hour sightseeing junket up to a mountain meadow and back. At $100–200 per hour per person, that's a pretty expensive picnic – the mountain flight is a better deal (see p.37). More commonly, though, these services are used by trekking parties with more money than time, who charter a chopper for upwards of $1000 to pick them up at a prearranged spot to save them several days' backtracking. Companies are supposed to charter only entire aircraft, but in practice if a helicopter is returning empty from a trekking landing strip to Kathmandu or Pokhara, the pilot will take on individual passengers for about the same price as a seat on a plane. You can arrange this informally yourself at airstrips, or go through local agents.

Driving and cycling

It's really liberating to have your **own wheels** in Nepal. Besides being faster and more comfortable than a bus, a car (or jeep) will enable you to get to places you'd never go by bus, stop wherever and whenever you like, and carry more cargo. **Rented vehicles** always come with a driver in Nepal, which means you don't have to grapple with the country's chaotic roads. However, if you rent a motorcycle or bring your own vehicle to Nepal, you'll find that **driving** is sometimes fun, sometimes terrifying, and always challenging. Most advice can be summed up in two words: **drive defensively**. Whether it's because of inexperience or exuberance, lack of driving instruction or sheer Hindu fatalism, Nepali drivers can pull some dangerous stunts.

The hairiest driving is in Kathmandu, where the roads are incredibly congested not only with vehicles but also pedestrians, cyclists, cows, pushcarts and street vendors. Observance of traffic regulations is fairly lax, with drivers constantly jockeying for position irrespective of lane markings or traffic signals. On **roundabouts**, confusion arises (for visitors) because priority officially goes to vehicles *entering* the intersection, not those already going around it. Drivers use horns rather

than indicators to signal a manoeuvre, and only haphazardly at that: tempos and minibuses will often pull over without warning, so you have to learn to anticipate their moves.

Follow local practice and use your **horn** liberally: to alert other vehicles and pedestrians that you're there, when rounding sharp corners, when overtaking (hence the "Horn Please" sign painted on the back of most trucks) and whenever overcome with morbid exhilaration. Most vehicles you want to overtake will want you to wait for their signal – a hand wave or – confusingly – a right-turning indicator.

Watch your **speed** on the highways, which are rarely free of unmarked hazards: potholes, landslides, washed-out bridges, speed bumps, grain spread out to dry, goats and the like. For this and other reasons, don't drive after dark if you can help it. Drunk drivers may be encountered at all hours of the day, and even the sober ones often try to overtake on blind curves. Cyclists can be particularly erratic. Take special care around pedestrians, who, even in cosmopolitan Kathmandu, sometimes behave as if they've just walked out of the jungle – a case of Nepalese fatalism at its most fatal. If you're on a bike, children may try to throw things under your wheels. Dogs and chickens frequently behave suicidally. And watch out for those **cows**: the penalty for killing a cow is up to twelve years in prison, the same as for killing a person.

Finally, **filling stations** can be found on main roads at the outskirts of all major towns. Fuel is *tel*, but some sell only diesel (*dizel*), but they'll show you where you can get petrol (*petrol*) – in smaller towns it's dispensed unofficially by small shops. At the time of writing, the cost of petrol was just under Rs50 per litre.

Cars and jeeps

In Kathmandu and Pokhara, chartering a **taxi** by the day is the cheapest option for short or medium-distance journeys – worth considering to get to certain trekking trailheads with your wits intact. The going rate for trips within the Kathmandu or Pokhara valleys is about $20 a day, including petrol. Most taxis aren't roadworthy for long distances, and usually aren't permitted to travel beyond certain checkpoints anyway. If you do take a taxi on a longer trip, **petrol** becomes a more significant expense, so the driver will probably prefer to quote a price for a particular destination or itinerary, plus an extra $8 or so for every night he's away from home to cover meals and accommodation.

Jeeps (or Land Rovers) are better for longer journeys and larger parties, and also for toting kayaks, bikes or other bulky gear. They can be rented through some travel agents in Kathmandu, Pokhara and the bigger Tarai cities, and cost proportionately more than cars. Prices for all vehicle rentals are by negotiation, so it's a good idea to have your lodge owner help. Avis and Hertz have representatives in Kathmandu, but renting a vehicle through them is much more expensive (about $50 a day).

Motorcycles and scooters

A **motorcycle** requires more nerve than a car, but it's also more versatile. You'll want to have had plenty of riding experience and you should of course have a licence, though it's unlikely to be checked. You may be expected to leave an air ticket, passport or large sum of money as a deposit. Check brakes, oil and fuel level, horn, lights and indicators before setting off, and make sure to get a **helmet**.

Indian-made street bikes can be rented in Kathmandu and Pokhara; you'll **pay** about $5 a day, and petrol is extra. These small (100cc or 135cc) two-stroke models aren't suitable for covering hundreds of kilometres a day but are quite sufficient for doing day-trips or even touring the country at a leisurely pace. Top speed is about 70kph, which is faster than you really want to be going on Nepali highways anyway. Two people can share a bike – you'll see three or even four Nepalis riding together – but doubling up can be rather nerve-racking over long distances and on rough roads. Riding solo, you can handle just about anything a four-wheel-drive vehicle can. Some places also rent dirt bikes, though these are quite a bit more expensive, and the only reason to take one would be to really tear up the trails, which isn't appropriate in Nepal.

Quite a few travellers bring 350cc or 500cc Enfields into Nepal from India, where they can easily be purchased and later resold to other travellers. These bikes have a lot more heft for long-distance cruising, and can easily carry two riders and gear, but are heavy and hard to handle off-road.

Motorcycling carries some **risk**; the safety tips above apply doubly for motorcyclists. Also note that rented bikes carry no insurance – if you break anything, you pay for it. Stick to back roads (they're more pleasant anyway), and take care on wet dirt roads, which can be extremely slippery.

By bicycle

A rented **bicycle** (*saikal*) is the logical choice for most day-to-day getting around. One-speeders (usually Indian-made Hero models) are good enough for most around-town cycling, and **cost** Rs150–200 per day, though you may be able to negotiate a deal for a longer period. They're incredibly heavy and their brakes are poor, but they're sturdy and have built-in locks.

For more money, a **mountain bike** will get you there in greater comfort, and is essential for longer distances or anything steep. Even a one-speed mountain bike, with its fatter tyres, better geometry and grabbier brakes, makes an improvement over the old sit-up-and-beg design. A few shops in Kathmandu and one in Pokhara rent top-quality mountain bikes, but most of the models available are cheap Indian and Taiwanese imitations of their Western namesakes that don't stand up well to rough roads or off-road use. (More tips on mountain-biking and bike rental are given in Chapter Nine.)

Bike rental shops are rare outside of Kathmandu, Pokhara and Chitwan, but you can often strike a deal with a lodge owner or cycle repairman. Check brakes, spokes, tyres and chain carefully before setting off – the last thing you want is for something to break on a remote mountain road. A bell is pretty well essential. Repair shops are everywhere, but they won't have mountain bike parts. **Theft** is a concern, especially with a flashier bike – be sure to take it inside your guesthouse compound at night.

City transport

Taxis, identified by black number plates, are confined mainly to Kathmandu and Pokhara, and you'll find details on their idiosyncrasies in the relevant sections of the guide. A metered ride will cost about Rs15 per kilometre but, on popular tourist routes, fixed fares work out to be around twice that. You can hire a taxi by the day (see p.39).

Tempos – three-wheeled, passenger-carrying scooters also known as autorikshas or tuk-tuks – are sometimes the best way to get from A to B. They come in two forms. Metered tempos have room for two or three passengers (only one if you've got a lot of luggage). In Kathmandu they're as common as taxis, though only slightly cheaper and quite a bit less comfortable; they're rarely found outside the capital. Fixed-route "Vikram" tempos fit eight or ten (or more), set off when they're full, stop at designated points, and usually charge only a few rupees per head. Both kinds are noisy and put out noxious fumes, although battery-powered safaa ("clean") tempos make a more pleasant alternative in Kathmandu.

Pedal-powered cycle **rikshas** are slow and bumpy, but may come in handy for short distances through Kathmandu's narrow, crowded streets. In Tarai cities they're an invaluable way to get around without breaking into a heavy sweat. Be sure to establish the fare before setting off (Rs5–20 per kilometre, depending on how touristy the place is).

Few cities in Nepal are so large that you're dependent on public transport. Where available, **city buses**, minibuses and microbuses are usually too crowded, slow or infrequent to be worthwhile, but you may find yourself using them to visit certain sights in the Kathmandu Valley. Fares are just a few rupees.

Accommodation

Finding a place to sleep is hardly ever a problem in Nepal, although only the established tourist centres offer much of a choice. Friendly and well-managed guesthouses are found almost anywhere that attracts tourists. If you go trekking or visit a wildlife park, you'll find a greater variety of accommodation, from rude lodges along the trail to luxurious tented camps in the jungle. A handful of village-stay schemes allow you to taste traditional rural life.

Prices vary considerably, depending on where you stay and when. You can pay anything from literally a few pennies per night in a trekking lodge to over $150 in a wildlife-viewing resort, but guesthouses, where most travellers stay, typically charge between $3 and $20. Outside the October to December high season, or if things are unusually quiet, prices can drop by up to fifty percent: the simple question "*discount paunchha?*" (any discount?) will often do the trick. Nearly all guesthouses have a wide spread of rooms in different classes, from budget, shared-bath boxes to rooms with televisions and an attached bathroom. In the Tarai, prices depend on whether the room has a fan, a basic air-cooler or full air-conditioning (a/c).

Hotels and the more popular guesthouses in the Kathmandu Valley, Pokhara and Chitwan take **bookings**, and reservations are worth considering in the busy seasons, during local festivals or if you expect to arrive late in the day. Otherwise it's rarely worth the bother, especially in the cheapest places, which may have a hazy notion of how to take bookings, or even how to use the telephone. Nevertheless, listings in the guide give phone numbers for all lodgings that have them, and sometimes fax or email too.

Single rooms are usually doubles offered at between half and two-thirds of the price.

Accommodation price codes

All accommodation listed in this guide has been graded according to the **price codes** below, which are based on the cost of the least expensive double room in the October–November high season, and are inclusive of ten–twelve percent tax where it applies. At other times, proprietors are usually more amenable to bargaining, and you may be able to negotiate a drop of as much as fifty percent. In budget places, the code may relate to rooms with a "common" (shared) bathroom; expect to pay a bit more – say in the ❸ range instead of ❷ – for a room with an attached bathroom. Where there's a real spread of rooms available in different classes and at very different prices, we've given prices as a range, such as ❷–❺.

❶ Less than Rs200 ❹ US$5–10 ❼ US$40–75
❷ Rs200–300 ❺ US$10–20 ❽ US$75–150
❸ Rs300–400 ❻ US$20–40 ❾ Over US$150

Lodges

Off the beaten track, **lodges** are geared for Nepali travellers, and are usually known as "hotel and lodge" (confusingly, the "hotel" bit means there's a diner). Some are luxurious – in bigger Tarai cities there will usually be at least one upscale place with creature comforts (even a/c) – but for the most part Nepalis are more concerned about the quality of the rice than the cleanliness of the bathrooms, so you may have to settle for something less salubrious. Stark concrete floors, cold-water showers and smelly squat toilets are the rule, and you'll rarely pay more than Rs150, often half that. Often not much English is spoken. Sheets and cotton quilts are usually provided, but it's a good idea to bring your own sleeping sheet to protect against bedbugs and lice. Noise is always a problem: consider earplugs. In the Tarai, mosquito netting (or mosquito coils) and a ceiling fan that works are crucial.

This is not to say that Nepali lodges are to be avoided. Often the most primitive places – the ones with no electricity, where you sit on the mud floor by a smoky fire and eat with your hosts – are the most rewarding. **Trekking lodges** can take this form (though there are some remarkably comfortable lodges out there too), and are described in Chapter Seven.

Guesthouses

Most tourist-oriented places to stay in Nepal call themselves **guesthouses**. This category covers everything from primitive flophouses to fairly well-appointed small hotels. Many places offer a spread of rooms at different prices, and inexpensive dorm beds are sometimes available too. By and large, those that cater to foreigners do so very efficiently: most innkeepers speak excellent English, and can arrange anything for you from laundry to bus tickets to trekking/porter hire. Those that serve a mainly Nepali clientele are usually (though not always) more basic, and are less attuned to the peculiar needs of Westerners.

Despite assurances to the contrary, you can't necessarily count on constant **hot water** (many rely on solar panels) nor uninterrupted electricity (power cuts are common). If constant hot water is important to you, ask what kind of water-heating system the guesthouse has – best of all is "geyser" (pronounced "geezer"), which means an electric immersion heater or backup.

All the really cheap guesthouses will have a safe for **valuables**, and better places have lock-boxes in each room. It's a good idea to leave your passport, air ticket and most of your money there; a photocopy of the relevant pages of your passport will suffice for moneychanging (but not for getting visas or trekking permits).

The cheeriest and most efficiently run guesthouses are highlighted throughout the guide, but remember that recommendations are often self-defeating and can result in instant price hikes. Also, watch out for name changes, which suggest a change in ownership or an attempt to escape a bad reputation.

Budget guesthouses

Kathmandu and Pokhara have their own tourist quarters where fierce competition among **budget guesthouses** ensures great value. In these enclaves, all but the very cheapest places provide hot running water (though perhaps only sporadically), flush toilets, foam mattresses and (usually) clean sheets and quilts – a sleeping bag should not be necessary. Elsewhere in Nepal, expect rooms to be plainer and maybe scruffier, and the innkeepers to be less savvy about what you might want. In the Tarai, a room fan is normally provided. Most guesthouses also offer some sort of roof-terrace or garden, a supply of (supposedly) boiled and filtered water and a phone. They're never heated, however, which makes them rather cold in winter.

Rooms in most budget places **cost** Rs200–400 (❷–❸), and standards can vary considerably. It's well worth remembering that there's usually a choice of **shared bathroom** or en-suite. Rooms that cost less than about Rs300 are likely to be "common bath"; pay more and you can be fairly sure of "attached". The advantages of attached baths are obvious: you don't have to lock up your valuables, walk up and down halls in partial undress, or wait until the bathroom becomes free (a disaster if you've got the runs). In cheaper places, however, attached bathrooms aren't necessarily an asset, as they can make the room damp and smelly.

Midrange guesthouses

Midrange guesthouses (for lack of a better term) are becoming increasingly popular. These tend to be more-spacious buildings where there's a lobby of sorts (often with a TV), the rooms have carpeting, nicer furniture, a fan and maybe a phone, toilet paper is provided in the bathrooms, the hot water is more reliable and daily maid service is available. The better ones will provide a portable electric heater in winter. Most quote their prices in dollars, though you can pay in rupees. Some may add ten percent VAT on top and many even accept payment by credit card.

Figure on **paying** $5–20 (❹–❺) for a double room of this sort. Even if everything is listed as attached bath, there may be a couple of cheaper rooms with common bath, so it's well worth asking what's on offer; this is a good way to open up price negotiations, too.

Hotels and resorts

It's hard to generalize about the more expensive **hotels and resorts**. Some charge a hefty premium to insulate you from the Nepal you came to see, while others, in their own way, offer unique experiences of the country. Prices for international-type features begin around the $40 mark (❼) but expect to pay more like $75 a night (❽) or more for a genuinely classy experience.

This guide also recommends several smaller resort hotels that offer something unique, like a breathtaking view – or the only hot shower for miles around. After a trek or a long spell of roughing it, a night or two in one of these places can be just what the doctor ordered.

Jungle lodges and **tented camps** inside the Tarai wildlife parks are the most expensive options of all. A stay in one is indeed the experience of a lifetime, but if $100 or more per night is beyond your reach, there are plenty of more affordable outfits just outside Chitwan and Bardia national parks.

Camping

Perhaps surprisingly, **camping** doesn't come high on the agenda in Nepal. Much of the country is well settled, every flat patch of ground is farmed, and rooms are so cheap that camping offers little saving. The only developed commercially operated campground is in Pokhara.

It's a different story, of course, if you're **rafting or trekking**, and camping is also possible in certain jungle areas near the Tarai wildlife parks. Long-distance cyclists might find it useful to bring a tent along to avoid spending nights in roadside fleapits en route to more interesting places. Between October and May, many terraces in the hills are left fallow, and you can pitch a tent if you ask permission and keep out of the owner's way. Set up well away from villages, unless you want to be the locals' entertainment for the evening. Don't burn wood – the locals need it more than you do. An unattended tent will probably be safe if zipped shut, but anything left outside is liable to disappear.

Village stays and homestays

Nepal is a predominantly rural society, and its rich culture and ethnic diversity are best experienced in its villages. A growing number of programmes enable visitors to stay overnight in private homes in traditional villages far from the tourist trails. **Village stays** (or village tourism, as it's called in the business) offer a unique opportunity for comfortable cultural immersion, and could become a good way to disperse visitors and spread the economic benefits of tourism into rural areas. The idea is that a tour operator contracts with a whole village to accommodate and entertain guests; rooms in local houses are fitted with bathrooms and a few tourist-style comforts, host families are trained to prepare meals that won't disturb delicate Western digestions, and a guide accompanies the guests to interpret. Participating villages tend to be located a couple of hours' walk from the nearest road – close enough to be easily accessible for less-than-fit visitors, yet far enough to receive less outside influence than even the smallest village on a trekking route.

Village tourism was pioneered by Nepal Village Resorts (℡01/430187, ⊛www .nepalvillage.com) in Sirubari, a Gurung settlement southwest of Pokhara. Another Gurung village, Chisapani, southeast of Pokhara near Rupa Tal, is the venue for programmes run by the Pokhara-based Child Welfare Scheme (℡061/22892, ⊛www .naturesgracelodge.com/chisapani.html). Another operator, Lama Adventure Treks and Expeditions, runs programmes in two Tamang villages southeast of Kathmandu; details of this and Kathmandu-based schemes can be found on p.170. Most village tourism schemes prefer groups of at least three or four people, so if you're an individual or couple you should contact the companies well in advance and adjust your schedule to co-ordinate with already-scheduled departures.

A few language institutes and other organizations in Kathmandu also organize **informal homestays** with individual families in and around the valley. Most of these are intended specifically to provide Nepali language immersion, but it's a great way to make local friends, whatever the official motive. At least one programme is set up for tourists just wanting to spend a weekend with a Nepali family; see p.170.

Eating and drinking

Nepal – specifically Kathmandu – is renowned as the budget eating capital of Asia. Sadly, its reputation is based not on Nepali but pseudo-Western food: pizza, chips (fries), "sizzling" steaks and apple pie are the staples of tourist restaurants. Outside the popular areas, the chief complaint of travellers is lack of variety in the diet, though with a little extra willingness to experiment, an extraordinary range of dishes can be found.

Indeed, a vast range of flavours can be found just in **daal bhaat tarkaari**, the national dish of white rice, lentils, lightly curried vegetables and pickles; it can also be disappointingly bland, though. In the Kathmandu Valley, the indigenous Newars

have their own unique cuisine of spicy meat and vegetable dishes, while *roti* (bread) and the vast range of Indian curries, snacks and sweets comes into play in the Tarai; in the mountains, the traditional diet is essentially Tibetan, consisting of soups, pastas, potatoes and toasted flour. Noodle dishes are available everywhere as snack foods, giving a taste of China's proximity.

Cheap as it is, food tends to be the biggest daily **cost** for budget travellers. A tourist dinner will cost Rs150–300 per person; double that in a really posh place. *Daal bhaat*, which usually has the advantage of coming with unlimited refills, costs roughly Rs50 anywhere except in tourist restaurants (where it'll cost at least double), and you can fill up on road snacks like noodles or *momo* dumplings for pennies.

Where to eat

Tourist restaurants in Kathmandu, Pokhara and a few other well-visited places show an uncanny knack for sensing exactly what travellers want and simulating it with the most basic ingredients. Some specialize in particular cuisines, but the majority attempt to do a little of everything. Display cases full of extravagant cakes and pies are a standard come-on.

Local **Nepali diners** (*bhojanalaya* or, confusingly enough, *hotel*) are traditionally humble affairs, offering a limited choice of dishes or just *daal bhaat*. Menus don't exist, but the food will normally be on display or cooking in full view, so all you have to do is point. Utensils should be available on request, but if not, try doing as Nepalis do and eat with your hand – the right one only. (See "Cultural hints", p.74, for more on social taboos relating to eating.) In towns and cities, eateries tend to be dark, almost conspiratorial places, unmarked and hidden behind curtains. On the highways they're bustlingly public and spill outdoors in an effort to win business. Tarai cities always have a fancy (by Nepali standards) restaurant or two, patronized by businessmen and Indian tourists, and lots of *dhaba* (the Indian equivalent of *bhojanalaya*).

It might take some time before you start appreciating the fine differences between *bhojanalaya* and other traditional establishments. **Teahouses** (*chiya pasal*) really only sell tea and basic snacks, while the simple **taverns** (*bhatti*) of the Kathmandu Valley and the western hills put the emphasis on alcoholic drinks, but also serve basic Nepali meals. Trailside, both *chiya pasal* and *bhatti* are typically modest operations run out of

family kitchens. **Sweet shops** (*mithai pasal*), found in bigger towns and identified by their shiny display cases, are intended to fill the gap between the traditional midmorning and early evening meals; besides sweets and tea, they also do South Indian and Nepali savoury snacks.

Street vendors sell fruit, nuts, roasted corn, fried bread and various fried specialities. As often as not, food will come to you when you're travelling – at every bus stop, vendors will clamber aboard or hawk their wares through the window.

Vegetarians will feel at home in Nepal, since meat is considered a luxury. Meatless dishes get more interesting the closer you get to India, with some orthodox Hindu restaurants in the Tarai and in Kathmandu billing themselves as "pure vegetarian". Tourist menus invariably include veggie items.

Nepali food

Daal bhaat tarkaari isn't just the most popular meal in Nepal – for many Nepalis it's the *only* meal they ever eat, twice a day, every day of their lives, and they won't feel they've eaten properly without it. Indeed, in much of hill Nepal, *bhaat* (rice) is a synonym for food and *khaanaa* (food) is a synonym for rice. The *daal bhaat* served in restaurants ranges from excellent to derisory – it's a meal that's really meant to be eaten at home – so if you spend much time trekking or travelling off the beaten track you'll probably quickly tire of it.

That said, a good **achhaar** (a sort of relish or pickle made with tomato, radish or whatever's in season) can liven up a *daal bhaat* tremendously. And once you've entered the world of *daal bhaat*, you'll learn that there are endless subtle variations in the textures, flavours and grades of rice (basmati is just for beginners – try *pokhreli* or *mansuli*) and in the tastes and colours of good *daal* – from the buttery, yellow gunge of *raharko daal*, to the king of winter lentils, *maasko daal*, which starts off green but is cooked in an iron pot until it turns black. Among the vegetable accompaniments, look out for *tama*, a sour, soup-like dish made with bamboo shoots, and *gundruk*, the tangy national dish of fermented vegetables – it's a staple in homes that can't afford lentils. Salty spinach and cauliflower with potatoes are other standards.

Daal bhaat is often served on a gleaming steel platter divided into compartments; add the *daal* and other condiments to the rice in the main compartment, a little at a time, knead the resulting mixture into mouth-sized balls with the right hand, then push it off the fingers into your mouth with the thumb. One price covers unlimited refills, except in tourist-savvy establishments that have adopted the "plate system".

Unlike India, where the British influence means that many people eat three meals of breakfast, lunch and dinner, traditional **eating times** have never changed in Nepal. Most Nepalis begin the day with a cup of tea and little else, eating *daal bhaat* some time in the mid-morning (often around nine or ten o'clock) and again in the evening, with just a snack of potatoes, *makkai* (pop corn) or noodles in between. *Daal bhaat* times in Kathmandu are pushing later and later towards something like lunchtime and evening meals, but outside the city, especially on trekking routes, it's worth remembering that if you turn up for your *khaanaa* at noon it'll either be cold or take a long time to cook from scratch.

You'll usually be able to supplement – or replace – a plate of *daal bhaat* with small side dishes of *maasu* (meat) – chicken, goat or, in riverside bazaars, fish – marinated in yogurt and spices and fried in oil or *ghiu* (clarified butter). In Indian-influenced Tarai towns you can often get *taareko daal*, fried with *ghiu* and spices to produce a tastier variation, and *roti* instead of rice. **Sokuti** (dried, spiced meat fried in oil) is popular in eastern hill areas. You could make a meal out of rice or *chiura* (beaten, dried rice) and **sekuwa** (kebabs of spicy marinated meat chunks) or **taareko maachhaa** (fried fish), both common in the Tarai. If you're invited into a peasant home in the hills you might be served **dhedo** (a dough made from water mixed with toasted corn, millet or wheat flour) instead of rice. Some say it's *dhedo* with *gundruk*, not *daal bhaat*, that's the real national food of Nepal, though you'll never see it in a restaurant.

Nepali **desserts** include *khir* (rice pudding), *sikarni* (thick, whipped yogurt with cinnamon, raisins and nuts) and versions of Indian sweets (see opposite).

Newari food

Like many aspects of Newari culture, **Newari food** is all too often regarded as exotic but too weird for outsiders. It's like no other cuisine on earth: complex, subtle, delicious and devilishly hard to make: most dishes require absolutely fresh ingredients and/or very long preparation times.

Most specialities are quite spicy, and based around four mainstays: buffalo, rice, pulses and vegetables (especially radish). The Newars use every part of the buffalo: **momocha** (meat-filled steamed dumplings), **choyila** (buff cubes fried with spices and greens), **palula** (spicy buff with ginger sauce) and **kachila** (a paté of minced raw buff, mixed with ginger and mustard oil) are some of the more accessible dishes; others are made from tongue, stomach, lung, blood, bone marrow and so on. Because of caste restrictions, Newars rarely eat boiled **rice** outside the home. Newari restaurants therefore serve it in the form of **baji** (*chiura* in Nepali) – rice that's been partially cooked and then rolled flat and dried, looking something like rolled oats – or **chataamari** (a sort of pizza made with rice flour, usually topped with minced buff). Pulses and beans play a role in several other preparations, notably **woh** (fried lentil-flour patties, also known as *baara* in Nepali), **kwati** (a soup made with several varieties of sprouted beans), **musya palu** (a dry mix of roasted soya beans and ginger) and **bhuti** (boiled soya beans with spices and herbs). Various vegetable mixtures are available seasonally, including **pancha kol** (a curry made with five vegetables) and **alu achhaar** (boiled potato in a spicy sauce). Radish turns up in myriad forms of *achhaar*. Order two or three of these dishes per person, together with *baji*, and share them around.

International food

Kathmandu and Pokhara form twin poles of a scene that has grown progressively more surreal over the years: a free-market free-for-all of tourist restaurants offering a taste of every cuisine under the sun, often as not on the same menu. There's no denying that this **international food** is tasty, especially after a trek, but the sheer range of choice (in a country where most people struggle to put rice on the table twice a day) can seem fairly grotesque, and has the unfortunate side effect of isolating many visitors from Nepalese cooking.

. Sizzling steaks (usually buffalo meat), as well as lasagne and pizza have been the mainstay of the trade for years, but many restaurants have moved upmarket into dedicated cuisines, notably Chinese, French, Italian, Japanese, Korean, Mexican, Swiss and Thai. At their best, such places can be an excellent way to sample foreign foods at knock-down prices. At their worst, you'll just make yourself homesick – or plain sick, especially if you're ordering the sort of food that gets reheated. Monosodium glutamate is used almost universally, and this tends to make all tourist food taste the same after a while, and of course can cause allergic reactions (if MSG gives you trouble, try asking for food without "tasting powder").

Tourist restaurants are notoriously hard to recommend, as chefs are forever jumping ship and taking their menus with them. And don't assume that a crowded place must have good food: tourists tend to judge restaurants by their ambience, and in any case the more diners there are, the slower the service will be. (That said, a popular restaurant's high turnover should ensure fresher ingredients.)

Nepalis don't eat **breakfast**, but most tourist restaurants and guesthouses fill the gap with set deals of eggs, hash browns and toast. Porridge or muesli with curd make healthy alternatives. Out in the sticks, you'll have to adjust your eating schedule to mid-morning *daal bhaat*, or make do with a greasy omelette or packet-noodles.

Indian food

A full description of Indian dishes isn't possible here, but the ones you're most likely to encounter in Nepal are from **northern India**, such as **Mughlai** curries (thick and mildly spiced, often topped with boiled egg) and **tandoori** meats (baked in a clay oven called a *tandoor*, with special spices). **Roti** (bread) is the accompaniment to North Indian cuisine: *chapati* (round, flat pieces of unleavened bread) are always available in Indian restaurants, *naan* (bigger, chewier versions of the same), *paratha* (fried bread) and *puri* (puffy

fried *chapatis*). In the Tarai the best bets are **masaala** (with perfumed spices) curries, and you generally can't go wrong with **kofta**, spiced vegetable dumplings in curry.

In Kathmandu you'll also run across **South Indian** canteens, which serve a completely different and predominantly vegetarian cuisine. The staple dish here is the **dosa**, a rice-flour pancake rolled around curried potatoes and vegetables, served with **sambar** (a savoury tamarind sauce) and coconut chutney. You can also get *idli* (mashed rice, usually accompanied with *sambar*), *dahi vada* (lentil-flour dumplings in curd) and various vegetable curries.

And as for the incredible array of Indian **sweets**, well, that could fill a book in itself. A selection: *laddu*, yellow-and-orange speck-led semolina balls; *jelebi*, deep-fried pretzels of battered treacle; *barphi*, fudgy diamonds made from reduced milk, often decorated with edible silver leaf; *koloni*, a softer version of the same; *lal mohan*, brown spongy balls of flour in sweet syrup; *gulab jamun*, white spongy balls in rose-flavoured syrup; and *ras malai* and *ras maduri*, curd cheese blobs in sweet spiced cream. Really good sweets are found only in the bigger towns.

Tibetan food

Strictly speaking, "Tibetan" refers to nationals of Tibet, but the people of the Nepal Himalaya, collectively known as Bhotiyas, together with the people of several other highland ethnic groups, all eat what could be called **Tibetan food**.

Momo, arguably the most famous and popular of Tibetan dishes, are available throughout upland Nepal. Distant cousins to ravioli, the half-moon-shaped pasta shells are filled with meat, vegetables and ginger, steamed, and served with hot tomato *achhaar* and a bowl of broth. Fried *momo* are called *kothe*. Put the same stuffing ingredients inside a flour pastry shell, fry it and you get *shyaphaglo*, a sort of Tibetan meat pie. Tibetan cuisine is also justly celebrated for its excellent hearty soups, usually called **thukpa** or **thenthuk**, consisting of noodles or home-made pasta strips, meat and vegetables in broth.

For a special blowout, try **gyakok**, a huge meal for two that includes chicken, pork, prawns, fish, tofu, eggs and vegetables, and which gets its name from the brass container it's served in; *gyakok* is only found in tourist restaurants and has to be ordered several hours ahead. In trekking lodges you'll encounter pitta-like Tibetan **bread**, which, though unappealing on its own, can be made more interesting by the addition of honey or peanut butter.

The average Bhotiya peasant seldom eats any of the above: the most common stand-bys in the high country are **potatoes**, which you peel hot and dip into salt or chilli; they're also made into pancakes (*riki kur*). **Tsampa** (toasted barley flour) is often mixed with milk or tea to make a sort of paste, and makes an excellent breakfast substitute for imported porridge.

Road food

There's certainly no need to go hungry when you're travelling – **fast food and snacks** are available at every stop, and rarely cost more than Rs30 or so, usually half that. Since these dishes are prepared ahead of time, what you see is what you get. Common sit-down fare includes **pakauda** (fried, bready nuggets of battered vegetables, served with hot sauce), and **tarkaari ra roti** (vegetable – usually bean – curry served with *puris*). Another refreshing possibility is **dahi chiura**, a mixture of yogurt and beaten rice that isn't so different from the "muesli curd" served in tourist restaurants. If you're in more of a hurry, you can grab a handful of **samosa**, fried pyramids of pastry filled with curried vegetables, or carry away *papar* (*pappadums* – crispy fried discs made from chickpea flour), *baara* (fried lentil patties), *chap* (potato and garlic, battered and fried), *chana* (curried chickpeas), *taareko phul* (boiled egg, battered and fried) or other titbits on a leaf plate.

In the hill towns, especially in and around Kathmandu, huge aluminium steamers sitting by the restaurant door advertise Tibetan **momo** or the smaller, harder Newari version, **momocha**. Hugely popular as lunchtime snack, they're served with a hot and sour tomato sauce.

If nothing else, there will always be **noodles**. The Nepali word is *chao-chao*, but you'll quickly learn the brand names of the instant, packet variety from the ubiquitous painted advertising hoardings. As many as thirty local brands are in fierce competition: RaRa are a longstanding favourite, but WaiWai and YumYum were hot property at the time of writing. They can either be boiled as a soup, stir-fried as **chow mein**, or (with the exception of RaRa), eaten straight from the packet, the method favoured by children all over Nepal. Roadside vendors peddle **chat** (a mixture of peas or soya beans, radish, chilli, salt and lemon, all whisked together and served in a paper cone or on a leaf), roasted peanuts, coconut slivers, corn on the cob, *sel roti* (doughnuts) and lots more.

Other snacks

Imported **chocolates** are sold in tourist areas, and waxy Indian substitutes can be found in most towns. **Biscuits** and cheap boiled sweets (confusingly enough, called *chocolet* in Nepali) are sold at roadside stalls everywhere. **Ice cream** brands such as Kwality and Vadilal, available throughout the Kathmandu Valley and Pokhara, are safe, but steer well clear of unbranded varieties, and of water-based ice-pops or ice-lollies, nicknamed "cholera sticks" by expats. **Cheese**, produced from cow, buffalo and occasionally yak milk, comes in several styles and is sold in tourist areas and "factories" along trekking routes. (In the hills you might also come across *churpi*, a native version of cheese made from dried buttermilk or yogurt – it's inedibly hard, and is normally softened by being added to soup.)

Fruit

Which fruits are available depends on the season, but there's usually a good choice imported from India. Lovely **mandarin oranges**, which ripen throughout the late autumn and winter, grow from the Tarai up to around 1200m and are actually sweetest near the upper end of their range. Autumn and winter also bring **papaya** in the Tarai and lower hills, **Asian pears**, **apples** (grown in higher valleys but widely sold lower down), and **sugar cane**, a low-elevation crop that requires strong jaw muscles to appreciate. **Mangoes** from the Tarai start ripening in May and are available throughout most of the summer, as are **lychees**, **watermelons**, pineapples and guavas. Bananas are harvested year-round at the lower elevations and are sold from bicycles everywhere: sweet little stubbies are most commonly available.

Drinks

Water (*paani*) is automatically served with food in Nepali restaurants – sometimes it's been boiled, but verification is difficult, so it's best to pass. Various brands of bottled water are widely available and usually safe, although some tests have found unhealthy levels of germs in supposedly sterilized water; check that the seal is intact, too. You can always **purify your own** water (see p.27).

Soft drinks (*chiso*) are safe and sold in "cold stores" just about everywhere for around Rs15, but prices rise steadily as you move into roadless areas; Coke, Sprite (pronounced *isprite*) and Fanta orange or lemon are all fairly common. Fresh lemon soda, made with soda water and a squeeze of lemon or lime juice, makes a good alternative if you want to cut down on sugar, as does Frooti, a small green carton of mango juice that's sold everywhere.

Tea (*chiya*), something of a national beverage in Nepal, is traditionally brewed by boiling tea dust with milk (*dudh*) and water, along with heaps of sugar (*chini*) and a bit of ginger, cardamom or cinnamon. In tourist restaurants you'll be offered the choice of "black" or "milk" (pronounced *mlik*) tea, both usually brewed from a bag – you have to specify "Nepali" or "*masaala*" tea if you want it made the traditional way. You can also ask for lemon tea or "hot lemon". Tibetans and Bhotiyas take their tea with salt and yak butter, which is definitely an acquired taste.

Locally produced **coffee** is increasingly available in Nepal, and the beans aren't bad, though most restaurants just do a very milky instant. Indian-made espresso machines are getting to be in vogue, but they're usually only used to boil the milk.

Roadside stalls and tourist restaurants serve freshly squeezed **fruit juices**, according to the season, but the practice of adding water and sugar is widespread even among reputable restaurants – if the water comes from the tap, as is usually the case with roadside vendors, your chances of catching something are high. Tinned juice and fruit drinks in cartons are sold in many shops. A **lassi**, a blend of yogurt, water or ice (beware), sugar and fruit (or salt), always goes down very easily, but has the unpleasant habit of going through you in much the same way.

Alcohol

Beer (*biyar*) makes another fine accompaniment to Nepali and Indian food. Foreign brands brewed by local joint ventures – notably San Miguel, Carlsberg and Tuborg, which all taste much the same – have all but entirely squeezed out the domestic lagers. All beers come in 650ml bottles and cost a fairly standard Rs110. Non-recyclable aluminium cans are becoming more common.

An amazing and amusing selection of **spirits** is bottled in Nepal, ranging from the classic Khukuri Rum (dark and raisiny) to Ye Grand Earl whisky ("Glasgow – London – Kathmandu"). They're cheap and often rough, but tolerable when mixed with soft drinks. Shops sell them in convenient quarter-litre bottles, restaurants by the "peg" (30ml). Look out for regional specialities like the apricot and apple brandies of Marpha, north of Pokhara, and the aniseed-based *dudhiya*, or "milky one" (so-called because it goes cloudy when added to water) of the eastern Tarai. Imported spirits and **wine** are available in supermarkets and convenience stores at practically duty-free prices; many tourist restaurants and bars serve wine by the glass, and make **cocktails** with local or imported spirits.

Nepalis are avid **home brewers** and distillers, though Maoists have enforced severe restrictions and even bans on drink in areas under their control (alcoholism is rife in the hills). *Jaar* is the Nepali term for home-brewed beer, but it's commonly referred to by the Tibetan or hill word, *chhang*. Most often made from rice or millet, it can vary from a thin, sour brew to a powerful porridgey concoction. **Raksi**, which is ubiquitous in hill Nepal, is a distilled version of the same and bears a heady resemblance to tequila. The acrid taste of the cheaper "rum cocktails" found in Kathmandu bars give away their high raksi content. Harder to find,

Tobacco and paan

Nepalis love their **cigarettes** (*churot*). Even if you don't smoke, consider carrying a pack, as cigarettes are much appreciated as tips. Factories in Janakpur and Birganj manufacture dozens of cheap brands, most of them from a mixture of Nepali and Indian tobacco. Cheapest and roughest of all are **bidi**, rolled single leaves of the poorest tobacco, tied together in bundles of twenty (ask for *ek muthaa*). The cheaper packeted cigarettes, non-filters like Bijuli and Deurali, are as harsh as you'd expect for the price, while the filter on the Yak brand doesn't seem to help much. Khukuri are surprisingly smooth for the price, while the more expensive Shikhar are tasty but strong for most Western tastes. Marlboro (Reds and Lights) are available in tourist areas, but you could also try the luxury domestic brand, Surya, which is fairly similar in taste and strength. After the evening meal, old men may be seen smoking tobacco in a **hookah** (hubble-bubble), or occasionally passing around a **chilam** (clay pipe).

Many Nepali men make quite a production of preparing **chewing tobacco** (*surti*), slapping and rubbing it in the palm of the hand and mixing it with lime before placing a pinch behind the lower lip. *Surti* comes in little foil packets hung outside *kiraana pasal*, village stalls that sell cigarettes, matches, biscuits and the like.

At least as popular, particularly near India, is **paan**, the digestive and mild stimulant that Westerners often wrongly call "betel". *Paan* sellers sit like priests in their little booths, and ordering *paan* is a hallowed ritual. The *paan* wallah starts with a betel leaf, upon which he spreads four basic ingredients: *katha* (a paste that produces *paan*'s characteristic red colour), *supaari* (chopped or shredded areca nut), *mitha masaala* (a mixture of sweet spices) and *chuna* (slaked white lime, to leach the other ingredients). After that, the possibilities are endless, although in general most *paan* will be either of the *jharda* (tobacco) variety, in various grades of overpowering, or *mitha* (sweet). For those who haven't got time for the whole performance, *paan* wallahs also sell foil packets of *paan parag*, a simple, ready-made mix.

---

but perhaps the most pleasant drink of all, is a brew-it-yourself highland concoction called **tongba**. The ingredients are a jug or tankard of fermented millet, a straw and a flask of hot water: you pour the water in, let it steep, and suck the mildly alcoholic brew through the straw until you reach the bottom; you repeat the process four or five times until the flavour and the alcohol run out. Two *tongba* can easily lubricate an entire evening.

☎ Communications

Nepal isn't nearly as isolated as it once was. Private telecommunications centres have sprouted in Kathmandu and other tourist areas like glittering electronic oases, offering internet access, international direct dialling, e-phone and fax services. The post is as slow and patchy as ever, though, and you can still walk days away from a phone if you want to.

Mail

Post takes at least ten days to get to or from Nepal – if it arrives at all. Postcards and aerogrammes go through fine, but envelopes or parcels that look like they might contain anything of value may go astray; even sending things registered offers no guarantees. During holiday times, when backlogs develop, postal service employees are rumoured to throw out what they don't have time to process.

Letters can be sent to a hotel or a friend's home, or care of **poste restante** in Kathmandu and (less reliably) Pokhara. Mail should be addressed: Name, Poste Restante, GPO, Kathmandu (or Pokhara), Nepal. To reduce the risk of misfiling, your name should be printed clearly with the surname underlined or capitalized. Mail is held for about two months, and can be redirected on request. In Kathmandu, American Express handles mail for cardholders and those carrying Amex cheques, and US citizens can receive mail c/o the Consular Section of the American Embassy.

When **sending mail** in Nepal, there's rarely a need to deal directly with the postal system; hotels and most guesthouses will take mail to the post office for you. Book and postcard shops in tourist areas sell stamps for a nominal extra fee, and many also have their own, largely reliable, mail drop-off boxes. Where no such services exist, take your letters or cards to the post office yourself and have the stamps franked before your eyes, or wait to send them from Kathmandu, where they've got a higher probability of reaching their destination. Never use a public letterbox: the stamps will be removed and resold, and your correspondence used to wrap peanuts.

Sending parcels

Parcels can be sent by air or sea. Obviously sea mail is cheaper but takes a lot longer (three months or more) and, as it first has to go by land to Calcutta, there are more opportunities for it to go missing. Again, the private sector is much easier to deal with than the official postal service. **Shipping agents** and **air freight services** in Kathmandu will shield you from much of the frustration and red tape, and they provide packing materials to boot, but for this they charge almost twice as much as the post office. Be sure you're dealing with a reputable company, though (a few are recommended on p.175). Don't entrust shipping to a handicrafts shop.

Telephones

Nepal may have one of the least-developed **telephone** networks in the world, but it could hardly be easier for visitors to make calls. All tourist areas and major towns have glitzy **telephone/internet shops** that offer a variety of ways to make cheap international calls. Many accept payment by credit card, too. Simpler telephone-only outfits, which advertise themselves with the acronyms ISD/STD/IDD (international subscriber dialling/standard trunk dialling/international direct dialling), can be found almost everywhere there's a phone line. Most district headquarters have government-operated telephone offices, which are slightly cheaper but considerably less user-friendly.

Domestic calls

Private phone shops charge Rs15–50 per minute for **trunk** (domestic long-distance) calls, depending on the distance. Your hotel or guesthouse, and any shop with a phone on the counter, will let you make **local calls** for a few rupees. Public phones in Nepal are practically nonexistent, though coin-operated **payphones** can be found inside some tourist businesses in Kathmandu. Coins are so rare, however, that it's much easier to use an ordinary phone and pay at the end of your call.

While this guide gives local **phone numbers** where they exist, be aware that numbers in Nepal change frequently. (Nepalis, accustomed to phone numbers being changed on them without notice, often start conversations with the phrase *Kaahaa pariyo?* – "Where have I reached?"). If the number has changed, **directory enquiries** (☎197 throughout Nepal) might be able to help, but have a Nepali translate.

Nepali numbers are always eight digits long: in the Kathmandu Valley the ☎01 area code is followed by a six-digit number; elsewhere, a three-digit area code is followed by a five-digit number. You don't need to dial

> The international code for Nepal is 977. When dialling a number in Nepal from abroad, drop the "0" at the beginning of the area code, which will leave a seven-digit number.

the area code when you're calling from within that area. Numbers in the Kathmandu chapter of this guide are listed with codes, but note that you'll need to remove ☏01 when dialling from within the Valley.

International calls

Most telecommunications shops offer a choice between conventional and internet phone services. Conventional **international calls** are expensive from Nepal: about Rs140–170 per minute from Kathmandu. Calls to North America are usually the cheapest, followed by Europe and Australia/New Zealand.

You can save money using the **"callback"** system, however, for which you pay the full whack for the initial call to tell your party the number where you can be reached, but then only Rs5–10 per minute for the incoming call – some places will allow you to receive calls for free. You can also call **collect** to many countries, but the per-minute charge to you is the same as with a callback, and much higher for the person at the other end.

Internet calls (also known as e-phone or VOIP – Voice Over Internet Protocol) run at between Rs5 and Rs50 per minute from Kathmandu (there's room for haggling). The catch is that the connection is unstable and there's a wicked delay, so you end up making long speeches and then saying "over", like on a walkie-talkie.

Mobile phones and faxes

At the time of writing, Nepal wasn't connected up to any international networks, so unless you plan to make a lot of calls in Kathmandu and Pokhara, and are prepared to queue for a local SIM card, there's little point in packing your phone. There are rumours of a private company bidding for a domestic network franchise, which may transform the situation, but don't hold your breath. In any case, Nepal's topography will probably continue to restrict coverage to the few urban centres.

Sending a **fax**, you'll be charged by the minute of transmission time, plus about Rs10 per page. A standard page takes less than a minute to go through. It should cost Rs10 per page or so to collect an incoming fax (**fax back**).

Calling home from Nepal

USA and Canada: 00 + 1+ city code
Australia: 00 + 61+ city code
New Zealand: 00 + 64+ city code
UK and Northern Ireland: 00 + 44 + city code
Republic of Ireland: 00 +353+ city code

Email

Email is huge in Nepal because it's much cheaper than phoning and faxing, and much quicker and more reliable than the post. Sign up for a free address from an **internet mail provider** such as ⓦ www.yahoo.com or ⓦ www.hotmail.com, and then use their site to pick up and send mail from anywhere with internet access.

In tourist areas, there are abundant places to go online, ranging from little family shops with a single PC to swish all-purpose communication centres. Even out-of-the-way bazaar towns may have a single shop with **internet connection**. Outside Kathmandu and Pokhara, and even within them, don't expect trouble-free connection, however. Phone networks are old and decrepit, processors slow, and power cuts not unknown. It's often worth copying mails to Wordpad or a similar program, and reading them while the next message downloads. Alternatively, use Hotmail's or Yahoo's instant messenger or chat services (installed on most internet-shop computers), which usually give access to your inbox at a faster speed than the main website.

Charges are given in the relevant chapters, but range from less than Rs1 per minute in Kathmandu to Rs7 in out-of-the-way places. Prices can be expected to come down outside Kathmandu as competition increases.

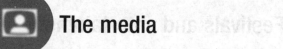

The media

Nepal's news traditionally comes in the form of the *gaine* musician, who sings the news and gossip of the day accompanied by his *sarangi*. Modern Nepalis, however, are more likely to listen to Radio Nepal, which reaches even the most rural areas. Television is spreading rapidly in the wake of electricity, newspapers are widely read in urban areas and, where there are phone lines, the internet is providing a unique point of contact with the outside world for those that can afford the connection.

Newspapers and magazines

Despite a literacy rate of less than thirty percent, Nepal boasts more than a thousand **newspapers** – an outgrowth of two noble Brahmanic traditions: punditry and gossip. Several are published in English, the most readable and incisive being the weekly *Nepali Times* (its *Yak Yeti Yak* cartoon is good, too). Of the dailies, the *Kathmandu Post* remains the frontrunner, overshadowing *Space Time Today*, *The Himalayan Times* and the government mouthpiece *Rising Nepal*. All are hard to find outside the Kathmandu Valley, but you can find them online at ⓦ www.nepalnews.com, along with various magazines and the Nepali-language press.

A number of **magazines** are published in English, the most interesting and easy to find being *Himal*, a bimonthly journal of environmental and development issues that's published in Kathmandu but covers all of south Asia. *Spotlight*, a weekly, tries to be a sort of Nepali *Time* or *Newsweek*, and actually carries some good features on Nepalese current affairs.

A wide range of **international publications** such as the *International Herald Tribune*, *Time* and *Newsweek* are available from bookshops in Kathmandu and Pokhara, as is the occasional foreign newspaper, usually at least two days old.

TV and radio

You can gauge the pace of local change by the programming of **Nepal TV**: only a few years ago it coughed into life with an amateurish daily hour of domestic news that focused on royal engagements and pronouncements; these days, it features discussions of current affairs and a burgeoning Nepali pop-video scene.

The rapid spread of **cable and satellite TV** is sending tremors through Nepalese society – Indian pop videos, Hollywood movies and all the advertising broadcast with them are challenging attitudes to traditional values. At any rate, more and more hotel and guesthouse rooms have TVs, and you can catch CNN, BBC World and movies and sitcoms in both English and Hindi. There's even a fledgling Nepali-language satellite station, Channel Nepal.

The government-run **Radio Nepal** (ⓦ www.radio-nepal.com), on 103 FM, is probably still the most influential of the nation's media, catering to the illiterate majority of Nepalis and reaching villages well beyond the circulation of any newspaper. With a daily format of traditional and pop music, news bulletins, English-language lessons, dramas and development messages, it has been a powerful force for cultural and linguistic unity, though in recent years various ethnic groups have pressured the government to provide programming in their native tongues. The station carries English-language news bulletins daily at 8pm.

There are also local FM stations, including a couple of English-language ones in the Kathmandu Valley, trendiest of which is Kantipur 96.1 FM. If you're travelling with a short-wave radio, you can pick up the **BBC World Service:** ⓦ www.bbc.co.uk/worldservice lists the frequencies.

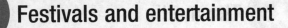

Festivals and entertainment

Stumbling onto a local festival may prove to be the highlight of your travels in Nepal – and given the sheer number of them, you'd be unlucky not to. Though most are religious in nature, merrymaking, not solemnity, is the order of the day, and onlookers are always welcome. You're even more likely to come across Nepalese music and dance, which are passions for many Nepalis, and form an integral part of most festivals. The language barrier means that few tourists seek out Nepalese cinema, for all its popularity among Nepali urban youth. For more detailed coverage of music, see Contexts, p.525.

Festivals

Festivals may be Hindu, Buddhist, animist or a hybrid of all three. **Hindu events** can take the form of huge pilgrimages and fairs (*mela*), or more introspective gatherings such as ritual bathings at sacred confluences (*tribeni*) or special acts of worship (*puja*) at temples. Many involve animal sacrifices and jolly family feasts afterwards, with priests and musicians usually on hand. Parades and processions (*jaatra*) are common, especially in the Kathmandu Valley, where idols are periodically ferried around on great, swaying chariots.

Buddhist festivals are no less colourful, typically bringing together maroon-robed clergy and lay pilgrims to walk and prostrate themselves around stupas (dome-shaped monuments, usually repainted specially for the occasion), and sometimes featuring elaborately costumed dances.

Many of Nepal's **animist** peoples follow the Hindu calendar, but local nature-wor-shipping rites take place across the hills throughout of the year, many of them unrecorded by the outside world. **Shamanic rites** usually take place at home, at the request of a particular family, although shamans themselves have their own calendar of fairs (*mela*) at which they converge on a particular holy spot, often high in the mountains. You'll have to travel widely and sensitively to have the chance to witness a shaman in action.

Jubilant (and public), Nepali **weddings** are always scheduled on astrologically auspicious days, which fall in the greatest numbers during the months of Magh, Phaagun and Baisaakh (see opposite). The approach of a wedding party is often heralded by the sound of a hired *band baajaa* or brass band – one of colonialism's stranger legacies, sounding like a Dixieland sextet playing in a pentatonic scale – and open-air feasts go on until the early hours. The bride usually wears red – an auspicious colour – and for the rest of her married life she will colour the parting of her hair with red *sindur*.

Funeral processions are understandably sombre and should be left in peace. The body is normally carried to the cremation site within hours of death by white-shrouded friends and relatives; white is the colour of mourning for Hindus, and the eldest son is expected to shave his head and wear white for a year following the death of a parent. Many of the hill tribes conduct special shamanic rites to guide the deceased's soul to the land of the dead.

Festival dates

Knowing when and where festivals are to be held will not only enliven your time in Nepal, but should also help you avoid certain annoyances such as closed offices and booked-up buses. Unfortunately as most are governed by the **lunar calendar**, **festival dates** vary from year to year, and determining them more than a year in advance is a highly complicated business best left to astrologers. Each lunar cycle is divided into "bright" (waning) and "dark" (waxing) halves, which are in turn divided into fourteen lunar "days". Each of these days has a name – *purnima* is the full moon, *astami* the eighth day, *aunshi* the new moon, and so on. Thus lunar festivals are always observed on a given day of either the bright or dark half of a given Nepali month. Confused? The festival calendar (see below) gives projected dates (where available) for the upcoming major festivals. Check one of the Nepali calendars on the **web** (try ⓦwww.visitnepal.com or ⓦwww.nepalhomepage.com) for more precision, or for dates in 2005 and beyond.

Nepal's major festivals

The following list details Nepal's most widely observed festivals, plus a few notable smaller events worth trying to coincide with. Many other local ones are described in the relevant chapters. The names of the months are given as spoken – spellings and the official written forms may differ. Few festivals fall in the months of Jeth (May–June), Asar (June–July) and Pus (Dec–Jan).

Magh (Jan–Feb)

Magh (or **Makaɲ) Sankranti** Marking a rare solar (rather than lunar) event in the Nepali calendar – the day the sun is farthest from the earth – the first day of Magh (Jan 14 or 15) is an occasion for ritual bathing at all sacred river confluences, especially at Devghat and Sankhu. The day also begins a month-long period during which families do daily readings of the *Swasthani*, a uniquely Nepali compilation of Hindu myths, and many women emulate Parvati's fast for Shiva, one of the *Swasthani* stories.

Basanta Panchami This one-day spring festival is celebrated on the fifth day after the new moon in most Hindu hill areas. The day is also known as Saraswati Puja, after the goddess of learning, and Shri Panchami, after the Buddhist saint Manjushri. School playgrounds are decorated with streamers and children have their books and pens blessed; high-caste boys may undergo a special rite of passage. Many people do *puja* to the famous image of Saraswati near Kathmandu's Swayambhu temple, which Buddhists also worship as Manjushri. The king attends a special ritual in the old royal palace.

Phaagun (Feb–March)

Losar Tibetan New Year falls on the new moon of either Magh or Phaagun, and is preceded by three days of drinking, dancing and feasting. The day itself is celebrated most avidly at Boudha, where morning rituals culminate with horn blasts and the hurling of *tsampa*. A time for families to be together, Losar is the highlight of the calendar in Buddhist highland areas, as well as in Tibetan settlements near Kathmandu and Pokhara.

Major festival calendar

Note that as this book went to press, no dates were available for Seto Machhendranath Jaatra or Raato Machhendranath Jaatra.

	2002	2003	2004
Magh Sankranti	Jan 14	Jan 15	Jan 15
Basanta Panchami	Feb 17	Feb 6	Jan 26
Losar	Feb 12	Feb 1	Feb 20
Shiva Raatri	Mar 12	Mar 1	Feb 18
Faagun Purnima (Holi)	Mar 28	Mar 18	Mar 6
Ram Nawami	Apr 21	Apr 11	Mar 30
Nawa Barsa/Bisket Jaatra	Apr 14	Apr 14	Apr 13
Chait Dasain	Apr 20	Apr 10	Mar 29
Buddha Jayanti	May 26	May 16	May 4
Janai Purnima	Aug 22	Aug 12	July 31
Gaai Jaatra	Aug 23	Aug 13	Aug 1
Krishna Janmasthami	Aug 30	Aug 19	Sept 6
Tij	Sept 9	Aug 30	Sept 16
Indra Jaatra	Sept 18–21	Sept 7–10	Sept 25
Dasain	Sept 7–15	Sept 27–Oct 5	Sept 14–23
Tihaar	Nov 2–6	Oct 23–27	Nov 10–14
Chhath	Nov 10	Oct 30	Nov 19

Shiva Raatri Falling on the new moon of Phaagun, "Shiva's Night" is marked by bonfires and evening vigils in all Hindu areas, but most spectacularly at Pashupatinath, where tens of thousands of pilgrims and sadhus (holy men) from all over the subcontinent gather for Nepal's best-known *mela* (religious fair). Fervent worship and bizarre yogic demonstrations can be seen throughout the day throughout the Pashupatinath complex. Children collect firewood money by holding pieces of string across the road to block passersby – foreigners are considered easy prey. Nepalis say the festival is usually followed by a final few days of winter weather, which is Shiva's way of encouraging the Indian sadhus to go home.

Holi Nepal's version of the springtime water festival, common to many Asian countries, is an impish affair lasting about a week, and commemorates a myth in which the god Krishna, when still a boy, outsmarted the demoness Holika. During this period, anyone – bus passengers included – is a fair target for water balloons and coloured powder (usually red, the colour of rejoicing). It culminates in a general free-for-all on Phaagun Purnima, the full-moon day of Phaagun.

Chait (March–April)

Chait Dasain Like its autumn namesake, the "little Dasain", observed on the eighth day after the new moon, involves lots of animal sacrifices. The goriest action takes place at goddess temples, such as the one at Gorkha, and in the Kot courtyard near Kathmandu's Durbar Square, where the army's top brass come to witness the beheading of numerous buffalo and goats.

Ram Nawami The birthday of Lord Ram is observed on the ninth day after the full moon at all temples dedicated to Vishnu in his incarnation as the hero of the *Ramayan*, one of the great Hindu epics. By far the biggest and most colourful celebrations take place in Janakpur, where thousands of pilgrims flock to the Ram temple.

Seto Machhendranath Jaatra Kathmandu's answer to Patan's Raato Machhendranath Jaatra (see below), this sees a lumbering wooden chariot containing the white mask of the god Machhendranath pulled through the narrow lanes of the old city for four days, starting on Chait Dasain. The chariot's progress is slow, but with occasional exciting and terrifying lurches. At each of the overnight stopping places, locals come to perform *puja* to the image.

Baisaakh (April–May)

Nawa Barsa Nepali New Year, which always falls on the first day of Baisaakh (April 13 or 14), is observed with localized parades. Culminating on Nawa Barsa, Bhaktapur's five-day celebration, known as Bisket or Biska, is the most colourful, combining religious processions with a rowdy tug-of-war (see p.229); the nearby settlements of Thimi and Bode host similarly wild scenes.

Raato Machhendranath Jaatra Nepal's most spectacular festival: thousands gather to watch as the image of Machhendranath, the Kathmandu Valley's rain-bringing deity, is pulled around the streets of Patan in a swaying, sixty-foot-high chariot. It moves only on astrologically auspicious days, taking four weeks or more to complete its journey. For more detail, see p.147.

Buddha Jayanti The anniversary of the Buddha's birth, enlightenment and death is celebrated on the full-moon day of Baisaakh at all Buddhist temples, but most visibly at Swayambhu, where the freshly repainted stupa is decorated with thousands of lights the night before; on the day, ritual dances are performed here by priests dressed as the five aspects of Buddhahood. Processions are also held at the Boudha stupa and in Patan. Observances at the Buddha's birthplace, Lumbini, are rather sparse.

Saaun (July–Aug)

Janai Purnima The annual changing of the sacred thread (*janai*) worn by high-caste Hindu men takes place at holy bathing sites throughout the country on the full-moon day of Saaun. Men and women of any caste may also receive a yellow-and-orange "protective band" (*raksha bandhan*) around one wrist, which is then worn until Tihaar, when it's supposed to be tied onto the tail of a cow. Mass observances are held at Gosainkund, a holy lake high in the mountains north of Kathmandu; Pashupatinath, outside Kathmandu; and most prominently at Patan's Kumbeshwar temple, where priests sit cross-legged tying strings and bestowing *tikas*, and *Jhankri* (hill shamans) perform sacred dances.

Gaai Jaatra Newari tradition has it that Yamraj, the god of death, opens the gates of judgement on the day of the full moon, allowing departed souls to enter. Falling on the day after the full moon, Gaai Jaatra honours cows (*gaai*), who are supposed to lead departed souls to Yamraj's abode. Processions in Kathmandu, Bhaktapur and other Newari towns are both solemn and whimsical: an occasion for families to honour loved ones who have died in the past year, but also for young boys to dress up in fanciful cow costumes or masquerade as sadhus. In Bhaktapur, where the festival is known as Gunhi Punhi and starts a day earlier (coinciding with Janai Purnima), men parade around town in humorous costumes. Satirical street performances are less common nowadays than they once were, but newspapers and magazines publish caustic Gaai Jaatra specials.

Nag Panchami On the fifth day after the new moon, Kathmandu Valley residents quietly propitiate the *nag* (snake spirits), who are traditionally held to control the monsoon rains and earthquakes, by pasting pictures of *nag* over their doorways with cow dung and offering milk, rice and other favourite *nag* foods to the images. Wells are cleaned only on this day, when the *nag* are believed to be away worshipping their ancestral deities.

Ghanta Karna On the fourteenth day after the full moon, residents of Kathmandu Valley towns celebrate the victory of the gods over the demon Ghanta Karna ("Bell Ears") by erecting effigies and then burning or tearing them down, to childrens' delight.

Bhadau (Aug–Sept)

Krishna Astami (also called Krishna Jayanti or Krishna Janmastahmi) Krishna temples such as Patan's Krishna Mandir throng with thousands of worshippers celebrating the god's birth on the seventh day after the full moon. Vigils are also held the night before.

Tij The three-day "Women's Festival", which starts on the third day after the new moon, sees groups of women clad in red (the colour of rejoicing and domestic harmony) singing and dancing through the streets. Letting their families fend for themselves for once, they start with a girls' night out, feasting until midnight when they begin a day-long fast. On the second day they queue up to worship Shiva at the Pashupatinath temple outside of Kathmandu, and break the fast and ritually bathe to remove their sins on the final day.

Indra Jaatra A wild week of chariot processions and masked-dance performances in Kathmandu, held around the full moon of Bhadau. On the last day, which is also known as Kumari Jaatra, the king receives a special *tika* (an auspicious mark on the forehead) from the "living goddess" and beer flows from the mouth of an idol in Durbar Square (for more detail see p.112).

Yartung A swashbuckling fair held at Muktinath, in the Annapurna trekking region, centred around the full-moon day and featuring horse-racing, dancing, drinking and gambling.

Asoj (Sept–Oct)

Dasain (known as Dashera near India) Although Hindu in origin, Nepal's longest and greatest festival is enthusiastically embraced by members of almost all religious and ethnic groups. It stretches over fifteen days, from the new moon to the full moon of Asoj, with the liveliest action taking place on the seventh, ninth and tenth days. Normally falling just after the summer rice harvest is in, Dasain is a time for families to gather (buses get extremely crowded with homeward-bound passengers), children to be indulged (with kites, makeshift swings and miniature ferris wheels), and animals to be sacrificed (the markets are filled with doomed goats).

On the first day, known as **Ghatasthapana**, people plant *jamura* (barley) in a *kalash* (sanctified vessel), representing Durga, Dasain's honoured goddess; the seedlings will be picked and worn in the hair on the tenth day. Devotees congregate at local goddess temples throughout the next nine nights. A separate festival, **Panchali Bhairab Jaatra**, which entails raucous late-night processions between the Bhairab's shrine and the Kumari Ghar in Kathmandu, always coincides with the fourth and fifth days of Dasain.

On the seventh day, **Fulpati**, a bouquet of sacred flowers (*fulpati*) is carried in a procession from Rani Pokhari to the Hanuman Dhoka Palace in Kathmandu, with the king and queen and many VIPs in attendance. The ninth day, **Navami**, begins at midnight with tantric buffalo sacrifices inside the forbidden Taleju (a form of Durga) temples of the Kathmandu Valley; throughout the day, animals are ritually beheaded publicly in the Kot Courtyard near Kathmandu's Durbar Square, and in every village and city of Nepal; their blood is sprinkled on tools, vehicles and even aircraft to impart Durga's *shakti* (power). These rituals commemorate Durga's slaying of the demon Mahisasur, and more generally, the triumph of good over evil.

Bijaya Dasami, the "Victorious Tenth Day", celebrates Ram's victory over the demon Ravana – with Durga's help – and is a day to visit elders to receive blessings and *tika*. The king and queen bestow *tika* to all comers at the Royal Palace, as does Kathmandu's Kumari (Living Goddess) at her house in Durbar Square, while various processions and masked-dance troupes ply the streets. The final days of Dasain are for low-key family visiting, feasting and gift-giving.

Kartik (Oct–Nov)

Tihaar (Diwali near India) Lasting for five days, starting two days before the new moon, the "Festival of Lights" is associated with Yamraj, the god of death, and Lakshmi, the goddess of wealth and good fortune. On the first day, Nepalis set out food on leaf plates for crows, regarded as Yamraj's messengers;

on the second, they honour dogs as Yamraj's gatekeepers, giving them *tika*, flower garlands and special foods; and on the third, they garland cows both as the symbol of Lakshmi and as the soul's guide to Yamarj's underworld. The festival's most picturesque event, Lakshmi Puja, comes on the evening of the third day, when families throughout Nepal ring their homes with oil lamps, candles or electric lights to guide Lakshmi to their homes so she can bless them with prosperity for the year. Trusting in her, many Nepalis gamble on street corners, and student groups make the rounds singing "Diusire", a form of musical fundraising. Firecrackers have also become a big part of the fun for kids. To Newars, the fourth day is known as **Mha Puja** ("Self-Worship"), an occasion for private rituals, and also their New Year's Day, marked by banners, well-wishing and motorcycle parades in the Kathmandu Valley's three main cities. On the fifth day, **Bhaai Tika**, sisters recall the myth of Jamuna, who tricked Yamraj into postponing her brother's death indefinitely, by blessing their younger brothers and giving them flower garlands, *tika* and sweetmeats.

Chhath Coinciding with the third day of Tihaar, this festival honours Surya, the sun god, and is one of the most important for the Maithili-speaking people of the eastern Tarai. Chhath is celebrated most ardently in Janakpur, where women gather by ponds and rivers to greet the sun's first rays with prayers, offerings and ritual baths.

Mangsir (Nov–Dec)

Ram-Sita Biwaha Panchami As many as 100,000 pilgrims converge on Janakpur for this five-day gathering, beginning on the new moon of Mangsir. The highlight is the re-enactment of the wedding of Ram and Sita, the divine, star-crossed lovers of the *Ramayan*, one of the great Hindu epics. Janakpur's stature as a holy city rests on its having been the location of the original wedding.

Mani Rimdu Held at Tengboche and Chiwong monasteries in the Everest region around the full moon of the ninth Tibetan month (usually Oct/Nov), this colourful Sherpa masked dance dramatizes Buddhism's victory over the ancient Bon religion in eighth-century Tibet. A similar event is held in May or June at Thami.

Music and dance

Music is as common as conversation in Nepal. In the hills, travelling minstrels (*gaaine*) make their living singing ballads and accompanying themselves on the *sarangi*, a hand-carved, four-stringed fiddle. Teenagers of ethnic groups from the hills traditionally attract the attention of the opposite sex by exchanging teasing verses. After-dinner singalongs are popular, even in Kathmandu, and of course music is indispensable in all festivals.

Traditional Nepali music often gets drowned out by the rising tide of **Indian film music**, with its surging strings and hysterically shrill vocals, yet the mercifully calm and villagey **Nepali folk music** still gets a good airing, and there's a burgeoning **Nepali pop** scene that adds varying degrees of Nepaleseness to a broadly rock sound. Restaurants and bars in the tourist quarters of Kathmandu and Pokhara host free performances by local folk groups, and weekend-night gigs by Nepalese rock- and reggae-covers bands.

Nepali music is inseparable from **dance**, especially at festivals. Nepali dance is an unaffected folk art – neither wildly athletic nor subtle, it depicts everyday activities such as work and courtship. Each region and ethnic group has its own distinct traditions, and during your travels you should get a chance to join in a local hoedown or two, if not a full-blown festival extravaganza. Look out, too, for the stick dance of the lowland Tharus, performed regularly at lodges around Chitwan National Park.

Staged **culture shows** in Kathmandu and Pokhara are a long way from the real thing, but they do provide a taste of folk and religious dances, and hint at the incredible cultural diversity contained in such a small country. Most troupes perform such standards as the dance of the *jhankri* (shaman-exorcists still consulted by many, if not most, hill-dwelling Nepalis); the sleeve-twirling dance of the Sherpas; the flirting dance of the hill-dwelling Tamangs; the Tharus' fanciful peacock dance; perhaps a formal priestly dance, to the accompaniment of a classical *raga* (musical piece); and at least one of the dances of the Kathmandu Valley's holiday-loving Newars.

Cinema

Nepal's love–hate relationship with India is perhaps best illustrated by its **cinema**: Nepalis might grouse about India's cultural imperialism, but that doesn't stop them rushing to see the latest schmaltz and pyrotechnics from Bollywood. Though Nepali films are still the exception, and are less slick than Indian productions, they're much more popular when they're on. You won't, of course, find English subtitles, but an expedition to a Nepali screening (cinemas are found in every major town) makes a lively antidote to the usual impressions of Nepali culture given by festivals, folk-dances and the like. **VCD/DVD** rental shops are commonplace in the main cities. Some tourist restaurants screen Hollywood flicks on video, many of them amazingly current – bootleg tapes and DVDs often hit the streets in Kathmandu long before their official release.

Opening hours and public holidays

The Nepalese government is in the process of changing to a five-day, Monday-to-Friday week. In the Kathmandu Valley, government offices and post offices are now open Mon–Fri 9am–5pm (4pm in winter). Offices elsewhere are eventually supposed to switch to the same schedule, but for now most still keep to the old a six-day week: Sunday to Thursday 10am to 5pm (4pm in winter), and Friday 10am to 3pm. "Winter" in this context means mid-November to mid-February. These schedules often get truncated at either end.

Museum closing days vary (usually either Sat, Sun, Mon or Tues); opening times are fairly similar to office hours. Shops keep long hours, from early morning (usually at some point in the hour after dawn), to seven or eight at night, and in tourist areas usually stay open seven days a week. **Money-changers** and some **banks** in tourist areas are generous with their hours, but elsewhere you'll have to do your transactions Mon–Thurs & Sun 10am–2pm, Fri 10am–noon. **Travel agents** tend to work from an hour or so after dawn to an hour or more after dusk, but it varies; **airline offices** are open roughly the same hours as government offices, and may well be closed for lunch between 1pm and 2pm. **Embassy** and consulate hours are all over the place, so it's impossible to generalize.

Nepal's hectic calendar of **national holidays** can shut down offices for up to a week at a time. Dates vary from year to year – Nepal has its own calendar, beginning in mid-April and consisting of twelve months that are a fortnight or so out of step with the Western ones. (The Vikram Sambat calendar began in 57 BC: thus the Nepali year beginning in April 2003 is 2060 VS.)

Complicating matters further are religious **festivals**, which are calculated according to the *lunar* calendar, while Tibetan and Newari festivals follow different calendars of their own (see p.54).

In times of political unrest, offices, shops and transport can sometimes be shut down by a "Nepal *bandh*", an organized **strike** designed to close down the Kathmandu Valley (or even the entire country), usually for a single day. On the whole, tourist enclaves and rural areas are less affected than the cities, but if the strike is successful it's all but impossible to find transport or get anything done. Everybody tends to know when one will happen at least a few days in advance, so you'll usually have time to prepare yourself for an enforced rest day. During major strikes, especially those said to have Maoist backing, you'd be wise to take advantage of a day off, and not indulge in any potentially "political" sightseeing.

National holidays

Prithvi Narayan Shah's Birthday January 10 or 11

Basanta Panchami late January or early February

Shiva Raatri late February or early March	**King's Birthday** July 6 or 7
Democracy Day February 18 or 19	**Janai Purnima** late July or early August
Nawa Barsa (Nepali New Year) April 13 or 14	**Krishna Asthami** late July or early August
Chait Dasain late March or early April	**Dasain** late September or early October (5–6 days)
Ram Nawami late March or early April	**Tihaar** late October or early November (3 days)
Buddha Jayanti late April or early May	**Constitution Day** – November 8 or 9

Outdoor activities

Nepal has always been about trekking – in the absence of roads, after all, it's how the majority of Nepalese get around. These days, however, Nepal is developing into one of the world's leading adventure sports destinations, and as well as trekking and climbing, you can also go rafting, kayaking, hydrospeeding, mountain-biking, canyoning and paragliding, or do a bungy jump.

Kathmandu and Pokhara are alive with adventure operators and agents (as well as places which rent out the adventure sports equipment). Some of the packages on offer are built around instruction for first-timers (with all equipment provided), while others can take you about as extreme as it's possible to go. On top of that, prices are quite cheap by international standards. (For tours booked from home, see pp.13–17.)

Nepal's roster of outdoor activities aren't just about altitude or adrenaline highs, however. The jungly wildlife parks of the low-lying Tarai are rich in bird and plant life, and serve as vital sanctuaries for the subcontinent's most endangered mammals, the tiger and the one-horned black rhino. Guided jungle walks, elephant rides and even jeep and canoe excursions can take you deep into Nepal's national parks, and offer some of the most rewarding **wildlife** viewing in the world.

Most of these activities are described in greater detail in later chapters on trekking (p.413), rafting and kayaking (p.457), and mountain-biking (p.471). Other adventure activities are dealt with at relevant points in the guide – this section just gives an overview of the possibilities.

Trekking and climbing

Almost everyone who doesn't go **trekking** ends up regretting it. It's the only way to get *into* the Himalaya, as opposed to looking at it from a distance, and it's by far the best way to experience the traditional life of Nepal's many ethnic groups. If you stick to low elevations and take it slowly, trekking doesn't have to be physically demanding, either – though you can, of course, plan routes that are about as tough as they come.

A trek normally lasts at least four or five days, but you'll get more out of it if you can set aside two or more weeks. Most people don't trek with a group, and wait until they get to Kathmandu or Pokhara before making any arrangements.

Day-hikes are described throughout the guide. While the scenery will seem rather tame compared with a trek, the cultural interactions on these uncommercialized trails are often more genuine. If you're up for a bigger challenge and can afford to go with a group, consider a **trekking peak** (see p.421). Or learn to **climb** – at least one

The golden anniversary of the **first ascent of Everest** falls in 2003, and the Nepal Mountaineering Association has set up an array of adventure sports competitions to celebrate the event, from whitewater rafting to the famously lung-busting Everest Marathon. See ⓦwww.mteverestgolden50.com.

company offers courses in the Everest region.

Rafting and kayaking

Of all the outdoor activities on offer in Nepal, **rafting** tops the list for adrenaline. Nepal's rivers are truly world-class – the scenery certainly is, too – and outside of the monsoon, the whitewater is fine for first-timers. Rafting is also a good way to get in among Nepal's lower hills and valleys, providing fresh angles on villages and religious gatherings at sacred confluences.

You'll almost certainly do your river-running with a **rafting** company, all of which offer standard one- or four-day trips, and provide the gear. Some organize longer trips on remoter rivers, and raft/wildlife or raft/trek packages. On most trips, the guide steers the raft while the crew – that's you – provides the paddle-power. Nights are spent camping on riverside beaches, usually far from roads or commercial centres.

Kayaking is another popular river activity. If you already know how to kayak, you can rent gear in Pokhara or Kathmandu and take off on your own; novices can join kayak schools on the Seti River, near Pokhara, or the Bhote Koshi, north of Kathmandu. Kayaking is also an option on rafting trips, since the more reputable companies use safety kayaks for support.

Mountain-biking

Nepal is a joy on a **mountain bike**: there are plenty of uncrowded and spectacular backroads, the riding is challenging, and the alternative mode of getting from A to B – buses – can be unpleasant. A degree of fitness is required, but if you can handle a one-speed cycle, you should have no trouble with a mountain bike.

Like trekking (and unlike rafting) mountain-biking can be done **independently**. Good bikes can be hired in Kathmandu and Pokhara, but you may want to consider bringing your own. There are plenty of **tours** on offer, however, ranging from easy one-day cultural jaunts and downhill road-rides to strenuous off-road cycle treks and multiday, long-distance trips taking in hill stations and/or Tarai wildlife parks.

Adventure sports

Canyoning – rock climbing and abseiling (rappelling) in and around waterfalls – is a European sport that's just starting to catch on in Nepal. Adventure sports resorts along the Arniko Highway, near the Tibet border, run trips to some superb canyons, with trained guides and all the equipment. One operator also offers Nepal's first **bungy jump**, one of the world's highest and surely one of the most beautifully situated.

A company in Pokhara offers **paragliding** courses for experienced pilots and beginners, while a neighbouring operator does short piloted trips around the valley in **ultralight** aircraft. Yet another company in Kathmandu offers early-morning **balloon flights**.

Nepal occasionally hosts **triathlons** and marathons (notably the unbelievably strenuous Everest Marathon), and mountain-biking and rafting events are becoming annual fixtures. The best way to find out about them is to check with clubs in your home country, or check out the major Nepalese operators' websites.

Conventional sports

Volleyball, **badminton** and **table tennis** are Nepal's staple sports, since they don't require large playing areas, and equipment can be improvised. Where there's flat land, **football** (**soccer**) is catching on, and teams often square off at the National Stadium in Kathmandu – check the English-language daily papers for news of upcoming matches. Since it was never part of the British empire, Nepal has no historical connection with **cricket**, but the sport is enjoying a huge rise in popularity thanks to satellite TV and the unprecedented success of the youth team in reaching the 2002 World Cup. **Elephant polo** is a joke sport invented by and for expats, but the "world championships" each December at Chitwan certainly make for a fun spectator event.

The big tourist hotels in Kathmandu have **swimming** pools and **tennis** courts, and nonguests can often use them for a fee. Nepal's **golf** courses are being heavily promoted within Asia, and as well as the old courses in Dharan, Pokhara and alongside

Kathmandu airport, there are flashy new ones just outside Kathmandu and Pokhara.

Wildlife-viewing

The wildlife parks of the Tarai, near the border with India, offer jeep and even boat safaris, but you'll probably find that the most rewarding **wildlife-viewing** excursions are on foot, or from the top of an elephant. You're likely to see the one-horned black rhino, while monkeys and various species of deer abound. You may see the occasional bear, too, but tigers are spotted only rarely.

Just six hours from Kathmandu by bus, **Chitwan** (p.327) is the easiest National Park to get to and the one most heavily used by budget travellers. The density of animal species, including one-horned black rhinos, is such that you can almost guarantee a large number of sightings, but in the high-season winter months, you may find that you spot other tourists just as often. However, if you're willing to make your own travel and guiding arrangements, you can easily sidestep the crowds, and luxury lodges within the park offer seclusion for those who can afford it. **Bardia National Park** (p.364) offers a similar range of habitats and animals, but its location (a twelve-plus-hour bus ride west of Pokhara) means that it requires a certain amount of determination to get to. As a result, it's far less developed, and offers a much more rustic experience than Chitwan. In the far west of Nepal, **Sukla Phanta Wildlife Reserve** (p.374) sees very few visitors, and has a

more open aspect than Chitwan or Bardia, its airy forests and grasslands sheltering mostly deer and birds.

You'll see less wildlife away from the national parks. Mammals aren't as easy to see in the hills and mountains, most of the interesting ones being nocturnal or extremely reclusive, but while trekking you'll often see monkeys, deer, various small rodents and (if you're lucky) goat-like *tahr* or blue sheep. Don't even think about spotting a snow leopard. The best wildlife viewing in the mountains is to be had at isolated national parks such as Rara Lake, Khaptad and Dhorpatan Hunting Reserve, but these require a trek, often combined with an internal flight, to get to.

Nepal is also famous for its huge number of **bird** species – 852 at the last count, among them 29 globally threatened species – though new migrants and seasonal visitors are always being added to the list. Many of the most colourful birds, such as kingfishers, babblers and ibises, are found in **forest habitats**. **Riverine areas** of Bardia and Chitwan national parks are obvious birding hotspots, but you'll also see plenty of species on the wooded slopes of Phulchoki, on the edge of the Kathmandu Valley. **Wetland** birds such as ducks and waders flock to the Koshi Tappu Wildlife Reserve (p.395) in the eastern Tarai region, and trekkers can look out for a host of **mountain species**, including eagles, partridges and the gorgeously coloured *danphe* or Impeyan pheasant (Himalayan Monal), Nepal's national bird.

Photography

With mountains, wildlife, temples, ethnic peoples and festivals all providing winning subjects, everyone's a National Geographic photographer in Nepal. But beware of experiencing your trip through a lens. The camera can provide great memories, but don't hesitate to put it away when it's getting in the way of the real thing.

Cameras and accessories are reasonably priced in Kathmandu, but you'll pay roughly the same as you would at home for up-to-the-minute technology. If you're bringing

your own, remember that a good **zoom** is well worth it for mountain shots and close-ups of wildlife. **Disposable cameras** are sold in tourist areas and are good for things like raft trips, when you don't want to carry big and expensive equipment.

Most major brands of **film** (*reel* or *filim*), including slide film, are easily obtainable in tourist areas, and prices are cheaper than back home. Off the beaten track, though, the selection is pretty thin, and stock may be old or improperly stored. Labs in the main cities and towns **process** most types of film; city labs usually do a fair job and may give substantial discounts if you have a few films done. **Batteries** (*battery*) are sold everywhere, but domestic brands are hopeless: stock up on imported long-lifes in a tourist area, particularly if you need something more unusual like a lithium battery. Remember that batteries go flat more quickly in cold temperatures.

People always make good photos, but be sensitive. Always ask first, and if they say no, or ask for money, perhaps better not. Polaroids make wonderful gifts, but don't make empty promises to send photos from home. **Light levels** and **contrast** can be higher than you might be used to at home, so consider filters, if they fit your camera, and plan on doing much of your shooting in the early morning or late afternoon. Tones are especially mellow at these times, producing the best results, and in any case some of the most interesting scenes occur just after dawn. In certain seasons, haze can spoil landscape shots except at dawn and dusk. For snow shots, meter off (or focus on, if you don't have a light meter) something of a neutral shade, like your hand or the darkest part of the sky.

Note that you have to pay a steep extra fee to bring a **video camera** into certain parks and sights. Nepal's electricity is 220V/50 cycles, which means North Americans need to use an adapter (available locally) to recharge battery packs.

Crime, hustle and hassle

Nepal is one of the most crime-free countries in the world, which is all the more remarkable when you consider the huge gulf between rich and poor. However, theft is on the rise, and political instability seems to be bringing about a general rise in lawlessness.

The main concern is **petty theft**. Store valuables that you're not using in your hotel or guesthouse safe, and carry the rest in a money belt or pouch around your neck. In a dormitory, keep your bag locked and any expensive items with you. A padlock can be purchased cheaply in Nepal; it doesn't have to be big, as deterrence is the main thing. Some public bus routes have reputations for baggage theft – see "Getting Around" (p.35) for advice. **Pickpockets** (who are often street children) operate in crowded urban areas, especially during festivals, and tend to home in on unprotected tourist wallets and handbags; best advice is to keep vigilant.

If you're robbed, report it as soon as possible to the **police** headquarters of the district in which the robbery occurred. Policemen are apt to be friendly and consoling, if not much help. For **insurance** purposes, go to the Interpol Section of the police headquarters in Durbar Square, Kathmandu, to fill in a report; you'll need a copy of it to claim from your insurer once back home. Bring a photocopy of the pages in your passport containing your photo and your Nepalese visa, together with two passport photos. Dress smartly and expect an uphill battle – they're jaded by stolen travellers' cheque scams.

Violent crime is extremely rare, and the possibility of getting raped or assaulted in a populated area is statistically insignificant. A very occasional concern is a certain amount of hooliganism or sexual aggression in the

Kathmandu tourist bars; fortunately the government is ploughing back some tourist tax revenue into maintaining an evening police presence in those areas. The countryside is for the most part equally safe, although a few Western women have been raped by trekking guides over the years (see p.421). There has always been a small risk of violent attack by bandits on remote trekking trails, and this risk is somewhat higher these days due to Nepal's **Maoists** (see p.498), so don't walk alone. Maoist leaders have explicitly stated that they have no quarrel with tourists, even to the extent of welcoming them into Maoist-held areas, though visitors are obviously unwelcome in conflict zones, and travellers staying in the international-class hotels owned by the royal family and its associated businesses have been warned that these are considered legitimate targets. To date, travellers encountering Maoists have almost universally reported being treated with courteousness and even curiosity. Some, however, have been approached for "donations" with a degree of firmness that's worth respecting – though real Maoists have been known to give receipts! Often as not, however, any such encounters will be with opportunist criminals rather than political revolutionaries; so-called *khaobaadis* ("eatists") rather than *maobaadis* (Mao-ists). If you're unlucky enough to have such an experience – and they're rare – you probably won't care to make enquiries about political ideology in any case.

There are several ways to get on the wrong side of the law, none of them worth it. **Smuggling** is the usual cause of serious trouble – drugs and gold are the big no-no's, and if you get caught with commercial quantities of either you'll be looking at a more or less automatic five to twenty years in prison (see p.126 for a description of that edifying experience). While it would be incredibly stupid to go through customs with **drugs**, discreet possession inside the country carries virtually no risk; flash dope around, though, and you could conceivably get shopped by an innkeeper.

In Nepal, where government servants are poorly paid, a little **bakshish** sometimes greases the wheels. Nepalese police don't bust tourists simply in order to get bribes, but if you're accused of something it might not hurt to make an offer, in an extremely careful, euphemistic and deniable way. This shouldn't be necessary if you're the victim of a crime, although you may feel like offering a "reward".

The worst trouble you're likely to run into is one of Nepal's all-too-common **civil disturbances**. Opposition political parties, student organizations, Maoist-sympathizing groups or anyone else with a gripe may call a *chakka jam* (traffic halt) or *bandh* (general strike). In either case, most shops pull down their shutters as well, and all motorized vehicles stay off the roads after about 8am to avoid having their windows smashed – you'll have great difficulty making any travel connections. Demonstrations sometimes involve rock-throwing, tear gas and *lathis* (Asian-style police batons), but you'd have to go out of your way to get mixed up in it.

Hustle and hassle

Indian-style **hustle** is on the rise in Nepal. You'll get a major dose of it at the airport or any major bus station, where **touts** bearing guesthouse cards lie in wait to accost arriving tourists. They also cruise the tourist strips of Kathmandu, offering drugs. For the most part, though, Nepali touts aren't as parasitic as their Indian brethren, and if you're entering Nepal from North India, where aggressive touts have to be dealt with firmly, adjust your attitude. Ignore them entirely – try to look occupied with something else – and they're likely to ignore you. If that doesn't work, most touts will leave you alone if asked nicely, whereas they'll take a rude brush-off personally.

The tourist zones are full of other lone entrepreneurs and **middlemen** – touts by any other name. Ticket agents (see p.34), riksha wallahs, innkeepers and guides are ever-anxious to broker services and information. Naturally they take a cut, but as with touts, they usually get their commission from the seller; your price is bumped up correspondingly. If you don't know where to spend the night or change money, a tout's services are certainly worth a few rupees, but in general, cutting out the middleman gives you more control over the transaction. You should find, without being too mercenary about it, that a few rupees (and smiles) given to people whose services you may require again will smooth the way and make your stay much more pleasant.

Beggars

As in most developing countries, dealing with **beggars** is part and parcel of travelling in Nepal. The pathos might initially get to you, as well it should, but you will probably adjust to it fairly quickly. A thornier dilemma is how to cope with panhandling kids.

A small number of bona fide **beggars** make an honest living from *bakshish* (alms). Hindus and Buddhists alike have a long and honourable tradition of giving to lepers and the disabled, as well as to sadhus and monks. Destitute women make up another large contingent of the begging population: it's terrifyingly easy for a Nepali woman to find herself alone in the world, either widowed or divorced – perhaps for failing to bear a son or because of a dowry dispute. There are no unemployment benefits in Nepal, and the state pension for senior citizens is just Rs100 a year; anyone who can't work and has no family for support generally turns to begging (or prostitution). Few would choose to do so if they had an alternative.

In the hills, ailing locals will occasionally approach foreigners for **medicine**, knowing that they usually carry first-aid kits. It's probably best not to make any prescriptions unless you're qualified to diagnose the illness. However, before leaving the country you can donate unused medicines to the dispensary at Kathmandu's Bir Hospital, which distributes them to the destitute, or to the Himalayan Buddhist Meditation Centre in Kathmandu, which gives them to monks.

Children

Throughout Nepal – but principally along the tourist trails – **children** will hound you. Shouting *"namaste"* or "hello" at the weird-looking stranger is all but universal, but just as often kids will ask you for "one rupee", "sweet" or "pen". Sometimes they're cute, sometimes they're a pain. They're not orphans or beggars, just ordinary schoolkids who've seen too many well-meaning but thoughtless tourists handing out little gifts wherever they go.

A laugh and a firm-but-gentle *hoina holaa!* ("I don't think so!") is usually enough. Few children would ever ask a Nepali for money, so reacting like one will quickly embarrass them into leaving you alone. But kids will sometimes tag along for hours, giving you the Chinese water-torture treatment. In groups, after school, they can be unbearable. Remember that they're not seriously expecting you to give them anything, just having some fun. The best defence is a sense of humour: better that they laugh with you than at you.

Street children are another matter. They're begging for real, but you should still think twice before giving to them – see p.120.

Shopping

Nepal's handicrafts are as rich and varied as its culture, having been influenced by hundreds of years of trade and religious exchange with Tibet and India. In addition, the influx of Tibetan artisans since 1959 has enriched the marketplace immeasurably, while tourist demand has helped fuel something of an artistic renaissance. You can pick up distinctive gifts, souvenirs and clothes for a song or, if your budget runs to it, spend a fortune on carpets and *objets d'art*.

Where to shop

Ninety-nine percent of **crafts outlets** are concentrated in the Kathmandu Valley and Pokhara: this is where the buyers are, and where just about all of the mass-produced stuff is actually made. Competition is intense. You can't stroll the tourist strips without being importuned by **curio sellers** or beckoned from the sidelines by operators of makeshift **stalls**; their overheads are low and so, at least in theory, should be their prices. More reputable **shops**, galleries, "emporiums" and boutiques have better selections and aren't so hard-driving (many have fixed prices). In Patan – Nepal's handicrafts capital – you'll also find **"factory" showrooms**, where you can watch the wares being made. Numerous **nonprofit** (or "fair trade") shops in Kathmandu and Patan claim to provide outlets for women, disadvantaged people and workers' cooperatives; some do exactly that, but not all – we list the better outlets in Chapter One (p.165).

Quite a few items sold in tourist areas are made elsewhere, and needless to say it's more fun (and cheaper) to pick them up at source. Best buys are noted in the relevant sections of the guide, along with a few local specialities that can't be found anywhere else.

No matter what the seller says, very few items are older than last week. Genuine **antiques** – anything over 100 years old, or anything customs officials might think is that old – have to be cleared for export by the Department of Archaeology in Kathmandu (see p.162). Get the dealer to take care of the paperwork.

Bargaining

Except where prices are clearly marked as fixed (and sometimes even then), you'll be expected to **bargain**. In Nepal it's always lighthearted, never acrimonious. Sellers speak English in tourist areas, but prices are generally cheaper for those who speak a few words of Nepali.

There's no firm guide as to what to expect to have knocked off, although prices are usually softer on the street than in shops. The initial asking price may be anywhere from 10 to 1000 percent over the going rate, depending, to a certain extent, on how much like a tourist you look. All the old chestnuts still hold true: never show too much interest, let alone enthusiasm; and walking away will usually cut the price dramatically. But far more important is to know what you want, its approximate value, and how much you're prepared to pay. Never start to haggle for something you don't intend to buy – it'll end in bad feeling on both sides. Similarly, don't suggest a figure that you're not prepared to pay – having mentioned a price, you're obliged to pay it.

If you're contemplating making a big purchase, hiring a knowledgeable **guide** may save you money many times over what you spend on the fee – but make absolutely sure you're getting independent counsel, and not just being taken on a tour of brother-in-laws' shops.

Statues and metalware

Artisans of the Kathmandu Valley have been casting bronze, brass and copper **statues** of Buddhist and Hindu deities for at least 1300 years – an unbroken artistic tradition with few parallels worldwide. The images are produced by the lost-wax process, in which a model is carved out of wax, surrounded by clay and then fired, melting the wax and leaving a terracotta mould. Small statues can be cast from a single mould, but larger ones have to be assembled from up to a dozen pieces, the joins concealed by ornate embellishments.

Statues are cast mainly in the **style** of Tibet (Nepal's main customer for centuries), depicting a tremendous variety of Buddhas, *bodhisattva* and defenders of the *dharma*, as well as Hindu and indigenous deities. Each is characterized by a certain posture, weapon or other identifying feature. If you're shopping for a metal statue, the Handicraft Association of Nepal's inexpensive booklet, *A Short Description of Gods, Goddesses and Ritual Objects of Buddhism and Hinduism in Nepal*, sold in some Kathmandu bookshops, can help in figuring out the iconography.

Patan is the traditional casting centre (see p.162). **Prices** depend on size, metal and workmanship, but are never cheap – at least Rs3000 for a 20cm-tall image. The best-quality pieces will cost double that; fingers and eyes will be carefully detailed, and the metal without pits or spots.

Many brass **pots and vessels** are wonderful pieces of design. *Ghada*, the brass water jugs that Nepali women cradle against one hip, may be too big to tote home, but small incense holders, *raksi* pourers, *puja* trays, oil lamps and *jal* urns are all attractive and relatively cheap. And if the classic *pittal-* or *kaash-ko taal* (a bronze-alloy bowl used for rice), is too heavy, the *kachora*, or accompanying goblet (for *daal*) makes an excellent alternative.

So-called **"singing" bowls** are popular both as domestic and ritual objects. Made from an alloy of various (traditionally seven) metals, they produce a continuous harmonic ringing when rubbed around the rim with a wooden pestle. When held near the navel, the singing bowl is said to resonate with the body and aid meditation.

Jewellery

Every hill bazaar has its metalsmiths who sell **gold and silver** at the going rate and, for a modest charge, will tap it into an earring, nose ring, necklace clasp, bracelet or any other form in which a woman wants to display the family wealth. Common to almost all hill women are *malla*, necklaces consisting of strands of glass beads drawn together with a cylindrical gold ornament called a *tilari*; most jewellers will either make these to order, or sell them ready-made. Shops in Kathmandu sell **jewellery** made of silver, white metal and semiprecious stones, which, though designed entirely for the tourist market, are nonetheless attractive.

Gem sellers in Kathmandu deal in a wide range of cut and uncut stones at reasonable prices. Garnet, tourmaline, ruby, aquamarine, citrine ("golden topaz") and cats' eye come from mines in Nepal's Ganesh Himal and eastern hills; turquoise, amethyst and sapphire come from Tibet; coral from India; and lapis lazuli from Afghanistan. Most stones are cut and polished in India. Take care when buying, as gem quality and cut can make a vast difference to value. Turquoise is often fake (bite it to see if the colour comes off).

Wood and papier-mâché

Nepali **woodcarving** reaches its apex in Bhaktapur, where you'll find everything from modest Buddha busts and Ganesh figures to exquisite, full-size window frames. Miniature replicas of Bhaktapur's famed Peacock Window are ubiquitous, and artisans are increasingly turning out non-traditional items such as animals, CD boxes and chess sets. Pieces are carved with mallet and chisel out of one of several types of wood, most of them from the Tarai. The most common are *sal*, a hard, heavy, chocolate-coloured wood like teak; *sisu*, similar but with more grain to it; *chaab*, cheaper, softer and honey-coloured; and *korma*, also light in colour but harder than *chaab*. **Prices** depend not only on size but also the type of wood and the quality of carving: Rs1000 should get you a finely detailed 20cm figure. Sandalwood figures, carved in extremely intricate designs after the Indian style, are considerably more expensive.

Wooden masks are used by Tibetans and highland Nepalis in religious dances and shamanic rituals. The genuine articles are rarely sold, but replicas are widely available in tourist areas; in the never-ending battle for tourists' attention, craftsmen are now souping-up their masks with overlaid metal designs.

Thimi is famous for its **papier-mâché masks**, copies of those used in the masked dances of the Kathmandu Valley in which dancers take on the persona of the deity represented. The Nawa Durga (Nine Durgas) and their attendant deities Ganesh, Shiva and Bhairab are the ones most commonly re-created for tourist consumption, ranging from full-size down to bite-size. The Nawa Durga also take the form of **puppets** with papier-mâché or clay heads and multiple wooden arms.

Separately, Kashmiri shops sell little lacquered papier-mâché boxes, incense holders, napkin rings and ornaments – they're not Nepali, but they make great cheap gifts.

Paper items

Items made from *lokta*, an indigenous form of handmade **paper**, make excellent, lightweight purchases. Traditionally *lokta* was made by hill people in winter, when there was nothing going on, and was valued for official documents because of its strong, cross-fibrous texture. In the past decade or so, many aid organizations have seized on *lokta* as a year-round opportunity to generate income, and it has blossomed into a thriving industry carried out by an internationally famous UNICEF operation in Bhaktapur, and increasingly in other places too.

Lokta is often confused with rice paper. It's actually made from the bark of a shrub (genus *Daphne*) that grows wild in Nepal's eastern and central hills between the elevations of 2000 and 3000 metres (it's not cultivated, so the increasing popularity of *lokta* products may eventually lead to its depletion). The fibrous bark is boiled, beaten to a pulp, mixed with water, poured into floating frames, and finally sun-dried on fallow terraces. The result is a rough but richly textured parchment which may be block-printed, painted or interwoven with leaves to produce beautiful greeting cards, lampshades, calendars, gift wrapping, boxes and a growing range of other products, none of which cost more than a few hundred rupees.

Carpets

Tibetan-style handwoven **carpets** have come a long way from their folk roots. What started out, thirty years ago, as a modest income generator for Tibetan refugees has become Nepal's biggest export item – and a multiethnic creative collaboration. The traditional Tibetan form has been reinvented, with a unique look and a lustrous, hard-wearing texture brought about by the use of synthetic dyes, blended Tibetan and New Zealand wool, standardized manufacture and modern chemical washing processes. In recent years the field has also been enlivened by an explosion of contemporary colour schemes and designs.

Many foreigners prefer carpets in earthy, pastel **colours**, assuming them to be traditional and presumably coloured with vegetable dyes. Actually, traditional Tibetan carpets come in bright, almost gaudy hues – earth tones are in vogue because of foreign demand. Synthetic dyes can produce any colour or shade, whether muted or bright, whereas vegetable dyes have a more limited range. Carpets made of all-Tibetan lamb's wool and/or vegetable dyes are less common, and more expensive.

Traditional Tibetan **designs** are bold and simple – angular dragons, flowers, clouds or various auspicious symbols, usually against a plain field and contained within a geometric border. Many carpets being produced these days are further simplified, using large, open fields, and combining traditional motifs with abstract patterns.

Carpets are woven throughout the Kathmandu and Pokhara valleys. Compared to Middle Eastern makes, Tibetan-style carpets have deeper, more luxuriant pile, but lower knot densities and coarser patterns. One of the best **shopping** areas is in Patan (there's more about their manufacture on p.164). The choice is vast, so take your time. Start by getting an idea of what different **knot counts** (usually 60, 80, 100 or 144 per square inch) and wool mixes (50-, 80- or 100-percent Tibetan wool) and sizes look like. Sizes aren't standardized, but many carpets are 3x6 feet; 18-inch squares, which make fine seat covers, are also common. Make sure the ratio of vertical to horizontal knots isn't less than 2:3. **Prices** are of course subject to bargaining, and you can pay anything from $30 to $100-plus per square metre, depending on quality. Note that Nepali carpets are often made with child labour. At least one organization based in Kathmandu (Rugmark) certifies that its carpets aren't, and some others say theirs aren't, though you have no way of verifying their claims.

Local carpet factories are increasingly imitating **Kashmiri and Afghan styles**, though these tend not to be as fine as the originals. Imported Kashmiri carpets are sold in many boutiques run by traders fleeing the tourist meltdown in Kashmir. These rugs are among the world's finest, but Kashmiri rug salesmen are among the world's wiliest, so proceed with great caution. A *pukka* carpet is a major investment, costing $500–2000 for a decent 3x5, depending mainly on knot count. It should have a label on the back stating that it was made in Kashmir, as well as what it's made of (wool, silk, or "silk touch" – wool combined with a little cotton and silk to give it a sheen), its size, number of knots per inch, and the name of the design. To tell if it really is silk, scrape the carpet lightly with a knife and burn the fluff: real silk shrivels to nothing and leaves a distinctive smell.

Textiles and clothing

Nepali designers are applying their creative talents to **textiles** and, as with carpets, adapting indigenous designs in stylish new ways. Most of these items are produced by tiny cottage-industry outfits and have yet to find their way overseas, but the fleeting success of certain fashions shows there's a receptive market.

Dhaka, a brightly patterned cotton weave made on hand looms in the eastern and western hills, has long been used to make *topi* (men's caps), *cholo* (women's half-length blouses) and shawls. Palpali *dhaka*, the preferred make for *topi*, comes from Tansen (Palpa), and you'll find more about it in that section (p.318). Women's co-operatives are now producing *dhaka* in colour schemes and patterns aimed squarely at Western tastes, and turning it into scarves, ties, place mats, jackets, handbags – you name it. Other cotton weaves, including *khadi* (traditional homespun) and many

forms of sari material, are produced locally all over Nepal. These, too, turn up in innovative incarnations – block-printed, quilted and hand-stitched – from pot holders and tea cosies to cushion covers and bedspreads.

Hemp products are appearing in many outlets. For clothing, hemp fibres are usually mixed with cotton, wool or silk to produce linen-look garments (pure hemp is rather rough on the skin). Hemp is also being used in handbags, totes, caps and hats, and even shoes and slippers. At least one group also markets **allo**, a wool-like material woven from the pounded bark of nettle stems.

Pashmina, a cashmere-like wool gleaned from the softest hair of goats, is made into shawls which are worn by many Kathmandu Valley residents in winter. These are good purchases, but be sure you're not buying acrylic and watch out for dyes that aren't fixed properly. Rub off some fibres and burn them: pashmina will smell like burning hair, acrylic won't smell of anything. A scarf can be had from Rs300 and up; shawls sell for around Rs2000 for a large one, or Rs1500 for a medium-sized version; you can get weaves in seventy-percent pashmina and thirty-percent silk for about half that. Kashmiri shops sell more elaborate embroidered shawls and various items decorated with chain-stitch patterns, including cushion covers, tea cosies and garments far too magnificent to wear in public. You can also pick up nice **leather** jackets and other clothing items at reasonable prices.

Silk is a relatively new industry in Nepal, with a few manufacturers in the Kathmandu Valley producing thread and raw material. Others weave Indian thread into *dupian*, which looks like raw silk but is softer, shinier and more expensive, or fine *crepe de Chine*.

Nepal's burgeoning **garment industry** has been quick to experiment with all these materials and more, producing everything from cheap readymade Punjabi trouser suits to designer fashions purchased by foreigners and a growing clientele of wealthy Nepalis. Boutiques in Kathmandu and Patan display some stunning original pieces melding Western and local influences; in global fashion terms, these are quite cheap, and all the more exciting for their obscurity.

Tibetan wraparound dresses, called

chuba, can be bought off-the-peg, and are also custom-made at shops in Kathmandu and Boudha; in the same areas, you'll also find specialist shops selling intricate Tibetan and Bhutanese **brocade**.

Sweaters, socks and other **woollens**, knitted in the home by women, are amazingly cheap and sold all over tourist areas. The cheaper ones suffer from quality-control problems – many will quickly fall apart at the seams. Ask which grade of wool the garment is made from. For more durability and better styling, it's worth paying more at one of the pricier boutiques in Kathmandu or Patan.

Other **cheap clothes** sold in tourist areas are usually of very poor quality, but they'll do for holiday wear – cotton dresses are good choices for trekking. Lots of travellers seem to think they're "going native" by wearing baggy, brightly coloured and totally un-Nepalese wools, distressed cottons and the like, which amuses Nepalis. Machine-embroidered T-shirts are inescapable. Tibetan-style black felt with rainbow trim is another budget-wear staple, finding its way into caps, jackets and bags.

Paintings

Like so many things in Nepal, **thangka** – Tibetan ritual paintings – are now cranked out for the tourist market, yet the best ones remain undiminished by commercialization, and even the cheapest can't hide the dense Buddhist symbolism inherent in the form. The production process and subject matter of these vibrant, intricate paintings is discussed on p.163.

Thangka are produced not only by Tibetans but also by Tamangs and, increasingly, by artisans of other Nepali ethnic groups. In addition, **poubha** – paintings in the style of the Kathmandu Valley's Newars – are undergoing a modest revival after near extinction in the early twentieth century. *Poubha* are created in much the same way as *thangka*, but they tend to contain less background detail, focusing instead on a central deity, who may just as easily be Hindu as Buddhist. Some *thangka* dealers also carry other Tibetan-style paintings depicting herbs, animals, medical charts and so on.

Before **buying** a *thangka* or *poubha*, first watch a painter at work – Patan and Bhaktapur are the main centres – to get an appreciation for how painstaking the art is; try to get someone to explain the imagery and the meanings behind it. When you see one you like, examine the detail of the eyes, facial expression and fingers of the main figure; background figures should also stand up to scrutiny. Many paintings aimed at tourists make a great show of their "gold" paint: real gold won't come away when a moist finger is pressed against it. Most "old" *thangka* have been aged with wood smoke. As with carpets, the brighter, more garish colours are in fact the traditional ones; *thangka* in muted browns or deep, dark blues are made to tourist tastes. Small, ill-made souvenir models can sell for as little as Rs100, but a good, small (say 15x30cm) *thangka* will **cost** ten times that. If you can find one – most dealers only stock real quality in large sizes. A full-size painting, using microscopic brushstrokes and genuine gold paint, will cost hundreds of dollars.

So-called **"Maithili"** art has caught on in the past few years. These brightly coloured folk paintings, which keep alive age-old religious and fertility symbols, are created by women in the villages surrounding Janakpur in the eastern Tarai (for more on them, see p.393). However, they're most easily bought in the nonprofit shops of Kathmandu or Patan, where Maithili motifs are reproduced not only on paper but also pottery and papier-mâché.

Other nontraditional artforms are gaining in popularity. Notable are the *thangka*-influenced **naive maps** of Nepal and the Kathmandu Valley that are found primarily in Patan, and the watercolour (and occasionally acrylic or oil) **street scenes** and **ethnic portraits** sold in all the tourist areas. **Batiks**, depicting typical Nepali scenes, are an inexpensive artform introduced in the past two decades as an income-generator for disabled people in the Kathmandu and Pokhara valleys.

Miscellaneous crafts

Khukuri, the all-purpose tool of the hillman and the deadly weapon of the Gurkha soldier, is Nepal's most ubiquitous souvenirs. Bhojpur, in the eastern hills, is the traditional forging centre, but knives are heavily peddled in Kathmandu. An authentic one will have a moon-shaped notch at the base of the blade to channel the blood away, and its sheath will contain two small tools for sharpening and honing. Prices start at Rs200, but a city-slicker model with a buffalo-horn handle will cost several times that.

Kathmandu Valley and Pokhara are awash with **Tibetan curios**, though the vast majority of these are manufactured in Nepal or India. The range of items is formidable: prayer wheels, amulets, charm boxes, bracelets (usually inscribed with the mantra, *Om mani padme hum*), prayer-flag printing blocks, *chhang* pots, *phurpa* (ritual daggers), masks, turquoise and coral jewellery, musical instruments and many other religious artefacts. Much of it has been artificially aged, and the turquoise is often fake. Tibetan chests and other furniture, if genuine, are quite expensive. The sale of human skulls and skull bowls (which are quite real), ornamented with metalwork and baubles and traditionally used for tantric purposes, is illegal and such items are now sold only in secret; decorated goat skulls are easy enough to come by.

Some shops in Kathmandu sell nothing but **musical instruments**, including *sarangi* (Nepal's version of a fiddle), *murali* (flutes) and *jhankri* (shaman) drums. Tibetan instruments can be purchased in Boudha.

Simple, unglazed **pottery** is produced by *kumal* (potters) throughout the hills. Very little of it rises above the level of mundane implements, but the potters of Bhaktapur and Thimi turn out ornamental items – candlesticks, elephant-shaped plant pots and so on. Some of the nonprofit shops sell nontraditional, glazed pieces.

Other items

Attractive embroidered pouches and wooden "caddies" of Nepali **tea** make great presents or souvenirs. They're sold mainly in the Kathmandu Valley, but the tea itself is cultivated in the eastern hills around Ilam (just over the border from Darjeeling), and you'll find an account of processing and grading in that section (p.407). Two principal varieties are grown for export: Ilam, which has a full flavour much like Darjeeling, and Kanyam,

smokier but considered superior by many. If you're not bothered about presentation, loose tea is much cheaper than the packaged stuff and can be sealed in plastic for travelling.

Dozens of varieties of **incense** manufactured in Nepal (and others imported from India) are available in every bazaar. Tibetan mixtures, made in Nepal and sold mainly in Tibetan neighbourhoods such as Boudha and Swayambhu, are redolent of juniper. **Essential oils**, used for aromatherapy, massage and other purposes, come in a wide variety in tourist-quarter shops – like incense, they're extracted from plants in India and Nepal.

There's no need to lug a library along when travelling in Nepal: Kathmandu and Pokhara each have dozens of **bookshops** devoted to travel, fiction and classics. You can get new and used books in English and other European languages, usually as Western imports but sometimes in cheaper Indian imprints. Most shops will buy or trade books as well.

A burgeoning number of music stores stock **CDs and cassettes**. The Western discs sold in tourist shops are mostly pirated versions manufactured in Singapore, Pakistan and even Ukraine, and consequently they're quite cheap (about Rs250 each); Indian and Tibetan CDs are comparably priced, while Nepali discs unfortunately cost the most (about Rs550). Nepalese tapes are usually of poor quality, but so cheap that it won't hurt to take a chance on a few. Asian VCDs are riskier, as many refuse to play on European and North American DVD machines. See "Music and dance" in Contexts for a recommended discography.

Things **not to take home** include ritual objects made from human bones (or even animal bones that a customs officer might mistake for human ones), and anything made from a rare or protected species (including ivory, certain furs and peacock feathers). These are illegal to export from Nepal. So are *shaligram* (fossil-bearing stones), though nobody seems to care much about their export. As for **drugs**, see "Crime, hustle and hassle", p.64.

Spiritual pursuits and alternative therapies

Nepal is a great place to go to challenge your assumptions, study other systems of thought and open yourself to other ways of experiencing life. The tolerant atmosphere encourages experimentation and provides several traditional disciplines to delve into.

Moreover, Nepal has emerged as quite a **spiritual supermarket**. The past decade has seen an explosion of outfits teaching yoga and meditation in the Kathmandu Valley, and centres are starting to pop up in the other tourist watering-holes as well. The allied health fields of ayurvedic and Tibetan medicine are also attracting a growing interest among travellers in Nepal. Many programmes are designed for those who are just starting out and don't require a lengthy commitment, although some do. Note that it's advisable to book any residential courses well in advance – website or email addresses are given in the guide where possible.

This section provides a quick introduction to a few major practices. For general background on Hinduism and Buddhism, which provide their philosophical bases, be sure to read the "Religion" section in Contexts.

Yoga

Contrary to what's often put about in Western manuals, **yoga** is not just exercises – it's a system of spiritual, mental and physical self-discipline, designed to bring about mastery of the self and true awareness of the self's oneness with the universe. There are several classical schools of yoga, but the ones that fit most easily into Western lifestyles come under the category of **raja yoga**, and share eight "limbs" or steps (*astanga*) which represent an ascending path to self-control. The first two are the moral limbs, divided into do's and don'ts; after that come the three external limbs, *asana* (correct posture), *pranayama* (correct breathing) and *pratyahana* (control of the senses); followed finally by the three internal limbs, *dharana* (concentration), *dhyana* (meditation) and *samadhi* (super-consciousness).

Yoga's reputation for headstands and the like comes from **hatha yoga**, which places special emphasis on the three external methods to purify the body as an aid to developing the self. The term comes from the syllables "*ha*" and "*tha*", representing inhalation and exhalation, since breath-control techniques, along with various postures, form an important part of this practice. Another popular variant, **kundalini yoga**, stresses meditation. The individual visualizes the process of enlightenment as a serpent, coiled near the base of the spine, rising through six psychic centres (*chakra*) in an ascending progression of consciousness, finally reaching the seventh, highest level.

Several **yoga centres** are located in and around Kathmandu, and are rounded up on p.172.

Buddhist meditation and study

Meditation is closely related to yoga, and the two often overlap: much of yoga (kundalini, for example) involves meditation, and Buddhist meditation draws on many Hindu yogic practices. However, meditation centres in Nepal generally follow the Buddhist – particularly Tibetan Buddhist – tradition.

Buddhist meditation is a science of mind. To Buddhists, mind is the cause of confusion and ego, and the aim of meditation is to transcend these. **Vipassana** ("insight") is the kernel of all forms of Buddhist meditation; related to hatha yoga, it emphasizes the minute observation of physical sensations and mental processes to achieve a cool, clear understanding of mind. Another basic practice common to most schools of Buddhism, **shamatha** ("calm abiding" – co-opted by New Agers as "be here now") attunes and sharpens the mind by means of coming back again and again to a meditative discipline (breathing, visualization, etc). Theravada Buddhists consider *vipassana* to be sufficient for the attaining of enlightenment. At least two centres in the Kathmandu Valley run rigorous residential courses in this practice – see p.171 for details of one that caters to foreigners.

Tibetan Buddhist centres start students out with *vipassana* and *shamatha*, which form the foundation for a large armoury of meditation practices. An adept (novice) will cultivate Buddha-like qualities through visualization techniques – meditating on the deity that manifests a particular quality, while chanting the *mantra* and performing the *mudra* (hand gesture) associated with that deity. The Tibetan Buddhist path also involves numerous rituals, such as prayer, offerings, circumambulation and other meritorious acts; committed followers will take vows, too. Kathmandu has several centres offering introductory courses (see p.171).

A big part of Tibetan Buddhism is the teacher–disciple relationship. More advanced students of the *dharma* will want to **study** under one of the lamas at Boudha (see p.198), some of whom give discourses in English.

Ayurveda

Ayurveda (often spelled "ayurved") is the world's oldest form of medicine still being practised. Dating back five thousand years, the "knowledge of life" is a holistic medical system that assumes the fundamental sameness of self and nature. Unlike the allopathic medicine of the West, which is all about finding out what's ailing you and then killing it, *ayurveda* looks at the whole patient: disease is regarded as a symptom of imbalance, so it's the imbalance that's treated, not the disease.

Ayurvedic theory holds that the body is controlled by **three forces** (*tridosha*), which are a reflection of the forces within the self: *pitta*, the force of the sun, which is hot and rules the digestive processes and metabolism; *kapha*, likened to the moon, the creator of tides and rhythms, which has a cooling effect and governs the body's organs, fluids and lubricants; and *vata*, wind, which relates to movement and the nervous system. The

healthy body is one that has the three forces in balance. To **diagnose** an imbalance, the ayurvedic doctor goes not only by the physical complaint but also family background, daily habits and emotional traits.

Treatment of an imbalance is typically with **herbal remedies** designed to alter whichever of the three forces is out of whack. Made according to traditional formulas using indigenous plants, ayurvedic medicines are cheaper than imports, which is why the Nepali government encourages their production. In addition, the doctor may prescribe various forms of **yogic cleansing** to rid the body of waste substances. To the uninitiated, these techniques will sound rather off-putting – for instance, swallowing a long strip of cloth, a short section at a time, and then pulling it back up again to remove mucus from the stomach.

You'll find **ayurvedic doctors** and clinics throughout the Hindu parts of Nepal, but those who are able to deal with foreigners are confined mainly to Kathmandu (see p.173).

Tibetan medicine

Medicine is one of the traditional branches of study for Tibetan Buddhist monks, and **Tibetan medicine** is based on the same philosophical and magical principles as Tibetan Buddhism.

Like ayurveda, from which it derives, Tibetan medicine promotes health by maintaining the correct balance of **three humours**: *beken*, inert matter or phlegm, which when out of balance is responsible for disorders of the upper body; *tiba*, heat or bile, which is associated with intestinal diseases; and *lung*, meaning wind, which may produce nervousness or depression.

Tibetan medicine is as much a spiritual discipline as a physical one. Part of a Tibetan doctor's regular practice is to meditate on the "medicine Buddha", a manifestation of the Buddha's compassion, wisdom and healing power. The physician **diagnoses** the patient's imbalance by examining the tongue, pulse and urine, and by determining the patient's psychological state through questioning. He'll then prescribe a **treatment** to counteract the imbalance, which initially may only be a change of diet or behaviour (for instance, "cold" disorders – those to do with wind – are treated with "hot" foods and activities). For quicker relief, he'll prescribe one of a range of herbal–mineral tablets, which have been empowered by special rites.

Recommended **clinics** specializing in Tibetan medicine are listed in the Kathmandu (p.173) and Boudha (p.201) sections.

Massage and therapies

Nepal, like many Asian countries, has its own indigenous form of **massage**. So-called Nepali "hard" massage is a deep, therapeutic treatment that works mainly on the joints and insertions (the places where muscles meet bones). It's not all that relaxing, but it

can be just the job for sore shoulders after a trek. Nepalis themselves rarely receive massages after the age of about three, and would find it hard to conceive of paying for one, but numerous masseurs ply their services to foreigners in Kathmandu and Pokhara. A few practitioners also offer yogic, shiatsu, Swedish or Thai massage.

Dubious-looking signs in the tourist areas frequently advertise "Yoga & Massage", which has become a sort of shorthand for a long menu of un-Nepali services: steam baths (usually a makeshift box with a hole in the top for your head to stick out), reflexology, herbal treatments and the like. Some of these serve as fronts for prostitution (see p.173). Caveat emptor.

Cultural hints

Customs and traditions run deep in Nepal. Few Nepalis get the chance to travel abroad, so their only exposure to the outside world is through travellers. This puts a great responsibility on visitors to be sensitive to Nepali ways and values, and to project a favourable image of foreigners – though in tourist enclaves like Kathmandu's Thamel district and Pokhara's Lakeside, they've seen it all before.

Many different ethnic groups coexist in Nepal, each with their own complex customs. In the Kathmandu Valley, where they mix the most, there's a necessarily high degree of **tolerance** toward different clothes and lifestyles – a fact that travellers sense, and often abuse. Away from the tourist areas, however, ethnic groups are quite parochial, and foreign ways may cause offence. That said, many taboos relax the further and higher you head into the mountains, as Hindu rules of behaviour are only partially shared by Buddhist and animist ethnic groups.

The do's and don'ts listed here are more **flexible** than they sound. You'll make gaffes all the time and Nepalis will rarely say anything. The list is hardly exhaustive, either: when in doubt, do as you see Nepalis doing.

Common courtesies

Giving the Nepali greeting, **namaste** (nah-

mah-*stay*), with your palms held together as if praying, is one of the most attractive and addictive of Nepalese customs. It means "I salute the god within you", and isn't used freely or casually: think of it as "how do you do?" rather than "hello!" Returning a *namaste* with the appropriate word and depth of bow is a complex social calculation, but as a foreigner you need not worry too much about it. For informal greetings, most Nepalese throw out a rhetorical question, usually something like "have you eaten?", or "where have you come from?", but just saying "hello" in English will do fine. If you want to show great respect, *namaskar* is a more formal or subservient variant.

Another particularly delightful aspect of Nepali culture is the familiar **forms of address** that Nepalis use when speaking to each other: it's well worth learning *didi* ("older sister"), *bahini* ("younger sister"), *daai* ("older brother"), *bhaai* ("younger brother"), *buwa* ("father") and *aamaa* ("mother") for the warm reaction they'll usually provoke. To be more formal or respectful, just add *"ji"* to the end of someone's name. You may find people doing this with your own name, as in *"namaste*, John-*ji"*.

The word *dhanyabaad* is usually translated as **thank you**, but you'll rarely hear Nepalis use it, except in Kathmandu, where they've copied it from tourists. Saying thank you in this way is normally reserved for a person of higher rank or someone who has gone above and beyond the call of duty – it's inappropriate to toss it around casually, say when someone brings you a plate of food. If you feel like you have to say something, "thank you" in English is widely understood, or you could try the untranslatable *la* ("so!").

The gestures for **"yes"** and **"no"** may also cause confusion, since Nepalis don't nod or shake their heads. To indicate agreement, rock your head slightly to one side and then back the other way. To tell a tout or a seller "no", hold one hand in front of you, elbow pointing towards the ground, and swivel your wrist subtly, as if you were adjusting a bracelet. (Shaking the head in the Western fashion looks too much like "yes".)

Caste and status

In Nepal, where Hinduism is tempered by Buddhist and other influences, caste doesn't dominate social interactions to quite the extent that it does in India. Nevertheless, caste *is* deeply ingrained in the national psyche, as even non-Hindus were historically assigned places in the hierarchy based on ethnic affiliation or occupation. Following India's lead, Nepal "abolished" the official caste system in 1963, but a millennia-old system cannot be dismantled overnight. For most Nepalis, **caste and status** continue to determine what they do for a living, whom they may (or must) marry, where they can live and with whom they can associate.

In a Hindu society, foreigners are technically **casteless**, and their presence is polluting to orthodox, high-caste Hindus. In Nepal, this is really only a big deal in traditional households in the remote far western hills, but wherever you travel you should be sensitive to minor caste restrictions: for example, you will not be allowed to enter the kitchen of a high-caste Hindu home.

However, status (*ijat*) is an equally important factor in Nepalese society, and as a foreigner you have a lot of it: you are fabulously wealthy, relative to most Nepalis, and your culture dominates the world. Status adds extra complexity and nuance to interactions between strangers. Meeting for the first time, Nepalis observe a ritual of asking each other's name, home town, education, profession and age, all to determine relative status and therefore the correct form of address and level of deference.

Eating

Probably the greatest number of Nepali taboos – to an outsider's way of thinking – have to do with **food**. One underlying principle is that once you've touched something to your lips, it's polluted (*jutho*) for everyone else. If you take a sip from someone else's water bottle, try not to let it touch your lips (and the same applies if it's your own – you're expected to share). Don't eat off someone else's plate or offer anyone food you've taken a bite out of, and don't touch cooked food until you've bought it.

Another all-important point of etiquette is eat with your **right hand** only. In Nepal, as in most Asian countries, the left hand is reserved for washing after defecating; you can use it to hold a glass or utensil while you eat, but don't eat, wipe your mouth, pass food or point at someone with it. It's considered good manners to give and receive everything with the right hand. In order to convey respect, offer money, food or gifts with both hands, or with the right hand while the left hand cups the right elbow.

Clothing and the body

Nepalis are innately conservative in their attitudes to **clothing**. Clearly, you're not Nepali, but it's worth knowing how you may come across. Visitors can flout local traditions, but doing so will only shut you off from the happy encounters with locals that make travelling in Nepal so pleasant. The following hints apply especially in temples and monasteries.

Men should always wear a shirt in public, and long trousers if possible (men who wear shorts are assumed to be of a low caste). For **women**, a dress or skirt that hangs to mid-calf level is traditional, though trousers are acceptable these days. Women in shorts or a short skirt run the risk of being seen as if they were sexually available. More surprisingly, perhaps, shoulders should also be covered up – a T-shirt is much more appropriate than a vest. Looking clean and well groomed shows respect – many Nepalis reckon that travellers are rich, and ought to look the part.

Nudity is a sensitive issue. Only women with babies or small children in tow bare their breasts. When Nepali men bathe in public, they do it in their underwear, and women bathe underneath a *lungi* (sarong). Foreigners are expected to do likewise. Nepal has some idyllic hot springs, but most are heavily used as bathing areas; don't scare the locals off by stripping. Paradoxically (many villages have no covered toilets), it's deemed okay to defecate in the open – but out of sight of others, in the early morning or after dark. Men may urinate in public away from buildings – discreetly – but women have to find a sheltered spot.

Still other conventions pertain to **the body**. In Nepal, the forehead is regarded as the most sacred part of the body and the feet the most unclean. It's impolite to touch an adult Nepali's head, and it's an insult to kick someone. (The Nepali equivalent of tarring and feathering is to force a person to wear a garland of shoes.) Don't put your feet on chairs or tables, and when sitting, try not to point the soles of your feet at anyone. On a related note, it's bad manners to step over the legs of someone seated: in a crowded place, Nepalis will wait for you to draw in your feet so they can pass.

Nepali views about **displays of affection** are the opposite of what most of us are used to. It's considered acceptable for friends of the same sex to hold hands or put their arms around each other in public, but not for lovers of the opposite sex. Couples who cuddle or kiss in public, or in front of a Nepali host, will at best draw unwelcome attention. At worst, you've offended everyone around you and reinforced the dangerous notion that foreign women are sex objects. Don't shake hands with a Nepali woman, as this form of contact is not traditional.

Temples and homes

Major Hindu **temples** or their inner sanctums are usually off-limits to nonbelievers, who are technically outside the caste system (traditionalists may even see foreigners as "untouchables"), and therefore a possible cause of ritual pollution. Being debarred for being non-Hindu may feel like unfair discrimination, but respect the rule, which is just a small part of a complex and highly structured set of beliefs that pervades Nepalese society. In a country where nearly everything is open to inspection by outsiders, some things must remain sacred. In most cases, you can see everything from outside anyway.

Where you are allowed in, be respectful, take your shoes off before entering (it's worth wearing slip-ons if you're doing a lot of temple- or monastery-visiting), don't take photos unless you've been given permission, and leave a few rupees in the donation box. Leather is usually not allowed in temple precincts. Don't touch offerings or shrines (usually covered in rice, flowers or red powder), nor people when they're on their way to shrines or are in the process of worshipping. The front of a shrine is usually marked by a pedestal supporting the deity's carrier, and/or a lotus-carved stone embedded in the ground: these define the territory of the shrine, where it's particularly important to be reverent.

Similar sensitivity is due at Buddhist temples and monasteries. If you're granted an audience with a lama, it's traditional to present him with a *kata* (a ceremonial white scarf, usually sold nearby). Walk around Buddhist stupas and monuments clockwise – that is, keep the monument on your right.

If invited for a meal in a private **home**, bring something appropriate such as fruit or sweets, but don't expect effusive thanks as gifts tend to be received without much fuss. Take your shoes off when entering, or follow the example of your host. When the food is ready you may be expected to serve yourself first, so you won't be able to follow your host's lead. Don't take more than you can eat – asking for seconds is the best compliment you can give. The meal is typically served at the end of a gathering; when the eating is done, everyone gets up and leaves.

Sherpas and some other highland groups regard the family **hearth** as sacred, so don't throw rubbish or scraps into it.

Casual encounters

Nepalis grow up constantly surrounded by other people (and noise); local people like to be with others, and may assume you do, too. And as a foreigner, you're likely to be an object of great curiosity to anyone who rarely has the chance to leave their home town, let alone travel abroad. You may be joined in the street or on the trail by someone who just wants a walk and a chat, and Nepalis will constantly be befriending you, wanting to exchange addresses and extracting solemn promises that you will write to them. (Sometimes they will ask you point-blank to help them travel to your country; more often than not, such a request is designed to tease you.)

Many travellers become frustrated or embarrassed by their interactions with Nepalis: it's hard to meet people who aren't trying to do business with you (see p.64), it's harder still to meet Nepali women, and everyone seems to ask the same stock **questions**, usually beginning with "what's your country?" and "how do you like Nepal?" Some questions are surprisingly intimate, such as asking how much you earn, but, as ever, there's a good reason for what may seem like rudeness. Less cosmopolitan Nepalis simply won't know how or where to place you (see the hints on status above), and giving you what feels like the third degree is a way of trying to understand who you are.

Try to convey an accurate impression of your home country, even in such casual encounters – a lot of myths go round about foreigners and you're a rare firsthand source of information. You may well be asked about exchange rates, and how it is that your currency is so much more valuable than theirs. (While this probably isn't the time to give a lecture on purchasing power, telling people how much rice costs back home is sure to provoke surprise and interest.) Another favourite question is how much your air ticket cost; it's likely to be more money than

your interrogator earns in a year, but lying isn't a good idea – Nepalis who meet a lot of tourists tend to know the answer anyway and may be teasingly testing how genuine your responses are, or just titillating themselves with the thought that anyone could have so much money.

Other hints

You may be dismayed by the amount of **rubbish** in the streets. There are few rubbish bins in Nepal (and currently, nowhere to dump city garbage at all), so people throw their litter on the ground, where it may or may not be swept up or burnt by other people whose job it is to do so. If you're uncomfortable throwing your litter on the street, don't buy things that cause it, or find a big pile that's already there and add your handful to it.

Where they exist, **toilets** range from "Western" (sit-down) flush jobs to two planks projected over a stream. In lodges – tourist ones aside – the norm is a squat toilet, usually pretty stinky and flyblown. When travelling by bus, there will almost always be a bathroom available at rest stops, but sometimes the public toilet will be nothing but a designated field. When in doubt, ask *Toilet kahaa chha?* ("Where is the toilet?"). Don't flush **toilet paper**: put it in the basket provided. It's not provided in more basic guesthouses and restaurants, so buy your own. Nepalis use a jug of water and the left hand (try it yourself – it's no more or less disgusting than the toilet paper method, and somewhat cleaner).

Finally, **be patient**. Nepal is a developing country and things don't always work or start on time. It's unrealistic to expect things to be like they are at home, even if the menu or brochure makes it sound as if they will be. If a restaurant is slow in filling your order, it may be because they've only got one stove. Getting angry or impatient will only confuse Nepalis and won't resolve the problem. The local way of dealing with setbacks isn't to complain, or even to keep a stiff upper lip, but to shrug, saying *ke garne?* ("what can one do?").

You can't change Nepal, and even if you could, it is not yours to change. Many things in Nepal are slow, inefficient or downright nutty, but that's just the way things are.

Taking the attitude that "somebody's got to teach them a lesson" or "if nobody complains it'll never change" will only make you and everyone around you miserable. Go with the flow.

To get by with a minimum of disappointment, the best strategy is to scale back your expectations, always double- and triple-check important arrangements, take all assurances with a pinch of salt (Nepalis will sometimes tell you what they think will make you happy rather than the truth), and find something interesting to do while you're waiting.

Travelling with children

Kids always help break the ice with strangers, and in Nepal they unleash even more than the usual hospitality (although the lack of privacy may prove to be a problem). Children can also open a door into the often closed world of Nepali women. Nepal is a pretty magical place to be a child. Kings and queens, fantastical tales of elephant-headed gods and superhero babies, a living goddess who gets to play the coolest kind of dress-up, snake charmers, elephant rides, cows, chickens and goats in the streets, festivals and pageantry and amazing sights on every corner: it's like being right inside a fairy tale or adventure story, and kids drink it up.

Arranging **childcare** is no problem, since labour is cheap and Nepalis generally love kids. Often you don't need to make arrangements – your offspring will be taken in hand by the nearest adult or older child. Some children (especially those with fair skin and blond hair) may be uncomfortable with the unaccustomed attention, however.

Parents will of course have to take extra **precautions** in the light of Nepal's poor sanitation, dogs, crowds, traffic, pollution, bright sun, rooftops and steep slopes. It may be hard to keep hands clean and yucky stuff out of mouths. You'll have to keep a firm grip on small children while out and about; drum home the necessity of keeping away from dogs and only drinking clean water. If your child comes down with diarrhoea, it's extremely important to keep him or her hydrated and topped up on salts – have oral rehydration formula on hand.

Naturally you'll want to plan a more modest itinerary and travel in greater **comfort** with children than you might on your own. Nepal's winding, bumpy roads are likely to make kids travel-sick, so take bus journeys in very small doses, or rent a car. Most cheap lodgings will be out of the question on account of their bathroom arrangements. In tourist areas it should be no problem finding **food** that kids will eat, but elsewhere they're bound to turn their noses up at "spicy" food and anything too wildly unfamiliar. Few restaurants have high chairs. Baby food and disposable **nappies/diapers** are available in Kathmandu and Pokhara, but are hard to come by elsewhere. Some toys and books can be purchased in Nepal, but bring a supply of your own. Carry small tots in a backpack or papoose – a stroller or pushchair will be virtually useless.

Trekking with children is generally a wonderful experience (see p.416), though it can be logistically awkward if they're too old to ride in a backpack and too young to hike on their own. You'll need one or more porters for all the kiddie paraphernalia; porters can also carry young ones in modified *doko* (wicker baskets). Trekking with an agency can alleviate some of the hassles – ask what special facilities they provide for children.

Travellers with disabilities

Although disability is common in Nepal, it's a poor country without the means to cater for disabled travellers. If you walk with difficulty, you'll find the steep slopes, stairs and uneven pavements hard going. Open sewers, potholes, crowds and a lack of proper street crossings will all make it hard for a blind traveller to get around. That said, guides are readily available and should be prepared to provide whatever assistance you need. Nepalis are also likely to be very helpful.

With a companion, there's no reason why you can't enjoy many of Nepal's activities, including elephant rides, scenic mountain flights and sightseeing by private car. If you rent a taxi for the day, the driver is certain to help you in and out, and perhaps around the sites you visit. A safari in one of the Tarai wildlife parks should be feasible, and even a trek, catered to your needs by an agency, might not be out of the question. Try Himalayan Holidays (☎01/427705, ⓦwww.himholidays-nepal.com), which has experience in tours for clients with disabilities.

Basic **wheelchairs** are available for use in the Kathmandu airport, and smaller airports, including Pokhara, are mostly at ground level. Generally, however, facilities for the disabled are nonexistent, so you should bring your own wheelchair or other necessary walking aids or equipment. Hotels aren't particularly geared up for disabled guests,

though the most expensive ones have lifts and ramps.

Contacts for travellers with disabilities

Australia Australian Council for Rehabilitation of the Disabled, PO Box 60, Curtin, ACT 2605 ☎02/6282 4333.
Ireland Irish Wheelchair Association, Blackheath Drive, Clontarf, Dublin 3 ☎01/833 8241, ⓔiwa@iol.ie.
New Zealand Disabled Persons Assembly, 4/173–175 Victoria St, Wellington, New Zealand ☎04/801 9100.
UK Royal Association for Disability and Rehabilitation, 12 City Forum, 250 City Rd, London EC1V 8AF ☎020/7250 3222, Minicom ☎020/7250 4119, ⓦwww.radar.org.uk.
USA Mobility International USA ☎541/343-1284, ⓦwww.miusa.org; Society for Accessible Travel and Hospitality ☎212/447-7284, ⓦwww.sath.org.

Women's Nepal

In most parts of the country, women will be of interest mainly as foreigners rather than as women, but a few specific tips are given below.

Life as a Nepali woman can mean years of unrelenting toil with little recognition. For **women travellers**, however, most parts of Nepal are relatively easy: the atmosphere is tolerant and inquisitive rather than threatening or dangerous. Nepali society is on the

whole chaste, almost prudish; **men** are almost universally respectful to and perhaps a little in awe of, foreign women. **Sexual harassment** is unlikely to upset your travels: staring and catcalling happen sometimes, but it's nowhere near as bad as in India, or indeed most of the world, and it seldom goes any further than words. Your chief danger comes from the rare predatory trekking guide (see p.421).

However, wearing revealing **clothes** will up the chances of receiving unwelcome advances. It's easy for Nepali men to get the idea that foreign women are wanton – relatively speaking, they are. Wearing a short dress, shorts or a top or skirt that's made of thin material may reinforce this stereotype for some men. That doesn't mean you have to wear Nepali clothes, it just means that you ought to wear more modest things that don't reveal thighs or shoulders. In tourist areas you can buy cheap calf-length dresses and skirts that fill the bill. If you trek on one of the popular routes and see how many trekkers wear skimpy clothes, you might wonder whether this is obsolete advice. It isn't. It's true that Nepalis along the main routes have seen everything by now, and in any case they're too polite to say anything. So you can get away with it, but you'll definitely widen the distance between you and the Nepalis you meet, and you can pretty much forget about any rewarding cross-cultural interactions.

A woman travelling or **trekking alone** won't be hassled so much as pitied. Going alone (*eklai*) is most un-Nepali behaviour. Locals (of both sexes) will ask if you haven't got a husband – the question is usually asked out of genuine concern, not as a come-on. Teaming up with another female stops the comments as effectively as being with a man.

If you find yourself without a reserved seat on a **public bus**, you can make your way to the front compartment, where preference is usually given to women and children. About the only form of discrimination you'll encounter is during toilet stops, when you'll have to hunt around for a sheltered place while men are free to pee by the side of the road (yet another reason to wear a long skirt).

Tarai cities and border towns are another matter, unfortunately. Some men here, as in northern India, have some real misconceptions about Western women, and may try for a surreptitious grope or even expose themselves. Travelling with a man generally

shields you from this sort of behaviour. If that isn't possible, or if you resent having to do so, don't be afraid to make a public scene in the event of an untoward advance – that's what a Nepali woman would do. Though he'll pretend it wasn't him, all eyes will be upon him and he won't try it again.

Of course, you may find you want to strike up a **relationship** with a Nepali man. If so, you should have no trouble finding eligible candidates in the tourist bars. Quite a few women travellers fall for trekking or rafting guides – the men of highland ethnic groups, such as Sherpas, have very similar views to Westerners on sexual equality – and Kathmandu has a small but growing community of women who have married and settled there. However, be aware that Nepali men are not without their own agendas: exotic romance, conquest, perhaps even a ticket out of Nepal. If you suspect ulterior motives, let him down gently but firmly and he'll usually retreat gracefully. Be aware also that AIDS is a growing and largely concealed problem.

Meeting women

A frustrating aspect of travelling in Nepal is the difficulty of making contact with **Nepali women**. The tourism industry is controlled by men; women, who are expected to spend most of their time in the home and are given fewer educational opportunities, have little contact with foreigners and speak much less English. If you're lucky enough to be invited to a Nepali home for a meal, chances are the women of the house will remain in the kitchen while you eat, only emerging to clear the plates and eat the leftovers. Upper class women are free of these restrictions and are often well educated, but of course they don't have to work so they, too, have few dealings with travellers.

Sexual politics are different among highland ethnic groups, which is as good a reason as any for going **trekking**. Along trekking routes, many women run teahouses single-handedly while their husbands are off guiding or portering. Proud, enterprising and flamboyant, these "*didis*" are some of the most wonderful people you're likely to meet anywhere. Language may be a problem off the popular trails, but that doesn't rule out all communication. On buses, women will be much more approachable in the front compartment. And anywhere you go, having a child with you will always open doors.

For more on **women's issues** in Nepal, see "Development dilemmas" (p.541). Rough Guides' *Women Travel* gives one Western woman's account of travelling in the country.

Living and working in Nepal

Working or studying while in Nepal can add a satisfying focus to your trip, and deepen your understanding of another way of life. It's certainly the best way to meet and get to know Nepalis.

Unfortunately, you can't stay longer than 150 days in any calendar year on a tourist **visa** without special permission (though that means you can stay almost a year if your trip straddles two calendar years). To **stay longer**, you have to get a longer-term visa (such as the business, residential or study visas), but they're nearly all more expensive than the standard tourist visa and require an accredited organization to apply on your behalf to the relevant Nepalese government ministry.

Working

If you feel you've received a lot from Nepal, **volunteering** is a good way to give something back. You can volunteer on a less formal, shorter-term basis through a couple of organizations in Kathmandu that match willing foreigners with projects (p.175). The old people's hospices in Pashupatinath and Chabahil run by Mother Teresa's Sisters of Charity welcome walk-in help on a day-to-day basis. The Kathmandu Environmental Education Project, Himalayan Explorers Connection and Himalayan Rescue Association offices in Kathmandu can always use volunteers.

Postings with the Peace Corps, VSO and other **voluntary agencies** abound, providing you've got the relevant skills and the determination to stay two or more years. People with experience in education, health, nutrition, agriculture, forestry and other areas are preferred. Many other aid agencies (such as Action Aid, Save the Children, CARE and

Oxfam) operate in Nepal and occasionally take on specialists. See "Development dilemmas" (p.530) for an idea of what to expect.

If you just want an open-ended arrangement for a few weeks or so, **teaching English** is a good option. Language schools in Kathmandu and Pokhara occasionally take people on, although the pay is negligible. A certificate or even experience isn't always necessary. Numerous organizations run longer, more formal teaching programmes (see overleaf), often aimed at young people, but you'll pay for the privilege, once you've factored in training and support fees.

Paid work is almost impossible to find locally, and it's against the law to work on a tourist visa. Some people find jobs as trekking and rafting/kayaking guides, but it's becoming harder to find work as more and more Nepalis become trained. In any case, the pay will be low and you may want to question the ethics of taking a job that could be done by a Nepali who can't leave the country to find alternatives. Qualified masseurs and yoga/meditation instructors may be able to find work in Kathmandu or Pokhara – try contacting the places listed towards the end of those sections.

If you can persuade the Department of Industry that you've got a good business idea that will help Nepal's development, and you have a Nepali business partner, you may qualify for a **business visa**. If you've got upwards of $100,000 dollars to invest, you may even qualify for a **residential visa**.

Studying

A few **language schools** in Kathmandu offer intensive courses in Nepali, Newari or Tibetan (see p.175). Opportunities to study yoga and Tibetan Buddhism are summarized in "Spiritual pursuits and alternative therapies", on p.72. Several American universities run **study programmes** in Nepal; see the list below.

For anything longer-term or more formal you'll need to apply in writing to Tribhuwan University (Campus of International Languages, PO Box 4339, Exhibition Rd, Kathmandu, Nepal ☎01/258132 or 226713, ℱ255738), which runs courses in Nepali, Tibetan, Sanskrit and Newari. Nepali courses are usually offered for either three years (six semesters) or six weeks (sixty hours), but tailored courses can be offered to groups of students, and the campus has run one-year courses in the past. Each semester costs $527; a six-week course costs $150. The university will find you a study visa, which costs $40 per month.

Study and work programmes

Campus of International Languages Tribhuwan University ☎01/258132, ⓦwww.yomari.com/nepali -language/nepali-language.html. Kathmandu's first and most highly regarded university.
Educate the Children ⓦwww.etc-nepal.org. Three-month teaching stints.
Global Action Nepal ⓦwww.gannepal.org. Small, friendly Nepal-based organization offering structured six-month English-language teaching placements in schools across Nepal. Mostly aimed at UK-based young people.

Himalayan Explorers Connection ⓦwww.hec.org. Information on more than fifty programmes and opportunities. The club also runs its own volunteer programme for teachers in the Khumbu region.
Himalayan Rescue Association ⓔhra@aidpost .mos.com.np. Accepts four doctors each autumn and spring to staff its high-altitude aid posts; the waiting list is two or three years long, but it can't hurt to write.
Naropa Institute ⓦwww.naropa.edu/studyabroad/. Colorado institution that runs a thirteen-week course on Tibetan Buddhism each autumn at Boudha.
Peace Corps ☎1-800/424-8580, ⓦwww.peacecorps.gov. Places US citizens with specialist qualifications or skills in two-year postings.
School for International Training ⓦwww.sit.edu. Based in Brattleboro, Vermont, the School has its own campus in Kathmandu.
School of South Asian Studies ⓦwww.wisc .edu. Full-year study programmes with the University of Wisconsin–Madison.
Students Partnership Worldwide ⓦwww.spwnepal.org.np. Six-month schoolteaching placements and environmental education programmes. Foreign volunteers are paired with Nepalis. Relatively expensive, but training is thorough.
Study Abroad.com ⓦwww.studyabroad.com. Good list of contacts and programmes for study and volunteer opportunities in Nepal.
Volunteer Nepal ⓦhttp://web1.pipemedia.net /nepal. Small UK organization offering teaching programmes of two- to six-months' duration.
VSO (Voluntary Service Overseas) ⓦwww.vso.org .uk. Highly respected charity that sends qualified professionals from the UK, US and EU (in the fields of education, health, community and social work, forestry, engineering, information technology, law and media) to spend two years or more working for local wages on projects beneficial to developing countries. Special programmes for young people and over-60s, too.

Directory

AIRPORT DEPARTURE TAX Rs1100 (Rs900 if flying within south Asia). Domestic tax, for internal flights, is Rs165 from Kathmandu and Pokhara, and Rs137.5 from anywhere else.

ADDRESSES Many streets in Nepal don't even have names. In cities, intersections (*chowk*) and neighbourhoods (*tol*) usually do, and these are often applied, confusingly, to any or all of the streets nearby. There is some sort of arcane street-address system in Kathmandu, but it's of no use to travellers.

CONTRACEPTIVES Condoms and birth-control pills are available in pharmacies everywhere. Consult one of the Kathmandu clinics listed on p.174 for other contraceptive advice.

CUSTOMS Officers are fairly lax on entry, but they might note fancy video gear in your passport so you can't sell it in Nepal.

Checks are more thorough on departure, mainly to make sure you're not smuggling antiques out.

DRUGS Illegal, of course. However, cannabis grows wild throughout hill Nepal, and old folks sometimes smoke it as an evening tonic. Touts in Kathmandu – shady characters, but not informants – mostly peddle local hash, and also whisper offers of opium and heroin from the Golden Triangle.

What to bring

As a rule, travel light. You can buy or rent most things in Kathmandu and you may need extra space in your pack to bring home the shopping. This box goes over the essentials that are worth bringing from home or picking up specially in Nepal. If you think you might go trekking, rafting or mountain-biking, see the relevant chapters for an additional list of recommended items.

A **backpack** is probably best for heaving your things around on buses and rikshas, especially if you're also travelling in other parts of Asia as well; try to find one which you can secure with a padlock. A lightweight **daypack** also comes in handy for short excursions.

The **clothes** you bring will depend very much on the time of year, and where you expect to be going. For warm weather you'll want lightweight cotton garments – loose-fitting but modest, and covering enough to ward off sun, bugs and stares. Shorts and a swimsuit are worth bringing (especially for rafting), but heed the advice given in "Cultural hints", p.75. A lightweight wind- and waterproof jacket is advisable at any time of year. For cooler seasons, try to dress in layers: a T-shirt, long-sleeved shirt, sweater or fleece jacket and shell will set you up for almost any weather. A down jacket is fantastically warm but expensive, and must be kept dry.

Any sort of durable, lightweight **footwear** will be adequate for most conditions in Nepal, but you'll want something with a sturdy sole for trekking. You'll also need a backup pair of shoes in case those get wet. Flip-flops, available locally, will do in warm weather and are useful for protecting your feet in the shower; sport sandals are better, and perfect for rafting.

For the **sun**, bring sunscreen, lip balm, sunglasses and a brimmed hat; an **umbrella** (available locally) acts as an effective parasol at low elevations, and is indispensable during the monsoon. If you're heading to the Tarai, especially between April and October, bring **mosquito repellent** and/or mosquito **netting** (you can buy coils locally). **Toiletries** are pretty easy to come by, but bring anything out of the ordinary. Alcohol-based antibacterial soap is good for keeping hands clean, as you don't need to use water.

Carry valuables in a **money belt** or neck purse. **Earplugs** are good for shutting out the ubiquitous honking vehicles, barking dogs and general commotion at night. In cheap lodgings, a **sleeping sheet** is an insurance policy against bedbugs and the like (and a good extra liner for your **sleeping bag** if you're going trekking). A **musical instrument** or **photos of home** will help break the ice and while away some idle hours. **Binoculars** (or a long zoom lens) are great to have in the Tarai wildlife parks.

And finally, some odd essentials (all of which can be purchased in Nepal): a **flashlight** (torch); small **towel** (a *lungi* – a Nepalese woman's sarong – makes an attractive and lightweight substitute); **sewing kit**; pocket **alarm clock** for early-morning departures; sealable **plastic bags** for keeping things separate in your pack; **passport-size photos** for visa and trekking applications; and **photocopies of the pages in your passport** containing personal data and your Nepalese visa.

ELECTRICITY 220 volts/50 cycles per second, when you can get it: virtually all power in Nepal is generated by hydroelectric projects, so power cuts ("load shedding") are common, especially in spring when water levels get low. Most places tourists go are now electrified.

EMBASSIES AND CONSULATES All are in Kathmandu: see p.174.

EMERGENCIES Where there's a phone, dial ☏100 for the police. Hospitals have their own telephone numbers for an ambulance, but get a Nepali-speaker to do the talking. Registering with your embassy can expedite things in the event of an emergency.

GAY AND LESBIAN NEPAL Nepalis will tell you that gays and lesbians don't exist in Nepal. Openly, they don't: there are no gay bars or meeting places or any support network whatsoever, even in the capital. Yet in a society where the sexes are kept well apart before marriage, and men routinely hold hands and sleep in the same bed, it obviously goes on. Gay couples may feel a certain freedom in being able to be close in public, but otherwise the same advice on sexual behaviour in public applies as for heterosexual couples (see p.76). The only approach a gay traveller is likely to get is from touts who might offer, at the end of a long inventory of drugs, "nice Nepali girls", and if that doesn't work, boys. But it's nothing like the scene in, say, Thailand.

LAUNDRY Tourist guesthouses will generally send laundry out for you, although the turnaround time depends on the weather. Rates are reasonable. If you're doing your own, detergent is sold in inexpensive packets in cities, or you can buy a cheap cube of local laundry soap almost anywhere.

LEFT LUGGAGE Guesthouses will always store bags for you, an invaluable service if you go trekking or if you just want to travel light. The usual charge is a few rupees per item per day, but some places waive this, especially if you take a room when you return.

TIME Nepal is fifteen minutes ahead of India – just to be contrary, one suspects. That makes it five hours 45 minutes ahead of London, ten hours 45 minutes ahead of New York, thirteen hours 45 minutes ahead of Los Angeles, and nineteen hours 45 minutes ahead of Sydney. Nepal doesn't observe daylight saving time, so daylight saving time elsewhere reduces the time difference by one hour.

TIPPING Tipping isn't compulsory, but rather a reward to be bestowed for good service or withheld for bad. It has become standard to tip waiters in tourist restaurants (it may be their only pay), but Rs20 or so should be sufficient in all but the fanciest places. Don't tip taxi drivers, except maybe to round up the fare to the nearest Rs5 or Rs10. Trekking porters and guides have their own expectations – see Chapter Seven. Don't tip anyone until full completion of the service.

guide

guide

Kathmandu and Patan

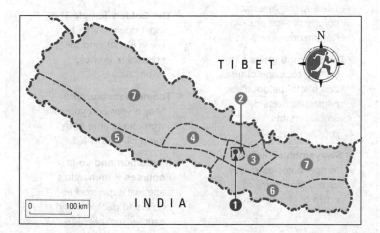

CHAPTER 1 # Highlights

✳ **Kathmandu Durbar Square** An old royal palace, a living goddess, temples, statues, vegetable sellers and curio hawkers commingle in this touristy yet vibrant hub. See p.108

✳ **Asan** This ancient waystation on the trade route to Tibet epitomizes traditionally prosperous old Kathmandu. See p.118

✳ **The Bagmati ghats** Little-visited relics and cremation platforms dot these neglected riverside embankments. See p.123 and p.145

✳ **Swayambhu** This hilltop temple complex serves as a profound microcosm of Nepali culture. See p.127

✳ **Baber Mahal Revisited** A converted Rana palace, now housing an Aladdin's cave of shops and restaurants. See p.136

✳ **Patan Durbar Square** The apex of Newari architecture, crowned by the classy Patan Museum. See p.139

✳ **The Golden Temple** The most opulent little temple in Nepal, and the spiritual hub of old Patan. See p.143

✳ **Thamel's restaurants** Stay a year and you still won't have time to try them all. See p.152

✳ **Meditation and yoga courses** Kathmandu's spiritual supermarket caters to dabblers and serious seekers alike. See p.171

Kathmandu and Patan

How to describe **KATHMANDU**? A medieval time capsule? An environmental disaster area? A pleasure dome? A tourist trap? A holy city? A dump? All of the above. There are a thousand Kathmandus, all layered and dovetailed and piled on top of one another in an extravagant morass of chaos and sophistication. Though its population barely tops 700,000, Nepal's capital is far and away its biggest and most cosmopolitan city: a melting pot of a dozen ethnic groups, and the home town of the Newars, Nepal's master craftsmen and traders extraordinaire (see p.507). Trade, indeed, created Kathmandu – for at least a thousand years it controlled the most important caravan route between Tibet and India – and trade has always funded its Newar artisans. Little wonder, perhaps, that the city has so deftly embraced the tourist business.

The Kathmandu most travellers experience, **Thamel**, is like a thumping, Third World theme park, all hotels and hoardings and promises, promises, with croissants and cakes beckoning from restaurant windows and touts flogging tiger balm and hashish to holiday hippies. The **old city**, though squeezed by traffic and commercial pressures, is still studded with ageless temples and splendid architecture. Its narrow lanes seethe with an incredible crush of humanity, echoing with the din of bicycle bells, religious music, construction and car horns, and reeking of incense, spices, sewage and exhaust fumes. Sacred cows still roam the streets, as do holy men, beggars, street urchins and coolies. To the south, the separate municipality of **Patan** was once the capital of an independent kingdom; though now subsumed into the greater Kathmandu conurbation, it has its own quieter and better-preserved historic district, marked by numerous Buddhist *bahal* (monastery compounds, some of them still active), proud artistry, and a laid-back tourism industry.

These quarters represent only a few facets of a complex and eccentric city that also encompasses squatter shantytowns, decrepit ministry buildings, swanky five-star shopping streets, sequestered suburbs and heaving bazaars. Perhaps the predominant images of contemporary Kathmandu are those that pass for progress: hellish traffic jams and pollution; a jostling skyline of rooftop water-storage tanks and obsolete satellite dishes; suburban sprawl, cybercafés, discos and trash heaps; power cuts and backup generators; chauffeured Land Cruisers and families on motorbikes. The city hasn't abandoned its traditional identity, but the rapid pace of change has produced an intense, often over-whelming, urban environment. Anyone visiting Nepal for its natural beauty is likely to be disillusioned by Kathmandu.

Nevertheless, Kathmandu is likely to be your first port of call in Nepal – all overseas flights land in the capital, and most roads lead to it – and you probably won't be able to avoid spending at least a couple of days here. It's the obvious place to sort out your affairs: it has all the **embassies** and airline offices, Nepal's best-developed **communications facilities**, and a welter of **trekking and travel agencies**. At least as important, in the minds of long-haul travellers anyway, are the capital's **restaurants** and the easy **social scene** that surrounds them, all of which makes Kathmandu the natural place to get your bearings in Nepal.

All things considered, though, you'd be well advised to get your business here over with as quickly as possible. If you're intending to do any sightseeing around the valley, consider basing yourself in the healthier surroundings of Bhaktapur or Boudha (see Chapter Two), or even further out in Nagarkot or Dhulikhel (see Chapter Three). These days, the smart money is on staying *outside* Kathmandu and making day trips *in*, not vice versa.

A little history

People must have occupied what is now Kathmandu for thousands of years, but chroniclers attribute the city's founding to Gunakamadev, who reigned in the late ninth century – by which time sophisticated urban centres had already been established by the **Lichhavi** kings at Pashupatinath and other sites in the surrounding valley. Kathmandu was originally known as Kantipur, but it later took its present name from the Kasthamandap ("Pavilion of Wood") that was constructed as a rest-house along the main Tibet–India trade route in the late twelfth century, and which still stands in the city centre.

The city rose to prominence under the **Malla** kings, who took control of the valley in the thirteenth century and ushered in a golden age of art and architecture that lasted more than five hundred years. All of Kathmandu's finest buildings and monuments, including those of its spectacular Durbar Square, date from this period. At the start of the Malla era, Kathmandu ranked as a sovereign state alongside the valley's other two major cities, Bhaktapur and Patan, but soon fell under the rule of Bhaktapur. The cities were again divided in the fifteenth century, and a long period of intrigue and rivalry followed.

Malla rule ended abruptly in 1769, when Prithvi Narayan Shah of Gorkha, a previously undistinguished hill state to the west, captured the valley as the first conquest in his historic unification of Nepal. Kathmandu fared well in defeat, being made capital of the new nation and seat of the new **Shah** dynasty. The Shahs rule to this day, although from 1846 to 1951 they were politically out-manoeuvred by the powerful **Rana** family, who ruled as hereditary prime ministers and left Kathmandu with a legacy of enormous whitewashed Neoclassical palaces. The capital remains the focus of all national political power – the 1990 democracy movement led, inevitably, to the palace gate – while its industrial and financial activities continue to fuel a round-the-clock building boom.

Note that when dialling Kathmandu Valley numbers from within the area, you must omit the initial 01 area code. All local numbers listed in this chapter are inclusive of area code, separated from the number by a forward slash.

Orientation and arrival

Despite chaotic first appearances, Kathmandu is surprisingly easy to get to grips with; the touts, like everything else, become much more manageable once you've dumped your bags. The following, along with the map on overleaf, should help with **orientation**.

Tradition has it that old Kathmandu (1290m) was laid out in the shape of a *khukuri* knife. Positioned at what would be the hilt of the knife is **Durbar Square** – a nonstop carnival set amidst temples, monuments and the former royal palace – while the oldest neighbourhoods stretch northeast and (to a lesser extent) southwest. **New Road**, the city's best-known shopping street, runs east from the square. The minaret-like **Bhimsen Tower** provides a useful landmark south of New Road. Kathmandu's budget hotels are concentrated in two areas: **Thamel**, north of Durbar Square in a newer part of town, and **Jhochhe**, better known to tourists as **Freak Street**, immediately south of the square.

Suburban Kathmandu sprawls mainly east of **Kantipath**, the main north–south thoroughfare, and is dominated by two landmarks, the **Royal Palace** and the **Tudikhel** (parade ground). Many of Kathmandu's expensive hotels, restaurants, boutiques and airline offices are located along **Durbar Marg**, the broad boulevard running south from the main palace gate. West of the Bishnumati River, the hilltop temple of **Swayambhu** is close enough to be reached easily on foot.

The separate municipality of **Patan** lies just across the Bagmati River to the south. It also has a **Durbar Square** at its heart, with most of its important temples to the north and south of the square. **Patan Dhoka** – the gate to the old city – lies northwest of the square, while **Mangal Bazaar**, an important crosstown route, skirts its southern edge. Broader, more conventional boulevards running from the Bagmati bridge to the big roundabout of **Jawalakhel Chowk** and from there to the Lagankhel bus park effectively divide the old city from its suburbs to the west and south.

Kathmandu and Patan are encircled by a none-too-scenic **Ring Road**, which pretty much defines the boundaries of this chapter.

Arriving by air

All international flights land at **Tribhuwan International Airport**, just 5km east of the city centre. While extensive improvements to facilities have been made in recent years, it's still a very provincial airport at heart, with no more than a couple of dozen international flights in and out per day. Locals still graze livestock on the grassy areas, and animals occasionally stray onto the runway. Pilots must also contend with a dangerous concentration of birds in the surrounding airspace, attracted by a landfill that was formerly situated just north of the airport in violation of international air-safety regulations. The landfill has now been closed, but many birds – mostly pariah kites, a common sight in the valley's skies – continue to scavenge among the many local rubbish piles.

Arriving, you'll first have to deal with **immigration**. If you've already got a visa, head for the relevant channel. If not, fill out an application form and join the first of three queues to obtain a visa. You'll need one passport-size photo and the exact amount (see p.20) of cash in US dollars – you can get dollars at the **exchange counter** in the immigration hall. Be sure to change money before you leave the immigration hall, as the exchange counter downstairs is currently not accessible to arriving passengers. The **duty-free** shop in the

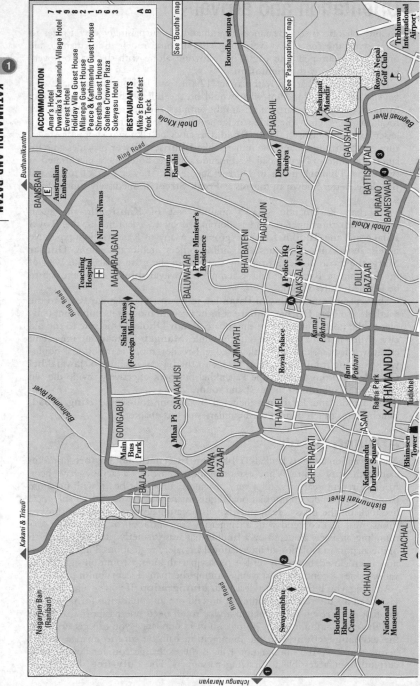

ACCOMMODATION
Amar's Hotel   7
Dwarika's Kathmandu Village Hotel   4
Everest Hotel   9
Holiday Villa Guest House   8
Milarepa Guest House   2
Peace & Kathmandu Guest House   1
Shrestha Guest House   5
Soaltee Crowne Plaza   6
Sukeyasu Hotel   3

RESTAURANTS
Mike's Breakfast   A
Yeok Teck   B

Sankhu & Sundarijal

Tribhuwan International Airport

Boudha stupa

See 'Boudha' map

See 'Pashupatinath' map

Royal Nepal Golf Club

Pashupati Mandir

Bagmati River

GAUSHALA

CHABAHIL

Dhando Chaitya

BATTISPUTALI

PURANO BANESWAR

Dhobi Khola

Dhobi Khola

Budhanikantha

Australian Embassy

BANSBARI

Ring Road

Dhum Barahi

Nirmal Niwas

MAHARAJGANJ

Teaching Hospital

HADIGAUN

BHATBATENI

Prime Minister's Residence

BALUWATAR

Police HQ

NAKSAL   NAFA

DILLI BAZAAR

Ring Road

Shital Niwas (Foreign Ministry)

Bishnumati River

LAZIMPATH

Kamal Pokhari

Royal Palace

Rani Pokhari

Ratna Park

KATHMANDU

Tudikhe

Kakani & Tristuli

GONGABU

Main Bus Park

BALAJU

Mhai P⁴

SAMAKHUSI

THAMEL

NAYA BAZAAR

CHHETRAPATI

ASAN

Kathmandu Durbar Square

Bhimsen Tower

Bishnumati River

Ring Road

Nagarjun Ban (Ranibari)

Swayambhu' map

Buddha Bharma Center

National Museum

CHHAUNI

TAHACHAL

Swayambhu

Ichangu Narayan

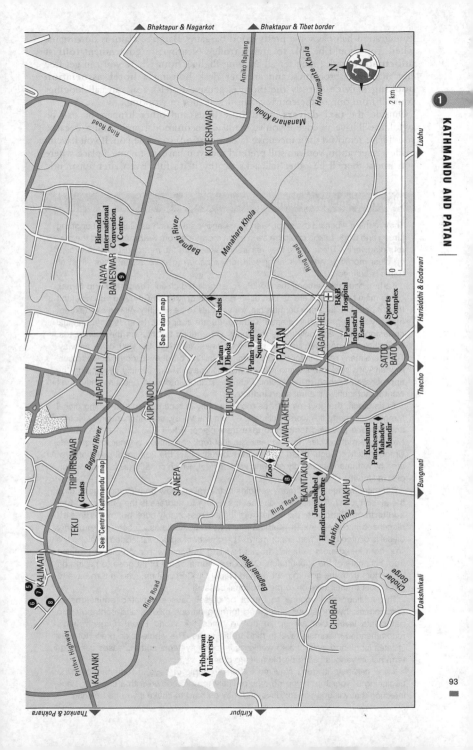

Bhaktapur & Nagarkot

Bhaktapur & Tibet border

KOTESHWAR

Arniko Rajmarg

Hanumante Khola

Manahara Khola

N

Lubhu

Ring Road

Bagmati River

Manahara Khola

Ring Road

Birendra
International
Convention
Centre

NAYA
BANESWAR

9

See 'Patan' map

Ghats

Harisiddhi & Godavari

B&B
Hospital

Patan
Industrial
Estate

Sports
Complex

2 km

0

Patan Durbar
Square

PATAN

LAGANKHEL

THAPATI-ALI

Patan
Dhoka

SATDO
BATO

TRIPURESWAR

KUPONDOL

PULCHOWK

Thecho

Bagmati River

Ghats

JAWALAKHEL

See 'Central Kathmandu' map

SANEPA

Zoo

8

EKANTAKUNA

Kushunti
Pancheswar
Mahadev
Mandir

Bungmati

TEKU

Ring Road

Jawalakhel
Handicraft Centre

NAKHU

Nakhu Khola

KALIMATI

5

6   7

8

Ring Road

Bagmati River

Chobar
Gorge

Dakshinkali

Prithvi Highway

CHOBAR

KALANKI

Tribhuwan
University

Thankot & Pokhara

Kirtipur

immigration hall has some pretty good bargains. Baggage claim is downstairs, where you should be able to grab a trolley. Nearby is a government **tourist information** desk (open for all arriving flights), from where you can get free city maps and brochures, and another desk housing a **hotel association booking service** (mostly the more expensive hotels). You can call lodgings yourself from one of the courtesy phones, if they're working.

Outside, the **taxi drivers**, guesthouse touts and other hangers-on can be awful. You'll have an edge if you've made an accommodation booking, because you'll have removed their incentive (a commission) to hassle you. If you haven't made a reservation, you can still pretend that you have: just name a place where you know there'll be other fallbacks nearby if it's full. Even after apparently

Where are the mountains?

They're there – behind the smog. Ten years ago, peaks such as Ganesh I, Langtang Lirung and Dorje Lakpa could be seen most mornings from Kathmandu and the surrounding valley. These days, they're rarely visible from the metropolitan area except on clear mornings after a soaking rain, or on *bandh* (general strike) days when all traffic is banned.

Kathmandu ranks among the world's most polluted cities. The **traffic and fumes** on its main boulevards are as bad as in Bangkok or Mexico City, and you wouldn't think it possible, let alone permissible, for vehicles to be so filthy. All vehicles (except motorcycles) registered in greater Kathmandu are supposed to undergo an annual **emissions test**, and only those that pass are entitled to drive on the main roads. Nevertheless, most vehicles pass, and as fines are trivial the rest drive anyway. There are many reasons for the programme's failure, but they all come down to corruption – it's said that anyone can get a green pass sticker simply by slipping the appropriate *bakshish* to the tester. Politicians don't intervene because they don't want to antagonize the transport industry.

To its credit, the government has moved boldly in recent years, banishing diesel tempos – formerly the worst polluters – from the valley, and encouraging electric- and propane-powered tempos to take their place; it has also banned the sale of two-stroke motorcycles, forcing their gradual replacement by cleaner four-strokes. Unfortunately, though, these moves have barely offset the additional pollution created by Kathmandu's rapidly growing vehicle fleet, which constitutes half of all vehicles in Nepal.

But there still aren't *that* many vehicles in the valley. How do they manage to dirty the air so much? The issue no one seems willing to address is the practice of **fuel adulteration**. Petrol entering Nepal from India is reasonably pure, but by the time it's dispensed into fuel tanks in Kathmandu it typically contains 25 percent kerosene; diesel is diluted by 45 percent or more. The cheaper kerosene is added all along the line, from fuel depots to tanker trucks to filling stations, with each player profiting from his share of the substitution. Of course, some of the profit goes to paying off inspectors from the government-owned Nepal Oil Corporation, who in turn have to pass most of their take on to their political bosses.

This addition of kerosene to petrol or diesel causes elevated **emissions** of carcinogenic hydrocarbons and smog-forming nitrous oxides, and contributes to particulate levels that are up to twelve times the World Health Organization's recommended maximum level in high-traffic areas. The whole toxic brew not only irritates lungs and eyes, it also weakens immune systems and increases the long-term risk of various health problems (see p.546).

If you can help it, don't stay more than a couple of days in Kathmandu at the beginning of your trip. If you do, you're likely to come down with a chest or sinus infection that will dog you for days and may be hard to shake if you go trekking.

agreeing to take you to your stated destination, a taxi driver may try to deliver you to a guesthouse that happens to be offering an especially handsome commission – some hoteliers go so far as to stake a TV or motorcycle to the cabbie who brings in the most business in a year. If all else fails, entertain offers from touts, choose one, and see what kind of room you end up with (you can always change the next day). A further unpleasant wrinkle to the airport arrival experience is the leech-like young men who crowd around and render all sorts of unasked-for assistance and then demand a tip. If you don't want their help, say so and make it clear that you will be giving no money, and then be prepared to stick to your word. If you do want help, Rs20 should be more than enough.

Most **taxis** at the airport operate on a voucher system. Vouchers are sold from the drivers' syndicate booth just inside or just outside the arrivals exit. Prices are fixed in the high season and are posted on a board; at the time of writing they were Rs200 to most parts of Kathmandu, Rs250 to Patan and Rs400 to Bhaktapur (all fares are fifty percent higher after 8pm). If you're up for haggling directly with a driver or tout, you can probably ride for half that. Touts may offer a "free" ride if you stay in their lodge, but of course the fare and the tout's commission will just get added on to the room charge – this will roughly double the price of a budget room, which is why you'll probably end up moving the next day.

Local **buses** offer a cheap (Rs5) but inconvenient alternative. They depart from the main intersection at the end of the airport drive – a 200m walk – and terminate at the City Bus Park, nearly 2km from most guesthouses. Forget it.

Arriving by bus

Tourist **buses** from Pokhara and Chitwan let passengers off on Kantipath near Tridevi Marg (for Thamel) and near Bhimsen Tower (for Jhochhe/Freak St). That's if they get to Kathmandu before the afternoon rush hour starts – if your bus enters the city after about 3.30pm it may be redirected to Balaju, further northwest of Thamel. Coming from the Indian border or Pokhara by public bus, you'll arrive at the New (Naya) Bus Park, located at Gongabu at the extreme north end of the city; taxis and tempos (see overleaf) charge Rs100–125 to most tourist destinations. If you happen to be travelling by Sajha (government cooperative) bus, stay on board and the bus will continue on to Bhimsen Tower. Buses from the Tibet border, Jiri and towns along those roads terminate at the City Bus Park, also known as the Old (Purano) Bus Park, east of the city centre and a Rs75 taxi ride to most lodgings.

Information and maps

The **Kathmandu Tourist Service Center** (Mon–Fri 9am–5pm) has a few more freebies than the airport desk and a more knowledgeable staff, but it's located in Bhrikuti Mandap, the public exhibition ground east of the Tudikhel, which isn't very close to anything else.

Free **magazines** such as *Nepal Traveller* and *Traveller's Nepal* are probably the best all-around sources of information on tourist services and upcoming events. They're distributed to the bigger hotels, travel agents and supermarkets. For even more current information, as well as advertisements for courses, trekking partners, stuff for sale and the like, check the **notice boards** in many tourist guesthouses and restaurants.

Three nonprofit organizations that specialize mainly in trekking matters may also be able to help with other travel questions: the **Kathmandu Environmental Education Project**, or KEEP (trekking seasons Mon–Fri & Sun 9am–7pm; off-season Mon–Fri 10am–4pm), located on Jyatha Thamel; the **Himalayan Explorers Connection** (Mon–Fri 10am–5pm), which shares offices with KEEP; and the **Himalayan Rescue Association** (Mon–Fri & Sun 10am–5pm), north of the Royal Palace. All three also have useful trekking-related notice boards.

The advertiser-supported city **maps** given away by the tourist offices at the airport and in town are less detailed than the ones in this book. Bookshops and street vendors sell better versions, ranging from the basic *Kat Map* to the splendid (and expensive) maps published by Mapple/Karto Atelier and Shangri-La; Nepa's modestly priced "pocket" map of Kathmandu and Patan is quite good value. Maps of trekking routes and other areas are recommended, where relevant, elsewhere in the guide.

Getting around

You'll probably find that you do most of your exploration of the old city on foot. Here's a rundown of transport options for sights further afield.

Taxis, tempos and rikshas

Taxis are fairly cheap, and are the most comfortable way to travel longer distances in Kathmandu and around the valley – though they don't work well in the crowded old city. A couple of companies operate fleet taxis, which can be requested by phone (have your guesthouse make the call for you). Freelance cabs tend to wait in designated areas such as Tridevi Marg, the main Thamel intersection, along Dharma Path, at the Jamal end of Durbar Marg, at the Mangal Bazaar side of Patan Durbar Square, and Jawalakhel Chowk. Both types have meters, and drivers are supposed to use them. However, it's standard practice to negotiate a flat rate for destinations beyond the Ring Road, including the airport, or for trips involving a lot of "waiting time". Drivers stationed in really touristy spots, such as the main Thamel intersection, will usually demand a flat rate even for shorter journeys, and those waiting inside hotel compounds always will. If you can't find a driver willing to use the meter, try walking a bit (say, to Tridevi Marg), or surprise them with a bit of Nepali (*Meter-maa januhunchha?* – "Will you go by the meter?"). Fares are fifty percent higher after 8pm. Taxis start getting scarce around then, too – try the night taxi service (☎01/244485 or ☎224375).

Metered tempos (also known as tuk-tuks or autorikshas) are slower, bumpier and less roomy than taxis, though their meter rates work out to be somewhat cheaper. **Fixed-route tempos** ply various routes throughout the city, generally following the main radial arteries; many originate from two locations along Kantipath, just north of Rani Pokhari and just north of the GPO, but you can get on at any of their frequent stopping points. Most are battery-powered Safaa ("clean") tempos nowadays, though some are powered by propane or petrol.

Cycle **rikshas** are really only worthwhile for short distances on narrow, crowded streets (where you'll feel every bump). The price should be about the same as for a metered tempo, but the wallahs charge whatever they can, so establish terms before setting off.

Local buses, minibuses and microbuses

Local **buses** and **minibuses** cover some of the same city routes as the fixed-route tempos, but they're really meant for longer journeys around the valley. They're cheap (usually no more than Rs10 for any journey), but slow and can be extremely crowded (avoid them at rush hour), so they're easiest to cope with if you get on at the starting point. The newer "**microbuses**" are more comfortable passenger vans, although the ones that run on bottled propane tend to stink of gas inside. Refer to the box below for useful routes; this also gives the numbers of bus, minibus and microbus services.

Bicycles

Cycling is still a good way to get to many sights in the surrounding valley, but traffic and pollution make it fairly miserable work on Kathmandu's main roads.

Useful local transit routes

Buses and minibuses
From City Bus Park to:
1. Chabahil and the airport
2. Gaushala (for Pashupatinath) and Boudha
3. Sundarijal
4. Sankhu
5. Budhanilkantha
6. Bhaktapur
7. Sano Thimi and Bhaktapur

8. Banepa and Panauti
9. Godavari
10. Patan (Lagankhel)
11. Swayambhu
12. Kirtipur
13. Pharping and Dakshinkali
14. Balaju and New Bus Park
15. Patan (Patan Dhoka)

Microbuses
Shahid Gate to:
2. Purano Baneswar and Sinamangal (airport entrance)

14. Patan (Mangal Bazaar)
22. Chobar

Ratna Park to:
5. Maharajganj and Budhanilkantha
14. Patan (Pulchowk and Lagankhel)

23. Lekhnath Marg, Balaju and Gongabu (Main Bus Park)

Fixed-route tempos
Shahid Gate to:
2. Petrol tempos go to Gaushala and Boudha; electric tempos to Purano Baneswar and Sinamangal (airport entrance); and propane tempos to Naya Baneswar and Koteswar

14. Patan (Mangal Bazaar)
22. Chobar

Ratna Park to:
5. Maharajganj and Budhanilkantha
14. Patan (Pulchowk and Lagankhel)

23. Lekhnath Marg, Balaju and Gongabu (main bus park)

Kantipath (near RNAC building) to:
1. Naya Baneswar
2. Gaushala and Chabahil (some continue to Boudha)
5. Maharajganj and Budhanilkantha

14. Patan (Sanepa)
19. Swayambhu (via Kalimati)
21. Kirtipur, Chobar and Pharping
23. Balaju (via Lekhnath Marg)

Consequently rental bikes are hard to find, especially in Thamel, where most of the cycle wallahs have been pushed out by redevelopment – there's one just north of Thamel Chowk, and a couple of cheaper places just south of Chhetrapati Chowk. In Jhochhe (Freak St), try the place in Basantapur Square. Some guesthouses have their own bikes for rent, or can arrange them.

Old-fashioned **one-speed bikes** rent for Rs75–150 a day, depending on condition of the machine and location of the rental outlet (and your bargaining skills). **Mountain bikes**, often of disappointing quality (see p.40), range from Rs100 a day for a one-speed model to Rs200–300 for an eighteen-speeder without helmet. Thamel mountain-bike operators (see p.169) may be able to set you up with something better for Rs300–500, including helmet. Shop for bikes early, or the night before, and bargain for a multiple-day discount. If riding on the main roads, consider wearing a mask (sold in pharmacies) or a dampened handkerchief.

The lane south of the National Theatre, just west of Kantipath, is the place to go to **buy a new bike**. An Indian-made gear-bike will cost you upwards of Rs6000, depending on quality.

Motorcycles and vehicles

Riding a **motorcycle** isn't much fun inside the Ring Road, but it's a great way to explore the Kathmandu Valley and beyond. Several operators in Thamel rent 125cc motorcycles for Rs400–600 a day, not including petrol. Again, you should be able to get a discount for multiple days. You'll need to leave a plane ticket or passport as security, and you're supposed to show a driving licence. Refer to the driving tips on p.39 of Basics.

The cheapest way to rent a **car** is to hire a taxi with driver by the day, which will cost about $20 for touring around the valley (petrol included). Prices for longer journeys are based on the distance to be travelled, or are quoted exclusive of petrol; make sure the taxi has permission to travel where you want to go, since many are restricted. **Jeeps** and **vans** can also be hired for about $30 a day (petrol excluded) through their owners or agents – ask around. Car rental agencies are more expensive: Yeti Travels (T01/226153) and Gorkha Travels (T01/224896), both on Durbar Marg, represent Avis and Hertz respectively.

If you've driven your own car or van to Nepal, beware: central Kathmandu is a nightmare for driving. You'd have to be very brave or very foolish to enter with a camper or other large vehicle. The streets are narrow and crowded, and you'd be constantly defeated by the one-way system. Aim for a hotel or guesthouse off a main road that has parking.

Accommodation

Kathmandu is well stocked with all kinds of **accommodation**. The lists below highlight the best in each price bracket, but you'll soon discover that there are literally hundreds of other options, and they're almost all perfectly fine.

The most popular budget lodges fill up early in the high season (especially in Oct). Book ahead if you can, but if that's not possible (phone numbers and email addresses change frequently), then just show up: Thamel and Jhochhe guesthouses are all cheek by jowl, so if one's full you can just try the next. If you plan to stay in a midrange or high-end hotel, you'll probably already have a booking with free airport pickup. If not, you can book through the Nepal Hotel Association's reservation desk at the airport.

See Basics p.42 for a rundown of the sort of **facilities** to expect for your money. Note that during the winter, when Kathmandu can be quite chilly, even cheap guesthouses will provide cotton quilts, but you'll probably have to pay at least $20 a night to get a portable heater in your room; only the more expensive hotels have central heating. Try to get a room that doesn't overlook the street: Kathmandu's barking dogs, banging pots and clattering shutters are enough to wake the dead. Note that price code spreads (ie ❺–❾) denote rooms with varying degrees of luxury; the higher code relates extras such as a/c or private bathroom.

Bear in mind that **you don't have to stay in Kathmandu or Patan**. You can just as easily ask the taxi driver to take you to Boudha (p.201), Bhaktapur (p.225), Dakshinkali (p.215) or Godavari (p.219).

Thamel

Tourist ghettos like **Thamel** follow a sort of circular logic. Most people stay there because, well, most people stay there. And the more people stay there, the more Thamel turns itself into what it thinks foreigners want it to be, which perversely increases its popularity. Especially in the high season, there's so much hype, and so little that has anything to do with Nepal, that you may wonder why it remains as popular as it does.

That said, if you've just arrived and your brain is still six time zones out to sea, Thamel can help ease you into things until you feel ready to sally forth. It's painting by numbers here, with scores of restaurants, bookshops, souvenir stalls, travel agencies, trekking-gear shops and other tourist services and touts vying for your business. But don't think that this is Nepal – you're still in the transit lounge.

"Thamel" nowadays refers to a large area containing a ridiculous number of guesthouses. To make the listings easier to navigate, we've broken them up into three geographic groupings. "**Central Thamel**" comprises the strips immediately north, south and east of the *Kathmandu Guest House*, where tourist development began and where it's now reached its unholy zenith. What we're calling "**North Thamel**" includes Paknajol, Bhagwan Bahal and Kaisher Mahal – neighbourhoods that are no longer distinct from Thamel proper, but are at least a bit less circusy. "**South Thamel**" spans the areas of Chhetrapati, Thahiti and Jyatha, which while similarly in thrall to tourism manage to pre-serve more of the architecture and culture of the old city.

For locations, see the Thamel map (p.100) unless otherwise indicated.

Central Thamel

Hotel Excelsior Narsingh Camp ☎01/411566, ⓦwww.excelsiornepal.com. Established hotel in a central location, providing excellent service and comfortable facilities; some air-conditioned rooms, which cost a little more. Helpful with trekking and travel logistics. ❻–❼

Hotel Garuda Thamel Northwest ☎01/416340, ⓦwww.garuda-hotel.com. A very professional hotel that has served as Kathmandu headquarters for many a mountaineering expedition. Centrally located, with rooftop seating, small library, helpful service and snug rooms with or without a/c. ❺–❼

Kathmandu Guest House Thamel Northwest ☎01/413632, ⓦwww.ktmgh.com. Thamel's origi-nal and best-known guesthouse is set well back from the noisy street, with a gorgeous garden. Efficiently managed, it's a huge and social place: exciting or pretentious, depending on your outlook. There are a few quite cheap common-bath rooms, as well as midrange and air-conditioned ones. They're always in demand, so book well ahead during the high season. ❹–❼

Mom's House Lodge J.P. School Rd ☎01/266897, ⓔasia@excursion.com.np. The way Thamel guesthouses used to be, before everything got so fashionable: small, funky, sociable and basic. Some rooms with attached bath. ❸

Hotel Pacifist Narsingh Camp ☎01/258320. A bit stark, but rooms are spacious – the more expen-sive ones have attached baths and separate sitting areas. ❶–❷

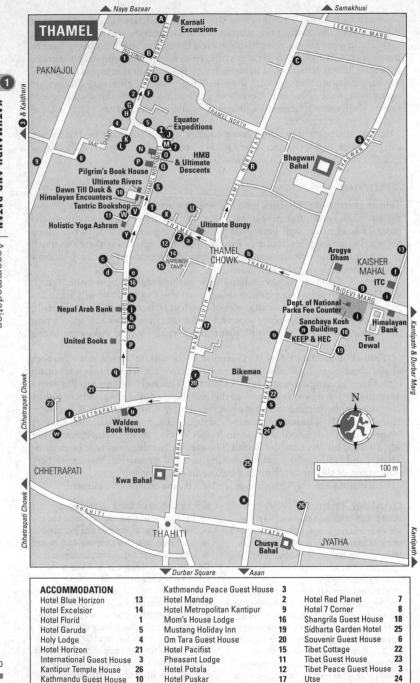

▲ Naya Bazaar   ▲ Samakhusi

THAMEL

PAKNAJOL

Karnali
Excursions

Equator
Expeditions

HMB
& Ultimate
Descents

Pilgrim's Book House
Ultimate Rivers
Dawn Till Dusk &
Himalayan Encounters
Tantric Bookshop
Holistic Yoga Ashram

Ultimate Bungy

THAMEL
CHOWK

Bhagwan
Bahal

Arogya
Dham

KAISHER
MAHAL

ITC

Nepal Arab Bank

United Books

Dept. of National
Parks Fee Counter

Sanchaya Kosh
Building
KEEP & HEC

Himalayan
Bank

Tin
Dewal

Bikeman

Walden
Book House

Kwa Bahal

CHHETRAPATI

THAHITI

Chusya
Bahal

JYATHA

N

0   100 m

▼ Durbar Square   ▼ Asan

ACCOMMODATION		Kathmandu Peace Guest House	3		
Hotel Blue Horizon	13	Hotel Mandap	2	Hotel Red Planet	7
Hotel Excelsior	14	Hotel Metropolitan Kantipur	9	Hotel 7 Corner	8
Hotel Florid	1	Mom's House Lodge	16	Shangrila Guest House	18
Hotel Garuda	5	Mustang Holiday Inn	19	Sidharta Garden Hotel	25
Holy Lodge	4	Om Tara Guest House	20	Souvenir Guest House	6
Hotel Horizon	21	Hotel Pacifist	15	Tibet Cottage	22
International Guest House	3	Pheasant Lodge	11	Tibet Guest House	23
Kantipur Temple House	26	Hotel Potala	12	Tibet Peace Guest House	3
Kathmandu Guest House	10	Hotel Puskar	17	Utse	24

RESTAURANTS, BARS & CLUBS

Aji Siru	r
Annapurna	R
B.K.'s Place	E
Café des Trekkers	s
China Town	c
Dechenling	f
Delima Garden Café	L
Didiko Baba Bhojanalaya	U
La Dolce Vita	T
Everest Steak House	w
Fire and Ice	l
Full Moon	M
Green Leaves	q
Helena's	k
Himalayan Java	i
Hot Breads	V
Jewels of Manang	A
Jump Club	J
Just Juice & Shakes	M
Kathmandu	m
Kilroy's of Kathmandu	n
Koto	p
Krua Thai	D
Laxmi Narayan's Steak House	u
Lhasa	I
Maya Cocktail Bar	Z
Nepalese Kitchen	t
New Orleans	S
Nirmala	G
Northfield Café	N
Omei	o
Over the Rainbow	Q
Pilgrims Feed 'n Read	P
Pink Palace	d
Pub Maya	W
Pumpernickel Bakery	a
Roadhouse Café	e
Rum Doodle	K
Sam's Bar	F
Shalimar	b
Solu	x
Studio 54	g
Tashi Deleg	X
Thakali Bhanchha	B
Thamel House	C
Tom and Jerry Pub	O
Tongues 'N Tales	h
Tripti	d
Tunnel Club	H
Utse	v
Weizen Bakery	j
Yin Yang	Y

Pheasant Lodge Off J.P. School Rd ☎01/417415. A very cheap, basic, traditional outfit tucked away in a quiet yet central cul-de-sac. Shared baths only. ❶

Hotel Potala Narsingh Camp ☎01/419159. Centrally located and run by a friendly Tibetan family. Clean (though small and darkish) rooms with shared bathrooms, and there's a small roof terrace. ❶

Hotel Red Planet Thamel Northwest ☎01/432879, ✉telstar@wlink.com.np. Comfortable rooms with attached baths and balconies. Located right in the heart of Thamel's nightlife area, so you can just stagger home. Rooftop seating too. ❹

North Thamel

Hotel Blue Horizon Kaisher Mahal ☎01/421971, ⓦwww.visitnepal.com/bluehorizon. A quiet, friendly hotel in a surprisingly leafy neighbourhood. Rooms (all with bath) range from standard to very well-appointed, and discounts are available for students. ❹

Hotel Florid Zed St ☎01/416155, ⓦwww.catmando .com/hotel-florid. Located on a quiet cul-de-sac. Rooms range from decent with common bath, to splendid with a/c and all mod cons. Small garden area, and good service. ❸–❻

Holy Lodge Saat Ghumti ☎01/416265, ✉holylodge @wlink.com.np. Reliable and relaxed, with a wide range of rooms with or without bath. The location strikes a happy balance between central and quiet. ❹–❺

International Guest House Paknajol (see Central Kathmandu map) ☎01/252299, ⓦwww.ighouse.com. Spacious, ornate hotel with plenty of balcony, roof and garden seating. Popular with Japanese, hence the restaurant's Japanese menu. ❻

Kathmandu Peace Guest House Paknajol (see Central Kathmandu map) ☎01/439369, ✉ktmpeacegh@visitnepal.com. Secluded, friendly guesthouse with a garden, parking and excellent views north and west from the rooftop. Rooms with or without bath. ❷–❻

Malla Hotel Lekhnath Marg (see Central Kathmandu map) ☎01/418383), ✉malla@htlgrp .mos.com.np. Attractive facilities such as a pool and health club; all rooms have a/c, but it's located at the ugly fringe of Thamel. ❾

Hotel Mandap Thamel Northwest ☎01/413321, ⓦwww.hotelmandap.com. Comfortable, reason- ably priced hotel in a popular part of Thamel – good if you want to be in the heart of things. All rooms have a/c. ❻

Hotel Metropolitan Kantipur Paknajol ☎01/251558, ⓦwww.go2kathmandu.com/ kantipur. An unexpected oasis of greenery, and with good views from the roof. Rooms are unex- ceptional, but all have private bathroom. ❻

Hotel 7 Corner Saat Ghumti ☎01/439405, ✉sevencorner@hotmail.com. Nicely furnished rooms (all with bath and phone, some with TV and a/c) and a small sheltered courtyard. Located on an uncommercial lane. ❹–❺

Souvenir Guest House Bhagwan Bahal ☎01/418255, ⓦwww.webnepal.com/souvenir. Unusually low-rise guesthouse with a small courtyard garden, roof terraces and tidy rooms with or without bath. Friendly management. ❷–❹

Tibet Peace Guest House Paknajol (see Central Kathmandu map) ☎01/415026, ⓔtpghouse@wlink .com.np. A nice little haven with gardens, funky layout, cosy restaurant and good views. Rooms with or without bath. ❹–❺

South Thamel

Hotel Horizon J.P. School Rd ☎01/220904, ⓔhorizon@hons.com.np. Down a quiet side lane, this is very secluded, with decent rooms (all with bath) and plenty of rooftop seating. ❸

Kantipur Temple House Jyatha ☎01/250131, ⓔkantipur@tmplhouse.wlink.com.np. An architecturally interesting tower-like building with a nice traditional-modern feel. Pleasant lawn seating area. ❼

Mustang Holiday Inn Off Jyatha Thamel ☎01/249041, ⓦwww.mustangholidayinn.com.np. A long-standing favourite with a quiet location, well-appointed en-suite rooms, garden and roof seating, and professional management. ❹

Om Tara Guest House Thamel South ☎01/259634. Small but pleasant courtyard, central location, and basic rooms with or without bath. ❸–❹

Hotel Puskar Thamel South ☎01/262956, ⓔthamelnepal@hotmail.com. A bit of a monolith, but economical, central, and with a small courtyard restaurant. Rooms with or without bath. ❷–❹

Shangrila Guest House Off Jyatha Thamel ☎01/250188, ⓔganesh_gana@hotmail.com. Quiet location and plenty of balcony and roof space. Basic rooms with or without bath. ❹

Sidharta Garden Hotel Jyatha Thamel ☎01/222253, ⓦwww.sidhartagardenhotel.com. Under French management, this features stylish rooms with private bath, a peaceful courtyard shaded by pomelo trees, and continental touches including a patisserie. ❺–❻

Tibet Cottage Jyatha Thamel ☎01/226577, ⓦwww.yomari.com/tibetcottage. Serene haven run by a nice Tibetan family, and popular with Peace Corps volunteers. Cheapest rooms have common baths. ❹–❻

Tibet Guest House Chhetrapati ☎01/254888, ⓔtibet@mail.com.np. A big operation with two tall buildings, the older one with cheaper rooms and a lovely roof garden, the newer one with air-conditioned rooms, a rooftop restaurant and great views. ❺–❼

Hotel Utse Jyatha Thamel ☎01/257614, ⓔutse@wlink.com.np. Neat as a pin with comfortable Tibetan decor, private baths, helpful staff, great restaurant and a roof garden. ❻

Jhochhe (Freak Street)

Jhochhe (aka **Freak Street**) and its immediate area beats Thamel in many ways: it's quieter and less touristy, much more authentically Nepali, and closer to the sights of the old city (it's actually *part* of the old city). And everything's cheaper here – food, provisions, services and so on as well as lodging.

However, Jhochhe has considerably fewer of the restaurants and other facilities that make Thamel so convenient. It's a much smaller area for a start, and its tiny landholdings, fragmented by generations of inheritance disputes, make redevelopment difficult; it hasn't got the critical mass to compete with Thamel. Unable to move with the times, it is comprised mainly of older traditional buildings and somewhat poky family-run businesses. But that's precisely what makes it an interesting place to stay.

For locations, see the Jhochhe map opposite.

Annapurna Lodge Jhochhe ☎01/247684. The biggest of the old Freak Street pack, with a large in-house restaurant. ❷–❸

Century Lodge Jhochhe ☎01/247641. The building has a nice, lived-in feel and some fine traditional features, with a mix of traditional low-ceilinged rooms and newer ones with attached baths. Peaceful courtyard and a library. (If it's full, try the similarly priced *Pagoda Lodge*, which shares the same courtyard. ❶–❸

Hotel Eden Jhochhe ☎01/258380. Originally conceived as a posh hotel (it has an elevator), this has come down a bit in the world but so have its prices. All rooms have private bathrooms, and there's a good rooftop restaurant. ❺

Friendly Home Between Jhochhe and Chikamugal ☎01/248690, ⓔfrentrav@ntc.net.np. Kathmandu's longest-running guesthouse, and invariably packed in high season. Pretty basic, but friendly and social. ❶

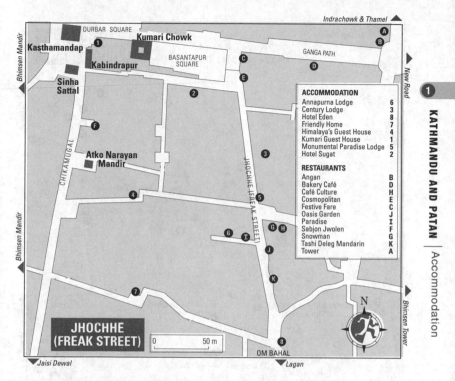

ACCOMMODATION

Annapurna Lodge	6
Century Lodge	3
Hotel Eden	8
Friendly Home	7
Himalaya's Guest House	4
Kumari Guest House	1
Monumental Paradise Lodge	5
Hotel Sugat	2

RESTAURANTS

Angan	B
Bakery Café	D
Café Culture	H
Cosmopolitan	E
Festive Fare	C
Oasis Garden	J
Paradise	I
Sabjon Jwolen	F
Snowman	G
Tashi Deleg Mandarin	K
Tower	A

Himalaya's Guest House Between Jhochhe and Chikamugal ☎01/246555, ⊜himalgst@hotmail.com. Secluded location, helpful management, passable in-house restaurant and small rooms (some of those with baths also come with TVs). ③–④

Kumari Guest House Opposite the Kasthamandap ☎01/263498. Staying here is an intensely Nepali experience: it's a traditional, decrepit old building with a dynamic *didi* and views right onto Durbar Square. Common bath only. ③

Monumental Paradise Lodge Jhochhe ☎01/240876, ⊜mparadise52@hotmail.com. A spiffy new place with eager staff and a nice rooftop restaurant. The well-appointed rooms have attached baths. ③

Hotel Sugat Basantapur ☎245824, ⊜mary-man@mos.com.np. Great location overlooking Basantapur Square, big rooms with or without bath, and an in-house bar/restaurant. ③

Durbar Marg and Lazimpath

Accommodation elsewhere in the city is more diffuse. Running south from the Royal Palace, **Durbar Marg** holds a handful of Kathmandu's poshest hotels (which all have air-conditioned, en-suite rooms), as well as many upscale restaurants and boutiques. Just about all the airline offices are located within walking distance, and it's not a long hike to Thamel. A less attractive boulevard running north from the Royal Palace, **Lazimpath** is within easy reach of many embassies and consulates, and boasts a few high-end hotels as well as a better selection of midrange ones.

Durbar Marg hotels are shown on the Kantipath and Durbar Marg map (p.104). For Lazimpath hotels, see the Central Kathmandu map (p.107).

Hotel de l'Annapurna Durbar Marg ☎01/221711, ⊛www.taj-annapurna.com.np.

Established and well-located, but a bit past its prime. Pool, sauna, tennis courts and casino. ⑧

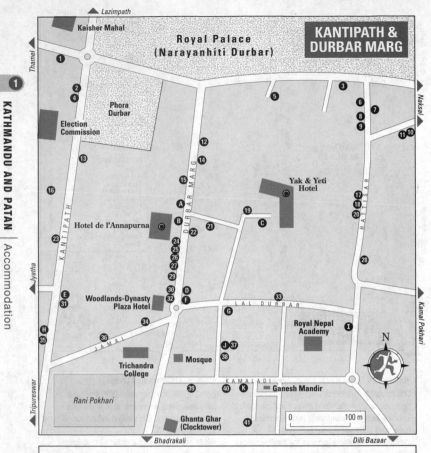

KANTIPATH &
DURBAR MARG

Lazimpath

Kaisher Mahal

Royal Palace
(Narayanhiti Durbar)

Thamel

Phora
Durbar

Election
Commission

Yak & Yeti
Hotel

Naxal

Kantipath

Hotel de l'Annapurna

Woodlands-Dynasty
Plaza Hotel

Jyatha

Kamal Pokhari

Royal Nepal
Academy

Jamal

Trichandra
College

Mosque

N

Tripureswar

Rani Pokhari

Kamaladi

Ganesh Mandir

0   100 m

Ghanta Ghar
(Clocktower)

Bhadrakali

Dilli Bazaar

RESTAURANTS & CLUBS

Bhanchha Ghar	K	Bishwa Jyoti Cinema	36	Lufthansa	26
Bhoe Chhen	C	British Airways	25	Mandala Book Point	31
Club X Zone	G	Buddha Air	8	Mountain Air	7
Delicatessen Center	E	Cathay Pacific	39	Nepal International Clinic	5
Dudh Sagar	H	China Southwest Airlines	33	Nepal Vipassana Center	16
Ghar-e-Kebab	B	CIWEC Clinic	21	PIA	9
Koto	A	Cosmic Air	37	President Travel & Tours	32
Moon Sun Disco	J	Dragon Air	14	Qantas	30
Moti Mahal & Godavari	D	Druk-Air	12	Qatar Airways	23
Raj Gharana	I	Emirates	35	Shangri-la Air	28
Tansen	F	Everest Travel Service	13	Singapore Airlines	15
		Gorkha Airlines	18	Skyline Airways	20
AIRLINE OFFICES &		Green Line bus depot	1	Standard Chartered Bank	4
OTHER SERVICES		Gulf Air	6	Thai Airways	24
Aeroflot	40	Himalayan Buddhist Center	41	Transavia	38
Air France	27	Indian Airlines	17	Yeti Travels	29
Air India	17	Japan Air Lines	22		
American Express	34	Jaya Nepal Cinema	3		
Austrian Consulate	10	Kathmandu Mountain Bikes	2		
Belgian Consulate	19	Kuwait Airways	13		
Biman Bangladesh	11	Lauda Austrian Airlines	39		

Hotel Manaslu Lazimpath ☎01/410071, ⓦwww.south-asia.com/manaslu. Pleasant oasis with a nice front lawn; popular with aid workers and their visitors. Some rooms have a/c. ⑥–⑦
Radisson Kathmandu Lazimpath ☎01/423888, ⓦwww.radisson.com/kathmandune. Massive hotel with pool, health club and chain reliability. ⑨
Hotel Shangri-la Lazimpath ☎01/412999, ⓦwww.hotelshangrila.com. Tucked away in embassyland. Pool, health club and a children's playground. ⑧
Hotel Shanker Lazimpath ☎01/410151, ⓦwww.shankerhotel.com.np. Unique: a magnificent Rana palace refitted for semi-luxury. ⑧
Hotel Yak & Yeti Durbar Marg ☎01/248999, ⓦwww.yakandyeti.com. Kathmandu's most prestigious hotel: lots of history, opulent restaurants, two pools, a health club and a casino. ⑨

West of the Bishnumati

There's only one real reason to stay **west of the Bishnumati**, and that's to be near the popular Swayambhu stupa. There aren't many hotels and guesthouses in that vicinity, though – a few more can be found in the bland but peaceful neighbourhood of **Tahachal**, just off the ugly main drag that runs through Kalimati and Kalanki.

For locations, see the Kathmandu map (pp.92–93) unless otherwise stated.

Amar's Hotel Tahachal ☎01/283493, ⓦwww.visitnepal.com/hotelamar. Quiet suburban location, a garden and comfortable rooms with attached bath. Popular with Dutch trekking groups. ⑥
Holiday Villa Guest House Tahachal ☎01/275682, ⓔholiday@ntc.net.np. On a quiet suburban lane near the *Soaltee*, this is more of a long-stay place, offering comfortable suites with fridges; a/c is available in the more expensive rooms. ⑥
Milarepa Guest House Swayambhu ☎01/275544. Currently the only accommodation right at Swayambhu, it's a big, rather stark building, but the rooms, all with attached bath, are nice enough and there's a meditation hall and great views from the roof. Run by the adjacent monastery; all profits support Tibetan resettlement projects. ⑤
Peace & Kathmandu View Guest House About 1km west of Swayambhu ☎01/281434. Far-flung location near Tibetan monasteries, with good views of Swayambhu, a modest garden and spacious rooms (all with common bath). More for long-staying dharma bums; simple meals available. ②
Shrestha Guest House Tahachal ☎01/271336, ⓔsghtahachal77@hotmail.com. Quiet and out of the way, so might be a good choice if you've got kids with you. Big, bright rooms, all with phone and attached bath; TVs are available. ④
Soaltee Crowne Plaza Tahachal ☎01/272555, ⓦwww.soaltee.crowneplaza.com. Kathmandu's biggest hotel, with top-notch rooms and restaurants, a health club, pool, tennis courts and casino. ⑨
Hotel Vajra Bijeshwari (about 1km east of Swayambhu; see Central Kathmandu Map) ☎01/271545, ⓦwww.hotelvajra.com. Unquestionably the best in its class: beautifully appointed, with a library, theatre and art gallery, and views of Swayambhu from the roof terrace. Wide range of rooms – the common-bath ones in the old building are excellent value. ⑤–⑧

Eastern neighbourhoods

The **east side of Kathmandu** is lacking in interest, and the city is small enough that there's no particular advantage to staying near the airport. However, the proximity of the Pashupatinath temple complex provides an incentive to stay in the nearby neighbourhood of **Battisputali**. Note that we list another option near the complex in Chapter Two, p.195.

For locations, see the Kathmandu map (pp.92–93).

Dwarika's Kathmandu Village Hotel Battisputali ☎01/479488, ⓦwww.dwarikas.com. A hidden gem: this is without doubt the most beautifully traditional of Kathmandu's deluxe hotels, incorporating bricks and woodwork salvaged from temple and house renovations. Excellent restaurant. ⑨
Everest Hotel Airport Rd, Naya Baneswar ☎01/488100, ⓦwww.everesthotel.com. Big hotel with pool, tennis, gym, good restaurants, disco and casino. ⑨
Sukeyasu Hotel Battisputali ☎01/472481, ⓔymtrek@ccsl.com.np. Long-established place in a quiet location within walking distance of Pashupatinath, with a well-kept garden, tidy, attached-bath rooms and helpful staff. ⑤

Patan

Patan offers a pleasant alternative to the Kathmandu scene. Its culture is more intact, yet it has sufficient restaurants and facilities, and easy enough access to those in Kathmandu to ensure that you won't feel way off the beaten track. However, there's a distinct lack of accommodation in the old part of Patan, and what there is fills up early, so it's important to book ahead. Several budget guesthouses are less ideally situated in the **Kumaripati** and **Man Bhawan** areas, southwest of the centre, and are run mainly by ex-Gurkhas who've settled close to the brigade headquarters there. Nearly all the pricier hotels are located in the newer western part of the city, either along the busy **Kupondol–Pulchowk–Jawalakhel** corridor or in much quieter **Kupondol Heights**.

For locations, see the Patan map (p.138) unless otherwise noted.

Café de Patan Guest House Mangal Bazaar ☎01/537599, ⓔpcafe@ntc.net.np. Friendly and centrally located, with well-maintained rooms (common or attached bath), rooftop views and a very competent restaurant. ❹

Hotel Greenwich Village Kupondol Heights ☎01/521780, ⓔgreenwich@wlink.com.np. Located in the quiet northwestern part of town, with a pool and good views. ❽

Hotel Himalaya Kupondol ☎01/523900, ⓔhimalaya@lalitpur.mos.com.np. Big, posh hotel on a horrendous thoroughfare, but with nice grounds, swimming pool and tennis courts. ❾

Hong Kong Guest House Man Bhawan ☎01/534337. The better rooms are spacious and have attached baths, TVs and phones, but the place has a vaguely disreputable feel. Snooker club, restaurant. The nearby *Hungry Treat Home* is similar but cheaper. ❸–❹

Mahabuddha Guest House Uku Bahal ☎01/540575, ⓔnfosterm@wlink.com.np. Great location just opposite the Mahabuddha temple, though it's a bit of a hike to the nearest eateries. Only six rooms, all with shared bath. ❸

Mountain View Guest House Kumaripati ☎01/538168. Run by a colourful ex-serviceman, this has well-kept rooms with or without bath, and a decent little rooftop garden. Only a short walk to the old city. ❷–❸

Hotel Narayani Pulchowk ☎01/525015, ⓦwww.go-nepal.com/Hotel-Narayani/hotel-narayani.html. A somewhat less deluxe alternative to the *Himalaya*, also with air-conditioned rooms and a pool. ❼

Okura Guest House Patan Dhoka ☎01/537299, ⓔokura@info.com.np. A new place without much character, but friendly enough. Spacious rooms with TV, plus a pseudo-Japanese in-house restaurant and roof seating. ❹

Summit Hotel Kupondol Heights ☎01/521810, ⓦwww.summit-nepal.com. Traditional Nepalese architecture, terrific view, beautiful grounds and a pool. The cheapest rooms only have common baths, but are comfortable; only the most expensive wing has a/c. ❻–❽

Third World Guest House Durbar Square (see Patan Durbar Square map) ☎01/522187, ⓔdsdp@wlink.com.np. Unbeatable location – all rooms look directly out on the square – and traditional decor, though a bit scruffy. ❺

The old city

The scene on Thamel avenue today: a very pretty pale-brown cow standing on the sidewalk, between a cigarette stand and an umbrella repairman, her head lifted straight up, perpendicular with the ground, while a ten-year-old boy heading home from school stood there, reaching up and scratching the animal's neck. Meanwhile all the tourists pointing to the fruit-bats hanging in the trees. The smell of bat shit and garbage and day-old murk, literally Another Shitty Day in Paradise. Shangri-la's getting wasted, but you can still stand on the street corner in Kathmandu and scratch her heavy velvet throat.

Jeff Greenwald, *Mister Raja's Neighborhood*
Daniel and Daniel

The Kathmandu most travellers come to see is the **old city**, a tight tangle of narrow alleys and numerous temples immediately north and south of the central

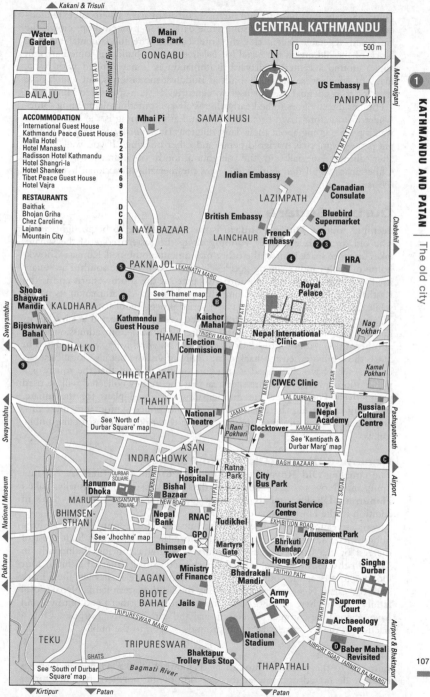

Durbar Square. It's a bustling and intensely urban quarter, where tall extended-family dwellings block out the sun, while dark, open-fronted shops crowd the lanes and vegetable sellers clot the intersections. The fundamental building block of the old city is the *bahal* (or *baha*) – a set of buildings joined at right angles around a central courtyard. Kathmandu is honeycombed with *bahal*, many of which were originally built as Buddhist monasteries, but which have reverted to residential use during two centuries of state-sponsored Hinduism.

Though the city goes to bed early, there's always something happening somewhere from before dawn to around 10pm. Early morning is the best time to watch people going about their daily religious rites (*puja*), adorning idols with red paste (*abhir*), rice, marigold petals and other offerings. If you walk around after dinner, especially in the neighbourhoods of Indrachowk, Asan or Chhetrapati, you'll frequently run across mesmerizing devotional hymn-sings (*bhajan*).

Durbar Square

Teeming, touristy **Durbar Square** is the natural place to begin sightseeing. The old royal palace (*durbar*), running along the eastern edge of the square, takes up more space than all the other monuments combined. Kumari Chowk, home of Kathmandu's "living goddess", overlooks from the south. The square itself is squeezed by the palace into two parts: at the southwestern end is the Kasthamandap, the ancient building that probably gave Kathmandu its name, while the northern part is taken up by a varied procession of statues and temples.

Tourists must pay a Rs200 **entrance fee**, which is collected at checkposts guarding the main approaches to the square (daily 8am–5pm; admission is free at other times). Hold onto the ticket, because it's good for a week. Enacted in 2001, the fee has raised the hackles not only of visitors but also local business owners, who have challenged it in court on the ground that the square is a public thoroughfare. Many are sceptical that the money collected will be used productively. For its part, the municipality has grand plans for the square, including converting the adjacent schools and police station into museums, creating a courtyard for traditional craftsmen to work, and constructing public toilets.

Hanuman Dhoka (Old Royal Palace)

The rambling **Old Royal Palace** (mid-Feb to mid-Nov Tues–Sat 9.30am–4pm; mid-Nov to mid-Feb same days 9.30am–3pm) is usually called **Hanuman Dhoka**, after its main entrance. Admission is Rs250 – that's in addition to the Durbar Square entry fee.

Its oldest, eastern wings date from the mid-sixteenth century, but in all likelihood there was a palace on this spot before then. Malla kings built most of the rest by the late seventeenth century, and after capturing Kathmandu in 1768, Prithvi Narayan Shah added (in characteristically martial fashion) four lookout towers at the southeastern corner. Finally, the Ranas left their mark with the garish Neoclassical facade along the southwestern flank. Nepal's royal family last lived here in 1886, before moving to the northern end of town, and have retained the complex for ceremonial and administrative purposes. Only a fraction of the five-acre palace and grounds is open to the public.

The entrance

Entrance to the palace is through *the* Hanuman Dhoka (Hanuman Gate), a brightly decorated doorway at the east side of the northern part of Durbar

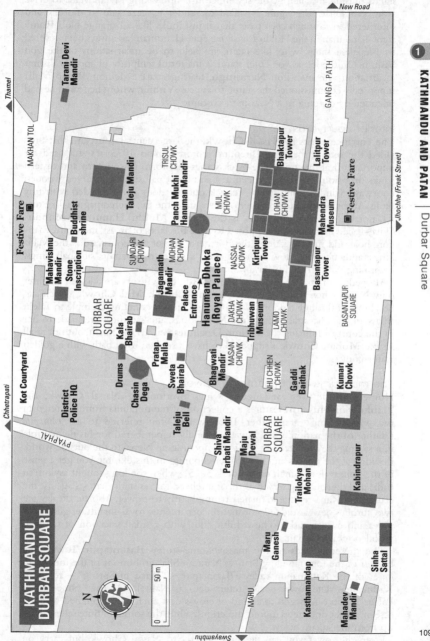

KATHMANDU
DURBAR SQUARE

N

0   50 m

New Road ▲

Thamel ▲

MAKHAN TOL

Tarani Devi Mandir

Festive Fare ▣

Mahavishnu Mandir
Stone Inscription
Buddhist shrine

Taleju Mandir

TRISUL CHOWK

Panch Mukhi Hanuman Mandir

GANGA PATH

Bhaktapur Tower

Lalitpur Tower

Festive Fare ▣

Jhochhe (Freak Street) ▶

MUL CHOWK

LOHAN CHOWK

Mahendra Museum

DURBAR SQUARE

Kala Bhairab

Jagannath Mandir

Palace Entrance

Hanuman Dhoka (Royal Palace)

SUNDARI CHOWK

MOHAN CHOWK

NASSAL CHOWK

Kirtipur Tower

Basantapur Tower

BASANTAPUR SQUARE

Pratap Malla

Sweta Bhairab

DAKHA CHOWK

Tribhuwan Museum

LAMO CHOWK

Chhetrapati ◀

Kot Courtyard

District Police HQ

Drums

Chasin Dega

Taleju Bell

Bhagwati Mandir

MASAN CHOWK

NHU CHHEN LCHOWK

Gaddi Baithak

Kumari Chowk

PYAPHAL

Shiva Parbati Mandir

Maju Dewal

DURBAR SQUARE

Trailokya Mohan

Kabindrapur

MARU

Maru Ganesh

Kasthamandap

Mahadev Mandir

Sinha Sattal

Swayambhu ▼

109

Square that's named after the popular monkey god **Hanuman**, whose statue stands outside. Installed by the seventeenth-century king Pratap Malla to drive away evil spirits, the figure is veiled to render its gaze safe to mortals, and smothered in so much *abhir* paste that it just looks like an orange blob. Ram's right-hand man in the Hindu *Ramayana* epic, Hanuman has always been revered by Nepalese kings, who, like Ram, are held to be incarnations of the god Vishnu. On the left as you enter stands a masterful sculpture of another Vishnu incarnation, the man-lion **Narasingh**, tearing apart a demon. Pratap Malla supposedly commissioned the statue to appease Vishnu, whom he feared he had offended by dancing in a Narasingh costume.

Interior courtyards

The entrance opens to **Nassal Chowk**, the large central courtyard that provided the setting for King Birendra's coronation in 1975; it's still used for important royal functions. The brick wings that form its southern and eastern flanks date from the sixteenth century and boast painstakingly carved wooden doorways, windows and struts – check out the door jambs beaded with tiny skulls. At the northeastern corner of the square, the five-tiered pagoda-like turret, notable for its round roofs, is the **Panch Mukhi Hanuman Mandir**: "Five-Faced Hanuman" is supposed to have the faces of an ass, man-bird, man-lion, boar and monkey. Along the northern side of the courtyard is the Malla kings' audience hall, now adorned with a series of portraits of Shah kings, beginning with Prithvi Narayan Shah.

Altogether the palace boasts ten courtyards, but visitors are allowed to enter only Nassal Chowk and one other, **Lohan Chowk**. **Mul Chowk**, which can be glimpsed through a doorway off Nassal Chowk, contains a temple to Taleju Bhawani, the ancestral deity of the Malla kings, and sacrifices are made to her in the courtyard during the autumn Dasain festival. To the north, but not at all visible, **Mohan Chowk** is supposed to have a sunken royal bath with a golden waterspout.

The museums and Basantapur Tower

Housed in the west and south wings overlooking Nassal Chowk, the **Tribhuwan Museum** features a collection of memorabilia from the reign of the present king's grandfather, Tribhuwan. Often referred to as *rashtrapita* ("father of the nation"), Tribhuwan is fondly remembered for his pivotal role in restoring the monarchy in 1951 and opening up Nepal to the outside world. Looking at the photos and newspaper clippings in this exhibit, you get a sense of the upheavals and high drama of 1950–51, when the king sought asylum in India and then, having served as the figurehead for resistance efforts against the crumbling Rana regime, returned triumphantly to power. Also on display are two thrones, jewel-studded coronation ornaments, royal furniture, guns, trophies and even a casket. The exhibit ends with a small selection of salvaged wooden temple carvings.

The museum leads to the massive nine-storey **Basantapur Tower**, the biggest of the four raised by Prithvi Narayan Shah in honour of the four main cities of the Kathmandu Valley. (Basantapur – "Place of Spring" – refers to Kathmandu. The tower is also referred to as Nautele Durbar, "Nine-Storey Palace".) You can ascend to a kind of crow's nest enclosed by pitched wooden screens to get fine views in four directions, while the sound of flute sellers drifts up from the square below.

From the tower you can descend directly to Nassal Chowk, but carry on through labyrinthine corridors to the **King Mahendra Memorial Museum**, dedicated to the present king's late father. Like the Tribhuwan exhibit, this one marches chronologically through the life and times of a monarch, the exhibits including a hunting scene and re-creations of Mahendra's office and cabinet room. The museum exits onto Lohan Chowk. The adjoining **King Birendra Museum**, dedicated to Mahendra's successor and late brother of the present king, is being reworked following his assassination in 2001 (see p.496).

For background information on the various gods, their symbols and styles of worship, see "Religion" on p.512. Definitions of various Nepali religious terms are also given in the glossary on p.580.

Kumari Chowk

At the southern end of the square stands **Kumari Chowk**, the gilded cage of Kathmandu's Raj Kumari, the pre-eminent of a dozen or more "living goddesses" in the valley. In case there was any doubt, Kumari Chowk proves Kathmandu is no stuffy, dead museum: no other temple better illustrates the living, breathing and endlessly adaptable nature of religion in Nepal, with its freewheeling blend of Hindu, Buddhist and indigenous elements.

The cult of **the Kumari** – a prepubescent girl worshipped as a living incarnation of the goddess Taleju – probably goes back to the early Middle Ages. Jaya Prakash, the last Malla king of Kathmandu, institutionalized the practice when he built the Kumari Chowk in 1757. According to legend, Jaya Prakash, who is remembered as a particularly paranoid and weak king, offended Taleju by lusting after her in the flesh, and to atone for his sin she ordered him to select a virgin girl in whom the goddess could dwell. He also established the tradition – continued to this day – that each year during the festival of Indra Jaatra, the Kumari should bestow a *tika* (auspicious mark) on the forehead of the king who was to reign for the coming year. In 1768, the hapless Jaya Prakash was driven into exile on the eve of Indra Jaatra, and the conquering Prithvi Narayan Shah slipped in and took the *tika*.

Although the Kumari is supposed to be a Hindu goddess, she is chosen from the Buddhist Shakya clan of goldsmiths, according to a **selection process** reminiscent of the Tibetan Buddhist method of finding reincarnated lamas. Elders interview hundreds of Shakya girls, aged three to five, shortlisting those who exhibit 32 auspicious signs: a neck like a conch shell, a body like a banyan tree, eyelashes like a cow's and so on. Finalists are placed in the courtyard of the Taleju Mandir at midnight, surrounded by freshly severed buffalo heads, while men in demon masks dance around making scary noises. The girl who shows no fear and can correctly identify belongings of previous Kumaris, and whose horoscope doesn't clash with the king's, becomes the next Kumari. She lives a cloistered life inside the Kumari Chowk and is only carried outside on her throne during Indra Jaatra and four or five other festivals each year; her feet are never allowed to touch the ground. The goddess's spirit leaves her when she menstruates or otherwise bleeds, whereupon she's retired with a modest state pension. The transition to life as an ordinary mortal can be hard, and she may have difficulty finding a husband, since tradition has it that the man who marries an ex-Kumari will die young. The present Kumari was installed in 2001, when she was three and a half years old.

Non-Hindus aren't allowed past the Kumari Chowk's *bahal*-style **courtyard**, which is decorated with exquisitely carved (if weathered) windows, pillars and doorways. When someone slips enough cash to her handlers, the Kumari, dressed in auspicious red and wearing heavy silver jewellery, her forehead painted red with an elaborate "third eye" in the middle, shows herself at one of the first-floor windows. (Your chances of a sighting are higher in the morning or late afternoon, when she's not busy with her studies.) She's believed to

Indra Jaatra: eight days of pomp and partying

According to Kathmandu Valley legend, **Indra**, the Vedic "King of Heaven", wanted to buy some flowers for his mother. Unable to find any in heaven, he descended to the valley and stole some, but was caught and imprisoned. When Indra's mother came looking for him, the people realized their mistake and were mortified: to appease him, they commenced an annual festival in his honour.

Usually held in late August or early September (see p.55), **Indra Jaatra** is an occasion to give thanks to the god for bringing the monsoon rains that make the all-important summer rice crop possible. Yet Indra's humiliation is a parallel theme of the festival, as straw effigies of the god, his arms outstretched as if bound, are placed in "jails" at various locations around the old city. Another local legend has it that an invading king, calling himself Indra, was defeated by the indigenous people of the valley, and some anthropologists believe such an event may have provided the historical impetus for the festival.

Indra Jaatra features eight days of almost nonstop spectacle. It begins with the ceremonial raising of a fifty-foot-tall **pole** in front of the Kala Bhairab statue by members of the Manandhar (oil-presser) caste. In Indrachowk, the famous blue mask of **Akash Bhairab**, a god sometimes identified with Indra, is displayed throughout the festival period, as are lesser Bhairab images in other neighbourhoods. Locals do *puja* to them by day, and light lamps by night in memory of deceased relatives. Masked dancers perform around the old city, and one group stages a tableau of the *das avatar* (the ten incarnations of Vishnu) at the base of the Trailokya Mohan.

Indra Jaatra is the fusion of two festivals, and the second, **Kumari Jaatra**, begins on the afternoon of the third day. From midday on, Durbar Square steadily fills up with spectators, battalions of soldiers in vintage uniforms, military bands and, in the balcony of the Gaddi Baithak, politicians, military brass and foreign dignitaries dressed in formal attire. (Tourists are herded into an area around the Shiva Parbati Mandir, where it's hard to get a decent view unless you're right behind the police cordon; however, women can sit on the elevated steps of the Maju Dewal.) Dancers, who are believed to be possessed by the deity whose mask they wear, entertain the crowd: the one in the red mask and shaggy hair is the popular **Lakhe**, a demon who's said to keep other spirits at bay so long as he's properly appeased. Eventually, the king and queen arrive and the procession can begin. The Kumari and two attendants, representing Ganesh and Bhairab, are pulled in wooden **chariots** around the square past the Gaddi Baithak, from where the royals pay homage by throwing coins. They then make a circuit of the southern old city, as far as Jaisi Dewal and Lagan, before returning to the square after dark.

After their departure, the formal state ceremony gives way to all-out partying. **Dance troupes** from around the valley perform near the entrance to the old royal palace, and a **pantomime elephant** – Indra's mount – careers through the streets. Young men gravitate toward **Sweta Bhairab** where, after lengthy ritual preliminaries, rice beer flows from a pipe sticking out of the idol's mouth.

Without the VIPs and ceremonial pomp, the chariots are again pulled the next afternoon, past Nardevi and Asan. On the eighth and final day of the festival, after a few days of relative calm, the chariots are pulled for a third time to Kilagal. According to legend, this last procession was added by King Jaya Prakash Malla to allow his concubine, who lived in Kilagal, to see the Kumari. When the chariots return to Durbar Square later that evening, His Majesty comes before the Kumari to receive the **royal tika** that assures his right to rule for another year. The ceremonial pole is then pulled down, and people take pieces of it as amulets against ghosts and spirits.

answer her visitors' unspoken questions with the look on her face. Cameras are okay inside the courtyard, but photographing the Kumari is strictly forbidden.

The chariot that carries the Kumari around during the Indra Jaatra festival is garaged next door to the Kumari Chowk. The big wooden chariot-yokes from past processions, which according to tradition may not be destroyed, are laid out nearby. The broad, bricked area to the east is **Basantapur Square**, once the site of royal elephant stables, where souvenir sellers now spread their wares.

Other temples and monuments

Dozens of temples (*mandir*), *dewal* (stepped platforms) and statues litter Durbar Square. The following stand out as highlights.

The Kasthamandap

If legend is to be believed, the **Kasthamandap**, standing at the southwestern end of the square, is Kathmandu's oldest building, and one of the oldest wooden buildings in the world. It's said to have been constructed from the wood of a single tree in the late twelfth century (Sinha Sattal, the smaller version to the south, was made from the leftovers), but what you see today is mostly the result of several renovations since 1630. An open, pagoda-roofed pavilion (*mandap*), it served for several centuries as a rest-house (*sattal*) along the Tibet trade route, and probably formed the nucleus of early Kathmandu. This corner of the square, called Maru Tol, still has the look of a crossroads, with vendors hawking fruit, vegetables and flowers. Many of the city's indigents sleep in the Kasthamandap at night.

The Shah kings converted the Kasthamandap into a temple to their lineage deity (see box below), **Gorakhnath**, whose statue stands in the middle of the pavilion. A Brahman priest usually sets up shop here to dispense instruction and conduct rituals. In four niches set around are shrines to Ganesh, the elephant-headed god of good fortune, which supposedly represent the celebrated Ganesh temples of the Kathmandu Valley (at Chabahil, Bhaktapur, Chobar and Bungmati), thus enabling Kathmandu residents to pay tribute to all four at once.

The building to the southeast of the Kasthamandap is **Kabindrapur**, a temple built in the seventeenth century for the staging of dance performances. Also known as Dhansa, it's dedicated to Shiva in his role as Nasa-dyo ("Lord of the Dance" in Newari), and is mostly patronized by musicians and dancers. Opposite Kabindrapur, occupying its own side square, is a brick *shikra* (Indian-style, corncob-shaped temple) to Mahadev (Shiva).

> A word about the confusing matter of royal deities: Gorakhnath, a mythologized Indian guru, is revered as a kind of guardian angel by all the Shah kings, and Taleju Bhawani, to whom many temples and bells are dedicated in the Kathmandu, Patan and Bhaktapur Durbar Squares, played a similar role for the Malla kings. The kings of both dynasties have worshipped the Kumari, but mainly as a public gesture to secure her *tika*, which lends credibility to their divine right to rule.

Maru Ganesh and Trailokya Mohan

Immediately north of the Kasthamandap stands yet another Ganesh shrine, the unassuming but ever-popular **Maru Ganesh**. A ring on Ganesh's bell is usually the preliminary act of any *puja*, and this shrine is the first stop for people intending to worship at the other temples of Durbar Square, royalty included. Ganesh's trusty "vehicle", a rat, is perched on a plinth of the Kasthamandap, across the way. The lane heading west from here used to be called Pie Alley –

in its heyday in the 1970s it boasted many pie shops, but they've now gone the way of hash shops and hippies.

The three-roofed pagoda between the Kasthamandap and the Kumari Chowk is the seventeenth-century **Trailokya Mohan**, dedicated to Narayan (a Nepali name for Vishnu). A much-photographed statue of the angelic Garud, Vishnu's man-bird vehicle, kneels in his customary palms-together *namaste* position in front of the temple.

Gaddi Baithak

The part of the Royal Palace facing the Trailokya Mohan is the **Gaddi Baithak**, a ponderous early-twentieth-century addition that pretty much sums up Rana-era architecture. If you didn't know Nepalese history you might say it had a whiff of the Raj about it, and in a way you'd be right: while India was under British rule, Nepal was labouring under its own home-grown colonialists, the Rana line of isolationist prime ministers. Some purists bemoan the Neoclassical building's distorting effect on Durbar Square's proportions, but you've got to admit it adds a bit of spice to the mix. The west-facing balcony serves as the royal reviewing stand during Indra Jaatra (see box on p.112).

The antiquity of the Durbar Square area was confirmed during the construction of the Gaddi Baithak, when workers uncovered what is believed to be remnants of a Lichhavi-era temple. The find spot is enclosed by a small grate in the middle of the road near the southwest corner of the Gaddi Baithak.

Maju Dewal and Shiva Parbati Mandir

North of the Trailokya Mohan, the huge seventeenth-century **Maju Dewal** sits high atop a pyramid of nine stepped levels. Climb to the top for a god's-eye view of the square and all its hubbub, but don't expect to escape the would-be guides, roving bangle-sellers and students anxious to practise their English.

From this height you can look straight across at the rectangular **Shiva Parbati Mandir**, erected in the eighteenth century by one of the early Shah kings. Painted figures of Shiva and his consort Parbati lean out of the first-floor window, looking like they're about to toss the bouquet and dash off to the honeymoon suite. Despite the temple's popular name, the actual objects of worship inside are nine images of the mother goddesses associated with the nine planets. The exterior woodwork is especially fine.

Around the Taleju Bell

North of the Shiva Parbati temple, the square narrows and then opens out to another temple-clogged area. Ranged along the left (western) side are the eighteenth-century **Taleju Bell**; the octagonal, seventeenth-century **Chasin Dega**, dedicated to Krishna the flute player; and a pair of ceremonial **drums** from the eighteenth century. The bell and drums were historically sounded as an alarm or call to congregate, but are now used only during the festival of Dasain.

Next to the palace opposite the bell, a small bas relief depicts **Jambhuwan**, the legendary teacher of Hanuman the monkey god. Just to the north of this, look up to see the **Kun Jhyal**, a gold-plated window frame flanked by two ivory ones, once used by Malla kings to watch processions in the square below.

Sweta and Kala Bhairabs

Just beyond, set against the palace wall but not very visible behind a wooden screen, is the snarling ten-foot-high gilded head of **Sweta Bhairab** (White Bhairab), a terrifying, blood-swilling aspect of Shiva. The screen comes down during the eight days of Indra Jaatra (see box on p.112), when men jostle to drink rice beer flowing out of Bhairab's mouth. The column nearby supports a gilded statue of **King Pratap Malla** and family, a self-congratulatory art form that was all the rage among the Malla kings of the late seventeenth century.

North of this, on the other side of the small Degu Taleju Mandir, the massive, roly-poly image of **Kala Bhairab** (Black Bhairab) dances on the corpse of a demon. Carved from a single twelve-foot slab of stone, it was found in a field north of Kathmandu during the reign of Pratap Malla, but probably dates to Lichhavi times. It used to be said that anyone who told a lie in front of it would vomit blood and die. One story has it that when the chief justice's office stood across the way, so many witnesses died while testifying that a temple had to be erected to shield the court from Kala Bhairab's wide-eyed stare.

The Jagannath Mandir and erotic carvings

East of Pratap Malla's column stands the sixteenth-century pagoda-style **Jagannath Mandir**, dedicated to the god whose runaway-chariot festival in India gave us the word "juggernaut". The struts supporting the lower roof of this temple contain Kathmandu's most tittered-about **erotic carvings**, although such images are actually quite common in Nepali temples: once you know where to look, you start noticing them everywhere.

Scholars can't seem to agree on the significance of these little vignettes, which often feature outrageous athletics, threesomes and bestiality. Some suggest that sex in this context is being offered as a tantric path to enlightenment, and as evidence they note that such scenes generally appear on the lower portions of struts, separated from the gods and goddesses above by lotuses (symbolic of transcendence). A more popular belief is that the goddess of lightning is a chaste virgin who wouldn't dare strike a temple so decorated. In any case, Hanuman, who guards the nearby palace entrance, is spared the sight by the veil over his eyes.

Nearby, along the palace outer wall, is a **stone inscription** in fifteen languages, carved in 1664 by King Pratap Malla, the prime architect of Durbar Square's temples, who also fancied himself something of a linguist. The inscription is a poem to the goddess Kali, and the story goes that if anyone can read the whole thing, milk will gush from the tap. There are two words in French and one in English.

The Taleju Mandir

Set atop a twelve-tiered plinth and rising 40m above the northeast end of the square, the magnificent **Taleju Mandir** looks down on you with haughty grandeur. Kathmandu's biggest temple, it was erected in the mid-sixteenth century by King Mahendra Malla, who decreed that no building should exceed it in height – a ban that remained in force until the middle of the twentieth century. It's open only on the ninth day of Dasain, and then only to Nepalis, who make sacrifices to Durga in the courtyard.

Taleju Bhawani, a South Indian goddess imported in the fourteenth century by the Mallas, is considered by Hindus to be a form of the mother goddess Durga, while Buddhist Newars count her as one of the Taras, tantric female deities. Behind the Taleju Mandir, reached by a doorway from Makhan Tol, sits the brick god-house of **Tarani Devi**, Taleju's "older sister".

The rest of the northern square

Other minor temples dotting the northern square belong mainly to Shiva. Inside each the god is worshipped as a *linga*, the stone phallus that to a Shaiva (follower of Shiva) is as potent a symbol as the cross is to a Christian. Two exceptions are the nineteenth-century **Mahavishnu Mandir**, destroyed in the 1934 earthquake and now being attractively restored, which enshrines an image of Vishnu; and, in front of the Taleju temple, a rare little **Buddhist shrine**, engulfed by a *bodhi* tree and containing a modest stone pedestal depicting the feet of Manjushri.

The infamous **Kot Courtyard**, which once lay northwest of the square, is now taken up by a walled army compound. It was here that the Machiavellian general Jang Bahadur Rana engineered a grisly massacre of 55 of the king's top brass in 1846, thereby clearing the way to proclaim himself prime minister and establish the hereditary line that was to rule Nepal until 1951. Blood again flows here each year on the ninth day of Dasain, when soldiers attempt to sever the heads of sacrificial buffaloes with a single sword stroke.

North of Durbar Square

Kathmandu's oldest, liveliest streets lie north and northeast of Durbar Square. You could make a more or less circular swing through the area (as this section does), but you'll almost certainly be diverted somewhere along the way. At any rate, the sights described here are only a backdrop for the old city's fascinating street life.

Indrachowk

The old trade route to Tibet passes through Durbar Square and becomes a narrow lane after it rounds the Taleju Mandir. Passing through **Makhan Tol** – the name harks back to a time when butter (*makhan*) was sold here – it runs a gauntlet of *thangka* (Buddhist scroll painting) sellers and then takes a northeasterly bearing towards Kathmandu's traditional goldsmiths' neighbourhood.

The first big intersection you reach is **Indrachowk**, named in honour of the Vedic (early Hindu) king of the gods. A sort of Asian Zeus, complete with thunderbolt, Indra fell from grace in India centuries ago, but in the Kathmandu Valley he still rates his own festival (see p.112). The newly-renovated house-like temple on the west side of the crossroads is that of **Akash Bhairab** (Sky, or Blue, Bhairab), who is considered to be equivalent to Indra and is represented by a large snarling blue head. Newars also call this deity Aju-dyo, and claim the idol is what's left of a native king who was beheaded in the *Mahabharat* epic. The upstairs temple is out-of-bounds to non-Hindus, but the great blue image is displayed outside on a bier of flowers during Indra Jaatra. In a pragmatic arrangement, the downstairs is rented out to shopkeepers to fund the temple's upkeep.

Shopping is good around Indrachowk. Pashmina (and acrylic) shawls are sold from the steps of shrines in the intersection, there's a courtyard full of fabric shops to the northeast of the square, and colourful bead necklaces (*pote*) and tassels (*dhaago*) hang in curtains from the stalls of the **Pote Bazaar**, a small market area to the east. *Pote*, worn by virtually all married women of Nepal's middle hills, typically consist of numerous strands of coloured glass beads drawn together with a cylindrical gold ornament known as a *tilhari*. Many married women also weave red *dhaago* into their hair – the colour indicates married status. The stalls here are owned mainly by Muslims, descendants of Kashmiri traders who migrated to the valley three centuries ago. You can watch them deftly making *pote*, using a big toe or a nail to anchor each strand while stringing it.

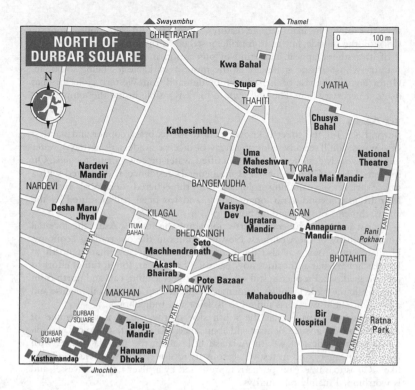

NORTH OF
DURBAR SQUARE

Kel Tol and Seto Machhendranath

The tumultuous street heading north from Indrachowk is the direct route to Thamel, but the old Tibet road continues diagonally to the small square of **Kel Tol** and the seventeenth-century temple of **Seto** (or Sweta) **Machhendranath**, one of two main shrines to the protector god of the Kathmandu Valley. Like his "red" cousin in Patan (see p.146), "White" Machhendranath is feted in a great chariot festival during the month of Chaitra (March–April).

Newars know this god as Karunamaya Lokeshwar, the *bodhisattva* of compassion, while Tibetans consider him Jowo Dzamling Karmo, White Lord of the World. Yet another name, **Jama-dyo**, traces back to a legend in which the white mask of Machhendranath was stolen by marauders from the west during ancient times. The invading king's family is said to have been afflicted with incurable diseases for six generations, until one of them took the idol back to Kathmandu and buried it in a field in Jamal, near what is now Durbar Marg. When a farmer rediscovered the image in the fifteenth century, it was immediately hailed as Jama-dyo – God of Jamal – and installed in this location, which is accordingly known as **Jamal** (or Jana) **Bahal**.

The entrance to the well-concealed courtyard is a gate at the west side of Kel Tol. Among the many votive *chaityas* and figures is a weathered old stone figure of Amitabha (one of the *panchabuddha*, the five personifications of Buddhahood), a Victorian bronze statue converted into an incense holder, three Tara figures on pillars, and the Kanaka Chaitya, a Lichhavi-era stone hemisphere that was the original centrepiece of this *bahal* before Machhendranath stole the show. The main temple features some beautiful gilt-copper repoussé work on the outside, but an iron grille, installed to thwart temple thieves, robs it of its aesthetic appeal. This kind of precaution is still unusual in Nepal, a country whose artistic riches are all the more remarkable for being so public. Unfortunately, the risk of theft, driven by demand from Western collectors, has made it necessary here. The god's white mask is visible inside the temple.

To Asan

Beyond Kel Tol, the street is known mainly for its brass, copper and stainless steel wares: you'll see a bewildering array of incense holders, *thaal* (trays), water jugs, and vessels designed to hold sanctified water or cow's urine for *puja*. On the left, **Tilang Ghar**, a former Rana general's residence, is decorated with a stucco frieze of marching soldiers. The three-tiered octagonal **Krishna Mandir** just beyond is no longer active, and has been half obscured by the encroachments of surrounding buildings.

The last and most exuberant intersection along this route is **Asan**, the ancestral home of many of the wealthiest Newar families in the old trading economy. Until recently Asan was also the main fruit and vegetable market north of Durbar Square, but authorities now bar such trade in an (often futile) effort to prevent gridlock. Produce is still sold in the streets leading east and north from here, while the trade in spices, homemade balls of soap, candles, oil, incense and other household wares has shifted to Kel Tol and Indrachowk.

The gilt-roofed pagoda at the south side of the square is the temple of **Annapurna**, the goddess of grain and abundance, and a manifestation of Lakshmi, the popular goddess of wealth. A lavish little affair, the pagoda bristles with icons and imagery, and in festival seasons its roof is strung with electric bulbs like a Christmas tree. Annapurna is represented by a silver *kalash*, or vessel, and is worshipped mainly on Sundays.

Mahaboudha and Bangemudha

From Asan, the trade route angles up to Kantipath and the modern city, while an alley heading south leads to **Mahaboudha**. Stuck in a rather unattractive square and said to date back to the sixth-century king Basantdev, this plain white stupa takes its name from the big statue of the Buddha in an adjacent brick shelter. The square is a wholesale grain and spice depot, and day labourers congregate here for jobs, or wait with their rubber-wheeled flatbed carts (*thela*) for hire. Like hill porters, they are often of the Tamang tribe.

Walk westwards from Asan and you'll first pass the small three-tiered pagoda of **Ugratara**, a goddess believed to cure eyesight problems, before returning to the main Indrachowk–Thamel lane at **Bangemudha**. Just south of this square is a somewhat odd shrine to **Vaisya Dev**, the Newar toothache god. Commonly billed as the "Toothache Tree", it's actually the butt end of a log, embedded in the side of a building, and it used to be common practice to seek the god's help with dental problems by banging a nail in the log. (Bangemudha – "Crooked Stick" – refers to the legendary tree from which the log was cut.) Nowadays, many dentists advertise their services with grinning signs nearby.

At the north end of Bangemudha, a priceless fifth-century **Buddha figure** stands all but neglected in a tacky, tiled niche. Continuing north another 100m, a lattice doorway on the right opens to a small niche housing a ninth-century **Uma Maheshwar**, a standard motif depicting Shiva and Parbati as a cosy couple atop Mount Kailas. The private house across the lane boasts fine woodwork and, it's said, Kathmandu's first glass window panes.

Kathesimbhu and Thahiti

Central Kathmandu's biggest stupa, **Kathesimbhu** stands in a square off to the left about 200m north of Bangemudha. The temple is only a modest replica of the more impressive Swayambhu stupa (its name is a contraction of "Kathmandu Swayambhu"), but for those too old or infirm to climb to Swayambhu (see p.127), rites performed here earn the same merit. According to legend, it was built with earth left over after Swayambhu's construction; Lichhavi-era sculptures hereabouts attest to the antiquity of the site, but the stupa itself probably dates to the late seventeenth century. Like its namesake, Kathesimbhu has an associated shrine to the smallpox goddess Harati, located in the northwestern corner of the square. The square doubles as the playground for a local school, so watch out during playtime.

Traffic circulates around another stupa at **Thahiti**, the next square north on the way to Thamel. Because they're continually replastered, stupas never look very old and are hard to date, but this one probably goes back to the fifteenth century. The name Thahiti apparently comes from Thane Hiti: this northern fringe of the old city was once known as Thane, and the story goes that a *hiti* (public water tap) here flowed with golden sand until it was covered by the stupa.

One of Kathmandu's finest old *bahal*, the seventeenth-century **Chusya Bahal** stands about two blocks east of Thahiti. It's recognizable by the two stone lions out in front and a meticulously carved wooden *torana* (decorative shield) above the doorway, both standard features of a *bahal*. The building is now privately owned.

Thamel

In the **Thamel** tourist zone north of Thahiti, old buildings are scarce and about the only sights are the goodies in the restaurant windows. **Kwa Bahal**, a traditional courtyard tucked away just off the touristy main drag, is one of several *bahal* in Kathmandu and Patan that have their own Kumaris. **Bhagwan Bahal**, which lends its name to an area north of Thamel Chowk, is home to a little-used pagoda whose most notable feature is a collection of kitchen pans and utensils nailed to the front wall as offerings to the deity. ("Bikrama Sila Mahabihar", the name on the sign in front, refers to a moribund monastery contained within the complex.) During the spring festival of Holi, a portrait of the *bahal's* eleventh-century founder is displayed to celebrate his slaying of demons on his return from a trade delegation to Lhasa.

Mhai Pi

Rarely visited by foreigners, the shrine of **Mhai Pi** sits atop a small, wooded hill twenty- to thirty-minutes' walk north of Thamel. Local people ascend the hill in early morning to do *puja* and sing hymns at the modest temple, which honours a local manifestation of Ajima, the Newar grandmother goddess. However, these low-key rituals belie this Ajima's importance in the Kathmandu Valley's religious protocol, for tradition dictates that the clay used to refinish the mask of Raato Machhendranath and certain other idols must be collected from seven sacred points around the shrine's hill. Mhai Pi is also believed to be the patron deity of witches. A colourful *jaatra* (festival) takes place here around the full moon of Bhadau (Aug–Sept).

The shrine is reached by either of two long flights of stairs, a steep one from the west and a newer one with switchbacks from the south. The western approach is reminiscent of Swayambhunath's main staircase, and monkeys in the trees add to the similarity.

Kathmandu's street children

A boy was pleading as pathetically as possible, "Master, I'm so hungry."
A tall, rough-looking boy among them cried, "Sleepy-eyed bastard, is that any
way to beg?" And he slapped the pleading boy.
The boy whimpered, "How do you do it then?" Gore saw that he was on the
verge of tears and felt sorry for him.
"Watch." While the other children looked on, the rough boy made a forlorn,
pitiable face. Innocent shadows began to darken his eyes as he whined, "They
hacked my father in Chobhar village, my mother ran off with another man…Sir,
I'm hungry, so hungry."
His acting was perfect. His cries filled the whole street with tones of lament,
and within moments a passing gentleman placed a five paisa coin in the boy's
hand. The boy's expression immediately changed. His eyes sparkled with success and his lips curled into a smirk. He turned contemptuously towards his
friends. "See!".
Ministers of the Sidewalk (Mandala Book Point, 1968), Ramesh Vikal, trans. Manjushree Thapa

Like so many urban problems, the plight of **street children** is a relatively modern
phenomenon in Kathmandu. Ground down by rural poverty and domestic violence,
and aided by new roads and bus services, many children run away to the capital in
search of a better life. Some are lured there by men promising high-paying jobs in
tourism; such promises often prove false. The charity Child Workers in Nepal (CWIN)
estimates that 400 children – some as young as five, and overwhelmingly male – live
on Kathmandu's streets at any one time. That's down from 1000 in the mid-1990s,
thanks to intervention programmes by CWIN and other groups, but about 300 more
join the ranks each year. Most are lone runaways or orphans, though some live with
their squatter families. The young beggars who roam Thamel and Durbar Marg,
barefoot and clutching dirty cloths for warmth, are the more conspicuous face of
homelessness in Kathmandu. Living relatively well off tourist handouts, they spurn
training programmes and education, and grow up illiterate, unskilled and unemploy-
able – perhaps to join the next generation of touts offering drugs to tourists. Your
alms will do more good if given to a charity working with beggars, rather than to the
beggars themselves. The majority of street children scrounge more anonymous and
meagre existences, though. Some scavenge in rubbish piles, pick pockets or drift
into prostitution – about the best a kid with no parental help can hope for is to find
steady work as a domestic servant, *kanchha* (errand boy), labourer or perhaps a bus
conductor. But even employment has its risks, and indeed many children take to the
streets to escape exploitive employers.

In a country where nearly half the population is living below the poverty line, it's
easy to overlook the plight of street kids. Yet the conditions they endure are arguably
more debilitating than rural poverty. Homeless, they sleep in doorways, *pati* (open
shelters) or unfinished buildings. Hungry, they often subsist on food thrown out by
tourist restaurants, and many suffer from malnutrition. Weakened by a poor diet and
contaminated water, few are without disease (CWIN reports that twenty percent
have tuberculosis). Craving stimulation, many sniff glue or become addicted to harder drugs. They're regularly beaten by the police, who regard them as bad for tourism,
and during visits by foreign delegations they may be rounded up and jailed. And
perhaps most damaging of all, they are deprived of the traditionally supportive
environment of family and community, and of the schooling essential for any kind of
career.

CWIN operates a **"common room"** near the *Soaltee Crowne Plaza* to provide
food, education, health care and play for street children; volunteers and donations
are needed. For more information, contact CWIN (☎01/282255, ✆www.cwin-nepal
.org). Another organization, Bisaune (☎01/230671), located just west of Thahiti, provides similar drop-in facilities for street children in the Thamel area.

Chhetrapati and Nardevi

At the southwestern fringe of Thamel lies boisterous **Chhetrapati**, a six-way intersection of almost perpetual motion. Though the neighbourhood lacks any ancient monuments, it supports a central *pati* (open shelter) resembling an Edwardian bandstand, around which religious processions and impromptu musical jamborees are frequent occurrences. During Shiva Raatri in February, sadhus build fires on the platform and light up their chilams, and during Tihaar the iron railings are decorated with oil lamps.

From Chhetrapati it's a straight run south to the Kasthamandap; this street is favoured as an assembly point for protest marches, since the police can't easily secure it. On the right if you're walking south, the **Nardevi Mandir** is believed to have been established by the ninth-century founder of Kathmandu, Gunakamadev, though the present structure is merely medieval. The temple's deity, known as Sweta (White) Kali or Neta Ajima, is said to have received human sacrifice in ancient times; visible inside the temple are three silver images of Kali. The area to the west of the temple has a reputation as an important centre of ayurvedic medicine, with a college, hospital and many doctors' practices and pharmacies.

Kilagal, Bhedasingh and back to Durbar Square

A short walk east of Nardevi, **Kilagal** is marked by a widening in the road with a handsome central *chaitya* and a bas relief of Bhairab. A small passage nearby leads to the large, flagstoned piazza of **Itum Bahal**, a remarkable sanctuary from the noise of the modern city. Though many of the buildings surrounding Itum Bahal have been modernized, the neighbourhood still has a villagey atmosphere, especially at harvest time when grain is spread out to dry. At the southern end of the square, a doorway surmounted by a weathered but still splendid *torana* leads to the fourteenth-century Kichandra Bahal, now privately owned.

Bhedasingh, the next junction east of Kilagal, is the domain of fruit, vegetable and spice sellers, and a few potters who sell their wares from the steps of a squat Mahadev temple erected in memory of King Tribhuwan. The name Bhedasingh, which means "Sheep Horn", is a legacy of the days when livestock was traded here.

From Bhedasingh you can return to Durbar Square either via Indrachowk (see p.116) or by backtracking to Nardevi and heading south from there along Pyaphal. The latter route soon re-enters atmospheric eighteenth-century neighbourhoods, with several large *bahal* dating back as far as the fourteenth century tucked away down dark alleys. Keep an eye out on the east side of the street for the **Desha Maru Jhyal** – literally, the "Country Nowhere Window" – a window grille of staggering complexity which, even in a country abounding in outstanding woodwork, is considered unique. Carved from a single block of wood, it obviously predates the house in which it's now set.

South of Durbar Square

The old city **south of Durbar Square** is home mainly to working-class castes – service providers, artisans and some farmers – and, increasingly, immigrant squatters. With fewer traders, it's less commercial and less touristed than the quarters north of the square, although New Road, which bristles and throbs with high-end consumerism, is as lively a street as any in Kathmandu.

Bhimsensthan

A small square southwest of the Kasthamandap, down a lane leading to the Bishnumati River, **Bhimsensthan** is named after one of Nepal's favourite

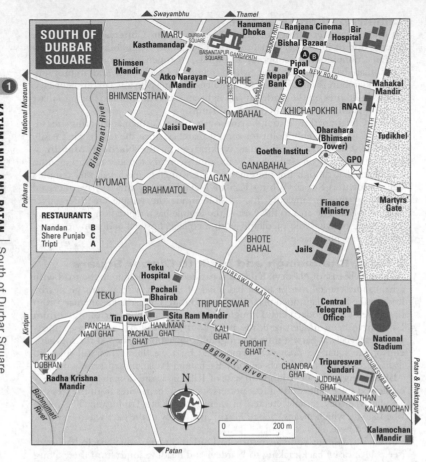

SOUTH OF DURBAR SQUARE

RESTAURANTS
Nandan B
Shere Punjab C
Tripti A

gods. Bhimsen, the strongman son of Vayu the wind god, is one of the famous five brothers of the Hindu epic *Mahabharat* who has been adopted as the patron saint of Newar merchants: you'll see pictures of him in shops everywhere. According to local legend, Bhimsen came to Kathmandu as the manservant of a bride from eastern Nepal, who was married off to a farmer who lived on the west bank of the Bishnumati. Unaware of his new servant's identity, the farmer put him to work in the fields; Bhimsen proceeded to work miracles with the rice, and the farmer, finally recognizing the god, granted him a plot of land he could reach in three strides. Bhimsen bounded across the river and settled at Bhimsensthan.

The Bhimsen temple here was founded in the twelfth century, and the current structure was built in the eighteenth, but is frequently renovated to look much newer. The shrine on the upper floor is open only to Hindus, while the ground floor is, fittingly, occupied by shops.

Jaisi Dewal to Tripureswar Marg

Jaisi Dewal, a seventeenth-century Shiva temple, stands in a square several blocks south of the Kasthamandap in the Chikamugal area. A three-tiered pagoda without much ornamentation, it's made more impressive by being set on an eight-level foundation. *Linga*-spotters can ogle the eight-foot-high monster at the foot of the temple, which, though only a raw, uncarved stone, has to be the biggest in the kingdom.

A *bahal* just to the southwest of the Jaisi Dewal contains a small **Ram Chandra Mandir**, surrounded by higgledy-piggledy brick buildings and stables. Hanuman, Ram's monkey helper, kneels before the temple. Further to the south, **Tukum Bahal** and its newly restored Swayambhu-style stupa are reached through a passage on the left. The road continues south to **Tripureswar Marg**, an important east–west thoroughfare and one of Kathmandu's strongest entries in the Bangkok lookalike sweepstakes.

Pachali Bhairab

The most interesting part of south Kathmandu begins with **Pachali Bhairab**, an open-air shrine marooned among the city's maintenance facilities. To find it, head west on Tripureswar Marg and then south on the back road to Patan; finally, bear left at a fork marked by a small park.

Compared to the awfulness of what you've just walked through, it feels very peaceful here. The tiny gilded idol of Bhairab stands in a sunken sanctuary, dwarfed by a huge pipal tree and a life-sized human figure laid out like a pharaoh's casket. The repoussé figure is a **betal**, Bhairab's vehicle and a likeness of death which, in Nepali Hinduism, is believed to protect against death (the old principle of fighting fire with fire). *Betal* normally take the form of miniature skulls or skeletons at temple entrances, so this one is unusual for being so large and fleshed out.

According to legend this shrine was established by Kathmandu's founder, the ninth-century King Gunakamadev, to protect the city's southern gate. For many centuries, all treaties were signed with Pachali Bhairab as witness, in the belief that the god would strike dead anyone who broke the agreement. A procession starts here on the fourth and fifth nights of Dasain before moving on to Durbar Square.

The Bagmati ghats

A path from Pachali Bhairab leads to the **ghats** of the Bagmati River, which stretch as far as the eye can see in either direction. Statues, temples and all manner of artefacts are jumbled along these stone-paved embankments – especially to the west, where the Bishnumati joins the Bagmati – and you could easily spend several hours picking around among them. The entire area is the subject of a proposed restoration project, so maybe someday (probably around the time the rivers run clean) it will enjoy a much-deserved renaissance. For the time being, though, it's in a pretty sorry state of neglect.

Pachali Ghat

The path forks before reaching the river, but both ways lead to **Pachali Ghat** and its remarkable collection of Hindu and Buddhist statuary. If you take the right fork, you'll enter an area that's like a primer of the Newar pantheon of gods. Statues set in niches along the right-hand wall depict (from right to left) Hanuman, Saraswati, the green and white Taras, Bhairab, Ganesh, a *linga/yoni*, a standing Vishnu, the Buddha, Ram, Shiva as sadhu, and a flute-playing Krishna. On the left are many more, concluding with depictions of the ten incarnations (*das avatar*) of Vishnu: fish, tortoise, the boar Baraha, the man-lion Narasingh, the dwarf Vaman, the Brahman Parasuram, the mythical heroes Ram and Krishna, the Buddha, and finally Kalki, the saviour yet to come.

Off to the right, the three-tiered **Lakshmishwar Mahadev Mandir** occupies a crumbling *bahal* that's been taken over by a language school. The temple's construction was sponsored by the late-eighteenth-century queen Rajendra Laskhmi Devi Shah, who apparently considered Shiva (Mahadev) her lord (*ishwar*).

Pancha Nadi Ghat

Continuing downstream (westwards), you pass under an old footbridge and a modern motorable one, both leading to Patan's northern suburb of Sanepa. Beyond, **Pancha Nadi Ghat** used to be one of Kathmandu's most important sites for ritual bathing, but no longer, as the Bagmati has receded from the embankment: the river is literally shrinking as its water is siphoned off for ever-growing industrial and domestic needs. Consequently the several pilgrims' shelters (*sattal*) and rest-houses (*dharmsala*) along here have been taken over by squatters.

A small **sleeping Vishnu** in this area recalls, in miniature, the great statue at Budhanilkantha (see p.204). Cremations are infrequently held at the nearby **burning ghats**. Butchers slaughter animals down by the river in the early morning – the buffalo you see here today could turn up in your *momo* tomorrow.

The confluence area

The embankment ends just short of **Teku Dobhan**, the confluence (*dobhan*) of Kathmandu's two main rivers, the Bagmati and the Bishnumati. The spot is also known as Chintamani Tirtha – a *tirtha* is a sacred place associated with *nag*, snake spirits.

The confluence area is ancient, and feels it, though none of the temples or buildings is more than a century old. The most prominent is the **Radha Krishna Mandir**, a brick *shikra* built in the 1930s; flute-playing Krishna in the middle of three figures inside. The rest-house behind the temple, **Manandhar Sattal**, is named after a wealthy nineteenth-century trader who was forced to retire here after his property was confiscated by the prime minister. The next-door building is an electric crematorium built in the 1970s, but never used.

The riverbank from here downstream to the Ring Road is currently serving as a temporary landfill – an appalling tactic in a long-running political stand-off over what to do with Kathmandu's solid waste. This dumping site, like an earlier one further upstream near the Pashupatinath temple complex, is certain to leach toxins into the river for decades to come. So much for sacred places.

Tin Dewal

Returning to Pachali Ghat and heading upstream (eastwards), you reach the atmospheric **Tin Dewal** ("Three Temples") by an entrance from the riverside. The temple's popular name refers to its three brick *shikra* sharing a common base and ground floor – an unusual combination of Indian and Nepali styles, with some fine brick detailing.

A sign identifies the site by its official name, which is transliterated into English as Bomveer Vikalashora Shibalaya. The complex was erected in 1850 by Bom Bahadur Kunwar, brother of Jang Bahadur Rana, who'd seized power in a bloody coup four years earlier. A *shivalaya* is a shrine containing a *linga*, one of which can be seen behind each of the temple's three lattice doors.

More ghats

A statue of Hanuman the monkey god, wearing his customary gold-trimmed robe and coating of vermilion paste, overlooks **Hanuman Ghat**, just to the east. Behind him is a newish and relatively popular **Sita Ram Mandir**.

Things get less interesting further east. Past the unremarkable Kali Ghat, **Purohit Ghat** is marked by another small Hanuman statue and a fine old *bahal* now used as a residence. Beyond that there's a 300-metre break in the embankment, as a path makes its way through a semi-permanent shantytown. Its residents – landless rubbish-pickers, day labourers and street vendors – have moved in as the river has receded, but they still take their chances each monsoon. An estimated 10,000 squatters live in Kathmandu, most in riverside settlements like this.

The embankment resumes at **Chandra Ghat**, where former pilgrims' quarters have been converted into a school. **Juddha Ghat** is flanked on the north by a long police barracks, and to the south, where the river used to flow, by a shady park. Another large Hanuman statue gives its name to **Hanumansthan**, a settlement dating to Lichhavi times. An Uma Maheshwar statue and a few old *linga* are also grouped here. Dying people used to be laid out on the angled, tombstone-like slab here so that their feet touched the Bagmati's holy water.

Tripureswar Sundari and Kalamochan Mandir

From Hanumansthan a path leads away from the river to Tripureswar Marg via the **Tripureswar Sundari**, a derelict quadrangle that has been squatted by a collective of low-caste families. The square's central temple, a massive three-tiered pagoda dedicated to Mahadev (Shiva), was erected in the early nineteenth century by Queen Lalit Tripura Sundari in memory of her husband Rana Bahadur Shah, who was assassinated in one of the period's many episodes of court intrigue.

Continuing north on this path brings you back to the buzzing, sputtering crosstown traffic of Tripureswar Marg. To the southeast lies the marvellously hideous **Kalamochan Mandir**, a study in Rana excess. Resembling a grotesque white wedding cake, it was completed in 1852 by the first of the Rana prime ministers, the ruthless Jang Bahadur, who is said to have buried the ashes of those killed in the Kot massacre beneath its foundation. The gargoyles snarling at its four corners are fitting testaments to his ambition.

New Road, Jhochhe and Bhimsen Tower

Rebuilt after a disastrous 1934 earthquake, **New Road** cuts a swath of modernity through the old city east of Basantapur Square. Wealthy Nepalis and Indian tourists regard it as a magical duty-free bazaar and swarm its shops for perfume, jewellery, kitchen appliances, consumer electronics and myriad other imported luxury goods. Security guards stand sentry in front of department store entrances, well-heeled matrons stroll the pavements with shopping bags, and peasants visiting the capital stand transfixed at the sight of snapshots rolling off automatic photo-processing machines. This is what economic prosperity looks like in one of the world's poorest nations: materialistic, elite and very localized.

The statue at the west end of New Road commemorates Prime Minister Juddha Shamsher Rana, who is credited with rebuilding the road (and much of Kathmandu) after the 1934 earthquake. **Pipal Bot**, a venerable old tree about midway along the road's south side, provides a natural canopy for shoeshiners and newspaper and magazine vendors, and is a favourite gathering place for Kathmandu's intelligentsia and gossipmongers.

1

Immediately south of Basantapur Square, **Jhochhe** (**Freak Street**) isn't prime sightseeing territory, but it does have unique historical associations. For a few foggy years in the late 1960s and early 1970s, this was an important station along the hippy trail through Asia. In those days, before the invention of Thamel, Jhochhe was *the* place to hang out. Grass and hash were legal and sold openly, and "freaks" had the freedom of the city. It all ended suddenly in 1974, when the young King Birendra passed a series of stricter immigration and drug laws. To catch a whiff of that halcyon time, kick back a while at the *Snowman*; the Freak Street pie shop in which Cat Stevens is said to have written his classic (and now all but forgotten) song *Kathmandu* was probably much like this one.

A lane heading east from Jhochhe leads to Kathmandu's main fish market and on to **Dharahara**, the tall minaret-like tower overlooking the GPO. Commonly known as **Bhimsen Tower**, it was built in 1832 by the prime minister, Bhimsen Thapa, possibly in imitation of Calcutta's Ochterlony Monument, which had been erected only four years earlier. A story is told that Bhimsen Thapa, sitting astride his horse, leapt off the tower, creating the nearby **Sun Dhara** (Golden Water Tap) where he landed; in reality the *mandala*-shaped sunken bathing area was created by Thapa in 1821.

Three of Kathmandu's four **jails** (see box below) are located south of here, down a side street off Kantipath – bear right just after the Ministry of Finance.

Kathmandu's jails

One of the more thought-provoking things you can do while in Kathmandu is to visit Westerners held in the capital's four **jails**. Most are held in one of the jails south of the GPO (Central, Badragol or Women's); a fourth facility is located in Dilli Bazaar. Since families are expected to provide for most of the prisoners' needs, foreigners may be particularly badly off.

At any given time, as many as half a dozen foreigners are imprisoned or awaiting trial in Kathmandu, usually on drug smuggling charges, but most of their cases never come to trial, since the government basically waits for someone to buy the accused out of jail. Nepalis receive the same rough justice, plus they are liable to be imprisoned for political reasons. Although human rights in Nepal have generally improved since the establishment of democracy, the police are known to detain protesters illegally and to torture and ill-treat prisoners, and the Maoists' "People's War" (see p.498) has prompted the government to give the police sweeping emergency powers to arrest suspected revolutionaries.

Conditions in the jails are grim. For food, inmates receive a half-kilo of "black" (fermented) rice and *daal* each day, plus a few rupees with which to buy vegetables at the prison shop. They sleep on the floor, with up to fifty to a room; no clothes or bedding are provided. Still, the prisoners here can consider themselves lucky they aren't locked away in provincial jails, beyond the normal range of human rights organizations.

Daily **visiting hours** are 8am–5pm (but check: times may vary). You must first sign in with the duty officer, in a building on the left side of the lane heading south from the Ministry of Finance. Ask for prisoners by name – there should be a list of foreigners on the wall of the duty officer's room, or check posters around Thamel and Freak Street. Inmates appear at a barred doorway, while visitors must stand behind a chain, so conversations are far from private. Don't go unless you're prepared to offer assistance, such as making telephone calls, passing along messages or bringing supplies. Food, vitamins, toiletries, reading materials, clothes, blankets and cash are all appreciated.

West of the Bishnumati

Most of Kathmandu **west of the Bishnumati River** was settled relatively recently, with much of the development focused on the ugly Kalimati–Kalanki corridor and the suburbs on either side of it. The only real antiquities are the famous **Swayambhu** stupa and a few shrines and temples that can be visited en route, plus the exhibits preserved in the **National Museum**. All of these sights are within fairly easy walking distance of central Kathmandu or Thamel, but to make a circuit of all of them it's more pleasant to go by bike or take taxis partway (taxis usually wait at Swayambhu, but are hard to find near the museum).

Swayambhu and around

Even if temple-touring makes your eyes glaze over, don't miss **Swayambhu** (or Swayambhunath), magnificently set atop a conical hill 2km west of Thamel. To begin with, it's a great place to get your bearings, geographically and culturally, in your first few days in Nepal: the hill commands a sweeping view of the Kathmandu Valley, and the temple complex, overrun with pilgrims and monkeys, is a real eye-opener.

But there's much more if you dig for it. The ancient stupa is the most profound expression of Buddhist symbolism in Nepal (many *bahal* in the valley contain a replica of it), and is the source and central location of the valley's creation myth. Inscriptions positively date the stupa to the fifth century, and there's reason to believe the hill was used for animist rites even before Buddhism arrived in the valley two thousand years ago. Tantric Buddhists consider it the chief "power point" of the Kathmandu Valley; one chronicle states that an act of worship here carries thirteen billion times more merit than anywhere else. To call it the "Monkey Temple" (its tourist nickname) is to trivialize it, as if the monkeys were its most noteworthy feature.

Since the Chinese invasion of Tibet in 1959, the area surrounding Swayambhu has become home to hundreds of Tibetans in exile. You'll see them and many other Buddhist pilgrims making a full circumambulation (*kora*) of

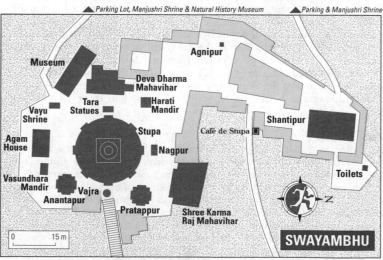

▲ *Parking Lot, Manjushri Shrine & Natural History Museum*   ▲ *Parking & Manjushri Shrine*

Museum

Agnipur

Deva Dharma
Mahavihar

Tara
Statues

Harati
Mandir

Vayu
Shrine

Shantipur

Agam
House

Stupa

Café de Stupa

Nagpur

Vasundhara
Mandir

Vajra

Anantapur

Toilets

Pratappur

Shree Karma
Raj Mahavihar

0   15 m

SWAYAMBHU

▼ *Main (Eastern) Entrance*

the hill, queuing up to spin the gigantic fixed prayer wheels and the 6000 smaller ones that encircle the perimeter, and frequently twirling their own hand-held ones. The place is so steeped in lore and pregnant with detail that you'll never absorb it all in a single visit. Try going early in the morning at *puja* time, or at night when the red-robed monks pad softly around the dome, murmuring mantras and spinning the prayer wheels. Make a final visit before you leave Nepal and see how your perceptions of it differ from your initial trip.

Swayambhu's main **festivals** are Buddha Jayanti (April or May) and Losar (in Feb or March), when pilgrims throng around the stupa and monks splash arcs of saffron paint over it in a lotus-flower pattern. Many also flock here each morning during the month-long Gunla festivities (Aug or Sept) to mark the "rain's retreat" with music and offerings to the monks.

A visit to Swayambhu can be turned into a longer hike or bike trip by continuing on to Ichangu Narayan (see p.207).

Getting there

The main entrance is at the eastern foot of the hill, and **getting there** is a simple matter on foot or cycle. From Thamel, the easiest way is via Chhetrapati, from where a small road heads straight towards Swayambhu, passing the *Hotel Vajra* en route. From Jhochhe or Durbar Square, take the lane running northwest from the Maru Ganesh shrine. Either way, it should take about twenty minutes to walk it. If you're cycling, the local kids will expect you to cough up a few rupees' protection money for your bike. Buses run at irregular intervals between the City Bus Park and the eastern entrance, but they're unlikely to be of much help except for the journey back. A taxi can drive you all the way up to a small car park near the top, just west of the stupa. **Admission**, paid at booths at the main entrances, is Rs50.

A paved road circles the base of the hill. Although there are several other ways up, the steep main path from the **eastern entrance**, with its 300-odd centuries-smoothed steps, is the most dramatic. The **Buddha statues** near the bottom are from the seventeenth century, while a second group further up was donated in the early part of the twentieth century. The chiselled slates sold by entrepreneurs along the path are *mani* stones, inscribed, in Tibetan script, with the ubiquitous Buddhist mantra *Om mani padme hum* ("Hail to the jewel in the lotus").

You can get **food** at a few lunch/snack places near the eastern entrance (*Pilgrim's Terrace* is decent) and at the far (northwestern) side of the stupa precinct (*Café de Stupa* has good views). There are also several Nepali–Tibetan eateries at the southern base of the hill, among them the *Iko* and *Classic* cafés, sedate descendants of the hippy hangouts that once thrived here. If you eat in the open, beware of the monkeys: they'll snatch at anything that even looks like food.

The stupa

According to Buddhist scriptures, the Kathmandu Valley was once a snake-infested lake (geologists agree about the lake: see "Natural history" in Contexts). Ninety-one aeons ago, a perfect, radiant lotus flower appeared on the surface of the lake, which the gods proclaimed to be Swayambhu ("Self-created"), the abstract essence of Buddhahood. **Manjushri**, the *bodhisattva* of knowledge, drew his sword and cut a gorge at Chobar, south of Kathmandu, to drain the lake and allow humans to worship Swayambhu. As the water receded, the lotus settled on top of a hill and Manjushri established a shrine to it, before turning his attention to ridding the valley of snakes (see Contexts,

△ Whitewashing Swayambhu stupa

p.522) and establishing its first civilization. Another legend tells how, when Manjushri cut his hair at Swayambhu, the strands that fell on the ground grew into trees, and the lice turned into monkeys.

The apparently simple structure of the **stupa** belies an immensely complex physical representation of Buddhist cosmology, and the purpose of walking round it is to meditate on this. The solid, whitewashed dome (*garbha*) symbolizes the womb or creation. Set in niches at the cardinal points, statues of **dhyani** (meditating) **Buddhas** correspond to the four elements (earth, air, fire and water) and a fifth, placed at an angle, to the sky or space. Like the rainbow colours produced by the refraction of pure white light, each represents a different aspect of Buddhahood: the hand positions, colours and "vehicles" (the animal statues below) of each are significant. The *dhyani* Buddhas are the same characters who appear on virtually every *chaitya* around the Kathmandu Valley. At each of the sub-cardinal points sit **female counterparts**, who in tantric Buddhism represent the wisdom aspect that must be united – figuratively speaking – with the compassionate male force to achieve enlightenment.

The gilded **cube** (*harmika*) surmounting the stupa surrounds a thick wooden pillar, which may be considered the phallic complement to the female dome. The **eyes** painted on it are those of the all-seeing Adi-Buddha (primordial Buddha), staring in all four directions. Between the eyes is a curl of hair (*urna*), one of the identifying features of a Buddha, and the thing that looks like a nose is a miraculous light emanating from the *urna* (it can also be interpreted as the Nepali figure "one", conveying the unity of all things). A **spire** of gold disks stacked above the pillar represents the thirteen steps to enlightenment, while the *torana*, or gold plaques above the painted eyes, also show the five *dhyani* Buddhas, known collectively as the *panchabuddha*. Finally, the umbrella at the top symbolizes the attainment of enlightenment: some say it contains a bowl filled with precious gems.

Shrines around the stupa

The stupa is surrounded by an incredible array of shrines and votive items, most of which have been donated over the past four centuries by merit-seeking kings and nobles. The bronze sceptre-like object at the top of the steps is a vastly oversized **vajra**, a tantric symbol of power and indestructibility; its pedestal is carved with the twelve animals of the Tibetan zodiac. The twin bullet-shaped *shikra* on either side of this, known as **Pratappur** and **Anantapur**, were installed by King Pratap Malla during a seventeenth-century dispute with Tibet, on the advice of an Indian guru. The story of the king's gift, and his subsequent victory over the Tibetans, is engraved on the twin bells in front of the *shikra*.

Moving around clockwise, as is the custom at all stupas, the brick hut to the south of Anantapur is **Vasundhara Mandir**, dedicated to the earth goddess Vasundhara, who's more or less synonymous with Annapurna and Lakshmi, the goddesses of grain and wealth respectively. Further on – past the priests' quarters and a number of *chaitya* – is a small marble-faced shrine to **Vayu**, the Vedic god of wind and storms.

The **museum** behind (Mon, Wed–Fri & Sun 10am–5pm; donation) contains a formidable range of bas-relief statues of gods, Hindu as well as Buddhist, which are beautiful to look at but are so tersely identified that they'll leave you hopelessly confused by the Nepali pantheon. Next door and up a flight of steps, the **Deva Dharma Mahavihar** is a small, uneventful monastery that's open to the public. In front of this, close to the stupa behind protective caging, stand two acclaimed bronze statues of the **White and Green Taras**, deified princess wives of an eighth-century Tibetan king.

A few paces further on squats a gilt-roofed temple built to appease **Harati** (also known as **Ajima**), traditionally the goddess of smallpox but now regarded as governing all childhood diseases. Like many Newar deities, Harati/Ajima is both feared (as a bringer of disease) and revered (as a protectress, if properly appeased). A Buddhist legend relates how Harati was originally an abductor of children: when the people complained to the Buddha, he stole one of Harati's own children, forcing her to realize the pain he caused and repent of her ways. Harati/Ajima's shrine is extremely popular, and you'll see queues of mothers with kids in tow, waiting to make offerings. The nineteenth-century idol was carved to replace an earlier one smashed by King Rana Bahadur Shah after his wife died of smallpox. Following rites observed throughout hill Nepal, petitioners toss handfuls of flower petals and rice at the image, sprinkle a bit of consecrated water (*jal*) onto the image and themselves, and finally receive a *tika* from the resident priest.

Agnipur, an insignificant-looking lump on the pavement in the extreme northwest corner of the complex, marked by two tiny lions in front, is a seldom-visited shrine to the Vedic fire god Agni, the relayer of burnt offerings to heaven. **Nagpur**, a bathtub-sized tank at the north point of the stupa, propitiates the valley's snake spirits, and when it's not filled with water you can see the idol (looking more like a draught excluder than a snake) at the bottom. Finally, the **Shree Karma Raj Mahavihar**, an active monastery at the northeast corner of the compound, contains a big Buddha and numerous butter candles, which Tibetan Buddhists light in much the same way Catholics do. You can catch the sonorous chanting of the monks at around 3 or 4pm every day.

Shantipur

A 1500-year-old mystery surrounds **Shantipur**, the otherwise plain, box-like building northwest of the stupa. Shanti Shri, a fifth-century holy man, is supposed to have sealed himself in a vault beneath the temple to meditate, vowing not to emerge until the valley needed him. Commentators write that he subsequently attained a mystic state of immortality, and according to devout believers he's still in there.

King Pratap Malla, who entered the chamber in 1658 to seek magical help in ending a drought, experienced adventures worthy of Indiana Jones. According to scholar Keith Dowman, the king recounted how he entered alone and descended to the second subterranean level. In the first room "bats as large as kites or hawks came to kill the light", while in the second room "ghosts, flesh-eating spirits and hungry ghosts came to beg", clutching at anyone who failed to pacify them. Of the third room he said, "if you cannot pacify the snakes by pouring out milk, they chase and bind you. Having pacified them you can walk on their bodies". Finally, Pratap Malla found the saint in an almost skeletal form, and was rewarded with a *nag* rain-making emblem.

Faded frescoes on the walls of the outer sanctum show scenes from the *Swayambhu Purana*, a recent (seventeenth-century) scripture that recounts the story of Manjushri's sword act and other creation myths. Shantipur, also known as Akashpur ("Sky-place"), completes a cycle of shrines to the five elemental spirits: earth, air, fire, water (snakes) and sky.

The Manjushri Shrine

The **Manjushri Shrine**, located on a prayer-flag-spangled spur of the hilltop to the west, comes second only to the main stupa in antiquity – the canopied *chaitya* is reckoned to be 1500 years old. Manjushri, the Buddhist god of wisdom and founder of civilization in the valley, is traditionally depicted by an empty niche in the *chaitya*, but an image of Saraswati, the Hindu goddess of learning, was placed in the niche three hundred years ago, and so the shrine is now on the pilgrimage circuit for Hindus as well. Schoolchildren make a special trip here on Saraswati Puja, in late January or early February, to have their books and pencils blessed.

Other monuments and monasteries

The Swayambhu area is littered with other monuments, including a controversial twenty-metre-tall **seated Buddha** figure overlooking the Ring Road west of the hill, constructed in the last few years by wealthy Manangis from the Annapurna region, and a *chaitya* located at the base of the north side of the hill containing the ashes of **Babu Chhiri Sherpa**, the ten-time Everest summiteer and holder of various records, who died on the mountain in 2001.

In addition, several **Tibetan monasteries**, which as a rule welcome visitors, have been built in the area since 1959, and more seem to be going up all the time. Some Westerners study Tibetan Buddhism at the Buddha Dharma Center south of Swayambhu (see p.171).

The Natural History Museum

The morbidly amusing **Natural History Museum** (Mon–Fri & Sun 10am–5pm; Rs20) also lurks nearby, on your right as you follow the road from the car park down the south side of Swayambhu hill. Its jumbled collection of stuffed birds and shrivelled animals in old-fashioned display cases looks like it was cobbled together from the trophy rooms of hoary old Rana hunters. The weirdness is fun for its own sake, though, and the specimens might give you an idea of what to look for when you get to the mountains or jungle.

Bijeshwari and Shoba Bhagwati

Bijeshwari, along the west bank of the Bishnumati on the way to Swayambhu, used to be Kathmandu's execution ground; Henry Ambrose Oldfield, one of the few Europeans allowed to tour Nepal in the nineteenth century, attended a beheading here and pronounced the place "a regular Golgotha". While Tibetans and other immigrants broke the taboo against settling near the cursed ground a generation ago, a fear of ghosts still endures, as do two important but little-visited temples.

Bijeshwari Bahal, perched at the top of a flight of steps above the river, is the centre of worship of an esoteric Buddhist goddess, Bijeshwari (Lord of Victory), who is also known as Akash (Sky) Yogini and sometimes counted as the fifth of the valley's Bajra Yoginis, the wrathful aspects of the tantric Tara goddesses. The inner courtyard is thick with *chaitya* and stone figures, and doors around the perimeter are painted with probing pairs of eyes – a reminder to worshippers that the Buddha is watching, and an injunction to look inward.

Just upstream stands a new cremation pavilion, and beyond that, the Hindu **Shobha Bhagwati Mandir**. Bhagwati is a common Nepali name for the mother goddess, and this idol of her is considered to be among the most powerful manifestations in the valley: early in the morning you might see political candidates, students preparing for exams, or anyone requiring quiet strength coming here to do *puja* to her. According to legend, the sculptor of the Shobha Bhagwati image here carved it with his feet, his hands having been cut off by a jealous king to prevent him from reproducing an earlier masterwork in the king's collection.

The National Museum

Given the wealth of heritage displayed out in the open, museums may seem redundant in Nepal, but theft and modernization are forcing a belated move to safeguard national treasures, many of which can be seen in the **National Museum**, based in an old Rana armoury 1km south of Swayambhu (mid-Feb to mid-Nov Tues–Sat 9.30am–4pm; mid-Nov to mid-Feb same days 9.30am–3pm; Rs50, Rs50 extra for camera). It's no curatorial coup, and shouldn't be considered a substitute for the valley's countless living exhibits, but you'll come away with a better appreciation of the intertwining of religion, art, myth and history in Nepal.

The art building

Count on spending most of your time in the **art building**, the white plaster one to the left as you enter. The collection of **stone sculptures** showcases an amazing artistic consistency spanning almost two thousand years, from the Lichhavi period (second to ninth centuries) through the tantric-influenced Malla dynasties (thirteenth to eighteenth centuries): though motifs and styles change, the common element is a wild diversity of gods and themes inspired by the vast and imaginative canon of Hindu mythology. The images seem to celebrate not only the power of the deities, who loom up in their "universal" forms or act out Herculean labours, but also the divinity that resides within each worshipper. The oldest is a life-size statue of King Jaya Varma from 184 AD (derived from the Lichhavi date clearly inscribed on the pedestal). The most recent additions to the collection are four pieces – a ninth-century Buddha, a tenth-century Vishnu, a twelfth-century Saraswati and a fourteenth-century Surya – stolen from Nepal in the 1980s, and returned by an American art collector in 1999 after seeing their pictures in the book *Stolen Images of Nepal*.

The **metalwork** exhibit pays tribute to a later art form which blossomed under patronage from Tibet. A trio of stunning fourteenth-century bronzes of tantric deities form the centrepieces. To Western eyes, the tantric *yab yum* (sexual intercourse) motif and its gory attendant imagery (skull cups, daggers, blood) may seem pretty peculiar, yet on an intuitive level it's a powerful celebration of life in all its creativity, weirdness and danger. More accurately, it's meant to be symbolic of the necessary union of wisdom (*prajna*), associated with the female aspect, and compassion (*upaya*), the male.

Other exhibits include exceptional images, window frames and *torana* (ornate shields mounted over the doors of temples) carved from **wood**, as well as terracotta images and a few Tibetan Buddhist ritual objects. A final room on the ground floor displays a couple of dozen rare **paubha** (Nepali scroll paintings) from the sixteenth century on, and a later series of Indian-style miniatures depicting scenes from the Puranas (chronicles of Hindu myths). Upstairs is a half-hearted collection of Tibetan Buddhist images and more ritual objects.

The Buddhist Art Gallery

The red-brick building at the back of the museum compound houses the **Buddhist Art Gallery**, which gives a patchy overview of artistic traditions from three distinct parts of the country. The **Tarai section** represents the most ancient and archeologically important area in Nepal: the environs of Lumbini, the Buddha's birthplace. Its contents are rather meagre and short on explanation, but photos of recent archeological work there give a feel for the place. The **Kathmandu Valley section** is much better, surveying the valley's considerable artistic contributions in brass, stone and painting from a Buddhist perspective; among its treasures is an eighth-century bas relief of the Buddha's birth. Finally, the small **Northern Himalayan section** contains *thangka*, bronzes and ritual objects – the same sort of stuff that you see in all the souvenir shops, only authentic.

The history building

A Rana-style mansion on the right as you enter the compound, the **history building** is aimed mainly at school groups. The downstairs natural history section is a terrible hodgepodge of animal carcasses, bones, dolls (check out the embarrassing specimens donated by your country!) and a moon rock. Upstairs, endless displays of weaponry do little to dispel the stereotype of the Nepalis as a "martial" race (although a pair of leather cannon, captured during a skirmish with Tibet in 1792, are genuine rarities). More interesting than what's included, perhaps, is what's left out. This is Nepalese history as written by the Shahs and Ranas, who've ruled Nepal for the past two centuries; the country's lower classes and ethnic groups, and any history prior to the Shah conquest, receive hardly a mention.

The top floor houses the **National Numismatic Museum**, displaying coins representing the reign of every Nepali king from the Malla and Shah dynasties, as well as Lichhavi specimens going back to the fifth century and some undated ones from Kapilvastu that presumably date from the Buddha's time (fourth century BC).

East of Kantipath

Old photographs of Kathmandu show the area **east of Kantipath** dominated by the palaces and residences of the ruling Rana family, with villages – Hadigaun, Dilli Bazaar, Baneswar – surrounded by farmland beyond. Today, the palaces have mostly been taken over by government ministries, while the boulevards around the current Royal Palace are lined with airline offices and high-end hotels, the old villages have become tinny, congested bazaars, and the farmland subdivided into walled suburban compounds. You'll probably come here to do errands or window shop – as you do, notice how the old buildings and development patterns have been integrated into the new.

Pashupatinath, which lies just east of the Ring Road, is covered in Chapter Two.

Kaisher Mahal

On the corner of Tridevi Marg and Kantipath, **Kaisher Mahal**, the former residence of Field Marshal Kaisher Shamsher Rana (1891–1964), now serves as the compound of the Ministry of Education and Sports. Inside, the **Kaisher Library** (mid-Feb to mid-Nov Tues–Sat 10am–5pm; mid-Nov to mid-Feb same days 10am–4pm; free) looks like a featured spread in the Nepali edition of *Better Homes and Gardens*. Long shelves of European books, cabinets of Sanskrit manuscripts, a suit of armour, a stuffed tiger and portraits of all the famous people the field marshal ever shook hands with shed intriguing light on a member of Nepal's pre-1951 ruling elite.

A man who appreciated the good things in life, Kaisher Shamsher Rana is said to have laid out the grounds of his mansion as a "dream garden" with areas devoted to each of the six seasons. Trees were planted to ensure that different fruits ripened year-round. Although the garden has gone downhill over the years, it still attracts thousands of **giant fruit bats**, which, in the daytime, can be seen hanging like handbags from the taller trees here and across the way at the royal palace.

Another sort of colonial landmark, Fora Durbar, the swish R&R compound for American expats, hides behind high brick walls at the southeastern corner of the Tridevi Marg–Kantipath roundabout. Across Kantipath is the former palace of Prince Basundhara, the present king's late uncle, now serving as the vastly oversized office of Nepal's Election Commission.

The Royal Palace (Narayanhiti Durbar)

An architectural travesty from the 1960s, the creepy **Royal Palace** looks like something out of Buck Rogers, with echoes of the Mormon Tabernacle. Built in front of an earlier palace dating from around 1900, it was inaugurated in 1970 for then Crown Prince Birendra's wedding. Its Nepali name, **Narayanhiti Durbar**, refers to a water tap (*hiti*) east of the main entrance.

Many Nepalis now avert their eyes when they walk past the palace, or avoid passing it altogether, for it evokes painful memories as the scene of the inexplicable **royal massacre** of June 1, 2001, when Crown Prince Dipendra killed his entire immediate family – King Birendra, Queen Aishwara and his younger brother and sister – and five other relatives before apparently turning the gun on himself (see p.496). Tribhuwan Sadan, the building where the carnage took place, was demolished a few weeks later on orders of the Queen Mother. As of this writing, the new King Gyanendra and Queen Komal and their son, Crown Prince Paras, continue to reside at Nirmal Niwas in Maharajgunj, and it's not clear whether they will ever move in to Narayanhiti Durbar.

Around Rani Pokhari

Rani Pokhari (Queen's Pool), the large square tank east of Asan, is older than it looks. It was built in the seventeenth century by King Pratap Malla to console his queen after the death of their favourite son; the shrine in the middle, which is opened one day a year during the Tihaar festival, is more recent. The pavements around the pool and nearby **Ratna Park** are active centres for small-time trade (including prostitution).

West of Rani Pokhari stands the mouldering edifice of **Durbar High School** (now renamed after the Nepali poet Bhanu Bhakta Acharya), established in 1853 to educate the children of the Rana aristocracy and their hangers-on for jobs in a nascent bureaucracy. To the east rise the c.1900 **Ghanta Ghar** (clock tower) – like Bhimsen Tower, a landmark only in the functional sense – and Kathmandu's two **mosques**. Muslims first settled in Kathmandu as traders five centuries ago, and now represent only a tiny fraction of Nepal's half-million "Musalmans".

Nearby Trichandra College's students have a reputation for militancy. During the 1990 People's Movement, the college was a flashpoint for government riots, and nowadays Maoist slogans can often be seen spray-painted on its walls.

Around the Tudikhel

Kathmandu's **Tudikhel** is the biggest military parade ground in Nepal. Percival Landon, an early twentieth-century traveller, proclaimed it "level as Lord's" (one of London's cricket grounds), and indeed the expanse seems quixotically flat in so mountainous a country. An institution rooted in Nepal's warring past, the *tudikhel* is a feature of every town of consequence throughout the hills. The king turns out to review occasional displays of pomp and circumstance here (notably during Ghoda Jaatra, an equestrian festival that falls in March or April), and bronze statues at each corner of the parade ground depict past Rana prime ministers on horseback, striking suitably swashbuckling poses. Unfortunately, although Kathmandu's Tudikhel provides a sizeable chunk of open space in the middle of the city, it's no green lung: it has few trees, and it actually adds to the city's pollution problem by forcing traffic to bottleneck around it.

On the Kantipath side of the Tudikhel stands the **Mahakal Mandir**, whose modern surroundings have in no way diminished the reverence of its worshippers: passing pedestrians and motorists commonly touch a hand to the forehead. Mahakal – to Hindus a form of Bhairab, to Buddhists a defender of *dharma* – is depicted here trampling a corpse (signifying ignorance), holding a skull-cup of blood and wearing what look like glacier goggles.

East of the Tudikhel, **Bhrikuti Mandap** serves as an amusement park and part-time exhibition ground. The nearby **Bhadrakali Mandir** has been turned into a traffic roundabout, but remains a popular venue for weddings and political sit-ins. Newars know the goddess Bhadrakali as Lumari Ajima, a powerful protectress whose image is set in a sunken open-air shrine here. The nearby **Martyrs' Gate** commemorates the four ringleaders of a failed 1940 attempt to overthrow the Rana regime.

Singha Durbar and Baber Mahal Revisited

Undoubtedly the most impressive structure ever raised by the Ranas, **Singha Durbar** dominates the governmental quarter in the southeastern part of the city. Once the biggest building in Asia, the prime ministers' palace of a thousand rooms was built in 1901 by Chandra Shamsher Rana, who employed workers round the clock for two years to complete the pile and fill it with such European extravagances as Carrara marble floors, crystal chandeliers and gilt mirrors, all for the then unconscionable sum of Rs2.5 million. It's said that the entire population of Kathmandu abstained from *daal*, an ingredient in traditional mortar, during the construction. While it was in use as a palace, up to 1500 servants were required to keep the prime minister and his household in the style to which they were accustomed.

The palace was mostly destroyed by fire in 1973, and only the main wing was restored for use as parliamentary offices. Numerous governmental ministries, departments and the Gallery Baithak (home of Nepal's parliament) now occupy new buildings and original outbuildings elsewhere in the vast complex. You can peek at the main wing's colonnaded facade through the sweeping front (western) gate, but if you want to go inside and experience the bastion of Nepalese political power firsthand, you'll have to queue up at the plebes' gate on the south side (Mon–Fri 2–5pm).

If you're down this way, make a point of calling in at **Baber Mahal Revisited**, located off a tree-lined street south of the Singha Durbar complex. A restored Rana palace with shops, restaurants and peaceful courtyards, it's a heavenly retreat where you can grab lunch, hang out in the courtyards, and check out before-and-after photographs of temple restorations around the valley.

Eastern neighbourhoods

While Kathmandu's eastern and northeastern neighbourhoods don't have much of scenic interest, they do provide insights into contemporary life in the capital.

Crowded **Bagh Bazaar** and **Dilli Bazaar** pretty much sum up one end of the spectrum, with their computer institutes, lawyers' cubbyholes and shops selling office furniture and "suitings and shirtings". ("Fine Art", incidentally, means sign-painting – there's always work for sign-painters in ever-changing Kathmandu.) Dilli Bazaar is also the home of Nepal's budding stock exchange. The other extreme is found further north in the shady lanes of **Bhatbateni**, **Baluwatar** and **Maharajganj**, where old money, new money and foreign money hide in walled compounds, along with embassies, aid organizations and corporate mansions.

Between the two lie the hopeful settlements of a burgeoning middle class, who build their houses one floor at a time, as funds allow, and send their children off in uniforms to "English boarding schools" with names like "Bright Future" and "Little Flower". An "English" education is almost universally viewed as the key to success in the capital.

Hadigaun and Dhum Barahi

Like most ancient cities, Kathmandu was formed by the gradual merging of what were once separate villages. Archeological excavations suggest that **Hadigaun**, now a northeastern suburb, is one of the oldest of Kathmandu's original settlements, though it has now been pretty well absorbed by the metropolis.

Evidence of Hadigaun's age comes from the overgrown shrine of **Dhum Barahi**, located in a schoolyard a further 1km northeast (head north out of Hadigaun, and when in doubt always take the right fork). Inside the small brick shelter, which is completely engulfed in the roots of an enormous pipal tree, a whimsical fifth-century image illustrates the tale of Barahi (Vishnu in his incarnation as a boar) rescuing the earth-goddess Prithvi from the bottom of the sea. Scholars rave about this sculpture because it dates from a time when there were no established rules for depicting Vishnu as a boar, nor for how a boar should look while fishing the earth from the sea. Locals say the shrine was built at the same time as the nearby Boudha stupa to appease Vishnu, who out of jealousy had caused the stupa's spire to collapse while under construction.

Patan (Lalitpur)

Although now largely absorbed by greater Kathmandu, **Patan** was once the capital of a powerful independent kingdom, and still maintains a defiantly distinct identity. Compared to Kathmandu it's quieter, less frenetic and more Buddhist (there may be a correlation). Sophisticated and, in a Nepali sort of way, bohemian, it's Kathmandu's Left Bank: while Kathmanduites are busy amassing power and wealth, Patan's residents appreciate the finer things of life, which perhaps explains Patan's poetic alternate name, **Lalitpur** ("City of Beauty"). Above all, it remains a proud city of **artisans**. Patan produces much of Nepal's fine metalwork (the sounds of tapping and filing ring out from workshops all over town), and its craftspeople have created some of the most extraordinarily lavish temples, *hiti* and *bahal* in the country. *Bahal* – their doorways here always guarded by cuddly stone lions with unscary overbites – are a particular feature of Patan, and a few still function as active monasteries. In the past two decades, Patan has also emerged as the de facto **foreign aid** capital of Nepal: the UN offices and diverse smaller organizations are scattered around the western suburbs, as are the residences of many expats who commute to the big USAID headquarters just across the river.

In legend and fact, Patan is the oldest city in the Kathmandu Valley. **Manjushri**, the great lake-drainer, is supposed to have founded Manjupatan, the forerunner of Patan, right after he enshrined Swayambhu, while the so-called Ashokan stupas, earthen mounds standing at four cardinal points around Patan, seem to support the legend that the Indian emperor **Ashoka** visited the valley in the third century BC (historians are sceptical). More reliable legend ascribes Patan's founding to **Yalambar**, second-century king of the Kirats, an ancient tribe that provided the original stock for the valley's Newar population

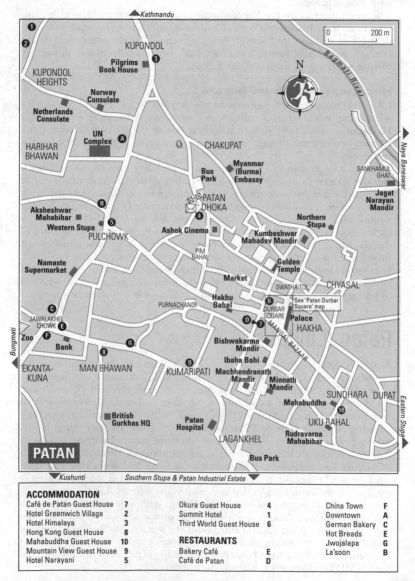

PATAN

ACCOMMODATION

Café de Patan Guest House	7	Okura Guest House	4	China Town	F
Hotel Greenwich Village	2	Summit Hotel	1	Downtown	A
Hotel Himalaya	3	Third World Guest House	6	German Bakery	C
Hong Kong Guest House	8			Hot Breads	E
Mahabuddha Guest House	10	**RESTAURANTS**		Jwojalapa	G
Mountain View Guest House	9	Bakery Café	E	La'soon	B
Hotel Narayani	5	Café de Patan	D		

(which explains the traditional Newar name for Patan, **Yala**), or to the Lichhavi King **Arideva** at the end of the third century. Under the long-running Lichhavi dynasty, Patan emerged as the cultural and artistic capital of Nepal, if not the entire Himalayan region. It maintained strong links with the **Buddhist** centres of learning in Bengal and Bihar – thereby playing a role in the transmission of Buddhism to Tibet – and when these fell to the Muslims in the twelfth century, many scholars and artists fled to Patan, setting the stage for a renaissance under the later **Malla** kings. Patan existed as part of a unified valley kingdom until the late fifteenth century, then enjoyed equal status with Kathmandu and Bhaktapur as a sovereign state until 1769, when Prithvi Narayan Shah and his Gorkhali band conquered the valley and chose Kathmandu for their capital.

One of Patan's charms is that its historic core is frozen much as it was at the time of defeat. However, see it while you can. Although a number of temples and public monuments have been skilfully restored in the past decade, the city has lost many of its older private buildings. Here, as in Kathmandu, most owners of traditional old houses hope to replace them with more comfortable, modern concrete ones, and to finance the redevelopment by selling off their antique wooden window and door frames.

Getting there

A **taxi** from Thamel or central Kathmandu to Patan should cost no more than Rs120 on the meter. A much cheaper way to go is by fixed-route **tempo** or **microbus**: #14 services from Shahid Gate to Mangal Bazaar (Patan Durbar Square) are the best bet, assuming your destination is the old city; #14 from Ratna Park take a longer route to Lagankhel via Pulchowk and Jawalakhel Chowk. From the City Bus Park, #15 **buses** go to Patan Dhoka.

Don't **bike** to Patan via the main Bagmati bridge and Kupondol – you'll expire from the fumes. A better alternative is to cross the river from the Teku area of Kathmandu, south of Durbar Square, entering Patan through its northwestern suburbs. It's even quieter coming from the international convention centre in Naya Baneswar (on the Airport Rd), crossing the footbridge to Sankhamul Ghat, but getting to Naya Baneswar is anything but quiet. There aren't any **bike rental** shops in Patan, but you can probably arrange something informally with your guesthouse. Patan itself has plenty of taxis and metered tempos, but within the old part of town you can easily get around on foot.

Durbar Square

While smaller and less monumental than Kathmandu's, Patan's **Durbar Square** comes across as more refined, not to mention less touristy. Maybe it's because the city of artisans has a better eye for architectural harmony; or because Patan, which hasn't been a capital since the eighteenth century, has escaped the continuous meddling of monument-building kings. That said, the formula is similar to that in Kathmandu, with a solemn royal palace looming along one side and assorted temples grouped in the remaining public areas.

Foreign non-residents must pay a Rs200 **admission charge** (at a desk next to the Royal Palace) to visit the square between 9am and 5pm. The ticket is good for one week.

The Royal Palace

Patan's richly decorated **Royal Palace** was largely constructed during the second half of the seventeenth century, but substantially rebuilt after both the

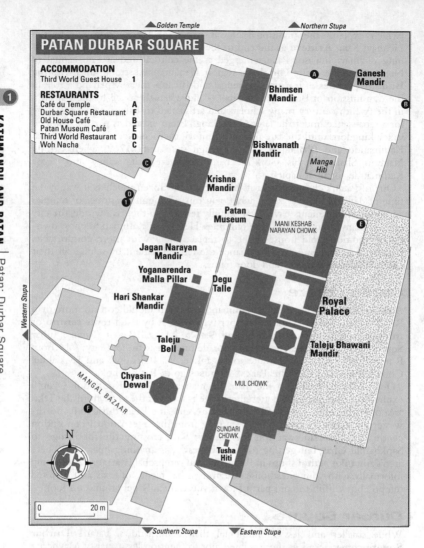

PATAN DURBAR SQUARE

▲ Golden Temple   ▲ Northern Stupa

ACCOMMODATION
Third World Guest House   1

RESTAURANTS
Café du Temple   A
Durbar Square Restaurant   F
Old House Café   B
Patan Museum Café   E
Third World Restaurant   D
Woh Nacha   C

Ganesh Mandir

Bhimsen Mandir

Bishwanath Mandir

Manga Hiti

Krishna Mandir

Patan Museum

MANI KESHAB NARAYAN CHOWK

Jagan Narayan Mandir

Yoganarendra Malla Pillar

Degu Talle

Hari Shankar Mandir

Royal Palace

Taleju Bell

Taleju Bhawani Mandir

Chyasin Dewal

MANGAL BAZAAR

MUL CHOWK

SUNDARI CHOWK

Tusha Hiti

N

0   20 m

◄ Western Stupa

▼ Southern Stupa   ▼ Eastern Stupa

Gorkhali invasion of 1769 and the 1934 earthquake. It consists of three main wings, each enclosing a central courtyard and reached by a separate entrance.

The courtyard of the small, southernmost wing, **Sundari Chowk**, contains what must surely be one of the grandest bathtubs in the world, although it seems to be closed indefinitely for renovations. **Tusha Hiti**, the seventeenth-century sunken royal bath, is done up like a hall of fame of Hindu gods and goddesses. Its brass spout is decorated with Shiva and Parbati, while the bath itself is shaped like a *yoni*, the symbol of female sexuality, and ringed with serpents. The courtyard is covered in ornate woodwork, including many fabulous carved doorways, windows, *torana*, and images of deities individually set into niches.

Mul Chowk, the next wing to the north, served as the actual royal family residence until Patan's fall in 1769. A sadly deteriorated gilt door in the right-hand wall of the courtyard, leading to the private Taleju Mandir, is flanked by statues of the Indian river goddesses **Ganga** and **Jamuna**, the latter riding a *makana* – a mythical cross between a crocodile and an elephant, whose curling snout decorates almost every public water spout in Nepal. Behind and to the left of Mul Chowk rises the octagonal, three-tiered **Taleju Bhawani Mandir**.

Yet another Taleju temple, the monolithic **Degu Talle** towers just north of Mul Chowk. Seven storeys high and the tallest building on the block, it was erected in 1640 by Siddhi Narsingh Malla, during whose reign much of the palace and square were built, and had to be completely rebuilt after being razed in the 1934 earthquake. The tower is kept locked except during the autumn Tihaar festival, when a priest is supposed to refill a pipe with ganja for the departed king.

The Patan Museum

The palace's northernmost wing, Mani Keshab Narayan Chowk, once served as the palace of another noted seventeenth-century king, Yoganarendra Malla. It, too, suffered in the 1934 quake and at the time was only clumsily rebuilt. With assistance from the Austrian government, it has been restored to house the splendid **Patan Museum** (daily 10.30am–5pm; Rs250; ⓦ www.asianart.com /patan-museum), a tasteful space that does honour to this city of artisans.

The museum displays a well-curated **permanent collection** of important bronzes, stone sculptures and woodcarvings, a gilded Malla throne and an assortment of archival photographs. Among the stone idols is a twelfth-century image of Uma-Maheshwar that was returned by Berlin's Museum of Indian Art after having been stolen from Dhulikhel and sold to a German collector in the 1980s. The exhibits are arranged thematically to lead you through Hindu, Buddhist and Tantric iconography, temple construction, ritual objects and met-allurgical processes, all supported by excellent explanatory text. If that's not enough, there's the building itself, which, with its newly stuccoed walls and art-ful lighting, suggests the royal palace Yoganarendra Malla might have built had he reigned at the beginning of the twenty-first century. From the interior bal-conies you can look out on the courtyard below and its central Lakshmi shrine, and watch the *kinkinimali*, leaf-shaped tin cut-outs hanging from the eaves, fluttering in the breeze. A stunning gold window above the exterior main entrance depicts Vishnu and a heavenly host.

There's a great **café** in the courtyard behind the museum, and a **gift shop** near the entrance.

Temples and monuments

Starting at the newer – eighteenth-century – southern end of Durbar Square, the stone **Chyasin Dewal** (opposite Sundari Chowk) is the lesser of the square's two Krishna temples. Some say the octagonal temple was raised in memory of the eight wives that committed *sati* on a king's funeral pyre, although Krishna temples almost always have eight sides to commemorate his role as the eighth *avatar* (incarnation) of Vishnu. The cast-iron **Taleju Bell** was the first to be erected in the valley, in 1736; keen civic rivalry among the three valley capitals prompted Bhaktapur and Kathmandu to follow suit with their own bells. Nearby, a Victorian-looking statue is of a Rana prime minister's wife, erected in 1905 to commemorate the arrival of piped water in Patan.

North of here, the finely carved **Hari Shankar Mandir** is dedicated both to Vishnu (sometimes called Hari) and Shiva (alias Shankar), while the statue mounted on a pillar and praying to the Degu Talle depicts **Yoganarendra**

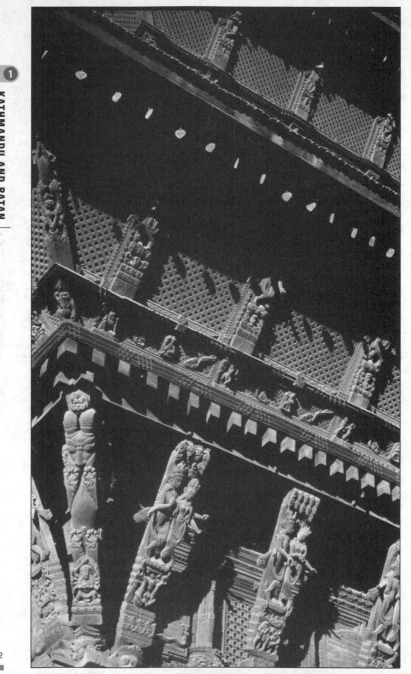

△ Woodcarving on the Royal Palace, Patan

Malla. An angry cobra rears up like a halo behind the king, and atop the cobra's head perches a gilded bird. Like all god-fearing rulers of the valley, Yoganarendra would have made sure to appease the *nag*, animist snake spirits who deliver or withhold the valley's rains. As for the bird, chroniclers state that the king, upon abdicating the throne to become a *sunyasan* (hermit) after the untimely death of his son, told his subjects that as long as the bird remained they would know he was still alive. To this day, the people of Patan keep a light burning and a bed ready for the absent king in an upper chamber of the palace.

Continuing northwards, the next temple is the two-tiered **Jagan Narayan**, built in 1565; if this is the oldest temple in the square, the most unusual and popular one is its neighbour, the seventeenth-century **Krishna Mandir**. Its central structure, a Mughal-style *shikra*, is girdled by three levels of stone verandas, with detailed scenes from the great Hindu epics, the *Mahabharata* and *Ramayana*, carved along the lintels. An incarnation of Vishnu, Krishna is one of Hinduism's best-loved characters: superhuman baby, mischievous lad, seducer of milkmaids and divine counsellor in the *Bhagavad Gita*. Worshippers gather here every morning for *puja*, and every evening butter lamps flicker on the temple's railings and the sound of *bhajan* drones on the air. On Krishna's birthday, in August or early September, the queue of worshippers at this temple stretches around the block.

The **Bishwanath Mandir** contains a copy of the Shiva *linga* of the same name in Varanasi, India. The temple collapsed in 1990, but has been seamlessly restored. Last but not least, on the northwest corner of the square, the seventeenth-century **Bhimsen Mandir** is dedicated to the ever-popular god of Newar traders. Non-Hindus aren't allowed inside, but you can often see and hear *puja* being performed in the open upstairs sanctuary. Across the way, one of the valley's largest sunken public bathing tanks, **Manga Hiti**, has been operational since the sixth century.

North and west of Durbar Square

Some of Patan's most interesting sights – the Golden and Kumbeshwar temples and the ghats – lie **north of Durbar Square**, but there's also plenty of serendipitous exploring to be done among the back alleys **west of the square**. For more detail on this area, pick up a copy of *Patan Walkabout*, an informative booklet available at the bookshop at Patan Dhoka (Rs75).

Hiranyavarna Mahavihara (The Golden Temple)

The **Hiranyavarna Mahavihara** – that's Sanskrit for "Golden Monastery", but all the tour guides call it the **Golden Temple** – is the most opulent little temple in Nepal. The three-tiered pagoda occupies one side of the cramped courtyard of Kwa Bahal, a still-active twelfth-century Buddhist Newar monastery and the spiritual hub of old Patan. During early-morning *puja*, the *bahal* is a fascinating theatre of Nepali religion in all its perplexing glory. **Admission** is Rs25 (no set hours); note that you're not allowed to bring anything made of leather inside.

The temple's gilt facade, embossed with images of Buddhas and Taras, is regarded as the pre-eminent example of large-scale repoussé **metalwork** in Nepal, while in the middle of the courtyard, a small, lavishly ornamented shrine contains a priceless silver and gold Swayambhu *chaitya*. Both the shrine and the main temple are further decorated with what look like long metallic neckties: these *pataka* are supposed to provide a slide for the gods when they descend to answer the prayers of their worshippers. The *bahal* is so crammed with images, ornaments and fine details that a full account of all its wonders would fill a book. For descriptions of some of the main features, including the deities enshrined in alcoves around the courtyard, refer to the **brochure** that comes with the price of admission.

Sakyamuni Buddha is the temple's *kwapadya* (main image). According to **legend**, it was made homeless in the twelfth century when the temple it formerly resided in collapsed. When King Bhaskardev built it a new temple, the image informed him in a dream that it wished to move to a new place where *mice* chased *cats*. One day the king saw a golden mouse chasing a cat here at Kwa Bahal, and so he set about building a new, golden temple on the spot. Rats are allowed to run free here in deference to the deity's wishes, as are tortoises, for in myth the universe rests on the back of a tortoise.

Though no longer a residential monastery, the *mahavihara* is an important centre of lay worship, following well-established Buddhist rituals and iconography that draw from both the Newar and Tibetan traditions. Its principal priest, a boy who must be no older than twelve, tends the main shrine. A Tibetan-style *gompa* upstairs on the northeastern side of the courtyard, which you can visit, is evidence of the spiritual ties forged between Patan and Tibet through centuries of trade.

Swatha Tol

Swatha Tol, an attractive intersection one block east of the Golden Temple, lies poised between Durbar Square and the more traditional neighbourhoods to the north, and seems to combine the best of both worlds. The square's centrepiece, the three-tiered **Radha Krishna Mandir**, has been restored by the Kathmandu Valley Preservation Trust, an organization that has now moved on to saving several other derelict temples and residences in Patan. The lovers Krishna and Radha, to whom this temple is dedicated, are a favourite subject for Indian sandalwood carvers.

The Kumbeshwar Mahadev and Bagalamukhi temples

Patan's oldest temple, and one of only two freestanding five-tiered pagodas in Nepal (the other is in Bhaktapur), the **Kumbeshwar Mahadev Mandir** was built as a two-roofed structure in 1392, and despite the addition of three more levels in the seventeenth century it remains well proportioned and, to all appearances, sturdy. Shiva is the honoured deity here: inside you can see a stone *linga* and a brass one with four faces; Nandi, Shiva's patient mount, waits outside. The temple apparently owes its name to an episode in which a pilgrim at Gosainkund, the sacred lake high in the mountains north of Kathmandu, dropped a pot (*kumbha*) into the water there. Much later, the same pot appeared in the water tank here, giving rise to the belief that the tank is fed by an underground channel from Gosainkund, and adding to Shiva's roll of titles that of Kumbeshwar – Lord of the Pots.

Thanks to this connection, Kumbeshwar's water tank is regarded as an alternative venue during Gosainkund's great annual **festival**, **Janai Purnima**, which takes place on the day of the late July or early August full moon, and sees Brahmans and Chhetris formally changing the sacred thread (*janai*) that distinguishes them as members of the "twice-born" castes. Thousands come to have their threads renewed and pay respect to a *linga* erected in the middle of the tank, while Tamang *jhankri* (shamans) perform ritual dances and young boys dive and splash in the water.

Though smaller and less to look at, the **Bagalamukhi Mandir**, occupying the southern end of the same compound, inspires far more day-to-day devotion. Considered a powerful wish-fulfilling manifestation of the goddess Kali, Bagalamukhi traditionally appeals to women seeking domestic harmony and anyone requiring strength to overcome adversity. Thursdays and Saturdays are the most popular for worshipping her – especially Thursday evenings, when Patan's teens and twentysomethings flock here more to flirt with each other than to worship the goddess.

Just north of the compound, the **Kumbeshwar Technical School** provides vocational and literacy training for poor women, orphans and other disadvantaged people, supported in part by sales from its small retail space.

The Northern Stupa and on to the ghats

Just northeast of the Kumbeshwar Mahadev, the **Northern Stupa** is the smallest and most central of the Ashokan mounds, and the only one that's been sealed over with plaster. Although it doesn't look wildly interesting for a supposedly 2200-year-old monument, you can let your imagination dwell on what treasures or relics Ashoka might have buried here – the contents are unlikely ever to see the light of day, since archeological digs are prohibited in the valley.

The stupa stands at the edge of the city. From here the road south plunges back between brick tenements and neglected temples to Durbar Square. Northwards, it wends through receding farmland towards Patan's **Sankhamul Ghat**, a half-kilometre-long embankment near the junction of the Manohara and Bagmati rivers. Confluences are regarded as auspicious locations, and Sankhamul Ghat serves as Patan's main cremation site and, during the festival of Magh Sankranti (usually Jan 14), an important spot for ritual bathing.

The ghat stretches on either side of a footbridge leading to the Naya Baneswar area of Kathmandu. Cremations are held to the west of the footbridge, where the putrid Bagmati still flows near the ghat. However, there's more to see east of the bridge. Flanked by sagging pilgrims' shelters and statues of Hanuman and Ganesh, a path leads under an arch and up to the exotic **Jagat Narayan** temple complex, named after its builder, the nineteenth-century prime minister Jagat Shamsher. The brick *shikra* shares a compound with monolithic stone statues of Garud, Hanuman and Ganesh, and a second gilt statue of Garud that makes Vishnu's man-bird vehicle look like a kendo warrior.

West to Pulchowk

From **Mangal Bazaar**, which these days sells mainly cloth and tourist odds and ends, central Patan's main drag heads out towards the Western Stupa. One of Patan's less-touristed former monasteries, **Hakhu Bahal** (also known as Ratnakar Mahabihar), rises on the left after 300m. Its courtyard crowded with lotus pedestals, indicative of divinity, the *bahal* is the seat of Patan's Kumari.

Though little more than a grassy mound beside a busy intersection, the **Western Stupa** comes alive on one day a year when the great chariot procession of Raato Machhendranath (see box on p.147) gets started just to the south. An open shelter here displays retired *ghana* – long, upward-curving chariot yokes – from past festivals. Chariot parts are considered sacred and may not be destroyed, so you'll often see them stowed next to temples or recycled into pillars or struts. Just to the right of the stupa, a whitewashed arch and a set of steps lead to the hilltop **Aksheshwar Mahabihar**, a working monastery that's not normally open to the public; the views from the terrace in front are good, though.

Northwest to Patan Dhoka

The northwestern quarter of old Patan is a jumble of *bahal* – the lane leading from the Golden Temple west to Patan Dhoka takes you past quite a few. The next lane further south, which parallels the main road to the Western Stupa, skirts Patan's small fruit and vegetable **market** and eventually opens out into **Pim Bahal** and its large and less-than-glamorous *pokhari* (pond). An inscription in front of the Swayambhu-style stupa here says it was built in the fourteenth century and restored a few years later, after Muslim invaders damaged it.

Another few blocks to the north, **Patan Dhoka**, a small bazaar area and bus park surrounding an unremarkable city gate, had its finest hour during the 1990 *jana andolan* (people's movement), when it stood on the front line of an all-out revolution. Nearly a month before the government's final capitulation, Patan was declared "liberated", with ditches dug across every road into the city, and defiant residents vowing to kill any opponent of the *andolan* who dared enter. Several police cars met their end at narrow Patan Dhoka.

South and east of the square

South of Durbar Square, you essentially have two choices. The southbound street passes the **Machhendranath temple** and other sights en route to the Lagankhel bus park, while the continuation of Mangal Bazaar leads southeast to **Mahabuddha**. The area directly east of Durbar Square, though short on specific sights, is an active **artisans' quarter**.

Bishwakarma Mandir and Ibaha Bahi

One of Patan's most charming streets runs parallel to Mangal Bazaar, a block to the south. This is an area of metalworkers and sellers of metal household wares, which perhaps accounts for the **Bishwakarma Mandir**'s facade of hammered gilt-copper and froggy copper lions standing guard. Unfortunately the facade is now unphotographable due to a railing recently installed to deter thieves. The name Bishwakarma refers both to the god of artisans and to members of the occupational caste of blacksmiths (more commonly known as Kami).

Patan's second-oldest monastery, **Ibaha Bahi**, stands one block further to the south. Founded in 1427, the *bahal* was recently restored with assistance from the Nippon Institute of Technology, and is supposed to be relaunched as a fully functional Buddhist centre and school.

Machhendranath Mandir

Outwardly, Patan's **Machhendranath Mandir** resembles many others: a huge seventeenth-century brick pagoda adorned with beautifully carved, gaudily painted struts and *torana*. It stands in an extra-large compound called Ta Bahal, about 300m south of Durbar Square and reached by following a narrow lane west from the main street and ducking under an arch next to a catering service.

What makes this temple extraordinary, however, is its idol, **Raato Machhendranath** ("Red Machhendranath"), a painted shingle of sandalwood which, for several weeks beginning in late April, is the object of one of Nepal's most extraordinary festivals (see box opposite). Older than his white counterpart in Kathmandu, Raato Machhendranath is a god of many guises. To Newars he's Bunga Dyo, the androgynous god of agricultural prosperity and a manifestation of the great cult figure Karunamaya. To Buddhists of other ethnic groups he's Avalokiteshwara or Lokeshwar, the *bodhisattva* of compassion. As

Raato Machhendranath's big ride

The Kathmandu Valley's oldest, lengthiest and most exciting festival, the **Machhendranath Raath Jaatra** begins the day after the full moon of Baisaakh (April–May), when priests ritually bathe Raato Machhendranath's sandalwood idol outdoors in Patan's Lagankhel square. Moved back to its temple at Ta Bahal, the idol then spends the next ten days undergoing the life-cycle rituals of Buddhist Newars, both male and female. Meanwhile, just south of the Western Stupa at Pulchowk, Machhendranath's chariot (*raath*) – actually it's more like a mobile temple – is assembled and its sixty-foot-high tower of poles and vegetation constructed. A smaller chariot to carry Minnath is built at its temple.

After a few more preliminaries, the idols are installed in their chariots and the great **procession** begins. It's an electrifying event. Scores of men heave at the ropes; Machhendranath's unwieldy vehicle rocks, teeters and suddenly lurches forward, its spire swaying and grazing buildings as it passes. The crowd roars, people leap out of the way, and the chariot comes to a stubborn stop until the pullers regroup and try to budge it again. Separately, local children pull Minnath's chariot. It goes on like this, in stages, for four or more weeks, until the chariots reach Jawalakhel Chowk, a journey of about 4km. At three designated resting spots – Hakhu Bahal, Sundhara and Lagankel – neighbourhood residents celebrate the gods with offerings, music and other auspicious acts.

At Jawalakhel, the stage is set for the dramatic **Bhoto Jaatra**. A huge crowd begins assembling before noon on a day ordained by the astrologers – usually the fourth day after the chariots' arrival at the *chowk*. Tension mounts until around 4pm or 5pm, when Patan's Kumari is carried in by palanquin, and the king and queen arrive in their motorcade and take their seats in a special viewing pavilion. Local VIPs then climb aboard Machhendranath's chariot and take turns holding aloft the god's magical jewelled vest, a relic of some ancient dispute. The king then pays homage to the gods and departs, after which the crowd charges the chariots for *prasad* (consecrated food offerings). Since the procession culminates during the showery pre-monsoon, Machhendranath usually obliges with rain: bring an umbrella.

Machhendranath's idol is then carried to Bungmati, 6km to the south (see p.215), where it is welcomed "home" with great fanfare – the cult of Raato Machhendranath is believed to have originated in Bungmati, accounting for the god's Newar name, Bunga Dyo ("God of Bunga"). The idol spends the summer months in Bungmati before being transported back to Ta Bahal, but once every twelve years it's kept in Bungmati all winter and the chariot procession begins and ends there. That will next happen in 2003.

Machhendranath, the progenitor of the *nath* (lord) cult, he's the spirit of a seventh-century Hindu guru who once taught the Shah kings' beloved saint, Gorakhnath. Legend has it that Gorakhnath once visited the valley and, offended that he wasn't accorded a full reception, caused a drought by rounding up all the rain-bringing snakes. The locals sent a posse to Assam to fetch Machhendranath, who came to their rescue in the form of a bee. Wishing to pay tribute to his guru, Gorakhnath had to release the snakes, whereupon the rains returned and Machhendranath came to be revered as a rain-maker.

Minnath and on to the Southern Stupa

Set behind a *hiti* (sunken bathing tank) across the street from the Machhendranath Mandir entrance, the smaller sixteenth-century **Minnath Mandir** is dedicated to yet another mythologized Indian saint. Historically supposed to have been Machhendranath's guru, Minnath has been transmuted by popular tradition into his sister, brother or even daughter, and his likeness follows Machhendranath in a smaller chariot of its own during the annual festival.

South of here, the main road widens to include a busy open-air bazaar and the chaotic **Lagankhel** minibus park, then jogs left; straight ahead lies an army barracks and a pair of overgrown water tanks that feed Patan's many *hiti*. It's not really worth travelling another kilometre south to visit the grassy **Southern Stupa** – the biggest of the four – although if you're going to the Patan Industrial Estate (see the "Shopping" section), you'll pass right by it.

Southeast to Mahabuddha

Mangal Bazaar gets quieter and better for walking east of Durbar Square. After 300m it reaches **Sundhara**, a sunken bathing area with four golden (*sun*) spouts (*dhara*), which gives its name to a picturesque intersection with a number of rest shelters and temples used for evening *bhajan*. East of here is **Dupat**, whose close, dark alleys are brimming with atmosphere. To the south is **Uku Bahal**, Patan's main metalsmithing area and home of the famed Mahabuddha temple.

Nicknamed "Temple of a Thousand Buddhas", **Mahabuddha** is not your average Nepali temple. Constructed entirely of terracotta tiles – each one bearing the Buddha's image – this remarkable Rococo structure mimics the famous Mahabodhi Temple of Bodhgaya in India, where its builder, an enthusiastic seventeenth-century Patan architect, had previously meditated for several years. Although the likeness is only approximate, the temple introduced the Indian *shikra* form to Nepal, which to this day remains prevalent around Patan. Reduced to rubble during the 1934 earthquake, it was put back together rather like Humpty Dumpty; the smaller temple beside it was built from the spare parts. The structure is so tightly hemmed-in by residences that you'll need to go up into one of the surrounding metal handicrafts sellers' buildings to get a decent view of it – looking is free, but of course they'll put the retail moves on you.

The name of this neighbourhood, Uku (or Oku) Bahal, comes from the now-defunct Buddhist monastery at the next intersection to the south, which also goes by the handle **Rudravarna Mahabihar** ("Red Monastery"). Though it's undergone a recent renovation, it's believed to be Patan's oldest – the wooden struts on the north side of the courtyard date from the thirteenth century. The ornate principal temple is surrounded by a small menagerie of bronze animals and mythological beasts, and its *kwapadya* (main image) is Aksobhya Buddha, one of the *panchabuddha*, who collectively represent the five aspects of Buddhahood.

Jawalakhel and around

The name **Jawalakhel** (pronounced *Jowl*-akel) is generally applied to a wide area around the big Jawalakhel Chowk roundabout and south from there down to the Ring Road. The southern part of it – often referred to as **Ekantakuna** ("Lonely Corner"), after a former Rana mansion now occupied by the Swiss development agency – is Patan's Tibetan ghetto. Nepal's only real **zoo** occupies another former Rana estate just off the *chowk*.

Ekantakuna

The former Tibetan refugee camp at **Ekantakuna** is arguably the best place in the valley to watch carpets being made (see "Shopping" on p.164). As a Tibetan cultural experience, though, it doesn't really compare with Boudha or

Swayambhu: there's no big temple or power place here, only one small monastery, and – except for the carpet-weaving centre (Mon–Fri & Sun 8am–noon & 1–5pm; free) and nearby carpet shops – not a lot of commercial vitality.

Tibetans started pouring into the Kathmandu Valley immediately after the Chinese annexation of Tibet and the flight of the Dalai Lama in 1959. By 1960 their plight prompted the International Red Cross to set up a transit camp at Jawalakhel, later assigned to the Swiss Red Cross, which in turn formed the Swiss Association for Technical Assistance (SATA) to help Tibetans on a long-term basis. SATA encouraged carpet-making and other cottage industries, and by 1964 the Jawalakhel "transit camp" was a registered company. A generation and a half on, Jawalakhel's Tibetans are prospering from the booming **carpet industry**, and many have left the centre to establish businesses and live closer to the Buddhist holy places.

Those who remain, and a steady trickle of new arrivals, have created a small suburb of solid brick residences east of the weaving and sales centre. About the only sight worth seeing in this neighbourhood is a small **gompa** with a big prayer wheel right beside the main road; wander beyond it and someone will probably take you to their house and show you carpets or woollens, which is likely to be more memorable than visiting a monastery.

The zoo

Nepal's only **zoo** (mid-Feb to mid-Nov Tues–Sun 10am–5pm; mid-Nov to mid-Feb same days 10am–4pm; adults Rs100, children ten and under Rs50, camera extra) – often rendered "jew" by Nepali-speakers – lies just south of Jawalakhel Chowk, on the way to Ekantakuna. It's probably the best attraction for young children in the entire Kathmandu Valley: besides looking at the animals, they can take elephant rides through the grounds and pedalo around the central lake. **Food** is available from a café and a couple of snack bars, and there are plenty of places for picnicking.

Most of the animal species kept here are indigenous to Nepal, and almost all have at least a South Asian connection. Many are hard to spot in the wild, so the zoo offers a chance to see them close up. Highlights include a **tiger** (a man-eater from Chitwan, now serving a life sentence here), **rhinos**, **blackbuck antelope**, **gharial crocodiles**, two species of **bear**, *nilgai* (**blue bull**) and a bevy of big **birds**. Conditions for the animals aren't brilliant, but they've improved somewhat since management of the zoo was handed over to the King Mahendra Trust for Nature Conservation, a non-governmental organization respected for its work in the Annapurna area and Nepal's lowland parks.

For background on Nepal's wildlife, see "Natural history" in Contexts.

Kushunti and Pancheshwar Mahadev Mandir

Kushunti, a suburb of Patan just south of the Ring Road, held little interest until 1997, when it became the site of a latter-day miracle. Kalyani Thapa, a poor widow seized by a vision sent by Shiva, instructed villagers to start digging under a local dump. The excavation revealed a *linga* and images of an ox and snakes that devotees believe are emblems of Shiva. A modest brick-and-concrete temple, the **Pancheshwar Mahadev Mandir**, was quickly erected on the spot, and Mata Kalanyi (as she is now known) has become a local celebrity.

The temple receives a fair number of worshippers in the mornings and on Saturdays, and given the large amount of money being raised by Mata Kalanyi's followers, its fame seems certain to increase. To get to it, head south from Jawalakhel Chowk, make a left after the staff college, cross the Ring Road, and after 200m make a right on a road heading downhill.

Eating

Scores of **restaurants** and **cafés** line the lanes of Kathmandu's tourist quarters, and more spring up after each monsoon. Quite a few carry on in a funky, student-coffee-house style – they're like relics from the early 1970s – but a growing number have gone upmarket, even emulating French bistros, American diners or English pubs.

While **Tibetan**, **Chinese** and **Indian** food have long been taken for granted in Kathmandu, all-purpose "**Continental**" menus predominate nowadays. These cater to Western travellers, and they're all pretty samey, featuring "buff"

Ethnic restaurants in Kathmandu and Patan

A good way to experience a culture is through its cuisine. Here's a quick index of restaurants that specialize in **ethnic cuisines** of Nepal and the surrounding region. For more information on a given restaurant, go to the section indicated after its name.

Nepali and Newari

Several of the restaurants recommended here are geared for tour groups and are on the **expensive** side, but worth it. At the other extreme are the city's many **dirt-cheap** *bhojanalaya* (diners) and *bhatti* (taverns), which advertise themselves with a curtain hung over the entrance and are impossible to recommend by name. Most are merely the Newar equivalents of a greasy spoon, but the best ones are fantastic. Ask your innkeeper for suggestions, or try your luck in the area north of Asan or north and west of Patan's Durbar Square. If you go to one of the tourist-savvy places first, you can familiarize yourself with the offerings before taking on the (menuless) local eateries. Many tourist restaurants advertise "special Nepali meals", which usually turn out to be rather ordinary *daal bhaat*. See Basics (p.45) for a rundown of Nepali and Newari dishes.

Baithak Kantipath, Durbar Marg and beyond
Bhanchha Ghar Kantipath, Durbar Marg and beyond
Bhoe Chhen Kantipath, Durbar Marg and beyond
Bhojan Griha Kantipath, Durbar Marg and beyond
Didiko Baba Bhojanalaya Central Thamel
Festive Fare Jhochhe and New Road
Jewels of Manang North Thamel
Jwojalapa Patan: west side
Lajana Kantipath, Durbar Marg and beyond
Nepalese Kitchen South Thamel
Sabjon Jwolen Jhochhe and New Road
Thakali Bhanchha North Thamel
Thamel House North Thamel
Woh Nacha Patan: Durbar Square and around

Indian

Perhaps the best measure of the Indian population in Kathmandu is the number of **Indian restaurants** – they're everywhere. The more expensive ones serve food steaks, pasta and pizza, and even a few pseudo-Mexican and Greek dishes, plus, of course, ever-popular **pies and cakes**. A few restaurants specialize in **Japanese**, **Thai** and **Korean** dishes, highlighting Nepal's connections to the rest of Asia. Sometimes the food is ingeniously authentic, sometimes you have to use your imagination. Terms like "French onion soup", "enchilada" and "moussaka" get thrown around pretty casually here.

The best news of all is that fine **Nepali** and **Newari** food – not just *daal bhaat*, but also special dishes traditionally only served in homes or during festivals or private rituals – are increasingly available in tourist restaurants as well as in reasonably sanitary local eateries, and are slowly taking their place among the other distinguished South Asian cuisines.

Not many tourist restaurants are all-**vegetarian**, but quite a few of the Indian ones are and, needless to say, every Nepali restaurant does *daal bhaat* (which is vegetarian unless you specifically request meat). For that matter, almost every restaurant serves at least a few meatless dishes, and even Tibetan places will usually do vegetable *momo*.

every bit as good as you'll find in India, and it comes with *ghazal* (see p.159) and five-star service. Even the cheapies (mostly around New Rd) do some fine pure-vegetarian dishes. Indian cuisine is also summarized in Basics.

Angan Jhochhe and New Road

Annapurna North Thamel

Dudh Sagar Kantipath, Durbar Marg and beyond

Ghar-e-Kebab Kantipath, Durbar Marg and beyond

Moti Mahal Kantipath, Durbar Marg and beyond

Nandan Jhochhe and New Road

Pilgrim's Feed 'n Read Central Thamel

Shalimar Central Thamel

Shere Punjab Jhochhe and New Road

Tansen Kantipath, Durbar Marg and beyond

Tripti Central Thamel; Jhochhe and New Road

Tibetan and Chinese

Tibetan restaurants offer some of the cheapest tourist food in Kathmandu. Cheaper still are the many *momo* kitchens throughout the old city – just look for the big aluminium steamers, or listen for the roar of the propane cookers. Tibetan places usually do some Chinese dishes as well; proper Chinese restaurants tend to be more expensive, but still reasonable. Again, see Basics for descriptions of popular Tibetan dishes.

China Town Central Thamel; Patan: west side

Da Hua Central Thamel

Dechenling North Thamel

Lhasa Central Thamel

Mountain City North Thamel

Omei South Thamel

Solu South Thamel

Utse South Thamel

Yeok Teck Patan: west side

Five-star dining

If you can't afford $150-plus a night to stay in one of Kathmandu's five-star hotels, the next best thing is to have dinner in one. For not much more than the cost of a meal at a good Thamel restaurant – which, remember, is peanuts – you'll have an experience unavailable back home at almost any price. The best of the **hotel restaurants** offer sumptuous food, unusual specialities (they often bring in chefs from other regional countries for temporary stints), opulent decor, over-the-top service and music and/or dance performances.

The *Yak & Yeti's* (☎01/248999) **Naachghar** does top-flight Nepali, Indian and Western set dinners in a palatial setting, with a resident dance troupe performing on its own little stage. Its less formal **Chimney Room** was founded by Boris Lissanevitch, the legendary Russian adventurer who opened Kathmandu's first hotel in the 1950s, and preserves his memory with borscht and other Russian and continental dishes.

At the *Soaltee Crowne Plaza* (☎01/272555) – another hotel with storied associations, having once been the palace of Prince Basundhara, the late uncle of the present king – you can choose between **Burkhara** (featuring Pakistani tandoori cuisine), **China Garden** (food ranging from Vietnamese to Mongolian, served in an elegant space) and **Himalchuli** (Nepali and Indian set meals, accompanied by a nightly culture show).

Dwarika's (☎01/479488), which boasts the greatest collection of historic Nepali woodwork of any hotel, goes the whole hog with its **Krishnarpan** restaurant: the tables are made of antique latticework, and the excellent Nepali food is served on traditional tableware. Finally, the *Everest Hotel's* (☎01/488100) **Far Pavilions** serves Indian and Nepali food with fine views of the city from its seventh-floor windows.

It's all too easy to overemphasize food in Kathmandu, however – it can also be the greatest peril of staying here. More travellers get **sick** in the capital than anywhere else, more often than not as a result of placing too much trust in the hygiene of tourist restaurants. Indeed, Nepali restaurants are arguably safer, since chefs know what they're doing when they prepare Nepali food. The places listed here are generally reliable, but heed the words of caution given in Basics (p.26).

Prices are reasonable. As a guide, places described here as cheap will charge less than Rs150 per person for a full dinner, not including alcohol (proportionately less for breakfast or lunch). Inexpensive restaurants will run to Rs150–250, moderately priced ones Rs250–500, and expensive ones Rs500 and up. Unless you're on a really tight budget, have at least one special meal at one of the posh restaurants to get the full maharaja experience. Phone numbers are given for restaurants where it's advisable to book ahead for dinner.

For picnic ingredients and other **provisions**, corner stores in Thamel sell just about everything you could want – chocolate, bread, cheese, biscuits, fruit, beer and so on. For a wider selection of imported goods, go to the Bhatbhateni Supermarket (north of *Mike's Breakfast* in Bhatbhateni), the Bluebird supermarkets in Lazimpath and Tripureswar Marg, or Namaste Supermarket or Gemini Grocer in the Jawalakhel section of Patan.

Thamel

As with lodgings, **Thamel** has all the newest, trendiest and most professional budget restaurants – though some have become so stylish that they've priced themselves out of the budget category. There are so many good ones that you'll never be able to try them all, and sampling them is one of the great pleasures of staying in Thamel.

Unless otherwise noted, the restaurants below are marked on the Thamel map (see p.100).

Central Thamel

China Town J.P. School Rd. Quality preparations of dishes representing many Chinese regional cuisines, including some interesting chef's seafood specials. Inexpensive–moderate.

Didiko Baba Bhojanalaya Off Thamel. Homestyle all-you-can-eat *daal bhaat* is all they do – there's no menu, and virtually no wait. The vegetarian *thaali* comes automatically; ask if you want meat too. Cheap.

La Dolce Vita Thamel. Pretty-close-to-the-mark Italian food in a big restaurant on three floors: choose from the trattoria, bar or rooftop terrace. Moderate.

Hot Breads Thamel. A bakery/café offering big-time people-watching from its terrace overlooking the main Thamel intersection. *Le Bistro*, next door, has the same view and a greater range of food. Inexpensive.

Just Juice & Shakes (aka JJ's) Thamel Northwest. Reliable smoothies, shakes and fresh juice, as well as coffee and pastries. Cheap.

Lhasa Thamel Northwest. Excellent Tibetan soups, *momo* and *tongba* (do-it-yourself millet beer). Cheap–inexpensive.

New Orleans Thamel Northwest. Improvised but tasty cuisine, running the gamut from Thai and Indian to Cajun. Tremendous atmosphere after dark – sort of like an American bar transported to a Nepali courtyard. Moderate.

Northfield Café Thamel Northwest. A somewhat less-accomplished Thamel version of *Mike's Breakfast* (see p.155). Inexpensive–moderate.

Over the Rainbow Thamel Northwest. Hearty American-style sandwiches, subs and fajita wraps, as well as terrific veggie *momo*. Will be of special interest to Judy Garland fans. Inexpensive.

Pilgrim's Feed 'n Read Thamel Northwest, behind Pilgrim's Book House. Pretty good South Indian and tandoori entrees, as well as Tibetan food and a good range of sandwiches and burgers for lunch. Inexpensive.

Pumpernickel Bakery Thamel. Overrated but ever popular for croissant sandwiches, baked goods and ice cream, with seating in a pleasant garden out back. Queuing for food is a drag, though. Cheap.

Roadhouse Café J.P. School Rd. Fancy appetizers, soups and salads, quality Italian and Indian entrees (wood-oven pizzas a speciality) and gourmet desserts. Stylish decor, though no outside seating. Moderate.

Shalimar Thamel. A *hallal* (Muslim) restaurant patronized by the many Kashmiris in the area, with extensive veg and non-veg offerings. Cheap–inexpensive.

Tashi Deleg Thamel. A cheap and cheerful formica-table kind of place with an all-rounder menu – the food isn't great, but it's reliable and good value. Cheap–inexpensive.

Tripti J.P. School Rd. Lively little pure-vegetarian place serving North and South Indian fare. Cheap.

Yin Yang J.P. School Rd ☎01/425510. Very popular for its combination of authentic Thai food and sophisticated atmosphere. Expensive.

North Thamel

Annapurna Thamel Northeast. An authentic, unpretentious tandoori diner, just like the *dhabas* found throughout Nepal's Tarai and in North India. Inexpensive.

B.K.'s Place Thamel North. Open-air snack bar serving what many claim to be Kathmandu's best chips (fries) and other takeaway food. Cheap.

Dechenling Two locations – the garden restaurant north of Tridevi Marg is much nicer in warm weather than the indoor one south of Tridevi Marg (next to *Fire and Ice*). Unique in Kathmandu, they serve fiery, cheesy Bhutanese dishes, as well as a full range of Tibetan ones. Moderate.

Delima Garden Café Off Saat Ghumti. A lovely garden sanctuary, ideal for breakfast or lunch. Offers a range of cuisines, with good value on Indian dishes. Inexpensive.

Himalayan Java Tridevi Marg. A slick Nepali version of *Starbuck's*: fresh ground coffees and lattes, speciality teas, impressive pastries and muffins. Also does sandwiches, chips and salsa, soups and even fajita wraps. Inexpensive–moderate.

Jewels of Manang *Hotel Manang*, Thamel Northwest. Unusual Nepali curries – of the ilk normally served only in upper-class homes – and a few Newari dishes, all delicious; the basement ambience is a bit depressing, though. Live Nepali music nightly. Moderate–expensive.

Krua Thai Thamel Northwest. The food won't astound anyone who's just flown in from Bangkok, but the Thai dishes at this sprawling, multilevel, indoor/outdoor facility are tasty and reasonably authentic. Expensive.

Mountain City In the *Malla Hotel* on Lekhnath Marg (see the Central Kathmandu map). Delicious Chinese food; Szechuan a speciality. Moderate.

Nirmala Thamel Northwest. Vegetarian restaurant serving consistently tasty meals from a varied menu. Inexpensive.

Rum Doodle Saat Ghumti. Trusty steaks, chicken, vegetarian dishes, pizzas and pasta, salads, desserts and cocktails. Famous bar upstairs. Moderate.

Thakali Bhanchha corner of Thamel Northwest and Zed St. Unpretentious place specializing in dishes of the Thakali people of the Annapurna region. The *phing* (clear noodles in spicy tomato sauce) and *dhok-dhok* (spiced buckwheat-flour fritters) are excellent. *Chhang* (as creamy as a lassi) and buttered salt tea are available. Inexpensive.

Thamel House Thamel Northeast ☎01/410388. Excellent nonstandard Nepali dishes, and great ambience in a lovely old building. Moderate–expensive.

South Thamel

Aji Siru Thamel South. Quite proficient food for the price, but without a lot of the standard Japanese-restaurant decorations. Inexpensive–moderate.

Café des Trekkers Jyatha Thamel. Improvised crepes and other French cuisine, but as good as you can expect for the money; some Tibetan dishes are also available, as are wine, aperitifs and coffee. By night, the candlelit roof terrace has a nice atmosphere. Moderate.

Everest Steak House Chhetrapati. Renowned as the home of Thamel's best steaks. Inexpensive–moderate.

Fire and Ice Tridevi Marg. Really good pizza from an authentic pizza oven, plus homemade ice cream and other fancy desserts. Moderate.

Green Leaves J.P. School Rd. Organic salads are the main attraction; also Indian and some Tibetan dishes. Lovely outdoor seating and nightly live music. Inexpensive.

Helena's J.P. School Rd. One of Thamel's oldest establishments, now in its own new seven-storey building (including two levels of rooftop seating). The cake display window here is one of Thamel's most popular tourist sights; the usual steaks-pasta-pizza menu otherwise. Inexpensive.

Kathmandu J.P. School Rd. Continental, Indian and Nepali food, all of it consistently good. The indoor hall lacks atmosphere, but the rooftop seating is nice on a warm evening. Moderate.

Kilroy's of Kathmandu Jyatha Thamel. A gourmet restaurant owned by a highly credentialled (and avidly self-promoting) chef, set in a secluded courtyard with a waterfall. Imaginative and eclectic entrees, decadent desserts, extensive wine and spirits list. A good option for a romantic meal. Expensive.

Koto J.P. School Rd. A full range of Japanese dishes, all excellently prepared. Probably the best value for money in town on the Japanese front. Moderate.

Laxmi Narayan's Steak House Chhetrapati. Popular for steaks, pasta and pies. Inexpensive–moderate.

Nepalese Kitchen Chhetrapati. A serviceable budget restaurant demonstrating that there's more to Nepali cuisine than *daal bhaat*. Outdoor seating, a fireplace and live music some evenings. Inexpensive.

Omei Jyatha Thamel. Convincing Beijing and Cantonese cuisine on white linen. Moderate.

Solu Jyatha Thamel. A Sherpa locals' hole-in-the-wall: undistinguished but enjoyably typical. Cheap.

Utse Jyatha Thamel, in *Hotel Utse*. An old standard, with reliable and reasonably priced Tibetan and Chinese food. Cheap–inexpensive.

Weizen Bakery J.P. School Rd. A spin-off of the *Pumpernickel* – better bakery booty, and less of a scrum. Cheap–inexpensive.

Jhochhe (Freak Street) and New Road

Jhochhe is noticeably cheaper than Thamel for eating, but it's got a smaller and less interesting selection of tourist restaurants – most are second-rate all-rounders. More interesting are the area's Nepali places, and the Indian establishments that dominate in the lanes on either side of **New Road**. Unless otherwise noted, see the Jhochhe map (p.103) for locations.

Angan corner of Ganga Path and Shukra Path. Divine Indian-style sweets (buy them by the piece), as well as ice cream and Indian and Nepali snacks. Inexpensive.

Bakery Café Ganga Path. Nepali yuppie hangout, churning out serviceable pizza, *momo*, ice cream and the like. Inexpensive.

Café Culture Off Jhochhe. Various all-veggie combinations of potatoes, cheese and tasty home-made pasta. Relaxed atmosphere (cosy in winter), good tunes and backgammon boards. Cheap–inexpensive.

Cosmopolitan Jhochhe. Tolerable pasta and steaks, but good crepes and a hip Freak St atmosphere. Inexpensive.

Festive Fare corner of Jhochhe and Ganga Path (with another branch at Makhan Tol – see the Durbar Square map). Good introductory Nepali and

Newari food, with excellent rooftop views of Durbar Square. Moderate (though the set menu is expensive).

Nandan Off New Rd (see South of Durbar Square map). A pure-vegetarian restaurant patronized by semi-well-off Indians. Good food from both North and South India, including an excellent Marwari *thaali* and to-die-for *ras malai*. Inexpensive.

Oasis Garden Jhochhe. Probably the most pleasant outdoor dining spot in this area, with standard Western fare and Nepali snacks. Cheap–inexpensive.

Paradise Jhochhe. A venerable Freak St institution, perhaps more popular than it deserves, serving tasty vegetarian food, mainly of the claggy, creamy variety. Cheap–inexpensive.

Sabjon Jwolen Chikamugal. Lively Newari restaurant offering not only standard items (*chatamari*, *choela*, *bara/wo*) but also preparations of tongue, intestines and brain. The "tucha set" is a good starting point if you're new to Newari food. Cheap.

Shere Punjab Off New Rd (see South of Durbar Square map). Basic in-and-out Punjabi canteen. Cheap–inexpensive.

Snowman Jhochhe. Operating continuously since 1968, this is the only original Freak St pie shop still going, and it's got a kind of cool that doesn't go out of fashion. Superior pies, cakes and crème caramel. Amazingly eclectic tunes (donate your tapes to the proprietor and your legacy will play on). Cheap.

Tashi Deleg Mandarin Jhochhe. Cramped but cosy all-rounder, with passable Chinese and Tibetan dishes. Cheap.

Tower On the roof of the *Hotel Classic*, Shukra Path. A nice rooftop haven. The Indian and Chinese food is okay, but you come here mainly for the elevation. Inexpensive–moderate.

Tripti Off New Rd (see South of Durbar Square map). Lively little pure-vegetarian place serving North and South Indian fare. Cheap.

Kantipath, Durbar Marg and beyond

Durbar Marg is famous for its fine restaurants, especially Nepali and Indian ones. It also harbours a few fast-food outfits, which is about the only type of place found along nearby **Kantipath**. Of the many restaurants scattered around the city east and north of these streets, those worth mentioning are generally of the upscale variety – the kind you take a taxi to and make an evening of it.

Unless otherwise noted, see the Kantipath and Durbar Marg map (p.104) for locations.

Baithak Baber Mahal Revisited, off Airport Rd (see Central Kathmandu map) ☎01/267346. A stunning dining room in a converted Rana palace, with formal furnishings and gilt-framed portraits, although the Nepali specialities don't quite live up to the atmosphere. Expensive.

Bhanchha Ghar Kamaladi ☎01/225172. Nepali nouvelle cuisine, featuring such delicacies as wild mushroom curry and buckwheat chapatis, served in a beautifully converted Newari house. Nightly culture show. Expensive.

Bhoe Chhen Off Durbar Marg in front of the *Yak & Yeti*. Varied and quite good Newari food in a small, traditionally decorated dining room. Moderate (but the set menu is expensive).

Bhojan Griha Dilli Bazaar (see the Central Kathmandu map) ☎01/416423. A culture show with dinner: the Nepali food is only average, and the music and dancing gets in your face, but it's all done very professionally, and the ambience – the building is a restored Rana priest's mansion – is fabulous. For after-dinner drinks there's the *Kama Sutra Bar*, with wink-wink woodcarvings. Expensive.

Chez Caroline Baber Mahal Revisited, off Airport Rd (see Central Kathmandu map). A classy French café/patisserie, serving crepes, quiche, soups and sandwiches for lunch (moderate) and fancier main courses for dinner (expensive).

Delicatessen Center Kantipath. A cornucopia of European-style deli meats, cheeses, breads, pastries, cakes, pies and ice cream. Soups and basic hot dishes are also available. Inexpensive–moderate.

Dudh Sagar Kantipath. Quick South Indian meals, snacks and excellent Indian sweets (including killer *ras maduri*). Cheap.

Ghar-e-Kebab Durbar Marg in front of *Hotel de l'Annapurna* ☎01/221711. Superlative North Indian food, nightly *ghazal*, and strange nightclub interior. Expensive.

Koto Durbar Marg ☎01/226025. A full range of Japanese dishes, excellently prepared. Alongside its sister-branch in Thamel, this offers the best value for money on the Japanese front. Moderate.

Lajana Off Lazimpath (see Central Kathmandu map). Competent group-oriented restaurant that does a wide range of Newari dishes, ranging from the accessible (*woh, chatamari, choela*) to the adventurous (lung, brain, "parts of head"). Nightly live music. Expensive.

Mike's Breakfast Naksal (see Kathmandu map). Absolute bliss for breakfast: garden tables, classical music and spot-on food. Americans' eyes will mist over at the *huevos rancheros*, waffles and fresh coffee. Moderate.

Moti Mahal Durbar Marg. Tandoori food rivalling that of the expensive places, though the decor isn't as swanky. *Godavari* is a sister all-vegetarian restaurant in the same building. Moderate.

Tansen Durbar Marg ☎01/224707. Top-notch tandoori and other Indian dishes served on burnished copper in minimalist surroundings. Expensive.

Patan

A number of restaurants and cafés cluster around **Patan Durbar Square** to target the day-trippers. They're often packed at lunchtime, but at night you'll feel like you've got the place to yourself. Sitting at a table overlooking the square on a balmy evening, with the temples lit from within, it can be magical. A separate category of restaurants, found mainly in the newly settled **west side** of Patan, are patronized mainly by expats and well-heeled locals.

Unless otherwise noted, see the Patan Durbar Square map (p.140) for locations of places in the "Durbar Square and around" listings; see the main Patan map (p.138) for places in the "Patan: west side" listings.

Durbar Square and around

Café du Temple North side of Durbar Square. All-rounder menu, featuring good Indian food. Head for the roof for great views. Inexpensive.

Durbar Square Restaurant Mangal Bazaar. A lively locals' joint where you can sample Newari specialities, including a few acquired-taste items (when in doubt, start with the set menu) as well as less-accomplished Indian and Continental dishes. Cheap.

Old House Café Northeast corner of Durbar Square. Romantic dining in a traditional old building with open balconies overlooking the square. The food is mainly sizzlers and other standard tourist fare. Inexpensive.

Patan Museum Café Royal Palace. Superb snacks, lunches and daily specials in a peaceful back courtyard. You can eat here without paying to enter the museum. Moderate.

Third World Restaurant West side of Durbar Square. Run-of-the-mill tourist food, but with the best views of Durbar Square. Inexpensive–moderate.

Woh Nacha Immediately west of the Krishna Mandir (there's no sign). The most famous of Patan's many *woh* eateries, this is a dark, cavelike little room where foreign customers inevitably attract stares and interest. Very cheap.

Patan: west side

Bakery Café Jawalakhel Chowk. One of a chain of semi-fast-food restaurants, serving burgers, pizza, hot dogs, *momo* and the like. Employs hearing-impaired staff (no worries, just point at the menu). Cheap–moderate.

Café de Patan *Café de Patan Guest House*, Mangal Bazaar. Consistently good (tourist) food plus phenomenal lassis, and Newari dinner specials on weekends. Courtyard and roof-terrace seating. Inexpensive–moderate.

China Town Jawalakhel Chowk. Upmarket decor, a vast menu including some interesting chef's seafood specials, and fairly authentic preparations. Moderate.

Downtown Pulchowk. Trusty Indian and Chinese food, packed at lunchtime by staff from the nearby UN complex. Cheap–moderate.

German Bakery Jawalakhel Chowk. The place that started the whole "German" bakery fad: it has only a limited range of items, notably croissants and whole loaves. Cheap.

Hot Breads Jawalakhel Chowk. Pastries and hot snacks. Cheap.

Jwojalapa Man Bhawan. An excellent place to try authentic Newari food: the waiters can guide you through the menu. The evening dance performances are kind of fun, but loud. Cheap.

La'soon Pulchowk. Another popular lunch spot for NGO workers, offering sandwiches, pastas and an interesting African peanut soup. Inexpensive–moderate.

Yeok Teck West of Ekantakuna (see the Kathmandu map). Vegetarian Malaysian/Chinese restaurant serving amazing mock-meat stir-fry dishes – the taste isn't exactly like meat, but something wonderful in its own right. It's in a strange location, but worth going out of your way for. Inexpensive.

Nightlife and entertainment

For a capital city, Kathmandu is pretty sleepy: most restaurants start putting up their chairs around 9.30pm, and except in a few designated nightclubs, drinking is supposed to stop at 10pm. Given that, you might just decide to retire early and rise early the next morning, when the city is at its best.

However, there are things to do if you're up for them. What follows is an overview of **permanent attractions**, from bars and clubs to cultural shows and cinema – check the noticeboards to find out about special events in the high season.

Bars and nightclubs

Thamel's **nightlife scene** is growing. The area around the *Kathmandu Guest House* has mutated into quite a throbbing little quarter in the evenings, with duelling sound systems blaring across the alleyways, noisy bands of revellers looking for action, and the cops and the riksha wallahs waiting outside for closing time.

As with the tourist restaurants, Thamel's **bars** are more like a Nepali's imagined idea of what a bar must be like than the real thing, but on the whole they're fine for meeting, mixing and prolonging an otherwise short evening. Many advertise "happy hours" – which generally means free popcorn – lasting just about all night. A number of nightspots have **pool** or **snooker** tables, which provide congenial common ground for foreigners and Nepalis to mix. In the high season, bar owners bribe the police to let them keep serving until the wee hours, usually behind drawn curtains and locked doors.

The Thamel bars attract mainly budget travellers, and a few young Nepali men hoping to hook up with Western women. A handful of fancier **nightclubs** elsewhere in the city attract a more diverse clientele – Nepali men and women, expats, upmarket tourists – and are busiest at weekends. They're kind of cheesy, stay open late, and typically have a modest cover charge.

Reputations rise and fall from season to season, but the establishments listed below appear to be in for the duration. Unless otherwise noted, see the Thamel map (p.100) for locations.

Bars

Full Moon Thamel Northwest. A small, cosy, sit-cross-legged kind of place. Eclectic music: techno, trance, etc.

Jump Club Thamel Northwest. Popular for dancing: a DJ plays intelligent new music most nights. Pool tables.

Maya Cocktail Bar Thamel. Two small bars on two floors, with a good atmosphere for social drinking. Latin and other world musics. Mexican snacks.

New Orleans Thamel Northwest. Terrific, sociable atmosphere with outdoor seating and tasteful blues/jazz (sometimes live bands).

Pub Maya J.P. School Rd. Small and intimate, retro decor, and rock oldies.

Rum Doodle Restaurant's "40,000 ½ -Foot Bar" Saat Ghumti. Kathmandu's oldest nightspot, cultivating a cluttered *après trek* atmosphere. The story behind the name is a long one (a novel, in fact).

Sam's Bar Thamel Northwest. A small place with a range of seating choices, from bar to terrace.

Tom and Jerry Pub Thamel Northwest. An established and surprisingly bar-like bar. Pool tables and classic rock music.

Tongues 'n Tales J.P. School Rd. Laid-back and uncommercial, like the bleary end of a frat party. Older rock music.

Tunnel Club Thamel Northwest. A relatively big place that often doesn't reach critical mass. Two levels, with dancing on one and pool tables and terrace seating on the other.

Nightclubs

Club X Zone Kamaladi (see Kantipath and Durbar Marg map). The choice of Kathmandu's rich young things. Fancy sound system, lighting, big dance floor, games. Cover charge.

Moon Sun Disco Heritage Plaza, Kamaladi (see Kantipath and Durbar Marg map). Dancing, snooker and video games.

Studio 54 Tridevi Marg. A shabby disco with a mainly young Nepali clientele; admission charged when busy, but usually not for white faces.

Culture shows

Music and dance are essential parts of Nepali culture, and perhaps nowhere more so than in Kathmandu, where neighbourhood festivals and parades (not to mention weddings) are an almost daily occurrence. Touring other regions of the country, you'll encounter other, markedly different styles of music and dance, and while it's more fun to see these performances in their native context, it might be worth checking out a **culture show** before you leave the capital to get a sampler of Nepal's folk and performing arts.

Several Thamel restaurants host free regular folk music performances in the high season, and most of the deluxe hotels do pricey dinner shows. Infrequent cultural evenings are held at the Royal Nepal Academy, off Kamaladi, and other venues such as the Patan Museum, although they're not well publicized; ask around and check notice boards.

Kathmandu's festivals

Your chances of coinciding with a **festival** while in Kathmandu are good, since the capital spends about a month out of every year partying. Those listed here are just the main events; there are many others centred around a local temple or neighbourhood. See p.55 for dates and longer descriptions of the major festivals.

Magh (Jan–Feb)
Basanta Panchami The spring festival is marked by a VIP ceremony in Durbar Square on the fifth day after the full moon. Children celebrate Saraswati Puja on the same day at Swayambhu.

Faagun (Feb–March)
Losar Tibetan New Year, observed at Swayambhu on the full moon of February, but more significantly at Boudha (see p.196).

Shiva Raatri "Shiva's Night" is celebrated with bonfires in Kathmandu on the new moon of Faagun, but the most interesting observances are at Pashupatinath (see p.190).

Phaagun Purnima (Holi) Youths bombard each other and passers-by with coloured powder and water. The festival lasts a week, but peaks on the day of the full moon.

Chaitra (March–April)
Chaitra Dasain On the morning of the eighth day after the new moon, the army's top-ranking officers gather at the Kot compound, at the northwestern end of Durbar Square, for the beheading of dozens of buffalo and goats and to troop their regimental colours.

Seto Machhendranath Jaatra A flamboyant chariot procession in which the white idol of Machhendranath is placed in a towering chariot and pulled from Jamal to an area south of Jhochhe in at least three daily stages. The festival starts on Chaitra Dasain, with the action getting under way at about 4pm each day.

Ghora Jaatra Equestrian and gymnastics displays, and military demonstrations at the Tudikhel on the afternoon before the full moon.

Baisaakh (April–May)
Nawa Barsa On Nepali New Year (April 13 or 14), there are parades in Kathmandu, but Bhaktapur's festivities are more exciting (see p.229).

Raato Machhendranath Jaatra An amazing, uniquely Newar extravaganza in which an immense chariot is pulled through old Patan over a period of several weeks (see box on p.147).

The following groups do regularly scheduled shows. Admission is about Rs400; call for times.

Everest Cultural Society *Hotel de l'Annapurna*, Durbar Marg ☎01/221711. Conventional folk performances with or without dinner, nightly in high season.

Gandarbha Cultural and Art Organization Thamel Northwest. A group of hot folk musicians who perform nightly in a small, stuffy upstairs room behind the *Lhasa* restaurant. Unlike more formal groups, these guys put on a spontaneous, intimate show that feels like an after-dinner singalong on a trek, only much more professional.

Funded by donation and sales of CDs. Instruction available.

Hotel Vajra Bijeshwari ☎01/271545. The *Vajra's* resident Kala Mandapa ensemble does a superb classical Nepali dance and dance-drama programme on Tues and Fri evenings in high season. Private dance, vocal and instrumental instruction available.

New Himalchuli Cultural Group At a space opposite the Israeli embassy in Lazimpath ☎01/415280. Nightly folk performances in high season.

Ghazal and "dance"

As it has with so many other cultural imports from south of the border, Kathmandu has been quick to embrace **ghazal** (an Indian style of popular

Buddha Jayanti The anniversary of the Buddha's birth, enlightenment and death, celebrated on the morning of the full moon at Swayambhu: thousands come to do *puja*, and priests dressed as the *panchabuddha* perform ritual dances around the stupa.

Saaun (July–Aug)

Janai Purnima The annual changing of the sacred thread worn by high-caste Hindu men (and of temporary wrist bands that may be worn by men and women of any caste), on the day of the full moon, at Patan's Kumbeshwar Mandir and other temples.

Ghanta Karna Demon effigies are burned on street corners throughout the city on the fourteenth day after the full moon of Saaun.

Gaai Jaatra Held on the day after the full moon, the "Cow Festival" is marked by processions through the old city, led by garlanded boys costumed as cows. A good place to watch is in front of the entrance to the old Royal Palace in Durbar Square.

Bhadau (Aug–Sept)

Krishna Astami (Krishna Jayanti) Krishna's birthday, in which thousands of women queue for *puja* at Patan's Krishna Mandir.

Tij A three-day "Women's Festival", starting on the third day after the full moon: the most public aspects take place at Pashupatinath (see p.190), but women may be seen singing and dancing anywhere.

Indra Jaatra A wild week of chariot processions and masked-dance performances held around the full moon of Bhadau (see box on p.112).

Ashoj (Sept–Oct)

Dasain A mammoth ten-day festival celebrated in most parts of Nepal, concluding on the full moon of Ashoj. In Kathmandu, mass sacrifices are held at the Kot courtyard near Durbar Square on the ninth day, Durga Puja, and the king bestows *tika* on all and sundry at the Royal Palace on the last day.

Khattik (Oct–Nov)

Tihaar The Festival of Lights, celebrated here (as in most places) with masses of oil lamps throughout the city and five days of special observances. Lakshmi Puja, falling on the full moon of Khattik, is the highlight. Newars celebrate the fourth day as their new year.

music). Troupes tend to work the better Indian restaurants, where they provide dinnertime accompaniment from a platform over to the side somewhere. A typical ensemble consists of amplified tabla, guitar, harmonium and/or synthesizer. The singer, who gets top billing, croons in a plaintive voice. Love is the theme, and the sentimental lyrics – typically in Urdu or Hindi, but increasingly in Nepali – draw from a long tradition going back to the great Persian poets.

To catch a *ghazal* act, try *Amber*, *Ghar-e-Kebab* or *Moti Mahal* in Durbar Marg; *Raj Gharana* at the top of the Kathmandu Plaza Building on the corner of Lal Durbar and Kamaladi; or *Ghoomti* in the Bishal Bazaar on New Road.

Another curious recent trend in Kathmandu is the popularity of so-called **dance** restaurants. The words "with dance" on a restaurant's sign telegraph a very specific ambience that includes women dancing under lights on a makeshift stage to loud Nepali pop music. They're fully clothed, and the dancing is more traditional than suggestive, but the customers are almost always men and some apparently arrange for private services after hours. It's one of those only-in-Nepal phenomena that's worth experiencing for the length of time it takes to drain an (overpriced) beer. Check out the *Pink Palace*, off J.P. School Road, a rare spot of native soil in touristland.

Theatre, cinema and other performances

Outside the tourist arena, scheduled performances of the arts are rare, but that's hardly surprising considering how much goes on all the time in public. The *Hotel Vajra's* resident **theatre** group, Studio 7 (℡01/271545), does an annual run each April; past performances have been adaptations of everything from Shakespeare to Hindu epics.

Despite stiff competition from cable TV and videos, Kathmandu's several **cinemas**, showing the latest Indian blockbusters in Hindi, are still popular. The easiest ones to get to are the Bishwa Jyoti on Jamal, the Ranjana north of New Road, and the Ashok near Patan Dhoka. Showtime is generally noon, 3pm and 6pm daily and tickets cost just pennies.

The Russian Cultural Center (℡01/415453) in Kamal Pokhari is known for screening films from Southern Asian countries, and hosts two superb festivals biannually, Film South Asia in October (odd years) and the Kathmandu International Mountain Film Festival in December (even years). The Alliance Français (℡01/411076), in Thapathali, and the Goethe Institut (℡01/220528), in Khichapokhari, also show films in their respective languages.

Some Thamel restaurants show pirated Hollywood **videos** and DVDs to bring in customers. They're often of poor quality, but they're free with a meal. For recent English-language releases on a bigger (video) screen, go to Kathmandu Mini Vision in the Kathmandu Plaza building at the east end of Lal Durbar (℡01/253140).

In the high season, the *Kathmandu Guest House* hosts **slide shows** by visiting authors and adventurers. The rafting companies do their own promotional shows, and the Indigo Gallery at *Mike's Breakfast* does impromptu slide shows on various subjects – ✉indigo@wlink.com.np to get on their mailing list.

Casinos

You may not have come to Nepal to gamble, but a night at one of Kathmandu's **casinos** is a weirdly memorable experience. They're frequented mainly by avid Indians and bored Westerners staying at the affiliated deluxe hotels (quite a few Nepalis also play, even though they're legally barred from entering). Admission is free, but to play you have to purchase a minimum of Rs1000 worth of chips.

Players can get a voucher for a complimentary all-you-can-eat buffet meal – the food is great, but served only at set times. As usual, higher-rollers get free drinks and transportation to their lodgings.

There are casinos at the *Soaltee Crowne Plaza*, *Hotel de l'Annapurna*, *Yak & Yeti* and *Everest Hotel*.

Shopping

Kathmandu and Patan are obvious places to do some serious **shopping**, especially if this is your last stop before leaving the country. The sheer volume of stuff on sale in Kathmandu, and the fierce competition among sellers there, makes it possible to get very good deals, especially if you're good at bargaining. Many of the items sold in Kathmandu are actually made in Patan, however, so shopping there will enable you to watch pieces being made and (maybe) get an even lower price by buying from the source.

Thamel offers Nepal's largest gathering of shops selling handicrafts and other tourist paraphernalia. **Durbar Marg** is equally well known for shopping, but its boutiques are posher and specialize in high-end crafts, antiques, jewellery and fashions. Other more modest handicraft shopping areas include **Jhochhe**; the area north of **Patan Durbar Square**; and the Tibetan-influenced **Ekantakuna** (Jawalakhel) section of Patan. The busy boulevards of Kupondol and Lazimpath aren't very pleasant for strolling, but they boast many designer clothing boutiques and nonprofit outlets selling Nepali-styled home furnishings and contemporary crafts.

If you want to shop where Nepalis do, check out the **old city** around **Asan** and **Indrachowk**, **New Road** and the lanes north and south of it, Patan's **Mangal Bazaar** and the street running south to Lagankhel, and the so-called

---

Other shopping meccas

If you're into shopping – or just window shopping – don't miss **Baber Mahal Revisited** an upscale shopping mall set in a beautifully restored former Rana Prime Minister's palace. The shops are Aladdin's caves of fine and unusual crafts, which typically cost no more (and sometimes less) than less-interesting or lower-quality equivalents in Thamel. Many taxi drivers are unfamiliar with Baber Mahal Revisited, and will assume you mean Baber Mahal, a ministry building off the Airport Road, just to the south. Fortunately, it's only a short walk around.

Despite its forbidding name, the **Patan Industrial Estate** is industrious in the nicest possible way. Located just beyond the Southern Stupa, the laid-back "estate" includes (in addition to more mundane industries) a dozen or so handicraft factory showrooms. They're primarily pitched at tour groups, which means that independent travellers are generally left to mosey round the work areas without too much pressure. The main reason to come here is to learn about Nepali handicrafts and the processes used to make them – especially woodcarving and metalsmithing, and to a lesser extent rug-weaving and *thangka*-painting. It's also kind of handy to have such a wide selection of crafts gathered together in one place – a couple of the outlets are like handicraft department stores, selling everything from shawls to gemstones. Prices are competitive, but not necessarily better than elsewhere; you can bargain, even in places with supposedly fixed prices. The estate is within walking distance of old Patan, but along a dreadful corridor, so consider taking a taxi or tuk-tuk.

Most shops in both these areas are open Monday to Friday and Sunday, from 9am to 5pm.

Hong Kong Bazaar, a canopied flea market encircling the Bhrikuti Mandap exhibition ground.

For more detail on many of the handicrafts mentioned below, including buying tips, see Basics.

Metal and jewellery

Patan has always been renowned for its metalsmiths, who produce religious (mainly Buddhist) **statues** by the lost-wax and repoussé processes. Uku Bahal – the area around the Mahabuddha temple – is their traditional neighbourhood, and you'll find dozens of retail outlets-cum-workshops there. Pieces run the gamut of size and price, from crude little statuettes to magnificent large-scale works of art. Simple statuettes, bells, singing bowls, bracelets and other metal items are sold throughout the city.

If you're in the market for a **khukuri** knife, you won't have to go far: street vendors and shops sell them wherever there are tourists, and there are several shops in Thamel devoted exclusively to them. Brass sets of **bagh chal**, Nepal's own "tigers and goats" game, are almost as common. Stalls and shops between Indrachowk and Asan sell all manner of household and ritual **brassware**.

Gold- and silversmiths in the old city (mainly north and west of Indrachowk) produce fine traditional **jewellery**; tourist shops sell cheaper but perhaps more wearable ornaments, usually made with white metal. **Gem** sellers are grouped mainly at the east end of New Road, while the Pote Bazaar near Indrachowk is the place to go for traditional **glass beads**.

Wood and paper

Many Nepali carved-**wood** crafts – picture frames based on Newar window designs, statues of deities and animals – are best bought in Bhaktapur (see p.233), although several shops north of Patan Durbar Square also deal in these items. For exquisite (and expensive) non-traditional Nepali-style furniture, mirror frames and windows, visit the **Woodcarving Studio** (☎01/38528, ✆asianart@mos.com.np) in Patan, located just west and north of the main Ekantakuna intersection, up the hill from the Tibetan area. Handmade wooden **toy** trucks, jigsaw puzzles, doll houses, rocking horses and the like are sold in many tourist shops; Educational Wooden Toys, about 100m south of Patan Durbar Square on the left, has a good selection, and you can visit their nearby workshop.

Many shops in Thamel are now devoted exclusively to beautiful handmade **paper** products: journals, calendars, lampshades, wrapping paper and so on. You can buy colourful **papier-mâché masks** and **puppets** all over the place, but these are produced in Bhaktapur and Thimi (see pp.233 and 238) and are better represented there.

Old stuff

Because so many of Nepal's antiquities have been looted over the years, His Majesty's Government is hypervigilant about the export of **antiques** more than one hundred years old. Not being experts, customs officials at the airport and the post office tend to err on the side of caution and reject any item that looks like it might be old. To avoid difficulties, take any suspect items to the Department of Archaeology on Ram Shah Path and have them tag it as okay for a modest fee. The process is quick but you may have to queue for up to an hour. If possible, have the dealer do it for you.

Thangka, poubha and other fine art

It's hard to say where to look for bargains on **thangka** and **poubha** (ritual scroll paintings in the Tibetan and Newari styles, respectively), since there are so many standard depictions and levels of quality that any comparison of prices is an apples-and-oranges exercise. There are many dealers in Makhan Tol (at the north end of Kathmandu Durbar Square), around Thamel Chowk and north of Patan Durbar Square. Some also sell paintings based on traditional Tibetan medical texts, and a few in Patan display *thangka*-influenced naive **landscape paintings** of Nepal and the Kathmandu Valley – they're mass-produced for the tourist market, but they still make nice souvenirs.

Some Kathmandu artists are starting to produce more individualistic works, usually in **watercolours**. Shops in the tourist areas sell mostly quaint street scenes and ethnic portraits – quality ranges from naff to impressive.

Kathmandu also has a growing number of **fine-art galleries**, including Indigo Gallery, Naksal (inside *Mike's Breakfast*), which hosts temporary shows and has a small permanent display of interesting nonstandard *thangka*, *poubha* and other indigenous fine art; Siddhartha Gallery, Baber Mahal Revisited, shows contemporary works by Nepali and expat artists; and Woodmaster Gallery, Naksal, specializes in high-quality traditional woodcarving.

Carpets

Kathmandu **carpet**-sellers offer some good deals, but you shouldn't buy until you've had a chance to see carpets being made. The easiest place to do so is in

About thangka

A good **thangka** is the product of hundreds – or even thousands – of hours of painstaking work. A cotton canvas is first stretched across a frame, and gessoed and burnished to a smooth surface that will take the finest detail. The desired design is next drawn or traced in pencil using a grid system and precise proportions; there is little room for deviation from accepted styles, for a *thangka* is an expression of religious truths, not an opportunity for artistic licence. Large areas of colour are then blocked in, often by an apprentice, and finally the master painter will take over, breathing life into the figure with lining, stippling, facial features, shading and, finally, the eyes of the main figure. Mineral- and vegetable-based paints are still used for the best paintings, but most nowadays are acrylic. Gold paint is also used, often to excess.

For discussion purposes, *thangka* can be grouped into four genres. The **Wheel of Life**, perhaps the most common, places life and all its delusions inside a circle held firmly in the clutches of red-faced Yama, god of death. The wheel's "rim" depicts the twelve causes of misery, while its "spokes" show the six sensual realms, where dwell the damned, ghosts, animals, humans, demigods and gods. All are caught in Yama's grip – even the gods – and only the Buddha exists outside the wheel. A second standard image is the **Buddha's life story**, tracing the major events starting in the upper right and proceeding clockwise, and dominated by an enlightened Buddha in the centre. Many *thangka* feature tantric **deities**, either benign or menacing; Avalokiteshwara, the Lord of Compassion, and the Taras, Tibetan Buddhist goddesses, are favourites. Such an image serves as a meditation tool in visualization techniques, in which the subject identifies with the deity's godly attributes or recognizes its demonic ones in him or herself. **Mandala**, too, are used in meditation. Symbolically, the subject moves through the three rings of the outer circle (representing the three parts of human nature that must be controlled), through the inner hexagram, towards the figure of the Buddha at the centre.

That's just the tip of the iceberg. A full exposition of *thangka* iconography would fill volumes – ask a dealer or artist to lead you through a few images step by step.

the former Tibetan refugee camp in the Ekantakuna section of Patan, Nepal's oldest and most famous carpet-weaving centre. You might as well start by paying an obligatory visit to the Jawalakhel Handicraft Center (Mon–Fri & Sun 8am–noon & 1–5pm), where you can see workers spinning, dyeing and weaving. The complex includes a fixed-price sales showroom, where profits benefit elderly and poor Tibetans, and a couple of souvenir shops. However, there are many more private shops out on the road leading back to Patan, and prices are, by and large, quite a bit cheaper.

The nonprofit Kumbeshwar Technical School Showroom, just north of the Kumbeshwar temple in Patan, is one of the few places in Nepal to buy 100-percent Tibetan-wool carpets. Nepal Rugmark, a charity that supports child-labour-free carpet manufacture, operates a retail outlet in the Sanchaya Kosh Building on Tridevi Marg.

Other souvenirs and curios

Vendors in Basantapur Square and Thamel flog a vast array of **Tibetan-style curios**, while a few Thamel and Durbar Marg boutiques sell genuine antique

Tibetan carpets: made in Nepal

If you've read the section on shopping in Basics (p.64), you'll know that Tibetan **carpets** made in Nepal have evolved significantly from their traditional forebears. Nonetheless, they do have their origin high up on the Tibetan plateau, where sheep are bred for their unusually long, high-tensile wool. Brought into Nepal by yak and mule train over passes in the far west, the Tibetan wool is blended with processed New Zealand wool and then carded and **spun** into yarn. Although carding machines are increasingly being used, spinning is still done exclusively by hand to produce a distinctive, slightly irregular look. The yarn is then taken to a **dyeing plant**, where it's dipped in vats of boiling dye (chemical dyes are used almost exclusively nowadays) and sun-dried before being rolled into balls, coded for colour and batch, and stored in warehouses. Weavers can then order up their colours by number, as instructed by a pattern or their carpet master.

As throughout Asia, **weavers** sit on benches in front of tall looms. However, Tibetan-style carpets are produced by the **cut-loop** method, which bears little relation to the process employed by Middle Eastern and Chinese artisans. Rather than tying thousands of individual knots, the weaver loops the yarn in and out of the vertical warp threads and around a horizontally placed rod; when the row is finished, the weaver draws a knife across the loops, freeing the rod. The loops, cut in half, form the pile. This method enables relatively speedy production – one person can produce a 3x6-ft carpet in as little as seven working days – but it results in a rather low density of 60 to 144 "knots" (cut loops) per square inch. Rather than beating each row down with an iron mallet, which in Middle Eastern carpets helps to create a tight weave, Tibetan-style weavers deliberately use wooden mallets for a looser, blanket-like feel.

The weaving done, carpets are taken off the looms and trimmed with shears to give an even finish. **Embossing**, an optional shearing stage, subtly separates the colours to highlight the design. Finally, carpets must be **washed** to remove dirt and excess dye, an industrial process which, in the absence of effective controls, pollutes local streams with chemicals that have been linked with birth defects.

Marketing is more sophisticated than it might at first appear. The carpets so haphazardly displayed in tourist shops represent only a fraction of those produced – most are in fact made to order for the export market and air-freighted to wholesalers in Frankfurt and London. A handful of export traders, led by the Carpet Trading Company, handle international distribution.

For background on the carpet industry's troubles, see p.544.

Tibetan chests and dressers. Countless shops in the tourist areas carry identical ranges of **Kashmiri**, **Rajasthani** and **Afghan** handicrafts; others sell Nepalese **tea** in boxes or embroidered bags, packaged **incense**, **essential oils** and relatively inexpensive saffron and other **spices**.

Small shops in Thamel, Chhetrapati and Khichapokhari (south of New Rd) stock Nepalese **musical instruments**, while hack minstrels doggedly peddle *sarangi* (traditional fiddles) around Thamel, and cheap bamboo flutes in Durbar Square. **Kites** and accompanying thread-spools are sold in the old city in the runup to Dasain.

Nepali artisans are turning out an ever-expanding range of **contemporary crafts** that adapt traditional materials or motifs to foreign tastes: cushion covers and other household furnishings made out of unusual forms of *dhaka* and other textiles, beautiful handmade paper products, Maithili-style paintings and papier-mâché items, toys, dolls in ethnic dress, ready-made clothes, woollens, leather goods, batiks, scented candles, and ingenious articles made out of bamboo and pine needles. The impetus for many of these innovations has come from a few income-generation projects supported by aid organizations, which operate their own sales outlets (see box below), although many products are now widely imitated.

Clothing and fashion

Thamel and Jhochhe are full of shops selling **wool** sweaters, jackets, mittens and socks, which are among Nepal's best bargains. **Cotton garments** and T-shirts are particularly cheap, in both senses of the word, but might be just the ticket for short-term travel needs. Similarly inescapable around the tourist areas are **kit bags**, **caps** and other fashion items with Tibetanoid rainbow fringes. Tailors, usually found inside the T-shirt shops, are skilled at machine-**embroidering** designs on clothing.

Ethical shopping

A number of shops in the tourist areas claim or imply that they're outlets for women's skill-development programmes. There's no doubt that they employ women – the question is on what terms. The following shops exist either to fund charitable causes or to sell crafts made by income-generation projects.

Dhankuta Sisters Kupondol. Small charity store that represents village women in the eastern hills, selling mainly *dhaka* clothes.

Dhukuti Kupondol, north of *Hotel Himalaya*. Run by a village and low-income project marketing association, Nepal's biggest nonprofit shop stocks a wide variety of cotton and quilted-cotton crafts, wool sweaters, dolls, copper vessels, basketry and leather.

Kumbeshwar Technical School north of Kumbeshwar Mandir, Patan. Carpets and woollen garments made by the school's students.

Ladybird Gift Shop J.P. School Road. Dolls, paper products and T-shirts sold in support of an organization for at-risk girls.

Mahaguthi branches in Kupondol and Lazimpath. Aided by Oxfam, this supports a home for destitute women, and sells a good selection of textiles, crafts, jewellery, toys and musical instruments.

Maheela Thamel South. Small shop in aid of the Women's Foundation, selling *dhaka* clothing and crafts.

Sana Hastakala branches in Kupondol and Lazimpath. Good selection and display of woollens, *dhaka*, pashmina, quilted cottons, ceramics, paper, Mithila art, toys and general gift items. Supports projects mainly run by and for women producers.

Now that the **pashmina** fad has run its course in the West, shops in all the tourist areas are offloading scarves and shawls at bargain prices – try the places at the Kwa Bahal end of Thamel. **Topi**, the caps that Nepali men wear in much the same way Westerners wear ties, are sold around Asan. You'll find **sari material** in New Road and around Indrachowk, and you can have cotton *shalwar kurtas* made to order from shops east of Asan. Other textiles are sold in the non-profit shops (see the box on the previous page).

A number of boutiques sell **designer fashions** with a Nepali flavour, usually in silk or other natural materials. A few worth highlighting are Chrysalis, Thamel South; Fashion Den, Lazimpath; Nepalese Handloom Silk, J.P. School Road; Rage, Durbar Marg; and Wheels, Durbar Marg. Bespoke tailors make **men's suits** to order – try Le-Baron House of Silk & Boutique, Thamel Northwest; and Mode Collection, J.P. School Road.

Books and maps

Kathmandu has one of Asia's greatest concentrations of English-language **bookshops**, and browsing them is one of the city's main forms of nightlife – many stay open till 10pm. Most are nameless holes-in-the-wall, but the listings below cover the bigger ones, along with a couple of places that specialize in maps.

Mandala Book Point Kantipath (under the *Delicatessen Center*). Good selection of reference, fiction and children's books.

The Map Shop J.P. School Rd and Jyatha Thamel. An outlet for Nepa/Himalayan Map House, with an extensive selection of their products.

Maps of Nepal Airport Rd (about 300m west of the *Everest Hotel*). The primary sales outlet for the high-quality FINNAID area maps.

Pilgrim's Book House Branches in Thamel Northwest and Kupondol. Extensive reference sec-

tions on all things Nepali, Indian and Tibetan: religion, mysticism, health, travel, language, development; also maps, postcards, paper, CDs, cassettes and incense. The Kupondol branch is good for children's books.

Tantric Bookshop Thamel Northwest. Thousands of used paperbacks, good for crime fiction.

United Books J.P. School Rd. Strong on fiction and discounted new releases.

Walden Book House Chhetrapati. Good selection of fiction, both new and used.

Music

There's no lack of **music** around Kathmandu to keep your Walkman humming. Many shops in Thamel sell cheap pirated rock/pop CDs, as well as East–West mood music, contemporary releases and folk compilations from Nepal, Tibet and India. Countless shops and stalls throughout the city sell Nepali folk and pop, and Indian pop and movie soundtracks. Prices at these stalls will be less than half what the tourist places charge, but finding what you're looking for will be harder if you don't speak (or read) Nepali. See Contexts for more on Nepali music.

Outdoor equipment

You can buy or rent almost any sort of **outdoor equipment** in Kathmandu. Most of the **new gear** is locally produced and of low quality (see box opposite). You'll also find some legitimate name-brand stuff made in the Far East, but it's not necessarily of export quality. For example, many trekking shops sell Korean-made lightweight hiking boots, which are cheaper here than back home, but they're not very durable and they delaminate easily. Go to the tailors in Jyatha if you want something made or copied in nylon.

A few shops specialize in quality **secondhand** stuff – generally expedition cast-offs (given to guides as tips and promptly resold) and stuff sold by other

Is it really Gore-Tex?

In Kathmandu, as in many Asian cities, authentic name-brand items and **counter-feits** exist side by side in a disorienting jumble. Except that here, the fakes aren't watches or handbags, they're backpacks and sleeping bags.

The tailors of Kathmandu are ingenious – give them any garment and they can copy it, and a few years ago they realized there was a business opportunity in making cheap knockoffs of imported trekking gear for the local tourist market. The idea took off, and a considerable cottage industry has developed. The designs are loosely based on actual name-brand products, but in a fanciful sort of way, sort of like the relationship between Thamel's pseudo-Western food and the real thing. Logos for Lowe Alpine, North Face, Patagonia and other well-known brands – often pathetically bogus – are brazenly stitched onto the items.

Does it do the job? Yes, but not as well. Things have too little padding or don't hang quite right. The zips are of poor quality, and you can't trust the stitching. The fleece quickly pills, the down loses its loft. The "Gore-Tex" isn't – it's just a generic waterproof layer with no particular breathable properties. Still, it'll probably do for a standard trek in the autumn or spring, and you can't beat the price.

trekkers. You can pick up climbing hardware, gas stoves, water bottles, glacier glasses, plastic boots, authentic name-brand clothing, packs and so on. Except for the climbing hardware, it will cost at least as much as in your home country.

Gear can be **rented** in Thamel or Jhochhe, and for most people this is a better way to go. Shona's, in Jyatha Thamel (under *Omei* restaurant), is a fixed-price, no bull shop that does a full range of trekking and climbing gear to buy or rent. Figure on Rs25–40 per day for a good sleeping bag, pack or parka.

For a full trekking equipment checklist, see p.424.

Other bargains

With close trading links to the Far East, Kathmandu has relatively cheap prices on consumer gadgets. **Cameras** and accessories cost about half what they do in Europe, and somewhat less than in North America, so if you're planning to buy any gear for your trip you might as well wait till you get here. New Road is the place to go – there are at least a dozen little camera shops in and around the Bishal Bazaar. **Camcorders**, **personal stereos** and other electronic devices are likewise available at competitive prices. The selection is patchy and models may be a year or two out of date, but if one shop doesn't have what you're looking for they'll send a guy down the street to get it from somewhere that does. You'll pay more for equipment with an international warranty (ie one that's valid in your home country).

Sunglasses and **glasses frames** are also a good deal in shops in and around New Road. European models are quite a bit cheaper than they are in Europe, and Chinese ones are cheaper still. Charges are very reasonable for **prescription lenses**, too, but leave plenty of time for your order to be filled in case a mistake needs to be rectified.

Trekking, rafting and other activities

Most people book organized outdoor activities like trekking, rafting, mountain-biking and wildlife-viewing in Kathmandu because that's where most of the operators and agents are. You don't have to join an organized trip, of course, but here's a rundown of recommended Kathmandu-based companies should you choose to do so. A list of companies that arrange village tourism and homestays is also included.

If you want to do, say, a mix of rafting and trekking, you don't necessarily have to book through two different outfits: most can organize **multiactivity adventures** in partnership with other specialists. Consolidation has been a recent trend, and a few companies – Adventure Centre Asia (which includes Ultimate Descents Nepal and Himalayan Mountain Bikes), Equator Expeditions, Himalayan Encounters and Ultimate Rivers – now offer one-stop shopping for a variety of outdoor experiences.

You should be aware that the confusing similarity between two prominent companies is not accidental. Ultimate Descents Nepal and its sister operation, Borderland Resort, pioneered a certain kind of slickly marketed multiactivity package, and had the field pretty much to themselves until a nasty management bust-up a few years ago. Since then, one of the former partners has continued to run Ultimate Descents Nepal and Borderland, while the other has founded two competing operations, Ultimate Rivers and The Last Resort. Thoroughly confusing matters, Ultimate Rivers markets trips overseas under the name Ultimate Descents.

Trekking companies

For a full discussion of the pros and cons of trekking with a group versus doing it independently, see Chapter Seven. As explained there, individual budget trekking companies can't be recommended because the quality of their service can vary so much from year to year (or trip to trip). Most of the following are more expensive outfits that have reputations for maintaining high standards or that offer unique services.

Above the Clouds Trekking & Mountaineering Thamel North ☎01/416909, ⊛www.visitnepal.com /abovetheclouds. Scheduled and custom teahouse treks, remote-area treks (such as Jaljale Himal), and expeditions.

Ama Dablam Trekking Kamal Pokhari ☎01/410219. Scheduled and custom treks – mostly teahouse routes, plus a few trips to more remote areas and trekking peaks.

Asian Trekking Bhagwan Bahal ☎01/424249, ⊛www.asian-trekking.com. A wide range of scheduled treks on standard and remote routes, as well as expedition support treks and rafting. Affiliated with Asian Airlines Helicopters, so flights are no problem.

Equator Expeditions Thamel Northwest ☎01/415782, ⊛www.equatornepal.com. Runs a

mountaineering school in the Khumbu (see p.422).

Guiding and Trekking Expedition Services (GATES) Gairidhara ☎01/410417, ⊜gates@mos .com.np. Specializes in short, custom treks – especially good for treks with children.

Himalaya Expeditions Kantipath ☎01/226622, ⊛www.himexnepal.com. Nepal operator for Classic Nepal, Karakoram Experience and others. Scheduled and custom teahouse treks, fully supported treks, trekking peaks and expeditions.

Journeys Mountaineering & Trekking Baluwatar ☎01/412898, ⊜journeys@mos.com .np. Nepal operator for US-based Journeys International, offering scheduled teahouse and remote-area treks such as Mustang, Dolpo and Kanchenjunga.

Trekking red tape in Kathmandu

Trekking permits are now required only for a few sensitive areas, and are obtainable only through a trekking agency – for more detail see Chapter Seven. However, if your trek passes through any of Nepal's national parks or conservation areas, it's advisable to buy your **entrance ticket** before departure. In Kathmandu the ticket counter is in the basement of the Sanchaya Kosh Building on Tridevi Marg (Mon–Fri 9am–3pm; plus Sun 9am–3pm for Annapurna Conservation Area permits only).

Karnali Excursions Thamel Northwest
☎01/430383, ⓦwww.trekkinginnepal.com.
Specialists in Humla and Kailash treks.
Nirvana Treks and Expeditions Durbar Marg
☎01/424822, ⓔnirvana@hilltrek.wlink.com.np.
Itineraries for disabled trekkers.

Sherpa Co-operative Trekking Durbar Marg
☎01/224068, ⓔsherpaco@trekk.mos.com.np.
Long-established outfit that does numerous scheduled treks in standard and remote areas.
Sherpa Trekking Service Kamaladi
☎01/222489, ⓔsts@wlink.lcom.np. Runs treks in
many areas and with a range of difficulties.

River operators

Because of the extra safety considerations when rafting (see Chapter Eight), it's
even riskier to recommend budget **river operators**. The ones listed here are
more reputable, hence more expensive. All raft the most popular rivers (scheduled departures in season) and can organize trips on other rivers on demand.

Equator, Ultimate Descents, Ultimate Rivers and Drift Nepal have **kayaks**
available on all their trips. These companies also run four-day **kayak schools**
on the Seti River, near Pokhara (see p.303), and several other river operators
are expected to follow suit. They'll rent kayaks at slow times of year for $15–20
a day (including skirt, paddle and helmet), but you might have better luck in
Pokhara.

Drift Nepal Thamel Northwest ☎01/425797,
ⓔdriftnepal.wlink.com.np. Small Nepali-run company.
Equator Expeditions Thamel Northwest
☎01/415782, ⓦwww.equatornepal.com. Well-
respected, medium-sized rafting operator and
kayaking specialist, concentrating on longer multiday trips. Experienced guides, good equipment.
Himalayan Encounters Thamel Northwest, in the
forecourt of the *Kathmandu Guest House*
☎01/417426, ⓔrafting&trekking@himenco.wlink
.com.np. Nepal's longest-serving rafting operator,
with experienced guides.
Shiva's River Adventure Thamel Northwest
☎01/417685, ⓦwww.shivasrafting.com. Affordable

Nepali-run outfit that runs some out-of-the-way
rivers.
Ultimate Descents Nepal Thamel Northwest
☎01/419295, ⓦwww.udnepal.com. Nepal's
biggest river operator, concentrating on longer and
more remote rivers and kayaking. Good equipment, safety record and guides, but relatively
expensive. Affiliated with Borderland Resort and
Himalayan Mountain Bikes.
Ultimate Rivers Thamel Northwest ☎01/439526,
ⓔinfo@urnepal.wlink.com.np. A spinoff from
Ultimate Descents, offering similar trips, standards
and prices. Affiliated with The Last Resort and
Ultimate Bungy.

Mountain-bike tours

The following companies operate **mountain-bike tours** out of Kathmandu.
Advice on tours, independent biking, equipment and routes is given in
Chapter Nine. For information on renting bikes in Kathmandu, see p.98.

Bikeman Jyatha Thamel ☎01/240633,
ⓦwww.bikenepal.com. A small outfit that runs
tours of the Kathmandu Valley, Nagarkot,
Dhulikhel/Namobuddha and Daman. Pretty beat-up
equipment.
Dawn Till Dusk Thamel Northwest, in the forecourt
of the *Kathmandu Guest House* ☎01/418286,
ⓦwww.nepalbiking.com. A seasoned operator
offering Kathmandu Valley backroads, Nagarkot,
Dhulikhel/Namobuddha, customized off-road itineraries. Good bikes and repair facilities.
Himalayan Mountain Bikes Thamel Northwest
☎01/437437, ⓦwww.bikingnepal.com. Nepal's

original mountain-bike operator, with the most
highly developed range of itineraries: day-trips
around the valley; Nagarkot, Kathmandu Valley rim,
Pokhara–Kathmandu off-road, Lhasa–Kathmandu,
and Ladakh, Sikkim and Bhutan. Good equipment
and repair shop.
Kathmandu Mountain Bikes Kantipath
☎01/226622, ⓔinfo@himexnepal.com. A relatively new entrant to the field, offering Kathmandu
Valley and rim rides, Pokhara–Kathmandu off-road,
Lhasa–Kathmandu, Kangchenjunga foothills and
(cringe) heli-biking.

Wildlife package-tours

Although most of the **budget lodges** near Chitwan and Bardia national parks are represented by agents in Kathmandu, their packages are not recommended for the reasons given on p.328. See the Chitwan and Bardia sections (pp.327 and 364) for full details on doing it yourself.

For **luxury jungle lodges and tented camps**, you *do* need to book ahead. See the relevant listings for Chitwan National Park (p.335), Bardia National Park (p.368), Sukla Phanta Wildlife Reserve (p.376) and Koshi Tappu Wildlife Reserve (p.397).

Victoria Travel & Tours (℡01/226130, ✆explore@mos.com.np), with offices in Kamaladi, specializes in **birdwatching** itineraries.

Other outdoor activities

It's impossible even to pass through Thamel without catching the buzz about **bungy jumping**. Ultimate Bungy at The Last Resort (℡01/439525, ⊛www .visitnepal.com/thelastresort) offers jumps off a 160-metre-high suspension bridge over the Bhote Koshi, a three-hour drive northeast of Kathmandu near the Tibet border; it's claimed to be the highest commercial bungy jump in the world. Packages, including transportation and food, start at $80.

Both The Last Resort and the nearby Borderland Resort (℡01/425894, ⊛www.udnepal.com/beyond.htm) run **canyoning** programmes, more or less as an add-on to their bread-and-butter rafting, bungy-jumping and so on. Cost is about $80 for a two-day package, including transportation, food and overnight accommodation.

Balloon Sunrise Nepal (℡01/424131, ⊛www.view-nepal.com/balloon) does early-morning flights from points in the Kathmandu Valley. The price is $195 per person ($150 if you're willing to go standby) – an expensive way to get above the smog.

Sports and recreation

The National Stadium, at the southern end of Kantipath, hosts frequent **football** (soccer) matches, and is also the headquarters for various martial arts clubs. **Cricket** is played at the Institute of Engineering campus in Patan and other venues. The *Soaltee*, *Everest* and *Yak & Yeti* hotels all have **tennis** courts, open to nonresidents for a fee. For **golf**, there's the Royal Nepal Golf Club, a nine-hole course near the airport, where hazards include monkeys from nearby Pashupatinath (℡01/472836; temporary memberships available). For an international-standard eighteen-hole course, head out to Gokarna (p.202).

The *Hotel de l'Annapurna*, *Woodlands-Dynasty Plaza* and *Yak & Yeti* all allow nonguests to use their **pools** for a modest daily charge, and offer weekend buffet-pool deals. *Shaligram Apartment-Hotel*, south of the zoo in Patan, does a Rs250 daily membership for swimming and sauna. The *Royal Hana Garden*, a Japanese restaurant near the French embassy in Lazimpath, offers **hot-spring baths** in a green secluded grotto (Tues–Sun 3–9pm; Rs250).

Village tourism and homestays

A few Kathmandu-based organizations run **village tourism** and **homestay** programmes (see p.44), in which participants stay in a private home living and eating with the family. This is a great way to connect directly with local culture, and it's of particular interest to foreigners wanting to learn Nepali. Host families are trained in health standards for foreigners. See also "Volunteer opportunities", p.175.

Himalayan Explorers Connection Jyatha Thamel ☎01/259275, ⊛www.hec.org. Keeps a file of families that accommodate club members in their homes for $3–7 per day (depending on the family), including two meals daily.

ITC On a lane leading north of the Tin Dewal on Tridevi Marg ☎01/414490, ⊜itc@mail.com.np. Another homestay programme intended mainly for people studying Nepali.

Lama Adventure Treks and Expeditions Thamel ☎01/413959, ⊜late@mos.com.np. A village tourism programme in two Tamang settlements near Dhulikhel; four-night packages cost $160–200 per person, depending on group size.

Nepal Village Resorts Naksal ☎01/430187, ⊜village@ecomail.com.np. The pioneer of village tourism in Nepal. Organizes stays in Sirubari, a Gurung village near Pokhara, and is developing other programmes in Junbesi (along the trail to Everest) and in the Annapurna area. A two-night all-in package costs $72–132 per person, depending on group size.

Meditation, yoga and astrology

Not surprisingly, Kathmandu is an important centre for **spiritual pursuits**. This section sketches out the general possibilities, concentrating on established outfits that cater specifically for Westerners; a scan through the posters in the popular lodges and restaurants will no doubt turn up others. See also the organizations listed in the next section on alternative therapies, as there's a lot of overlap between all these disciplines. You'll find brief introductions to meditation and yoga in Basics (p.72).

Meditation

The **Himalayan Buddhist Meditation Centre** (☎01/221875, ⊛www .dharmatours.com/hbmc) conducts regular meditations and introductory dharma talks, hosts a revolving schedule of day-long workshops and courses on Tibetan Buddhist meditation and related Tibetan arts, and offers multiday courses and retreats (about $15 per day, including food and lodging). The centre's restful headquarters is located in Kamaladi, down a lane running south from the Ganesh temple. HBMC is affiliated with Kopan Monastery, north of Boudha (p.200), and another monastery in Pokhara (p.304).

Nepal Vipassana Centre (☎01/250581, ⊜nvc@htp.com.np) runs twelve-day courses on *vipassana* at its centre in Budhanilkantha. These aren't for the frivolous: daily meditation begins at 4.30am, and silence is kept for the duration. To register or pick up a pamphlet on the course, visit the centre's Kathmandu office (Mon–Fri & Sun 10am–5.30pm) in the courtyard of Jyoti Bhawan, behind Nabil Bank on Kantipath. All courses are funded by donations.

For those interested in residential study of Tibetan Buddhism, the **Buddha Dharma Center** (☎01/282744), located on a high point south of Swayambhu, offers instruction under the direction of Lopon Tsechu Rinpoche. Many more opportunities exist in Boudha.

If you're of the Rajneesh persuasion, you'll be pleased to learn that Kathmandu supports a thriving Osho industry which includes a travel agency, a bimonthly magazine and two meditation centres. The **Asheesh Osho Meditation Centre** (☎01/274126) in Tahachal conducts one-hour dynamic meditation sessions every morning; these are open to all and the fee is a donation. The second venue, **Osho Tapoban Forest Retreat Centre** (☎01/353762, ⊛www.oshotapoban.com.np), located in a beautiful setting north of Nagarjun Ban, hosts occasional retreats as well as daily meditations and discourses, and can provide accommodation (❸–❺) and meals.

Yoga

Patanjali Yoga Center (☎01/276670, ⓦwww.saptayoga.com), in Tahachal near *Hotel Shrestha*, offers daily drop-in classes and private tuition in pure astanga yoga, a balance of the eight traditional yoga systems. Contact the centre for information on residential study and its month-long teacher-training programme in Pokhara. Patanjali staff also lead daily introductory yoga sessions at the **Healing Hands Center** (see "Massage", opposite).

The Yoga Studio (☎01/417900, ⓔchrissieg@wlink.com.np) teaches hatha yoga in the Iyengar method, a gradual path espoused by B.K.S. Iyengar, a key figure in bringing yoga to the West. The resident instructors teach a regular schedule of classes, as well as occasional longer courses. The studio is located in Tangal, about a ten-minute bike ride east of Thamel, but it's hard to find – pick up a map and schedule at *Fire and Ice* in Tridevi Marg. Beginner classes are also offered at the *Summit Hotel* in Patan.

The **Himalayan Buddhist Meditation Centre** (see "Meditation" overleaf) does one-day beginners' workshops on hatha yoga.

Of the many yoga outfits in Thamel, only two pass the giggle test. **Holistic Yoga Ashrama** (☎01/419334, PO Box 4783), off J.P. School Road on the lane leading to *Pheasant Lodge*, and **Arogya Dham Yoga and Nature Cure Center** (☎01/421193, ⓔarogyadham@hotmail.com), north of Tridevi Marg, offer daily yoga/meditation sessions and various yogic therapies.

Astrology

It's best not to single out **astrologers** in the Kathmandu area, partly because few of them speak English, but mostly because they all have their own flocks to look after and it wouldn't be fair to rain hordes of foreign horoscope-seekers down on them. Try offering your innkeeper or a guide a commission to take you to his astrologer and to translate for you – you'll get a fascinating glimpse into an extremely important but behind-the-scenes aspect of Newar life (see p.520).

To have a **horoscope** prepared you'll need to make an appointment first, and when you go you'll be expected to provide the exact time and place of birth (if you don't know the time, the astrologer may be able to improvise by reading your palm). It'll then take up to a week to produce an annual chart, even longer for a full span-of-life chart. You'll need to schedule a separate session for the astrologer to interpret it for you and answer any questions. The fee for the entire service may run to Rs500 or more. Whatever you may think of astrology or your particular reading, at the least you'll come away with a beautiful and unique work of art, hand-calligraphed and painted on a parchment scroll.

Alternative therapies

Many of what we in the West call **alternative therapies** are, of course, established practice in Nepal. The full range of remedies is actually quite a bit greater than what you see in this section, which, like the previous one, focuses on what's accessible to the average visitor. Again, refer to "Spiritual pursuits" in Basics for a bit of background on these practices.

Ayurvedic medicine

For private consultations, contact **Dr R.R. Koirala** at the Ayurveda Health Home & Research Centre (℡01/414843, ✉ayurveda@wlink.com.np), a group practice located north of Tridevi Marg near *Hotel Blue Horizon*, or **Dr Mana Bajracharya**, a world-famous practitioner whose office is in a hard-to-find courtyard off the street running from Asan to Mahaboudha. **Dr Ram Narayan Shah** at the Ayurvedic Hospital in Nardevi, about 200m west of the Nardevi Mandir on the left, will also treat foreigners.

To fill ayurvedic prescriptions, visit the **Gorkha Ayurved Company**, south of Chhetrapati Chowk, or if your Nepali is up to it, try any of the ayurvedic *pharmas* lining the lane running west from the Nardevi Mandir.

Tibetan medicine

Kunphen Tibetan Medical Centre (℡01/251920; Mon–Fri 10am–noon & 2–5pm), north of Chhetrapati Chowk, is basically a front office for a Tibetan medicine company, whose products it sells, but its diagnostic services come highly recommended. **Kailash Medical and Astro Society** (℡01/251994), with outlets in Dhobichaur (the road leading northwest from Chhetrapati Chowk) and Boudha, offers a similar range of treatments and keeps similar hours.

Massage

A few legitimate **masseurs** practise in Thamel and other tourist/expat areas, though they come and go – again, check the notice boards. Some are Westerners here temporarily on a tourist visa, others are Nepalis who have received professional training at a certified yoga school. Ask to see their credentials. The price of a Nepali massage should be somewhere around Rs200 per hour; other types of massage (shiatsu, Thai, etc) may cost more.

The **Healing Hands Center** near the Russian embassy in Maharajganj (℡01/9810-38447, ⓦwww.ancientmassage.com) offers multiday courses in Thai massage, as well as instruction in t'ai chi, reiki and other healing arts. Some of the deluxe hotels have their own in-house masseurs.

Most of the "Yoga and Massage" signs around Thamel have been put there by charlatans attracted by the princely sums tourists will pay to have their bodies rubbed. Some offer "special" massages. **Prostitution** isn't very obvious in places like Thamel because the police keep it in check with periodic raids, but it happens and it seems to be on the increase. The same factors that fuel the sex industry in countries like Thailand (rural poverty, low status of women, tourism) are also present in Nepal. Fortunately, Nepali society doesn't condone it so openly, so Thamel is unlikely to become another Patpong.

Listings

Airlines, domestic Buddha Air, Hattisar ℡01/542494; Cosmic Air, Kamaladi ℡01/246882; Gorkha Airlines, Hattisar ℡01/436576; Mountain Air, Hattisar ℡01/489065; Necon Air, Sinamangal ℡01/480565; Royal Nepal Airlines (RNAC), corner of New Rd and Kantipath ℡01/220757 (tourist sales office handles flights to Bharatpur, Lukla and Pokhara; domestic sales office, located down the lane running along the west side of the building, handles all other internal flights); Shangri-la Air, Kamalpokhari ℡01/410026; Skyline Airways, Hattisar ℡01/488657; Yeti Airlines, Lazimpath ℡01/421215.

Airlines, international Aeroflot, Kamaladi ☎01/227399; Air France, Durbar Marg ☎01/223339; Air India, Hattisar ☎01/415637 (flights from Kathmandu are handled by Indian Airlines); Biman Bangladesh Airlines, off Hattisar ☎01/434982; British Airways, Durbar Marg ☎01/222266; Cathay Pacific, Kamaladi ☎01/248944; China Southwest Airlines, Lal Durbar ☎01/419770; Dragon Air, Durbar Marg ☎01/223502; Druk-Air, Durbar Marg ☎01/225166; Emirates, Kantipath ☎01/220579; Gulf Air, Hattisar ☎01/430456; Indian Airlines, Hattisar ☎01/410906; Japan Airlines, Durbar Marg ☎01/222838; KLM, Lekhnath Marg ☎01/410089; Korean Air, Kantipath ☎01/252048; Kuwait Airways, Kantipath ☎01/249884; Lauda/Austrian Airlines, Kamaladi ☎01/223331; Lufthansa, Durbar Marg ☎01/223052; Northwest Airlines, Lekhnath Marg ☎01/410089; Pakistan International Airways (PIA), Hattisar ☎01/439324; Qantas, Durbar Marg ☎01/220245; Qatar Airways, Kantipath ☎01/257712; Royal Nepal Airlines (RNAC), corner of Kantipath and New Rd ☎01/220757; SAS, Kupondol, Patan ☎01/524232; Singapore Airlines, Durbar Marg ☎01/220759; Swissair, Hattisar ☎01/434607; Thai Airways, Durbar Marg ☎01/223565; Transavia, Kamaladi ☎01/247215.

American Express The office is on Jamal (Mon–Fri & Sun 10am–1pm & 2–5pm). You can receive mail at the office if you can produce an Amex card or travellers' cheques.

Banks and money Moneychangers can be found all over Thamel, and are scattered in other tourist areas (Jhochhe, Durbar Marg, Patan Durbar Square); they're typically open daily 8am–8pm. Banks worth changing money at include the ones at the airport (open whenever the airport is), and Nepal Bank on New Rd (daily 10am–4pm, limited service available 7.30–10am & 4–7.30pm). The latter has the best rates anywhere, but requires you to show your purchase receipt for travellers' cheque trans- actions. Nepal Grindlays Bank operates several ATM machines in Thamel that give cash advances against Visa or MasterCard in rupees (Rs250 transaction fee), and other banks are likely to fol- low suit. Himalayan Bank on Tridevi Marg makes cash advances against a credit card (Mon–Fri 8am–8pm), as does Nepal Arab Bank on J.P. School Rd (Mon–Fri & Sun 10am–7pm). See p.33 for information on having funds wired to Nepal.

Email, internet, faxing and computer services Communication centres providing internet access are located throughout Thamel and Jhochhe, and just about every commercial street has one or two. Most hotels have business centres with computers and faxes, and even many budget guesthouses

have a computer they'll let guests log on to. Typical charges are Rs1 per minute or Rs25–50 per hour for internet access; Rs10 per page for printouts; and Rs20 for photo scans.

Embassies and consulates Australia, Bansbari ☎01/371678; Austria, Hattisar ☎01/434891; Belgium, Durbar Marg ☎01/228925; Canada, Lazimpath ☎01/415193; Denmark, Baluwatar ☎01/413010; Finland, Lazimpath ☎01/417221; France, Lazimpath ☎01/418034; Germany, Gyaneswar ☎01/416832; Israel, Lazimpath ☎01/411811; Italy, Baluwatar ☎01/412280; Japan, Panipokhari ☎01/426680; Mexico, Baluwatar ☎01/412971; Netherlands, Kupondol Heights, Patan ☎01/523444; New Zealand, Dilli Bazaar ☎01/412436; Norway, Kupondol Heights, Patan ☎01/538746; Poland, Ganabahal ☎01/250004; Russia, Baluwatar ☎01/412155; South Korea, Tahachal ☎01/270172; Spain, Battisputali ☎01/470770; Sweden, Khichapokhari ☎01/220939; Switzerland, Jawalakhel, Patan ☎01/538488; UK, Lainchaur ☎01/411590; US, Panipokhari ☎01/411179. For India, Tibet (China) and other countries in the region, see "Moving on", pp.179–181.

Emergencies For an ambulance, call ☎01/244121 (or better still, take a taxi). See also "Police", opposite.

Hospitals, clinics and pharmacies Two Western-standard clinics in Kathmandu do inocu- lations, stool tests and other diagnostics. Unquestionably the best is CIWEC Clinic, off Durbar Marg on the way to the *Yak & Yeti* (Mon–Fri 9am–4pm; ☎01/228531, ⊛www.ciwec- clinic.com), which has very proficient Western and Nepali staff, and is a great source of information on all matters pertaining to health in Nepal. Charges are very high by Nepali standards – at least $50 for a basic consultation. The Nepal International Clinic (NIC), a block east of the Royal Palace entrance (daily 9am–5pm; ☎01/434642), is also good, and a bit cheaper. Several other clin- ics in Thamel offer more hit-or-miss care and can't be recommended. Medicines can be purchased at *pharma* (pharmacies) everywhere, with or without prescription. CIWEC and NIC can refer you to a specialist physician if need be. A number of small private hospitals operate in the valley; B&B Hospital (☎01/531930) has a good reputation among expats, although it's located in Patan, way down near the southern edge of the Ring Road. Of the public facilities, Patan Hospital (☎01/522266) is reasonably modern but again fairly far from Kathmandu, while Bir Hospital (☎01/221119) is central but very Third World. If you're in really bad shape, you'll be sent to Bangkok anyway.

Language courses The ITC School (☎01/414490, ✉itc@mail.com.np), located up a lane north of the Tin Dewal on Tridevi Marg, is professional and has enough teachers to offer scheduling flexibility. They offer short-term one-on-one sessions (about Rs200 per hour), longer intensive courses, and homestays with Nepali families. Language schools come and go in Thamel; the Kathmandu Institute of Nepali Language, on Jyatha Thamel (☎01/220295), has been around for a while. The Peace Corps (☎01/410019) might be able to suggest other language teachers. For long-term study opportunities, see "Staying on" in Basics.

Newspapers and magazines Tourist bookshops stock a wide variety of international newspapers and magazines, including the Asian editions of the *International Herald Tribune*, *USA Today*, *Time*, *Newsweek* and the like, and many glossy magazines imported from Europe and North America. The local English-language dailies sell out early at the main bookstores, supermarkets and at pavement vendors on New Rd.

Police If you're the victim of a crime, first contact the Tourist Police (☎01/247041), in back of the Tourist Service Center in Bhrikuti Mandap, which is supposed to have an English-speaking officer on duty from 11am to 5pm. They also staff little booths in the centre of Thamel, in Durbar Square and in other tourist areas. Outside regular hours, have a Nepali-speaker call ☎01/100. You'll need to report thefts to the district police headquarters, which in Kathmandu is on the west side of Durbar Square and in Patan at Jawalakhel Chowk. Ask for the Interpol section. The national police HQ and Interpol office is in Naksal.

Post and shipping The Poste Restante section at Kathmandu's GPO (General Post Office) is open Mon–Fri 9.30am–4pm. Letters are filed alphabetically in self-serve pigeonholes; it's always a good idea to check under both your first and last initial. You can buy stamps and aerogrammes and have outgoing mail franked at the GPO (windows open Mon–Fri 9.30am–6pm), but it's more convenient to use one of the book- or postcard shops in the tourist areas, which also sell stamps (for a small surcharge) and take mail for franking. Hotels and many guesthouses will also do this. Shipping agents can take the headache out of sending parcels home. A few that can be recommended are Atlas de Cargo, Hattisar ☎01/419416; Ritual Freight, Thamel ☎01/220842; Sharmasons Movers, Kantipath ☎01/249565; and Speedway Cargo, Thamel North ☎01/410595. Air-freight services include DHL International, Kamaladi ☎01/222358; United Parcel Service, Exhibition Road ☎01/241100; and Federal Express,

Ramshah Path ☎01/418008; all of these have agents in Thamel. Sending parcels through the Foreign Post Section (Mon–Fri 9.15am–2pm), around the corner from the GPO on Kantipath, is cheaper but completely exasperating – set aside the whole morning.

Radio and TV Numerous FM radio stations operate in the Kathmandu Valley, including the bilingual Namaste Kathmandu/Hits 100, Kantipur 96.1, Hits FM 92.1 and Sacred Valley Radio 94.3. Radio Nepal, heard on several medium-wave frequencies, reads English-language news bulletins at 8am and 8pm. Cable TV services carry CNN, BBC World Service, and English-language movie and sports channels, as well as Nepal TV and plenty of Indian programming. Programme schedules are given in the daily papers.

Telephones Small, red payphones can be found inside select businesses and public buildings – they only work for local calls and only take Rs2 coins, which are very hard to come by. Many local shops will let you use their phone for about Rs5 per call. For trunk (long-distance) and international calls, there are countless telecommunication centres and ISD/STD/IDD places (see p.51) in the tourist zones. They're generally open daily 8am–11pm, and many accept credit cards. You'll pay about Rs5–50 per minute for international calls by internet (depending on country, internet service used, etc); Rs165–180 per minute for conventional international calls; and Rs5–10 per minute collect calls and callbacks.

Tours Grayline (☎01/413188) does half-day tours to various sites around the Kathmandu Valley for about Rs300.

Travel agents Everest Travel Service, Kantipath ☎01/249216, ✉air@ets.com.np; Natraj Tours and Travels, in the forecourt of the *Kathmandu Guest House* ☎01/222014, ✉natraj@ccsl.com.np; President Travel and Tours, Durbar Marg ☎01/220245, ✉preintl@mos.com.np; Wayfarers, J.P. School Road ☎01/264851, 🖰www.wayfarers .com.np.

Visa extensions Apply at the Department of Immigration, in the Tourist Service Center (mid-Feb to mid-Nov Mon–Fri 9am–3pm; mid-Nov to mid-Feb same days 9am–2pm). You should be able to collect your passport later the same day. See p.20 for general information on visa extensions. Instant passport-sized photos are available nearby for Rs150.

Volunteer opportunities Gift for Aid Nepal, in Jyatha Thamel opposite *Kilroy's* (☎01/259122, ✉gift@infoclub.com.np; Mon–Fri & Sun 10am–5pm), acts as a referral agency to match up willing volunteers with non-governmental organizations in Nepal. Volunteers are needed to help with computing, teaching, editing and other tasks, for a few days or longer. Inside Nepal Friendship Organization (INFO), in Paknajol (☎01/413408, ✉infonp@ntc.net.np) is similar, but prefers a minimum three-month commitment (the first month of which is language training).

Moving on

Life in Kathmandu is easy – too easy. Get out before you start gathering moss; later, you'll wonder why you stayed so long. What follows is a full rundown on buying tickets, arranging transport and trips, and getting visas. If you can't find what you're looking for here, try the "Listings" above.

Travel within Nepal

For better or worse, most people make Kathmandu their base for **travels within Nepal**. The country is so centralized, with Kathmandu its transport hub, that a grand tour easily becomes a series of trips out from the capital and back again. This, admittedly, has its advantages: you can make good use of the tourist bus services and choose from the most reputable trekking, rafting and cycle-touring companies. It's also easy to leave luggage with your guesthouse in Kathmandu, allowing you to travel lightly around the country.

For advice on renting a private vehicle, see p.98.

Buses

Various companies operate regular **tourist buses** or minibuses to Pokhara, Nagarkot, Dhulikhel, Sauraha (for Chitwan National Park) and Thakurdwara (for Bardia National Park). The Pokhara and Chitwan services are worth considering if your destination lies anywhere along the routes to those places. Even though tickets cost roughly double the public bus fare, they're still cheap (Rs200–600 to Pokhara, Rs200–400 to Chitwan, around Rs150 to Nagarkot). Some buses are operated by guesthouses, so price and availability may depend on whether you're willing to commit to staying in that establishment. Minibuses cost more because they're a bit faster and more comfortable. Tickets for tourist services are available through any agent (although not every agent will be able to sell tickets for every bus). Most buses depart from Kantipath near Tridevi Marg, usually in the early morning.

Most privately operated **express and night buses** depart from the Naya (New) Bus Park in Gongabu, 3km north of Thamel on the Ring Road. Those serving destinations along the Arniko Highway (such as Dhulikhel, Barhabise, Tatopani and Jiri) leave from the City Bus Park (also known as Purano "Old" Bus Park) on the east side of the Tudikhel. You'd have to be a real do-it-yourselfer to go to the bus park to buy your own ticket – book through an agent, and consider his commission as money well spent. See the box opposite for approximate frequencies and journey times.

Local buses (including buses to all destinations in the Kathmandu Valley) originate at the City Bus Park. Get on there to have any hope of getting a seat. See the box on p.97 for routes.

Internal flights

Internal flight schedules are seasonal and fairly volatile, so you're better off making bookings through one of the travel agents listed on p.175. Local contact information for airlines is given on p.173. The box on p.178 gives details

Bus services from Kathmandu

See also "Useful local transit routes" box, p.98.

Tourist buses

	Frequency (per day)	Time (minimum)
Dhulikhel	0–1*	2hr
Nagarkot	0–2*	2hr
Pokhara	2–10*	7–8hr
Sauraha/Chitwan	0–3*	6hr

*Frequencies vary from low to high season.

Express buses

	Day service		Night service	
	Daily frequency	Time	Daily frequency	Time
Barhabise	10	7hr	–	–
Besisahar	5	8hr	–	–
Bhairawa	15	8hr	10	8hr
Biratnagar	1	10hr	8	14hr
Birganj	8	8hr	12	12hr
Butwal	8	8hr	14	12hr
Dhangadhi	–	–	3	16hr
Dhankuta	–	–	1	17hr
Dharan	1	14hr	10	15hr
Dhunche	3	8hr	–	–
Dipayal	–	–	1	24hr
Gorkha	5	6hr	–	–
Hetauda (via Daman)	2	8hr	–	–
Hetauda (via Narayangadh)	6	7hr	–	–
Hile	–	–	1	18hr
Ilam	–	–	2	20hr
Janakpur	4	11hr	18	11hr
Jiri	5	10hr	–	–
Kakarbhitta	3	14hr	13	15hr
Lumbini	1	10hr	1	12hr
Mahendra Nagar	1	13hr	4	17hr
Meghauli	2	7hr	–	–
Narayangadh	12	5hr	–	–
Nepalganj	3	12hr	4	15hr
Pokhara	12	8hr	11	8hr
Tadi Bazaar (Chitwan)	5	6hr	–	–
Tansen (Palpa)	1	10hr	1	14hr
Tatopani	5	8hr	–	–
Taulihawa	1	12hr	1	14hr
Trisuli	12	4hr	–	–

on services to the airstrips that can be reached directly from Kathmandu (others require plane changes and layovers, often overnight). The private-sector airlines all concentrate on a few lucrative routes and the mountain flight; for more out-of-the-way destinations, your only choice will be Royal Nepal, the unreliable and nearly defunct government-owned carrier.

Internal flights from Kathmandu

The following is a list of the most common direct flights from Kathmandu; indirect flights to Dunai, Jumla and Simikot (via Nepalganj), Taplejung (via Biratnagar) and Jomosom (via Pokhara) are also available. For a map showing all domestic routes, see p.37. Fares will vary slightly by airline. Note that services are subject to cancellation and change.

	Frequency	Time	One-way fare (US$)
Bhadrapur	5 daily	50min	99
Bhairawa	6–8 daily	40min	72
Bharatpur	4–5 daily	25min	55
Biratnagar	10–12 daily	40min	77
Dhangadhi	1 weekly	1hr 45min	149
Janakpur	1 daily	30min	55
Lamidanda	4 daily	40min	66
Lukla	4–14 daily	40min	83
Meghauli	1 daily	30min	72
Mountain flight	up to 20 daily	1hr	99
Nepalganj	4–9 daily	1hr	99
Phaplu	4 daily	30min	77
Pokhara	18–28 daily	30min	61
Simara	5–10 daily	20min	50
Tumlingtar	2 daily	45min	65

Note that there's an airport departure tax of Rs165 for domestic flights out of Tribhuwan Airport.

Leaving Nepal

Overland **connections from Nepal** to India and Tibet are well developed, not to say comfortable. Kathmandu is the usual setting-off point, since it's the only place in Nepal to get Indian visas and to join Tibet tours. For other countries you'll almost certainly fly: see p.175 and p.174 for details of recommended travel agents and international airline offices. It's worth shopping around, as even supposedly standard airfares may vary from one agent to the next.

By air

If you're flying out of Nepal, don't forget to **reconfirm** your flight at least 72 hours prior to departure or you may lose your seat. You can usually do it by phone (airline contacts are given on p.174), but you may have trouble getting through, or staff may tell you to do it in person at their office. A travel agent will reconfirm for you for about Rs100. While you're at it, find out the baggage allowance on your flight: on routes over the Pacific it's usually two bags of up to 70lbs each, but on flights to Europe it's only 20kg total.

When checking in at Tribhuwan Airport (☎01/471933), first join the queue to pay your **passenger service charge** (departure tax) – it's an astronomical Rs1100 (Rs900 if you're flying within South Asia). The PSC counter is also a **bank**, so you can pay the charge in any currency, and you can change back any leftover rupees at the same time. Next comes **security** and **check-in**, where personnel have been known to hit travellers with trumped-up overweight charges. After that, head upstairs and pass through **immigration**, after which there's a modest **duty-free** shop and an overpriced **snack bar**.

Overland to India

If you're travelling on to **India**, you can arrange your transport in one of two ways: buy a bus ticket to the border and then make your own onward arrangements from there; or book a package deal from a ticket agent that takes you all the way to your first Indian destination.

The first way is cheaper, more reliable and usually no more difficult. Seven **border crossings** between Nepal and India are open to foreigners. The most popular are Sonauli and Birganj, which are served by day-buses from Kathmandu. Other border crossings can be reached by night buses, but unless you're in a big hurry you'll probably want to stop at other places en route. See the relevant sections in Chapters Five and Six for details on the various border crossings.

The second way has been known to cause a lot of heartache, especially where reserved train tickets are involved. Given that a typical **bus–train package** to India involves three different tickets and as many as six companies or agents, the chances of something going wrong are high. Ticket sellers in Kathmandu know that few travellers will come back to complain.

If you need the assurance of an advance booking, be sure to make arrangements at least a week ahead of time to allow for delays and mistakes (accidental or otherwise), and if the agent tells you your ticket is being held at the border, demand your money back. Be particularly careful when booking first-class sleepers, as there's a racket in replacing them with second-class sleepers or first-class seats. Never surrender your receipt to anyone – without it, you've got no proof of what you paid for.

Bus-only deals to Darjeeling, Delhi and a few other Indian cities are less chancey. On the other hand, there's less reason to book an Indian bus so far in advance. At least one company runs a regular **direct bus** to Delhi; other outfits lay on occasional direct services to Goa and such places, but they're overpriced and must be horrendously long journeys. Agents will take care of bookings.

Just a handful of **companies** package tickets to India from Nepal, and all other agents deal through them. The most reliable appear to be Pagoda Travels and Tours, Basantapur Square (℡01/252266), and Shikhar Nepal Tours and Travels, J.P. School Road (℡01/241669).

The Indian visa two-step

Applying for an Indian **tourist visa** in Kathmandu has to be one of the world's most convoluted processes – allow *one week* to work your way through it.

Apply in person at the **Indian Embassy** (℡01/410900), which is northeast of Thamel, off Lazimpath – take a left at *Hotel Ambassador*. Application hours are 9.30am to noon, Monday to Friday (with lots of holidays). Bring a passport-sized photo and a black pen. Read the signboard instructions before you do anything else. The time-consuming part is obtaining "clearance" from your home country, which is needed before your visa application can even be considered. Just getting your hands on a clearance form, filling it in and paying the fee will kill the better part of a morning. After waiting a week for the clearance, you must then come back to pay for the visa, which you'll finally be able to collect later that day. A six-month tourist visa costs Rs3050 for most nationalities (the fee may vary depending on what your country charges Indians for visas), plus Rs300 for the clearance telex or fax.

A fifteen-day **transit visa** can be obtained on the same day. Note, however, that a transit visa is not extendable, and its validity starts on the date of issue (not the date that you enter India). The cost is Rs800.

Travelling to Tibet

China's official policy is that foreigners wanting to enter **Tibet** from Nepal must join a **tour**. The Chinese embassy in Kathmandu issues only group visas through official tour agents, and doesn't deal with individuals. Some daring travellers have reported getting into Tibet independently on a Chinese visa issued in another country, but others have been turned back at the border or the airport check-in counter, and enforcement of the tour-only policy seems to be getting stricter over time. Check locally to see if the position has changed.

Tour prices start at $250, which gets you an English-speaking guide, basic transportation to Lhasa and four-nights' dorm accommodation along the way: you buy your own food, and once you reach Lhasa you're on your own. (This entails "splitting" the group visa, a not-quite-legal operation that some operators aren't willing to do.) If you want all your lodging taken care of and a ride both ways by minibus or Land Cruiser, the cost will be $600–1000, depending on calibre of accommodation, for a week's bed-and-breakfast tour. Flying adds another $100 or so each way. Including side trips to Rongbuk (base camp for Everest on the Tibet side) or other sights in central Tibet will bump up the cost further. More adventurous itineraries, such as trekking around holy Mount Kailash or cycling from Lhasa to Nepal, take at least two weeks and start at around $1500. These are fixed-departure prices – small custom groups cost more. The Chinese visa (about $45, depending on your nationality) may or may not be included in the price. Visa processing normally takes a week unless you pay a rush fee. If you don't have a multiple-entry visa for Nepal, you'll get hit with an additional $50 charge for a re-entry stamp.

The Tibet high **season** is from May to September; monsoon landslides make the overland route less predictable in the latter part of that period, but there's almost always a way to get through. Tours aren't run between the middle of December and early March – the roads are usually okay, but the operators don't want to risk groups getting stranded in a snowstorm for days without proper facilities. China Southwest Airlines also suspends its three-times-a-week flights to Lhasa between late November and early March.

Travelling by road between Kathmandu and Lhasa is an exciting but gruelling four- or five-day trip, so most people elect to fly at least one way. Flying to Lhasa and overlanding back is preferable because it allows you to acclimatize to Lhasa's 3700m elevation before going over the 5000m passes. Another reason some tour operators discourage clients from flying back from Lhasa is that flights are heavily overbooked between July and November, so that even with a confirmed reservation you can't really be sure of flying on a particular day. See p.260 for advice on crossing the border.

Nepali travel agencies subcontract most arrangements in Tibet to the state-run China International Travel Service, and when things go wrong many will simply pass the buck. The following agencies have reasonably good reputations to uphold. Some trekking companies and mountain-bike tour operators (see p.168 and 169) also run trips in Tibet.

Arniko Travel Baluwatar ☏ 01/439906, ⊛ www.arnikotravel.com.
Explore Nepal Richa Tours and Travels J.P. School Rd ☏ 01/423064, ⊛ www.explorenepalricha .com.
Green Hill Tours Thamel Northwest, just north of the *Kathmandu Guest House* ☏ 01/414803, ⊛ www.greenhilltours.com.
Shiva Travels Chhetrapati ☏ 01/260356, ⓔ travel @mail.com.np.
Tibet Travels and Tours Thamel South ☏ 01/249140, ⊛ www.tibettravels.com.

Visas for other Asian countries

If you're moving on to other parts of Asia, the following embassies and consulates in Kathmandu issue **visas**. Call ahead to find out application times and procedures, as they change from time to time.

Bangladesh Maharajganj, on the Ring Road ☎01/372843.

India Lainchaur ☎01/410900. See "The Indian visa two-step", p.179.

Myanmar (Burma) Chakupat, Patan ☎01/521788.

Pakistan Tangal ☎01/374024.

Thailand Bansbari, north of the Ring Road on the way to Budhanilkantha ☎01/371410.

The Kathmandu Valley

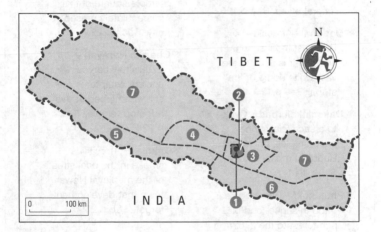

CHAPTER 2   # Highlights

✳ **Flying into the Valley** –
As the plane tops the
last hill ridge, the elevat-
ed bowl of the lush
Valley opens out below.
See p.185

✳ **Pashupatinath** – The
most sacred of Nepal's
Hindu temple complexes
is veiled by the smoke of
funeral pyres. See p.190

✳ **Boudha** – At dusk,
Buddhist monks, nuns
and pilgrims flock to the
vast white dome of the
stupa. See p.196

✳ **Dakshinkali road** – Cycle
to a sacrificial shrine,
past temples, pools and
Buddhist monasteries.
See p.211

✳ **Phulchoki** – Hike or bike
through shrine- and bird-
rich forest to the 2762m

summit of the "Place of
Flowers". See p.220

✳ **Bishanku Narayan** – This
peaceful Hindu shrine is
modestly hidden in a
still-rural fold of the
Valley. See p.220

✳ **Bhaktapur** – Taste Newari
cuisine in the stunning
temple square of this
immaculately preserved
city. See p.222

✳ **Changu Narayan** –
Exquisitely carved
ancient sculptures are
still worshipped at this
ridgetop temple. See
p.234

✳ **Thimi** – Pottery kilns
smoke in the backstreets
of the medieval Newar
town that development
forgot. See p.238

The Kathmandu Valley

Once you've experienced Kathmandu, it should come as no surprise that the **Kathmandu Valley** is not the natural paradise it once was. It's the country's economic engine, after all, supporting numerous industries and with a smoggy capital city right in the middle of it. Yet this broad, undulating, fertile basin – so unlike the steep-sided hills that ring it – still displays a unique combination of natural and man-made beauty. Only a few miles outside the capital, traditional brick villages maintain their rural ways, and the countryside shimmers in an undulating patchwork of paddy fields – brown, golden or brilliant green, depending on the season.

But above all, it's the valley's incredible wealth of art and architecture that overwhelms visitors, just as it did the early explorers: "The valley consists of as many temples as there are houses, and as many idols as there are men," gushed William Kirkpatrick, the first Englishman to reach Kathmandu, and generations of travellers since have accurately (if patronizingly) described it as a "living museum". Its geography is largely spiritual: most of its places are named after gods, and many were literally put on the map by ancient myths. The valley's one-time name, Nepal Mandala, recalls how for millennia its pilgrimage sites have together formed a kind of gigantic meditation tool. If most of this chapter is devoted to temples and holy sites – there are no forts, you'll notice – it's because religion is the best and most fascinating window on Nepali culture.

Until two hundred years ago, this protected bowl *was* Nepal (and many hill people outside the valley still refer to it as such). At that time, Kathmandu was only one of three major city-states constantly battling for dominance: Patan, just across the Bagmati River, controlled the southern part of the valley, while **Bhaktapur** ruled the east, and these historical divisions remain profoundly ingrained in valley society and live on in distinct religious practices, festivals and even dress. Physically, however, Patan has now been absorbed within the concrete jungle that is speedily filling in all the open land within the ring road and is covered in the main Kathmandu chapter.

The sheer density of sights in the valley is phenomenal. Hindu holy places abound: the great pilgrimage complex of **Pashupatinath**, the sleeping Vishnu of **Budhanilkantha**, the sacrificial pit of **Dakshinkali** and the hilltop temple of **Changu Narayan** are the most outstanding. If Buddhism is your main

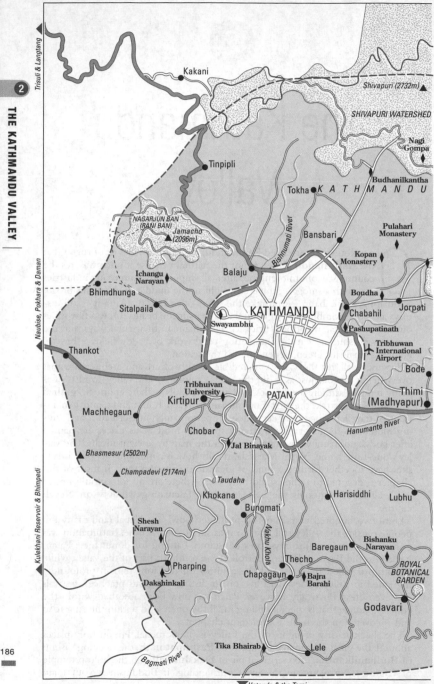

Trisuli & Langtang

Naubise, Pokhara & Daman

Kulekhani Reservoir & Bhimpedi

Shivapuri (2732m)

SHIVAPURI WATERSHED

Nagi Gompa

Kakani

Tinpipli

NAGARJUN BAN (RANI BAN)
Jamacho (2096m)

Bishnumati River

Budhanilkantha

Tokha
KATHMANDU

Pulahari Monastery

Bansbari

Kopan Monastery

Ichangu Narayan

Balaju

Boudha
Chabahil
Jorpati

Bhimdhunga

Sitalpaila

KATHMANDU

Swayambhu

Pashupatinath

Thankot

Tribhuvan International Airport

Bode

PATAN

Thimi (Madhyapur)

Tribhuvian University

Kirtipur

Machhegaun

Chobar

Hanumante River

Jal Binayak

Bhasmesur (2502m)

Champadevi (2174m)

Taudaha

Khokana

Bungmati

Harisiddhi

Lubhu

Shesh Narayan

Nakhu Khola

Baregaun

Bishanku Narayan

ROYAL BOTANICAL GARDEN

Pharping

Thecho

Dakshinkali

Chapagaun
Bajra Barahi

Godavari

Tika Bhairab

Lele

Bagmati River

Hetauda & the Tarai

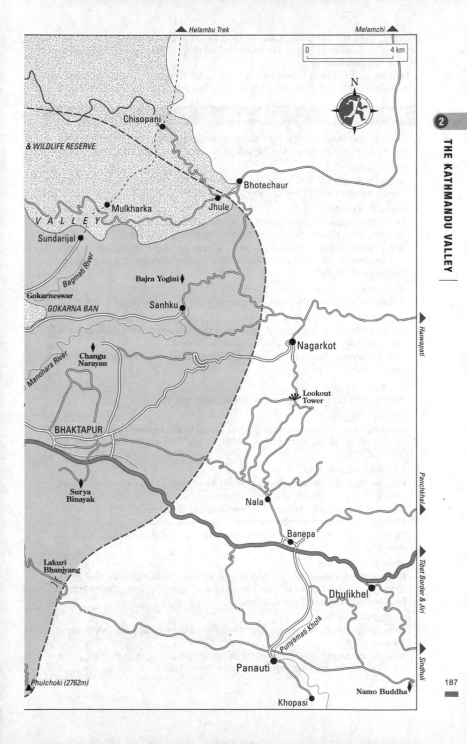

interest, head for the great stupa of **Boudha**, the centre of Tibetan Buddhist worship and study in Nepal. For medieval scenes, try **Kirtipur**, **Bungmati** or, best of all, **Bhaktapur**.

Hiking and **cycling** is best in the rural outer fringes of the valley floor and along the valley rim. Trails lead beyond the botanical gardens at **Godavari** to

Kathmandu Valley's major festivals

Some of the festivals listed in the Kathmandu chapter are also celebrated in the valley. Again, most are reckoned by the lunar calendar, so check locally for exact dates.

Magh (Jan–Feb)
Magh Sankranti The first day of Magh (Jan 14 or 15), marked by ritual bathing at Patan's Sankhamul Ghat and at Sankhu.

Faagun (Feb–March)
Losar Tibetan New Year, the new moon of February, celebrated at Boudha with processions, horn-blowing and *tsampa*-throwing on the big third day.

Shiva Raatri On the full moon of Faagun, the Pashupatinath *mela* (fair) attracts tens of thousands of pilgrims and holy men, while children everywhere collect money for bonfires on "Shiva's Night".

Chaitra (March–April)
Balaju Jaatra Ritual bathing at the Balaju Water Garden on the day of the full moon.

Baisaakh (April–May)
Bisket Bhaktapur's celebration of Nepali New Year (April 13 or 14) – see box, p.229. Thimi and Bode have their own idiosyncratic festivities.

Buddha Jayanti The anniversary of the Buddha's birth, enlightenment and death, celebrated at Boudha.

Asaar (June–July)
Dalai Lama's Birthday Observed informally at Boudha (July 6).

Saaun (July–Aug)
Janai Purnima The annual changing of the sacred thread worn by high-caste Hindu men, involving bathing and splashing at Patan's Kumbeshwar Mahadev on the day of the full moon.

Bhadau (Aug–Sept)
Krishna Jayanti Krishna's birthday, marked by an all-night vigil at Patan's Krishna Mandir on the seventh day after the full moon.

Gokarna Aunsi Nepali "Father's Day", observed at Gokarneswar with bathing and offerings on the day of the new moon.

Tij A day of ritual bathing for women on the third day after the new moon, mainly at Pashupatinath.

Khattik (Oct–Nov)
Haribondhini Ekadashi Bathing and *puja* on the eleventh day after the new moon. The main action takes place at the Vishnu sites of Budhanilkantha, Sesh Narayan, Bishanku Narayan and Changu Narayan.

Mangsir (Nov–Dec)
Indrayani Jaatra Deities are paraded through Kirtipur on palanquins on the day of the new moon.

Bala Chaturdashi All-night vigil at Pashupatinath on the night of the new moon, involving candles and ritual seed-offerings to dead relatives.

the shrine of **Bishanku Narayan,** and up through rich forests to **Phulchoki,** the highest point on the valley rim; cyclists can even continue south to **Tika Bhairab** and all the way to Hetauda, in the Tarai. For more woodland solitude and views, hike up **Shivapuri,** Nagarjun Ban's **Jamacho,** or any high point on the valley rim.

All of the places described in this chapter are within day-tripping range of Kathmandu, although in several cases you're urged to stay overnight. Some can be treated as stops along the longer, multiday routes described in the next chapter.

Depending on where you're going, certain ways of getting around the valley are definitely better than others – making the wrong choice can kill an otherwise fun outing. A **taxi** is probably the way to go if you're aiming for a specific destination, especially if the journey there is along a main road. Negotiate for a return trip with ample waiting time if your destination isn't one of the main tourist sites. **Buses** and fixed-route **tempos** are obviously cheaper and bring you into (very) close contact with real Nepal, but they're slow and uncomfortable. In the sections that follow, bus routes are mentioned where they exist (fares are usually just a few rupees) – see also the table of Kathmandu-originating bus services on p.97. A **bike** or **motorcycle** is best if you're touring around the rural parts of the valley and you want maximum flexibility to stop and go. However, getting out of Kathmandu is not part of the fun, so if you're cycling, consider loading the bike in a taxi at least to get beyond the Ring Road.

The Kathmandu city/valley **maps** sold in tourist areas will probably suffice for general sightseeing. For serious walking or biking, try to get your hands on the HMG/FINNIDA 1:25,000 sheets for the valley – Maps of Nepal, on Airport Road west of the *Everest Hotel*, is the main sales agent, but some Thamel bookshops also have them. Failing that, there are the excellent but dated Schneider map of the valley or other newer but rather inaccurate versions, such as the one published by Himalayan Map House.

The northern valley

Just beyond the Ring Road beat the twin hearts of Nepalese religion: the Shiva temple and sombre cremation ghats at **Pashupatinath,** the sacred centre of Nepalese Hinduism; and the vast, white stupa at **Boudha,** the hub of Tibetan Buddhism's small renaissance. You could visit both in a single day, but both have facilities for staying overnight, or longer, if the glitzy lights of Kathmandu suddenly seem to lose their glamour.

The roads snaking out towards the northern limits of the valley are increasingly blighted by traffic and rampant house construction. Step a few metres away from the tarmac, however, and you're in an older, slower world. The "Sleeping Vishnu" statues at **Budhanilkantha** and **Balaju,** and the Bajra Yogini temple at **Sankhu** provide moving reminders of the sacred geography that lies behind the concrete.

Pashupatinath and around

Nepal's holiest Hindu pilgrimage site, **PASHUPATINATH** (pronounced Posh-*potty*-not), is an amazing enclave of temples, cremation ghats, ritual bathers and half-naked sadhus. Often likened to India's Varanasi, many Nepalese claim that their site, while much smaller, is at least as holy, straddling as it does not only an ancient trading route from Tibet to India, but also a *tirtha*, or sacred crossroads. The sacred complex lies just beyond the Ring Road, 4km east of Kathmandu – incongruously close to the modern airport, but fortunately sheltered from it in a wooded ravine. For all Pashupatinath's myriad impressions of pilgrims, temples, rituals and myths, it is the sombre sight of public cremation that, for many, proves the most lasting image. Perhaps more than anywhere else in Nepal, this is a place to modestly cover legs and arms – women especially. It's also important to respect the privacy of bathers, worshippers and the grieving families at cremation pyres, particularly if taking photographs in the area.

Pashupatinath is a relatively short **taxi** ride from central Kathmandu (about Rs80). It's not a terrible **cycle**, either: from Thamel, follow Tridevi Marg east past the Royal Palace, take the first right after Durbar Marg, then a left on the

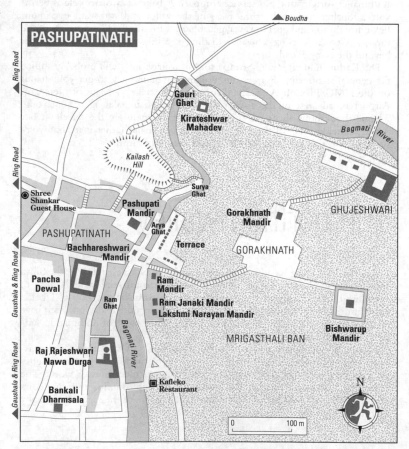

Sadhus

Sadhus, those dreadlocked holy men usually seen lurking around Hindu temples, are essentially an Indian phenomenon. However, Nepal, being the setting for many of the amorous and ascetic exploits of sadhus' favourite deity, Shiva, is a favourite stomping ground for them. Sadhus are especially common at Pashupatinath, which is rated as one of the subcontinent's four most important Shaiva pilgrimage sites. During the festival of Shiva Raatri, Pashupatinath hosts a full-scale sadhu convention, with the government laying on free firewood for the festival.

Shaiva sadhus follow Shiva in one of his best-loved and most enigmatic guises – the wild, dishevelled **yogin**, the master of yoga, who sits motionless atop a Himalayan peak for aeons at a time and whose hair is the source of the mighty Ganga (Ganges) River. Traditionally, sadhus live solitary lives, always on the move, subsisting on alms and owning nothing but what they carry. They bear Shiva's emblems: the *trisul* (trident), *damaru* (two-sided drum), a necklace of furrowed *rudraksha* seeds, and perhaps a conch shell for blowing haunting calls across the cosmic ocean. Some smear themselves with ashes, symbolizing Shiva's role as the destroyer, who reduces all things to ash so that creation can begin anew. The trident-shaped *tika* of Shiva is often painted on their foreheads, although they may employ scores of other *tika* patterns, each with its own cult affiliation and symbolism.

Sadhus have a strange role model in Shiva, who is both a mountaintop ascetic and the philandering god of the phallus. Some, such as the members of the Gorakhnath cult (which has a strong presence at Pashupatinath), follow the tantric **"left-hand" path**, a reference to the hand used for unclean tasks. Beyond the pale of orthodox Hindu practice, they employ esoteric and sometimes deliberately deviant practices to free themselves of sensual passions and transcend the illusory physical world. Occasionally sadhus may be seen here tying heavy stones to their penises in an effort to destroy the erectile tissues; of one famous sadhu it was said that he had so completely marshalled his sexual energies that he bled semen. **Aghoris**, the most extreme of the left-hand practitioners, subject themselves to horrific disciplines to overcome the fear of death: cremation grounds like Pashupatinath are their temples. Some also make a practice of eating every form of disgusting thing – including, it's said, human flesh – to experience the undifferentiated oneness of true reality.

Like Shiva, sadhus also make liberal use of **intoxicants** as a path to spiritual insight. It was Shiva, in fact, who supposedly discovered the transcendental powers of *ganja* (cannabis), which grows wild throughout hill Nepal. Sadhus usually consume the weed in the form of *bhang* (a liquid preparation) or *charas* (hashish, smoked in a vertical clay pipe known as a chilam). With each toke, the holy man intones *"Bam Shankar"*: "I am Shiva".

first main road (Kamal Pokhari), and follow that road over the Dhobi Khola and all the way to Gaushala, a busy, modern intersection on the Ring Road. The lane angling downhill from the northeast corner of Gaushala leads to a small built-up area (also known as Pashupatinath) at the western side of the temple complex. You'll probably have to pay a few rupees to have your bike "watched". Tempos and microbuses to Pashupatinath are both numbered #2 (which looks much the same in Devanagari as Roman numerals). Safaa ("clean") **tempos** originate next to RNAC on Kantipath; blue or white **microbuses** leave from Shahid Gate and Ratna Park. All will drop you at Chabahil, by the main gate to Pashupatinath, before continuing on to Boudha.

The Pashupatinath complex

The **temples** of Pashupatinath straddle the Bagmati River, which despite its filth is held by conservative Hindus to be the holiest in the Kathmandu Valley

– this specific stretch the most sacred of all. To die and be cremated here is to be released from the cycle of rebirths. Wives used to commit *sati* on their husbands' funeral pyres here, and although the practice was outlawed early in the twentieth century, it's still widely believed that husbands and wives who bathe here together will be remarried in the next life. **Bathing** is considered especially meritorious on full-moon days, on Magh Sankranti (usually Jan 14) and Bala Chaturdashi (late Nov or early Dec) and, for women, during the festival of Tij (late Aug or early Sept). The entire complex overflows with pilgrims from all over the subcontinent during the **festival** of Shiva Raatri (held on the full moon of Feb–March). Devout locals also come for special services on full moon days and on the eleventh lunar day (*ekadashi*) after each full and new moon.

In all probablility, Pashupatinath was once the site of a pre-Hindu animistic cult, its god being progressively incorporated into Hindu culture under the name of Shiva, a process that continues today among many of the ethnic groups in the hills. Traces of this prehistory can be seen in the form that Shiva takes – one of his more benign – as **Pashupati, Lord of the Animals**. The king of Nepal ends all his public addresses in this deity's name, and praises are sung to him on Radio Nepal at the start of each broadcasting day. Several tales are told of how Shiva came by this title. Nepali schoolchildren are taught that Shiva, to escape his heavenly obligations, assumed the guise of a one-horned stag and fled to the forest here. The other gods pursued him and, laying hold of him, broke off his horn, which was transformed into the powerful Pashupati *linga*. The *linga* was later lost, only to be rediscovered at its present site by a cow who magically began sprinkling the spot with her milk.

The Pashupati Mandir

Approaching from the west, a lane leads past trinket stalls and sweet shops to the main gate of the **Pashupati Mandir** – the holy of holies for Nepali Shaivas, followers of Shiva. As in many temples in Nepal, admission is for Hindus only (which in practice means anyone who looks Nepali or South Asian, but not Tibetan). From the outside, though, you can glimpse the two symbols that are found in front of almost every Shiva temple, their gargantuan proportions here a measure of the temple's sanctity: a two-storey-high *trisul* (trident), and the enormous golden backside of Nandi, Shiva's faithful bull, the latter yet another reminder of the god's procreative power.

Hidden inside, the famous **Pashupati linga** displays four carved faces of Shiva, plus a fifth, invisible one on the top (Buddhists claim one of the faces is that of the Buddha). The *linga* is a fourteenth-century replacement of the original one, which was damaged by Muslim crusaders. Hindus associate this *linga* with yet another Shiva myth, in which the god transformed his phallus into an infinite pillar of light and challenged Brahma and Vishnu – the other members of the Hindu trinity – to find the ends of it. Brahma flew heavenward, while Vishnu plumbed the depths of hell. Both were forced to abandon the search, but Brahma falsely boasted of success, only to be caught out by Shiva. Shaivas say that's why Brahma is seldom worshipped, Vishnu gets his fair share, and Shiva is revered above all.

The gold-clad pagoda dates from the late seventeenth century, but inscriptions indicate that a temple has stood here since at least the fifth century, and some historians suspect it goes back to the third century BC, when the ancient village of Deopatan is said to have been founded just west of here. The temple apparently emerged as a hotbed of tantric practices in the eleventh century and remained so for four hundred years, until King Yaksha Malla reined things in by importing conventional Brahman **priests** from South India, although the *bhandaris* (temple assistants) are always Newars born in the immediate area. This arrangement continues to this day, although there have been calls to end it since a scandal in which the *mul bhatta* (high priest) was forced to resign in 1998 amid charges that he had siphoned off millions of rupees in temple donations to build a resort hotel in his native Karnataka.

Wearing the ceremonial orange robes of the Pashupata sect, the priests array the *linga* in brocade silk and bathe it with curd, ghee, honey, sugar and milk. Hindu pilgrims are expected to distribute offerings to the priests and then make a circuit of the temple and the 365 *shivalinga* and other secondary shrines scattered about the precinct. Most also distribute alms to beggars lined along some of the nearby lanes. If you choose to give, arm yourself with a sufficient stockpile of small change (*saano paisa*), available from nearby vendors.

Along the west bank

Hindus exit the temple via a back way leading down to the west bank of the Bagmati, while tourists approach the river just to the south, where a Rs75 charge is levied at the gate by the twin footbridges. **Arya Ghat**, on the left, is a cremation area reserved for members of the higher "twice-born" castes. The platform furthest upstream (so placed for obvious reasons) is reserved for the royal family; next down, just above the bridge, is the ghat for "VVIPs" – prominent politicians, minor royals and, these days, anyone else who can afford it. After the royal massacre in June 2001 (see p.496), the army had to build a temporary ghat between the two to accommodate the body of the queen, as her husband, King Birendra, and her younger son, Nirajan, already occupied the platforms on either side. Two days later, kept indoors by an emergency curfew, a stunned Kathmandu watched the cremation of Crown Prince Dipendra, broadcast live from this spot.

Housed in a small stone reliquary beside the royal ghat is a famed seventh-century statue of **Virupaksha**, the "Three-Eyed Shiva", whose Mongoloid features are said to betray the figure's pre-Hindu origins. The image is also associated with Kalki, the tenth and final incarnation of Vishnu, a sort of messiah figure who will bring the present Kali Yuga (Age of Kali) to a close and usher in a new, virtuous cycle of history. The statue is half-submerged in the Bagmati: some claim that the idol is gradually sinking, and its final disappearance will mark the end of the age; others say that Virupaksha will be released from the waters when he has earned enough merit from visiting pilgrims.

Many of the buildings around the main temple, including the tall, whitewashed ones overlooking the river, are *dharmsala* (pilgrims' rest houses), set aside here for devout Hindus approaching death. In their final hour, the dying will be laid out on a sloped stone slab with their feet in the Bagmati and given a last drink of the holy river water, which probably finishes them off.

The small pagoda between the bridges is the **Bachhaleshwari Mandir**, dedicated to Shiva's consort Parbati in one of her mother-goddess roles. Next to it stands a newish ten-foot terracotta frieze of Narayan (alias Vishnu) and other sculptures of Ganesh and Gauri (Parbati). Cremations are held almost continuously at the next embankment downstream, **Ram Ghat**, which is used by all castes. The bank is lined by another string of metal-roofed *dharmsala*, which you can explore in a limited way. A small eleventh-century (some say fifth-century) **Buddha statue**, looking rather out of place in this Hindu Lourdes, sticks out of the embankment in front of the next-to-last building. Just beyond, a neglected bumper-sized *linga* ensconced in a round brick battlement is believed to date from the fifth century. The southernmost building shelters two temples in its courtyard, the oval **Raj Rajeshwari** and the gilded pagoda of **Nawa Durga**.

Behind the *dharmsala* broods the gothic bulk of **Pancha Dewal**, whose five Mughal-style cupolas are visible from high up on the opposite bank. This now serves as an old people's home, one wing of which is operated by **Mother Teresa's Missionaries of Charity** (the government runs the rest), and though emphatically not a tourist site, it is an excellent place to experience a different side of Nepal as a volunteer. The sisters need help each morning changing and cleaning sheets, helping residents wash, clipping nails, scrubbing pots and so on – humble work, but that's the whole idea of it. Arrive in the morning or evening if you're interested: the entrance to the compound is on the north side of Pancha Dewal; look for the sisters (who speak English) in their trademark white saris with blue trim.

The east bank

You can cross the river to the east bank just downstream of the *dharmsala*. As you head upstream, the walled-off forested area on your right is a **cemetery** set aside for Nepal's few "burying" groups, which include Rais and Limbus of the eastern hills and members of one Hindu sect.

Moving northwards and uphill, you'll enter a wide, paved enclosure, which during Shiva Raatri is chock-a-block with sadhus and other spiritual exhibitionists. Of the two small temples found here, the one with a statue of Garud in front is called **Lakshmi Narayan**, in honour of Vishnu (Narayan) and his wealth-bringing wife Lakshmi. The other is the **Ram Janaki**, containing statues of Ram – Vishnu's incarnation as a mortal in the *Ramayan* epic – and his whole family, including Hanuman the monkey king, who helped rescue Ram's wife Sita from the clutches of a Sri Lankan demon. Sita is popular among Nepali Hindus, since she was born in Janakpur in the eastern Tarai (see p.388). These temples, along with the **Ram Mandir** in the next compound, are disappointingly recent and un-Nepali, however. Temples at Pashupatinath are built and rebuilt often, renovations being the standard way of winning favour with gods and mortals, and wealthy Indian patrons are among the principal contributors to the development fund.

Further upstream, the fifteen great **shivalaya** (boxy *linga* shelters) were erected in the mid-nineteenth century by the Ranas and the royal family, in honour of women who committed *sati* on the pyres opposite; photo-me sadhus stake out lucrative perches around them. Great views of the whole area are afforded from the terrace above. At its northern end is a one-faced *shivalinga* from the fifth century, its serene beauty marred by modern vandals, who have hacked off its nose.

Gorakhnath

The main stairway up the east bank heads up past troupes of light-fingered and occasionally aggressive monkeys into Mrigasthali Ban, the forest where Shiva is supposed to have cavorted as a stag, to the mellow **Gorakhnath Mandir** at the top of the hill. Visiting this compound, after the sensory overload below, is like entering a soundproofed room. The temple itself, a medium-sized *shikra* structure dedicated to the patron deity of the Shah kings, isn't that interesting; what will amaze you is the sight of scores of **shivalaya** arranged in crumbling rows in the forest, mottled by shade and shafts of sunlight. The place has the romantic, ruined feel of an overgrown cemetery, with broken statuary lying undisturbed and stone inscriptions recording long-forgotten decrees. You could easily mistake the *shivalaya* for tombs, but their iconography – the *trisul*, statues of Nandi and Shiva (always with an erection), the *linga* atop the *yoni* – proclaims them to be Shiva shrines. It would be a fine spot for a picnic if it weren't for the monkeys.

The onion dome rising above the trees to the southeast of Gorakhnath is the **Bishwarup Mandir** (entrance only to Hindus), dedicated to Vishnu in his many-limbed "universal form". Dominating the sanctum, though you won't see it, is a six-metre-tall statue of Shiva and Parbati in the state of *yab-yum* (sexual union).

Ghujeshwari and back

The **Ghujeshwari** (or Ghuyeshwari) **Mandir** sits at the bottom of the path that continues downhill from Gorakhnath. Here, too, non-Hindus can only peek from outside. The legend behind this temple is one of the all-time masterpieces of Hindu surrealism. The story goes that Shiva's first wife, Sati, offended by some insult, threw herself onto a fire (giving rise to the term *sati*, or *suttee*). Shiva retrieved her corpse and, blinded by grief, flew to and fro across the subcontinent, scattering parts of the body in 51 sacred places. Ghujeshwari is where Sati's vagina (some say her anus) fell. As a consequence, the temple here represents the female counterpart to the Pashupati *linga* and is held to be every bit as sacred, its chief focus being a *kalash* (vessel) kept in a sunken pit and containing an "odiferous liquid". Buddhists consider Ghujeshwari to be one of the valley's four mystic Bajra Yoginis – powerful tantric goddesses – and the site to be the seed from which the Swayambhu lotus grew.

Just across the river from Ghujeshwari stands a controversial **sewage treatment centre**, the construction of which was delayed after arguments between the secular authorities, who planned to clean up the effluents entering the river from settlements upstream, and the *mul bhatta* of the temple, who objected to the treated water being reintroduced above the complex on the grounds that it wasn't holy. The dispute illustrates how Nepalis' ideas about cleanliness are changing, as modern hygiene competes with traditional concepts of ritual pollution. Meanwhile, a Chinese company is tunnelling 500m under the Mrigasthali hill in order to release the treated water downstream of the complex – a compromise that will further lower the water level in the river, already almost dry in the lead up to the monsoon.

From Ghujeshwari a lane follows the river downstream past the **Kirateshwar Mahadev Mandir**, which hosts Nepali classical music concerts at 4pm on full-moon evenings, and **Gauri Ghat**, a peaceful spot where the river enters the Pashupatinath ravine and monkeys leap from branches and cliffs into the water. The road crosses the river here and circles around to the village of Pashupatinath, while a path past the river crossing takes a more direct route up and over the grassy knoll of **Kailash Hill**. From the eastern edge of Kailash, a steep staircase leads down to **Surya Ghat**, the site of several caves hewn out of the cliffs. These caves have been used for meditation for centuries, and are sometimes still occupied by latter-day yogis.

Pashupatinath practicalities

There is a single **guesthouse** in Pashupatinath, making it possible to experience this amazing area much more intimately. The *Shree Shankar Guest House* (☎01/479866; ❷), just up from the main temple on a quiet lane, couldn't be better located, though the rooms leave something to be desired. For **food**, there's a small tourist restaurant, *Kafleko*, on the east bank of the Bagmati, and various *daal bhaat* and sweet shops in Pashupatinath village and around Gaushala.

Handicrafts peddlers sell the usual range of Tibetan curios and *khukuri* knives, most of which are totally irrelevant here. If you're looking for an authentic souvenir of Pashupatinath, check out the things Nepalis buy: cheap votive icons, statuettes, *linga* replicas, conch shells, *shaligram* (fossil-bearing stones), offertory vessels, *motimala* (pearl necklaces, supposed to be good for the health of the mind) and bangles. The *rudraksha* or "tears of Shiva" necklaces, made from the seeds of the Ultrasum tree, make an interesting buy – you'll see strings of them around the necks of the sadhus.

Boudha (Boudhanath) and around

To ancient travellers along the Kathmandu–Tibet trade route, the ten-kilometre corridor from Pashupatinath to Sankhu was known as the zone of *siddhi* (supernatural powers), where guardian deities dwelt and all wishes were granted. The biggest, most auspicious landmark along this route was – and still is – the

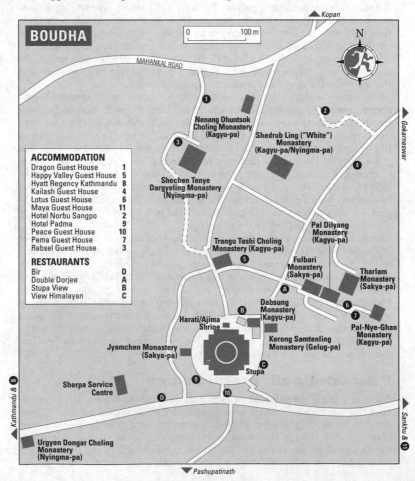

BOUDHA

0   100 m

Kopan

N

MAHANKAL ROAD

Gokarneswar

Nenang Dhuntsok
Choling Monastery
(Kagyu-pa)

Shedrub Ling ("White")
Monastery
(Kagyu-pa/Nyingma-pa)

ACCOMMODATION

Dragon Guest House	1
Happy Valley Guest House	5
Hyatt Regency Kathmandu	8
Kailash Guest House	4
Lotus Guest House	6
Maya Guest House	11
Hotel Norbu Sangpo	2
Hotel Padma	9
Peace Guest House	10
Pema Guest House	7
Rabsel Guest House	3

RESTAURANTS

Bir	D
Double Dorjee	A
Stupa View	B
View Himalayan	C

Shechen Tenye
Dargyeling Monastery
(Nyingma-pa)

Pal Dilyang
Monastery
(Kagyu-pa)

Trangu Tashi Choling
Monastery (Kagyu-pa)

Fulbari
Monastery
(Sakya-pa)

Tharlam
Monastery
(Sakya-pa)

Dabsung
Monastery
(Kagyu-pa)

Harati/Ajima
Shrine

Kerong Samtenling
Monastery (Gelug-pa)

Pal-Nye-Ghan
Monastery
(Kagyu-pa)

Jyamchen Monastery
(Sakya-pa)

Stupa

Sherpa Service
Centre

Kathmandu & 8

Urgyen Dongar Choling
Monastery
(Nyingma-pa)

Sankhu & 11

Pashupatinath

great stupa at **BOUDHA** (or **BOUDHANATH**), about 5km northeast of downtown Kathmandu.

One of the world's largest stupas, Boudha is generally acknowledged to be the most important Tibetan Buddhist monument outside Tibet. Tibetans simply call it Chorten Chempo – "Great Stupa" – and since 1959 it has become the Mecca of **Tibetan exiles** in Nepal. Tibetans now run most of the businesses along the main road and around the stupa, while the construction of monasteries has created a regular suburban sprawl to the north. Despite the tour groups and souvenir sellers, Boudha gives you a thorough dunking in Tibetan culture, past and present. Early morning and dusk are the best times to be here, when the resonant chanting of monks and the otherworldly cacophony of their music drifts from the upper rooms of the houses that ring the stupa, and pilgrims perform *kora*, shuffling and prostrating their way around the dome.

If you want an extra helping of Tibetan culture, go during the **festival** of Losar in February or March, when Boudha hosts the biggest Tibetan New Year celebration in Nepal. Other busy times are Buddha Jayanti (the Buddha's birthday), the full moon of April–May, when an image of the Buddha is paraded around the stupa aboard an elephant, and the full moon of March–April, when ethnic Tamangs – the original guardians of the stupa – converge here to arrange marriages, and hundreds of eligible brides are sat around the stupa for inspection. Full moon and new moon days in general attract more pilgrims, since acts of worship earn more merit on these days.

From Kathmandu, crowded **minibuses** and buses depart the City Bus Park frequently for Boudha, **tempos** from Kantipath near RNAC, and **microbuses** from Shahid Gate, but you're better off going by **taxi** (about Rs120). However you travel, you'll be dropped off close to the main gate, where a Rs50 charge is levied on tourists. Boudha is not a place to cycle to: the main road along here is one of the valley's busiest and most polluted.

The site

Assigning a reliable age to Boudha is impossible, and historians are left at the mercy of legends, which seem to fix its origins around the fifth century AD. A **Tibetan text** relates how a daughter of Indra stole flowers from heaven and was reassigned to earth as a lowly poultryman's daughter, yet prospered and decided to use some of her wealth to build a stupa to honour a mythical Buddha of the Previous Age. She petitioned the king, who cynically granted her only as much land as could be covered by a buffalo hide. Undaunted, the woman cut the hide into thread-thin strips and joined them end to end to enclose the area needed for the gigantic stupa, and the king was obliged to keep his word. Tibetans attach great importance to this tale because it's attributed to Guru Padma Sambhava, Tibet's first and best-loved evangelist. Interestingly, in the same manuscript the guru warns of an invasion by a giant enemy, which would scatter the Tibetan people to the lands of the south.

The **Newar legend** has a firmer historical grounding, involving a drought that struck Kathmandu during the reign of the early Lichhavi king, Vrisadev. When court astrologers advised that only the sacrifice of a virtuous man would bring rain, Vrisadev commanded his son Mandev to go to the royal well on a moonless night and decapitate the shrouded body he would find there. Mandev obeyed, only to find to his horror that he had sacrificed his own father. When he asked the goddess Bajra Yogini of Sankhu how to expiate his guilt, she let fly a bird and told him to build a stupa at the spot where it landed, which was Boudha.

Boudha's **Western community** is well established, though to become a part of it you need either an introduction or a lot of time, since serious Western students of *dharma* tend to regard tourists as spiritual interference. But as those in the know say, if you're ready you will find a teacher here. Many Westerners rate Boudha as the best place in the world to **study** Tibetan Buddhism, for although **Dharmsala** in India is better known because the Dalai Lama is based there, the presence of the Tibetan government-in-exile creates a politically charged atmosphere that can distract from serious study. Moreover, Dharmsala is heavily dominated by the Dalai Lama's Gelug-pa order, whereas at Boudha all four sects are well represented, making it easier to sample the different traditions.

Western monks wear the same maroon robes and have taken the same monastic vows as Tibetan monks but, partly because of visa restrictions, aren't expected to make the same commitment to a monastery. While Tibetan monks live at their monastery, maintaining the building and making visits to the local community, Westerners are free to come and go. Given a maximum five-month stay, most cram as much personal instruction as possible into their time, and then try to maintain a long-distance teacher–disciple relationship from home. Some follow their lama on speaking tours overseas, which are conveniently scheduled during the soggy monsoon months.

A separate wing of the *dharma* crowd consists of Westerners living in Boudha for a season of **individual study**. Some are just trying Buddhism on for size, others are earnestly shopping around for a teacher. Most teachers at Boudha give occasional open talks – with or without English translation – and normally agree to one-on-one meetings with anyone who shows a keen interest.

The Chinese occupation of Tibet killed or drove away an entire generation of lamas, and Boudha's line-up of **teachers**, though formidable, reflects this: most are either very old or rather young. Perennially popular among the *dharma* set is **Chokyi Nyima**, abbot of Ka Nying Shedrupling, the "White Monastery" (ⓦwww.shedra.com), who speaks excellent English and holds open teachings most Saturday mornings. He also runs meditation courses during the tourist season. His younger brother, **Tsokney Rinpoche**, who is abbot of a monastery near Swayambhu, is also accessible and frequently gives teachings at Ka Nying Shedrupling. The death in 1991 of **Dilgo Khyentse** of Shechen Tenyi Dargyeling, the "Bhutanese Monastery", has left a large gap, but it is being filled by his grandson, the current abbott, **Shechen Rabjam Rinpoche**, who teaches courses in English (ⓔshechen@wlink.com.np). He also acts as tutor to Dilgo Khyentse's *yangsi* (reincarnated successor), Urgen Tenzin Jigme Lhundrup, who was enthroned at the monastery in 1997 at the age of four.

Kopan Monastery (3km north of Boudha), whose **Yeshe Lama** passed away in 1986, remains as busy as ever with a full schedule of Gelug activities. A Spanish boy was recognized as Yeshe's *yangsi*, and still lives at Kopan. Pulahari Monastery, east of Kopan, is still a major centre for long-term Western Buddhists, despite the death in 1994 of its abbot **Jamgon Kongtrul Rinpoche** and the subsequent installation of his young *yangsi*. Other teachers include **Chogke Triaging Rinpoche**, who runs Jyamchen Monastery, and is also abbot of the Tibetan *gompa* at Lumbini, and **Kenpo Tsultrim Gyamtso** of the Marpa Institute on Mahakal Road (1km northwest of Boudha).

To find out about upcoming teachings, check out the restaurant notice boards around Boudha, or try asking some of the regulars at the *Bir* or the *Double Dorjee*. But if you've had no prior experience with Buddhism, you'll probably want to test the waters first by enrolling in a **meditation course**. The courses run by the Himalayan Buddhist Meditation Centre (☎01/221875, ⓔhbmc@mos.com.np) are the usual place to start, or you could head out to Kopan Monastery (☎01/481268, ⓦwww.kopan-monastery.com), which holds daily Discover Buddhism classes as well as longer retreats.

Around the stupa

While less embellished than Swayambhu, Boudha is in its own way more interactive: you can climb up onto the stupa's base from its northern end, and kids
sometimes even fly kites from it. The dome is elevated on three twenty-cor-
nered plinths of decreasing size, which reinforce the notion of the stupa as a
mandala, or meditation tool. As usual, the primordial Buddha's searching blue
eyes are painted on the four sides of the central spire, and above them rise the
thirteen golden steps to *nirvana*. Instead of five *dhyani* Buddhas, however, 108
(an auspicious number) much smaller images are set in niches around the
dome, describing a broad pantheon of Buddhas, lamas and protector deities.
Prayer wheels are mounted around the perimeter wall – it's said that each spin
of a prayer wheel here is the equivalent of reciting the *mantra* embossed on it
11,000 times.

The small **Ajima shrine** at the far side of the stupa shelters the ghoulish
image of the goddess Ajima literally sucking the guts out of a corpse, reflecting her malevolent aspect as the bringer of disease. More popularly known as
Harati, she was a much-feared abducter of children until, it is said, the Buddha
taught her a lesson by stealing one of her own brood. Buddhist Newars take
care to propitiate her suitably, however, in which case she acts as the revered
protectress of their children. Next door is a room-sized prayer wheel – all are
welcome to spin it – and on the other side of the shrine you'll see the tanks
where whitewash is mixed during festivals.

Boudha's **pilgrims** are arguably its greatest attraction, as the stupa is famed
throughout the Himalayan region for its wish-fulfilling properties. Prayer
wheels, heavy silver jewellery and rainbow-striped aprons are good general
indicators of a pilgrim's Tibetan origins. The men of Kham, in eastern Tibet,
wear red tassels in their long hair, as do the Dolpo-pa of northwest Nepal,
many of whom winter here. Nomads from the central Tibetan plateau wear
sheepskin *chuba* (coats) with extra-long sleeves. Bhutanese men and women
keep their hair cropped short and wear distinctive embroidered robes. Ladakhi
women are distinguished by their velvet dresses, and high-crowned silk hats
with small wings on either side. In addition, Nepali Bhotiyas (p.508) and
Tamangs (p.505) visit Boudha in force.

The monasteries and back lanes

A spate of monastery-building has transformed Boudha in the last twenty years,
and at the last count there were 28 *gompa* (monasteries) scattered around the
neighbourhood. Unlike Swayambhu (see p.127), which was traditionally sacred
to Newar Buddhists, Boudha has always been essentially Tibetan in culture.
While all four of the major Tibetan Buddhist sects (see "Religion" in Contexts)
are represented by at least two monasteries, most are Nyingma-pa, the oldest
order of Tibetan Buddhism and that of Nepal's ethnic Tamangs. Natives of the
hills around Kathmandu, Tamangs still own most of the land around Boudha,
though they are now outnumbered by Tibetan refugees. A complete and up-
to-date map of the monasteries is painted on a wall near the Ajima shrine.

The older, smaller **monasteries** around the stupa keep their doors open
most of the time, and welcome spectators during their morning and dusk *puja*.
Furnishings and icons are broadly similar in each. The gilded statues at the front
of the assembly hall (*lhakang*) vary, but often represent Shakyamuni (the historical Buddha), Chenrezig (or Avalokiteshvara, the Buddha of Compassion) and
the founder of the monastery's sect (in the case of the Nyingma-pa, this is
Padma Sambhava, the *Guru Rinpoche* or "Precious Teacher"), as well as various
bodhisattva. Spread out in front of these are likely to be oil lamps, which monks

and pilgrims continually replenish; heaps of rice piled onto three-tiered silver stands, which are objects of meditation; conical dough-cakes (*torma*) symbolizing deities; and offerings of fruit, coins, flowers and incense. Polychrome murals cover every inch of the surface of the the walls, and depict fearsome guardians of the faith, symbolic deities and historical figures, or, like *thangka* (see p.163), express the complex cosmology of Tibetan Buddhism.

If you follow either of the two lanes heading **north of the stupa**, the romance evaporates in short order: this is Boudha the boomtown, an unplanned quagmire of garbage-strewn lanes, unlovely new buildings, schools, carpet factories and the mansions of their nouveau riche owners. The area from Boudha to Gokarneswar accounts for the largest share of the valley's carpet manufacture, a dubious distinction that contributes to serious water pollution as well as the awful congestion out on the main road in front of the stupa. Yet the carpet industry has brought undreamt-of wealth to the Tibetans of the Kathmandu Valley, who are piously donating much of it for the construction of new monasteries here. Sequestered behind high walls and iron gates, these monasteries have been deliberately named after *gompa* in Tibet that were destroyed by the Chinese, and it's hoped that, besides keeping the flame of Tibetan Buddhism alight and preserving traditional art forms, they'll help bring about the resurrection of their namesakes. It's a telling picture of the bittersweet present – and foreseeable future – of the Tibetan diaspora. With each new carpet factory or monastery, Boudha's Tibetans find themselves more comfortable in exile, and more deeply enmeshed in the difficult development-related dilemmas of their hosts.

Further afield

Boomtown aside, Boudha makes a good springboard for several walks and bike rides in this part of the valley. **Kopan Monastery**, occupying a beautifully leafy ridge about 3km due north of the stupa, is an easy target. Further along this ridge to the east lies **Pulahari Monastery** (also accessible from Gokarneswar – see p.204), where a stupa containing the remains of the late Jamgon Kongtrul Rinpoche (see box on p.198) has the makings of an important pilgrimage stop. From either of these points, it's a pleasant two- or three-hour hike north along the ridge to **Nagi Gompa**, and another hour's descent to Budhanilkantha.

In the opposite direction, Pashupatinath (see p.190) is only about a half-hour's walk southwest of Boudha. A path sets off from the main road almost opposite the entrance to the stupa. Sankhu and Gokarneswar, described in the next section, can be reached by bike.

Straddling the Ring Road west of Boudha, the ancient settlement of **Chabahil** is unfortunately now blighted by traffic and characterless construction. However, Tibetans have long been drawn to its stupa (known locally as **Dhando Chaitya**), which despite its newish appearance dates to Lichhavi times. One chronicle states it was constructed by Dharmadev, a fifth-century king, although legend attributes it to Charumati, who settled here and married a local prince after accompanying her father Ashoka on his apocryphal pilgrimage to the Kathmandu Valley in the third century BC. The prince, Devapala, is credited with founding Deopatan, one of the valley's ancient capitals and now the site of Pashupatinath. In a brick shelter at the south end of the compound stands a sixth-century statue of Padmapani Lokeshwar, carved in black stone. Chabahil's Nepalis rally round the **Chandra Binayak Mandir**, one of the valley's four principal Ganesh temples, located in the reasonably atmospheric bazaar west of the main Chabahil intersection.

Boudha practicalities

Most tourist facilities – a moneychanger, a **bank** (though without, as yet, an ATM) and film, phone and internet shops – can be found in the vicinity of the stupa. For **Tibetan medicine**, there's a branch of the Kunphen Tibetan Medical Centre on the main road just opposite the stupa entrance, inside the *Boudhanath Guest House*.

Accommodation

There's a good range of moderately priced **accommodation** in Boudha, so it's well worth staying overnight to enjoy the place after the day-trippers are gone. Most lodgings are within easy walking distance of the stupa; those located away from the busy main road are preferable.

Budget

Dragon Guest House ☎01/479562, ℱ486744. A very comfortable little establishment in a quiet area with a friendly atmosphere, excellent views and a small garden. A good place to meet people. Call ahead, as it's often full. ❸

Kailash Guest House ☎01/480741. Overlooks a rather scruffy, noisy backroad, and the concrete rooms are somewhat dingy, but it's cheap and welcoming enough. The back rooms are quieter. ❷

Lotus Guest House ☎01/472432, ℱ478091. Clean, quiet, spacious and minimalist, with low-rise buildings arranged around a pleasant garden. Operated by the next-door monastery. ❸

Peace Guest House ☎01/496661. A tiny, cold-water flophouse above a restaurant, with a few dorm beds. ❶

1km west of the stupa. Offers everything you'd expect for the money including plentiful "heritage" detailing and a fashionable restaurant-bar. ❾

Maya Guest House ☎01/470266, ℱ470261, ⓦwww.maya-travels.de/nepal.htm. The ugly and inconvenient location, 400m east of the stupa on the main road, is almost redeemed by the garden and air of seclusion. Used by German tour groups. ❻

Hotel Norbu Sangpo ☎01/477301, ℱ488357, ⓦwww.norbusangpo.com. Palatial affair, right down to the swaths of white marble. Smart but unfussy rooms, as you might expect of a Buddhist-style three-star. Apartments available too. ❼

Hotel Padma ☎01/479052, ℱ481550, ⓦwww.hotelpadma@wlink.com.np. A quirky little *pension* directly overlooking the stupa – good for breakfast at the rooftop restaurant. The bedrooms all face the back, but they're well-appointed. ❻

Midrange and expensive

Happy Valley Guest House ☎01/471241, ℱ471876. Cavernous five-storey pile with fabulous views of the stupa (and the airport) from its rooftop terrace. ❼

Hyatt Regency Kathmandu ☎01/491234, ℱ490035, ⓦwww.hyatt.com. Nepal's biggest and swankiest five-star hotel dominates the skyline

Pema Guest House ☎01/495662, ℱ487545. A large, ornate tower in a quieter area, with an excellent lawn and balconies. ❹

Rabsel Guest House ☎01/479009, ℱ470215. Tucked away in a quiet area, with smart rooms pleasantly arranged around a small lawn, overlooked by the adjacent monastery. ❺

Eating

A handful of **restaurants** around the stupa plaza target day-trippers, with rooftop seating and standard tourist menus. Most are lacklustre, but stick to Tibetan food and enjoy the view and you can't go wrong. Other, more authentic Tibetan places – with trademark curtained doors and windows, dim lighting and white cotton seat covers – are tucked away in the back lanes and on the main road.

Bir Restaurant A popular meeting place for Tibetans and long-term Westerners, though the food is unremarkable.

Double Dorjee A cosy Tibetan den that's popular with insiders. Good Tibetan food – the largest plate of *momos* ever – and some Western choices.

Stupa View Boudha's premier restaurant, with prices to match. Vegetarian, with fairly imaginative

dishes (good pasta and tofu), plus there's a full bar and a roof terrace.

View Himalaya Restaurant The menu covers some ground, from China to India by way of Tibet and Nepal, plus Mexico, but most dishes are tasty enough, and the rooftop catches the evening sun and, sometimes, views of Ganesh Himal.

Shopping

Run-of-the-mill souvenirs at Boudha are notoriously overpriced, but this is
the place to come if you're seeking genuinely obscure or antique items. Keep
an eye out for tea tables, jewellery, flasks, butter-tea churns and prayer-flag
printing blocks. For **thangka**, Tushita Heaven Handicraft, on the main stupa
plaza in Boudha, is a co-operative of *thangka* artists, some of whom can be seen
at work in the shop. Most of their business is with local monasteries so it's an
excellent place to learn about what you're buying. The Tibet Musical Cultural
Center, on the northwest side of the stupa plaza, sells traditional **musical
instruments** and provides instruction.

Boudha is also a good place to buy prayer flags, brocade banners, Tibetan
incense, *chuba* (Tibetan wraparound dresses) and maroon monks' garb. For
books, however, Thamel is a much better option, as the few Boudha bookshops have mostly Tibetan-language stock; the traditional wood-block printed
texts might make good souvenirs in themselves. Try Boudhnath Book Store,
just down from *Bir Restaurant*, or Boudha Book Store, just next to *View
Himalaya Restaurant*. Cassettes and CDs, not only of music but also teachings
by local lamas, are sold at a couple of places around the stupa and on the main
road.

The Sankhu and Sundarijal roads

The paved road past Boudha – one of the old trade routes to Tibet – rolls eastwards as far as **Sankhu** and its Bajra Yogini temple, from where there are
unpaved tracks to points on the valley rim. A second road forks left at Jorpati,
1km east of Boudha, and makes for **Sundarijal** in the extreme northeastern
corner of the valley.

Both roads are rather blighted by carpet-industry build-up for some distance
past Jorpati, but the Sankhu road then becomes a fairly gentle ride on a **bicycle**, and it can be combined with visits to Nagarkot or Changu Narayan (for
which you'll need a mountain bike). The Sundarijal road is mainly of interest
for starting a **trek** in the Helambu region; its most interesting feature, the
Gokarna Mahadev temple, is better reached by bike or foot from the Kopan
and Pulahari monasteries (see p.200). Regular **buses** from Kathmandu's City
Bus Park ply both roads.

The road to Sankhu

Crossing the Bagmati River beyond noxious Jorpati, the Sankhu road first passes
Gokarna Ban, a former royal game reserve that is now the site of Nepal's most
prestigious eighteen-hole **golf course** (reservations ☏01/450444), designed
by the Gleneagles group. Green fees are around $50 a day, clubs can be hired
on site, and the inevitable luxury hotel will soon be complete. Further on, a
right fork leads to the controversial Gokarna **landfill**, which was the
Kathmandu Valley's main refuse dump until it was finally declared full, in 1999.
While the search goes on for a new, permanent site, toxic waste seeps from
Gokarna unchecked, and the dangerous levels of methane have caused it to be
described as a "timebomb", and not in a metaphorical sense.

About 5km from Jorpati, a trail to the south crosses the Manohara River on
a temporary bridge (dry season only) and ascends the ridge to Changu
Narayan (see p.234). The road carries on to **SANKHU**, an important trade and

spiritual centre in ancient times that now drifts on as a Newar backwater in a far corner of the valley. A large but unhurried town, it's not especially well preserved, but neither is it at all touristy. The oldest part is the bazaar area to the east of the main north–south road. Sankhu's main **festivals** are Magh Sankranti (Jan 14 or 15), observed with bathing just upstream of the town, and Sankhu Jaatra (the full moon of March–April), when the image of Bajra Yogini is paraded. **Food** is scarce here, but you should be able to get snacks in the bazaar and at the Bajra Yogini temple (see below).

Two roads connect Sankhu with Nagarkot (see p.244): the more travelled route leaves Sankhu from the old bazaar area, heading north, while a steeper back way branches off on a more easterly bearing. The main road from Boudha continues northwards partway to the Bajra Yogini temple.

Sankhu Bajra Yogini

Sankhu's main claim to fame is its temple to **Bajra Yogini**, whose gilded roof glints from a grove of trees on the sparsely wooded hillside north of town. To make the two-kilometre hike, follow the main road through the arch at the north end of town, then bear left after 400m on a cobbled path. If you're on wheels, continue on the road for another 1km to where it peters out at a cold-drinks stall, where you can leave your bike and walk up the remaining steps.

Sankhu Bajra Yogini is the most senior of a ferocious foursome of tantric goddesses specially venerated in the Kathmandu Valley. To Buddhist Newars – her main devotees – she is identified with Ugratara, the wrathful, corpse-trampling emanation of Tara, one of the female aspects of Buddhahood. Hindus identify her as Durga (Kali) or one of the eight mother goddesses. She's also known as Khadga Yogini, since her distinctive feature is a sword (*khadga*) held in the right hand. The main **temple** dates from the seventeenth century, but inscriptions elsewhere record that a shrine stood here a thousand years earlier. A smaller building next to it contains a replica of the Swayambhu stupa, whose natural stone dome may well be the original seventh-century object of worship at this site. The stone just to the right of the temple door is a *nag* (snake) shrine. In the back wall of the compound, a small square opening indicates a **cave** carved out of the rock where tantric yogins conduct long-term meditations. Another cave behind the *pati* west of the compound is known as Dharma Pap Gupha: those who can squeeze through the opening into the inner chamber demonstrate their virtue (*dharma*), and those who can't their vice (*pap*). The area is pleasantly shaded, but overrun by monkeys – the place literally stinks of them.

Steps lead up to a second compound, now occupied by a school, where more ritual objects relating to the temple, including a large **Buddha head** and an overturned **frying pan**, are still kept. The Buddha head is popularly said to be that of Vrisadev, whose legendary decapitation led to the founding of Boudha (see p.197). The frying pan is associated with another wonderful legend, in which an ancient king's great success aroused the jealousy of a rival. Wanting to learn the king's secret, the rival spied on him during his daily devotions and watched as the king offered his own body, fried in a pan, as a sacrifice to Bajra Yogini; the goddess then restored him to life and endowed him with supernatural powers. When the rival copied the trick, the goddess accepted his flesh as a one-time offering, with no resurrection, and then turned over the frying pan to indicate that she would no more require blood sacrifice. Animal sacrifices are now performed only in front of the triangular stone of **Bhairab**, beside the path up to the temple, and not to the goddess herself.

The road to Sundarijal

Located 4km up the Sundarijal road, **GOKARNESWAR** overlooks the Bagmati River where it cuts through a low ridge (Gokarna Ban is just across the river – see p.202). A tranquil spot, it has been an important cremation and pilgrimage site since ancient times, and is marked by the imposing **Gokarna Mahadev Mandir**, dedicated to Shiva. It's best known for its **festival** of Gokarna Aunsi, Nepali "Father's Day", held in late August or early September.

The recently restored fourteenth-century **temple** boasts excellent wood-carving along the top of the ground floor, around the doors and on the roof struts. Inside stands a beefy natural-stone *linga*, though non-Hindus aren't allowed to approach close enough to the door to get much of a look at it. The temple's most unusual feature is an outdoor gallery of stone **sculptures** representing an ecumenical cross-section of the Nepalese pantheon, including unusual depictions of Brahma and the Vedic gods Surya, Chandra and Vayu, as well as more standard iconographies. The building closest to the river, an open hall called the **Vishnu Paduka**, is used for special rituals such as *shradha* (the rite performed by a son for a deceased parent); at the height of the monsoon, the river rises right up to its base. Another, smaller temple in the compound contains an eighth-century statue of Parbati, Shiva's consort.

From Gokarneswar you can **hike** up to Pulahari Monastery on the long ridge to the west, and from there northwards to Nagi Gompa or westwards to Kopan.

Although **SUNDARIJAL**, 5km beyond Gokarneswar, isn't a brilliant destination in itself, it's the most accessible trailhead for treks in the Helambu region. The steep climb up alongside the cascading Bagmati River – a small, reasonably clean stream here – would be much prettier without the hulking iron pipe that criss crosses the trail: much of Kathmandu's water supply comes from the upper Bagmati. After a half-hour or so, the trail leaves the pipe and civilization behind and enters the forested Shivapuri National Park (see below).

Budhanilkantha and Shivapuri

A paved road leads 8km north from Kathmandu to **BUDHANILKANTHA** (pronounced *B*uda-nil-*kan*ta), site of a monolithic sleeping Vishnu statue that is one of the valley's most impressive reminders of its semi-mythic early history. The surrounding bazaar supports a lively trade in religious paraphernalia, sweets and tea, but the Vishnu statue, set in a walled compound, is the only real attraction of the place, which is rapidly being swamped by galloping suburbanization. Try to make it here in time for the morning *puja* (9–10am), when things are most interesting.

A visit to Budhanilkantha can be combined with a **hike** or **mountain-bike** ride in the Shivapuri Watershed. However, the ride from Kathmandu cannot be recommended, at least not on the main road – it's better via Tokha. **Buses** to Budhanilkantha (#5) leave from the City Bus Park every fifteen minutes or so. **Minibuses** leave from Kantipath, just north of Jamal, while **tempos** depart from Jamal, on the north side of Rani Pokhari.

The Sleeping Vishnu (Jalakshayan Narayan)

The valley's largest stone sculpture, the five-metre-long **Sleeping Vishnu** (**Jalakshayan Narayan**), reclines in a recessed water tank like an oversized astronaut in suspended animation. Carved from a type of basalt found miles away in the southern hills, it was apparently dragged here by forced labour during the reign of the seventh-century monarch Vishnugupta, who controlled the Valley under the Licchavi king Bhimarjunadev, much as the Ranas ruled in the name of the Shah dynasty in the early twentieth century. Many locals maintain that the Sleeping Vishnu was self-created, believing no human being could have fashioned such a masterpiece. According to legend the image was lost and buried for centuries, only to be rediscovered by a farmer tilling his fields – priests show worshippers the spot.

Hindus may enter the sanctum area to do *puja* before the Sleeping Vishnu; others may only view it from between concrete railings. Priests and novices continually tend, bathe and anoint the image and chant the thousand names of Vishnu.

Budhanilkantha's name has been a source of endless confusion. It has nothing to do with the Buddha (*budha* – or *burha* – means "old"), though that doesn't stop Buddhist Newars from worshipping the image as Lokeshwar, the *bodhisattva* of compassion. The real puzzler is why Budhanilkantha (literally, "Old Blue-Throat"), a title which unquestionably refers to Shiva, has been attached here to Vishnu. The myth of **Shiva's blue throat**, a favourite in Nepal, relates how the gods churned the ocean of existence and inadvertently unleashed a poison that threatened to destroy the world. They begged Shiva to save them from their blunder and he obliged by drinking the poison. His throat burning, the great god flew up to the range north of Kathmandu, struck the mountainside with his trident to create a lake, Gosainkund, and quenched his thirst – suffering no lasting ill effect except for a blue patch on his throat. The water in the Sleeping Vishnu's tank is popularly believed to originate in Gosainkund, and Shaivas claim a reclining image of Shiva can be seen under the waters of the lake during the annual Shiva festival there in August, which perhaps explains the association. Local legend maintains that a mirror-image statue of Shiva lies on the statue's underside.

Nonetheless, the Budhanilkantha sculpture bears all the hallmarks of Vishnu or, as he's often called in Nepal, **Narayan** (pronounced Nuh-*rai*-uhn). It depicts Vishnu at his most cosmic, floating in the ocean of existence upon the snake Sesh (or Ananta, which in Sanskrit means "never-ending"); from his navel will grow Brahma and the rest of creation. Each year the god is said to "awaken" from his summer slumber during the Haribondhini Ekadashi **festival** in late October or early November, an event that draws thousands of worshippers.

One person who never puts in an appearance here, as a matter of policy, is the king of Nepal. Some say the boycott goes back to the seventeenth-century king Pratap Malla, who was visited by Vishnu in a dream and warned that he and his successors would die if they ever visited Budhanilkantha. Others say it's because the king, who is half-heartedly held to be a reincarnation of Vishnu, must never gaze upon his own image.

The *Kathmandu Guest House* runs the luxury **hotel**, the *Park Village Hotel* (☎01/373935, ⓦwww.nepalhotel.com; ❽), on the main road about 200m short of the gate to the shrine, but it's hard to think of a reason to stay out here.

Up to Shivapuri

At 2732m, **Shivapuri** (or **Sheopuri**) is the second-highest point on the valley rim. It offers excellent views of the Himalaya off to the west, from Jugal and Ganesh Himal out to Himalchuli, and eastwards from Langtang Lirung to Dorje Lakpa, not to mention intense rhododendron blossoms in March and April. The summit can be reached in about four hours by one of at least two **trails** from Budhanilkantha. You'll need to pack a lunch and sufficient water, and the vertical gain, nearly 1200m, shouldn't be taken lightly. You can camp on the flat, grassy summit to catch the best views first thing in the morning; clouds often move in by lunchtime.

Shivapuri and the Shivapuri Lek (the ridge that forms the northern rim of the Kathmandu Valley) lie within the **Shivapuri National Park**, a huge walled area set aside to protect the valley's water supply and critical forest. As with several other parks and reserves in Nepal, this one was initially created without much regard for the needs of local people, who were summarily prohibited from gathering wood and other forest products. More recently, the government and foreign aid agencies have recognized the need to add social programmes to their original environmental agenda, but the residents of some villages are still irate that the reserve is preventing them from getting road access.

The road past Budhanilkantha continues steeply upwards for another 2km to the park gate, where you have to pay a Rs250 **admission charge** (likely to increase to Rs1000). From there, follow the dirt road to the right, contouring around and up the ridge to the east. Where the road finally rounds this ridge, take a trail up to **Nagi Gompa**, a former Tamang monastery now run by the renowned lama Urgyen Rinpoche, and continue along the ridge to Shivapuri (when in doubt, bear left). Near the top is the hermitage of Swami Chandresh, a Hindu sage who is following in the tradition of the celebrated Shivapuri Baba, who established the site in the early twentieth century and, it's said, lived to be 137.

It's also possible to hike to Shivapuri from Gokarna or by a more direct route from Budhanilkantha, and there are numerous possibilities on a mountain bike (see p.479).

Balaju, Nagarjun Ban and Ichangu Narayan

The road to Trisuli (see p.262) passes a couple of worthy sights before it climbs out of the valley. **Buses** (departing from the City Bus Park), **tempos** (from the Kantipath side of Rani Pokhari) and **microbuses** (from Ratna Park) follow fixed routes to **Balaju** (all #23) and almost as far as the Nagarjun Ban gate, but both of these destinations are within easy **cycling** distance of Kathmandu – and a mountain bike will stand you in good stead once you get to Nagarjun Ban.

Simple **food** – snacks, *momo* and *daal bhat* – is available from diners in Balaju. If you're cycling or walking to Nagarjun Ban, you can eat in more pleasant surroundings at a few outdoor cafés along the main road beyond the forest entrance.

Balaju

If **BALAJU**'s "Water Garden" isn't as ravishing as its name suggests, neither is the Balaju Industrial Estate as awful as it sounds. The water garden is where Kathmandu comes to picnic and paddle on Saturdays, and for the jaded traveller it can provide some welcome relief from the commotion of the city. The park is only 2km northwest of Thamel along the road to Trisuli, behind a municipal-looking fence at the foot of a wooded hill. Admission is Rs5, plus about the same to park your bike.

In the northeast corner of the grounds lies a **Sleeping Vishnu** statue now thought to be contemporaneous with, or possibly even earlier than the more famous and much larger seventh-century image at Budhanilkantha. An earlier theory held that this was only a copy, commissioned in the seventeenth century by King Pratap Malla when he was barred from visiting the original. As at Budhanilkantha, the attribution to Shiva is controversial. The iconography is obscure, but some art historians claim that the god is holding a conch and mace in his two left hands, and ashes and a rosary in his right (attributes of Vishnu and Shiva respectively), making the figure a Shankar-Narayan or half-Vishnu, half-Shiva. If so, the compromise may reflect the balancing act of the early Gupta rulers, who introduced Vaishnavism but continued to honour the more ancient, popular worship of Shiva. Balaju's other claim to fame – for Nepalis, at least – is **Baaisdhara**, a bathing tank fed by twenty-two (*baais*) stone spouts (*dhara*), which really rocks with bathing worshippers during the **festival** of Lhuti Punhi, observed on the day of the full moon of March–April.

Nagarjun (Rani) Ban and Jamacho

Once in Balaju, you might as well continue on up the road another 2km to the entrance of **Nagarjun Ban** (also known as **Rani Ban**), a large and surprisingly wild royal forest preserve (daily 6am–6pm; pedestrians and cyclists Rs10, motorcyclists Rs30, cars and elephants Rs100). An unpaved road winds to the summit of 2096m **Jamacho**, but you can hike more directly up the ridge along a five-kilometre trail starting at the entrance. The north side of this ridge is riddled with limestone **caves**, including one where the famous second-century Buddhist saint Nagarjuna meditated and died, or so it's said. At the summit, a **stupa** decorated with fluttering prayer flags and penetrating eyes marks the spot where the Buddha sat during an apocryphal visit to the Kathmandu Valley, and a small **lookout tower** commands a panoramic (but sometimes hazy) view of the valley and of Ganesh Himal, Langtang and the peaks to the east.

Several **alternative routes** return to the valley below. If you can find it, the most interesting one is an obscure trail that starts from the road southeast of the lookout tower and descends in a southeasterly direction through thick forest and past several limestone caves, one of which contains a large image of the Buddha. The trail eventually meets the Jamacho road, which you can either follow back to the entrance (3km), or part of the way to a military post (1km), from where you can leave the forest reserve for the village of Rani Ban and muddle back down to Balaju or Swayambhu. Another trail from Jamacho makes for the slightly higher summit 1km to the west, then curves south down to Ichangu Narayan (below). **Mountain-bike** routes are described on p.479.

Four kilometres or so beyond the entrance gate to Nagarjun Ban, on the main Trisuli road, the idiosyncratic *Osho Tapoban* **retreat centre** (T01/225525, W www.oshotapoban.com) runs short, residential meditation camps, and occasional classes in yoga, homeopathy and the like. The regime is fairly strict, but the forest location is lovely and the Rajneeshis' roadside restaurant, *Zorba the Buddha*, may provide some relief.

Ichangu Narayan

According to tradition, a Narayan temple occupies each of the four cardinal points of Kathmandu Valley. The western one, **Ichangu Narayan**, nestles in a small side valley at the southern base of Jamacho.

The newish temple is crudely fashioned and not particularly interesting, but it's a good excuse to get out into an area that's surprisingly rural considering how close it is to Kathmandu. Starting at the Ring Road west of Swayambhunath, the route quickly becomes quite rough before crossing a very steep little saddle at the village of Halchok, then descends past a rock quarry to reach Ichangu after about 3km. By backtracking to the base of the quarry, you can **hike** or **mountain–bike** westwards to Bhimdhunga and all the way to the Prithvi Highway near the valley rim.

The southern valley

Paved roads fan out from Patan (see p.137), the hub of the southern valley, to the hilltop outpost of **Kirtipur**, the holy places of **Chobar** and **Dakshinkali**, and the wilds (well, sort of) above **Godavari**. Things get more rural the farther south you go, and off the main routes you'll find some of the valley's best remaining countryside. Consider basing yourself in Patan; otherwise there are places to stay near Dakshinkali, Lele and Godavari, though few of them are particularly enticing.

Kirtipur

Once-proud **KIRTIPUR** ("City of Glory") occupies a long, low battleship of a ridge 5km southwest of Kathmandu. An historic stronghold commanding a panoramic view of the valley, the well-preserved old town is vehicle-free and great for wandering. However, its unpaved, narrow lanes and mainly low-income families seem out of place so close to the prosperous capital, and in recent years it has been singled out by some tour companies as an example of picturesque poverty. It's the kind of place that may make you question your own motives for coming to Nepal.

Established as a western outpost of Patan in the twelfth century, Kirtipur had gained nominal independence by the time Prithvi Narayan Shah began his final conquest of the Kathmandu Valley in 1767. The Gorkha king, who had himself been born and raised in a hilltop fortress, considered Kirtipur the strategic linchpin of the valley and made its capture his first priority. After two separate attacks and a six-month siege, with no help forthcoming from Patan, Kirtipur surrendered on the understanding it would receive a total amnesty. Instead, in an **atrocity** intended to demoralize the remaining opposition in the valley, Prithvi Shah ordered his troops to cut off the noses and lips of every man and boy in Kirtipur. "This order was carried out in the most exact way," wrote the early twentieth-century traveller Percival Landon, "and it adds rather than detracts from the savagery of the conqueror that the only persons spared were men who were skilled in playing wind instruments. The grim statistic is added that the weight of the noses and lips that were brought to Prithvi Narayan in proof that his order had been obeyed amounted to no less than eighty pounds." The rest of the valley fell within a year. Kirtipur's residents haven't forgotten that episode, and to this day they don't allow the king and queen of Nepal to enter their town.

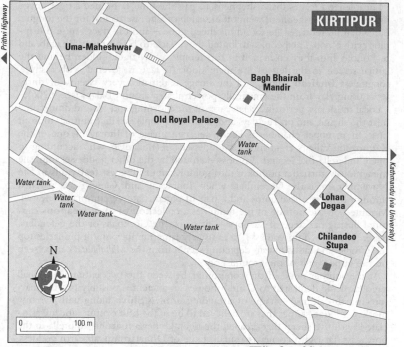

KIRTIPUR

Prithvi Highway

Uma-Maheshwar

Bagh Bhairab
Mandir

Old Royal Palace

Water
tank

Kathmandu (via University)

Water tank

Water
tank

Water tank

Lohan
Degaa

Water tank

Chilandeo
Stupa

N

0   100 m

▼ Naya Bazaar & Chobar

Kirtipur's hilltop position, once a strategic asset, has proved a serious handicap to development. The town has responded by shifting essentially all of its
commerce to **Naya Bazaar** (New Market) at the southern base of the hill,
which is why the upper town is so neglected. Many residents of the old town
are Jyapus (members of the Newar farming subcaste), who work the fields
below and in spring and autumn haul their sheaves up and thresh the grain in
the narrow streets. Others, whose land was appropriated for the building of
Tribhuwan University (Nepal's largest, with more than 5000 students), now
commute to jobs in Kathmandu or produce handicrafts behind closed doors.

Frequent **minibuses** run from the City Bus Park to a point just short of
Naya Bazaar, from where it's a ten-minute walk up to the village. **Cycling** to
Kirtipur is not a great experience, but a bike is useful for exploring the more
rural countryside beyond. The main way there is via Tribhuwan University, on
the Dakshinkali road (turn right at the red-brick gate and take the left fork
another 1km later). Other paths lead to Kirtipur from the Prithvi
(Kathmandu–Pokhara) Highway, the Ring Road and Chobar. For **food**, you
can't expect much more than samosas or chow mein in Naya Bazaar.

Bagh Bhairab Mandir

The road from the university ascends to the saddle of Kirtipur's twin-humped
ridge and deposits you in a weedy square outside the prodigious **Bagh
Bhairab Mandir**, which serves double duty as a war memorial and a cathedral
to Bhairab in his tiger (*bagh*) form. Dating from the early sixteenth century, it's
one of the oldest and best-preserved Newar pagodas in the valley.

Local legend relates that a shepherd, to pass the time, fashioned a tiger image out of burrs. The shepherd went off in search of a poinsettia leaf for the tongue, but when he returned he found his sheep gone – and the tiger's mouth dripping with blood. The people attributed the miracle to bloodthirsty Bhairab, and to honour him they enshrined in this temple a clay tiger, hidden behind the lattice screen to the left of the main door. Its face is covered with a silver, tongueless **Bhairab mask**, and the image is remade every twenty or thirty years using clay from the tantrically powerful area around Balaju (see p.206).

Local musicians perform *bhajan* early in the morning and around dinnertime near the shrine, and on Tuesdays and Saturdays people sacrifice animals in front of it. In an upper chamber is kept a separate image of Indrayani, one of the Kathmandu Valley's eight mother goddesses (*ashta matrika*), who, according to one Cinderella-like legend, was bossed around by the other goddesses until she miraculously turned a pumpkin into gold. Kirtipur's biggest **festival** is in late November or early December, when Indrayani and Ganesh are paraded through town on palanquins and a pair of pigeons are ceremonially released. Mounted on the outside of the temple is a collection of rusty **weapons** captured during the siege of Kirtipur – either by the Gorkhalis or the defenders, depending on whom you ask. An unusually large number of gilt pinnacles top the temple, and faded murals depicting scenes from the *Mahabharat* can be seen on the upper walls of the ground floor.

At the southern end of the compound, between the two entrances, a small pagoda shrine dedicated to Ganesh houses an ancient – possibly pre-Lichhavi (pre-fourth-century) – statue of a standing, armless **Shiva**, along with five tiny mother-goddess statues that are believed to be of the fifth century and are associated with five sheep that escaped the tiger. Under a metallic umbrella in the northeast (far right) corner is a small statue of **Dhartimata**, an earth goddess, shown in a graphic state of giving birth – to what, no one seems to know. Women do *puja* to this statue to aid against problems during pregnancy and childbirth.

Uma-Maheshwar Mandir and Chilandeo Stupa

Kirtipur is a pleasantly confusing maze of stony alleys, and navigating isn't hard so long as you stick to the ridgeline. The northwestern end of town is predominantly Hindu, the southeastern Buddhist.

At the top of the northern, Hindu hump stands the elephant-guarded **Uma-Maheshwar Mandir**, whose temple bell is a copy, cast in the unlikely setting of Croydon, England. The original bell tolled the hours in the old Kathmandu clock tower for many years, before the structure collapsed in the earthquake of 1934. Kathmandu's quaint **aerial ropeway** runs just beyond the town's northwestern gate; built in the 1940s, before any roads connected the valley to the outside world, it's now idle but kept on standby.

Heading southeastwards from the Bagh Bhairab temple first brings you to the Lohan Degaa, a stone *shikra* shared by both Hindu and Buddhist worshippers. Beyond, the atmospheric **Chilandeo Stupa** crowns the southern hill, its exposed brickwork lending a hoary antiquity generally lacking in better-maintained stupas. Chilandeo (also known as Chilancho Bahal) is commonly believed to have been erected by Ashoka – though if Ashoka really built every stupa attributed to him he would have had little time for anything else. The ridge that rears up so impressively to the southwest is Champadevi (see box opposite), one of the high points along the valley rim.

Naya Bazaar and the Theravada temple

Naya Bazaar's only attraction sits below the road where it rounds the south-east flank of the Kirtipur ridge. A Thai-style **Theravada temple**, the Nagara Mandapa Kirti Vihara, was completed in 1989 with money donated by the Thai king and an array of the great and good of Thailand. In the minimalist Theravada tradition, the main sanctuary is unadorned except for an altar groaning with assorted gilded Buddhas and *bodhisattva*. A statue outside honours the Venerable Pragyananda Mahasthavir, the now-deceased patriarch of Nepali Theravada Buddhists, who lived in Patan. A separate hall, brought to you by Thai Airways, displays four large images representing the turning points in Buddha's career. On the roof above are replicas of the four relevant holy sites: Lumbini, Bodh Gaya, Sarnath and Kushinagar.

The Dakshinkali road

The longest and most varied of the valley's roads begins at the Ring Road southwest of Kathmandu, just below Kirtipur, and ends high in a fold of the hills forming the valley rim at the famous sacrificial shrine of Dakshinkali, a distance of 18km. En route it passes several temples and Buddhist monasteries, and some beautiful stretches of forest as it rises more than 300m above the valley floor.

Buses for Dakshinkali (#22) depart from Kathmandu's City Bus Park roughly every half-hour (Rs15), while on Saturdays buses and minibuses leave as soon as they are filled. Kathmandu travel agents offer guided **tours** on

---

Hikes to Champadevi and Bhasmesur

Champadevi and Bhasmesur are high points on the prominent ridge that forms the southwestern rim of the Kathmandu Valley. Champadevi is easier to get to, Bhasmesur is higher. The views of the Himalaya from both knolls are excellent.

Champadevi

Trails to **Champadevi** start from near Taudaha, Pikhel and Pharping. A hike up one and down another will take four to six hours (bring plenty of food and water). It's also possible to drive within just over an hour of the summit. The first trail begins where the road makes an abrupt bend beyond Taudaha, climbing steeply southwestwards to gain the ridge and then more gradually along it to the stupa-marked summit (2278m). From Pikhel, a dirt road heads north to the ridge, entering a splendid pine forest and passing the four-star *Haatiban Resort* (see p.215), then tracks northwest to join the first trail. The Pharping route (best taken going down if you intend to get a seat on the bus) follows a dirt road up a valley south of the ridge as far as a small pond, where it veers northwards straight up to the ridge.

Bhasmesur

Bhasmesur (2502m) is another hour's walk along the ridge from Champadevi, separated from it by a saddle. It can also be reached from Kirtipur: start by following the dirt road southwest from Naya Bazaar and then west to Machhegaun ("Fishville"), from where a trail switchbacks up to a saddle on the ridge just north of the summit. In Hindu myth, Bhasmesur was a demon who extracted a boon from Vishnu that everything he touched would turn to ash. Emboldened by his apparent invincibility, the demon proceeded to make a heavenly nuisance of himself until Vishnu, having taken the form of a fair maiden, seduced Bhasmesur into imitating a dance. Vishnu concluded the dance by touching his forehead, and Bhasmesur, following suit, incinerated himself. This mountain is reputed to be the pile of ashes left by the demon's demise.

Tuesday and Saturday mornings (about Rs250), or you could hire your own **taxi** (about Rs700 return to Dakshinkali for a half-day). For real independence, though, go by **mountain bike**; the outward (upward) leg takes at least two hours, but you can put a bike on the roof of the ordinary bus for the price of a small tip. Traffic eases up after Kirtipur – except on Saturday, when the road is busy with sacrificial traffic.

Chobar

CHOBAR, a former outpost of Patan, stands at the top of a deceptively tall hill overlooking the Bagmati River. A paved road marked by a "Welcome to Chobar" sign leads only partway up – if you're cycling, follow the road to the northwestern side of the hill, where a dirt track through a quarry doubles back and eventually climbs to near the top. On foot, take the broad, stepped path under the arch, which leads straight to the central temple.

Chobar huddles around its idiosyncratic **Adinath Mandir**, the front of which is completely decorated with pots, pans and jugs. Various explanations are cited for the practice of offering kitchen utensils to Lokeshwar, the temple's deity: newlyweds will say it ensures a happy union, others claim it's a necessary rite to send a recently departed loved one off to a prosperous next life. Like so many traditions, the act has become independent of its origins, and may hark back to a time when metal implements were new technology and decorating a temple with them was a way to keep it looking spiffy and up-to-date – just as other temples are often graced by European tiles and photographs. Lokeshwar is worshipped here in the form of a red mask, which bears a close resemblance to Patan's Rato Machhendranath.

Chobar Gorge

When Manjushri drained the Kathmandu Valley of its legendary lake, **Chobar Gorge** was one of the places he smote with his sword to release the waters. As the Bagmati River slices through a wrinkle in the valley floor, 1km south of Chobar and just beside the Dakshinkali road, it really does look like the work of a neat sword stroke. However, though the gorge is a wonder of nature, it's not exactly a beauty spot. The Bagmati emerges from the chasm black with the accumulated gunge and sewage of the valley, and under a pall of smoke from the nearby Himal Cement Factory. This nightmarish, smoke-belching construction was Nepal's first cement plant, and is alleged to be responsible for over half the air pollution in the Valley. Its closure has long been rumoured, due to mismanagement and environmental concerns, but officials are reluctant to stop milking such a valuable cash cow.

Make a left just before the cement plant to reach **Jal Binayak**, a recently restored seventeenth-century Ganesh temple that stands at the mouth of the gorge. Built on a rocky outcrop, the tip of which is worshipped as Ganesh, it's full of the usual bells and bell-ringing. Just upstream, an iron **footbridge**, custom-cast by a Scottish foundry and assembled here in 1907, gives a good view of the chasm and Jal Binayak (and the cement plant).

A path along the west bank scrambles up to the main entrance of **Chobar Gupha** (Chobar Cave), which Hindus associate with Shiva and Tibetan Buddhists with the saint Guru Padma Sambhava. A Czech team explored it in 1985 for at least 1.2km before pronouncing it the third-largest cave in South Asia. Locals claim it's connected to Chobar's Adinath Mandir, the Shantipur temple at Swayambhu, or even Tibet or Varanasi. Needless to say, it's extremely dangerous to venture inside without a knowledgeable guide.

Taudaha

Beyond the cement plant, the road begins climbing and after 2km passes **Taudaha**, a duck pond with a legend. The story goes that when Manjushri drained the Kathmandu Valley he left Taudaha as a home for the snakes, and the belief persists that the serpent king Karkatnag still lives at the bottom, coiled around a heap of treasure. Jang Bahadur Rana, prime minister in the middle of the nineteenth century, is said to have tried (unsuccessfully) to dredge the lake for booty. Nowadays Taudaha is considered sacred and is off-limits to hunters and fishermen; though choked with water hyacinths, it's a popular stopping place for migrant water birds in winter. During the festival of Nag Panchami, in Saaun (July–Aug), the area is packed with devotees.

Shesh Narayan (Yanglesho)

From Taudaha the road ascends steadily for another 6km to its highest point, a little beyond Pikhel. Two kilometres beyond, the quiet and shady **pools** of **Shesh Narayan** crouch under a wooded hillside just off the road. Hindus worship Vishnu here as the mighty creator, who formed the universe out of the cosmic ocean; the snake Shesh (or Ananta), the "remainder" of the cosmic waters after Vishnu's creation, is symbolized by the four pools. A sculpture depicting Surya riding his twelve-horse chariot stands half-submerged in the semicircular pool. Steps from there lead to Narayan's **temple** at the base of a limestone overhang, whose serpentine stalactites are said by Vaishnavas to be the "milk", or blessing, of Shesh. A stone naturally eroded in the shape of a coiled snake, which was enshrined in the temple until its recent theft, provided a further association with Shesh. To the left of the temple is another hunk of eroded limestone known as Chaumunda – you're supposed to put your ear to it to hear the sound of running water.

To the right of the temple, a half-height wood latticed doorway conceals a cave that Buddhists call **Yanglesho**, where Guru Padma Sambhava, the eighth-century founder of the Nyingma-pa sect of Tibetan Buddhism, is supposed to have wrestled with a horde of *nag* and turned them to stone. This episode marked a turning-point in Padma Sambhava's career – allegorically, it probably refers to the saint's struggle to introduce his brand of tantric Buddhism from India – which accounts for the presence of a tiny **gompa** next to the Shesh Narayan temple.

Pharping

A few hundred metres beyond Shesh Narayan, **PHARPING** is unexpectedly large and lively for this distant corner of the valley. It's divided between an unattractive modern commercial strip along the road, the more villagey Newari centre (reached by a side road where the main road swerves left), and a Tibetan Buddhist boom town which seems to throw up another fantastically gilded *gompa* every year. Nepal's first hydroelectric plant was built just down-hill from Pharping, in 1911, but the power generated all went to light Singha Durbar.

A fifteen-minute walk uphill brings you to the Tibetan area, dominated by the huge white-and-gold stupa of Tharik Gompa, built in 1997 by followers of Tharik Rinpoche, a Sakyapa lama based in Boudha. Less grandiose but more significant is the golden-roofed **Pharping Bajra Yogini**, which sits above the newer monasteries and is one of the valley's four tantric temples dedicated to the angry female aspect of Buddhahood. Foreigners usually aren't allowed to enter, but the upstairs sanctum contains two prancing images of Bajra Yogini, each holding a skull-cup and knife.

A staircase just to the left of the Bajra Yogini temple entrance leads further up the hill to a monastery sometimes used as a retreat by Buddhist Westerners. Introduce yourself and the monks will show you the **Padma Sambhava Cave** (also known as Asura Cave) in the courtyard; the irrepressible guru, whose image stands among butter candles, apparently meditated in this grotto as well as at Yanglesho. Buddhists say the handprint to the left of the cave entrance and the "footprints" in the centre of the courtyard are those of Padma Sambhava (Hindus claim they were left by Gorakhnath). The site has grown to be a major pilgrimage stop for Tibetan Buddhists, and has spawned several other nearby *gompa* of Padma Sambhava's Nyingma-pa sect, all connected by strings of prayer flags that from a distance make the hillside look like it's covered in a gigantic spider web. Red-robed monks are a common sight around Pharping.

A couple of small **restaurants**, the *Asura Cave* and the *Snowland*, cater to the monasteries' residents and visitors. They're located just downhill from the Bajra Yogini temple, so if you find them you'll know you're on the right track for the temple and cave. The *Asura Cave* has basic **rooms** (❶).

Dakshinkali

The best and worst aspect of **DAKSHINKALI** is that everything happens out in the open. The famous sacrificial pit of Southern Kali – the last stop for hundreds of chickens, goats and pigs every week – lies at the bottom of a steep, forested ravine, affording an intimate view of Nepali religious rituals. The spectacle makes many people feel uncomfortable – if it's not squeamishness, it'll be the sense of prying. That said, the public bloodbath is quite a sight, and attracts busloads of camera-toting tourists early every Saturday morning. Asthami, the eighth day after a new or full moon, draws the largest crowds.

Motorists and motorcyclists have to pay a small fee before the final switchback descent into the ravine, and then pay again to park (cyclists pay a tiny "bike-watching" charge). From the car park a path leads to a small bazaar of stalls selling food, drinks and sacrificial accessories. The **shrine** is directly below the bazaar, positioned at the auspicious confluence of two streams. Tiled like an abattoir (for easy hosing down) and covered with a gilt canopy, the sacred area consists of little more than a row of short statuettes, Kali being the heavily decorated one under the canopy. From the back of the shrine, stone steps lead up through a pine wood to a small promontory where there's a subsidiary shrine to Mata, Kali's mother. You'll have to take your shoes off to step onto the small concrete viewing platform that surrounds the shrine, but it's well worth it for the views across to Pharping and beyond.

Dakshinkali is as much a picnic area as a holy spot. The sacrifice done, families make for the pavilions that surround the shrine and merrily cook up the remains of their offerings. If you didn't sacrifice anything, you can get a good sit-down **meal** at the *Dakshinkali Village Inn* (see opposite), or fried snacks from the "fast-food" restaurant across the way or from the stalls near the shrine.

A visit to Dakshinkali can be combined with a few different **hikes** or **bike rides**. A trail heading south from the shrine area goes for miles into lush hill country. The road that continues straight past the *Dakshinkali Village Inn* makes a great downhill descent into the valley of the lower Bagmati. You can hike to Champadevi (see box, p.211), or follow other trails westwards from there all the way to the Kulekhani Reservoir and Daman (p.267).

A note on Hindu animal sacrifices

Hindu animal **sacrifice** is superficially similar to what the Old Testament patriarchs did, but Hindus don't kill animals to prove their loyalty to a deity so much as to propitiate it. Kali, the usual recipient, doesn't care about the personal sacrifice her worshipper has made in order to get an animal, all she wants is the blood. Nepalis lead their offerings to the slaughter tenderly, often whispering prayers in the animal's ear and sprinkling its head with water to encourage it to shrug in assent; they believe that the death of this "unfortunate brother" will give it the chance to be reborn as a higher life form. Only uncastrated males, preferably dark in colour, are used. At Dakshinkali, men of a special caste slit the animals' throats and let the blood spray over the idols. Brahman priests (referred to as *baahun*, *pandit* or *pujari*) oversee the butchering and instruct worshippers in all the complex rituals that follow. However, you don't need to speak Nepali to get the gist of the explanations.

Accommodation

There's very little budget **accommodation** in this part of the valley, and what does exist is nothing special. However, it might be worth putting up with it, or spending a bit more, in order to visit Dakshinkali first thing in the morning, thereby avoiding the Saturday and Tuesday transport hassles. In addition to the options listed below, the *Asura Cave* and other eateries in Pharping usually have some fairly grotty rooms upstairs.

Ashoka Resort 200m before the Dakshinkali gate ☎01/290657. An unsightly concrete tower, but the rooms have excellent views and there are more attractive motel-like bungalows arranged around a rough garden. ❹

Dakshinkali Club Resort At Dollu, 2km off the road ☎01/710072, ✉qkitchen@ntc.net.np. Attractive chalet-style resort in a peaceful wooded valley below Shesh Narayan. ❻

Dakshinkali Fast Food and Lodge Beside the Dakshinkali gate ☎01/710041. Very basic, but it's inexpensive and conveniently located for an early start on Saturday. ❸

Dakshinkali Village Inn At the Dakshinkali gate ☎01/710553, ☏330889, Cosy brick and thatch bungalows, lovely garden dining area, excellent location. ❻

Haatiban Resort Above Pikhel, on the way to Champadevi ☎01/371397, ☏371561. Perched 500m above the valley floor, it has clean air and great views. Pony rides and guided hikes to Champadevi. Ring ahead to get picked up from the main road in a 4WD. ❼

The Bungmati and Chapagaun roads

These two paved but minor roads take parallel courses southwards from Patan. The first leads to the delightful village of Bungmati, summer home of Rato Machhendranath. The second has no particularly interesting towns along it, but it goes much further south into attractive countryside.

The main reason you'd come this way is to do a **bike** circuit of the southern valley: these two roads aren't themselves that great for cycling, but they give access to smaller tracks and trails that are. **Buses** for Khokana/Bungmati depart from the Ring Road just south of the Ekantakuna area of Patan (hourly). Chapagaun buses depart from Patan's Lagankhel bus park (at least hourly).

Bungmati and Khokana

From a distance, you could almost mistake **BUNGMATI** for a well-preserved Tuscan village: scrunched together on a hillock, its tall, brick houses, with their

Agriculture in the Valley

Agriculture employs two out of three residents of the Kathmandu Valley, the **farmers** a mixture of Newars, Baahuns, Chhetris and Tamangs (see Contexts pp.501–508 for background on these ethnic groups). Newar farmers, called Jyapus, dig their fields with two-handed spades called *kodaalo* (*ku* in Newari) – it's back-breaking work – and live in close, brick settlements on the valley floor, while the other groups tend to use bullock ploughs and build detached, mud-walled houses around the fringes. Many are tenant farmers and are expected to pay half their harvest as rent.

Low enough in elevation to support two or even three main crops a year, and endowed with a fertile, black clay – *kalimati*, a by-product of sediment from the prehistoric lake – the valley floor has been intensely cultivated and irrigated for centuries. **Rice** is seeded in special beds shortly before the first monsoon rains in June, and seedlings are transplanted into flooded terraces no later than the end of July. Normally women do this job, using their toes to bed each shoot in the mud. The stalks grow green and bushy during the summer, turning a golden brown and producing mature grain by October.

Harvest time is lazily anarchic: sheaves are spread out on paved roads for cars to loosen the kernels, and then run through portable hand-cranked threshers or bashed against rocks. The grain is gathered in bamboo trays (*nanglo*) and tossed in the wind to winnow away the chaff, or, if there's no wind, *nanglo* can be used to fan away the chaff. Some sheaves are left in stacks to ferment for up to two weeks, producing a sort of baby food called *hakuja*, or "black" rice. The rice dealt with, terraces are then planted with **winter wheat**, which is harvested in a similar fashion in April or May. A third crop of pulses or maize can often be squeezed in after the wheat harvest, and vegetables are raised year-round at the edges of plots.

The lot of valley farmers has improved in the past generation. **Land reform** in the 1950s and 1960s, which didn't work too well in most parts of the country, was more diligently implemented near the capital, helping to get landlords and moneylenders off the backs of small farmers. However, the traditional Newar system of **inheritance**, in which family property is divided up among the sons, means that landholdings get smaller with each generation. That presents a contrasting problem: farms that are too small to make mechanical equipment worthwhile, necessitating labour-intensive farming and keeping productivity low.

Meanwhile, Kathmandu's **prosperity** is bringing problems. In the past decade, while the valley's population has nearly doubled to 1.2 million, housing (and the brick "factories" that make it possible) has been chewing up farmland at a speedy rate – a trend that threatens to accelerate, as ever more hill people flock to the valley for a piece of the action. At the same time, high land prices and the declining quality of life in the capital are only adding to the pressure on farmland. Those who can are fleeing the inner city, just as they have every other city in the world, and are rapidly creating a **suburban** commuter culture. In the absence of any greenbelt regulations, valley farmers and *guthi* (temple trusts) are steadily selling out, as their valuable farmland becomes even more valuable as real estate.

tiled roofs sloping in different directions, look distinctly Romanesque. The bus stops along the road a short walk northeast of the town.

Close up, Bungmati is quintessentially Newar, and what at first looks like a tiny village quickly envelops you in its self-contained universe. All alleys eventually lead to the broad, teeming central plaza and the whitewashed *shikra* of **Machhendranath**, whose more ancient Newar name is Bunga Dyo ("God of Bunga"). According to legend, Bungmati marks the spot where Machhendranath, having arrived in the valley in the form of a bee to save it from drought, was "born" as the valley's protector-rainmaker. Each summer at

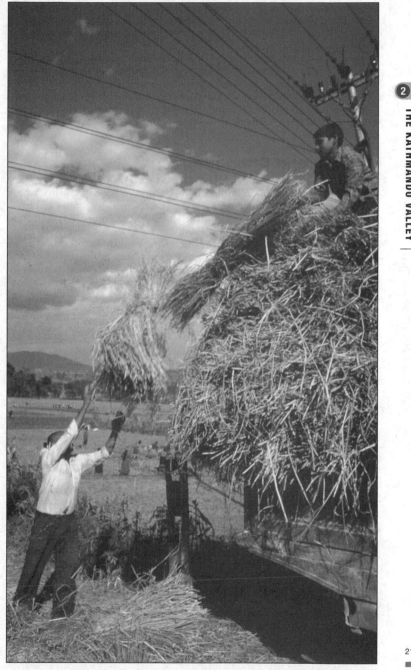

△ Wheat harvest, Bhaktapur

the end of Patan's Rato Machhendranath festival, the god's red mask is brought to the Bungmati temple for a six-month residency, but every twelfth year it is kept here through the winter and then pulled by lumbering chariot all the way to Patan (see p.147).

One kilometre to the north, **KHOKANA** resembles Bungmati in many ways, but somehow lacks the character and magnetism of its neighbour. It's locally renowned for its mustard oil, and in season the presses run full tilt. Khokana's pagoda-style **Shekali Mai Mandir**, a massive three-tiered job, honours a local nature goddess. Midway between Khokana and Bungmati stands the poorly maintained **Karya Binayak**, another of the valley's four Ganesh temples.

Thecho and Chapagaun

THECHO, 8km south of Patan, is the largest town in this end of the valley, while **CHAPAGAUN**, 1km further south, is a smaller but similarly brick-built settlement. Thecho has a touch more atmosphere, Chapagaun more to eat.

More attractive than either town, the seventeenth-century **Bajra Barahi Mandir** is secreted in a small wood 500m east along a track from Chapagaun. Despite Shiva imagery, the temple is dedicated to a tantric manifestation of the goddess Kali: like the Bajra Yoginis, Bajra Barahis represent the female, creative power of divinity. This goddess receives her share of worship and sacrifice on Saturdays, but most visitors come just to picnic in the park. The stone statue of Bajra Barahi kept in the sanctum is a recent replacement for an ancient image that was stolen; the stolen image was later recovered and is now on display at the National Museum.

Tika Bhairab and Lele

The road, unpaved after Chapagaun, continues south for another 4km to **TIKA BHAIRAB**, a quarrying centre named after a locally famous abstract mural of the god Bhairab painted on a wall at the junction of two small streams. This stretch of road can be fairly unpleasant because of the heavy-vehicle traffic generated by stone quarrying in the area. A much better route is to go east from Chapagaun past the Bajra Barahi temple (this track eventually meets the paved Godavari road), then strike south on a smaller track that crosses a steep, forested ridge and enters the **Lele** valley several kilometres upstream of Tika Bhairab.

Paths extend into the hills in all directions, but see few tourists. Mountain-bikers, however, have discovered this corner of the valley; the more intrepid can even pedal all the way to Hetauda (see p.383) and the Tarai, on a recently completed dirt road. Public transport, in the form of private shared jeeps, is likely to serve this route in the future, though at present the road is only passable in dry weather.

The Godavari and Lubhu roads

The greenest, most pristine part of the valley is its southeastern edge, where you'll find something now all too rare in Nepal, or at least around the Kathmandu Valley: virgin forest. Once the dominant feature of the middle hills, it has come under increasing pressure in recent years from an exploding population desperate for fuel and farmland.

The principal starting point for day-trips in this area is **Godavari** (usually pronounced Go-*dow*ri), home of the Royal Botanical Garden, 10km southeast of Patan. On foot from Godavari you can hike to Phulchoki, the highest point on the valley rim and a full day's outing, or make a more leisurely low-elevation circuit via the curious shrine of Bishanku Narayan. On a mountain bike or motorcycle, you can do either of those, or you can connect up with the Chapagaun route or with another road that reaches the valley's southeastern rim via Lubhu and the Lakuri Bhanjyang (see p.221).

Local **buses** depart very infrequently for the botanical garden from the City Bus Park in Kathmandu, but it makes more sense to make your own way to Patan's Lagankhel bus park, from where microbuses leave every fifteen minutes or so to the St Xavier School in Godavari, and hourly buses run direct to the gardens. Hourly local buses from Patan also stop at St Xavier's on their way to **Bishanku**, and there's another hourly service from Lagankhel to **Lubhu**.

Harisiddhi

The paved Godavari road starts rather inauspiciously, with heavy traffic fuelled in part by the many brick kilns around **HARISIDDHI**. Those bricks have built many a traditional Newar town, among them Harisiddhi itself. Despite its unimpressive appearance from the road, the village is actually a close-knit cluster of mostly old houses, a central temple, and a series of courtyards often occupied by local women spinning wool for Patan's carpet industry. It's reached by walking straight up a stepped path where the main road jogs left.

Harisiddhi's **Bal Kumari Mandir** received unwanted notoriety in 1997, when the *Sunday Telegraph* in London published an article implying that it was the centre of a child-sacrifice cult. The article was pure hack journalism, but it touched a nerve in Nepal because apparently human sacrifice *was* performed in the Kathmandu Valley not so very long ago. Though no historical proof exists, several nineteenth-century European visitors reported hearing of it, and some authorities claim the practice continued until the early twentieth century. Only a generation ago, parents in this part of the valley would jokingly warn their children to behave or they'd be sent to Harisiddhi.

Godavari and the Royal Botanical Garden

Somewhat quieter after Harisiddhi, the road climbs steadily past a number of plant nurseries to the botanical garden at **GODAVARI**, beautifully situated up against the forested valley rim. To reach it, follow the main road to the left of the Jesuits' St Xavier School for 1km, then turn left again just before a clump of local restaurants.

Kipling wrote that "the wildest dreams of Kew/Are the facts of Kathmandu", and the **Royal Botanical Garden** (daily: mid-Feb to mid-Nov 9am–5pm; mid-Nov to mid-Feb 9am–4pm; Rs25) might seem to be the obvious place to put his theory to the test. The garden is in fact more modest than wild, though it contains some idyllic paths, streams and picnic areas and an excellent orchid house. Curiously, it's a popular location for dance sequences in Nepalese films and pop videos. There's little worthwhile literature or information available on site, but *Enjoy Trees*, sold in most Kathmandu bookshops, makes an excellent stand-in.

Just a couple of hundred metres north and then west of the car park, the spring-fed water tank of **Godavari Kunda** hosts a big *mela* every twelve years during July and August (the next will be in 2003). The adjacent **Buddhist retreat centre**, which must have one of the most fabulous back gardens in the world, is an offshoot of Than *gompa*, in Pharping, and only for the serious seeker of enlightenment: minimum stay three years.

The only **accommodation** in these parts is the pricey *Central Godavari Resort* (☎01/560675, ⓦwww.godavariresort.com.np; ⑥), located about 2km northwest of Godavari. It has a nice rural setting and acres of gardens (plus a pool and health club), but it's not high enough for very good views. **Food** is available from the institutional *Tara Gaon Restaurant*, next to the entrance gate, and from the smaller eateries back at the intersection just before the car park.

Phulchoki

The road bearing straight ahead to the right of the St Xavier School switchbacks and spirals right to the top of **Phulchoki** – a 1200m ascent. Phulchoki itself means "**Place of Flowers**", which is entirely apt. If you know what to look for, you'll see orchids, morning glories, corydalis and, of course, rhododendrons (March and April are best for catching them in bloom). The whole mountain is covered by tall, luxuriant **forest**, and as you climb from its subtropical base to its temperate summit you pass through mixed stands of oak, chestnut, walnut, bamboo, laurel and rhododendron. It's a superb place for **birdwatching** – a trained eye is supposed to be able to spot a hundred or more species in a day – and also for **butterflies**, which are attracted to the flowers during spring. If the **summit** (2762m) isn't wreathed in clouds, you'll have a magnificent view of a wide swath of the Himalaya and practically the entire Kathmandu Valley (smog permitting). The effect is only slightly marred by the presence of a microwave relay station, erected with Canadian assistance, which is the only reason for the summit road's existence.

The only way to **get to the top** of Phulchoki early enough to be sure of views is to go by taxi (about Rs1800, if you can find a driver willing to take his car up there) or motorcycle. The road is partly paved in the early going, but higher up the loose gravel is quite tricky. There's essentially no traffic, except on Saturday. Given a lift to the top, you can hike down in three hours or less. You can also hike up and back – an all-day proposition – on a trail that starts behind the shrine to **Phulchoki Mai**, the mother goddess of these parts, 500m up the road and just opposite the entrance to an unsightly marble quarry. The trail crosses the road a few times, and can be very slippery after rain. You'd have to be a very strong rider to make it up this steep, rough road on a mountain bike, and it would take you all day from Kathmandu.

Just beyond the Phulchoki Mai shrine, hidden in woods to the left of the road, the temple and bathing place of **Nau Dhara** is a good place to draw breath. The name means "nine spouts" and that's exactly what you'll find, along with worshippers, pilgrims and local women washing clothes. The site is especially holy to the Silwar caste, who come here in huge numbers to worship their ancestral god in the full moon of the month of Bhadau (Aug–Sept). The main shrine is off to the left at the far end, and houses the remnants of a tree sacred to Buddhists and Hindus alike. You won't be able to see it, however, as the Hindu temple guardians have locked it behind metal doors, allegedly on the grounds that Buddhist pilgrims in search of relics were slowly chipping away at the holy wood.

Bishanku Narayan

A dirt road (served by buses from Patan's Lagankhel bus park) strikes left (north) from the Godavari road just beyond St Xavier School and contours around into a lovely, sheltered side valley that seems a world away from

Kathmandu. If you're on foot, you can access the valley more directly via a path that leaves the western (back) entrance of the botanical garden and joins the road coming down from St Xavier's – turn right just after the back gate at a large tree. Either way, it's a good hour's brisk walk to **Bishanku Narayan**, situated in a notch in the ridge on the far (northwest) side of the valley. Meandering trails leave the dirt road and thread their way along the raised borders of the paddy and mustard fields that line the valley floor. From the village of Bistachhap, on the other side of the valley, a number of obvious trails lead up to the shrine.

One of the valley's four main Narayan (Vishnu) sites, Bishanku is not a temple – rather, it's a small **cave** reached by a set of precarious steps. A chain-mail curtain protects the god's image inside the cave. If you're thin enough, you can descend through another narrow fissure; according to popular belief, those who manage to squeeze through it will be absolved of past sins. From Bishanku it's another 2.5km to the Godavari Road at Badegaun.

About 1km south of Badegaun, a quiet unpaved road leads westwards through farm country to the Bajra Barahi Mandir and Chapagaun (see p.218). The turning is impossible to miss because it's marked by a prominent sign for the *Central Godavari Resort* (see opposite).

Lubhu and Lakuri Bhanjyang

The thirty-kilometre road connecting Patan with Panauti (see p.249) is a superb intermediate-level mountain-bike ride that can be done in either direction. From Patan, ride out of town on the road past Sundhara and the Eastern Stupa. The first section to **Lubhu**, a brickmaking and handloom centre 6km beyond the Ring Road, is busy and uninteresting, but things get better shortly thereafter. The road, now unpaved, climbs gradually at first and then commences a serious 500m switchback ascent through a woodcutters' area to **Lakuri Bhanjyang**. On a clear day, the view of the valley and mountains from here is splendid. The second half of the ride is a sweet descent through the close, rural valley of the Bebar Khola and its scattered Tamang, Chhetri and finally Newar settlements.

From Lakuri Bhanjyang, it's possible to descend to Godavari or Bishanku Narayan on a track that branches off to the left.

Bhaktapur and the eastern valley

The valley's eastern arm maintains a discreet cultural, as well as geographical, distance from Kathmandu. Perhaps because it lay off the main India–Tibet trade route all those years, its Hinduism has scarcely been diluted by Buddhism. Creeping Westernization has been slower to take root here, too, and concrete has made fewer inroads against native brick. Fashions at this end of the valley remain conservative, especially among Jyapu women: most still wear the traditional black and red-trimmed *pataasi*, wrapped around the waist in tiers, giving the effect of a flamenco skirt. Hitched up in back, these often reveal tattoos above the ankles, believed to be necessary for a woman to enter heaven.

Bhaktapur makes an excellent base from which to explore this part of the valley. Roads and trails radiate from there in several directions, the temple complex of **Changu Narayan** making an immensely rewarding excursion, particularly for fans of Nepali sculpture. Bhaktapur is also a staging post for Nagarkot, and can serve as a springboard for trips up the Arniko Highway to Dhulikhel and beyond (see Chapter Three).

Bhaktapur (Bhadgaun)

In the soft, dusty light of evening the old city of Bhaktapur, with its pagoda roofs and its harmonious blend of wood, mud-brick and copper, looked extraordinarily beautiful. It was as though a faded medieval tapestry were tacked on to the pale tea-rose sky. In the foreground a farmhouse was on fire, and orange flames licked like liquescent dragon's tongues across the thatched roof. One thought of Chaucer's England and Rabelais's France; of a world of intense, violent passions and brilliant colour, where sin was plentiful but so were grace and forgiveness ...

Charlie Pye-Smith, *Travels in Nepal*

Kathmandu's field of gravity weakens somewhere east of the airport; beyond, you fall into the rich atmosphere of **BHAKTAPUR** (also known as **BHADGAUN**). Rising in a tight mass of warm brick out of the fertile fields of the valley, Bhaktapur appears something like Kathmandu must have been before the arrival of the modern world. It often feels more like a big village than a small city, a sensation intensified by the absence of traffic. Wandering about the herringbone-paved streets and narrow alleys, every turn of a corner brings a new wonder: a neighbourhood shrine, a sudden vibrant courtyard, a red-and-gold-skirted pagoda. And everywhere the burnt-peach hue of bricks is offset by the deep brown of intensely carved wood – the essential media of the Newar architects.

Even today, well over half of Bhaktapur's population is from the agricultural Jyapu caste of the Newars, and it may well be the city's tightly-knit, inward-looking nature that has saved it from the free-for-all expansion that overwhelms Kathmandu. Thanks to a long-term German-funded restoration and sanitation programme, and to the policies of its independent-minded municipal council, much of the city is pedestrianized. Temples and public shelters are being restored with the money raised from the controversial entrance fee, and new buildings are now required to follow traditional architectural styles. This is one Nepalese city that has got its act together, and it wears its status as a UNESCO World Heritage site proudly.

It's hardly surprising therefore that increasing numbers of travellers are heading to Bhaktapur straight from Kathmandu airport. During the day, travellers, tour groups and persistent "student" guides mill about enthusiastically in the beguiling main squares, but after hours, or in among the maze of backstreets, it would be hard not to feel the pulse of this quintessential Newar city.

Some history

The "City of Devotees" was probably founded in the ninth century, and by 1200 it was ruling Nepal. In that year Bhaktapur witnessed the launch of the Malla era when, according to the Nepalese chronicles, King Aridev, upon being

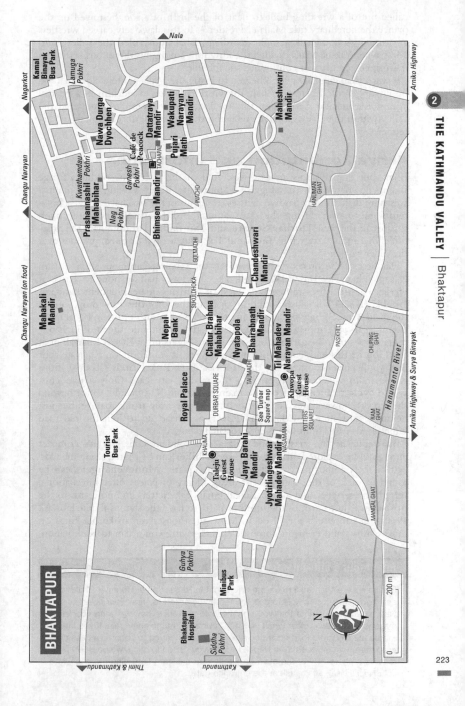

BHAKTAPUR

Nala

Nagarkot

Changu Narayan

Changu Narayan (on foot)

Arniko Highway

Kamal
Binayak
Bus Park

Lamuga
Pokhri

Nawa Durga
Dyochhen

Dattatraya
Mandir

Wakupati
Narayan
Mandir

Maheshwari
Mandir

Café de
Peacock

TACHAPAL

Pujari
Math

Kwathandau
Pokhri

Prashannashil
Mahabihar

Ganesh
Pokhri

INACHO

Nag
Pokhri

Bhimsen Mandir

IGULMADHI

Chandeshwari
Mandir

Mahakali
Mandir

SUKULDHOKA

Nepal
Bank

Chatur Brahma
Mahabihar

Nyatapola

Bhairabnath
Mandir

Til Mahadev
Narayan Mandir

PASIKHEL

CHUPING
GHAT

HANUMAN
GHAT

Royal Palace

DURBAR SQUARE

TAUMADHI

See 'Durbar
Square' map

Khwopa
Guest
House

POTTERS
SQUARE

RAM
GHAT

Hanumante River

Arniko Highway & Surya Binayak

Tourist
Bus Park

KHAUMA

Taleju
Guest
House

Jaya Barahi
Mandir

Jyotirlingeshwar
Mahadev Mandir

NASAMANA

MANGAL GHAT

Guhya
Pokhri

Minibus
Park

Bhaktapur
Hospital

Siddha
Pokhri

Thimi & Kathmandu

Kathmandu

Kathmandu

N

200 m

0

223

called out of a wrestling bout to hear of the birth of a son, bestowed on the prince the hereditary title Malla ("wrestler"). To this day, beefy carved wrestlers are the city's trademark temple guardians. Bhaktapur ruled the valley until 1482, when Yaksha Malla divided the kingdom among his three sons, setting in train three centuries of continuous squabbling.

It was a Bhaktapur king who helped to bring the Malla era to a close in 1766 by inviting Prithvi Narayan Shah, the Gorkha leader, to aid him in a quarrel against Kathmandu. Seizing on this pretext, Prithvi Narayan conquered the valley within three years, Bhaktapur being the last of the three capitals to surrender.

Arrival, orientation and information

Bhaktapur drapes across an east–west fold in the valley, its southern fringe sliding down towards the sluggish Hanumante River. Owing to a gradual westward drift, the city has two centres (residents of the two halves stage a boisterous tug-of-war during the city's annual Bisket festival) and three main squares. In the west, **Durbar Square** and **Taumadhi Tol** dominate the post-fifteenth-century city, while **Tachapal Tol** (**Dattatreya Square**) presides over the older east end.

Handiest of the **buses** to Bhaktapur is the "Express" minibus service from Kathmandu's City Bus Park, which takes just over half an hour to arrive at Siddha Pokhri, a five-minute walk west of Durbar Square. Frequent Banepa-, Dhulikhel- and Barhabise-bound buses from the City Bus Park drop you on the main Arniko Highway about ten-minutes' walk south of town. Local buses from Nagarkot terminate at Kamal Binayak, five minutes northeast of Tachapal; tourist buses from Nagarkot stop to drop passengers off at Kamal Binayak or at the "Tourist Bus Park" north of Durbar Square. If you come on a private tour bus you'll be deposited at the Tourist Bus Park. **Taxis** (Rs300 from Kathmandu) will take you only to the nearest city gate. Only a masochist would **cycle** to Bhaktapur on the main road from Kathmandu. Once beyond the airport, however, it's possible to turn off the busy trunk road (either just before or just after the Manchara River) and head up to join the old road which leads past Thimi (see p.238) to Bhaktapur.

Bhaktapur has no rikshas and just a few resident taxis, but it's compact enough to be explored on foot. One-speed **bikes** can be rented along the road east of the minibus park (west of Durbar Square). **Moneychangers** can be found in each of the main tourist areas. Plenty of places offer international **telephone** services, and a few also do email. Take letters and postcards to the **post office**, just north of the minibus park, to have the stamps franked, or ask at your guesthouse if they'll do it. Most guesthouses can make bookings on tourist **buses** and even on domestic flights, saving you a trip to Kathmandu.

Bhaktapur's entrance fee

Foreigners are charged $10 (or the equivalent in Nepali rupees) to enter Bhaktapur, and the regime is strictly enforced – you may be asked to show your ticket as you walk around town. Note that you only need to pay once, however long your stay: make your intentions clear when you buy your ticket at the entry gate. If you intend to visit the city more than once, the ticket can be extended to become a pass covering the length of your stay in Nepal. For this you'll need to bring two passport photos and a photocopy of the main pages of your passport (including the page with your Nepali visa); again, ask at the entrance gate.

Bhaktapur's **hospital** would not be a great place to have to go in an emergency. However, the **Bhaktapur International Homeopathic Clinic** (℡01/613197), with both Western and Nepali staff, is highly regarded throughout the valley. It's located up a lane going north from the Dattatreya temple; hours vary depending on individual staff schedules.

Accommodation

Most **guesthouses** in Bhaktapur are small, friendly and exceptionally well located in the area around Taumadhi and Durbar Square (though this means that early morning *puja* bells may prevent a lie-in). As a rule prices are somewhat higher than for comparable lodgings in Kathmandu, but Bhaktapur is worth it. The city doesn't have that many beds, so book ahead in busy times, or arrive as early as possible in the day. Refer to the "Durbar Square and Taumadhi Tol" map for locations. You might also consider staying at Changu Narayan (see p.234).

Bhadgaon Guest House ℡01/610488, ℻610481, ⓦwww.bhadgaon.com. A small but professionally run hotel – the classiest in Bhaktapur – with small but comfortable rooms. The decor is a high-class version of traditional Nepali, there's a calm central garden area and the high rooftop restaurant is unrivalled. ❻–❼
Golden Gate Guest House ℡01/610534, ℻611081, ⓔgoldengatge@unlimit.com. Relatively large concrete block house with faded rooms, but it's pleasantly secluded and has good views from the roof and upper (more expensive) rooms. ❸–❺
Khwopa Guest House ℡01/614661, ℻612388. Brand-new place with ten cosy, low-ceilinged rooms piled up over three floors, with pleasant wood fittings and terracotta tiles. Small rooftop terrace with views of the Nyatapola temple. ❹
Kumari Guest House ℡01/611323, ⓔkumari@craftcoll.wlink.com.np. Bright, spacious rooms, with comfortable, attractively carved beds, in a new guesthouse between Taumadhi Tol and Durbar Square. ❹
Namaste Guest House ℡01/610500, ℻225679, ⓦwww.bccinepal.org. Newer building without much character, but the rooftop rooms are worth going for. ❹

New Nyatapola Inn ℡01/611852, ℻612780, ⓔsaragha53@hotmail.com. Tiny, family-run hotel with dark but not unpleasant rooms somewhat cheered up by floor cushions. ❹
Nyatapola Rest House ℡01/612415. Small, dark, motel-like stalls on the ground-floor, but it's cheap and there's room to spread out in the rooftop restaurant. ❸
Pagoda Guest House ℡01/613248, ℻612685, ⓔpagoda@aol.com.np. Hugely friendly, family-run place with pretty rooms; the higher-priced ones come with phone, TV and heat. Overlooks the Nyatapola. ❹
Shiva Guest House ℡01/613912, ℻610740, ⓦwww.shivaguesthouse.com.np. Classic location overlooking the Pashupati Mandir, and reasonably cheerful inside, with a range of rooms and helpful management. Good food, too. ❹–❻
Taleju Guest House ℡01/611078, ⓔrush@col.com.np. Smart modern block just outside the western entrance gate. Rooms are clean and well-furnished – the beds are huge. ❹
Traditional Guest House ℡01/611057. The name says it all: spread across two floors of a Newari family house, it's cramped and poky. Traditional indeed, but clean enough. ❸

Durbar Square

Bhaktapur's **Durbar Square** hasn't got quite the same gusto as its namesakes in Kathmandu and Patan. Isolated near the old city's edge, it's neither a commercial nor a social focal point, and it has lacked a certain architectural harmony ever since the 1934 earthquake claimed several of its temples. Despite all that, it boasts one of Nepal's proudest artistic achievements – the Golden Gate – plus the National Art Gallery.

The square enjoyed one brief, magnificent renaissance during the shooting of the 1995 film **Little Buddha**, when it was used as the location for many of the ancient flashback scenes. Director Bernardo Bertolucci transformed the area beyond recognition: high, simulated brick walls were erected to block modern sightlines and the palace front was extended with false balconies and columns. Residents won't soon forget that Hollywood facelift – nor the handsome fees Bertolucci paid them for the use of their houses and shopfronts.

The Royal Palace

Bhaktapur's **Royal Palace** originally stood further east, near Tachapal Tol, but was shifted westwards (like the city) in the fifteenth century, and may have lost various wings along the way. It is said to have once had 99 *chowks* (courtyards), and while this number is almost certainly fanciful, there would have been many more than the five which are all that remain since the renovation and demolition works of 1934. Further structural works are planned in order to rescue the palace from serious subsidence problems, so some areas may be closed off. Worst affected is the palace's superbly carved eastern wing, known as the **Panchapanna Jhyale Durbar** ("Palace of Fifty-Five Windows"), which was raised around 1700 by Bupalendra Malla, Bhaktapur's great builder-king, whose *namaste*-ing figure kneels on a stone **pillar** opposite.

The Golden Gate and Mul Chowk

While the **Golden Gate** (Sun Dhoka) probably wouldn't be so famous if it were made of wood or stone – it is, in fact, gilt copper repoussé – its detail and sheer exuberance have ensured its current renown. The *torana* above the door features a squat Garud and a ten-armed, four-headed Taleju, the Mallas' guardian deity, but to locals the most powerful figures are those of Bhairab and Kali, situated chest-high on either side of the gate. These alone among the statues are covered in red *abhir* and yellow *keshori* powder, showing that they are still worshipped today.

Upon entry, you follow an outdoor passage around to another impressive doorway, depicting the goddess Taleju and her heavenly host in wood. Beyond it lies the ornate, polychrome **Mul Chowk**, which is probably the oldest surviving part of the complex, and is regarded by art historians as one of the most exquisite palace courtyards in the whole of the Valley. You can peer in through the door to catch tantalizing glimpses of the riotously elaborate metalwork, carvings and wallpaintings, but photographs are forbidden, and only Hindus can enter to see the metal *kalash* (vessel) representing the goddess. The actual Taleju idol hidden in the sanctum in the south wing – said to be a *yantra*, or mystical diagram – may be seen by initiates only. South Indian in origin, Taleju was brought here by the fourteenth-century king Harisinghadev, and was also adopted by the royal houses of Kathmandu and Patan. She was never much worshipped by commoners, however, and the dynasties that patronized her are long gone. Those who worship her today equate her with Bhagwati or Durga.

The door facing you across the courtyard leads into the fabled Kumari Chowk, said by the few who know it to be as old and as beautiful as Mul Chowk, though smaller. Turning back towards the Golden Gate, a doorway on the left leads through to **Naga Pokhari** ("Snake Pond"), a regal bathing tank dating from the early sixteenth century. The extraordinary waterspout writhes with images of thirsty animals in gilt copper, overlooked by two sinister gilt *nag* figures standing clear of the water.

The National Art Gallery

The palace's western wing houses the excellent **National Art Gallery** (Tues–Sat 9.30am–4.30pm; Rs20), displaying an extensive permanent exhibit of tantric *poubha* and *thangka* paintings that focus on the fierce local gods Bhairab and Kali, the latter seen in some of his 64 bloodcurdling forms – White

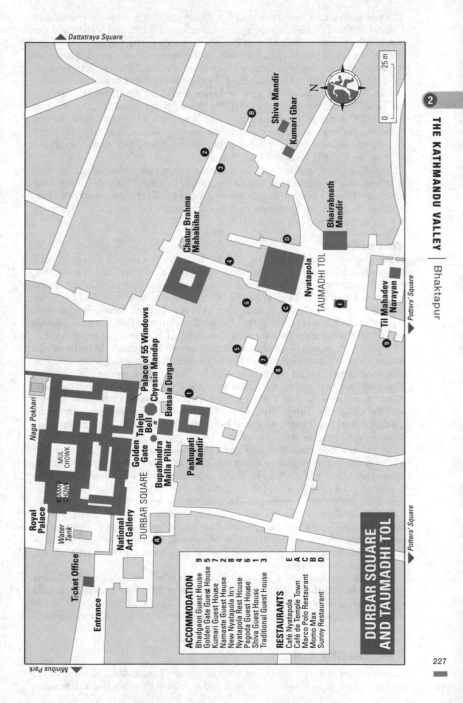

DURBAR SQUARE AND TAUMADHI TOL

ACCOMMODATION
Bhadgaon Guest House	9
Golden Gate Guest House	5
Kumari Guest House	7
Namaste Guest House	2
New Nyatapola Inn	8
Nyatapola Rest House	4
Pagoda Guest House	6
Shiva Guest House	1
Traditional Guest House	3

RESTAURANTS
Café Nyatapola	E
Café de Temple Town	A
Marco Polo Restaurant	C
Momo Max	B
Sunny Restaurant	D

Bhairab, Lion-faced, Fire-breathing … The main hall houses a depiction of Nritaswor, the dancing, copulating Tantric union of Shiva and Shakti, and the *Sata Chakra Darsan* (labelled "Yoga Purush"), a medical chart showing the location of the seven power points (*chakra*) of the human body; reproductions of the latter can be bought in various shops around town. In the gallery beyond, an eighteenth-century *paubha* labelled "Gorkha Palace" acts as a kind of botanical-zoological-topographical map of Nepal stretching from the Himalaya to the Tarai. The collection also includes illuminated pages of religious texts going back as far as the eleventh century, a few erotic miniatures, some wonderful stone images from the Malla dynasty and a single "Ladies Handbag" from the eighteenth century. Stone friezes at the entrance portray Vishnu Varahi and Narasimha, Vishnu's boar and man-lion *avatar*.

English-speaking **guides** may be available for private tours, which are well worth joining to get the most out of this rich collection. Otherwise, ask for the brochure (they don't hand it out automatically). Keep your **entry ticket**, because it's good for admission to two other, smaller museums in Dattatraya Square (see p.230).

The square

Durbar Square itself won't detain you for long; in any case, as a parade of regal set-pieces it never had much connection with the religious life of the town. Near the main gate at the west end you can admire a pair of multiple-armed statues of **Bhairab** and **Ugrachandi**, whose sculptor reportedly had his hands cut off by order of the Bhaktapur king to ensure that he wouldn't reproduce the images in Kathmandu or Patan. Among the clutch of minor temples opposite, a Shiva *shikra* showcases the often overlooked Newar art of brickwork.

In the entire square, only the fifteenth-century **Pashupati Mandir** at the busier, more touristy eastern end receives much in the way of reverence. The oldest structure extant here, the temple houses a copy of the exalted Pashupatinath *linga*, and its roof struts sport some wildly deviant erotic carvings. Next door stands the mid-eighteenth-century stone *shikra* of **Batsala Durga** and the obligatory **Taleju Bell**, plus a smaller replica known generally as the "**Bell of Barking Dogs**", so called because its toll evidently inflicts ultrasonic agony on local canines.

Behind the bell rises the **Chyasin Mandap**, the Pavilion of the Eight Corners, erected in 1990 as an exact replica of an eighteenth-century structure destroyed in the 1934 earthquake. German architects did a first-rate job of relocating original pillars and lintels and integrating them into a new, steel-reinforced structure, but they had to do without the original carved roof-struts, which have adorned the entrance archway leading into Kathmandu's New Road since 1934. East of here are another fine stone *shikra* to Durga and the platforms of other demolished and half-heartedly rebuilt temples. This end of the square is slated for renovation, and in the long term may even see the construction of new temples.

Rare for predominantly Hindu Bhaktapur, the well-preserved **Chatur Brahma Mahabihar**, east of the square, attracts Buddhist as well as Hindu worshippers, and is a gathering place for neighbourhood metalsmiths in the evening; you might also hear languorous music performed on harmonium and tabla.

Taumadhi Tol

One hundred metres southeast of Durbar Square, **Taumadhi Tol** is the nerve centre of Bhaktapur's Newari culture, and a livelier place to linger, if only to

Bisket: New Year, Bhaktapur style

While many Nepali festivals have their origins in religious myth, Bhaktapur's high-spirited **Bisket** festival is based on a fairy tale. Similar fables appear in Zoroastrian myth and in the biblical Apocrypha's Book of Tobit. According to the local version, a Bhaktapur king wanted to marry off his daughter, but each time he made a match, the groom would turn up dead in the marital bed the next morning. Eligible bachelors were soon thin on the ground, and the people prayed for deliverance from the curse. One day a stranger came to town and learned of the situation from his host, whose son was due to be the next groom, and offered to take the son's place. Forcing himself to stay awake after doing the act with the princess, the stranger watched as two deadly serpents slithered out of her nostrils. The hero slew the snakes, broke the spell and won the undying gratitude of the people, who now celebrate his deed with an annual festival. The festival's Newari name, Biska, is a contraction of two words meaning "snake" and "death".

Bisket also differs from most Nepali festivals in that its date is reckoned by the solar calendar, not the lunar one, which means it always starts on April 9 or 10. It kicks off with a raucous **tug-of-war** in Taumadhi Tol, in which residents of the upper and lower halves of the city try to pull a creaky, three-storied chariot containing the image of Bhairab to their respective sides; you can usually see the chariot's wheels lying beside the Bhairab temple. On the fourth day – the day before Nawa Barsa (Nepali New Year) – Bhairab and another smaller chariot are pulled to the sloping open area above Chuping Ghat. When they're in place, men of the city struggle to raise a 25-metre-high **ceremonial pole** with a crossbeam to which are attached two banners representing the two slain snakes – an exciting and sometimes dangerous operation.

The pole stays up until the next afternoon, when residents again take up a tug-of-war, this time trying to pull the mighty pole down to their side. (This is an even more dangerous performance: on one or two occasions people have been killed by the falling pole.) The pole's plunge marks the official beginning of the **new year**. Bisket continues for another four days, with a wild *khat* (deity litter) parade in the eastern part of the city, a candlelight procession to Dattatreya Square, an all-city display of temple deities, and a final tug-of-war over Bhairab's chariot.

admire the view from the balcony of one of the surrounding cafés. In mid-April this square serves as the assembly point for Bisket, Nepal's foremost New Year celebration (see box above).

Dominating Taumadhi and all of Bhaktapur, the graceful, five-tiered **Nyatapola** is Nepal's tallest and most classically proportioned pagoda. So obscure is its deity, a tantric goddess named Siddhi Lakshmi, that she apparently has no devotees, and the sanctuary has been barred to all but priests ever since its completion in 1702. Perhaps that's why the temple is named not for a deity but, uniquely, for its architectural dimensions: in Newari, *nyata* means "five-stepped" and *pola* means "roof". The Nyatapola's five pairs of temple guardians – Malla wrestlers, elephants, lions, griffins and two minor goddesses, Baghini (Tigress) and Singhini (Lioness) – are as famous as the temple itself. Each pair is supposed to be ten times as strong as the pair below, with Siddhi Lakshmi herself, presumably, being ten times as strong as Baghini and Singhini. Bisket chariot components, including the solid wooden wheels, can be seen near here.

The heavy, thick-set **Bhairabnath Mandir** is as different from the slender Nyatapola as one pagoda could possibly be from another. The most peculiar thing about this heavy-set building, in fact, is the tiny Bhairab idol mounted on a sort of mantel on the front of the temple (several other figures are kept inside, including the larger mask that leads the Bisket parade). A story is told that Bhairab, travelling incognito, once came to Bhaktapur to watch the Bisket festivities. Diving the god's presence and hoping to extract a boon, the priests bound him with tantric spells, and when he tried to escape by sinking into the ground they chopped off his head. Now Bhairab, or at least his head, gets to ride in the Bisket parade every year – inside a locked box on board the chariot. The *kinkinimalla*, or golden metal fringe at the very top of the temple, is held to be particularly fine.

Hidden behind recent buildings southeast of the square, the seventeenth-century **Til Mahadev Narayan Mandir** displays all the iconography of a Vishnu (Narayan) temple: a gilded *sankha* (conch), *chakra* (wheel) and Garud are all hoisted on pillars out in front, in a manner clearly imitating the great temple of Changu Narayan, 5km north of Bhaktapur. The temple's name, it's said, derives from an incident involving a trader from Thimi who, upon unfolding his wares here, magically discovered the image of Narayan in a consignment of sesame seeds (*til*).

A block northeast of the Bhairabnath Mandir stands Bhaktapur's **Kumari Ghar**. An image of the goddess is kept upstairs and is only displayed publicly during Bisket. The living goddess herself resides in another building north of Tachapal Tol.

West to the Potters' Square

Like a brick canyon, Bhaktapur's main commercial thoroughfare runs from Taumadhi west to the city gate. Roughly 150m along, you'll reach a kind of playground of sculptures and shrines, and a *shikra* that rejoices in the name of **Jyotirlingeshwar Mahadev**, freely translatable as "Great God of the Resplendent Phallus" – a reference to a myth in which Shiva challenges Brahma and Vishnu to find the end of his organ (they never do). Further west, where the street's brick cobbles temporarily give way to flagstones, the **Jaya Barahi Mandir** – one of many whose recent face-lift was paid for by the tourist entrance fee – commemorates the *shakti* (consort) of Vishnu the boar; you have to stand well back from this broad edifice to see its pagoda roofs.

Dark, damp alleys beckon on either side of the main road – north towards Durbar Square and south to the river. An obligatory destination in this area is Kumale Tol, the **Potters' Square**, a sloping open space southwest of Taumadhi Tol. Until recently, Bhaktapur's potters (*kumal*) worked here fairly anonymously, cranking out simple water vessels, stovepipes, disposable yogurt pots and the like. Nowadays the square has blossomed into quite a little tourist attraction, and as its output has shifted to tourist knickknacks, workaday pottery is increasingly being produced in other, smaller squares in the eastern part of the city, or in neighbouring Thimi. Ironically, the tourist market gives these potters an incentive to stick to mostly traditional methods. You'll see them kneading their clay by hand, and a few still form their vessels on hand-powered wheels. The finished creations are set out in soldierly rows to dry in the sun for a day or two before firing, which turns them from grey to brick red.

Tachapal Tol (Dattatraya Square)

From Taumadhi, the eastern segment of Bhaktapur's main artery snakes its way to the original and still-beating heart of the city, **Tachapal Tol** (or **Dattatraya Square**). Here again a pair of temples looms over the square, older than those of Taumadhi if not as eye-catching. More notably, though, Tachapal conceals Nepal's most celebrated masterpiece of woodcarving, the Pujari Math's Peacock Window, and a superb woodcarving museum. You'll also find the finest woodwork studios in Nepal here, which are well worth a browse, even if you haven't got room in your rucksack for an eight-foot, Rs100,000 peacock-window reproduction.

Just north of Tachapal, a second open space around Ganesh Pokhri is equally busy with *pasal* (shops) and street vendors. South of the square is also good for exploring, as Bhaktapur's medieval backstreets spill down the steep slope to the river like tributaries.

Dattatraya and Bhimsen temples

Rearing up behind an angelic pillar-statue of Garud, the **Dattatraya Mandir** (accent on the second syllable of Dattatraya) is Bhaktapur's oldest structure. The temple was raised in 1427 during the reign of Yaksha Malla, the last king to rule the valley from Bhaktapur. Like the Kasthamandap of Kathmandu, which it resembles, it was once a *sattal*, a three-storey loggia and public meeting-place, and is similarly reputed to have been built from the wood of a single tree. Dattatraya, a sort of one-size-fits-all deity imported from southern India, epitomizes the religious syncretism that Nepal is famous for: to Vaishnavas Dattatraya is an incarnation of Vishnu, while Shaivas hail him as Shiva's guru and Buddhists even fit him into their pantheon as a *bodhisattva*.

The oblong temple at the opposite end of the square belongs to **Bhimsen**, the patron saint of Newar merchants, whose territory Tachapal is. As usual for a Bhimsen temple, the ground floor is open and the shrine is kept upstairs.

The Pujari Math

Behind and to the right of the Dattatraya temple stands the sumptuous eighteenth-century **Pujari Math**, one of a dozen priests' quarters (*math*) that once ringed Tachapal Tol. Similar to Buddhist *bahal*, these *math* typically sheltered communities of Hindu devotees loyal to a single leader or sect. Like *bahal*, most have now also been converted to other, secular uses. Given the nature of the caste system, it's not surprising that the grandest houses in the city traditionally belonged to priests. The Pujari Math's awesome windows can be seen on two sides; the often-imitated **Peacock Window**, overlooking a narrow lane on the building's far (east) side, has for two centuries been acclaimed as the zenith of Nepalese window-lattice carving.

The woodcarving and brass museums

Don't miss the small **Woodcarving Museum** (Tues–Sat 9am–5pm; same ticket as National Art Gallery) inside the Pujari Math. Well displayed and lit, it enables you to inspect a small collection of exquisite temple carvings that in their normal surroundings are often too high up to fully appreciate. Highlights of the collection are an alluring fifteenth-century Nartaki Devi, a large, waist-up Bhairava (Bhairab) of the seventeenth century, several magnificent steles and *torana*, and various abstractly weathered temple struts. The tiny **courtyard** is a lavish, almost oppressive concentration of woodcarving virtuosity, and possibly the finest in the country.

Somewhat misleadingly, the **Brass and Bronze Museum** (hours and ticket as above) across the square contains none of the flamboyant religious art that one might expect, consisting instead of domestic and ritual vessels and implements. Still, by cataloguing the many esoteric forms of these items, the collection helps to suggest just how complex traditional Nepali culture is.

Nawa Durga Dyochhen and points east

North of Tachapal, the **Nawa Durga Dyochhen** looks like a haunted house, Nepali-style. A tantric temple only open to initiates, it honours the nine manifestations of Durga, who are especially feared and respected in Bhaktapur. According to legend, the Nawa Durga used to eat solitary travellers, turning the area east of Bhaktapur into a Bermuda triangle until a priest managed to cast a tantric spell on them. The Nawa Durga occupy a special place in Bhaktapur's spiritual landscape: the city is said to be delimited by symbolic Nawa Durga stones (*pith*), and most *tol* (neighbourhoods) have adopted one of the nine as their protector goddess.

Most famous of all are the **Nawa Durga dancers**, a troupe whose members are drawn from the caste of flower sellers. Each wears a painted clay mask which, empowered by tantric incantations, enables the wearer to become the very embodiment of the deity. Every September a new set of masks is moulded and painted, each with its own iconography – there are actually thirteen in all, the Nawa Durga plus four attendant deities. On Bijaya Dasami, the "victorious tenth day" of Dasain, the dancers and accompanying musicians gather at Brahmayani Pith, about 1km east of town, and dance all the way to the Golden Gate, where they re-enact the legend of Durga's victory over a buffalo demon. The troupe continues to perform at designated places on days determined by the lunar calendar throughout the winter and spring wedding and festival seasons. In the month of Bhadau (Aug–Sept) their masks are formally retired and burned, and the ashes saved to be added to clay to form the next year's masks.

West of the Nawa Durga Dyochhen, the **Prashannashil Mahabihar**, distinguished by its pagoda-style cupola, is another of Bhaktapur's few Buddhist institutions. East along the main road from Tachapal, the **Wakupati Narayan Mandir**, where local Jyapus worship Vishnu as a harvest god, displays no fewer than five Garuds mounted on pillars in a line.

Along the Hanumante Khola and beyond

The **Hanumante Khola** is Bhaktapur's humble tributary of the River Ganga, its name deriving from the monkey god Hanuman who, locals like to think, stopped here for a drink on his way back from the Himalaya after gathering medicinal herbs to heal Ram's brother in an episode of the *Ramayan*. Like all rivers in the valley, it's pretty disgusting, and doesn't exactly present Bhaktapur's best face, but several interesting bathing and cremation ghats flank the river as it curls along the city's southern edge. Unfortunately there's no riverside path connecting them.

The ghats

The most active site is **Hanuman Ghat**, located straight downhill from Tachapal Tol where two tributaries join to form the Hanumante. Morning *puja* and ablutions are a daily routine for many, while old-timers come here just to hang out. The area is reached by passing between two jumbo *shivalinga* hoisted on octagonal plinths. Behind the left hand one is the Ram temple that gives the ghat its Hanuman association: a statue of the monkey god outside the sanctum pays tribute to his master sheltered within. Another Hanuman, painted orange, keeps watch over a clutter of small *linga* and other Shiva imagery scattered around the confluence area.

Downhill from Taumadhi Tol, **Chuping Ghat**'s temple complex has been partially restored and taken over by Kathmandu University's Department of Music, and sometimes offers short courses in Nepali music. If it's open you can go in – there's a lovely garden, and students may be heard practising their instruments. The long, sloping area above the ghat is the focal point on New Year's Day (Nawa Barsa) in April, when a 25m *linga* pole is ceremonially toppled by the throng. This area is inhabited mainly by members of the sweeper caste, so much of Bhaktapur's rubbish ends up nearby.

Ram Ghat, below Potters' Square, has little to offer beyond a run-of-the-mill Ram temple, though it's a good place to hear evening *bhajan*. **Mangal Ghat**, further downstream, boasts a more atmospheric selection of neglected artefacts, and by following the trail of *linga* across the river you'll end up at a forbidding Kali temple in one of Bhaktapur's satellite villages.

Surya Binayak

Once south of the Hanumante, you can ramble up to the forested ridge overlooking Bhaktapur, where **Surya Binayak** makes a worthy target. This most pleasantly situated of the valley's four main Ganesh shrines – catching the valley's first rays of sun – is reached by a steep, kilometre-long paved road from the main highway, south of Potters' Square. The temple itself is just an ordinary plaster *shikra*, surrounded by the usual Ganesh trappings; smeared with red *sindur* paste, the god's image looks like a warm fire in an ornate Victorian hearth. Ganesh is regarded as a divine troubleshooter, and this particular image specializes in curing children who are slow to walk or speak.

If you're on a bike, keep going: you can round the ridge either to the east or the west and noodle around a seldom-visited rural corner of the valley.

Eating

Most of the guesthouses have their own **restaurants** with standard tourist menus. Meanwhile, several cafés overlooking the various squares cater mainly to day-trippers – they're great places for watching the goings-on below, but the food is usually undistinguished and overpriced.

For something more authentically Nepali, there are plenty of cheap *bhojanalaya* west of Durbar Square and around the bus park, and Newar *bhatti* are found throughout the old city. If nothing else, you can always load up on thick, presweetened yogurt (Bhaktapur's famed *juju dhau* – "king of curds"), available by the clay pot or glass from local stalls at a fraction of the price charged in tourist restaurants.

Café de Peacock You can't beat the surroundings – the restaurant occupies a former *math* overlooking Dattatraya Square – but the food is run-of-the-mill tourist grub.
Café de Temple Town Popular with day-trippers and tour groups. It's on the expensive side, but the food (especially the Indian) is quite good.
Café Nyatapola If it weren't for the inflated prices, the location – in a former temple in Taumadhi Tol – would be irresistible. Smart, however, and the food is fairly good.

Marco Polo Restaurant Enjoy the view over a cup of tea or simple but uninspired snack meals.
Momo Max Tiny and extremely characterful cave-like local restaurant with local prices and clientele. Good *momos*, chow mein and more.
Sunny Restaurant A cosy, hobbit-house of a place located in a low-ceilinged old building next to the Nyatapola. Great food, including decent Newari combo platters.

Shopping

Some of Bhaktapur's best buys are in **wood**: browse the workshops around the main squares to get a feel for different styles, woods and techniques, then haggle for bargains with the traders along the lane that contains the Peacock Window. See Basics for more on what's available.

Bhaktapur is also known for its Nawa Durga **puppets** and papier-mâché **masks**, which are associated with a local dance festival (see p.232). The puppets come in various sizes and with one, two or four faces. Masks also come in a range of sizes and in two qualities, but the selection is greater in Thimi (see p.238). Many of the **paper** products sold elsewhere in the valley are handmade here in Bhaktapur, at a UNICEF-supported factory near the Tourist Bus Park. And of course you can pick up cheap **pottery** at the Potters' Square: animal figures, planters, candlestick holders, ashtrays, piggy banks (called *kutrukke*, a word that imitates the sound of a coin being dropped in) and so on.

Nepalis recognize Bhaktapur for its traditional **textiles**, such as black-and-red *pataasi* material and black *Bhadgaonle topi*, formal headgear now worn mainly by traditionalists and government officials. Foreigners will be more attracted by the locally produced *dhaka* in original designs, as well as block-printed, quilted cotton items, woollens, *pashmina* shawls and Rajasthani-style tapestries.

Several shops around Taumadhi sell quality **thangka**, and artists can often be seen painting them. **Watercolours** of local scenes are popular. Some **metal** pieces, such as incense holders and traditional ritual objects, are produced here. Tea, incense and music CDs are also available.

Changu Narayan

The beautiful, tranquil site of **CHANGU NARAYAN** is a must. Perched at the abrupt end of the ridge north of Bhaktapur, the ancient temple complex commands a fine view of the valley in three directions. "One remembers all the wealth of carving of the rest of the Valley," wrote Percival Landon in 1928, "… but when all is recalled it is probably to the shrine of Changu Narayan that one offers the palm. Perhaps one drives back home from Bhatgaon more full of thought than from any other expedition to the many outlying places of this crowded centre of holiness and history and art." To recapture the spirit of Landon's visit these days you'll have to block out the competing attentions of the local souvenir industry, but that's not so hard to do, and the site retains its pensive, palpably ancient atmosphere – not to mention the finest collection of statues outside the National Museum.

You can approach the temple complex from Bhaktapur, the Sankhu road or Nagarkot – time permitting, the ideal itinerary is to walk from Nagarkot to Bhaktapur via Changu Narayan. An **entrance fee** of Rs60 is charged at the main gate by the bus park area immediately below the steps leading into the village.

Buses from Bhaktapur's tourist bus park run approximately every half-hour. If you're **cycling** you'll need a mountain bike because the last 2km or so are very steep. Two other roads set off from the north side of Bhaktapur towards Changu Narayan, but they soon converge and eventually become a trail that passes through rural villages before a steep ascent to reach the temple after 5km. The ten-kilometre **hike from Nagarkot** is described on p.244, while the trail from the Sankhu road is only 2km long, but it's hard to find at its lower end and the bridge over the Manohara River is only seasonal.

The temple

The valley's oldest Vaishnava site, Changu Narayan's documented history goes back to the fifth century AD, and its sculptures attest to continuous worship here ever since. Some historians suspect an even greater antiquity, postulating that the Lichhavi temple was built atop a much older animist site.

The **main temple**, rebuilt around 1700, stands in a quiet quadrangle of rest houses and pilgrims' shelters. A measure of the temple's importance is the exag-

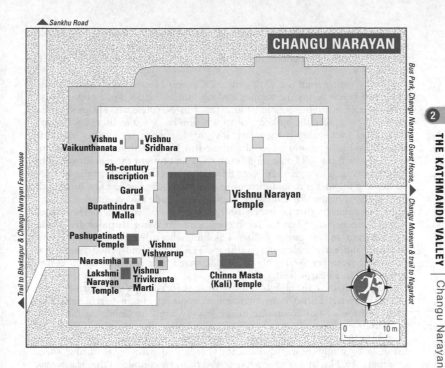

CHANGU NARAYAN

Sankhu Road

Bus Park, Changu Narayan Guest House, ▶ Changu Museum & trail to Nagarkot

Trail to Bhaktapur & Changu Narayan Farmhouse

Vishnu Vaikunthanata
Vishnu Sridhara
5th-century inscription
Garud
Bupathindra Malla
Vishnu Narayan Temple
Pashupatinath Temple
Narasimha
Vishnu Vishwarup
Lakshmi Narayan Temple
Vishnu Trivikranta Marti
Chinna Masta (Kali) Temple

N

0   10 m

gerated size of the four traditional emblems of Vishnu – the wheel (*chakra*), conch (*sankha*), lotus (*padma*) and mace (*gada*) – mounted on two pillars at its western corners. The repoussé work on the front (west side) of the building is as intricate as any you'll find in Nepal, as are the carved, painted struts supporting the roofs. The *torana* above the main door depicts Vishnu in his *sridhara* posture (see p.236), brandishing the four emblems in his four hands. The original fifth-century stone image of Vishnu, covered in a seventh-century gilt sheath, is allegedly kept inside the sanctuary, but only the temple priests are allowed to view it. From time to time, the statue is said to sweat miraculously, indicating that Vishnu is battling with the *nag* spirits, and the cloth used to wipe the god's brow is considered a charm against snake bites.

The base of the *chakra* pillar bears the **oldest inscription** in the valley. Dated 454 AD and attributed to the Lichhavi king Mandev, it relates how Mandev, upon the death of his father, dissuaded his mother from committing *sati*, saying "what use are the joys and pleasures of this world without you?" The face of the statue of Garud opposite (see p.236) is thought to be a portrait of Mandev.

Smaller temples in the compound are dedicated to **Chinna Masta** (a local version of Kali), Lakshmi (the goddess of wealth, Vishnu's consort) and Shiva. Some scholars speculate that Chinna Masta is the mother goddess who was worshipped at this site in prehistoric times. Her cult endures: a Chinna Masta Mai chariot procession is held here in the Nepali month of Baisaakh (April–May).

The statues

The courtyard of Changu Narayan is an outdoor museum of priceless works of art, displayed in an almost offhand manner and all the more exciting for it.

You'll find the oldest, famous statues grouped around the front of the temple (see map) plus loads of other, more recent (but still centuries-old) pieces in the vicinity. With few exceptions, they all pertain to Vishnu or his faithful carrier, Garud.

Probably dating from the sixth century, Changu Narayan's celebrated statue of **Garud** kneels before the temple, looking human but for a pair of wings and a cobra scarf – a representation found only in Nepalese art. He used to be mounted on a pillar, the broken base of which is lying just to his right. Garud's association with snakes is legendary. It's said that when his mother was kidnapped by his stepmother, Garud appealed to his serpentine stepbrothers to free her, which they did on condition that Garud brought them ambrosia from Indra's heaven. Although Indra later flew down and reclaimed his pot of nectar (leaving the snakes to split their tongues as they licked up the few drops spilt on the grass), Vishnu was so impressed that Garud hadn't been tempted to consume the ambrosia that he immediately hired him as his mount. The statues inside a screened cage next to Garud commemorate **King Bupalendra Malla** of Bhaktapur and his queen Bubana Lakshmi, who ruled during the late seventeenth and early eighteenth centuries. The king's gold-plated image was stolen in September 2001, only to be discovered by a cowherd the next day, half buried in a nearby field.

Though damaged, the eighth-century image of **Vishnu Vishwarup** (Vishnu of the Universal Form) is an awesome example of Hindu psychedelia. The lower portion of this composite image shows Vishnu reclining on the snake of infinity in the ocean of existence, echoing the sleeping statues of Budhanilkantha and Balaju. Above, the god is portrayed rising from the waters before a heavenly host, his thousand heads and arms symbolizing sheer omnipotence. The latter image is borrowed from an episode in the *Mahabharat* in which the warrior Arjuna lost his nerve and Krishna (an incarnation of Vishnu) appeared in this universal form to dictate the entire Bhagavad Gita by way of encouragement.

Two notable statues rest on the platform of the adjacent Lakshmi Narayan temple. The eighth-century **Vishnu Trivikranta Murti**, Vishnu of the Three Strides, illustrates a much-loved story in which the god reclaimed the universe from the demon king Bali. Disguised as a dwarf (another of his ten incarnations), Vishnu petitioned Bali for a patch of ground where he could meditate, which need only be as far as the dwarf could cover in three strides; when Bali agreed, Vishnu grew to his full divine height and bounded over the earth, sky and heavens. (An even older version of this statue is held in the National Museum.) The adjacent eleventh- or twelfth-century image depicts Vishnu in yet another of his incarnations, that of the man-lion **Narasimha**.

At the northwest corner of the compound, the twelfth- or thirteenth-century **Vishnu Vaikunthanata** – reproduced on the Nepalese ten-rupee note – shows a purposeful Vishnu riding Garud like some sort of hip space traveller. Nearby stands a **Vishnu Sridhara** of the ninth or tenth century, an early example of what has since become the standard Nepalese representation of Vishnu.

The Changu Museum

Small, eccentric, but definitely worth a look, the **Changu Museum** (daily 8am–6pm; Rs50) spreads across various floors of a Newari townhouse lying halfway between the entrance gate and temple. The collection is a beguiling mixture of traditional Newari utensils, all with English and Newari labels, and the owner's personal enthusiasms. You are led up and down narrow wooden

△ Changu Narayan

staircases, from the family kitchen and prayer room on the top floor to the rice storage cupboard and *raksi* still at ground level. The traditional guests' reception room on the middle floor is lined with a comprehensive collection of old and new Nepalese coins, including the world's smallest coin – an obscure medieval Nepalese minting – and a series of watercolours depicting the story of the foundation of the Changu Narayan temple. Other delights include an ingenious carved-wood plate drainer, a bowl of 220-year-old rice and a holy, hairy cow's gallstone.

Practicalities

The friendly little *Changu Narayan Guest House* (☎01/613242, ✉saritabhatta @hotmail.com; ❹) is the only **accommodation** option actually in town, and its location is pretty ideal, right next to the east side of the temple, with views across the valley to Bhaktapur. Down below the temple, on the steep west side, the *Changu Narayan Farmhouse* (❸) has decent rooms and a rooftop restaurant. For the best views you'll have to walk about 500m along the unpaved road to Nagarkot to the *Changu Narayan Hill Resort* (☎01/290691; ❸), which isn't as classy as it sounds, though the rooms are bright and clean.

All three guesthouses have acceptable **restaurants**, and there are also two tourist-oriented snack places by the entrance gate at the Changu Gaun parking lot. There are no other tourist facilities in town, although the legion of souvenir **shops** do a roaring trade in film, postcards, soft drinks, souvenirs and the like.

Thimi (Madhyapur) and around

THIMI, the valley's fourth-largest town, lies on a plateau 4km west of Bhaktapur. The name is said to be a corruption of *chhemi*, meaning "capable people", a bit of flattery offered by Bhaktapur to make up for the fact that the town used to get mauled every time Bhaktapur picked a fight with Kathmandu or Patan. Recently the town has revived its ancient name of **MADHYAPUR** ("Middle Place"), which recalls its midway location. Its mainly Newar inhabitants are indeed very capable craftspeople, and Thimi is the place to go for papier-mâché masks and pottery.

Any **bus** to Bhaktapur or beyond will drop you off at the southern end of Thimi, but you'll get a far more favourable introduction by **cycling** in along the old road to Bhaktapur, which skirts the town to the north. **Minibuses** from Bhaktapur and Kathmandu also ply this back route.

Several handicrafts shops – Thimi's only real attraction – are located along the north road. The **papier-mâché masks** seen in tourist shops all over the Kathmandu Valley originated here, and Thimi's Chitrakar family, famed for generations as purveyors of fine festival masks, still produces them in a range of sizes and styles. Snarling Bhairab, kindly Kumari and elephant-headed Ganesh are most commonly represented by the masks, which are based on those worn by Bhaktapur's Nawa Durga dancers. Compared to those now produced in Bhaktapur and elsewhere, Thimi masks are cheaper, lighter, and have a duller, rougher finish. **Pottery** is an even older local speciality, and you can see pots being fired under open heaps of smoking charcoal in back-alleys and courtyards in the north of town. However, Thimi's potters have largely abandoned traditional hand-powered methods for electric wheels and kerosene-fired kilns, and with help from a German project they're shifting from cheap terracotta housewares for the local market to export-quality glazed products.

The remainder of Thimi is grotty and unglamorously primitive. Thimi's only temple of note is that of **Balkumari**, a sixteenth-century pagoda located near the southern end of the main north–south lane. Couples pray to the "Child Kumari" for babies, presenting her with coconuts as a symbol of fertility. Balkumari's vehicle is a peacock, which stood upon a nearby pillar until it was stolen in 2001 – yet another victim of the voracious private collectors' market. The temple is the focus of the **Sindoor Jatra** festival for Nepali New Year (in April), when dozens of deities are ferried around on palanquins and red powder (red being the colour of rejoicing) is thrown like confetti.

Bode

A small, tight-knit Newar community, **BODE** is built on a bluff overlooking the Manohara River, 1km north of Thimi. The village's main shrine, the **Mahalakshmi Mandir**, stands at the northwest corner of the village, a modest and not particularly well-maintained two-tiered pagoda. The goddess of wealth, Maha ("Great") Lakshmi is feted during a three-day festival beginning on New Year's Day (here called Baisaakh Sankranti, meaning the first day of Baisaakh – April 13 or 14). The highlight of the proceedings comes on the second day, when a volunteer has his tongue bored with a thin steel spike and, thus impaled and bearing a disc-shaped object with flaming torches mounted on it, accompanies the goddess as she's paraded around the village. Volunteers believe that they won't bleed if they've followed a prescribed three-day fast and have sufficient faith, and that by performing this act they'll go directly to heaven when they die.

The central hills

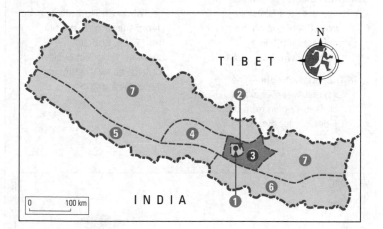

CHAPTER 3 # Highlights

✻ **Nagarkot** – A massive view of the Himalaya range, two hours from Kathmandu. **See p.244**

✻ **Panauti** – Perfect miniature pagoda complex at the holy confluence of two rivers. **See p.249**

✻ **Dhulikhel** – See the sun rise over the Himalaya from the hilltop shrine above this friendly Newar town. **See p.251**

✻ **The Bhote Koshi** – The whitest water of all, charging down from the Tibet border. **See p.257**

✻ **Jiri** – Travel to the end of the road, halfway to Everest, and persuade yourself to go trekking. **See p.261**

✻ **Nuwakot** – Historic fortress with stupendous views, one-hour's walk from the road. **See p.264**

✻ **The Tribuwan Rajpath** – Nepal's first road, built in the 1950s, and still the best and toughest cycle route of all, with stunning views. **See p.265**

The central hills

I t's only when you leave it that you appreciate just how extraordinary the Kathmandu Valley really is, surrounded by a 700-kilometre band of jumbled foothills that offer hardly enough flat land to build a volleyball court. Only a half dozen roads fight their way out of the Valley, but they are enough to make the **central hills** the most accessible area in the mostly roadless hill country – though not necessarily the most travelled. To the northeast, the **Arniko Highway** follows the old Kathmandu–Lhasa trade route through broad valleys and misty gorges to the Tibet border; northwestwards, the **Trisuli Road** snakes its way down into a subtropical valley nearly 1000m lower than Kathmandu; while west and then south, the **Tribhuwan Rajpath**, Nepal's first highway, takes a dramatically tortuous route up and over the hills on its way to the Tarai. If the scenery in this area is a shade less dramatic than you'll encounter further west, the land is nonetheless varied and rugged, only partially tamed by defiant terraces.

The majority of places described here can be treated as easy overnights from anywhere in the Kathmandu Valley. The most popular are those that involve mountain views: **Nagarkot** and **Dhulikhel**, with well-developed lodgings, are

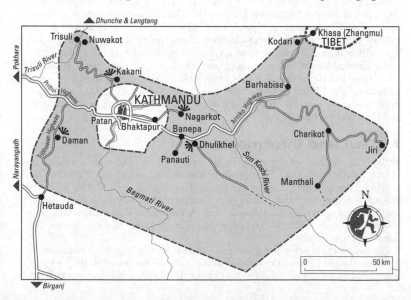

acknowledged classics. **Kakani** is equally scenic, though short on accommodation, and **Daman** is splendidly off the beaten track. These vantage points can't compare with what you'll see on a trek, but they provide a taste of the Himalaya and can also serve as springboards for hiking and mountain-biking explorations. The **Tibet border** area, meanwhile, is developing into something of a magnet for extreme sports. Although cultural attractions are relatively few outside the Kathmandu Valley, **Panauti** and **Nuwakot** are among Nepal's most intriguing small towns, and all the more because they're so seldom visited.

To an extent, the boundaries of this chapter are dictated by travel formalities: towns and **day-hikes** are described here, while backcountry **treks** that take you more than a day from a road are saved for Chapter Seven. Many of the places described in this and the previous chapters could even be strung together in one long quasi-trek or mountain-bike ride, a kind of grand tour.

Despite a relative abundance of roads, **buses** in the central hills are slow and infrequent, and indeed few travellers brave them except to get to the start of the Langtang/Helambu and Everest treks. All the more reason to go by mountain bike or motorcycle, for the region contains some of Nepal's most popular and rewarding **biking routes**.

Nagarkot

Set on a ridge northeast of Bhaktapur, **NAGARKOT** (1950m) is no quaint hilltop village. The straggling line of guesthouses and hotels is only here for one reason: the classic panorama of the Himalaya. While the view isn't as comprehensive as that from Daman, and the area not half as interesting as Dhulikhel, it's very easy to get to from Kathmandu and you don't have to stay in an expensive hotel to get a fantastic view from your window.

The first tourists are supposed to have been a troop of Punjabi mercenaries recruited to defend the Valley against Prithvi Narayan's troops. Stationed at the now-vanished ridgetop fort, they quickly succumbed to the "mountain air", and proved drunkenly incapable when the Gurkha invaders finally arrived. Since those times, numerous hotels have sprouted along some 2km of ridge, but the main attractions haven't changed all that much. Taking in the sunrise view, either from the hotel or from a view tower further back along the ridge, is the standard activity. Many visitors take the chance to just lie back and chill out – fairly literally, at that, as it gets pretty cold in winter – but there's a wealth of **hiking** and **biking** opportunities too. Since Nagarkot's located at a high point and easily reached on a good road, many people choose to get a lift up and then hike or bike down.

Arrival and information

In high season, two or three tourist **buses** depart each afternoon at around 1pm from the north end of Kantipath in Kathmandu and return the following morning. Book through any ticket agent (Rs100 each way). Public buses to Nagarkot depart from Bag Bazaar in Kathmandu every twenty minutes, stopping at Bhaktapur's Kamal Binayak area. A **taxi** from Kathmandu will cost about $12. Free transport should be provided if you're booked into one of the more expensive hotels.

The easiest **cycle** up is along the main road from Bhaktapur. It's consistently steep for the last 12km – the vertical gain is 650m – but paved all the way and relatively free of traffic. Unpaved and generally steeper roads and tracks head

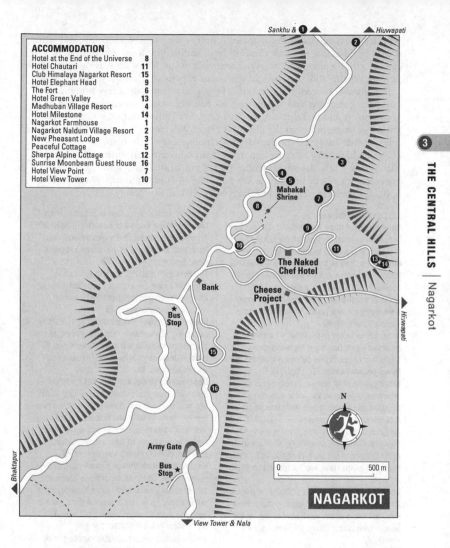

ACCOMMODATION

Hotel at the End of the Universe	8
Hotel Chautari	11
Club Himalaya Nagarkot Resort	15
Hotel Elephant Head	9
The Fort	6
Hotel Green Valley	13
Madhuban Village Resort	4
Hotel Milestone	14
Nagarkot Farmhouse	1
Nagarkot Naldum Village Resort	2
New Pheasant Lodge	3
Peaceful Cottage	5
Sherpa Alpine Cottage	12
Sunrise Moonbeam Guest House	16
Hotel View Point	7
Hotel View Tower	10

NAGARKOT

up from Changu Narayan, Sankhu, Nala and other points – see the "Routes down from Nagarkot" section, p.247. It's also possible to walk up any of these routes, but most people prefer to do that in reverse.

For **changing money**, Himalayan Bank has an efficient branch near the bus stop. Local shops sell films, batteries, soft drinks, chocolate and the like.

Accommodation

Nagarkot's soubriquet of "Thamel-on-the-Hill" isn't quite deserved, but there has been a similar boom in hotel construction, throwing up a rash of mostly rather overbearing guesthouses and "resorts" of varying standards. Our recommendations cover about half the hotels on offer, and more were under construction at the time of writing. Most hotels have offices or agents in Thamel who try to charge ridiculously inflated **prices** for prebooked rooms, and while it may be advisable to book ahead in high season, you'll get a better rate if you call direct. The price will be even lower if you just show up – as much as fifty percent off the published rate in the more expensive places, sometimes more.

The **view** is touted as the major selling point, but only a few hotels boast a complete panorama and in any case it's not necessarily a bad thing to have to get up for it and feel the sun on your face. Availability of hot water is another arbiter of price, but even the cheapest places will supply a bucket. Many hotels offer a wide range of rooms, often including cosy little bamboo or wooden chalets, which may be more expensive than conventional rooms with attached bathrooms. Only the most deluxe places are heated, and although quilts are provided, it's worth bringing a sleeping bag in colder months. A torch (flashlight) for walking between buildings after dark is also handy.

Inexpensive

Hotel Elephant Head ☎01/680031. Large, clean but ordinary rooms, and you'll have to head for the roof terrace to see the mountains. ❸

Hotel at the End of the Universe ☎01/680019. Characterful rooms, chalets and miniature Nepali houses, all done out in local style with lots of wood. At a high point of the ridge, though views from rooms are only partial. No hot water in the cheaper rooms. ❷–❺

Hotel Green Valley ☎01/680078. Excellent mountain views, but rooms are rather damp, and this corner of the ridge is becoming crowded. ❸

New Pheasant Lodge ☎01/680032. One of the best locations of all, looking directly out at the mountains over the valley, and in a relatively secluded spot accessed by a great little jungle trail. A couple of bamboo cottages and some plain ordinary rooms with hot showers "coming soon". ❸–❹

Peaceful Cottage ☎01/680077. Killer panorama of the mountains and the Kathmandu Valley from a high point on the ridge, and the rooms aren't bad either. ❸

Sherpa Alpine Cottage ☎01/680015, ⓔnagarkot @wlink.com.np. Not just an alpine cottage these days, but this is where you'll want to stay as the annexe wing is uninspiring. Well-managed and friendly. ❸

Sunrise Moonbeam Guest House (no phone). Last of a dying breed: a couple of basic rooms in a local family household. ❷

Midrange and expensive

Hotel Chautari ☎01/680075. Rather cosier than the more officiously upmarket joints. Most rooms are in semi-detached bungalows with partial views. ❼

Club Himalaya Nagarkot Resort ☎01/680080, ⓔclub@mos.com.np. Flashy international-class hotel, with an indoor pool and sauna and partial views from room balconies. ❽

The Fort ☎01/680069, ⓔfort@mos.com.np. Attractive rooms and cottages, excellent service, lovely gardens, traditional architecture, great restaurant and total views. ❽

Madhuban Village Resort ☎01/680114. Dinky Robinson Crusoe-esque bamboo A-frames, or brick bungalows with attached baths. Great views. ❻

Hotel Milestone ☎01/680088. Little brick huts with great views. ❹

Nagarkot Farmhouse ☎01/228087, ⓦwww .hotelvajra.com. Located nearly 2km north of the bus stop on the road to Sankhu (1km off the map). Run by the same folks who brought you the excellent *Hotel Vajra* in Kathmandu, this restful retreat places an emphasis on yoga and meditation. Lovely, secluded grounds with orchard. ❼

Nagarkot Naldum Village Resort ☎01/610963, ⓦwww.hotelharati.com. Great views from a mixture of chalets, some brick, some bamboo, some rather plush, some very ordinary. A good place to get away from the main build-up of hotels. ❻

Hotel View Point ☎01/680123, ⓦwww.hotelviewpoint.com. Big rambling brick complex of a place with nicely wood-panelled rooms. Unrivalled views from the top of its unmistakeable tower. ❻

Hotel View Tower ☎01/680122. Oddly, it's the *Hotel View Point* which has the view, and the tower, but there are compensations in the large, balconied rooms and friendly service. ❺

The view

Most guesthouses have good views of their own, but you'll get much better ones – with a glimpse of Everest, on clear days – from the **view tower** at the highest southern point of the ridge (2164m), an hour or more's walk from most hotels along a tarmac road. When you get to the tower you'll understand why Nagarkot has been the site of a fort (*kot*) since Rana times: this hilltop controlled the eastern entrance to the Kathmandu Valley and the vital trade route to Tibet. There's still a large army training base in the area around the tower, and you'll occasionally hear target practice, or see troops jogging along the roads.

The view itself is dominated by the Langtang range, which on good days looms alarmingly close at hand above a wall of dark rock. Haze usually obscures anything west of Ganesh Himal, though you can sometimes see Himchuli and even Annapurna. The view to the east is even more weather-dependent, and the mountains of Khumbu rarely appear as more than a rose-tinted dawn haze. On a good day, Everest can be seen, but only from high up, near the view tower: it's the second peak left of the rounded m-shaped mountain.

A predawn **bus** service (book through your hotel; Rs100) has turned the tower area into something of a circus, with crowds of tourists in season, fuelled by coffee brought up in thermos flasks by enterprising locals. For a bit more peace, and just as good a view, stop off short of the tower at the signpost to *Renuka Village Resort* and climb the small mound next to the turnoff. Nearer to the hotel area, there are good views from the tiny Mahakal shrine, from where the only obstructions are the ever-growing towers of *Hotel View Point* and *Peaceful Cottage* – good viewpoints themselves, and with the advantage of breakfast.

Eating

Food at the budget guesthouse dining rooms takes a long time to prepare and usually doesn't live up to expectations. You can always try seeing if the grass is any greener at other guesthouses or hotels, though eating dinner out means returning in the dark. Some of the expensive hotels can offer some pretty fine dining, and the restaurant at the *Naked Chef* hotel has an excellent, and very popular, restaurant serving anything from tuna niçoise to *gundruk* soup – the latter usually served only with the humblest Nepalese meals. At the other end of the scale, you can get cheap, standard fare from any of several "cafés" along the roadsides and in the small bazaar area around the bus stop.

Routes down from Nagarkot

Probably the most popular way down from Nagarkot goes **via Changu Narayan** (see p.234) to Bhaktapur, which can be reached in three or four hours on foot, or half that time on a mountain bike or motorcycle. The route follows the main road down to Phedi, where the road passes through a notch in the ridge (hikers can catch a bus here). At Phedi, take the dirt road to the right and follow it generally along the wooded ridgeline to Changu Narayan. It's another 6km from Changu down to Bhaktapur.

The descent **to Sankhu** (p.202), which starts by following the road past Nagarkot's northern lodges, is favoured by mountain-bikers. The road forks not far past the *Nagarkot Farmhouse* (off the map): the left-hand route is steep, rutted and good fun (vehicles rarely use it); the right-hand one is smoother and longer, contouring around the Kattike Daada, the next ridge north of Nagarkot, to enter Sankhu from the north.

A longer two-day trek **to Shivapuri National park** (p.205) initially follows the latter route, then bears to the right (north) on a rough motorable road that contours round into the Watershed. This trek can be done in numerous permutations, in either direction and on foot or by bike. Most hikers spend a night in a local teahouse in Bhotechaur, just north of the road, near the Jhule entry point to the Watershed (Rs250 entry fee). From there it's another easy day's walk along a wood road to Sundarijal or Nagi Gompa, and an optional hard third day up to the summit of Shivapuri and back to Kathmandu via Budhanilkantha. It's not possible to ride a bike up to the summit, but cyclists can make it from Nagarkot to Nagi Gompa or further in a day, and to Kakani (see p.262) in two days.

If you want to move on **to Nala** (see below), continue south from the view tower, from where it's a stiff 700m descent along any of three different routes. The road that bears right around the tower is the easiest for biking, providing a good intermediate-level ride for 7km to the Nala–Bhaktapur road. Two other hiking trails, via the villages of Tukucha and Ghimiregaun, descend from a track heading left from the tower. From Nala you can travel west to Bhaktapur or south to Banepa and Dhulikhel.

Yet another option is to descend eastwards **to Hiuwapati**, deep down in the valley of the Indrawati River. You can make this trip on either of two roads – one starting at the north end of the Nagarkot ridge, the other from near the bus stop – which join after only a couple of kilometres, or on the track that goes around the left (eastern) side of the view tower. If you walk, it'll take three to four hours and you should be able to catch a bus or some sort of vehicle from Hiuwapati to Panchkhal on the Arniko Highway, where there are connections to Dhulikhel and Kathmandu. On a bike it should be no trouble to reach Dhulikhel or return to Nagarkot via a different route in the same day.

A decent **map** will make route-finding on any of these excursions much easier. The best by far are the 1:25,000 sheets published by HMG/FINNIDA, but Himalayan Map House's *Nagarkot* (1:25,000) and *Kathmandu Valley* (1:50,000) will suffice.

Banepa, Nala and Panauti

Leaving the Kathmandu Valley through a gap at its eastern edge, Nepal's only road to the Tibet border is officially known as the **Arniko Rajmarg** (**Arniko Highway**). Constructed by the Chinese in the mid-1960s – to India's great distress – the highway is a busy conduit for lorry-loads of Chinese goods by way of Lhasa, despite frequent blockages by landslides higher up. Appropriately, it's named after the thirteenth-century Nepali architect who led a delegation to Beijing and taught the Chinese how to build pagodas. The first stop along the highway is **Banepa**, which together with **Nala** and **Panauti** once comprised a short-lived independent kingdom east of the Kathmandu Valley.

Loads of **buses** and minibuses ply the Arniko Highway as far as Banepa. However, it's much prettier and less stressful to enter this area by **mountain bike** or motorcycle from Bhaktapur (entering Nala from the west along a dirt road) or Patan (via Lubhu and the Lakuri Bhanjyang – see p.221). Other biking and hiking routes are discussed in the Panauti and Dhulikhel sections below.

Banepa and Nala

BANEPA, 26km east of Kathmandu, was for centuries an important staging post to Tibet, and now – such is progress – it's an obligatory and unattractive pitstop for buses heading up the Arniko Highway. Beginning at the first round-about north of the highway, a road leading northeastwards to Panchkhal (p.256) first passes by Scheer Memorial Hospital, established by the Seventh Day Adventists, and the **Chandeshwari Mandir**, overlooking a new set of cremation ghats beside a wooded ravine. The three-tiered temple, which is best known for the psychedelic fresco of Bhairab decorating its exterior, commemorates Bhagwati, who according to one of the *purana* (Hindu scriptures) slew a giant called Chand here, earning her the title Chandeshwari ("Lord of Chand"). The arch over the entrance to the temple compound depicts the scene. Chandeshwari's image is the object of a chariot festival here coinciding with Nepali New Year (April 13 or 14).

A second unpaved road heads 3km northwestwards to **NALA**, a quiet, parochial village near the head of the meandering Punyamati Valley. Fanning out at the base of a hill, the classically Newar houses look like a landslide of bricks, frozen in mid-tumble. Nala's main temple, a recently restored seventeenth-century pagoda dedicated to Bhagwati, is unusual for having four tiers – even numbers are usually avoided as they're considered unlucky. The weathered image of eighteen-armed Bhagwati is ferried around on a chariot on the third day of Indra Jaatra in August–September.

From Nala you can continue west along a wide dirt road, passing a Lokeshwar temple on the outskirts of town, to reach Bhaktapur in 10km. Three lesser tracks branching off from it ascend to Nagarkot via different routes (see p.247).

Panauti

Built on a single stratum of rock, **PANAUTI** is said to be the best place in the Valley to be when the next earthquake hits. It's an enticing enough place at any time, leading a self-sufficient existence in its own small valley 7km south of Banepa. The best-preserved Newar town after Bhaktapur, the centre is a perfect nugget of extended-family dwellings, temples and public meeting houses, all built in the Newar's signature pink brick and carved wood. At the bottom end of the old centre, a cluster of riverside temples and ghats makes a delightfully sleepy alternative to Pashupatinath's gaudier treasures. In the past few years, a French-aided restoration effort has greatly improved conditions in the old town by covering sewers, rebricking lanes and rehabilitating historic structures. Although most travellers pass through Panauti only briefly on their way between Namo Buddha and Dhulikhel, it's an enchanting place to spend the night: wandering among the temples and bazaars by low-watt light is quite special.

The most pleasant way of **getting there** is by bike, either from Lubhu (p.221), Banepa (above) or Dhulikhel (p.251) and Namobuddha (box p.254). The latter route is also feasible on foot. Another possibility is to walk from the summit of Phulchoki (p.220) – you'll need a good topo map and the whole day. Minibuses to Panauti depart from Kathmandu's City Bus Park approximately hourly, calling at Bhaktapur and Banepa en route.

The town

Wedged between the Punyamati and Roshi streams, Panauti forms the shape of a triangle, with a serpent (*nag*) idol standing at each of its three corners to protect against floods. Buses pull up at the newish northwest corner, but the oldest and most interesting sights are concentrated at the streams' confluence at the east end of town, approached through a distinctive entry gate.

The shrine area at the sacred confluence, known as the **Khware** or **Tribeni Ghat**, is one of those tranquil spots that can waylay you for hours. The large *sattal* (pilgrims' house) here, a favourite hangout for local seniors, sports an eclectic range of frescoes depicting scenes from Hindu (and some Buddhist) mythology: Vishnu in cosmic sleep, Ram killing the ten-headed demon king Ravana, and even Krishna being chased up a tree by a pack of naked *gopi* (milk-maids). Krishna is the featured deity of the pagoda temple next door, too, where he's shown serenading his *gopi* groupies with a flute. Other small shrines dotted around the complex are dedicated to just about every deity known to Hinduism.

The Khware has been regarded as a *tirtha*, a sacred power place, since ancient times, and on the first day of the month of Magh, which usually falls on January 14, it draws hundreds of people for ritual bathing. Beside the river, the tomb-stone-shaped ramps set into the ghats are where dying people are laid out, allowing their feet to be immersed in the water at the moment of death. Orthodox cremations are held at the actual confluence, but local Newars are cremated on the opposite bank, apparently to prevent their ghosts troubling the town. A footbridge crosses over to the recently restored seventeenth-century **Brahmayani Mandir**, from which the mythical Padmati Khola is said to flow during the town's *mela*, held every twelve years on the first day of Magh; the next occurrence will be in 2010. Brahmayani's *dyochhen* (god house) is located in Paumari Tol, in the heart of the old town.

Just west of the Khware, the massive, three-tiered **Indreshwar Mahadev Mandir** stands in the middle of a lovely walled quadrangle. The temple is ded-icated to Shiva, the "Lord of Indra" in several myths, who is represented by a magnificent brass four-faced *linga*. Some authorities believe this to be the orig-inal temple (albeit restored since a 1988 earthquake) that was raised here in 1294, which would make it the oldest surviving pagoda in Nepal. The grace-ful and sensuous roof struts have been dated to the fourteenth century, although they may have been recycled; each carved from a single piece of wood, they predate the Malla style of carving the arms separately and then attaching them to the strut figures. Sharing the compound is a smaller, rectan-gular temple of Unmatta Bhairab, distinguished by three carved wooden fig-ures occupying its upstairs windows. "Unmatta" refers to Bhairab's erotic form, in which he is depicted as a terrifying, red-bodied demon with a prominent hard-on.

Practicalities

There are no lodgings in the old part of town, but the most central **place to stay** is the *Hotel Panauti* (☎011/61055; ❸), on the left about 200m along the main road south from the bus park; it has clean **rooms**, pleasant gardens, a decent rooftop restaurant and the only hot water in Panauti. A friendly, though simple, alternative is the *Panauti Guesthouse* (❷), just out of town beyond Khware Ghat, on the road to Namobuddha.

There are more choices for **food**. The lovely *Cafe Indreni* lies just behind the Indreshwar Mandir compound and is good for snacks and some Western dishes, while *Aaphno Ghar Newar Kitchen*, overlooking the main drag from the entry gate down to Khware, offers up excellent Newari dishes on the open first floor of a traditional Newari *lamopaati* meeting-house.

Dhulikhel

DHULIKHEL is justly famous as a well-preserved Newar town, mountain viewpoint, and hiking and biking hub, but its popularity is waning as road-building and modernization take their toll. Located 5km east of Banepa, just beyond the Kathmandu Valley rim, it sits in a saddle at the relatively low elevation of 1550m, which makes it warmer than Nagarkot. A number of resort hotels and guesthouses are positioned along the highway to catch the mountain views, but there are more pleasant places to stay in the woods above town, on the way to a small summit from which the full Himalayan vista can be seen. Most visitors to Dhulikhel stay at least two nights, which allows time for a wander around the old town, a sunrise walk and a full-day circuit of the surrounding countryside and the cultural sites of Namobuddha and Panauti.

These days, Dhulikhel is something of a boom town, which isn't necessarily a good thing for visitors in search of tranquillity. The municipality donated a large tract of land below town to Kathmandu University, Nepal's first private campus, which opened in 1991, and the Dhulikhel hospital, established five years later, has earned a reputation as one of the best in Nepal. But the most significant development is yet to come, as a new 200-kilometre route to Sindhulimadi and the eastern Tarai snakes out from the town's western and southern flanks. Donated by Japan, the road is expected to draw as much as half of the traffic between the Kathmandu Valley and India, all of which currently has to squeeze through Thankot. At the time of writing, roads had been hammered out as far as Mangaltar (coming from the north) and Sindhulimadi (coming from the south). When the last 80km will be finished is anyone's guess, but a roughed-in route at least can be expected by 2003. Once the tarmac is down, Dhulikhel may become one of Nepal's principal transport junctions, with all the revving and tooting that that entails.

Arrival and information

Local **buses** to Dhulikhel (every half-hour from Kathmandu's City Bus Park or from Bhaktapur's trolley bus stop; Rs18) are exasperatingly slow. You can ask

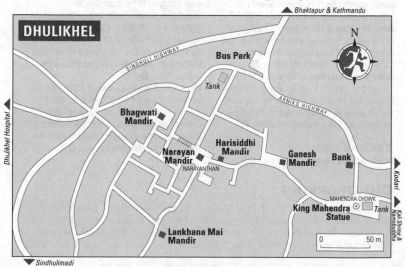

to be dropped off at any of the hotels along the highway, but for most of the cheap lodgings you'll want to stay on until the small bus park, a short walk away from the main square, Mahendra Chowk. A **taxi** will cost around Rs900 from central Kathmandu. On a **bike**, it's better to come one of the back ways – via Lubhu–Panauti, Bhaktapur–Nala or Nagarkot–Nala.

Apart from the postcards and primitive art for sale at the *Nawaranga Guest House*, and the usual range of bazaar goods, there's nothing to buy in Dhulikhel. Some shops stock a locally-produced booklet called *Ten Walks Around Dhulikhel*, which doesn't offer much beyond route descriptions but might be a good buy if you plan to stay a few days. You can change money at the lone Nepal Banijya **bank**. Dhulihel's **water** supply is among the safest in the country, though you'd be foolhardy to chance drinking it untreated. If you do, and you get sick, the **hospital** (☏011/61497), in the old town, is also said to be very good; again, these things are relative.

Accommodation

Dhulikhel used to get more independent travellers, but nowadays most of its **accommodation** is geared to upmarket tour groups, though only a handful of the numerous resort hotels ranged along the noisy highway ridge are worth considering. The older guesthouses along the route of the sunrise walk are much better located. More expensive places may offer substantial discounts to walk-in customers.

Budget and midrange

Hotel Gauri Shankar Mountain View Just off the highway ☏011/62079. Since the nearby *Mirabel Resort* obstructed the best of the view, the atmosphere has gone to seed, and the garden with it, but rooms are acceptable for the price. ❹

Nawaranga Guest House 300m east of Mahendra Chowk ☏011/61226. The last of Dhulikhel's original budget guesthouses still standing: fairly primitive, but it has a cult following thanks to the management's hippy chic, good food and rock-bottom prices. Partial view from the roof. ❷

Panorama View & Lodge Near the Kali temple ☏011/64358. Dynamite views, splendid isolation, though the place lacks atmosphere and it's a hassle to get to if you haven't got wheels. ❹

Snow View Guest House 1km east of Mahendra Chowk ☏011/61229. Quiet, friendly and in a great location, tucked away in woods on the way up to the Kali shrine viewpoint. Views from the rooms are limited but lovely, framed by the hills. ❹

Expensive

Dhulikhel Lodge Resort Just off the highway ☏011/61114. Well-managed; tasteful architecture and grounds. All rooms with view. ❽

Dhulikhel Mountain Resort On the highway 4km east of Dhulikhel – off the map ☏01/420774. Very scenic, private grounds with individual cottages, but nowhere near Dhulikhel. ❽

High View Resort On a side road 600m off the highway ☏011/61966, ✉hrvd@wlink.com.np. Well away from the highway, and every room has a great view from its balcony across the lush gardens and away to the mountains. ❼

Himalayan Horizon Hotel Sun-N-Snow On the highway ☏011/61296 or 01/225092, ⊛www .catmando.com/hotel-horizon. Spectacular views from the back terrace. The cheaper Newar-style buildings are more attractive than those in the modern block. ❼

Himalayan Shangri-La Resort 1.5km east of Mahendra Chowk ☏011/63244 or 01/427837, ✉himalayan@hsr.wlink.com.np. Sumptuously peaceful location, spread across the hillside in the woods below the Kali shrine. Beautiful rooms in Newar- and Gurung-style cottages. ❽

Old Dhulikhel

Old Dhulikhel starts immediately to the west of **Mahendra Chowk**, the main square at the new, east end of town, centred around a bust of King Mahendra. A close, traditional Newar settlement of remarkable architectural consistency, Old Dhulikhel is comprised almost exclusively of four- and five-storey brick

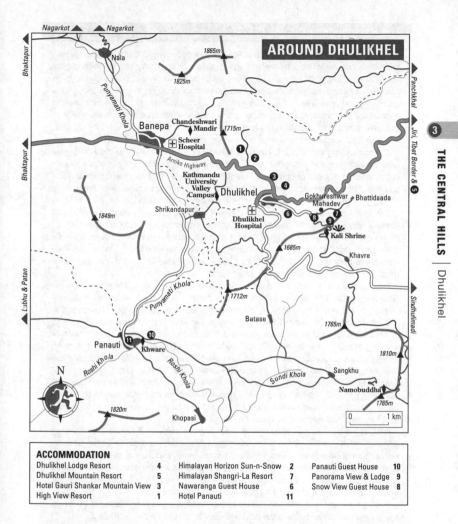

AROUND DHULIKHEL

ACCOMMODATION

Dhulikhel Lodge Resort	4	Himalayan Horizon Sun-n-Snow	2	Panauti Guest House	10
Dhulikhel Mountain Resort	5	Himalayan Shangri-La Resort	7	Panorama View & Lodge	9
Hotel Gauri Shankar Mountain View	3	Nawaranga Guest House	6	Snow View Guest House	8
High View Resort	1	Hotel Panauti	11		

mansions, many with ornate wooden lattices in place of glass windows, some affecting Neoclassical detailing imported from Europe during the Rana regime. These huge houses are extended-family dwellings: some Dhulikhel clans number fifty or more members. The older buildings, which are held together only by mud mortar, show some fairly serious cracks from the infamous 1934 earthquake; Dhulikhel also experienced some damage during the 1988 quake centred near Dharan in the eastern Tarai. Wandering around Dhulikhel is basically a matter of following your nose (and occasionally holding your nose), but highlights include the central square of **Narayanthan**, containing a temple to Narayan and a smaller one to Harisiddhi (both emanations of Vishnu), and the **Bhagwati Mandir**, set at the high point of the village with partial mountain views. Members of the Bhagwati temple association often do *bhajan* in the next-door building.

Hardened trekkers might sniff at the so-called "Namobuddha circuit", but it's a pleasant hike or bike ride. The scenery isn't spectacular, and the dusty, ungraded road gets some vehicle traffic, but the route takes you through mostly unspoiled countryside and there are some pleasant woods and interesting stops on the way. Although it's usually hyped as a hike, a **bike** will enable you to zip through the less interesting sections; if you **walk**, the advantage is that you can get onto some lesser trails in the latter half of the circuit. A full loop could be done in four or five hours on foot, but with food stops and side trips on the way round, it'll take much of the day.

It's worth trying to combine Namobuddha with a sunrise walk to the Kali shrine (see opposite), since the latter is on the way, although this requires a degree of organization that most people won't be able to manage first thing in the morning. Be advised that schoolchildren along the circuit have been known to taunt foreigners; it's a game you cannot win – just don't betray any exasperation.

The route follows the road beyond the Kali shrine, passing through the village of **Khavre** and crossing the new Sindhuli Highway after 2.5km, and contouring close to the crest of a ridge for another 7km to an intersection at a small saddle. True off-the-beaten-path riding can be found down any of the tracks off to the left in this section, particularly the one at this last junction – see the HMG/FINNIDA map series for details. For Namobuddha, though, bear right.

Resting on a red-earth ledge near the top of a jungly ridge, **Namobuddha** (or **Namura**) is for Tibetans one of the three holiest pilgrimage sites south of the Himalaya. It's like a hick version of Swayambhu – smaller and pretty uneventful, except during the February–March pilgrimage season, when Tibetans and Bhotiyas arrive by the vanload to circumambulate it. The stupa celebrates the compassion of a young prince (in some versions, the Buddha himself) who encountered a starving tigress about to devour a small child, and offered his own flesh to her – a sacrifice that ensured his canonization as a Bodhisattva. The Tibetan name of the stupa, Takmo Lujin ("Tiger Body Gift"), links it explicitly to the well-known legend. According to one Tibetan scribe, the name Namobuddha ("Hail to the Buddha") came into popular usage in the seventeenth century, when the superstition took hold that the site's real name should not be uttered.

Among the houses and teashops surrounding the stupa is a scruffy little Tamang *gompa*, which you can enter. Since the 1980s, however, the main Buddhist population at Namobuddha has been Tibetan. A steep path leads up to the ridge behind, which is festooned with chaitya, prayer flags and Tibetan monasteries in various states of completion, most of which are satellites of the mothership at Boudha; the latest effort looks set to be very grand indeed. In a small shelter near the top is preserved a famous stone relief sculpture of the Buddha-precursor feeding his flesh to the tigress. A hole near the base of the shelter is said to be the tiger's lair.

The road descends from Namobuddha to **Sangkhu**, where a right fork leads to Batase and eventually back to Dhulikhel along various roads or trails (refer to the "Around Dhulikhel" map on p.253). However, it's about the same distance – 9km – to Panauti (see p.249), and this is a preferable alternative if you have the time to spend the night there. From Panauti you can return to Dhulikhel a number of different ways by foot or bike, or by bus with a change at Banepa.

If you decide to stay along the way, the Trangu Tashi Choling Monastery above Namobuddha has a small **guesthouse** but it's mainly for long-term retreat participants. Simple rooms (❷) can be found at the smaller monastery at the farther end of the ridge; you'll be expected to eat with the monks. Down at Namobuddha itself, dorm beds (❶) can be had at the teahouses opposite and alongside the Tamang gompa. A luxury resort is being built about half an hour short (east) of Namobuddha: a kind of village of cottages built in traditional style, it looks as if it will be lovely, but the price tag is expected to fall, or rather soar, in the ❾ category.

The sunrise walk

The done thing in Dhulikhel is to hike to the high point southeast of town in time for sunrise over the peaks. To get to the top, take the road leading east from Mahendra Chowk for about 1km, passing a big recreation area on the left, and then go right at the next fork. Cyclists will have to stay on this graded road, but hikers can take a more direct, gullied path that branches left almost immediately. On foot, allow about 45 minutes from Dhulikhel to the top, plus any time spent gawking at the numerous birds and butterflies that have returned to the area since local reforestation programmes came to maturity. The **summit** (1715m) is marked by a small Kali shrine and, unfortunately, a small microwave tower. The peaks from Ganesh Himal to Everest are visible from here, and the sight of Dhulikhel's brick houses, salmon in the dawn light and perhaps wreathed in mist, is pretty wonderful, too.

On the way back down you can call in at a small, mossy temple complex, hidden down a flagstone path that angles off to the left just past the *Snow View Guest House*. The main temple, known as the **Gokureshwar Mahadev Mandir**, contains a large bronze *linga*. A couple of the adjacent Ram temple's marble statues have been lopped off at the ankles by temple-robbers – a persistent problem in Nepal, fuelled by demand from foreign collectors.

Eating

Dhulikhel has no tourist **restaurants**, other than those attached to guesthouses and hotels. Of the cheapies, *Nawaranga Guest House* does the best food (great custard pie). Both it and the *Snow View* have convenience going for them if you're looking for breakfast or lunch after a hard morning's mountain-viewing. Any of the hotel restaurants would be worth a splurge. For simple Nepali fast food, try the places around the bus park, or in the bazaar area east of the *Nawaranga Guest House*.

To the Tibet border and Jiri

Tour groups bound **for Tibet** follow the Arniko Highway to **Kodari**, the only official border crossing from Nepal, and a few individual travellers make the trip up to the border just to see it – or to chance their luck. Rafting, canyoning and even bungy-jumping parties also frequently pass this way en route to rafting trips on the Sun Koshi, or to the adventure resorts on the Bhote Koshi river. Trekkers on their way to **Jiri**, the main trailhead for the Everest region, follow the Arniko Highway for most of its length before heading off on a spectacular side road.

There are no scheduled tourist **bus** services in this area, but express public buses ply both the Arniko Highway and the Jiri road. Note that these services depart from Kathmandu's City (Purano) Bus Park, not the main one at Gongabu; you can also get on at Bhaktapur or Dhulikhel, but don't expect to get a seat. Both these routes make excellent adventures on a **bike**.

To the border

Traffic drops off beyond Dhulikhel, but **buses** are relatively frequent and increasing numbers of lorries and shared taxis ply the road to the border. Buses from Kathmandu to Barhabise run at least every half-hour, and are more

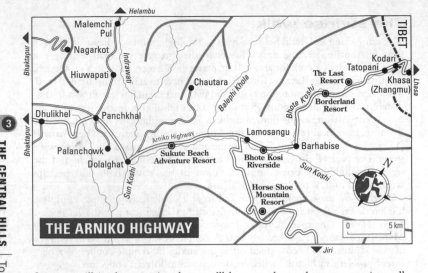

frequent still in the morning, but you'll have to change buses to continue all the way to the border.

Dhulikhel to Dolalghat

From Dhulikhel, the Arniko Highway descends 600m into the broad Panchkhal Valley, a lush, irrigated plain cultivated with rice paddy, sugar cane and tropical fruits. The village of **Panchkhal** is a minor gateway to the Helambu trekking region: an unpaved road, served by local buses, heads north past Hiuwapati (see p.248) to the trailhead at Malemchi Pul. Just past Panchkhal another rough road to the south leads 9km to **PALANCHOWK**, home of the famous black-stone Palanchowk Bhagwati, which draws pilgrims seeking protection in time of need. The Nepalese contingent to the UN Peacekeeping Force trains nearby. *Sunkoshi Adventure Retreat* (☏01/427496; ❺), located a few minutes' walk above the village, is more of a plain old resort hotel than a retreat, but makes a good base for exploring this rural area on foot, mountain bike and raft.

The highway reaches its lowest (and hottest) point 29km beyond Dhulikhel at **Dolalghat** (634m), a small market town clumped at either end of the bridge across the impressively vast and braided Indrawati River. This is the put-in point for rafting trips on the Sun Koshi, which joins the Indrawati just around the corner. A paved side road forks left just beyond Dolalghat to reach **Chautara** (1400m), a workaday Newar bazaar and an obscure trailhead for Helambu treks, after 25km. The town is served by direct buses from Kathmandu, but has only bare-bones Nepali inns; a Bhimsen temple at a high point of the ridge 3km further up the road offers good views.

The Sun Koshi Valley

The scenery begins to change after Dolalghat, as the highway bends north-eastwards up the deep, terraced **Sun Koshi Valley**. Nepal's terraces, while they're marvellous feats of engineering, are a sign of agricultural desperation: with so little flat land available and a growing number of mouths to feed, hill people have no choice but to farm ever steeper and less productive slopes. Terraces make good farming and environmental sense – they stabilize the topsoil and form a stopgap against erosion on deforested slopes – but maintaining them is a tremendously labour-intensive chore that detracts from the actual business of growing food, and building more terraces inevitably brings about further deforestation.

Having built the Arniko Highway, China has poured much of its aid to Nepal into infrastructure projects along the route. The first of these to come into view is a hydroelectric diversion, whose spillway and powerhouse are located just beyond the turning for Jiri. Human impacts to the valley are much in evidence for the next couple of kilometres to **Lamosangu** (740m), which is distinguished by a defunct magnesite processing plant, a ropeway and a big pile of castings.

Up the Bhote Koshi

A few kilometres upstream of **Lamosangu**, the highway proceeds up the larger of two tributaries, the **Bhote Koshi**, or Tibet River, which it follows to its source in Tibet. Taking advantage of both the highway and the river is a series

Adventure resorts on the Bhote Koshi

The raging Bhote Koshi's reputation as one of the most extreme **rafting** rivers in the country, and the fact that there's actually only about a day's worth of rafting to be done, attracts a young, fast-moving, thrill-seeking crowd to the area. The big rafting operators haven't been slow to develop the trend and, as well as the classic rafting trip, now offer **mountain-biking**, **abseiling** and **canyoning** expeditions, as well as one of the world's highest **bungy** jumps. Three major companies base their operations in attractive tented resort camps which – even if you're not intent on throwing yourself downriver on a raft, or off a bridge attached to an elastic rope – can make excellent bases for exploring the valley or just chilling out for a few days. In season, the atmosphere is rather transient, as clients arrive in groups and are bussed up and down the river to the various put-in and pull-out points, but there are usually a few travellers arriving from Tibet and expats escaping Kathmandu to leaven the mix of international adrenalin junkies. At relatively balmy altitudes of between 900m and 1200m, the valley is nearly as warm as Pokhara.

Equator Expeditions' **Sukute Beach Adventure Resort** (☎01/415782, ⊛www .equatornepal.com) is the closest to Kathmandu, sitting alongside a wider, gentler stretch of the Sun Koshi between Dolalghat and the Balephi bridge. The thatch-shaded tents have a regimented feel, but each has its own hammock and they do indeed overlook a broad sandy stretch of the riverbank.

Ultimate Descents was first in the area with the now well-established **Borderland Resort** (☎01/425836, ⊛www.borderlandresorts.com), set at the bottom of the gorge 9km north of Barhabise. It's a very relaxing, social place with thatched-roof tents, an open-air dining pavilion and lovely gardens.

Furthest north of the trio, Ultimate Rivers' **The Last Resort** (☎01/439525, ⊛www .tlr-nepal.com) has the most spectacular situation, accessed by a footbridge suspended 160m above the gorge that also serves as the launching point for their massive bungy jump ($80 including transport, lunch and been-there-done-that T-shirt). Comparing heights is a contentious game but it's certainly one of the world's top three jumps, and currently the only bungy in Nepal. The resort itself is probably the funkiest of the three – the full-moon parties are becoming notorious – and is set in beautifully landscaped gardens with plenty of sunny corners (and a sauna), but the river is some distance below. If you're fixed on that riverfront situation, Ultimate Rivers also run **Bhote Kosi Riverside**, a more basic tented camp 2km beyond Lamosangu that's a popular base for kayakers.

Prices for all of the above usually come as part of packages including activities, or at least meals, so it's worth shopping around for the best deal of the moment.

of **adventure resorts** (see box on p.257), which offer organized rafting and canyoning trips, and also make an attractive place to soak up the sunshine that penetrates the steep valley. **BARHABISE**, just beyond Lamosangu, straddles the river on either side of a hefty bridge and is the last town of any size before the border. Its bazaar is little more than a line of open shopfronts selling *daal bhaat* and Chinese goods, but the area around is still a traditional centre for the production of *lokta* paper, which is made from the bark of a type of shrub that's native to the hills above; you can visit any of the local operations, which are easily recognized by their rows of frames tilted to dry in the sun.

Buses to and from Kathmandu arrive and depart at least every half-hour from the south side of the bridge, while hourly buses bound for the border depart from the northern end of town, on the opposite bank – an arrangement that leaves the bazaar unusually peaceful. You're unlikely to be stranded here, as buses run continuously during daylight hours, but several **lodges** in Barhabise let cold-water rooms: *Bhote Koshi Guest House* (❷), right by the bridge on the east bank, is clean and has a terrace overlooking the river.

The permanent pavement ends north of Barhabise, as it's virtually impossible to maintain a permanent surface in the face of annual monsoon **landslides**. The Chinese who engineered this highway put it in the most unstable zone near the bottom of the valley, which made it easier to build but harder to maintain – to be fair, given the precipitous terrain between here and Tibet, they may not have had any other options. If you're entering or exiting Tibet along this route during the monsoon, there may be blockages where you'll have to transfer to another vehicle waiting on the other side; even in the dry season, journey times to the border can range from an hour to as long as three hours.

In the autumn, Nepal's famed honey-hunters may sometimes be seen clinging to the cliffs below the road in pursuit of hives. Afternoon rain is common up here, even in the dry season, and despite a general scarcity of trees near the river, everything is intensely green, with waterfalls splashing down cliff faces at every turn. As the road approaches Tatopani the scenery is interrupted by a series of hydroelectric plants that were developed by a private, US-based firm – a sign of changing times. Just before Tatopani is a police checkpost, where you may be asked to show your passport: from here up, the Bhote Koshi forms the border – Tibet is just across the river.

Tatopani to the border

Until the mid-1980s, **TATOPANI** (1530m) enjoyed a small following among Westerners, who came to gaze into forbidden Tibet and soak in the village's hot springs (*taato paani* means "hot water"), but it's fallen out of fashion now that Tibet is open. It remains a quiet, relaxing place – probably too dull for most, but kind of nice if you're into offbeat locales.

The village stretches along the highway for almost a kilometre, in two parts. Tamangs (see p.505) are in the majority at this altitude, and they maintain a small **gompa** five-minutes' walk above the southern bazaar. The building is modest, but it looks out on a fine view of the valley and, up at the head of it, the start of the Tibetan plateau. The signposted **hot springs** (Rs10) are at the northern end of the village, down steps towards the river. A hot tub it's not: the water splashes out of pipes into a concrete pool and is used strictly for washing, but it's a lovely spot to scrub away the grime and aches of travel, and soaping up alongside the locals can give a great sense of transnational solidarity. If you take the waters, remember that nudity offends in Nepal.

Western menus have virtually disappeared from Tatopani, but a few **lodges** limp on from the good old days: *Maiti Lodge* (❷), near the hot springs, is probably

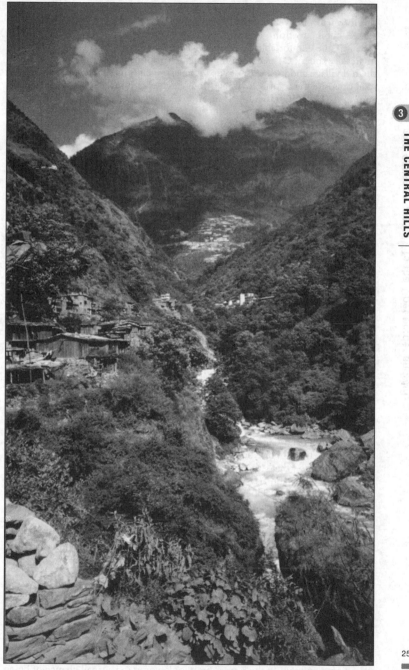

△ Bhote Koshi Valley

the best. Hints of China's nearness are everywhere: you'll see chopsticks and thermos flasks in every kitchen, and some places even sell Chinese beer.

One kilometre from Tatopani and just short of the village of **KODARI** (1600m), the comfortable Swiss-style *Kodari Eco-Resort* (☎01/480262, ⑩www .nvnet.de/kodari; ❼) perches on a bluff ten minutes above the road, close to the old village and its small Kagyupa *gompa*; the path up to the lodge leaves the road opposite the resort's *Roadhouse* lodge, which has less expensive rooms (❹) and meals. **LIPING** (1640m), 1km on from Kodari, is a scruffy agglomeration of shops, lodges and checkposts just short of the actual border, and is usually referred to as Kodari. You could do worse than stay at the Tibetan-run *Namgyal* or *Lhasa* (both ❷), which are right next to the immigration office and would give you an early start if you're crossing into Tibet.

Buses leave Liping at least every hour for Barhabise (Rs40), from where there is a frequent service to Kathmandu until around nightfall. The descent to Barhabise can take as little as an hour if the road is in good condition, but it's more likely to take double that, and journey times of three hours or more are not unknown during the monsoon. It's usually possible to commandeer a **taxi** direct to Kathmandu for around Rs1500 (Rs250 to Barhabise), but consider spending a night or two in the Valley towns of Dhulikhel (see p.251) or Bhaktapur (see p.222), which are much pleasanter places to wind down after China. Ask around: there's often someone willing to share the taxi ride.

The border

Disabuse yourself of any visions of high, snowy passes into Tibet. The border sits at the bottom of a deep valley, with nary a yak in sight. The lowest point along the Nepal–Tibet border, Kodari has always been the preferred crossing for traders between Kathmandu and Lhasa. Its low elevation isn't as extraordinary as it might seem, though: the main Himalayan chain, which the border generally follows, is breached in several places by rivers that are older than the mountains themselves (the watershed, in fact, runs not along the highest peaks but as much as 100km to the north). In the case of Kodari, the border was actually shifted further south after an ill-advised war with Tibet in 1792.

The actual frontier is marked by the so-called **Friendship Bridge**, which spans the Bhote Koshi at the top end of town, guarded at either end by lackadaisical Nepali and Chinese soldiers. Up at the head of the valley, 600m higher than Kodari, the Chinese buildings of **Khasa** (or **Zhangmu**) cling to the side of a mountain – that's the extent of the view of Tibet from here. A steady stream of Nepalis and a few Chinese cross the bridge during daylight hours. Officially, Nepalis and Tibetans living within 30km of the border are allowed to move freely to exchange goods, but in practice you won't see the Chinese border guards waving through any Tibetans. Nepalis from elsewhere in the country can usually travel as far as Khasa with a simple permit, and are allowed to bring back small amounts of stipulated goods such as electronics, garments, wool and shoes duty-free – noodles, flour and ghee go in the opposite direction.

Should you be **crossing the border**, the 9km between the Kodari and Khasa immigration posts is a precipitous no-man's-land which, when the road isn't washed out, will be traversed by some sort of shuttle vehicle. If the road is closed, you'll have to walk; you can hire a porter to carry your pack. Remember that Tibet is two hours and fifteen minutes ahead of Nepal, so you have to set off early if you want to catch the bank in Khasa before it closes, though reportedly there are plenty of people willing to exchange on the black market. Exchange rates are much the same either side of the border. Even if you've just come up to the border for a look, you stand a small chance of being

You can't officially enter Tibet (China) from Nepal without a visa and Tibet entry endorsement, which must be obtained in Kathmandu, and you must also be part of an official organized tour. There are always tales of travellers getting through with just the paperwork, but the rules have been strictly enforced in recent years. See p.180 for details.

allowed to cross and go up to Khasa if you leave your passport with the Chinese guards and promise to return in a couple of hours; if that doesn't work out then Nepalese immigration will usually let you walk halfway across the bridge.

If you're **entering Nepal** from Tibet, set off from Khasa as early as possible if you plan to make Kathmandu, as it's a full day's journey. Visas are available at Nepalese immigration, although there have been reports of travellers having trouble in the past.

To Jiri

The road **to Jiri** gives a marvellous foretaste of the immense country that's in store if you're on your way to Everest. It's very narrow and winding, with some unbelievable ups and downs, making it a gruelling **bus** journey of anywhere from ten to thirteen hours from Kathmandu. On a **mountain bike** it would be a marathon. On a **motorcycle**, though, it's an absolute magic-carpet ride – this has to be one of the world's great motorcycle journeys. In the past this route has had a bad reputation for theft from the roofs of buses, but the bus companies seem to have quelled this scam.

Along the Jiri road

Completed in 1985, the 110-kilometre-long **Jiri road** was financed by the Swiss government as part of its integrated development work at Jiri. It breaks off from the Arniko Highway at Khadichaur, 78km from Kathmandu, and immediately starts a merciless 1800m climb out of the Sun Koshi Valley. There's a delightful place to stay in **MUDE**, 28km into the climb and not far from the top: the *Horse Shoe Mountain Resort* (☎011/63174; ❼), run by a former riding instructor to the Crown Prince, has rooms done up in Tamang style. A short path from the resort leads to a fine viewpoint.

The first high point (2540m), reached after 32km, brings views of Phurbi Chyachu and nearby peaks, though they're a bit despoiled by the operations of a soapstone quarry straddling the road. After contouring around two small basins, the road reaches the Newar pitstop of **CHARIKOT**, just about at its midway point, where there are excellent views of Gauri Shankar and peaks to the east. A rough road to the left leads 5km to the older town of **Dolakha**, known for its temple to Bhimsen, the patron deity of merchants. The *Charikot Panorama Resort* (☎01/524209, ✉thapamaag@wlink.com.np; ❻), just above Charikot, makes a lovely base for exploring the area.

From Charikot the main road begins a long descent to the Tama Koshi (835m), then it's another long pull up a rhododendron-forested ridge to the road's highest point (2555m), and finally a dip into the Jiri Valley, at 1900m.

Jiri

Most people come to **JIRI** for the Everest trek, and are too eager to hit the trail or get back to Kathmandu to spend more than a night here. Set in a small, sloping valley, the bazaar is a busy place, with trucks dropping off supply shipments and porters assembling to carry impossibly heavy loads out into the hinterland of Solu and Khumbu: you can learn a lot about the local economy just by observing the composition of porters' loads. Saturday is particularly colourful, as Jirels (the local indigenous group), Sherpas, Tamangs and Newars descend from the hills for the weekly market in the old bazaar, about 3km back up the road.

Charlie Pye-Smith, in his book *Travels in Nepal*, called Jiri "the half-caste offspring of an impoverished Nepalese mother and a wealthy Swiss father". In 1958 the Swiss established the **Jiri Multi-Purpose Development Project**, a ground-breaking scheme based on the view that development needs – health, agriculture, education and so on – are interrelated and can't be tackled separately. The programme established a hospital, technical school, experimental farm, managed forests and other facilities, most of which have now been handed over to HMG. But it was the Swiss-built road that brought the greatest material boost to Jiri, and it has now been extended south via the major Khimti Khola hydroelectric project to the district capital of **Manthali**. It is currently being bulldozed on from there towards Okhaldhunga, an important bazaar town in the eastern hills.

At least a dozen trekker **lodges** are grouped around the western end of the bazaar – *Cherdung Lodge* (➊) is comfortable enough, but any one will do. Shops in the bazaar sell Nepali porter gear (small backpacks, jackets, socks, etc) in case you forgot anything. Lodge owners can arrange porters and guides. Be sure to book return bus tickets as soon as possible for the next day's departures, as seats go quickly.

The Trisuli road

One of Nepal's earliest forays into road-building, the **Trisuli road** was constructed in the mid-1960s as part of a hydroelectric project on the Trisuli River, northwest of Kathmandu. That's the official story, anyway, although the road probably owes its existence as much to historical nostalgia as progress: the route retraces the triumphal approach of Prithvi Narayan Shah, founding father of Nepal, from his fortress of Nuwakot to the Kathmandu Valley two centuries ago. It's since been extended north to a mining area in the Ganesh Himal. The majority of travellers passing this way are only concerned about getting to Syabrubesi (see p.442), the usual starting points for treks to Langtang and Gosainkund, yet **Nuwakot** is sorely underrated as a stopover, and **Kakani** makes a serviceable destination in itself.

From Kathmandu's Gongabu Bus Park, **buses** leave every half-hour for Trisuli (4hr). There are three morning buses to Dhunche (8hr), one of which goes on to Syabrubensi (outside the monsoon, at least). The road is slow and laborious by bus, especially after Trisuli, where the tarmac largely peters out, and its endless zigzagging, potholes, fords and light traffic are all better appreciated on a bike.

Kakani

KAKANI (*Kaa*-kuh-nee), the closest mountain viewpoint to Kathmandu, straddles the valley's northwestern rim at an elevation of 2070m. It's much less developed than Nagarkot, Dhulikhel or even Daman, and the views are somewhat inferior, but it's vastly more peaceful as a result.

Trisuli-bound **public buses** drop you off at a gap in the valley rim, 24km from Kathmandu, from where it's 4km up a paved side road (there are short-cuts) that passes a large training college for armed police en route. In the days of Prithvi Narayan Shah, the Kakani pass was the Kathmandu Valley's Achilles' heel – by controlling it, he was able to besiege the valley for two years – and this installation, like that of Nagarkot, is a vestige of the days of hand-to-hand combat, when hilltop positions provided military superiority.

For a **room** with a view you'll have to stay at the government-owned *Kakani Tara Gaon Resort* (☎01/290612; ❻), just beyond the police college. It's a bit cheerless, and overpriced if you pay full whack, but does feature a marvellous back lawn where you can lounge like a sahib, with Ganesh Himal splashed across the horizon and the Likhu Khola coursing through the valley 1000m below. Just below the *Tara Gaon* the trekking-style *Kakani Guest House* (❷) was the only alternative at the time of writing. For **food**, the *Tara Gaon* serves palatable lunches. You might be able to get your hands on the local strawber-ries, the commercial farming of which has transformed Kakani's economy in recent years.

Other than the mountains, Kakani is short on sights. The yellow building next door to the *Tara Gaon* is the former British Resident's bungalow, whose grounds once boasted a miniature golf course. During the Rana era, when Residents were prohibited from travelling outside the Kathmandu Valley, this was their window on the rest of Nepal; it's still owned by the British Embassy, and maintained for use by Gurkha officers. Occupying a high point further to the east, the well-tended Kakani Memorial Park honours those who died in a 1992 Thai airliner crash north of here.

From Kakani you can **walk back** to Balaju (see p.206) in three or four hours. Follow the dirt road east from Kakani past an agricultural station, then bear right and contour beneath the ridge before bending south and down along a spur. After passing a set of stupas, look for a fork to the left leading to Dharamthali and Balaju. **By mountain bike**, you can ride down to Budhanilkantha (see p.204).

Trisuli Bazaar

TRISULI BAZAAR (540m) is just 32km from Kathmandu as the crow flies, but 70km – and a good four hours – as the bus crawls. Curled at the bottom of a deep, subtropical (and once malarial) valley, it was put on the map by the construction of the Trisuli River hydroelectric project and flourished for a time as the trailhead for Langtang treks. The development bandwagon has moved on, and nowadays most trekkers don't stop in Trisuli for longer than it takes to swill a bottle of Coke and get back on the bus to Dhunche. Indeed, there's lit-tle to see in this ramshackle township, with the possible exception of the old, stair-stepped **bazaar** (reached through a passage at the west end of the bridge) and a small **stupa** perched above the opposite bank. That said, staying overnight at Trisuli permits a visit to nearby Nuwakot, which, if you find yourself with an extra day at the end of a trek, is a good deal more enjoyable than killing time in Dhunche or returning to Kathmandu early. You can also **trek** to Gorkha and Pokhara from Trisuli, starting up the Samri Khola, and there are a number of **mountain-biking** possibilities (see p.482).

Trisuli **buses** terminate in the main bazaar area on the west side of the bridge, and tickets for onward journeys are purchased there. Dhunche-bound buses usually stop in Dhunge, the smaller bazaar on the other side, near the turning for Dhunche. All of Trisuli's **accommodation** is on the west side of the river: *Hotel Ranjit* (❷) is as downmarket as the rest, but at least it has rooms overlooking the river.

Nuwakot

One of Nepal's proudest historical monuments, Prithvi Narayan Shah's abandoned fortress looms like a forgotten shipwreck on a ridge above Trisuli, casting a poignant, almost romantic spell over the tiny village of **NUWAKOT** (Noo–*aa*–kote). The **walk** from Trisuli takes less than an hour, although the trail is a tad tricky to find: climb a flight of steps starting at the Dhunge (eastern) side of the Trisuli bridge until you reach the Dhunche road, walk up the road for about 150m and make a right at the first group of houses. The path becomes wide and eroded as it climbs through a spindly forest of *sal* trees – the trees are coppiced for animal fodder – and reaches Nuwakot on the crest of a ridge about 400m above the valley floor. To **cycle**, take the (initially) paved road that leaves the main road about 1km south of Dhunge.

The **fortress** stands to the right as you enter the village, consisting of three brick towers rising like Monopoly hotels within a walled compound. The tallest one is open to the public, though you'll have to track down the caretaker to unlock it for you. The views from the top-floor windows are stupendous, looking out on Ganesh Himal and the pastoral Trisuli and Tadi valleys.

It was from this command centre that **Prithvi Narayan Shah**, the unifier of Nepal, directed his dogged campaign on the Kathmandu Valley from 1744 to 1769, and gazing out through these windows you can gain some insight into the mind of this obsessive but brilliant military tactician. In his determination to conquer the valley, Prithvi Narayan had **three other towers** built in the name of the three valley capitals, perhaps hoping to bring about their downfall by a kind of voodoo; the Kathmandu and Patan towers share the main compound, while the crumbling Bhaktapur tower stands on a rise just outside. After Kathmandu's fall, Nuwakot had just one more moment in the limelight. In 1792, attempting to extend Nepal's territory into Tibet, Prithvi Narayan's successor pushed his luck too far and was driven all the way back to Betrawati, the next village north of Trisuli. In the resulting **peace treaty**, signed at Nuwakot, Nepal ceded to Tibet the lucrative trading posts of Kyirong (north of Trisuli) and Khasa (north of Kodari), accounting for two southward lunges in the border that remain to this day.

Nuwakot's old main street runs south from the fortress along the spine of the ridge and suddenly dead-ends, the land falling away to reveal a lovely panorama of the Tadi and Trisuli valleys. In the late eighteenth century, when Nuwakot enjoyed a brief flowering as the winter residence of the Kathmandu court, the houses along this boulevard must have looked considerably posher. Several ornate old brick-and-wood buildings remain, notably the two-tiered **Bhairabi Mandir**. During the annual Bhairabi festival here, held in the Nepali month of Chaitra (March–April), the priest, under the influence of divine powers, drinks the blood of an entire buffalo straight from its severed neck. He immediately vomits it back up; not so many years ago it was the custom for worshippers to drink the vomited blood as a sacrament.

To Dhunche and beyond

Beyond Trisuli the road is unpaved, steep and agonizingly slow, buses taking four hours to cover this 40km stretch. You may prefer to close your eyes as the bus negotiates some of the switchbacks. Foreigners must show **trekking permits** at a couple of different army posts above Trisuli.

The road has replaced what used to be the first two days of the Langtang trek, and **DHUNCHE**, an unmemorable administrative centre, has boomed since its completion. Dhunche's guesthouses (all ❶–❷) are clustered around the main drag just past the town gate; *Hotel Langtang View* has a good restaurant and hot water. To return to Kathmandu, make sure to book your seat as early as possible the day before.

Beyond Dhunche, the road angles down to cross the Trisuli River, then climbs continuously to cross a ridge at around 3700m before descending slightly to the lead- and zinc-mining centre of **SOMDANG**, 34km northwest of Dhunche. Incredibly, there's a small hotel there, *Ganesh Himal Resort* (❹), but you can't book ahead because it has no telephone, and you have to bring all your own food.

The Tribhuwan Rajpath and Daman

Nepal's most magnificent and hair-raising highway, the **Tribhuwan Rajpath** (usually just called the Rajpath, which means "King's Way") heads west out of the Kathmandu Valley and then hurls itself, through an astounding series of switchbacks, straight over the Mahabharat Lek to the Tarai. En route it passes through lush stands of rhododendron and takes in superb views of the Himalaya. Mountain-bikers regard the road, and the culminating viewpoint of **Daman**, as something of a holy pilgrimage. The nearby **Kulekhani Reservoir** provides an interesting side trip.

Built by Indian engineers in the mid-1950s, the Rajpath was the first highway to link Kathmandu to the outside world – before that, VIPs were carried to the capital by palanquin, and the prime ministers' automobiles had to be portered from India, fully assembled, by 200-strong teams of coolies. The road is a perfect example of politically distorted aid. At the time, India was on the brink of war with China and preferred to make any route through Nepal as inconvenient as possible to reduce the risk of invasion. King Tribhuwan, who owed his crown to India, agreed to allow the road to be built right over the highest ridge in the entire area, rationalizing it by saying it would help in the development of remote villages. Since the faster Mugling/Narayangadh route was completed, however, the road has become something of a backwater – though its importance as the sole alternative route out of the valley was underlined during the monsoon in 2000, when the Prithvi Highway was closed by landslide.

The Rajpath is poorly served by public transport, with just one **bus** making the through trip between Kathmandu and Hetauda (see p.383) every day (plus another making the return trip). Another four buses do travel this route, but break the journey overnight in Markhu and Palung respectively – useful for getting to Daman from Hetauda, but not vice versa. From Kalanki, on the outskirts of Kathmandu, there are also five daily buses that travel as far as Palung, from where it's an hour's walk up to Daman. Infrequent trucks take on passengers, but nearly all of them are heading south to Hetauda after delivering their cargo to Kathmandu – fully laden vehicles bound for Kathmandu take the safer, quicker and less diesel-drainingly steep Prithvi Highway.

The lack of traffic makes the Rajpath a perfect route for a **mountain bike** (see p.482) or motorcycle: challenging, varied and scenic. A good time to do this route is in April, when the **rhododendrons** are in bloom. The Rajpath is also famed for its many varieties of **orchids**, most of which bloom in March–June or in September–October.

Along the Rajpath

For its first 26km, the Rajpath follows the heavily used Prithvi Highway towards Pokhara. Leaving the Kathmandu Valley through its ugliest and most industrial corridor, it slips over a low point in the rim (good views here of Manaslu, Boudha, Ganesh and Langtang) and descends to **NAUBISE** (945m),

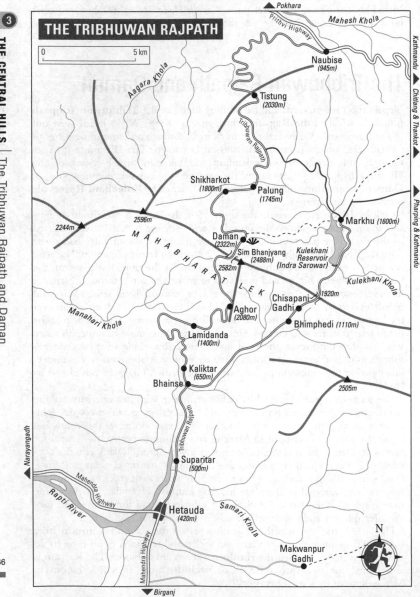

THE TRIBHUWAN RAJPATH

0   5 km

▲ Pokhara

Prithvi Highway

Mahesh Khola

Naubise
(945m)

Kathmandu ▶

Chitlang & Thankot ▶

Pharping & Kathmandu ▶

Aagara Khola

Tistung
(2030m)

Tribhuwan Rajpath

Shikharkot
(1800m)

Palung
(1745m)

Markhu (1600m)

2244m ◀

2596m

M A H A B H A R A T

Daman
(2322m)

Sim Bhanjyang
(2488m)

Kulekhani
Reservoir
(Indra Sarowar)

L E K

2582m

Kulekhani Khola

1920m

Chisapani
Gadhi

Bhimphedi (1110m)

Manahari Khola

Aghor
(2080m)

Lamidanda
(1400m)

2505m

Kaliktar
(650m)

Bhainse

Tribhuwan Rajpath

Narayangadh ◀

Suparitar
(500m)

Mahendra Highway

Samari Khola

Rapti River

Hetauda
(420m)

Makwanpur
Gadhi

N

Mahendra Highway

▼ Birganj

near the bottom of the deep, wrinkled Mahesh Khola Valley. This first stretch is a real drag: traffic is heavy, there are often long waits to clear police checkposts, and the descent to Naubise is a slow crawl behind smoke-belching trucks (punctuated by adrenalin-pumping manoeuvres to overtake them between switchbacks). Nepali restaurants are plentiful in Naubise and a few places have inexpensive rooms.

At Naubise the Rajpath leaves the Prithvi Highway and forks off to the left, climbing relentlessly for 30km to Tistung (2030m) before descending into the **Palung Valley** and its tidy terraces (spinach – *paalung* – and potatoes are local specialities). The turning for Markhu and the Kulekhani Reservoir (see p.268) appears on the left 4km past Tistung, and the Newar village of **Palung**, at 1745m, is 5km beyond that. Very basic food and lodging can be had in **SHIKHARKOT**, 2km further on, but unless you're desperate it's worth toiling up the final, tough 10km to spend the night in Daman (see below).

Three kilometres beyond Daman, the Rajpath crosses the pass of **Sim Bhanjyang** (2488m) – often icy in winter – where it enters a landscape of plunging hill country and begins a relentless, 2000m descent to the valley below. These south-facing upper slopes of the Mahabharat Lek are dramatically greener and wilder than those on the other side – they wring much of the moisture out of the prevailing winds, and are frequently wreathed in fog by afternoon.

The road passes through successive zones of mossy jungle, pine forest and finally terraced farmland until reaching the Bhimphedi turning (see p.269), 40km from Sim Bhanjyang. The electric transformers seen near here relay power from the Kulekhani hydroelectric dam north of Bhimphedi, an important source of power for Nepal. The devices that look like ski lifts are ropeways, one bringing quarried limestone down to the big cement plant in Hetauda and the other, now disused, for ferrying raw materials up to Kathmandu. Hetauda (see p.383) is 10km further on.

Daman

Set higher and farther back from the mountains than its rivals, **DAMAN** (2322m) is the most comprehensive of the Himalayan viewpoints surrounding Kathmandu, and about the quietest too. Sitting below the Rajpath's highest point, the hamlet overlooks the peaceful Palung Valley towards a magnificent spread of peaks. However, the mountains will probably be in clouds when you arrive: an overnight stay is obligatory to see them in their best morning light. Bring a sleeping bag in winter, unless you've got reservations at the deluxe *Everest Panorama Resort*.

The village and around

A signboard announces you're in Daman, but blink and you'll miss it. The village consists of a loose gathering of houses, a couple of agricultural research facilities, a seismic station and – its one unmissable landmark – an enclosed **view tower** that looks as if it might have been built for air traffic control purposes. Operated by the adjacent *Daman Mountain Resort*, the tower offers the best views in the village (admission Rs20 for nonguests). On good days you can see seven 8000m peaks from here, along with the closer and hence more prominent 7000m peaks of Himalchuli, Ganesh Himal and Langtang. Uniquely among the Himalayan viewpoints, the view of the entire range is unbroken by foothills. A couple of high-powered telescopes give awesome close-ups of the peaks from this angle: the magnified view of Everest is almost identical to the one you get from Kala Pattar, ten days into the Everest trek.

The view from the tower also gives you a good feel for the topography of the central hills and the Kathmandu Valley, from Phulchoki to the Trisuli Valley.

An even more sweeping (though unmagnified) vista can be had from the *Everest Panorama Resort*, a thirty-minute walk up the Rajpath, which also happens to be a fine spot for breakfast or lunch. One hairpin turn below the *Everest Panorama*, a signposted path winds through oak and rhododendron forest to a Buddhist **gompa** in another twenty minutes. Run by a Bhutanese lama, the monastery is small and unembellished, but the view from its meditation perch is awesome.

Practicalities

Daman lacks the facilities for travellers that Nagarkot and Dhulikhel have. For **accommodation**, there's not much choice, and all of it is expensive for what you get. At the budget end two nightspot-cum-truckstops face each other across the road: *Hotel Daman & Lodge* (❷) has a couple of dark rooms and cold water; while just above, the *Hotel Sherpa & Hill Side* (❷) is little more than trekking digs, but friendly enough. The *Daman Mountain Resort* (☎057/40387 or 01/269004; ❼) has cushy, safari-style tents and a few basic rooms, and can serve decent meals in the lookout tower. If you really want to go in style, book into the *Everest Panorama Resort* (☎057/40382 or 01/428500; ❽), 2.5km above Daman, which has heated rooms and thatched-hut tents, and runs activities ranging from hiking and mountain-biking to fishing and pony-riding. Both resorts may offer substantial discounts from the official price if you turn up at the door. In all likelihood, you'll **eat** wherever you're staying.

Moving on

Heading down **to Kathmandu** by public transport can be difficult, as the sole **bus** coming over from Hetauda is standing room only, and standing on a bus on this road is no fun. It passes through at around 10am, late enough for you to have enjoyed the sunrise view, but is sometimes so full it doesn't even stop. More buses may be added in time, but meanwhile, a useful alternative is to walk down to Palung, less than an hour below Daman, from where there are five daily buses, spread out through the day, to Kathmandu. Moving on **to Hetauda** you should be able to squeeze onto any of the four morning buses coming up from Kathmandu, Palung and Markhu, or failing that, hitch a ride with a truck.

These transport peculiarities make a good case for **walking** or **biking** down instead. Departing from the Rajpath about 500m down from the view tower, a walking trail descends to the western shore of the Kulekhani Reservoir (see below) in three to four hours, and continues from there to the Kathmandu Valley.

The Kulekhani Reservoir and Bhimphedi

Completed in 1982, Nepal's first major hydroelectric project dammed the Kulekhani Khola to form a sizeable lake east of Daman at an elevation of 1520m. The **Kulekhani Reservoir**, more commonly known as **Indra Sarowar**, is attractively nestled at the base of forested hills, and despite being a very deserving stopover on a couple of different itineraries from Daman, it remains completely undeveloped for tourism.

An unpaved but well-graded road leads 13km from the Rajpath to **MARKHU**, a small new village on the lake's northern shore settled by families displaced by the reservoir. Unfortunately, having been helped by an aid project to start a small-scale fishing industry here, their livelihood has been threatened by the Nepal Electricity Authority, which has banned commercial fishing on the lake. You can get simple accommodation and food here, though there are no English-language signs. Two buses a day connect the village with Kalanki on the outskirts of Kathmandu and a single daily bus travels up to Daman and over the Rajpath to Hetauda.

Walking down from Daman, you'll arrive at the western shore, where you can take a boat across to Markhu. From Markhu you can either catch a bus to Kathmandu the next morning or walk another full day to **Pharping** in the Kathmandu Valley (see p.213), or **Thankot** on the Prithvi Highway, from where it's a quick bus ride to Kathmandu.

You can also continue on a rough road all the way around the lake's eastern shore to the **dam**, and then follow a newly paved road up over the Mahabharat Lek to Bhimphedi (see below) via Chisapani Gadhi. Before the construction of the Rajpath, this was the main approach to Kathmandu from the Tarai – visiting dignitaries came this way by elephant and sedan chair – and there's a certain cachet to retracing the route. At the time of writing only private vehicles were plying the road between the dam and Bhimphedi, but it's probably only a matter of time before shared jeeps connect the gap.

Perhaps the new road link will restore some prestige to **BHIMPHEDI**, which was an important district capital until the government decamped to Hetauda. Connected to the Rajpath by an eleven-kilometre side road, it's a sleepy, traditional Newar bazaar in an attractive situation at the head of the valley. Seven daily buses connect with Hetauda but there's as yet no transport northwards, although locals claim that by walking over the hills to Thankot, on the Prithvi Highway, they can be in Kathmandu in time for an evening Hindi film. A small **museum** of howdahs (elephant-riding platforms) highlights one aspect of Bhimphedi's heritage from its heyday, but you'll have to ask around for the man with the key. You'll also have to ask around for the single local lodge, the unsignposted *KC Hotel and Lodge* (❶), which provides decent bed and *bhaat*.

4

The western hills

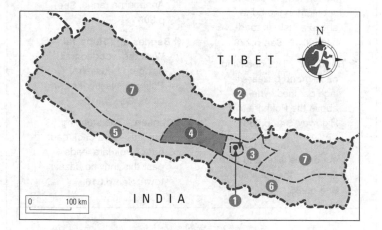

CHAPTER 4

Highlights

❋ **Gurkhas** – Retired Gurkha soldiers run many of Pokhara's lodges. **See p.274**

❋ **Manakamana** – Swoop up to this lofty, wish-ful-filling temple in Nepal's only cable car. **See p.277**

❋ **Gorkha** – Gorgeously carved temple-palace, set high on the ridge above a historic road-head town. **See p.279**

❋ **Bandipur** – This decaying, once-grand bazaar village perches eyrie-like above the Pokhara Highway. **See p.283**

❋ **Pokhara** – Take a boat out on the lake, and take it easy in the sunshine. **See p.285**

❋ **Gupteshwor Mahadev Gupha** – Feel the pulse of Hinduism in this womb-like underground cave-shrine. **See p.299**

❋ **Sarangkot to Naudaada** – Get the taste for trekking on this easy ridgetop walk, with classic views of the Annapurna range. **See p.309**

❋ **Begnas and Rupa Tal** – Walk the wooded trail rising up between Pokhara's lesser-known lakes. **See p.313**

❋ **Tansen** – The stunning but little-used backroad out of Pokhara leads past this thriving bazaar town. **See p.316**

The western hills

T he **western hills** are Nepal at its most outstandingly typical: roaring gorges, precariously perched villages and terraced fields reaching to unsupportable heights, with some of the most graceful and accessible peaks of the Himalaya for a backdrop.

In this, Nepal's most populous hill region, people are the dominant feature of the landscape. Magars and Gurungs, the most visible **ethnic groups**, live in their own villages or side by side with Tamangs, Hindu castes and the usual smattering of Newar merchants. Life is traditional and close to the earth, but relatively prosperous: the houses are tidy and spacious, and hill women are festooned with the family gold. For more on Gurungs, Magars and other ethnic groups, see p.501. The prosperity comes, indirectly, from an unlikely quarter, as the western hills were historically the most important recruiting area for **Gurkha soldiers**. Ex-Gurkhas command the highest respect within their communities, and young men look up to them as role models. They also speak English, happily, and wherever you go there will probably be an ex-Gurkha to help you over the language barrier.

The chief destination here by far is the cosmopolitan lakeside resort of **Pokhara**, Nepal's major trekking hub. Most visitors are understandably intent on heading straight for the mountains (trekking and rafting are described in Chapters Seven and Eight), but it's well worth side-stepping to the historic

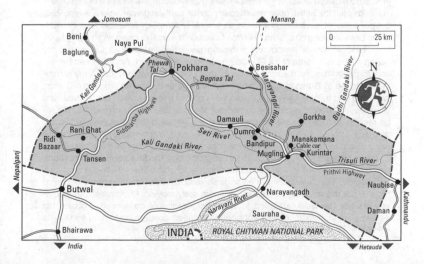

As I write these last words, my thoughts return to you who were my comrades: the stubborn and indomitable peasants of Nepal. Once more I hear the laughter with which you greeted every hardship. Once more I see you in your bivouacs or about your fires, on forced march or in the trenches, now shivering with wet and cold, now scorched by a pitiless and burning sun. Uncomplaining, you endure hunger and thirst and wounds; and at the last, your unwavering lines disappear into the smoke and wrath of battle. Bravest of the brave, most generous of the generous, never had a country more faithful friends than you.

Ralph Lilley Turner, *Dictionary of the Nepali Language* (1931)

Comprising an elite Nepalese corps within the British and Indian armies for over 180 years, the **Gurkha regiments** have long been rated among the finest fighting units in the world. Ironically, the regiments were born out of the 1814–16 war between Nepal and Britain's East India Company: so impressed were the British by the men of "Goorkha" (Gorkha, the ancestral home of Nepal's rulers) that they began recruiting Nepalis into the Indian Army before the peace was even signed.

In the century that followed, Gurkhas fought in every major British military operation, including the 1857 **Indian Mutiny** and campaigns in Afghanistan, the North-West Frontier and Somaliland. More than 200,000 Gurkhas served in the two world wars, and, despite being earmarked for "high-wastage" roles (16,000 have died in British service), earned universal respect for their bravery: ten of the one hundred **Victoria Crosses** awarded in World War II went to Gurkhas. Following India's independence after the war, Britain took four of the ten Gurkha regiments and India retained the rest. More recently, Gurkhas have distinguished themselves in Cyprus, the Falklands and as UN peacekeepers in Bosnia, Kosovo and Afghanistan.

Gurkhas hail mainly from the Magar, Gurung, Rai and Limbu ethnic groups, from Nepal's middle hills (for more on Nepal's ethnic groups, see Contexts, pp.501–511). Most boys from these groups have traditionally dreamt of making it into the Gurkhas, not only for the money, but also for a rare chance to see the world and return with prestige and a comfortable pension. Yet a Gurkha's pension – less than £100 a year for a corporal – is vastly lower than that of a British soldier of equivalent rank, a controversial matter in both Nepal and the UK, and the subject of court battles at the time of writing. Gurkhas were also excluded from compensation paid to ex-POWs in Japan and, in 1998, the widow of a Gurkha sergeant who had been killed by a mine in Kosovo received a fifth of the compensation awarded to the wife of a British officer. The outcry led the British government to announce parity in death-in-service gratuities, but pensions remain a thorny issue in an otherwise famously amicable arrangement.

The Gurkhas' long and faithful service to Britain is winding down. With Hong Kong (the Gurkhas' former headquarters) having been handed over to China and the Sultan of Brunei's contract for Gurkha protection now expired, Britain's need for military forces in Asia has declined – though, that said, the crisis in British Army recruitment has led to Gurkhas filling gaps in other, regular regiments. The main Gurkha recruiting and training centre in Dharan was handed over to civilian use in 1989, and all remaining operations are now carried out at the smaller facility in Pokhara. Would-be recruits can still try out for places in the lower-paid Indian regiments but the gradual loss of salaries and pensions – Gurkhas used to send home $40 million annually in remittances – is likely to take the steam out of many Nepali hill communities.

You won't learn much about such issues in the tiny **Gurkha Memorial Museum**, which is tucked away in one side of the compound of the flashy *Hotel Nature Land*, in Damside. The collection is mostly given over to dull old uniforms and photographs, but the small upstairs sanctum is strangely moving. Photographs of medal-winners line the walls, attached to short paragraphs of no-nonsense prose that describe act after extraordinary act of old-fashioned courage performed by Gurkha soldiers in British service.

hilltop fortress of **Gorkha**, the pilgrimage site of **Manakamana** and the charmingly neglected backwater of **Bandipur**. Beyond Pokhara, on the road to the Indian border, the laid-back bazaar town of **Tansen** lies at the southern edge of the hills. All of these make excellent bases for **day-hikes**.

Two main roads cut a swath through the hills: the **Prithvi Highway** (Prithvi Rajmarg), running west from Kathmandu to Pokhara, and the **Siddhartha Highway** (Siddhartha Rajmarg), which carries on from Pokhara to the Indian border. These and three spur roads (to Gorkha, Narayangadh and Baglung) are literally the only paved roads in this region, and they're not always paved. Elsewhere, most journeys are made on foot – and you don't have to go far in this area to appreciate how blurred the distinction between "travelling" and "trekking" can be.

Heading west: the Prithvi Highway

Weaving through the heart of the hills, the **Prithvi Highway** (Prithvi Rajmarg) is the easiest initiation into the pain and pleasure of Nepalese bus travel. You may find yourself on it several times, in fact, since besides linking Kathmandu and Pokhara it's also the best-maintained and fastest road between either city and the Tarai – a status that makes it all the more dangerous, as bus drivers compete to slice minutes off journey times. Nepal's second trunk road when it was built with Chinese assistance in 1973, the Prithvi Highway has played a crucial role in modernizing the country, opening up the western hills and enabling Pokhara to develop into Nepal's second tourist city.

The road stays near the bottom of deep valleys for most of its 200km, providing only intermittent views. If you travel directly between Kathmandu and Pokhara you might think there's nothing worth stopping for, since there are few towns of any consequence along the way, but actually there's a lot to do here. Many **rafting** parties come this way to paddle Nepal's most popular river, the Trisuli, which the highway parallels for about 50km, or to put in on the Seti, which it crosses at Damauli. **Trekkers** going around Annapurna get off at Dumre.

In addition, three **cultural destinations** just off the highway – **Manakamana**, **Bandipur** and especially **Gorkha** – offer further reasons to break the journey. Not many people visit them, because it means giving up their seat on the tourist bus, but continuing on by public bus is an experience in itself, and easily bearable given the short distances involved. If you want to stick with tourist services, you can always buy a separate ticket for a later date and arrange to be picked up at the nearest town along the highway. The danger from traffic puts off most potential **cyclists**, though it's easy enough to put your bike on the roof for the most trying leg, as far as Naubise.

Along the Prithvi Highway

After parting with the Tribhuwan Rajpath at Naubise (see p.266), the highway descends steadily along the south side of the Mahesh Khola, which soon joins the **Trisuli River** at Bhaireni, one of several rafting put-in points. Keep an eye out for magnificent, spidery suspension bridges and precarious ropeways spanning the river; you might also spot funeral pyres on the sandy banks, and rafting parties running the rapids. Lorries parked in the riverbed are collecting stones; these are then broken up by families of workers, attracted by the chance of earning as much as $2 a day. The high-water mark on the rocks shows how much the Trisuli, like all Himalayan rivers, swells and rages during the monsoon. The solid, three-storey farmhouses seen here generally belong to Baahuns and Chhetris, while the humbler mud-and-thatch huts are typical Tamang or Magar dwellings.

Most tourist buses make a mid-morning pitstop for *daal bhaat* at the relatively upmarket roadside town of **KURINTAR**, 102km from Kathmandu and just 3km short of the cable car to **Manakamana** (see opposite). Manjushree Thapa's novel, *The Tutor of History* (see p.563), lays open the elaborate social and political life of just such a Khaireni Tar ("the Ashen Flatlands"), but you'd be hard pressed to penetrate either in the twenty minutes the tourist buses allow you for lunch. Public buses break for lunch at **MUGLING**, a truly ghastly crossroads at the junction of the Trisuli and Marsyangdi rivers, that exists mainly to provide *daal bhaat* and prostitutes to long-distance drivers. At 280m, Mugling is the lowest point along the Prithvi Highway. Sugar cane is cultivated on a small scale around here, and you'll also see the tall, angular *simal* (the silk cotton or kapok tree), which produces red flowers in early March and pods of cotton-like seeds in May. Traffic bound for the Tarai turns south here for the gradual 34km descent to Narayangadh.

Just past Mugling, the Prithvi Highway crosses the Trisuli and heads upstream along the Marsyangdi, passing the massive **Marsyangdi Hydroelectric**

Farming in the hills

Most Nepalis live in countryside like that seen along this stretch of the Prithvi Highway, and the **farming** methods practised here are fairly representative of those employed throughout the hills. The land is used intensively but sustainably: trees and bamboo are pruned for fodder; livestock, fed on fodder, pull ploughs and provide milk and manure; and manure, in turn, is dolloped onto the fields as fertilizer (and used as fuel at higher elevations). Goats, chickens and pigs recycle scraps into meat and eggs, and even pariah dogs are tolerated because they eat garbage and faeces.

Nepali hill farmers have a harder go of it than their Tarai counterparts: the average hill family's half-hectare holding is fragmented into several plots located at different elevations, often a half-hour or more apart. The typical household owns only simple hand tools – its only beast of burden a buffalo or ox – and grows just seventy percent of the food it needs each year. Most farmers barter surplus grain for odd essentials such as salt, sugar, pots and pans, and have little to do with the cash economy. Some supplement their incomes with portering work or seasonal labour in the Tarai or India, while the unlucky or unenterprising fall into debt and often lose their land as a result. Growing numbers near the highway are starting to raise vegetables for sale, however, and several research stations in this area are experimenting with improved seeds, but tractors and chemical fertilizers will probably never be appropriate for the vast majority of farms in Nepal's hills.

Project powerhouse, which until recently generated nearly thirty percent of the country's electricity. (See p.537 for a discussion of Nepal's hydroelectric schemes.) The spur road to **Gorkha** (see p.279) leaves the highway at **Abu Khaireni**, 7km west of Mugling, while **DUMRE**, 11km beyond, is a drab roadside bazaar that's really only of interest as the turning for two side roads: one north to Besisahar, the starting point of the Annapurna Circuit, and one south to **Bandipur** (see p.283).

DAMAULI, 8km west of Dumre, is a nondescript administrative town marked out only by its position overlooking the confluence of the Madi and Seti rivers. This confluence, like so many others in Nepal, is highly venerated, and the large complex of shrines that has built up around it is one of those weird and wonderful places that you find only in the Indian subcontinent. To get there, follow the main street that runs perpendicular to the highway for about 500m, pass through an arch, bear left and descend a broad set of steps to the river. To the left is **Byas Gupha**, a cave where Byas (or Vyasa), the sage of the *Mahabharat*, is supposed to have been born and lived. It's really only a rock overhang with a concrete room containing a statue of Byas attached to it, but the attending priest ,will give you a *tika* and point you in the direction of an enclosed park area that's bursting with shrines, statues, rest houses and pilgrims.

After crossing the Madi, the Prithvi Highway rises and then descends gradually to rejoin the broad Seti Valley, finally reaching Pokhara 54km from Damauli. Begnas and Rupa lakes, off to the right of the highway on the approach to Pokhara, are described in the later "Pokhara Valley" section (p.313).

Practicalities

All of the roadside towns – Kurintar, Mugling, Dumre and Damauli – have plentiful **accommodation**, most of it noisy and insalubrious. Given that any stopover is likely to be an emergency overnighter it makes little sense to make particular recommendations for budget places, as standards are barely indistinguishable (they're low) and names change frequently. Generally speaking, Dumre, Kurintar and Damauli are all quieter and less unpleasant places to stay than Mugling.

There are, however, a few **resort hotels**, which make the best places to stay if you can't get to Gorkha, Manakamana (the cable car starts 3km west of Kurintar) or Bandipur, all of which are described below. Some resorts make the most of the warm riverside location, and are used mostly by rafting parties and expats escaping Kathmandu at the weekend. *River Side Springs Resort* (☏056/29429 or 01/434554, ⓦwww.nanglogroup.com/kurintar; ❼) provides the most luxurious **accommodation** anywhere between Kathmandu and Pokhara. The bungalows and dining area are nice, but what really makes the place is its palatial pool and long, sandy Trisuli River frontage. Nearby, the *Manakamana Village Resort* (☏01/252560, ⓔom@hons.com.np; ❻) represents a more affordable alternative, but it's rather close to the highway.

The same principles apply to **food** as budget accommodation: *daal bhaat* reigns king, but lots of places do chow mein, fried rice and all kinds of weird and wonderful snack foods.

Manakamana

Just about every Nepali has either been to **MANAKAMANA** (Ma-na-*kaa*-ma-na) or hopes one day to go. Located on a prominent ridge high above the confluence of the Trisuli and Marsyangdi rivers, the attractive village is home to Nepal's most famous "wish-fulfilling" temple. Each year over half a million people make the journey, the wealthier of them speeding up the hillside on a dramatic new **cable car** service. Completed in 1998, at a cost of $7.5 million, the line is one of the few developments targeted at Nepali tourists, who make up around two-thirds of the clientele. Sadhus and poorer pilgrims still toil up the walking route on the other side of the hill, but the cable car's slogan – "a pilgrimage with pleasure" – betrays the more genteel nature of many of Manakamana's visitors.

A visit to Manakamana can now be done in as little as an hour, thanks to the cable car (daily 9am–noon & 1.30–5pm; $12, children $7). Manufactured by the Austrian company Doppelmayr, the gondolas are just like those found in international ski resorts, with seating for six and plenty of windows for 360-degree views; the ride is smooth, silent and comfortable, and it takes just ten minutes to ascend the 2.8km-long line. Any bus will drop you off at the turning for the base station, which is marked by a big brick archway just off the Prithvi Highway about halfway between Kurintar and Mugling. Be prepared for long queues on Saturday mornings.

The village and around

From the cable car station at the top, a path leads between rows of Hindu souvenir stalls and *daal bhaat* restaurants up to the famous **Manakamana Devi** temple, set in a square near the top of the village and overlooked by a huge sacred magnolia, or *chaap*. Tradition has it that the goddess Bhagwati rewards those who make the pilgrimage to her shrine by making their wishes come true; she's especially popular with Newar newlyweds, who come to pray for sons. Animal sacrifices are an essential part of the ritual, and locals raise goats, chickens and pigeons specifically for the sacrificial market. The place goes into overdrive on Saturday mornings, when the vast majority of pilgrims come to perform animal sacrifices; the festivals of Dasain (in Sept–Oct) and Nag Panchami (in July–Aug) bring even greater numbers of celebrants. Visiting Manakamana is a very Nepali thing to do, and even if you don't sacrifice an animal you'll feel like you've received an initiation into the society.

Manakamana is also famous for its **mountain views**: from high points around the village you can see a limited panorama from Annapurna II and Lamjung Himal across to Peak 29 and Baudha of the Manaslu Himal. If you're game for more, you can continue 45 minutes further up the ridge to another temple, the **Bakeshwar Mahadev Mandir**, and then another fifteen minutes to **Lakhan Thapa Gupha**, a holy cave near the highest point of the ridge, from where the views are tremendous on clear mornings. The cave is named after the founder of the Manakamana temple, a seventeenth-century royal priest whose descendant – to seventeen generations – is still the chief temple *pujari* today, making offerings of eggs, rice, strips of cloth and the famous local oranges, which come into season in November and December.

Practicalities

At the time of writing, a flashy resort hotel was about to open next to the cable car base station, but it's far more interesting to head up to the fresh hill air of Manakamana itself, where dozens of **lodges** vie for pilgrims' business. You're unlikely to have any trouble finding a room, though on a Friday or Saturday night you should stake your claim early. Decent budget options include *Manakamana Lodge* (☎064/60125; ❸) and *Malla Lodge* (☎064/60056; ❷), both of which are reasonably far away from the noise of the temple bells. For a more exclusive experience, try *Manakamana Resort* (☎064/70088; ❻), which has an unrivalled position perched on the ridge just beyond the lower end of town. **Food** is mostly a matter of *daal bhaat* or Indian-style variations thereof, though in season the *Thakali Café*, just above the temple, has some more interesting Nepali dishes, as well as the usual "Continental" offerings.

Moving on from Manakamana, board any local bus plying the Prithvi Highway – it's only three bearable hours to either Kathmandu or Pokhara. Few pilgrims go by foot nowadays, but the old walking route, done in reverse, is a good way to approach Gorkha. The path leaves from the entrance gate to *Manakamana Resort*, descending steeply over 1000m to reach the busy junction town of **Abu Khaireni**, in the Marsyangdi valley. The descent should take less than two hours, and from Abu Khaireni there are frequent local buses to Gorkha, less than an hour away. A more ambitious hike would be to take the old porters' path that bends north along the ridge from the Bakeshwar Mahadev Mandir, reaching Gorkha in around four-hours' walking time from Manakamana.

Gorkha and around

Despite its status as the cradle of the nation, **GORKHA** remains strangely untouristed, even though the 24-kilometre paved road up from Abu Khaireni makes it a relatively painless half-day's ride from Pokhara, Kathmandu or Chitwan, and the new Manakamana cable car takes most of the sweat out of

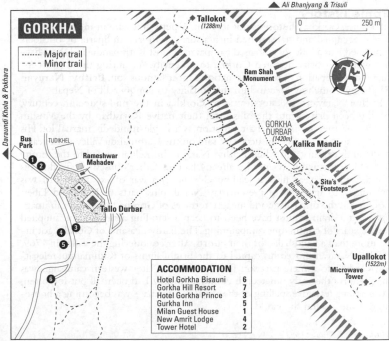

hiking here. Conscious of its tourist potential, the government has spruced up Gorkha's main monuments, but the minuscule lower town remains a fairly ordinary roadhead bazaar, its workaday atmosphere only leavened by a handful of hotels.

As the ancestral home of the Nepalese royal family, Gorkha occupies a central place in Nepalese history. Hunched on the hilltop above the bazaar is its link with that splendid past, the **Gorkha Durbar**, an architectural tour de force worthy of the flamboyant Gorkha kings and the dynasty they founded. Unless you're setting straight off on a trek or just finishing one (the old Pokhara–Trisuli trail passes through Gorkha), you'll have to spend the night here. Think about staying longer: the Durbar and environs could easily soak up a day, and hikes around the area could keep you busy for another day or two. The hill climate is agreeable, the pace is easy and, for the moment at least, there's not an apple pie or pizza in sight.

Direct **bus** services connect Gorkha with Kathmandu, Pokhara, Narayangadh, Sonauli and Birganj, but it's easy enough to take a tourist bus from Pokhara or Kathmandu to Abu Khaireni and ride a local bus from there. All buses terminate at Gorkha's modest bus park just west of the bazaaar. If you're pedalling, bear in mind it's a 900m ascent from Abu Khaireni to Gorkha, and it gets steeper as you go.

Note that the countryside around Gorkha is one of the strongholds of Nepal's **Maoist insurgents**, and Gorkha, being a district headquarters, has experienced some acts of violence. This is one district the government won't abandon easily, however, and at the time of writing, around six hundred Nepalese soldiers were quartered in and around town, making it as safe as anywhere in the country – if you like that kind of security.

Some history

In a sense, Gorkha's history is not its own. A petty hill state in medieval times, it was occupied and transformed into a sort of Himalayan Sparta by outsiders who used it as a base for a dogged campaign against Kathmandu and then, having won their prize, restored Gorkha to obscurity. Yet during those two centuries of occupation, it raised the nation's most famous son, **Prithvi Narayan Shah**, and somehow bred in him the audacity to conquer all of Nepal.

Prithvi Narayan's ancestors came to Gorkha in the mid-sixteenth century, having been driven into the hills from their native Rajasthan by the Muslim horde, and they soon gained a reputation as a single-mindedly martial lot. His father launched the first unsuccessful raid on the Kathmandu Valley in the early eighteenth century, and when Prithvi Narayan himself ascended to the throne in 1743, at the age of twenty, he already had his father's obsession fixed in his mind. Within a year, he was leading Gorkha in a war of expansion that was eventually to unify all of present-day Nepal, plus parts of India and Tibet. Looking at the tiny village and meagre terraces of Gorkha today, you can imagine what a drain it must have been to keep a standing army fed and supplied for 27 years of continuous campaigning. The hardy peasants of Gorkha got little more than a handshake for their efforts. After conquering the valley in 1769, Prithvi Narayan moved his capital to the bright lights of Kathmandu, relegating Gorkha to a mere garrison from which the later western campaign was directed. By the early nineteenth century, Gorkha had been all but forgotten, even as an alternative spelling of the name – Gurkha – was becoming a household name around the world.

In and around the town

Nestled on a shelf beneath a steep ridge, most of the bazaar stretches along two parallel lanes, separated by the old **Tallo Durbar** (Lower Palace). Built in around 1750, this imposing Newar-style edifice served as the kingdom's administrative headquarters, while the upper Durbar housed king and court. Seen from above, Tallo Durbar indeed looks like a mini-Pentagon, its restored brick and woodwork more stern than inspiring. It is eventually supposed to be opened up as a museum of the Shah dynasty leading up to Prithvi Narayan, but the only proposed exhibits are old royal letters and decrees, which in any case are proving hard to locate. Landscaped gardens surround the palace, one of the efforts of the rather lacklustre **Gorkha Conservation Area Project**.

The road joining the two main lanes runs past Gorkha's modest Tudikhel (parade ground) and a small temple precinct. The gilded figure kneeling atop a pillar facing the onion-domed **Rameshwar Mahadev Mandir** is Prithvi Pati Shah; grandfather of Prithvi Narayan Shah, he established most of the temples and shrines still in use around the town, including the Kalika temple in the upper Durbar.

The buildings of the **bazaar** itself are huddled close together to save space for farming. Most shops sell the usual imported bric-a-brac, though the jewellers are worth a look for their *maadbhari* (heavy gold earrings) and *tilari* (decorated gold tubes strung on a necklace), favourites of the Gurung people who farm the local hills. Typically, the bazaar itself is run by business-minded Newars.

The Gorkha Durbar

It's a brisk, 250m ascent up a steep stone stairway to the **Gorkha Durbar** from Pokharithok, the junction just east of Tallo Durbar (figure on half an hour). At the top of this route – once the royal approach to the palace – you can marvel at the grand staircase that's one of the Durbar's most distinctive features. Pure ostentation or cheeky bluff, either way it must have cowed visiting vassals into submission – a neat trick for a tinpot realm that could barely muster 150 soldiers at the time of Prithvi Narayan's first campaign. Entrance to the Durbar is now through a doorway on its western side, reached by a path to the left of the retaining wall. No leather is allowed in the compound, and photography is prohibited.

Conceived as a dwelling for kings and gods, the fortress remains a religious place, and first stop in any visit is the **Kalika Mandir**, probably the most revered shrine this side of Kathmandu. Occupying the left (western) half of the Durbar building, its interior is closed to all but priests and the king of Nepal (others would die upon beholding Kali's terrible image, say the priests). Plenty of action takes place outside, though: sacrifices are made in the alcove in front of the entrance, and after the twice-monthly observance of Astami, which is celebrated with special gusto in Gorkha, the paving stones are sticky with blood. Most worshippers arrive cradling a trembling goat or chicken and leave swinging a headless carcass. Chaitra Dasain, Gorkha's biggest annual **festival**, brings processions and more bloodletting in late March or early April, as does the tenth day of Dasain in October.

The east wing of the Durbar is the historic **palace**, site of **Prithvi Narayan's birthplace** and, by extension, the ancestral shrine of the Shah kings. This accounts for the king regular visits (the royal helipad is just west of the complex) and the government's spare-no-expense renovation of the Durbar's exceptional eighteenth-century brick- and woodwork. Though predating the

Gorkhali conquest of Kathmandu, the palace bears the unmistakable stamp of Newar craftsmanship: the Gorkhalis, who never pretended to have any art or architecture of their own, imported workmen from Kathmandu. The building is open only on the tenth day of Dasain, but if you look through a lattice window on the east side you can see what is claimed to be Prithvi Narayan's **throne**.

The remaining space within the fortress walls is fairly littered with other Hindu shrines. By the exit is a small temple built around the holy **cave of Gorakhnath**, the centre for worship of the shadowy Indian guru who gave Gorkha its name and is regarded as a kind of guardian angel by the Shah kings. As a young man, Prithvi Narayan Shah is said to have prayed to the guru for success, and was answered in a dream (some say he came in person, and at this spot) by an old man who offered the young prince a bowl of curd. Haughtily, Prithvi Narayan let it fall to his feet (though some say he spilled it by accident), whereupon Gorakhnath revealed himself, saying that the future king would conquer everywhere he set his foot. If he had accepted and eaten the curd, the guru admonished, he would have conquered the world. Sadhus of the Gorakhnath cult are known as *kaanphata* ("split-ears"), after an initiation ceremony in which they insert sticks in their earlobes – which is a walk in the park compared to some of the other things they get up to in the name of their guru. *Kaanphata* priests sometimes administer ashen *tika* from the shelter above the cave.

Viewpoints and forts

The views are good from the Durbar, but carry on for much better ones. Exit the compound through a door to the east and descend to **Hanuman Bhanjyang** (Hanuman Pass), a small notch in the ridge named after the valiant monkey king whose image guards the popular shady rest stop. Cross the main trail (a branch of the Pokhara–Trisuli porter route) and follow a steep, stone-paved path up for just a couple of minutes to an awesome vantage point where you can stand in a pair of stone "**footsteps**" (variously ascribed to Ram, his wife Sita, Gorakhnath himself and even – by Buddhists – to Padma Sambhava) and, weather allowing, snap a postcard picture of the Durbar and the mountains to the north. From this angle, the Durbar looks like Nepal's answer to Mad Ludwig's castle. The Himalaya seen from here stretch from the Annapurnas (and even Dhaulagiri, which from this angle is to the right of Annapurna I and Machhapuchhre) to Ganesh Himal, with the pyramids of Baudha and Himalchuli occupying centre stage. If you can manage it, come early to catch the sunrise.

From Hanuman Bhanjyang it's another half-hour hike to **Upallokot** (Upper Fort), a 1520m eyrie at the highest, easternmost point of the ridge. To get to it you have to walk through a fenced microwave relay facility, and views are unfortunately restricted by vegetation. Upallokot itself is more a hut than a fort, its thatched roof long gone. The small walled pen contains a grinding-wheel-shaped *yoni* and a set of stones laid out in the shape of a reclining human figure – obscure icons of Kali and Bhairab.

At the other end of the ridge stands **Tallokot**, another watch post with limited views. You can easily stroll there from the Durbar, passing a small Ganesh shrine and a new monument to **Ram Shah**, the seventh-generation ancestor of Prithvi Narayan Shah who is reckoned by some to have been the progenitor of the Shah title. The views from this monument are also excellent. A rough track descends directly from Tallokot to Gorkha, tripping down terraces past small clusters of farmhouses and the odd communal water tap.

Longer walks

If that circuit whets your appetite for longer walks, there are three main options. One with a unique cultural dimension is the route **to Manakamana** (see p.277), which starts on an unpaved side road off the main Gorkha road about 4km down from the town, and takes three to four hours. It's easily possible to return via the cable car and bus the same day.

The high road through Hanuman Bhanjyang gives access to the country east of the Durbar, descending gently for about an hour and a half to Ali Bhanjyang (where you can find tea and snack food), then ascending along a ridge with fabulous views **to Khanchok Bhanjyang** after about two and a half hours. This would be about the limit for a day-hike, but given an early start you could continue down to the subtropical banks of the Budhi Gandaki at Arughat, a long day's 20km from Gorkha, and find basic lodging there – at this point you'd be a third of the way to Trisuli. Other, less distinct trails from Upallokot and the Ram Shah monument take roundabout routes to Ali Bhanjyang.

Alternatively, follow the main trail west out of Gorkha village, which reaches the untrammelled **Daraundi Khola valley** after about an hour and a half. Continuing on for another three hours brings you to Khoplang, a beautiful hill village with lodgings. You could even do a two-day loop: Gorkha to Khanchok Bhanjyang, from there down to the Daraundi at Ulte, head downstream to Chorkate, and then back up to Gorkha. For trekking from here, see Chapter Seven.

Practicalities

There's little choice of **accommodation** in Gorkha. Two relatively fancy hotels vie for attention, both offering gardens and views across the valley. The better option is *Gurkha Inn* (℡064/20206 or 01/358953; ❺–❼), which has some really lovely rooms, and the nicer garden. *Hotel Gorkha Bisauni* (℡064/2 0107, ✉ghbisauni@wlink.com.np; ❺–❼, dorm beds ❷) is similar, but a touch more secluded and run-down. Both of these places will usually go way lower on their official prices for travellers turning up at the door, as they're rarely full. Facing each other across the main road are two more-basic places: *Hotel Gorkha Prince* (℡064/20131; ❷) is large, dingy and commercial, while *New Amrit Lodge* (℡064/20138; ❷) is little more than a couple of spare rooms in a friendly family home. The usual local lodges are found near the bus park: *Milan Guest House* and *Tower Hotel* (both ❶) are reasonably clean. Gorkha also has a more luxurious "resort", but it's not in town: *Gorkha Hill Resort* (℡064/20326 or 01/419798; ❼) is located 4km down the road, on the way to Manakamana.

For **food**, the choice is fairly limited. The restaurants at *Gurkha Inn* and *Gorkha Bisauni* do reasonably good Western fare, while plenty of places near the bus park serve up the usual *momo*, chow mein or all-you-can-eat *bhaat*. There's a **bank** on the main road, but it will usually exchange only US dollars cash.

Bandipur

Perched improbably on a ridge above the Pokhara highway, the tiny hilltop bazaar of **BANDIPUR** has been lapsing into romantic obscurity for the best part of fifty years, and is only now starting to appear on the tourist map. These days it's little more than a small village, but the grand houses facing each other along the single paved street hint at a more illustrious past, and evoke a close, half-derelict atmosphere that's oddly reminiscent of a spaghetti Western. Buses are infrequent but with a little extra commitment Bandipur makes an idyllic stopover between Kathmandu and Pokhara, and might well tempt you to stay longer.

From Pokhara, you can catch one of two daily direct **buses** to Bandipur, while another service leaves once daily from Narayangadh. From anywhere else, take any bus heading along the Prithvi Highway and get off at Dumre, from where you can pick up any of these three direct buses coming through – two in the morning and one in the early afternoon. At the time of writing the road to Bandipur was being black-topped, which may result in a more frequent service. Failing a bus, it may be possible to hitch a lift or hire a vehicle in Dumre, or you could always take the historic **trail** to Bandipur, immortalized in a poem by the late King Mahendra. The walk takes two to three hours, beginnning 500m east of the main Dumre intersection and climbing through shady forest punctuated by very civilized rest shelters and waterspouts.

The town and around

Bandipur was once a prosperous **trading centre**, and its substantial buildings, with their Neoclassical facades and shuttered windows, bespeak past glories. Originally a simple Magar village, it was colonized in the early nineteenth century by Newars from Bhaktapur, who took advantage of its malaria-free location to develop it into an important stop along the India–Tibet trade route. Bandipur hit its heyday in Rana times, when, as a measure of its power and prestige, it was granted special permission to have its own library (which is still going). However, the town began to lose its edge in the 1950s, when the eradication of malaria in the Tarai made travel easier there. In the 1960s, the district headquarters was moved from Bandipur to Damauli, and the completion of the Prithvi Highway in 1973 shifted commerce to Dumre, leaving Bandipur a semi-ghost town.

Sitting in a saddle at 1000m beneath dramatic limestone hills, Bandipur's quiet main **bazaar** is oriented from southwest to northeast. Vehicles enter at the southwestern end. Hiking up, you approach the bazaar from the northwest, first passing the **Tudikhel**, which is certainly one of the most dramatic in Nepal. Perched exhilaratingly on a rock outcrop with a sheer dropoff to the east, it looks like the perfect place to put a prison, but this being Nepal, it's used as a school playground. The view to the north is stunning: basically, you're looking at a map of the first half of the Annapurna Circuit, with the Marsyangdi valley straight ahead and the Annapurna and Manaslu ranges behind.

Bandipur has several temples, though none are very much to look at. The main **Khadga Devi Mandir**, reached by bearing left up the steps at the north end of the bazaar, looks like a one-room schoolhouse; it houses a holy sword (*khadga*) supposedly given to a local king by Lord Shiva himself, which is displayed on the seventh day of Dasain. The shrine of **Thani Mai**, Khadga Devi's "sister", is of more interest for its awesome views – it's at the top of Gurungche Daada, the limestone hill southwest of the bazaar.

Day-hikes around Bandipur could fill up several days. The obligatory destination is **Siddha Gupha**, Nepal's biggest cave, which incredibly was discovered only in 1987. It's 10m wide, 400m long and full of stalactites, not to mention a sizeable bat population. You'll need to bring your own torch/flashlight. It takes about an hour and a half to walk to the cave from Bandipur; a guide will cost around Rs150. A trail also leads up to it from the Prithvi Highway at Bimalnagar, 1km east of Dumre, and there are plans to build a road to it. A hike to Siddha Gupha can be combined with a visit to another cave, **Patale Dwar** ("Portal to the Underworld"), which is supposed to be a geologic wonder.

Other, longer hikes go through pretty, cultivated hills and traditional Magar villages, and are worth considering as alternatives to leaving Bandipur by bus. You can walk **to Damauli** via the Chabda Barahi Mandir in about four hours, the last part of it on a motorable road. Given an early start and all day, it's reportedly possible to walk south **to the Seti River** and then downstream to its confluence with the Trisuli, where there's a bridge across to the highway not far north of Narayangadh. With a guide, or a few words of Nepali, a three-day trek could be traced south down through Magar country to Gaighat, the so-called "Magar Trek".

Practicalities

Bandipur's numerous **guesthouses** are situated right in the main bazaar and offer similarly simple lodgings, usually with meals included. The proprietor of *Pradhan's Paying Guests' Accommodation* (☏065/20110; ❷) speaks excellent English, while *Bandipur Guest House* (☏065/20103; ❸) occupies a seventy-year-old Neoclassical mansion built by the owner's grandfather in memory of his house in Delhi. The upmarket *Old Inn* (☏065/20110; ❺) has beautifully restored rooms, all beams and slate floors; run by Himalayan Encounters (see p.169), it also serves as the overnight stop on their bus trip between Kathmandu and Pokhara. *Bandipur Mountain Resort* (☏01/220162, ⓔisland @mos.com.np; ❼), located at the beautiful northern end of the Tudikhel, offers pricey and very comfortable accommodation, some of it in posh tents, and can also arrange nature treks from here down to Chitwan National Park.

Moving on from Bandipur, morning buses leave for Pokhara and Narayangadh, and at the time of writing there was also an early afternoon service to Pokhara. It shouldn't be too hard to get down to Dumre, however, either on foot or by hitching a ride. Frequent buses pass through Dumre on their way between Kathmandu and Pokhara.

Pokhara

The Himalaya form the highest, sheerest rise from subtropical base to icy peaks of any mountain range on earth, and nowhere is the contrast more marked than at **POKHARA** (*Pok*-huh-ruh). Spreading down a warm, lush valley to the lake shore, on clear days it boasts a nearly unobstructed view of the 8000m-plus Annapurna and Manaslu *himal,* just 25km to the north. Dominating the skyline, in beauty if not in height, is the double-finned summit of Machhapuchhre ("Fish-Tailed") – so named for its twin-peaked summit, though only one is visible from Pokhara.

Basking in the sunshine, Nepal's main resort area lolls beside **Phewa Tal** (Phewa Lake), well outside the actual town of Pokhara. This is Nepal's little budget paradise: carefree and culturally undemanding, though extremely touristy, with a steaks-and-cakes scene rivalling Kathmandu's. Whatever you're looking for, it's a buyer's market here – everything comes so easily, the main challenge is sifting through the growing multitude of possibilities. New businesses pop up like mushrooms after each monsoon, and disappear just as quickly; cheap places have a habit of going upmarket, great views get blocked, and what's hot today may be dead tomorrow. No guidebook can hope to keep up with all the changes, so take all recommendations with a pinch of salt.

If you're spending more than a week in Nepal, chances are you'll touch down

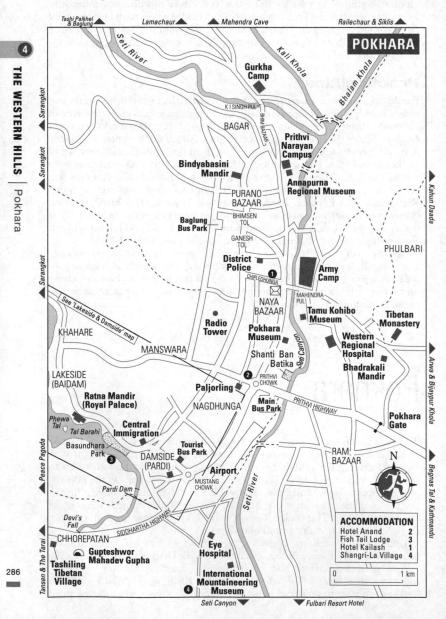

POKHARA

Tashi Palkhel & Baglung

Lamachaur

Mahendra Cave

Railechaur & Siklis

Seti River

Kali Khola

Bhalam Khola

Gurkha Camp

K I SINGH PUL

BHIM BAZAAR

BAGAR

Prithvi Narayan Campus

Bindyabasini Mandir

Annapurna Regional Museum

Kahun Daada

PURANO BAZAAR

BHIMSEN TOL

Baglung Bus Park

GANESH TOL

PHULBARI

District Police

Army Camp

CHIPLEDHUNGA

Sarangkot

Sarangkot

Sarangkot

Sarangkot

See 'Lakeside & Damside' map

KHAHARE

NAYA BAZAAR

MAHENDRA PUL

Tamu Kohibo Museum

Tibetan Monastery

Radio Tower

Pokhara Museum

Western Regional Hospital

MANSWARA

Shanti Ban Batika

Bhadrakali Mandir

LAKESIDE (BAIDAM)

Ratna Mandir (Royal Palace)

Paljorling

PRITHVI CHOWK

Arwa & Bijaypur Khola

Phewa Tal

Tal Barahi

NAGDHUNGA

Central Immigration

Main Bus Park

PRITHVI HIGHWAY

Pokhara Gate

Basundhara Park

Tourist Bus Park

RAM BAZAAR

Begnas Tal & Kathmandu

DAMSIDE (PARDI)

Airport

Peace Pagoda

Pardi Dam

MUSTANG CHOWK

Seti River

N

Devi's Fall

SIDDHARTHA HIGHWAY

CHHOREPATAN

Gupteshwor Mahadev Gupha

Eye Hospital

Tansen & The Tarai

Tashiling Tibetan Village

International Mountaineering Museum

ACCOMMODATION
Hotel Anand	2
Fish Tail Lodge	3
Hotel Kailash	1
Shangri-La Village	4

0   1 km

Seti Canyon

Fulbari Resort Hotel

in Pokhara at some point. As the main destination served by tourist buses and internal flights, it's usually the first place travellers venture to outside the Kathmandu Valley. For trekkers, Pokhara is the gateway to Nepal's most popular trails; for rafters and kayakers, it's Nepal's river-running headquarters; and for everyone else, it's the most relaxing place in Nepal that you *don't* have to trek or paddle to get to. Day-trips around the Pokhara Valley beckon, and if Pokhara town is short on temples and twisting old alleys, you might find that a relief after Kathmandu's profusion. Despite its shallow hedonism – which definitely gets cloying after a while – Pokhara is a great place to recharge your batteries, especially after a trek or time spent in India. At 800m above sea level it's both cooler than the plains in summer – though it stills gets hot from April onwards – and warmer than Kathmandu in winter. With lower foothills to the south, it's also less protected from the prevailing rains, and receives about twice as much precipitation as the capital.

Orientation, arrival and information

Pokhara's layout requires some explanation if you plan to do any sightseeing (an activity which, admittedly, isn't a top priority for most visitors here). To get your bearings, start with the tourist areas of **Lakeside** and **Damside**, set along the eastern and southeastern edges of **Phewa Tal**, where you'll find the vast majority of budget lodgings and restaurants. The **tourist bus park** lies at the northern edge of Damside, and the **airport** begins just to the northeast.

Northeast of the lake, **Pokhara Bazaar** is maddeningly diffuse, sprawling a good 6km along two main north–south roads and a ladder of cross streets – the map doesn't begin to suggest how interminably far it is to cycle the entire length of it. From **Mustang Chowk**, which can be considered the southernmost main intersection, it's nearly 2km north to **Prithvi Chowk**, home of the **public bus park**. A further 1.5km northwards, the bustling **Mahendra Pul** (Mahendra Bridge) area forms the heart of **Naya (New) Bazaar**, while the subdued **Purano (Old) Bazaar** and **Bindyabasini Mandir** occupy the highest ground still further north.

Arrival

Tourist buses arrive at their own bus park near Damside, called either the tourist bus park or the *naya* bus park; Greenline buses continue on to a depot at the southern end of Lakeside. It's a pretty easy walk from the bus park to most lodgings, but the touts, who go into a feeding frenzy at the arrival of Westerners, make this all but impossible. The only way to escape intact is to grab a taxi as quickly as possible and state your destination with great certitude. Don't be surprised if the touts insist that your guesthouse burned down last week or the owner died, or if your driver tries to take you to a different one where he can earn a commission. If you allow a tout to entice you with an offer of a free taxi ride, expect to be charged double for the room; otherwise, the fare should be Rs25–75, depending on your destination.

You'll be spared most or all of this hassle if you arrive by **public bus**. Public services entering along the Prithvi and Siddhartha highways all terminate at the main bus park, east of Prithvi Chowk. If you're coming off a trek in the Annapurna region and entering Pokhara along the Baglung Highway, you'll be dropped at a separate, smaller bus park on the west side of town. A taxi ride to Lakeside/Damside from either of these should cost about Rs100. It's also possible to **trek directly to Lakeside**, in which case you'll enter it from the north via the Bangladi and Khahare areas.

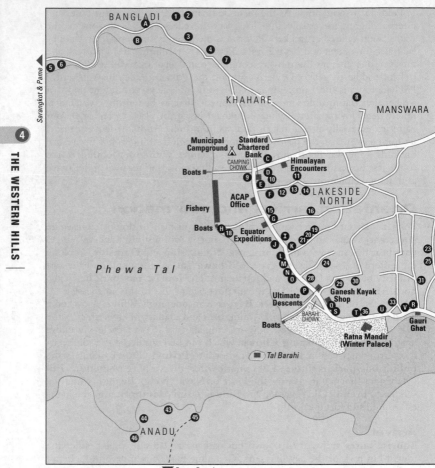

ACCOMMODATION

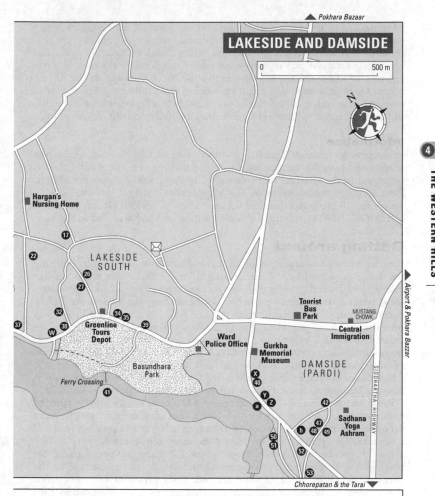

LAKESIDE AND DAMSIDE

▲ Pokhara Bazaar

0   500 m

N

Hargan's
Nursing Home

17

22

LAKESIDE
SOUTH

26

27

32

37   W 38

Greenline
Tours
Depot

34 35

39

Basundhara
Park

Ferry Crossing

41

▲ Airport & Pokhara Bazaar

Tourist
Bus
Park

MUSTANG
CHOWK

Central
Immigration

Ward
Police Office

Gurkha
Memorial
Museum

DAMSIDE
(PARDI)

X
40

Y
Z

a

42

47
b 48 49

Sadhana
Yoga
Ashram

50
51

52

53

Chhorepatan & the Tarai ▼

SIDDHARTHA HIGHWAY

RESTAURANTS & BARS

Sarowar Resort	**24**	
Shanti Guest House	**23**	
Snow Hill Lodge	**35**	
Hotel Snow Land	**28**	
Stay Well Guest House	**32**	
Temple Villa	**14**	
Trekkers Lodge	**39**	
Hotel Trek-O-Tel	**37**	
Hotel Twin Peaks	**53**	
Typical Guest House	**45**	
Hotel View Point	**48**	

Beam Beam	**J**	Lakeside Garden/	
Bistro Caroline	**N**	Pokhara Anrang	**B**
Blues Café	**F**	Le Panoramix	**A**
Caffe Concerto	**V**	Little Tibetan Tea Garden	**D**
Club Amsterdam	**O**	Loss Time	**Y**
Don't Pass Me By	**a**	Maya Pub	**K**
Everest Steak House	**M**	Mike's	**H**
German Bakery	**b**	Mamma Mia	**C**
Hungry Eye	**S**	Moondance Pub	**Q**
Fewa Park	**L**	Monsoon Garden Café	**T**
Koto	**P**	Nepali Kitchen	**Z**
Lan Hua	**U**	Once Upon a Time	**K**
Laxman	**R**	Rose	**X**
Lemon Tree	**I**	Tea Time	**G**
Lhasa	**W**	7-Eleven	**E**

Flying to Pokhara from Kathmandu cuts out some of the hardships of the journey (see p.176 for airline info) and the mountain views from aloft are stupendous. Take the earliest flight available, before clouds obscure the peaks, and book early for a seat on the right-hand side of the plane. At the time of writing, taxi fares from the airport were fixed at Rs70 for Damside and Rs100 for central Lakeside, though you might be asked to pay a little extra. The information desk in arrivals can confirm the prices and help with other basic enquiries, and there's a registered moneychanger alongside offering fairly decent rates.

Information

Innkeepers or even travel agents, notwithstanding the sales pressure, are the best sources of up-to-the-minute information. Anything else you might need is contained in the standard tourist **map** of Pokhara, sold in most bookstores. Better, though more expensive, are Mappa/Karto Atelier's *Pokhara Town & Valley* map (Rs650) and the very detailed series of 1:25,000 sheets published by HMG/FINNIDA, though the latter is almost impossible to find in Pokhara.

Getting around

Poor local transport makes getting around Pokhara time-consuming, widening the divide between lake and bazaar and making it that much harder to tear yourself away from the tourist fleshpots. A crosstown journey on one of Pokhara's **local buses** takes the better part of an hour, but things should improve slightly once the planned replacement of all full-size buses with minivan-like **microbuses** is complete – the big, old polluting buses were due to be banned from Lakeside at the time of writing. The four main routes will be the same for both, however: all start or end at the Prithvi Narayan Campus near the north end of the bazaar, and go to Lakeside (via Mahendra Pul), Damside (via Chipledhunga), Chhorepatan (via Mustang Chowk) and Mahendra Cave. Catch buses in Damside near the *German Bakery* and at various points in Lakeside.

Taxis wait at several spots in Lakeside and Damside, but it's usually easier to have your innkeeper call one for you. Some taxis are metered, but drivers are very reluctant to use them – expect to bargain if you're going to any standard tourist destination. For day-trips around the valley it might make sense to hire a taxi for the day, which should cost about $20 including petrol (more for overnights or longer journeys) – again, let someone at your guesthouse do the negotiations. Older, more beat-up **shared taxis** ply fixed routes between major points in the bazaar the same way that tempos do in Kathmandu; they cost just a few rupees per person.

A **bicycle**, rentable all over Lakeside and Damside, multiplies your mobility and flexibility tremendously. One-speed bikes go for about Rs50 a day. A **mountain bike** with gears is more practical for exploring the valley, which has a lot of slopes to it, although the ones for rent on the street aren't very good – for better quality, try Himalayan Mountain Bikes or From Dawn Till Dusk; both have offices in Lakeside and charge around Rs750 a day, depending on the quality of the bike. For speedier zipping around the valley, consider renting a **motorcycle**, available from many Lakeside outlets for about Rs250 a day (not including fuel), or a rarer **scooter**, which costs around Rs400 a day and is better suited to novices.

Accommodation

Pokhara is glutted with cheap and moderately priced **accommodation**, and these days you'll have to look a bit harder to find the laid-back, family-run lodgings that brought travellers here in the first place. Nearly every lodge owner has replaced his perfectly nice small building with an ugly new big one and the main accommodation districts are now fully fledged urban areas.

But looking on the bright side, you'll never have any trouble finding a room, and Pokhara's lodge-owners probably have a better idea of what travellers want than anyone else in Nepal. The majority of the **inexpensive** hotels have clean rooms, friendly staff and good breakfasts, and given the oversupply, you'll seldom have to pay the published rate, even in high season. Many also offer more expensive rooms that may be a better bet than those offered by the **midrange** "resort" hotels, where you risk getting little more for your extra money than a telephone and a lack of real welcome. That said, some of Nepal's classiest **luxury hotels** are found in Pokhara: these are grouped together on p.294, alongside a couple of Indian-oriented business hotels for the few travellers who'll want to stay in busy Pokhara Bazaar.

Just about all independent travellers stay in **Lakeside** or **Damside**. Awash with Western food, Western comforts and Western tourists, both areas certainly offer the easy life. If you're looking for the chilled-out lakeside retreat that made Pokhara's name, however, consider staying further along the lakeshore, in semi-rural **Bangladi**, or across the lake in **Anadu**.

Within a given establishment, the bigger, higher-up rooms with better views will always cost more; but it doesn't necessarily follow that the more expensive hotels have the best views. In general, the views are better the further south you go. The listings start with Lakeside, since that's the biggest and most popular accommodation area. It's so big, in fact, that it makes sense to divide it up into two parts: Lakeside North and Lakeside South are arbitrary divisions, not actual place names, but nevertheless they correspond to areas that have distinctive personalities.

Lakeside North

With its strip of high-rise guesthouses, thatched-roofed restaurants and curio shops, the **northern** portion of Lakeside is like Thamel all over again, though less urban and a lot more relaxing. Avoid guesthouses overlooking the main roads, as you'll be tormented by early-morning buses.

Inexpensive

Amrit Guest House ☎061/22882. If you really want to be on the strip, this is a relatively cheap, quiet option with big, clean, albeit boxy rooms. ❸

Lubbly Jubbly Guest House ☎061/22881. A small but shady banana garden and a little café make this place quite sociable. Worn at the edges, especially in the cheaper common-bath rooms, but generally good value. ❶–❹

Hotel Matterhorn ☎061/26734. Sort of unfinished-looking, but not bad, and the price is good for such a central location. ❷

Nepali Cottage Guest House ☎061/31637. Family-run place offering a few large rooms in a small but rather grand building shoehorned into the thick of the action. ❸

Pokhara Peace Home ☎061/24690. Quiet, restful grounds and big rooms on a less-developed back lane. ❷

Quiet View Lodge ☎061/22612. Small, simple, and boxed in by new construction, but you can't beat the price, and it's run by a friendly family. ❶

Sanctuary Lodge ☎061/32407. Tiny family-run place with traditional rooms and gardens. Very cheap for a place so close to the strip. ❶

Sarowar Resort ☎061/23037. Undistinguished facilities, but the premises include one of the last remaining oval Baahun farmhouses in Lakeside, at a special bargain rate, and the family is nice. ❶–❸

Midrange

Hotel Barahi ☎061/23017, ⊛www.barahi.com. Anonymously large, businesslike complex, but the sizeable swimming pool in the garden helps the atmosphere along. Rooms, some with a/c, are rather tired. ❻–❼

Butterfly Lodge ☎061/22892, ⊛www .butterflylodge.com. Lovely, spacious garden, and clean, homely rooms, the more expensive ones kitted out in traditional style. ❹–❻

Hotel Fewa T 061/20151, W www.trekinfo.com /mikes/mikefewa.htm. You pay through the nose for the lakeside location, but the faux traditional rooms are nice, if small. The rustic theme is developed in the new, eccentric little cottages, which have beds on a mezzanine floor. **6**

Little Tibetan Guest House T 061/31898, W www.littletibguesthouse.com. Set back behind a quiet garden, with sparkling new rooms furnished in characterful Tibetan style. **4**

Hotel Monal T 061/21459. Cool, clean and freshly furnished rooms set around a pleasant garden. Professional atmosphere. **5**

Nature's Grace Lodge T 061/27220, W www.naturesgracelodge.com. Small, tucked-away place with simply furnished rooms and an in-house pub. Profits go to the Child Welfare Scheme and treks can be arranged to visit projects. Also arranges village-stay programmes. **4**

Hotel Snow Land T 061/20384, E snowland @cnet.wlink.com.np. Efficient place right in the heart of the strip, with good views of the lake and a/c in more expensive rooms. **6–7**

Temple Villa T 061/21203, E templevilla_hotel @hotmail.com. Tranquil and decidedly swish, the exclusive tone is alleviated by the owners' friendliness. More expensive rooms have terraces overlooking the garden. Solar-heated hot water. **4–5**

Lakeside South

Things get quieter and less Disneyesque **south** of the Royal Palace. You can actually see the lake from the strip, and the mountain views are better, too. The flip side of all this is that the choice of restaurants, bars and shops isn't as great, so you may find yourself trekking up to Lakeside North a couple of times a day.

Inexpensive

Holy Lodge T 061/31422, E holylodge@bb.com .np. Big, leafy garden, thatch seating area with fireplace in winter. Clean rooms; the cheap ones are in a rustic old building. **1–3**

Nepal Guest House T 061/22692. Comfortable if slightly faded roooms with bathrooms and satellite TV, arranged around a small garden. Friendly management. **3–4**

New Star Lodge T 061/22478, E msnr@mos .com.np. Older building with simple, inexpensive rooms in a relatively uncommercialized area. **2–3**

Peace Eye Guest House T 061/31699. Funky, family-run place with a shady garden. Rooms are small but well-furnished; more expensive ones have attached bath. **3–4**

Pokhara Guest House T 061/21228, W www. pghphwa.com.np. Big, fairly well kitted-out rooms, some with attached bath. Service is attentive, and there are views from the roof. **3–4**

Shanti Guest House T 061/22645. Rooms with common baths are clean, white and spare; the en-suite rooms are more comfortable, with nice rugs. Small garden and a good little library. **2–4**

Midrange

Gurkha Lodge T 061/20798. The stone thatched bungalows are a perfect retreat, if a bit musty. Run by an ex-Gurkha and his English wife, with a fabulous garden. **5**

New Nanohana Lodge T 061/22478,

E msnr@mos.com.np. Spotless rooms, pleasant big balconies, lovely terrace garden. Popular with Japanese, partly for the deep Japanese-style bathtubs in the top rooms. **4–5**

Hotel Nirvana T 061/23332, E hotelnirvana @hotmail.com. Huge, thoughtfully decorated and spotlessly clean rooms overlooking spacious balconies and a garden. The friendly and knowledgeable owners also run treks. **4–5**

Pokhara Mount Resort T 061/22465, W www .accessnepal/pokharamt.htm. Modest place with pleasant small grounds. Not a great location, but good value for air-conditioned rooms. **5**

Sacred Valley Inn T 061/31792, E svalley@cnet .wlink.com.np. Very clean, balconied rooms with views in a homely modern block. **4**

Snow Hill Lodge T 061/22685. Pleasant sanctuary in a quiet part of the strip. Rooms are a bit run-down, but most have TVs. **4**

Stay Well Guest House T 061/22624. Friendly and quiet, in a cute little castle of a building. The deluxe rooms are lovely, with huge windows looking out on mountain views. **4–5**

Hotel Trek-O-Tel T 061/28996. Beautifully furnished, odd-shaped a/c rooms with terracotta floors in a tight little complex right on the lakefront. Classy act, with uniformed, much-namasteing staff. **6**

Trekkers Lodge T 061/21458. Ugly new building with pleasant garden views. A range of rooms, most with decent facilities and lots of light. **4–6**

Khahare, Bangladi and beyond

The area north of Camping Chowk (the main crossroads near the municipal campground) is well-known to long-termers, hippies, Israelis and other bargain-hunters. It's also convenient if you're trekking directly into Lakeside, since it's the first lodging area you'll come to. **Khahare**, the more southerly part of this area, is sort of a suburb of Lakeside – quieter and less commercialized, but still within its sphere of influence. **Bangladi**, further north, preserves some of the undeveloped ambience of old, with simpler facilities and mostly unmolested views of the lake. A few lodges in the farm country beyond Bangladi provide even more-rural settings.

Taxis can get to any of the guesthouses listed below, but they'll charge more than the standard fare to Lakeside.

Inexpensive

Banana Garden Lodge ☎061/21880. Bungalow rooms ranging from the monastic to the spartan, set among pleasant gardens. Friendly and inexpensive, hence often full. ❶

Buddha Guest House ☎061/31259. Tiny operation right at the end of the line. Tidy rooms in a single long bungalow with magnificent views of the lake and surrounding countryside. Hot water by the bucket only. ❶

Garden Yiga Chozin Buddhist Centre ☎061/22923. Peaceful but run-down place that doubles as meditation retreat centre and budget guesthouse. ❷

Green Peace Lodge ☎061/32780, @greenpeacelodge@hotmail.com. Basic but friendly, right by the lake, with its own boats and semi-resident traveller population. The new annexe, with more-plush rooms, is oddly isolated in a rice-paddy field round the next bend in the road. ❶

Lonely View Lodge ☎061/26994. A nice combination of rural location and proximity to town. Beautiful garden/orchard, excellent views, friendly family, and a cool atmosphere. ❷

Maya Devi Village ☎061/32293. The last word in seclusion: located at the extreme northern end of the lake, it's 3km beyond Camping Chowk (way off the map). Delightful little circular thatched bungalows, no electricity, set meals. ❸

Pleasure Home Lodge (no phone). Big, acceptable rooms, small garden and the aptly named *Mellow Fellow* restaurant. ❷

Midrange

Chhetri Sisters Guest House ☎061/24066, ⓦwww.3sistersadventure.com. Success has brought an extremely smart new guesthouse to the eponymous sisters, pioneers in trekking for women. Beautiful rooms in wood and brick, with paintings of local scenes. Cheaper rooms available in the old block. ❸–❺

Full Moon Lodge ☎061/21511. A unique place in an above-it-all location (access by a steep set of steps). The garden area is littered with Hindu shrines, statues and unusual touches. Good-sized rooms. ❺

Damside

Damside is like a quiet suburb, isolated both from the town and the tourist razzmatazz of Lakeside. The mountain views are better, but it's questionable whether they compensate for the limited choice of bars and restaurants. For some reason, Damside is very popular with Japanese tourists, which is an interesting cultural feature in itself.

Inexpensive

Hotel Anzuk ☎061/21845. Family-run guesthouse with a garden and terrace. Rooms on the upper floor are pretty and well-furnished; cheaper rooms downstairs are basic but acceptable. ❷–❺

Green View Hotel ☎061/21844. Looks like the worst kind of concrete mansion, but the flashy frontage conceals a friendly, family-run guesthouse. Secluded, very flowery garden and a roof view. ❸–❺

Hotel View Point ☎061/21787. Standard facilities, but a good view from the roof. ❷

Midrange

Hotel Dragon ☎061/22630, ⓦwww.himalayadragonhotel.com. Slightly overbearing complex, but there's a pretty garden and the rooms have cosy Tibetan furnishings. Also has more expensive rooms with a/c. ❺–❼

Hotel Garden ☎061/20870. Spacious, with a good location, greenery and view. ❹–❺

Hotel Jharna ☎061/21925. Ideal location overlooking the neck of the lake with the mountains behind. The lakeside rooms are pricier but, like the standard rooms, they're slightly boxy. ❹–❻

Hotel Lake City ☎061/21341, ⓔlakecity@cnet
.wlink.com.np. A bit pokey for the price, but the
grounds are great, there's a good in-house restaurant and the profits go towards training and education for street kids. ❺
Hotel Monalisa ☎061/20863. A bit more upmarket than the *Jharna*, in an equally good location. ❻

Hotel Twin Peaks ☎061/22867, ⓦwww
.hotelinpokhara.com. An ex-Gurkha's Gurung family run this cheery small hotel with plain, standard
rooms and more luxurious ones too. The "Fawlty
Towers Restaurant – But No Manuel!" is better
than it sounds. ❹–❻

Across the lake: Anadu

Anadu, directly across the lake from Lakeside, is not one of Nepal's friendliest
or best-kept villages, but it's certainly peaceful and there's a certain bohemian
attraction to staying in a place that can only be reached by boat. (Actually, you
can walk to Anadu from the highway on the other side of the ridge behind,
but let's not spoil the illusion.) Furthermore, the views from here are better
than they are from anywhere in Lakeside, the water is clean, and there's a great
hike (to the Peace Pagoda) right out your back door. The nearest of the places
listed here, the *Typical*, can be reached in about twenty minutes' rowing from
the palace area of Lakeside.

Fewa Resort ☎061/20885. Green, quiet and
roomy, with a fair restaurant and excellent views.
Free boat service. ❺–❻
Gurung Cottage (no phone). Awfully primitive
(cold water and *daal bhaat* only), but certainly
secluded. ❶

Kopila ☎061/28369. The clear winner in Anadu:
awesome views, shady (though unkempt) grounds,
good (though slow) restaurant, and hot water. ❷–❹
Typical Guest House ☎061/26978. Dingy and
depressing atmosphere, though the rooms themselves aren't too bad. Cold water only. Boat service
available on demand (small charge). ❷

Pokhara Bazaar and resort hotels

Most of Pokhara's poshest places are uninspiringly located in the vicinity of the
airport, though a couple of resort hotels aim high, and get it right. Busy
Pokhara Bazaar is at least honestly Nepali, unlike Lakeside, but otherwise has
little going for it: its lodgings, catering mainly to Nepali and Indian businessmen, charge more for less.

Hotel Anand Prithvi Chowk, Pokhara Bazaar
☎061/20029. Professional enough hotel in a
tumultuous area, with a rooftop garden and TV. ❹
Fish Tail Lodge Opposite Lakeside South ☎061/
20071 or 01/225242, ⓦwww.fishtail-lodge.com.
Lakeside's original deluxe hotel: fabulous grounds
and an unrivalled view of the lake and the classic
profile of the mountains behind. Access by rope
ferry. ❽
Fulbari Resort Hotel 4km south of the airport
☎061/23451 or 01/477305, ⓦwww.fulbari.com.
Humungous top-of-the-class complex overlooking
the Seti gorge, with a golf course, heated pool, six
restaurants, tennis courts, etc. ❾

Hotel Kailash Mahendra Pul, Pokhara Bazaar
☎061/21726. Clean commercial hotel with a roof
garden. ❷–❹
Rani Ban Retreat On the ridge 1km west of the
Peace Pagoda ☎061/31713 or 01/426481,
ⓦwww.raniban.com. Only four rooms, plus
cheaper (❺) tented camp. Pick-up service, or it's
a half-hour walk from Devi's Fall. Unparalleled
views, and you can rent mountain bikes. ❼
Shangri-La Village 1.5km south of the airport
☎061/22122 or 01/412999, ⓦwww.hotelshangrila
.com. Deluxe versions of Nepali houses scattered
through expensively landscaped grounds. Pool,
conference centre and eat-all-you-like weekend
buffet. ❾

Camping

Pokhara's **municipal campground** is right by the lake and not half bad.
Charges are Rs70–100 per vehicle (depending on size), Rs40 per tent, Rs50
for a hot shower, and Rs250 to use the kitchen facilities. It's popular with overland groups but you'd be better off working out a deal with one of the guesthouses along the back lanes of Lakeside.

Phewa Tal (Phewa Lake)

Visitors to Pokhara typically spend most of their time within arm's reach of apple pie, which means staying close to **Phewa Tal**. This is not fertile territory for cultural interaction, but a number of activities on the lake will at least help you to work off the calories. According to a local **legend**, the lake covers the area of a once-prosperous valley, whose inhabitants one day scorned a wandering beggar. Finding only one sympathetic woman, the beggar warned her of an impending flood: as the woman and her family fled to higher ground, a torrent roared down from the mountains and submerged the town – the "beggar" having been none other than the goddess Barahi Bhagwati. The woman's descendants settled beside the new lake and erected the island shrine of **Tal Barahi**; for local innkeepers and restaurateurs, who've done rather well out of the lake, a few alms at her shrine still don't go amiss.

Nautical pursuits

Boating (or just floating) on Phewa Tal is the easiest way to get away from the business of getting away from it all. Oversized **rowing boats** (*dungaa*), which hold six easily, can be rented all along the eastern shore. Prices are supposed to be fixed at Rs130 per hour or Rs400 per day, but "discounts" are possible, especially at Damside. If you've got a specific destination in mind, it might work out better to hire a boatman to take you there for a fixed price. Fibreglass **sailboats**, available from *Hotel Fewa* (see p.292) and from a couple of freelances nearby, cost Rs200 per hour or Rs950 per day; wooden ones are somewhat less. At least one operator rents **pedalos** (Rs250 per hour, Rs950 per day), and some rafting companies (see p.303) rent out **kayaks** for about Rs750 a day (without all the gear) if they have any going spare. Motorized boats aren't allowed on the lake – the tourist industry, to its credit, has reached a fairly firm consensus on that. You could also try your hand at catching the various carp and eels that swim in the lake: **fishing** rods go for about Rs50 per hour, but you'll need to find your own bait.

Swimming is best done from a boat, as much of the shore is muddy and bacteria counts are sometimes unhealthy due to sewage seeping from a couple of prominent Lakeside hotels and from the police camp just south of Basundhara Park. That said, Phewa Tal's water is fairly clean for a subtropical lake, largely because the monsoon rains flush it out each year. The stuff floating on the surface at certain times of year is pollen, not sewage (which it resembles when the wind balls it up). Stay away from the dam area, as the **current** is deceptively strong – an Irish woman drowned in 1996 when her boat capsized near the dam and she was sucked over the edge. The shore around the Royal Palace is off-limits; if you see gesticulating security guards, you're too close.

An obvious first destination is **Tal Barahi**, the island shrine located a few hundred metres offshore from the palace. While the temple itself is modern and not much to look at, it's a busy spot on Saturdays, when the lake goddess exacts a steady tribute of blood sacrifices. If that doesn't put you off your lunch, the island makes a fine place for a picnic. During the spring wedding months you might find yourself caught up in a flotilla of merrymakers headed for the island, where music, dancing and *raksi*-drinking go on until all hours.

From the island it's a little bit further again to the far shore which, with dense jungle, manic monkeys and few places to put ashore, is most easily observed from the water. If you want to walk around on the other side, make for **Anadu**, the diffuse Gurung village that covers the hillside directly opposite Lakeside, twenty- to thirty-minutes' row from the palace. Food is available from a few lakeside establishments. For some real exercise, you could row to the farthest (northwest) end of the lake and up the meandering Harpan Khola.

The other, geological explanation is that the entire Pokhara Valley, like the Kathmandu Valley, was submerged about 200,000 years ago when the fast-rising Mahabharat Lek dammed up the Seti River. Over time, the Seti eroded an ever-deeper outlet, lowering the water level and leaving Phewa Tal and several smaller lakes as remnants. Phewa was further enlarged by the installation of **Pardi Dam** in 1967, which brought electricity and irrigation to the valley, and gave Damside its name.

Like most Himalayan features, Phewa Tal is geologically very young and fast-changing, and may prove to be a short-lived phenomenon. Its watershed is steep and highly prone to erosion (a process that's hastened by agriculture and deforestation), so the streams that feed it carry massive quantities of suspended **sediments**. When the sediments reach the lake, they settle out: the Harpan Khola, the lake's main tributary, has already deposited a "delta" that covers the western third of the lake's former surface. Year by year, farmers who lost land to the dam are reclaiming it as rice paddy. Their gain will eventually be Lakeside's loss, for some experts have predicted that siltation will fill up the lake in as little as thirty years, in spite of the municipality's best efforts to dredge up the silt.

Lakeside (Baidam)

Next to eating, promenading along **Lakeside**'s pipal-shaded main drag is the favourite pastime in Pokhara. Despite the name, you'll have to walk some distance from the main strip to get near the lake, as new construction in this area (known locally as **Baidam**) has spoiled its former rural character: they've literally paved paradise. Shops and restaurants now crowd together so closely on the main strip that they block off any lake views between the Royal Palace and Khahare, and you can only reach the water on a couple of short access roads, all of which terminate at boat jetties rather than anything resembling a shoreline. It's actually illegal to build commercial structures along the lake side of the road, and these buildings are all theoretically under a demolition order, but the government has never shown the political will to enforce the law, and the buildings are now so numerous and valuable that it's hard to imagine the order ever being carried out.

Basundhara Park, Lakeside's biggest patch of open space, is the venue for the annual **Annapurna Festival** (usually held in April), a cultural event featuring music, dance and food, and for occasional other commercial expos. At other times it's quiet and not very interesting, though it has extensive shoreline. The main reason to enter it is to get to the **rope ferry** that leads across this narrow neck of the lake to *Fish Tail Lodge*. You don't have to be staying there to go across and have a look.

Further north at **Gauri Ghat**, where the Lakeside strip passes at its closest to the lake, a set of steps leads from a leafy *chautaara* down to a rocky outcrop marked by a *linga* shrine. Midway along the strip sits Ratna Mandir, the winter **Royal Palace**, a definite no-go area during the king's residence each winter or early spring. (Hima Griya, further south, is an annexe of the palace reserved for guests and lesser royals.) At the palace's northern edge, a road leads down to the lake at a shady spot known as **Barahi Tol**, where Nepalis and visiting Indians often go to escape the Western-dominated strip, and the main launching site for boats to Tal Barahi.

Numerous other lanes head back away from the lake into what was until recently lush farmland. The farmers have now all sold out to developers and speculators, although many of the family-run guesthouses retain their traditional vegetable plots, sugar-loaf haystacks and banana-palm borders. Traditional thatched oval houses – designed to be warm in winter and cool in summer – have almost all been replaced by rectangular concrete ones. North

Chautaara

A uniquely Nepali institution, the **chautaara** is more than just a resting place – it serves important social and religious functions as well. Every hill village has its *chautaara*, and you'll find them at appropriate intervals along any reasonably busy trail. The standard design consists of a rectangular flagstoned platform, built at just the right height for porters easily to set down their *doko*, and sometimes a smaller platform atop that. Two trees (a pipal and a banyan – see below) planted in the earthen centre provide shade for all who gather underneath: passing strangers, old friends, couples – they're particularly popular for village assemblies as it's said that no one can tell a lie in the shade of a pipal.

Chautaara are erected and maintained by individuals as an act of public service, often to earn religious merit or in memory of a deceased parent. Commonly they'll be found on sites associated with pre-Hindu nature deities, often indicated by stones smeared with red *abhir* and yellow *keshori* powder. The trees, too, are considered sacred. Invariably, one will be a **pipal**, whose Latin name (*Ficus religiosa*) recalls its role as the *bodhi* tree under which the Buddha attained enlightenment. Nepalis regard the pipal, with its heart-shaped leaves, as a female symbol and incarnation of Laxmi, and women will sometimes fast and pray before one for children, or for success for the children they already have. Its "husband", representing Shiva Mahadev, is the **banyan** (*Ficus benghalensis*, or *bar* in Nepali), another member of the fig genus, which sends down Tarzan-vine-like aerial roots which, if not pruned, will eventually take root and establish satellite trunks. A *chautaara* is incomplete without the pair; occasionally you'll see one with a single tree, but sooner or later someone will get around to planting the other.

of Lakeside in the area known as **Khahare**, the lake again becomes visible from the main road, which reverts to a dirt track that can be followed along the attractive and less developed northern shore. Side trails lead up to Sarangkot (p.308) from there.

Damside (Pardi)

In **Damside** (**Pardi**), go for mountain views – the classic scene, captured in a ubiquitous Ministry of Tourism poster, can be viewed from a small Vishnu shrine in the triangle of land between the spillway and the lake.

Pardi Dam is of no intrinsic interest, and unfortunately you can't walk across it, but from the footbridge that crosses the Pardi Khola, downstream, trails lead south to Devi's Fall (see p.299) or up the ridge to the west for phenomenal views. A pukka but sometimes smelly path connects Damside with Lakeside through Basundhara Park – it's not really a walk you'd do for pleasure, and it's awkward on a bike, but it chops a bit of the distance off getting to Lakeside restaurants.

Pokhara Bazaar

Until being linked to the outside world by the Prithvi Highway in 1973, **Pokhara Bazaar** was a small Newar market town along the trade route from Butwal to Mustang. The original bazaar has now grown into a city of over 100,000, with traffic, pollution and all the rest, yet it still rests lightly on the land – natural wonders are always near to hand.

The northern bazaar

Most of Pokhara was destroyed in a fire in 1949, but remnants of the original Newar quarter can still be seen in the **Purano Bazaar**, which runs from Bhimsen Tol up to Bag Bazaar. Perched on a hillock in the middle of this area you'll find the **Bindyabasini Mandir**, Pokhara's main cultural attraction, a quiet temple complex more noteworthy for its sweeping mountain views than its collection of shrines. The featured deity, Bindyabasini, is an incarnation of Kali, the mother goddess in her bloodthirsty aspect, who is carved from a *shaligram* stone (see p.321). Animal sacrifices are common at this temple, particularly on Saturdays and the ninth day of Dasain in October. Bindyabasini has a reputation as a bit of a prima donna: in one celebrated incident, her stone image began to sweat mysteriously, causing such a panic that the late King Tribhuwan had to order special rites to pacify the goddess. The 1949 fire allegedly started here, when an offering burned out of control.

Tucked away in one corner of the Prithvi Narayan Campus at the northeastern part of town, the **Annapurna Regional Museum** (daily except Sat 9am–12.30pm & 1.30–5pm, closes 4pm in winter; free) offers a feeble treatment of Nepal's natural history that's really meant for local schoolkids. The display of Himalayan butterflies is genuinely interesting, though, and useful for identifying some of the many species seen in the Pokhara area. An adjacent **information centre** (same hours), maintained by the Annapurna Conservation Area Project, contains some enlightening exhibits about wildlife, geology, ethnic groups and culture in the ACAP area – it's a pity it's way out here.

Along the Seti River

Immediately east of town lies the dramatic, sometimes almost invisibly narrow **Seti River gorge**, where the abrasive torrent has cut like acid though the valley's soft sediments. One of the best places to see it, amazingly, is just north of the ugly main bus park. Walk north past Shanti Ban Batika, a park/picnic spot that's slowly reverting to jungle, then make a right down a path. The river emerges from its narrow confines for about 1km here to produce a sizeable canyon, incongruously close to the bazaar, from which sand and gravel are extracted and carried up by porters for use in local construction. From here you can walk upstream to where the Seti's churning waters emerge from a dark, mossy, inaccessible ravine, or downstream to where they plunge back into another similar chasm (certain death if you slip). Several of Pokhara's bridges (*pul*), including Mahendra Pul, K.I. Singh Pul and the footbridge east of the airport, provide top-down views of some of the narrowest parts of the gorge.

Two nearby museums are definitely worth visiting if you're in the area. The **Pokhara Regional Museum** (daily except Tues 10am–5pm, Friday closes at 3pm; Rs10), located south of Mahendra Pul, is small but quite well done, with informative displays and commentary on Nepalese ethnic groups, rites, customs, crafts, trade, musical instruments and costumes. The tiny **Tamu Kohibo Museum** (daily 10am–4pm; Rs20) sits on the opposite side of the canyon, and is reached by a lane heading down from Mahendra Pul. Dedicated to the shamanic traditions of Gurung culture, it gives an intriguing introduction to an important aspect of Nepalese culture that's all too often ignored. Its distinctive building, based on the shape of the shaman's *kaidu*, a ritual object, looks like a garlic bulb split into four equal cloves and is easily spotted from just about anywhere in the canyon area. There are plans afoot to move the museum to the shaman training school next door, leaving the old building as a shrine. For more on Gurungs and Nepalese shamanism, see p.504 and p.523 respectively.

Other sights

Just west of Prithvi Chowk hides the smallest and least interesting of Pokhara's three former Tibetan refugee camps (see p.311). **Paljorling**, shown on some maps as the **Tibetan Handicrafts Centre**, is now not so much a community as a factory with on-site housing. The emphasis is on retail sales, and its inhabitants work over any foreigners who inadvertently fall into their web. There's little reason to actually enter the compound, as handicrafts are sold in shops along the main road outside.

When – if – it finally opens, the ambitious **International Mountaineering Museum** should make a worthwhile destination in the extreme southern end of the bazaar. It's set to house models of famous peaks, mannequins of renowned climbers, a historical exhibit of mountaineering equipment, and information on the geology, flora and fauna of the Himalaya and other ranges. A newly scheduled opening date of 2002 was already overdue at the time of writing, but backed by fees levied on trekking peaks, the Nepal Mountaineering Association should eventually bring it off.

If you're in this neighbourhood, especially on a mountain bike, set aside at least a little time to check out the dramatic **Seti canyon**. There's an access point near the mountaineering museum, and the road following the river southeastwards from there makes an excellent jaunt.

Chhorepatan

About 2km west of Damside, or ten minutes on a bike, a trio of sights in the roadside suburb of Chhorepatan might just tempt you away from the lake. **Devi's Fall** (Rs10) marks the spot where the Pardi Khola – the stream that drains Phewa Tal – enters a grottoed channel and sinks underground in a sudden rush of foam and fury. Given a good monsoon in the autumn it can be very impressive, as the green water thunders and corkscrews into the earth, forcing up a continuous plume of mist; in the spring it's a washout. The spot is perhaps more interesting as a source of pop mythology: known to locals as Patale Chhango (roughly, "Waterfall to the Underworld"), the sinkhole's name is supposed to be a Nepalification of Devin, the name of a Swiss woman who is said to have drowned while skinny-dipping with her boyfriend in 1961. The name "Devi" may be a a casualty of the transliteration system, or possibly part of the Nepali propensity to deify everything that moves – *devi* means "goddess". The whole story sounds like a fabrication to warn local youth to shun promiscuous Western ways.

On the opposite side of the highway, a signposted path leads for a few metres between houses and curio stalls to **Gupteshwor Mahadev Gupha** (Rs20), a cave-shrine dedicated to Shankhar, who incorporates both Shiva and his consort Parbati as male and female halves of one figure. Guided by a dream vision, a priest discovered the idol in 1992, since when the cave has attracted increasing numbers of devotees. There are plans to develop the site with a temple and ashram above ground, but for now, plain steps lead down underground into a large, womblike chamber, warmed by perfumed lamps and dripping with moisture. Enshrined in the centre is the black Shankhar figure, a natural rock form dolled up with a carved Naga (snake) crown, and surrounded by small images of Shiva, Parbati and their son Ganesh below. Local youths, who will act as guides, claim to have penetrated the low opening in the rock behind the shrine as far as Devi's Fall. Local religious authorities have prohibited photography inside the cave, whatever guides may say.

The adjacent Tibetan settlement of **Tashiling** has some 750 residents. Walk to the far end of the compound, past the school, *gompa* and curio stalls, to reach

Longer day-trips and overnights from Pokhara are covered in "The Pokhara Valley", p.306.

the community's small carpet-weaving hall and wool-dyeing shed; a short walk beyond brings you to an abrupt drop and a glorious panorama of the valley of the Phusre Khola, a Seti tributary.

Eating

Restaurants are everywhere in Pokhara, and food even sets the social agenda: there's not much nightlife after around 10.30pm, but the congenial restaurants and cafés around the lake are easy places to make friends and find trekking partners. Candlelight (often imposed by load-shedding) adds to the romance – unless it's a video night. Most tourist restaurants boast a more or less standard menu, featuring an implausible selection of improvised **non-Nepali** dishes and local fish prepared umpteen different ways. The recipes are very formulaic, since Nepali cooks all receive the same training and copy each other shamelessly.

If pseudo-Western food gets you down, many restaurants do good but expensive set **Nepali** meals and some pretty good **Indian** dishes. For something much cheaper, try one of the myriad **momo** shacks, where locals eat. For a real change of scene, Pokhara Bazaar has a number of Indian restaurants around the northwest corner of Prithvi Chowk (west of the public bus park), and a few others in Mahendra Pul, as well as the usual greasy spoons serving Nepali or **Tibetan** food, scattered throughout the city. Watch out for the **juice** sellers: they'll dilute the juice with (unsafe) water and sugar behind a curtain.

Restaurant **prices** are comparable to those in Kathmandu's Thamel area. Places described here as inexpensive will charge less than Rs150 per person for a full dinner, not including alcohol (proportionately less for breakfast or lunch). Moderate restaurants will run to Rs150–250, expensive ones Rs250–500. For a real post-trek splurge, the *Shangri-La Village Hotel*, outside town (see p.294), does an eat-as-much-as-you-like/can buffet for Rs500 at weekends, and you can use the swimming pool.

Lakeside North

Bistro Caroline Long, hard trek? Need some pampering? The food isn't quite as French as the atmosphere, but it's about as good as it gets in Pokhara, and there's a wine list – at a price. Expensive.

Everest Steak House Lively rooftop place serving beef in every conceivable form; the huge garden is pleasant for daytime seating. Moderate.

Fewa Park Unbeatable location, with thatched pavilions scattered around a lawn that slopes down to the lake. Better for breakfast or lunch, as insects can be troublesome at night. Moderate.

Hungry Eye A pricier, tour-group version of the other standard-menu restaurants on the strip, with reliable food. The nightly culture show is hardly discreet, but does at least feature genuine, and well-performed Nepali songs and dances. Expensive.

Koto Pleasantly minimalist restaurant serving reasonably authentic Japanese food, including sushi and sticky rice (grown in Nepal!). Expensive but excellent set menus. Moderate to expensive.

Lemon Tree Sophisticated atmosphere and good service, with one or two better-than-average dishes and excellent fish. Moderate.

Little Tibetan Tea Garden A good range of Tibetan food, along with the usual Western stuff, in a lovely little bamboo grove. Inexpensive.

Mamma Mia Relaxed wicker interior open to the street. Serves surprisingly good home-made pasta with fresh sauces, and great pizza. Inexpensive.

Mike's The ultimate tranquil spot, literally right beside the lake at the *Hotel Fewa*. Like the related Kathmandu restaurant of the same name, it's best for breakfast or lunch. Large portions of authentic American-style *huevos*, waffles, eggs Benedict, etc. Good margaritas, too. Expensive.

Monsoon Garden Cafe Lovely garden for relaxing and enjoying classy breakfasts and lunches, and afternoon cream teas. Open till 6pm. Moderate.

Moondance. The epicentre of Lakeside eating, with dishes you won't find elsewhere (wonderful quiche), great Thai food and a lively atmosphere. Moderate.

Once Upon a Time Another popular establishment that likes to pretend it's in Goa. The food is interchangeable with that of the neighbouring *Maya Pub*. Moderate.

Tea Time One of Lakeside's original bamboo joints, good for daytime people-watching, drinks and snacks. Moderate.

Lakeside South

Caffe Concerto Authentic pizza, lasagne, gnocchi and other Italian dishes (their tiramisu is the real McCoy), plus tolerable wine. Mellow atmosphere, with videos banished to a back room. Moderate.

Lan Hua Adequate Chinese food, and the tofu is quite good. Moderate.

Laxman Large indoor/outdoor hangout, one of the pioneers of the cosy-wicker decor now so prevalent around Lakeside. Steaks, pastas, serious cakes. Pool and snooker tables. Moderate.

Lhasa Good range of Tibetan specialities and excellent Indian food. Monotonous music. Moderate.

Khahare and Bangladi

Lakeside Garden or **Pokhara Anrang** Worth it just for the beautiful setting in a tranquil corner of the lake. Decent standard dishes, and great *momos*, but the real draw is the superb (pricey) Korean menu. Moderate to expensive.

Le Panoramix Simple outdoor restaurant serving bargain French foods like *momos*, spag bol and steaks to an eclectic, long-term-traveller crowd. Inexpensive.

Damside

Don't Pass Me By Really lovely patio seating right beside the lake. Competent all-round food, excellent for breakfast. Inexpensive.

German Bakery Tolerable croissants and Damside's premier cake display. Inexpensive.

Loss Time Passable all-rounder, better for Indian food. Moderate.

Nepali Kitchen Caters to the local Japanese traveller contingent with tasty soups, snacks and fish and noodle dishes. Dingy inside. Inexpensive.

Rose Great garden seating (unusual for Damside), nightly menu featuring Continental (especially Dutch) specialities. Shares premises with *Hotel Lake City*. Moderate.

Nightlife

While nightlife around Pokhara usually just means a second helping of pie and another pirated DVD, a good way to break the routine is to catch a **culture show**. The *Hungry Eye* and a few other tourist restaurants put on free dinner music performances by local folk troupes. *Hotel Dragon* and *Fish Tail Lodge* host more-elaborate music and dance programmes nightly in the high season. Tickets cost Rs100–200 and are available through agents. Lakeside's **bars** regularly push back the usual 10pm bedtime barrier, at least during the high season.

Full-moon **raves** take off every now and again in the vicinity of the lake: keep your ear to the ground for any stray talk escaping the self-contained Nepali-trendy or Israeli-traveller scenes.

Beam Beam Laid-back inside/outside affair with a nice belly-up bar. Occasional live music. Opens late.

Blues Café Popular with local (male, inevitably) youth and young traveller crowd. Nepali bands, pool and sometimes even dancing.

Club Amsterdam Well-stocked bar, pool table, satellite TV above the bar…all the trappings of a studenty bar back home.

Maya Pub Current after-hours favourite for cocktails and music. Serves good, moderately-priced

pastas, sizzlers and vegetarian dishes, too.

Moondance Pub A lively pub with eclectic music that centres around pool tables, darts and carom boards (an addictive subcontinental game that's a bit like pool played on a giant checkers board). The restaurant is good for quieter after-dinner drinks.

7-Eleven Cheesy lounge with authentic *ghazal* entertainment, popular with local Nepalis and visiting Indians.

Shopping

Shopping is still a mainly outdoor activity in Lakeside and Damside, where laid-back curio stalls make a welcome change from the hard-driving salesmen of Kathmandu, even if their prices and selection don't quite compare. Local specialities include **batiks**, wooden **flasks**, **dolls** in ethnic dress and fossil-bearing **shaligram** stones from the Kali Gandaki. Hand-stitched **wall hangings** in simple Tibetan designs are attractive. Persuasive Tibetans peddle their wares in Lakeside's cafés, but these aren't produced locally, and **carpets** are best purchased at the Tibetan villages. Hand-knitted woollen sweaters, socks and such aren't of very good quality here, but may fit the bill for **trekking**.

Kashmiris have colonized Lakeside, as they have Thamel, with boutiques touting "Asian" art: mainly high-priced carpets and cheap **papier-mâché** and soapstone widgets. Other than that, you'll find the usual range of tourist bait, most of it imported from Kathmandu: ritual masks, *thangka*, embroidered T-shirts (wear that trek!), cloth bags and hippie clothes. Stalls along the strip opposite the palace are extremely competitive. The **bookshops** and stalls around Lakeside and Damside are individually small, but collectively they can muster a good selection of secondhand books.

Activities

Pokhara has emerged as the outdoor-recreation capital of Nepal. If someone's been trekking in Nepal, chances are they based themselves here, and an increasing number of travellers are coming for rafting, kayaking and mountain-biking too. Pokhara is also a pleasant setting for meditation or yoga studies, though the options here are more limited than in the Kathmandu Valley.

Trekking

There are any number of ways to get to the start of a **trek** out of Pokhara. Most people, being in a hurry to get up into the mountains, take a taxi to **Suikhet (Phedi)**, **Naya Pul** or **Beni** (or maybe beyond Beni, depending on how quickly the road is extended). The fare to Naya Pul – the most popular gateway – should be about Rs500–600. Cheaper but much slower local buses depart hourly from the Baglung bus park. You can also enter the region by hiking straight in from Lakeside, via **Sarangkot** (see p.308), or by hiring someone to row you across the lake and upriver to a point below Naudaada. Those trekking the Annapurna Circuit typically start at Besisahar, reached by taking a bus to **Dumre** (on the way to Kathmandu – see p.277), from where buses and jeeps shuttle the rest of the way. An alternative trailhead is **Begnas Tal** (see p.313), reached by taxi or local bus from Chipledhunga in the bazaar.

Recommending **trekking agencies** in Pokhara is even riskier than in Kathmandu. Anyhow, you don't need an agency to trek the Annapurna region unless you're doing something unorthodox. **Guides** and **porters** can be hired through almost any trekking agency or equipment shop, though it's often a good idea to book through your guesthouse, where there's more of a chance to talk to guides or to trekkers who have just returned. Three Sisters Adventure Trekking, operating out of the *Chhetri Sisters Guest House* (℡061/24066, Ⓦwww.3sistersadventure.com), can arrange female guides and porters; book in advance in season.

If you're going trekking you'll almost certainly be heading into the Annapurna Conservation Area (**ACAP**), and will want to pay the **entry fee** (Rs2000) in advance, as it costs double when bought at an entry post. ACAP's Lakeside office is on the first floor immediately opposite Standard Chartered Bank (Mon–Fri & Sun 9am–4.30pm, closes 3pm mid-Nov to mid-Feb); you'll need a passport photograph. See Chapter Seven for full details on trekking preparations and routes.

To find a **trekking partner**, the ACAP office is a good place to meet people who are about to set off. You'll sometimes see messages at Lakeside restaurant notice boards as well, but don't worry too much if you don't hook up with anyone before you leave – you'll meet tons of people as soon as you start walking. Pokhara's selection of rental **trekking equipment** is as good as Kathmandu's, and you'll pay for fewer days by renting locally. Sleeping bags, packs, down jackets and even boots are easily obtainable (about Rs20–30 per day per item, depending on quality). Prices for rental and sale are mostly fixed by agreement between shopkeepers, at very reasonable rates – often cheaper than Kathmandu. Ex-expedition gear tends to be top quality but it's more lived-in than worn-in, while new kit, usually imported from farther east, looks better than it wears.

Rafting and kayaking

Pokhara is within striking distance of no fewer than four **rafting** rivers – the Kali Gandaki, Trisuli, Seti and Marsyangdi. The Kali is probably the most popular trip out of Pokhara; the Trisuli is better done out of Kathmandu, since the starting point is closer to there and the river flows towards Pokhara. The Seti is best known as the venue for **kayak** clinics, which are organized by several companies; kayaks can be rented from most of the places listed below (from $10 without gear). See Chapter Eight for more detail about rivers, rafting and kayaking. See the box on p.295 for information on **boating** on Phewa Tal.

Many **river operators** have offices in Lakeside but, as in Kathmandu, most don't have enough of a track record to be worthy of recommendation. Some are merely agents. The following are the more reputable companies.

Equator Expeditions ℡061/20688, ⓦwww .equatornepal.com. Rafting trips with kayak support, also four-day (registered) kayak courses on the Seti. Experienced Western and Nepali guides, good equipment.
Ganesh Kayak Shop ℡061/22657, ⓦwww .raftnepal.fsnet.co.uk. If you're in Nepal to kayak independently, this should be your first stop. The shop has a wide variety of kayaks and associated gear for rent, as well as hydrospeeds. Runs Seti kayak clinics, but these aren't as yet registered for certificates.

Himalayan Encounters ℡061/20873, ⓔrafting&trekking@himenco.wlink.com.np. Classy, professional and expensive. Nepal's longest-serving rafting operator, with experienced Nepali guides.
Himalayan Wonders ℡01/42670. Good, experienced Nepali guides from a long-established Kathmandu firm. Offers some kayak trips, but specializes in rafting.
Ultimate Descents ℡061/23240, ⓦwww.udnepal .com. Nepal's biggest river operator – operating as part of Adventure Centre Asia – has had its ups and downs, but is still good on the river. Also does Seti kayak clinics.

Other outdoor activities

Local **mountain-biking** possibilities are described in Chapter Nine (see p.483), and possible routes are also indicated briefly throughout the "Pokhara Valley" section, where appropriate. Himalayan Mountain Bikes (in the same office as Ultimate Descents – see above) and Dawn Till Dusk, both with offices in Lakeside, run organized day-trips and longer tours out of Pokhara, and also rent out good bikes for around Rs750 per day.

Sunrise Paragliding (℡061/21174, ⓦwww.nepal-paragliding.com) launches **paraglide jumps** from Sarangkot, the hill north of Lakeside, and offers an array of short courses for beginners and experienced gliders. Qualified jumpers can try out the para-treks, which involve hiking up to various local summits and floating back down. If only you could do it the other way round. Beginners' tandem jumps cost from $65; courses range from $230 for three days up to $650 for nine. Avia Club Nepal (℡061/25192, ⓦwww.avianepal .21bc.net) does short trips around the valley and up towards the mountains in **ultralight** aircraft, which carry one passenger at a time. The price is $50 for a fifteen-minute flight, $170 for an hour.

Kids and their parents will get the most out of **pony-trekking**. Many outfits run short rides beside the lake, half-day rides around the north shore to Pame, and full-day treks up to Sarangkot. Prices are around $12 for a half-day, $20 for a full day; book through any agent. If the season is right, you can pay to play **tennis** at the *Hotel Barahi* in Lakeside, **swim** at the *Shangri-La Village* or *Bluebird Hotel*, or play **golf** at the *Fulbari Resort Hotel*'s nine-hole course, or the eighteen-hole Himalayan Golf Course (☎061/21882), set up by an ex-Gurkha Major who saw it as a suitable investment for his pension; sheep keep the fairways trim.

Meditation and yoga

Many spiritual centres last only a season or two in Pokhara. One that appears to be permanent is **Garden Yiga Chozin Buddhist Centre** (☎061/22923), a very peaceful facility a short walk north of Lakeside, where teachers come up in season from Kopan monastery, outside Kathmandu, for regular residential courses and daily teachings, designed for mainly Western participants. Enquire about three-day retreats and daily yoga, t'ai chi and reiki sessions in high season. The **Nepali Yoga Centre** in Lakeside (☎061/28886) is run by women and has had very good reports. **Sadhana Yoga Ashram** (✉yogisanga@yahoo.com), operating out of *Hotel Orion Legend* in Damside, offers one-day yogic cleansing and hatha yoga sessions and longer residential courses.

Introductory classes are sometimes free, while short sessions usually **cost** a few hundred rupees. Expect to pay $10–20 per day for residential courses. Other courses can easily be found by checking notice boards around Lakeside and Damside.

Listings

ACAP For trekking permits in the Annapurna Conservation Area, the ACAP office (Mon–Fri & Sun 9am–4.30pm, closes 3pm mid-Nov to mid-Feb) is opposite Standard Chartered Bank, in Lakeside North; the permit costs Rs1000.

Banks and money Standard Chartered in Lakeside handles foreign exchange and credit card cash advances (Mon–Thurs & Sat 9.45am–4.15pm, Fri 9.45am–1.15pm) and has an ATM next to *Hotel Snowland*. The rates at Nabil Bank, also on the main drag, weren't as good at the time of writing. Many registered moneychangers operate in Lakeside and Damside and at the airport (generally 8am–7pm), and some hotels will change money as well, but you'll pay a higher commission for avoiding bank queues.

Email and internet Internet shops are now almost as ubiquitous as travel agencies. At the time of writing, prices stood at a standard Rs5 per minute, but are likely to drop significantly as soon as local-rate dial-in numbers become available.

Film and processing Films are available for about Rs100 and up, according to quality. A few places in Lakeside and Pokhara Bazaar do same-day processing, and other tourist shops can send film out.

Haircutting Pokhara has a preponderance of barbers, who do not only haircuts but also shaves and massages (see "Massage", below). A basic trim should cost from around Rs30, but establish the price and exact extent of services beforehand.

Hospitals, clinics and pharmacies Several pharmacies in Lakeside/Damside do stool tests, though incorrect diagnoses are common. One or two also offer ayurvedic medicine. In an emergency head for the new Manipal Teaching Hospital (☎061/26417), with a staff of Indian-trained doctors. Closer to hand, but more chaotic, is the Western Regional Hospital (☎061/20066), also known as the Gandaki Hospital – its ER looks terrible, but quite a few Western-trained doctors work there. Have your hotel phone ahead to make sure a doctor is on duty. Padma Nursing Home, on New Rd (ask a taxi to take you), is good for non-emergency treatment, and you'd probably be fine at the flashy, businesslike Hargan's Nursing Home in Lakeside (☎061/32271).

Laundry Most lodges take laundry for a few rupees per item. The places calling themselves "dry cleaners" return your clothes dry, but wash as wet as the others.

Massage Sanja Lama, who can be found at Rainbow Thanka Art Gallery (☎061/32132), is recommended for many types of massage and physical therapy (Rs1000 for a one-hour full-body massage). Many other uncertified masseurs charge less (typically around Rs300 per hour) – they're good for ironing out post-trek kinks, but not for professional therapy. Barbers, who mostly come from India, are well-versed in traditional head massage, and usually offer neck, back and even full-body massage too.

Media International newspapers and magazines are available in bookshops, usually one or two days late. The English-language Nepali papers mostly arrive around noon, on the morning flights from Kathmandu.

Post Tourist book- and postcard shops sell stamps – Europe Rs25, USA Rs30. Some shops and many hotels and guesthouses will take mail to the post office; they're mostly trustworthy. In any case, the trip to the main post office in Mahendra Pul (Mon–Thurs & Sun 10am–5pm or 4pm in winter, Fri 10am–3pm) is an eye-opener. They've got a tiny poste restante department, but it may not be as reliable as the one in Kathmandu – don't have anything of value sent to you here (and for that matter don't post anything of value *from* here).

Provisions Mini-supermarkets along the Lakeside strip anticipate your every need. Basically, everything you can get in Kathmandu, you can get in Lakeside/Damside: chocolate, tinned food, bread, cheese, wine, spirits, toiletries, batteries, etc.

Telephones As in Kathmandu, you'll find plenty of ISD/IDD businesses (most open 8am–10pm), plus many guesthouses have international dialling facilities. International calls are charged at around Rs160–200 per minute, depending on country and shop. Some places even pass on cheaper phonecard rates, and you could always struggle with the delay on an internet phone. Trunk calls to Kathmandu cost about Rs15 per minute. Callback (receiving an incoming call) is usually free for the first five minutes, Rs5 per minute thereafter.

Visa extensions For visa extensions, head north from Damside to the Department of Immigration office, 50m short of Mustang Chowk. Application hours are Mon–Thurs & Sun 10.30am–1pm (12.30pm in winter), Fri 10am–noon; visas are ready later the same day. Trekking or travel agents can handle the paperwork for a commission of about Rs300, but it's hardly worth it. Passport photos are available in minutes from photo shops around Lakeside and near the Immigration office (about Rs200 for four).

Moving on

Buses link Pokhara with Kathmandu via the Prithvi Highway, and with the Tarai and India via the Siddhartha Highway. All the major domestic airlines connect Pokhara with Kathmandu.

Buses

As many as a dozen companies operate tourist buses and minibuses from Pokhara to **Kathmandu**, which usually leave around 7am. The fare is around Rs200–250, which is about twice the price of public buses, but the tourist services are more comfortable and somewhat faster and safer, and they pick up passengers in Lakeside and Damside. More expensive ($10 or so) luxury coaches offer air conditioning and an alternative 8.30am departure; operators change from year to year, but Greenline, Sunny and Travelanes seem established. A handful of companies also run tourist buses to Sauraha (for **Chitwan** National Park); the fare is Rs200, or $8 for Greenline's luxury bus.

Buses and night buses to the Indian border at **Sonauli** aren't technically tourist services, but they do pick up passengers in Lakeside/Damside. There are no other tourist buses, and none to **Bardia** National Park: most people take the night bus to Dhanghadi or Mahendra Nagar, both of which leave Pokhara at or shortly after 1pm, and get off at Ambaasa (see p.366).

All tourist and night buses and some public buses can be booked through ticket agents, but shop around since not every agent represents every bus company, and prices vary quite a bit. The agent's fee for obtaining a public bus ticket may be more than the ticket itself, but it's well worth it to avoid an extra encounter with the bus park. Buses serving the Prithvi and Siddhartha highways depart from the **main bus park**, and tickets are sold from the booking hall at the top of the steps on the west side. For services along the Baglung Highway (including those to various Annapurna-region trailheads), you need to buy tickets from the separate **Baglung bus park**, located on the western side of the bazaar. However, Baglung buses have a reputation for reckless driving, so it's preferable to take a taxi to the start of a trek.

If you're heading **to India**, read the section on ticket agents in Basics (p.34) first.

Private vehicles

Long-distance travel by **private vehicle** works out to be more expensive than the usual daily rental rate, since you have to pay for the car and driver to return to Pokhara even if you're travelling only one way. For most journeys the most economical option will be a taxi; jeeps and vans can also be arranged. Rates for a taxi or similar are around $55 to Kathmandu, $45 to Chitwan, and $65 to Lumbini/Sonauli. Travel agencies can arrange rentals, but it's easier and probably more satisfactory all around to have your hotel or guesthouse do it.

Flights

There are **internal flights** from Pokhara to Kathmandu ($69) and Jomosom ($63), and in the past there have been flights to Manang in the trekking season as well. It's easier to use an agent than book direct, and many agents can also book or reconfirm **international flights** by phone to Kathmandu. Mountain-view excursions and flights to Dolpo) are usually available only on a charter basis.

The Pokhara Valley

Day-trips around the **Pokhara Valley** make excellent training for a trek, and serve as an effective antidote to lakeside idleness. Excursions generally entail a healthy amount of cycling or hiking, often both. Start early to make the most of the views before the clouds move in and the heat builds – it can get really sticky here in all but the winter months – and bring lunch and a full water bottle. If you're feeling adventurous (or running behind schedule), you can **stay overnight** at Sarangkot, Tashi Palkhel or Begnas Tal.

Many of the **ethnic groups** that make treks north of Pokhara so popular – Gurungs, Magars, and Baahun and Chhetri Hindu castes – are equally well represented around the valley, and less touched by tourism here. In addition, the **Tibetan settlements** in the area are less commercial, and in their own way more instructive about Tibetan culture, than those in the Kathmandu Valley.

The World Peace Pagoda and beyond

The newly constructed **World Peace Pagoda**, which crowns the ridge across the lake at an elevation of 1113m, provides one of the most satisfying short hikes in the Pokhara area. The views from the top are phenomenal, and since there are several routes up and back, you can work this into a loop that includes boating on the lake and/or visiting Chhorepatan. A basic up-and-back trip can be done in anything from two to three hours, so you can leave after breakfast and be back in time for lunch.

The easiest approach is by trail **from Damside**. Cross the river on a foot-bridge just downstream of the dam, then follow the path as it bears left and passes a small shrine before beginning a gradual ascent up the back (south) side

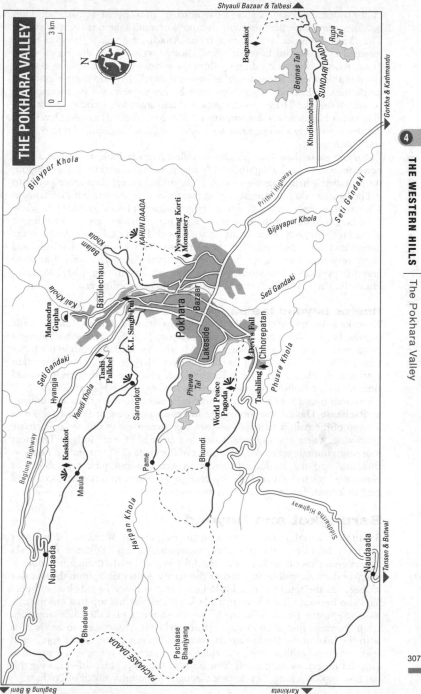

of the ridge. The way is somewhat obscure and littered at first, but soon becomes a fine wide path through chestnut forest until the final, steeper ascent. The climb is steeper and damper **from Anadu**, the village across the lake (reached by boat from Lakeside). A signposted trail starts at the *Typical Guest House*, though all trails heading up from the various put-ashore points eventually join this one. If descending this way, you should have no trouble getting a canoe back to Lakeside – you may even be intercepted by a boatman before you reach the lake. There's also a signposted trail ascending straight up from the Siddhartha Highway at **Chhorepatan** (see p.209), about 1km past Devi's Fall, but this is probably a better route for descending and continuing on to the falls and Tashiling.

Standing more than 40m tall, the so-called **pagoda** looks more like a cross between a stupa and a lighthouse. It seems rather grandiose for a religious shrine, but if it helps achieve its stated aim (world peace) then more power to it. The Japanese Buddhist organization that funded the monument maintains an adjacent monastery with a small meditation hall and monks' quarters. The **view** from here is just about the best wide-angle panorama you can get of this part of the Himalaya, and certainly the only one with Phewa Tal and Pokhara in the foreground. Over on the far left there's the towering hump of Dhaulagiri and its more westerly sisters, in the middle rises the Annapurna Himal and the graceful pyramid of Machhapuchhre, and off to the right are Manaslu, Himalchuli and Baudha. A small café-bar provides refreshment.

Routes beyond the pagoda

To make a day-trip of the walk you can **loop around Phewa Tal**. From the pagoda, keep walking along the ridgeline past *Rani Ban Retreat* and along a rough road to the village of Bhumdi, where another road descends to the highway and a trail leads down to the sluggish Harpan Khola at Pame, 3km upstream of Phewa Tal. For a longer hike, continue further west beyond Bhumdi to the end of the road before descending to the Harpan Khola.

A superb two-day trek offering supreme views climbs on from Bhumdi up to **Pachaase Daada**, the prominent forested ridge west of Phewa Tal. From the top of the path, a trail follows the ridge northwest to the col at Pachaase Bhanjyang, where you can stay at one of a handful of basic **lodges**. The next morning, continue up to the high point of the ridge (2509m) and on north to Bhadaure and the Baglung Highway, where you can pick up a bus past Naudaada back to Pokhara. Very few foreigners venture into this area, so a good map or knowledgeable guide is recommended.

Sarangkot and beyond

Sarangkot, a high point (1590m) on the ridge north of Phewa Tal, is by far the most popular of the mountain viewpoints around Pokhara. The peaks appear even closer from here than from the Peace Pagoda, though not quite as many of them are visible. Sarangkot's popularity stems mainly from the fact that it's been on the tourist map a lot longer than the Peace Pagoda has, and perhaps also because it has a substantial little village near the top that can provide lodging – many people hike up in the afternoon, spend the night and then catch the views first thing in the morning, when it's most likely to be clear. As with the hike to the Peace Pagoda, there are various routes to the top and at least one route further along the ridge once you're up there, so a number of different itineraries are possible. You can also cycle up, potentially making this the first stop on a longer cycle trek through the country north of Pokhara.

Getting there

There are two principal **hiking routes** up Sarangkot, a hard one and an easier one. The first entails walking straight up **from Lakeside**, which is quite a long, steep climb with no mountain views until the very top – if you're running late you might miss them altogether. Follow the road north from Lakeside as it bends around the lake, goes up and down a small hill and traverses a large cultivated area. Two kilometres beyond Camping Chowk the trail, marked by a painted stone, forks off to the right; when in doubt, stay on the flagstoned path and keep heading generally towards the summit. You'll be doing well to make it from the trailhead to the top in less than two and a half hours. The easier route starts near the **Bindyabasini temple** in the bazaar, a Rs80 taxi ride from Lakeside. A paved road goes from there to within a half-hour's hike of the top, so if you want to make this a really easy route you can have the **taxi** take you as far as the end of the road (Rs500 one way). Otherwise, walk westwards from the temple along the signposted road and then take the obvious shortcuts, which stick to the spine of the ridge and avoid the road for much of the way. Compared to the Lakeside approach this is a gentler ascent, and the scenery – both mountains and lake – gets better and better as you go. That said, it's also far more commercialized, with offers of cold drinks, curios and guide services all along the upper stretch. There are apparently other trails to the top, including one that starts about 200m north of the radio tower southwest of the main bazaar.

It takes a good **mountain bike** to get to Sarangkot and back down again in one piece, and a strong rider to do much more than that in a day; for a detailed description of the route, and continuing on to Naudaada, see p.483.

The village and summit

The **village** of **SARANGKOT**, nestled just below the summit, has tea shops, handicrafts sellers and something like a dozen **lodges** with views of the lake. All have electricity and most can provide hot washing water by the bucket. Names change often here, but *Lake View Lodge* (☎061/29363; ❷) and *Hotel Mountain Prince* (no phone; ❷) seem fairly well established. Several simple restaurants line the path up to the top, some with excellent views.

For the **summit**, continue another ten minutes up to the remains of a fort. (*Kot* means "fort" in Nepali, and you'll find that just about every hilltop in this region, which was once divided among many warring principalities, is called Something-kot.) If you've hiked up from Lakeside, and it's not too hazy or late in the day, the sudden view here will come as a staggering revelation. The peaks seem to levitate above their blue flanks, the gathering clouds add a quality of raw grandeur, while to the south, Phewa Tal shimmers in the hazy arc of the valley. If you hadn't been planning on trekking, this is where you might change your mind.

Routes beyond Sarangkot

A road connects Sarangkot with Naudaada, about 10km further west on the Baglung Highway, making possible all sorts of longer trips beyond Sarangkot. Contouring along the south side of the ridge, the road lets you make good time on foot or bike. A few villages are located along the way, notably Maula, the starting point of a flagstoned path up to **Kaskikot**, seat of the kingdom that once ruled the Pokhara Valley, perched on a craggy brow of the ridge with views as big as Sarangkot's. (Maula is therefore sometimes referred to as Kotmuni – "Below the Fort".) A stone enclosure and a house-like Kali temple are all that remain of the citadel of the Kaski kings, which fell to the Gorkhalis without a fight in 1781. **NAUDAADA** is another 4.5km west of Maula (it's not to be confused with the other Naudaada, which lies south of Pokhara on the road to Butwal), and the first place from which Machhapuchhre's true fish-tail profile can be seen. Two or three nice little lodges offer trekking-style accommodation along the road between Maula and Naudaada.

On foot, you'll probably catch a bus from Naudaada back to Pokhara. However, other interesting variations are possible, including walking down from Maula to Pame or west along the main road from Naudaada and then south to Pachaase Daada (see p.308). On a decent **bike**, you could even continue deeper along the Baglung Highway (see below), which is fast being extended into the hills beyond Beni, taking you into what was, until recently, trekking country.

The Baglung Highway and Tashi Palkhel

Heading northwest from the bazaar, the **Baglung Highway** provides the chief access for treks in the Annapurna region and rafting trips on the Kali Gandaki. Most people are only whizzing through on their way to their respective adventures, however, and other than a few mountain-bikers returning from Sarangkot, towns along the road see few foreign faces.

It was a different story up until the mid-1980s, when this was the main trekking trail north from Pokhara. But as has happened elsewhere, the construction of a new highway has introduced enormous changes to the local social order, bringing wealth and prosperity to a few – mostly outside developers – and luring young people away to the cities. The Yamdi Khola valley has been transformed, not only by vehicles, but also by a hydroelectric project and a roadside smattering of modern concrete dwellings emanating like a comet's tail from Pokhara Bazaar.

Tashi Palkhel (Hyangja)

With twelve hundred residents – eighty of them monks – **Tashi Palkhel** (also known as **Hyangja**, after the village 3km beyond) is the largest and also the least commercial of Pokhara's Tibetan settlements. The entrance is clearly marked, about 4km northwest of the north end of Pokhara Bazaar on the Baglung Highway. Get there by bike, taxi (Rs350) or a bus from the Baglung bus park. If you're doing the Siklis trek you can hit the trail not far from here.

A path past curio sellers draws you naturally to the community's large **gompa** (monastery), where resident monks usually gather for chanting at 6am and 4pm, and all day during festivals. The *gompa* is of the Kagyu-pa sect, and portraits either side of the Buddha statue inside the hall depict the Dalai Lama and the late Kagyu leader, the sixteenth Karma Lama; smaller figures behind represent the one thousand Buddhas believed to exist during the present age. Opposite the monastery, a broad quadrangle is the focal point of Tashi Palkhel's **carpet industry**, which is successful enough to employ local women from outside the Tibetan community as weavers. No one minds if you wander around; you can see the wool being dyed in huge copper basins that are warmed over wood fires, then dried, spun and finally woven. You can even specify your own designs, which can be turned into a workable pattern and woven within a fortnight – ready for when you come back from that trek. The community also has a school to which Tibetan children from all over Nepal come as boarders, an old people's home (many of the original refugees are now getting on in years), a clinic and community hall.

Tashi Palkhel's cooperative **guesthouse**, the *Tibetan Yak* (❷), can supply very

Tibetans in exile

Thirty years ago, Dervla Murphy worked as a volunteer among **Tibetan refugees in Pokhara**, and called the account she wrote about her experiences *The Waiting Land*. Pokhara's Tibetans are still waiting: three former **refugee camps**, now self-governing and largely self-sufficient, have settled into a pattern of permanent transience. Because Pokhara (unlike Kathmandu) has no Buddhist holy places, most Tibetans have remained in the camps, regarding them as havens where they can keep their culture and language alive. Many plainly don't see the point of moving out and setting up permanent homes in Nepal when all they really want is to return to their former homes in Tibet.

The settlements – Tashi Palkhel, Tashiling and Paljorling – are open to the public, and a wander around one is an experience of workaday reality that contrasts with the otherworldliness of, say, Boudha or Swayambhu. You'll get a lot more out of a visit if you can get someone to show you around – and if the tour inevitably finishes with a sales pitch back at your guide's one-room home, so much the better.

At the time of the **Chinese invasion** of Tibet in 1950, the Tibetans now living in Pokhara were mainly peasants and nomads inhabiting the border areas of western Tibet. The political changes in faraway Lhasa left them initially unaffected, but after the Dalai Lama fled Tibet in 1959 and the Chinese occupation turned genocidal, thousands streamed south through the Himalaya to safety. They gathered first at Jomosom, where the terrain and climate were at least reminiscent of Tibet, but the area soon became overcrowded and conditions desperate. Under the direction of the Swiss Red Cross, three **transit camps** were established around low-lying Pokhara and about two thousand refugees were moved down.

The first five years were hard times in the camps, marked by food rationing, chronic sickness and general unemployment. Relief came in the late 1960s, when the construction of Pardi Dam and the Prithvi and Siddhartha highways provided welcome work. A second wave of refugees began around the same time, after the United States' detente with China ended a covert CIA operation supporting Tibetan freedom-fighters based in Mustang. Since then, the fortunes of Pokhara's Tibetans have risen with the local **tourism** industry, and carpet-weaving and handicraft sales have become the main source of income, especially for women. Many of the men work seasonally as trekking porters or guides, where they can make better money than in the camps. A small but visible minority have become smooth-talking curio salespeople, plying the cafés of Lakeside and Damside, but whereas Tibetans have by now set up substantial businesses in Kathmandu, opportunities are fewer in Pokhara, and prosperity has come more slowly.

---

basic rooms; hot showers are sometimes available, and camping is possible. Get **food** at the guesthouse or at one of the smoky, buttery holes-in-the-wall nearby. **Handicrafts** can be purchased at the cooperative shop in the guesthouse compound, whose profits support community projects, as well as from private shops and freelance vendors. Even if you're perfectly healthy, the **Tibetan medicine centre** is worth a visit, as long as you can find someone to help you over the language barrier.

To Beni

The Baglung Highway is smoothly asphalted as far as **Baglung**, a zonal headquarters 72km from Pokhara, and well-roughed in to **Beni**, 10km further on. The road grows a little longer each year, however, and a seasonal dirt road now forces its way up the Thak Khola nearly halfway to Jomosom, and there are plans to extend the route right into Mustang. Most rafting trips on the Kali start at Baglung, but at certain times of year some companies put in farther up near Beni.

Combined with a visit to Sarangkot, the highway makes for an enjoyable two-plus-day bike ride or motorcycle cruise. It ascends seriously past Naudaada to its high point near **Kaare** (1770m), then descends into the valley of the Modi Khola, where you can overnight in **Naya Pul** or in one of the nice lodges at **Birethanti** (off the highway, at the boundary of the Annapurna Conservation Area). The downhill ends at **Kusma**, where the road leaves the Modi and bends upstream along the Kali Gandaki.

From Kusma, a thirty-kilometre road will eventually loop over to **Naudaada**, on the Pokhara to Tansen Highway (not to be confused with the Naudaada northwest of Pokhara), but at present there's a 6km gap between Kusma and Karkineta that's walkable only – though bold cyclists might try it.

Mahendra Gupha and the Kali Khola

While it just about scrapes a description as a geological wonder, **Mahendra Gupha** (Mahendra Cave; Rs15) is probably best thought of as a base from which to explore the snug hills and side valleys north of Pokhara. To get there by bike, cross K.I. Singh Pul (Bridge) at the top end of Pokhara and head north past the Gurkha camp, turn right up a paved road 600m beyond the bridge, and follow it for about 3km to the end. The climb is relentless and if you're on a one-speed bike you'll have to push some of the way (the reward comes on the way back). A taxi will charge about Rs250 return. Some city buses come up this way (change at Prithvi Narayan Campus).

Water percolating through the valley's limestone sediments has created a honeycomb of caves extending up to 2km from the main entrance, though a guided tour of the illuminated part only takes about ten to fifteen minutes. The cave used to be well known for its stalactites, but these have unfortunately been ransacked by vandals; a few surviving **stalagmites** are daubed with red *abhir* and revered as *shivalinga* because of their resemblance to phalluses. A café near the entrance serves food in a pleasant garden setting.

A more adventurous and more impressive trip is to **Chamere Gupha** (Bat Cave; Rs15 plus something for the guide), about ten-minutes' walk along a side road. It's a bit of a scramble up out of the main chamber, a big, dripping, sweating space with thousands of bats hanging from the ceiling – only in Nepal could you go into such a place with a stranger and not be worried about being bludgeoned to death. Bring your own torch/flashlight, or rent one from the ticket seller.

Eastwards from Mahendra Cave, a trail beckons up the **Kali Khola**, a minor tributary of the Seti, to the village of Armala. Adventurous types might want to forge on up the cultivated slopes on either side of the valley; by following the ridge to the south, you should be able to return to Pokhara the same day via the Bhalam Khola.

About 1km south of Mahendra Cave, the road from Pokhara passes through **BATULECHAUR**, a village locally famous for its **gaaine**. Wandering minstrels of the old school, *gaaine* are still found throughout the hills, earning their crust by singing ballads to the accompaniment of the *sarangi*, a four-stringed, hand-hewn fiddle: "I have no rice to eat/let the strings of the *sarangi* set to," runs the *gaaine*'s traditional opening couplet. These days, many find they can make better money down at Lakeside serenading tourists, spawning legions of inept imitators.

To vary the route on the way back, take a left onto a paved road just before K.I. Singh Pul and then look for a pathway off to the left. From there you can cross the Kali and Bhalam rivers by footbridges (you'll have to carry your bike a bit) to get to the Kahun Daada area (see opposite).

Kahun Daada and the Bhalam Khola

If the view from **Kahun Daada**, the hill east of Pokhara, is a shade less magnificent than Sarangkot's, a lookout tower near the top gives you a better crack at it, and trails up to it are totally uncommercialized. The easiest and most interesting starting point is the **Tibetan monastery** which stands on a hill 2km east down the main road from Mahendra Pul (the main bridge in Pokhara Bazaar). At the top of a breathless couple of hundred steps at the southern base of Kahun Daada, the Karma Dhubgyu Chhokhorling Nyeshang Korti Monastery occupies a breezy spot – always good for keeping the prayer flags flapping – with valley views east and west. Around thirty monks and monklets inhabit the monastery, which is modern and contains all the usual Vajrayana paraphernalia.

The trail to the lookout tower starts at the bottom of the steps, initially following a road that hugs the western base of the ridge for about 1km, and then climbs through several lazy settlements collectively known as **Phulbari**. Keep heading towards the tower (1444m), which is visible most of the way and can be reached in about an hour and a half from the monastery. From the half-finished concrete platform, you can contemplate the tremendous force of the Seti River and its tributaries, which tumble out of the Annapurna Himal clouded with dissolved limestone (*seti* means white) and, merging at the foot of the Kahun Daada, split the valley floor in a bleached chasm. Descending back to the monastery, paths bearing to the left may suggest a longer circuit via the valley and villages on the east side of the ridge.

Also eminently worth exploring is the tidily terraced side valley of the **Bhalam Khola**, immediately north of Kahun Daada. To get there directly from the tower involves some nasty bushwhacking, so it's better to backtrack towards the monastery until you pick up the first main northbound trail. It's also accessible by a rough (bikeable) track heading northwards on the east side of the Seti River. The power of erosion can readily be seen from this route as it passes the confluence of the Bhalam, Seti and Kali rivers, where they undercut old gravel beds, leaving sheer, mossy cliffs. The track continues at least another 3km to the village of Railechaur, and trails go further up the valley from there. This route can be linked with the one to Mahendra Cave (see opposite) by crossing two footbridges over the Bhalam and Kali rivers, but it's easier to visit the cave first.

Begnas and Rupa Tal

With Lakeside and Damside so overdeveloped, it's strange that **Begnas Tal** and **Rupa Tal**, twin lakes 15km east of Pokhara, haven't taken off as tourist destinations. Begnas Tal, the bigger and better-known of the two, is framed by meticulously engineered paddy terraces marching right down to its shore, while Rupa, on the other side of an intervening ridge, remains pristinely hidden in a bushy, steep-sided valley. Come prepared to spend the night: several lodges can put you up, and roads and trails open up a wealth of outstanding walking opportunities.

A **taxi** to Begnas Tal costs about Rs300 one way. **Local buses**, departing every fifteen minutes from the main bus park in Pokhara, take up to an hour and tend to be crowded. By **bike**, the first stretch along the Prithvi Highway is horribly polluted and fairly terrifying. After 10km, turn left at the signpost, and it's a pleasant three-kilometre ride down a straight, paved road to the end of the line. The dumpy hamlet of **KHUDIKOMOHAN** (often referred to simply as Begnas) is typical of so many roadhead towns; it seems to exist only as a conduit for corrugated roofing, bags of cement and other tools of progress for the surrounding hills.

Begnas Tal

Begnas Tal is just around the corner from the bazaar, up the road to the left immediately before the cul-de-sac where the buses stop. Just after the gate and ticket booth (Rs10 entrance fee), a plain block of basic lodge-restaurants looks across grassy sward to the southern shore of the lake – or would do if it wasn't for the decaying concrete sheds in the way. The dam stretches away to the left, below which the Ministry of Agriculture has built a big **fish farm** and research centre, consisting of concrete holding tanks fed by water from the lake. Fish farming is getting to be big business here, with Chinese carp and native *sahar* and *mahseer* packed off to restaurants in Pokhara and Kathmandu – those that the white *bhakula* (egrets) don't get, at any rate. Phewa-style **boats** are rented out beside the lake just beyond the dam (Rs250 per hour); with tent-shaped Annapurna II for a backdrop, the paddling here is at least as scenic as at Phewa Tal, and you'll practically have the lake to yourself. A good destination is the wooded peninsula at the north side of the lake, which is a **bird sanctuary**.

Rupa Tal and Paachbaiya Daada

Getting to **Rupa Tal** involves a little more effort than Begnas Tal, and the lake is far more secluded as a result. Every hour or two, in the dry season at least, **buses** from Begnas's bazaar negotiate the switchback road that leads along **Sundari Daada**, the ridge that separates the two lakes, but most people will prefer to **hike**. A handful of quirky, trekking-style **lodges** are scattered along the ridge, and any of them would make a great antidote to Pokhara's razzmatazz.

The rough road leads north from the far end of the bus park at Begnas bazaar and ascends the side of the ridge steeply. Hikers can turn left up to the ridge-top after about twenty minutes; cyclists and buses (just) stick to the road. Begnas Tal is visible first, on the left, and then Rupa Tal comes into view after the highest point is passed, about 45 minutes from the bus park. Local belief has it that the lakes are husband and wife, and that an object thrown into one lake will eventually appear in the other. The things that look like fences peeping above the water of both lakes are more fish farms – Rupa Tal is said to be particularly rich in nutrients. It's not such a good choice for swimming, however, as the lake margins are being progressively choked with mud and water hyacinths. In another ten minutes or so the trail rejoins the road as it descends to the half-dozen shops of the village called **SUNDARI DAADA**, after the ridge it sits on. This is the jumping-off point for just about all explorations in this area.

Just short of Sundari Daada, a trail to the left leads steeply down to Begnas Tal and *Begnas Lake Resort*, where you should be able to get a boat back to the dam area. A bit further along the road, a trail leading off to the right, signpost-ed "Karputar", descends to the north end of Rupa Tal and the village of Talbesi – this route makes an attractive alternative way into the Annapurna Circuit, and offers the possibility of a steep side trip to the hilltop viewpoint of **Rupakot**. Another 1km down the road, a trail to the left leads up to another village called Begnas and then to **Begnaskot** (about three hours from Sundari Daada), an even better viewpoint of the Annapurnas and lake from the grassy crest of the ridge; this trail is part of the Royal Trek (see p.439). The road itself swings around to Talbesi and Shyauli Bazaar (13km), and is being pushed all the way through to Besisahar, the starting point of the Annapurna Circuit. If the road is ever paved, expect this route to vie in popularity with the one from Dumre – but also to kill off the walking route.

Practicalities

A couple of **guesthouses** and snack joints are clumped near the dam, an easy walk from the bus stop – the location is good for access to the lake, but otherwise unattractive. At *New Begnas Lodge* (❶), below, you get what you pay for, but *Hotel Daybreak* (❷), perched on a bluff above the other buildings, has better views and cleaner, brighter rooms.

Far more idyllic are the indescribably peaceful **lodges** strung along the Panchbhaiya Daada trail. Be prepared to rough it at *Hotel Himalayan Range* (❶), reached first, which consists of just two tin-roofed mud huts overlooking Begnas Tal – a steep path leads down to the lake. The simple chalets of *Rupa Viewpoint* (❶), accessed by a path leading off to the right, just after the highest point of the road, are tacked onto a farmhouse home. Slightly more upmarket, *Dinesh's House* (❷), near the top of the ridge, is a sort of bed-and-breakfast in the home of the friendly owners, set among beautifully kept gardens; while *Robin's Nest* (℡061/60345; ❸), immediately above, is an ordinary guesthouse with a tourist menu and a fabulous view from its rooftop terrace.

Another steep path leads down from the ridge to the seriously posh *Begnas Lake Resort and Villas* (℡061/60030, ⓦwww.intertours_nepal.com/begnas; ❽), which spreads down through the forested southeastern shore of Begnas Tal and, oddly enough, has a swimming pool; most guests come by boat. An even fancier outfit run by the Tiger Tops people, *Tiger Mountain Pokhara Lodge* (℡061/ 27474, ⓦwww.tigermountain.com; ❾), is located along the Royal Trek on a ridge to the northwest of Begnas Tal, and offers naturalist-led treks.

The **food** served by the guesthouses is pretty unexciting compared to what's on offer in Pokhara, although you can usually get a few tourist items as well as the Nepali standards.

South of Pokhara

The only through road beyond Pokhara, the **Siddhartha Highway** (Siddhartha Rajmarg), points south: a slow, uncomfortable, but occasionally rewarding journey to the Tarai. In 160km the highway traverses four major river drainages, negotiates countless twists and turns, crosses many landslide paths, and often claims a tyre or an axle. Six hours would be a fast run. Although it's the most direct route between Pokhara and the Indian border, most buses travel via Narayangadh, to the east. Cyclists, however, will enjoy the variety and light traffic.

From Pokhara, the road labours 800m up to a divide before descending to **Naudaada**, a little-used alternative starting point for treks into the Kali Gandaki/Annapurna region (minibuses from Chipledhunga in Pokhara shuttle up here every half-hour or so). An old Kaski fortress guards the pass from the hill just to the east; to the west, a rough road makes its way to Karkineta, just 6km short of Kusma and the Baglung Highway.

Entering the Amdhi Khola watershed, the Siddhartha Highway wriggles tortuously across the side of the valley, purposely avoiding the flat, straight valley floor – in a country so reliant on agriculture, you don't put a road through the best farmland. After the bazaar of **Syangja**, the valley draws in and the hills rear up spectacularly in places. Signs of erosion are evident everywhere here: these hills are geologically very unstable, and slough their topsoil like a thin skin.

Public buses stop at **Waling**, a nondescript wayside that owes its existence to busloads of hungry travellers. Beyond, the highway ascends gradually and then begins its descent to the Kali Gandaki, first passing the access road to the huge new **Kali Gandaki "A" Project**, which has provided Nepal with surplus power for the first time. The $450-million, 144-megawatt hydroelectric diversion was the largest and most expensive project ever undertaken in Nepal – and like it or not, it's now the finishing point for rafting trips on the river. The Siddhartha Highway crosses the river at **Ramdi Ghat**, the site of many caves, before climbing almost 1000m to its highest point. A few kilometres beyond is the turning for **Tansen** (below), the only town of note in this area. From there it's an hour's descent to Butwal and the Tarai (covered in Chapter Five). This last forty-kilometre stretch is particularly prone to landslides and so is often in dreadful shape.

Tansen and around

Once the seat of a powerful kingdom, the hill town of **TANSEN** (Palpa) now seems little more than a bazaar town stranded in the hills. Tourism comes a low second to trading, yet slowly, almost reluctantly, Tansen yields its secrets: clacking *dhaka* looms glimpsed though doorways; the potters of Ghorabanda; the view from Srinagar Hill; the superb day-hikes and bike rides in the surrounding countryside. If you're coming from India, Tansen makes a far more authentic introduction to Nepal than Pokhara, and at an altitude of 4300m, it's usually pleasantly cool after the heat of the plains.

Tansen's **history** goes back to the early sixteenth century, when it was known as Palpa, and when the Sen clan of princes, already established at Butwal, chose it as a safer base from which to expand family holdings that soon covered the length of the lower hills, almost to Sikkim. Makunda Sen, Palpa's legendary second king, allegedly raided Kathmandu and carried off two sacred Bhairab masks, only to be cut down by a plague sent by the Pashupatinath *linga*. Chastened by the king's death, his successors settled for forming a strategic alliance with Gorkha, which bought them breathing space when the latter began conquering territory in the mid-eighteenth century. Aided by a friendly Indian rajah, Palpa staved off the inevitable until 1806, when it became the last territory to be annexed to modern Nepal. Tansen remains the headquarters of Palpa District, and many still refer to the town as Palpa.

The bazaar was set up by Newar merchants from the Kathmandu Valley to take advantage of the trade route between India and Tibet. That business was killed off by the road, which passes a few hundred metres below town, but the Newars have smoothly switched to retailing Indian-manufactured goods to the local Magar people, who walk in from villages lying as much as, or more than, a day's walk away. You may even hear the town called Tansing, which was its original Magar name.

Arrival and information

Public **buses** serve the Siddhartha Highway between Pokhara and Butwal, with a few services originating much further afield, including from Kathmandu. Coming from Pokhara or Sonauli/Bhairawa you've also got the option of taking a faster and more comfortable quasi-tourist bus. However, these buses don't leave the Siddhartha Highway, so you have to get off at Bartun, the village at the start of the three-kilometre Tansen spur road. Jeeps and buses shuttle almost nonstop from the roadside to Tansen, leaving as soon as they're full.

There are no taxis or rikshas in Tansen, although the better hotels can arrange **motorcycle** or **vehicle hire**. It should be possible to rent an ordinary bicycle through some guesthouses. One of the two **banks** on Bank Street, Rastriya Banijya or Nepal Bank (Mon–Thurs & Sun 10am–2pm, Fri 10am–noon), should be able to change US dollar and sterling travellers' cheques. There are **telephone** services all over, and a couple of expensive **email** boutiques.

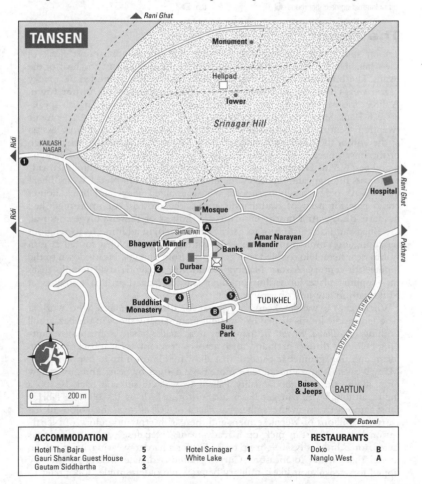

ACCOMMODATION				RESTAURANTS	
Hotel The Bajra	5	Hotel Srinagar	1	Doko	B
Gauri Shankar Guest House	2	White Lake	4	Nanglo West	A
Gautam Siddhartha	3				

Accommodation

You pay roughly double in Tansen what you'd pay for the same class of **accommodation** in Pokhara, though it's still not very expensive. There's nothing very fancy, though two places try. Hot water and electricity are always intermittent, and the town is under a permanent water shortage. Don't settle for the lodges near the bus park, which are noisy and a steep slog from the centre.

Hotel the Bajra ☎075/20443. A big place with decent, if slightly shabby, rooms and a friendly owner. Just far enough from the bus park to avoid the worst of the noise, but hardly secluded. ❶

Gauri Shankar Guest House ☎075/20150. A dreary place in a workaday corner of town, though the rooms are big and tolerably clean. ❷

Gautam Siddhartha Guest House ☎075/20280. A fairly primitive Nepali lodge in a relatively quiet but uninteresting neighbourhood. ❶

Hotel Srinagar ☎075/20045. Great location on Srinagar Hill, with views nearby, but the building is depressingly modern, and facilities and service are poor for the price – for the full price, anyway. It's a good twenty minutes above town, so call ahead to arrange transport. ❻

White Lake ☎075/20291. Pretty ordinary, but nevertheless the top hotel in Tansen itself, and used to dealing with foreigners. Decent restaurant too. ❸

The Town

Tansen spills down the flank of Srinagar Hill, the southernmost flank of the Mahabharat range and the first bulwark of the hills against the heat of the plains. The **bus park** occupies the lowest, newest level, surrounded by a tacky bazaar area. Things improve once you've found your way to the **upper town**. A direct footpath leads steeply up from *Hotel the Bajra* to what English-speakers call Bank Street, home of a modest bazaar. Across the street is the prosaic twentieth-century Durbar, slapped together by British architects from Calcutta at the end of the nineteenth century. Bank Street ends at **Shitalpati**, the hub of the busy upper town, overlooked by the only visible reminder of Tansen's grand past – **Mul Dhoka** (Main Gate), tall enough for elephants and their riders to pass through, and reputedly the biggest of its kind in Nepal. West of here lie Tansen's oldest neighbourhoods, whose cobbled alleys and brick houses could pass for parts of Kathmandu, minus the crowds. An undistinguished modern **Bhagwati Mandir** enshrines the hostess of Tansen's biggest festival, the Bhagwati Jaatra (late Aug to early Sept), which, in addition to its religious function, also commemorates an 1814 battle in which Nepal routed British troops near here. The cobbled lane going east from Shitalpati leads down to the nineteenth-century **Amar Narayan Mandir**, a pagoda-style temple that's the stopping place for sadhus on their way to Janai Purnima festivities at Muktinath in late July or early August.

Wherever you wander, keep an eye out for **dhaka weavers**, who work at wooden treadle looms shaped like upright pianos; many shops in the bazaar sell nothing but *dhaka*. Woven in many hill areas, *dhaka* fabric is created by shuttling coloured threads back and forth across a constant vertical background to form repeating, geometric patterns that allow for almost infinite improvisation. Many weavers know a hundred or more basic designs by heart, and invent new ones all the time. A good-quality Palpali weave will set you back Rs400 a metre, although you can get lesser quality for as little as Rs100. The fabric's most famous use is in the archetypal *dhaka* or *Palpali topi*, the colourful hat worn by millions of Nepalese men, and the garish crowning glory of Nepal's national dress. You can pick up a ready-made "Nepalese cap", as it's always called, for as little as Rs50 – or up to Rs400 for a harder-wearing, hand-woven model that's made to measure. Current fashions dictate wearing it smartly tipped forward, almost like a military beret, while older, simpler folk prefer to

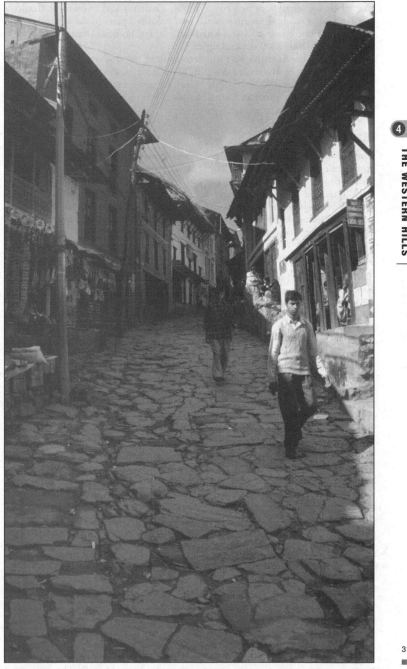

△ Tansen

sport their *topi* tilted back at a rustic angle. Tansen is also known for **thailo**, a woman's purse made from *dhaka* with two coloured pairs of drawstrings – one to close and one to open – and **karuwa** – heavy, bulbous brass water vessels, which cost Rs200–2000 depending on size.

Tansen's solitary **mosque** isn't much to look at, but does recall the somewhat surprising presence of a settled Muslim population, descendants of bangle-sellers who once roamed Nepal's hills – and, to some extent, still do. Even after centuries in Tansen, many still speak a dialect which blends Nepali with influences from North Indian languages.

Eating

Nanglo West, a branch of a Kathmandu-based **restaurant** chain, provides a welcome culinary oasis in Tansen. Overlooking Shitalpati, it has comfy indoor and outdoor tables, and serves excellent Nepali and Newari food. Only the *White Lake* hotel and *Hotel Srinagar* are alternatives in the tourist food department. *Doko Restaurant* serves a good range of *momo* and other Newari dishes, and there's the usual swarms of *bhojanalaya* around the bus park and in the old part of town for *daal bhaat* and road snacks.

Around Tansen: Srinagar Hill and beyond

The best thing about Tansen is getting out of it and exploring the outlying hill country and unaffected Magar villages. People on the trail will likely greet you with delighted smiles and the full palms-together *namaste* – a sign of gratitude for the assistance provided by foreign doctors at the nearby United Mission Hospital, which they will tend to assume you work for.

First stop on most excursions is **Srinagar Hill** (Srinagar Daada), north of town. The most direct route, which takes about half an hour on foot, starts from a small Ganesh temple above Shitalpati, but you have to zigzag a bit to get to the temple. From *Hotel Srinagar* it's an easy twenty-minute walk east along the ridge. The top (1525m) is planted with thick pine forest. catch the view from the helipad or the open area west of *Hotel Srinagar*. The peaks appear smaller and hazier from here than they do from Pokhara, but the Dhaulagiri and Annapurna ranges are still impressive; Machhapuchhre is less dominant, but its true "fishtail" profile is visible from this angle. On the southern side, beyond Tansen, lies the luxuriant Madi Valley, layered with paddy fields owned by Tansen's Newar landlords. On winter mornings the valley is filled with a silver fog. The area north of the helipad, just below the summit, has been turned into a large municipal park.

All three routes described below pass through farmland and are heavily used by villagers, so it's fairly easy to find your way with just enough Nepali to ask directions. You may prefer to take a guide – ask your innkeeper – or consult the HMG/FINNIDA maps for the area. *Hotel Srinagar* sometimes has some excellent route plans, which include detailed maps. Numerous other hikes are possible from Tansen, including taking the old trading route to Butwal, which passes the ruins of the old Sen palace at Nuwakot.

Rani Ghat

For walks beyond Srinagar there are at least two strong options, the first being the fourteen-kilometre round-trip to **RANI GHAT**, site of a fantastically derelict palace along the Kali Gandaki. The trail begins 200m east of *Hotel Srinagar* (locals call this intersection Kailash Nagar) and descends through an immensely satisfying landscape of farmland, trailside hamlets – Aule has a teashop – and, finally, a jungly gorge with impressive waterfalls. The walk itself takes at least four or five hours, but you'll want to set aside the whole day (it's quite an uphill climb on the way back). A road is eventually supposed to be built between Tansen and Rani Ghat, but it shouldn't interfere with the trail.

Set in a tranquil spot beside the turquoise Kali Gandaki, Rani Ghat is the site of occasional cremations. But the main attraction here is the spooky old **palace**, which was built in the late nineteenth century by a former government minister who, according to the custom of the day, was exiled to Palpa after a failed palace coup. Perched atop an outcrop directly overlooking the river, it was abandoned to the elements for many years. You get a great view of it from the distressingly long suspension bridge that crosses the river here. An alternative route, which could be combined into a circular walk, leaves from the Mission Hospital, and takes a parallel route to the east, passing through the village of Deurali, where there's another teashop. This path descends directly to the suspension bridge at Rani Ghat via a steep, twisting path.

Rani Ghat itself isn't really a village, just a couple of *chiya pasal* that offer only very limited food and emergency shelter. Bring a lunch and picnic on the tranquil, sandy beach.

To Ridi Bazaar

RIDI BAZAAR makes an equally eventful all-day outing, either on foot (13km one way, with the option of bussing back) or by bike (60km round-trip). From *Hotel Srinagar*, walk west to a fork at a police checkpost, bear right and in half an hour you'll reach Chandi Bhanjyang; turn left here and descend through a handsome canyon before rejoining the unpaved road for the last 7km. On a bike, stay on the main road all the way.

Set on the banks of the Kali Gandaki, Ridi is considered sacred because of the wealth of **shaligrams** – fossil-bearing stones associated with Vishnu – found in the river here. It used to be said that if a person were cremated at Ridi and his ashes sprinkled into the river, they would congeal to form a *shaligram*, and if the stone were then made into a likeness of Vishnu, the devotee would be one with his god. The spiral-shaped ammonite fossils typically found in *shaligram* are 150–200 million years old, dating from a time when the entire Himalayan region was submerged under a shallow sea.

Ridi has declined in importance over the years, but remains an occasional cremation ground and, during the **festival** of Magh Sankranti (Jan 14 or 15), a pilgrimage site for ritual bathing. Celebrations of the *ekadashi* of Khattik (the eleventh day of the bright fortnight of Oct–Nov) include processions and dancing. The colourful commercial end of town lies across a stream that joins the Kali Gandaki here, while the magical eighteenth-century **Rishikesh Mandir** is south of the stream, just above the bus stop. According to legend, the idol inside the squat temple, a form of Vishnu, was fished out of the river and originally bore the likeness of a young boy, but over the course of years has matured into adult form.

Several **buses** a day head back to Tansen, taking two and a half hours, but you may have to wait some time, as most ply the route in the morning only. You can stay overnight if you get stuck. The return journey can be combined with a visit to **Palpa Bhairab**, up a short path from the pretty Newar village of Bhairabsthan, 8km before Tansen. So many animal sacrifices are performed at this temple, especially on Saturdays and Tuesdays, that it's often compared with that of Dakshin Kali in the Kathmandu Valley. Its much-feared Bhairab image is kept in a small chamber at the far corner of the compound; the gilded *trisul* here is claimed to be the biggest in Asia, and pilgrims have left a large number of smaller replicas at its base.

Ghorabanda

The most interesting of the villages east of Tansen, **GHORABANDA** is locally famous for its **potters**. It's just off the Siddhartha Highway, 3km north of the Tansen turning, but without your own wheels you'll have to walk. Take the dirt road from the Amar Narayan temple towards the United Mission Hospital, bear right onto a trail after about 500m, descend and then contour through extensive paddy – if you've done it right, you'll drop down to the highway after about 2km, with Ghorabanda another 1km further along the road. Ghorabanda's notoriously drunken potters, members of the Kumal ethnic group, throw their almost spherical water jugs on heavy clay flywheels, shaping them and adding a stipple pattern with a wooden paddle, then sun-drying and finally kiln-firing them. The farmhouses and potteries of Ghorabanda spread down the hill from the highway.

Travel details

Day buses

Gorkha to: Abu Khaireni (every 30min; 1hr); Birganj (2 daily; 7hr); Kathmandu (5 daily; 6hr); Narayangadh (14 daily; 2hr 30min); Pokhara (2 daily; 3hr); Sonauli (1 daily; 7hr).
Pokhara to: Baglung (22 daily; 3hr); Bartun for Tansen (12 daily; 5hr); Begnas Tal (every 20min; 45min); Beni (8 daily; 4hr); Birganj (5 daily; 8hr); Butwal for Sonauli* (16 daily; 7hr); Gorkha (2 daily; 3hr); Jagatpur (2 daily; 7hr); Janakpur (2 daily; 11hr); Kakarbhitta (1 daily; 14hr); Kathmandu* (12 daily; 8hr); Narayangadh (every 30min; 4hr).
Tansen to: Butwal (every 30min; 2hr); Kathmandu (1 daily; 10hr); Pokhara (3 daily; 6hr).

* Tourist bus service also available.

Night buses

Pokhara to: Birganj (3 daily; 10hr); Butwal for Sonauli (4 daily; 10hr); Dhangadhi for Bardia (1 daily; 15hr); Janakpur (1 daily; 12hr); Kakarbhitta (3 daily; 16hr); Kathmandu (11 daily; 8hr); Mahendra Nagar (2 daily; 16hr); Nepalganj (3 daily; 14hr).
Tansen to: Kathmandu (1 daily; 14hr).

Flights

Pokhara to: Bhairawa (1 daily); Jomosom (3–9 daily); Kathmandu (18–28 daily); Manang (0–2 weekly).

The Western Tarai

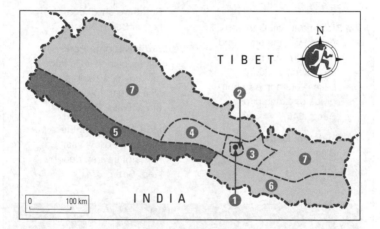

CHAPTER 5

Highlights

✳ **Chitwan National Park**
Spot the endangered
Asian one-horned rhino
from the back of an ele-
phant. **See p.327**

✳ **Sauraha, Chitwan** Watch
the sun go down over
the teeming jungle from
a "beach" bar. **See
p.328**

✳ **Bis Hajaar Tal, Chitwan**
Away from the tiger- and
rhino-hunting crowds,
the swampy "20,000
Lakes" are home to hun-
dreds of exotic birds.
See p.346

✳ **Ghatgain, Chitwan**
Blissfully simple and
untouristy, lodges here

overlook the river and
national park. **See p.334**

✳ **Devghat** Devout Hindus
come to die at this holy
confluence, spanned by
a dramatic suspension
footbridge. **See p.348**

✳ **Tilaurakot** Meditate
among the ruins of
Buddha's childhood
home. **See p.360**

✳ **Bardia National Park**
Take a guided walk into
the jungle, with no one
else around to disturb
the animals. **See p.364**

✳ **Sukla Phanta Wildlife
Reserve** Follow vast
herds of swamp deer by
jeep. **See p.374**

5

The Western Tarai

I n a country best known for Himalayas and Sherpas, the lowland, Indian-influenced **Tarai** gets short shrift from most guidebooks. A narrow strip of flatland extending along the entire length of Nepal's southern border – including several *dun* (inner Tarai) valleys north of the first range of hills – the Tarai was originally covered in thick, malarial jungle. In the 1950s, however, the government identified the southern plains as a major growth area to relieve population pressure in the hills, and, with the help of liberal quantities of DDT, brought malaria under control. Since then, the jungle has been methodically cleared and the Tarai has emerged as Nepal's most productive agricultural and industrial region, accounting for around half its GDP and supporting about half its population. The jungle barrier that once insulated Nepal from Indian influences as effectively as the Himalaya had guarded the north, making possible the development of a uniquely Nepali culture, has been replaced by the geographic and political equivalent of a welcome mat. An unmistakable quality of Indianness now pervades the Tarai, as evidenced by the avid mercantilism of the border bazaars, the chewing of betel, the Muslim mosques and orthodox Brahmanism, the heat and dust, the jute mills and sugar refineries, and the many roads and irrigation projects built with Indian aid.

Fortunately, the government has set aside sizeable chunks of the **western Tarai** in the form of national parks and reserves, which remain some of the finest **wildlife and bird havens** on the subcontinent. Dense riverine forest provides cover for predators like tigers and leopards; swampy grasslands make the perfect habitat for rhinoceros; and vast, tall stands of *sal*, the Tarai's most common tree, shelter huge herds of deer. Of the region's wildlife parks, the deservedly popular **Chitwan** is the richest in game and the most accessible, but if you're willing to invest some extra effort, **Bardia** and **Sukla Phanta** make quieter, more jungly alternatives.

The region's other claim to fame is historical: the Buddha was born 2500 years ago at **Lumbini**, and his birthplace – one of the four holiest pilgrimage sites for Buddhists – is an appropriately serene place. Elsewhere in Lumbini, important archeological discoveries have been made at **Tilaurakot** and several other outlying sites.

Four **border crossings** in the western Tarai are open to foreigners. As it's on the most direct route between Kathmandu and Varanasi, and fits in well with visits to Lumbini and Chitwan, **Sonauli** is still the most heavily used, though it's fairly horrid. Since the completion of the Mahendra (or East–West) Highway in 2000, the far western frontier at **Mahendra Nagar** looks set to change from backwater border post to the prime route into Nepal: it's roughly

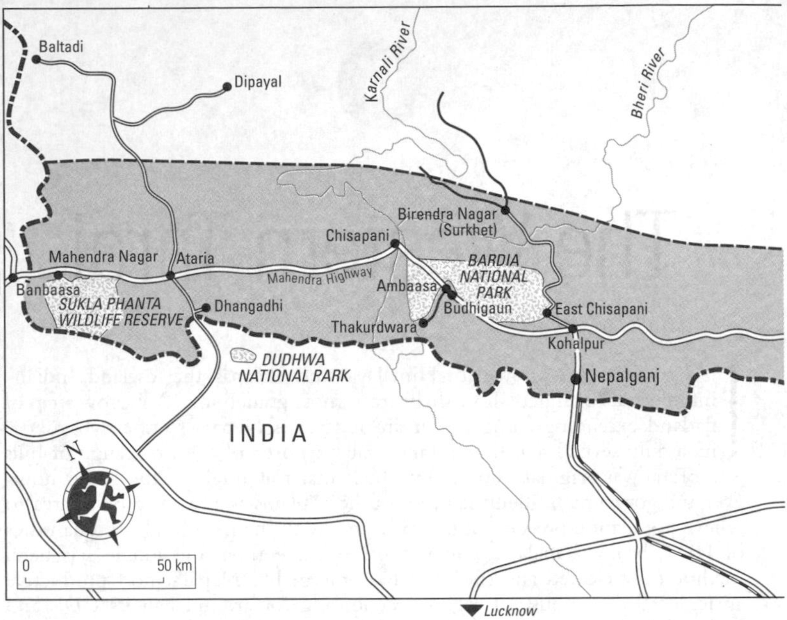

Baltadi
Dipayal
Karnali River
Bheri River
Almora
Pilibhit & Delhi
Mahendra Nagar
Ataria
Chisapani
Birendra Nagar (Surkhet)
BARDIA NATIONAL PARK
Banbaasa
SUKLA PHANTA WILDLIFE RESERVE
Dhangadhi
Mahendra Highway
Ambaasa
East Chisapani
Thakurdwara
Budhigaun
Kohalpur
DUDHWA NATIONAL PARK
Nepalganj

INDIA

N

0   50 km

Lucknow

twelve hours from both Delhi and Kathmandu, and the route from Delhi to Pokhara and Kathmandu takes you right past the wildlife parks at Bardia and Sukla Phanta. For a really obscure international experience, you can cross at points south of **Nepalganj** or Dhangadhi.

Bus connections to the Tarai from Kathmandu and Pokhara are well developed via Narayangadh. The Tarai itself is traversed by the **Mahendra Highway** (the Mahendra Rajmarg in Nepali), a thin line of tarmac stretching from the far west to the far east, with offshoot roads connecting to the district capitals in between. Traffic drops off dramatically west of Butwal, which makes for peaceful **cycling** and bus-window-gazing, but potentially long waits for bus connections. Internal **flights** aren't expensive, however, and can help you skip some of the longer bus rides. And although you'll be flying over the lowland plains, the mountains can look pretty close from five thousand metres up. Nepalganj is the air hub for western Nepal, and there are numerous less useful airstrips in the areas as well.

The **weather** in the Tarai is at its best from October to January – the days are more pleasantly mild during the latter half of this period, though the nights and mornings can be surprisingly chilly and damp. However, the wildlife viewing gets much better after the thatch has been cut, from late January on, by which time the temperatures are starting to warm up again. It gets really hot (especially in the far west) in April, May and June. The monsoon brings not only rain but mosquitoes, malaria and leeches, and many roads become impassable at this time,

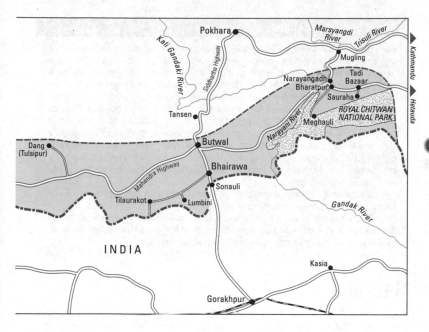

Chitwan

CHITWAN is the name not only of Nepal's most visited national park but also of the surrounding *dun* valley and administrative district. The name means "Heart of the Jungle" – a description that, sadly, now holds true only for the lands protected within the park and a few designated community forests. Yet the rest of the **valley**, though it's been reduced to a flat, furrowed plain, still provides fascinating vignettes of a rural lifestyle that's different again from the hill-clinging existence of upland Nepal. Really ugly development is confined to the wayside conurbation of **Narayangadh/Bharatpur** – and even this has left the nearby holy site of **Devghat** so far unscathed.

The best – and worst – aspects of **Chitwan National Park** are that it can be visited on the cheap, and that it's easy to get to. In recent years the park has risen meteorically on the list of "Things to Do in Nepal", so that these days, unless you go during the steamy season, you'll be sharing your experience with a lot of other people.

If you want to avoid crowds, and don't mind making a little extra effort to get into the park, try avoiding the much-touted tourist village of **Sauraha** and head instead for **Ghatgain** or **Meghauli**, a little further west. Or, if you've got the money – usually at least $100 a night per person, all-in – go for pampered seclusion at any one of half a dozen luxury lodges and tented camps that are actually inside the park.

About budget packages

The best advice is avoid them! A three-day Chitwan "safari" **package**, booked via any Kathmandu or Pokhara travel agency, gives you only a day and a half in the park, and you'll have little control over the "if-it's-8am-it-must-be-time-for-the-bird-walk" programme of activities. You'll be locked into staying at a lodge that has little incentive to work for your business (and every incentive to cut corners, since it has to give the booking agent between forty and sixty percent), you'll be served inferior set meals, and you probably won't get to choose your guide either. Finally, a $60 two-night package is likely to cost slightly more than doing the same thing on your own, and saves you hardly any trouble, since Chitwan is incredibly easy to visit independently. If you must be bound by an itinerary, at least book it directly through the lodge's own office in Kathmandu or Pokhara (contacts are given in reviews in relevant places in this chapter).

A package tour of Chitwan can also be combined with a **raft trip** on the Trisuli River, bookable through rafting operators in Kathmandu and Pokhara, but, for the reasons set out above, it's still a bad idea to book the Chitwan stay as part of the raft trip. And a raft won't take you all the way to the park no matter what the salesman says: Narayangadh is normally the end of the line.

Sauraha

Spectacularly situated on the banks of the Rapti River, opposite a prime area of jungle, **SAURAHA** (pronounced *So-ruh-hah*) is one of those unstoppably successful destinations at which Nepal seems to excel. In some lights it looks like the archetypal budget-safari village, its folksy guesthouses spread out along a few dusty roads at the edge of the forest; at other times, you could half-close your eyes and imagine yourself in a miniature, jungly Thamel. There's still a lot to recommend it, not least the ease of access into the park, but each year, Sauraha loses a little more of what once made it so enjoyable. Electricity has replaced lanterns and fire-light, resort hotels are displacing local lodges (not to mention village homes), and, when it's complete, the new tarmac road connecting Sauraha with the Mahendra Highway will just accelerate the pace of change.

Park practicalities, including details of permits and guides, as well as activities on offer both inside and outside the park, are covered in the main Royal Chitwan National Park section (p.336).

Getting there

Daily **tourist buses** serve Sauraha from Kathmandu and Pokhara; the fare is Rs150–200 (minibuses are more expensive) and the journey takes about six hours. At the time of writing, the last bridge before Sauraha had been washed away and buses were stopping at a place called Chitrasari, about 2km short of town. If the bridge is rebuilt, buses will probably arrive at the new **bus park** being built near *Osho Camp*, in Sauraha itself. Wherever you arrive, touts will have prepared the usual ambush and will take you by battered **jeep** to their own guesthouse, making every effort to win your business on the way. You don't have to stay at their place, of course, but – as they will argue – you may as well have a look. The jeep-ride rate from Chitrasari is fixed at Rs30 per person, and it'll probably be the same from the new bus park – though you should be able to walk from the latter.

The nearest **public bus** stop is Tadi Bazaar; though this isn't a final destination for most long-distance services, any bus passing by along the Mahendra

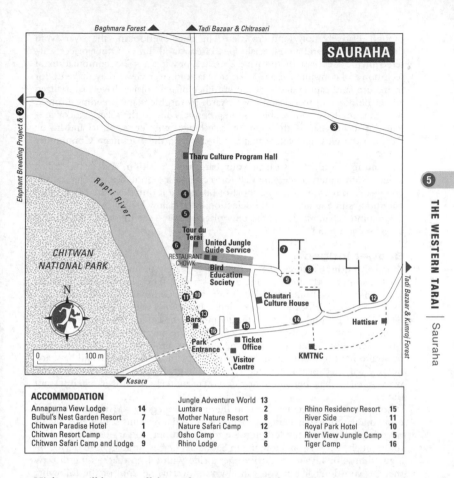

ACCOMMODATION

		Jungle Adventure World	**13**		
Annapurna View Lodge	**14**	Luntara	**2**	Rhino Residency Resort	**15**
Bulbul's Nest Garden Resort	**7**	Mother Nature Resort	**8**	River Side	**11**
Chitwan Paradise Hotel	**1**	Nature Safari Camp	**12**	Royal Park Hotel	**10**
Chitwan Resort Camp	**4**	Osho Camp	**3**	River View Jungle Camp	**5**
Chitwan Safari Camp and Lodge	**9**	Rhino Lodge	**6**	Tiger Camp	**16**

Highway will let you off there. If you arrive at Tadi by midday your chances of meeting up with a guesthouse jeep are pretty good (Rs50 to Sauraha). Otherwise, catch a cycle riksha or autoriksha to Chitrasari or the new bus park.

It's also possible to **fly** to Bharatpur (see p.348), about 15km west of Tadi Bazaar, though the journey to Chitwan isn't so taxing that this is really necessary, and it's mostly expensive tour groups that fly in. Booked independently, a flight from Kathmandu will cost around $50.

Accommodation

Sauraha has a great tradition of "camp"-style **accommodation**: the best guesthouses here are like rustic little country clubs, with simple mud-and-thatch bungalows, airy dining pavilions and shady gardens or open lawns. Unfortunately, many have forsaken traditional designs and natural materials for concrete, and some of the newer places, with their regimental rows of bunkers and little or no shade, look more like prison camps than jungle camps.

The deciding factor when choosing a place to stay in Sauraha is usually **location**. The largest share of lodgings line up shoulder to shoulder along the village's main north–south strip – handy for restaurants and the park entrance, though relatively noisy and crowded. The ones overlooking the river avoid those drawbacks, and are especially peaceful around sunset. Other places scattered in the area east of the park entrance provide a good combination of seclusion and convenience, and what they lack in river views they make up for in mature landscaping and shade. A number of new places have materialized along the peaceful road leading westwards to the Elephant Breeding Project, though many have had trouble winning business due to the relative inconvenience of staying here – the more upscale lodges will ferry you to and fro by jeep. On the plus side, you're that much closer to the Baghmara Community Forest.

Booking ahead may weaken your bargaining position, and if you call a lodge's Kathmandu office you'll almost certainly be quoted a package rate. If you just turn up, you won't be short of offers of a room; there are many more guesthouses in Sauraha than the selection listed below.

A reminder: Sauraha is not the only place to stay – see the later "Alternative bases" section (p.334).

Budget lodges

Sauraha's **budget lodges** (the places so aggressively promoted by the touts at the bus stop) mostly come in one of two varieties. The old-fashioned type has a row of cheap (**①**) mud-and-thatch huts with a common toilet/shower facility, and a separate block of bigger concrete bungalows with attached bathrooms (**③**). The more "modern" type typically just has the latter, as well as pretensions to higher standards and higher prices. Both are invariably arranged around attractively subtropical gardens. You pay more for a room with a ceiling fan, but mosquito netting should come with either type of room – use it, and have any holes sewn up. Solar hot-water systems are gradually replacing destructive wood-fired boilers, but in either case you're unlikely to miss it when it's not there.

Competition is extremely keen in the budget category, so **prices** will often drop dramatically when occupancy is low, and discounts can generally be negotiated. However the lodgings are too spread out, and it's usually too hot, to do much comparison-shopping in Sauraha. The best strategy is to decide on a guesthouse in advance and try to get a ride with a jeep that's going directly there; if you don't like it you can always move in the cool of the following morning. The following list is short but selective. Most of the others are perfectly adequate, but one or two seem to generate consistently bad reports, so keep an ear out for both negative and positive word of mouth.

Annapurna View Lodge ☏056/80024. Shabby huts and smarter concrete bungalows encircling a lovely garden. A short, shady walk from the park boundary. **①**

Bulbul's Nest Garden Resort ☏056/80079. Staying here, at the edge of Sauraha, you could almost believe you were in a Tharu village, and this is one of the few lodges that is actually Tharu owned, Tharu styled and Tharu run. **②**

Chitwan Resort Camp ☏056/80082 or 01/227711. Close to the village but reasonably insulated from it. Sun and shade in the garden. **④**

Chitwan Safari Camp and Lodge ☏056/80078. Locally owned lodge bordering the fields, with cosy, clean concrete bungalows or cheaper – and nicer still – wattle-and-daub versions, all set round a mature garden. **①–③**

Luntara ☏056/80145, ✉luntara@mail.com.np. Rather far from the action, set back from the river opposite the Elephant Breeding Centre, but transport is provided to the main park entrance and it's incredibly peaceful. The detached thatched cottages have attractive, quirky touches, and efforts are made to employ local women and encourage female guests. **②**

Mother Nature Resort ☏056/80008. Peaceful location at the edge of the village, with a large garden edging the fields. Mud-and-thatch or more expensive concrete chalets. **③–④**

Nature Safari Camp ☏056/80019. Somewhat

far-flung from the action, but this is a villagey and relatively untouristed corner of Sauraha. Large garden and decent thatched or concrete huts. ➊–➌

Rhino Lodge ☎ 056/80065. Rooms come in somewhat institutional two-storey blocks, but the garden leads down to the river and you can watch the resident elephant bathe in the evening. ➍
River Side ☎ 056/80009, ✉ hotelriverside@hot-mail.com. As a concrete blot on the previously pristine riverfront, it probably shouldn't be encouraged, but the rooms are lovely and the river view unrivalled. ➍

River View Jungle Camp ☎ 056/80096 or 01/524822. Only the back end of the garden actually has a view, but the camp is smart and attractive, with a choice of simple thatched huts or well-kept, semi-detached bungalows. ➌–➎

Moderate and expensive lodges

Price is not necessarily an indicator of quality in Sauraha. Some lodges charge deluxe prices for budget facilities, on the theory that package tourists will never know the difference. However, the ones listed here are a cut or two above the budget pack: you should be able to count on superior location and grounds, good (or at least better) food, reliable hot water, a jeep in good working order, experienced guides, and small touches like a library, slide shows and enough binoculars to go around. Full air-conditioning is fairly rare, but some places have simple air coolers.

These lodges get by mainly on expensive package business, but they'll usually take you on an accommodation–only basis if you just show up, with substantial discounts out of season.

Chitwan Paradise Hotel ☎ 056/80048, ✉ paradise@mos.com.np. Large, posh and beautifully manicured place, where the spacious rooms (with aircoolers) are arranged around a huge, rather formal lawn. Forty percent of profits go to projects aiding the local community. ➎
Jungle Adventure World ☎ 056/29364, ✉ jaw_resort@hotmail.com. Excellent location near the river and park entrance, with decent bungalows and a great array of labelled plants in the garden. ➎
Osho Camp ☎ 056/80067, ✉ mediarep@mos.com .np. Huge, shady and very peaceful grounds, but it's actually a Rajneesh retreat centre, so the emphasis is on meditation rather than safaris. ➍–➎
Rhino Residency Resort ☎ 01/220697, ⊛ www.rhino-residency.com. The swankiest place in Sauraha, with a meticulously tended garden centred on a small swimming pool, and hotel-standard, air-conditioned rooms. The manager is an experienced, committed naturalist. ➐
Royal Park Hotel ☎ 056/80061 or 01/412987, ⊛ www.royalparkhotel.com.np. Huge, airy and tastefully decked-out rooms in small blocks dotted around a pristine garden of park-like proportions. Excellent central location. ➎
Tiger Camp ☎ 056/80060 or 01/224318, ⊛ www .catmando.com/tiger-camp. Arguably the best location in Sauraha, overlooking the river right at the park entrance – the garden seating area is great for watching elephant-bathing and other river activity. Disappointing rooms (the ones with attached bathrooms are definitely overpriced), though there's a marvellous *machaan*-like hut. ➍–➏

The village

The fast-changing cluster of shops and hotels that make up Sauraha "**village**" constitute most of the action here. On a smaller scale, there's all the conveniences of Lakeside and Thamel, and similarly, there's nothing to do except shop, eat and plan excursions, though the national park **visitor centre** (daily 6am–6pm) has a modest but informative display on the ecology of the park and the local Tharu culture. If you want to get a flavour of Tarai village life, find yourself a bicycle (see box on p.332) and put as much distance between you and Sauraha as the heat allows.

Small **shops**, stalls and "German" bakeries stock basic food and other items (bottled water, film, batteries, toilet paper, postcards and so on), and there are a handful of fairly good bookshops. The **Community Souvenir Shop**, just opposite the park visitor centre, sells some useful books and maps, as well as the mementos; curio shops sell mainly geographically inappropriate items, but if

Tharu village tours and bike rides

Guided **Tharu village walks** out of Sauraha usually mean a loiter through the houses and villages nearest to Sauraha. It's all rather voyeuristic, especially when you consider how many tourists have trooped through before you, and the way guides point at residents and pick up their tools without asking is not something that should be encouraged. For cultural tours with more sensitivity, try Tour du Tarai (☎056/80030, ✉hlc@mos.com.np), just north of the main Restaurant Chowk.

You'll learn a lot more about real Tarai village life by hopping on a **bike** and just getting lost on the backroads to the east and west of Sauraha. Stopping at any village and asking *chiya paunchha?* ("where can I get a cup of tea?") will usually attract enough attention to get you introduced to someone, even if you're reduced to sign language.

In November, when the rice is harvested, you'll be able to watch Tharu and Baahun villagers cutting the stems, tying them into sheaves and threshing them – or, since it's such a busy time of year, piling them in big stacks to await threshing. January is thatch-gathering time, when you'll see people bringing huge bundles out of the park, to be put by until a slack time before the monsoon when there's time to repair roofs. In early March, the mustard, lentils and wheat that was planted after the rice crop is ready; maize is then planted, to be harvested in July for animal fodder, flour and meal. Rice is seeded in dense starter-plots in March, to be transplanted into separate paddy fields in April. During each of these harvest seasons you'll hear the rhythmic toot-toot of local mills, hulling or polishing grain, or pressing oil.

From Sauraha, the most fertile country for exploration lies to the east: heading towards Tadi along the eastern side of the village, turn right (east) at the intersection marked by the King Mahendra Trust health post and you can follow that road all the way to **Parsa**, 8km away on the Mahendra Highway, with many side roads to villages en route. Given a full day and a good bike or motorcycle, you could continue eastwards from Parsa along the highway for another 10km, and just before Bhandaara turn left onto a track leading to **Baireni**, a particularly well-preserved Tharu village. Another 10km east of Bhandaara lies **Lothar**, from where you can follow a trail upstream to reach the waterfalls on the Lothar Khola, a contemplative spot with a healthy measure of birdlife.

For a short ride west of Sauraha, first head north for 3km and take the first left after the river crossing, which brings you to the authentic Tharu villages of **Baghmara** and **Hardi**. If you're game for a longer journey, pedal to Tadi and west along the Mahendra Highway to Tikauli. From there, the canal road through Bis Hajaar Tal leads about 10km through beautiful forest to **Gita Nagar**, where you join the Bharatpur–Jagatpur road, with almost unlimited possibilities from there. A good route is to continue due west from Jagatpur on dirt roads all the way to Meghauli, though you may have to ford a river on the way – impossible on a motorbike until at least late November. Don't overlook the possibility of an outing to Devghat (see p.348). For more on Tharu culture, see Contexts, p.510.

you search around you can find some locally produced Tharu handicrafts such as woven-grass baskets and hats.

A couple of **moneychangers** have offices on the strip, though their rates are a couple of percent lower than what you can get in a **bank**. Tadi Bazaar, on the Mahendra Highway, 6km north of Sauraha, has a branch of Himalayan Bank with an ATM that accepts credit cards, and there are plans, which may yet come to fruition, to open a bank at "Restaurant Chowk", the crossroads at the centre of Sauraha. International **telephone** and **email** services are available, but again, charges here are significantly higher than in Kathmandu or Pokhara. The **post office** is at the intersection east of *Osho Camp* (off the map), but bookshops will take letters there for franking. The **pharmacy** on Restaurant

Chowk, can probably manage a stool test, and a private clinic in Tadi Bazaar has paramedics, but if you're really ill you'll want to make for the hospital in Bharatpur (see p.348)

Bikes can be rented from a few shifting stalls and private operators on the main strip for about Rs100 a day, and some guesthouses have their own. **Motorcycles** cost about Rs500 to rent for the day, not including fuel, and make a great way to get to park entry points further afield, such as Ghatgain or Meghauli (see pp.334 and p.335), or to make a day-trip to Devghat (see p.348).

Eating

Guesthouse dining rooms are okay for breakfast and hobnobbing with guides and fellow travellers, but their main meals are, by and large, not very appetizing, and the fact that three of the half-dozen **restaurants** on Sauraha's so-called Restaurant Chowk are called some variation on "Hungry Eye" says a lot about the differences between them. All offer attractive, airy first-floor terraces under thatch, and do a good job of the standard sizzlers, pasta, chips, noodles and local fish. You won't find the famous "special" or *bhang* (cannabis) lassis on the menu any more, but you might still get one if you ask. You could also visit one of the classier guesthouses for a nice meal – *Tiger Camp* is recommended – or go for inexpensive local fare at one of the *bhatti* on the main drags.

Nightlife

Some of Sauraha's rooftop restaurants advertise "happy hours" and are good for **evening drinks**, but nothing stays open very late. To avoid unplanned encounters with wildlife, you'll want to make your way back to lodgings before 10pm or so in any case. At **sunset**, head for the "beach" on the riverbank by the park entrance, where a few shifting bars spring up every season serving beers, cocktails and snacks on the sandy shore. Watching the sun go down over the jungle is one of Chitwan's more relaxing activities, but you'll have to get away from the bars to enjoy it in peace.

Sauraha's trademark entertainment is the **Tharu stick dance**, a mock battle in which participants parry each other's sticks with graceful, split-second timing. The original purpose of the dance, it's said, was simply to make a lot of racket to keep the wild animals away at night. It still forms a traditional part of Tharu celebrations of Phaagun Purnima (the full moon of Feb–March), but the version you're likely to see is a more contrived tourist show put on for package groups at Sauraha lodges; anyone is welcome to come along and watch.

The Tharu Culture Program Hall and Chautari Culture House (see map) put on nightly **culture shows** at around 8pm featuring regional music and dance for tourist consumption (Rs60). In addition, some lodges host informal folk-dancing sessions, where audience participation is expected, if not coerced.

Moving on

Leaving Sauraha is easy **by tourist bus**. For a small commission over the Rs150 or so ticket price, your guesthouse or an agent in the village on the main strip can arrange tickets, and a guesthouse jeep will get you to the departure point in time. Agents in Sauraha can also arrange **air tickets** from Bharatpur to Kathmandu; buses leave Tadi Bazaar for Bharatpur roughly every fifteen minutes.

If your next destination isn't Kathmandu or Pokhara you'll have to get yourself to Tadi, and from there catch any **public bus** heading in your direction, which may well mean standing – all public buses start their journeys elsewhere, so you can't usually book seats at Tadi. Long-distance buses pass roughly every half-hour in both directions; your guesthouse should be able to advise on the timings of relevant services. You could also ride a local bus to Narayangadh, the nearest transport hub, where there will be a greater selection of onward services and where you'll be able to book a seat.

When the new bus park is completed, there is likely to be transport available from there to Tadi. Until then, **getting to Tadi** means either walking (20min) or catching a ride with your guesthouse jeep to Chitrasari. From the bus park at Chitrasari you can pick up a cycle riksha (Rs20), autoriksha (Rs30) and sometimes a bus to Tadi, though you may have to wait. You can also get a jeep to take you all the way to Tadi (for at least Rs50), but the price may depend on whether or not the jeep is going there anyway and what you can negotiate.

Alternative bases

It's becoming increasingly easy (though still not very popular) for Chitwan Park visitors to avoid Sauraha altogether, and make a base in one of two villages along the park's northern boundary, just west of Sauraha. Both **Ghatgain** and **Meghauli** are much quieter and less developed than Sauraha, and yet they also have guesthouses, guides, elephants and entry checkposts. These villages are very much off the beaten track, though, so unless you're staying in one of the few upmarket, package-only places, don't expect highly developed services or lots of fellow travellers. If you're unsure about getting to either village under your own steam, or whether the isolation is what you're looking for, you can always go to Sauraha first and do a jungle trek (see p.344) from there to Ghatgain or Meghauli.

An option for those with deeper wallets is to seek seclusion in one of the **luxury lodges and tented camps** inside the park itself.

Ghatgain

Three simple, peaceful lodges and one upmarket resort hotel make up the sum total of tourist facilities in the sleepy, traditional village of **GHATGAIN**, on the north bank of the Rapti River, 16km west of Sauraha. All are within easy reach of a good patch of jungle, two interesting lakes (Lami Tal and Tamar Tal) and the Kasara park headquarters, 4km downriver, where there's a gharial crocodile breeding project (see p.345). The **park** starts on the other side of Rapti River from the village: guides (from your guesthouse) will take you across by dugout canoe and you pay your entry fee, if you haven't already got a ticket, to one of the soldiers at the army station, about 1km into the jungle on the other side. Currently only a couple of elephants are quartered in this area, but park officials are said to be planning to move more of Sauraha's animals here.

Most people come to Ghatgain on a jungle trek **with a guide** from Sauraha, but once here you might well want to stay more than one night. If you decide to make this your base, take any **bus** for Jagatpur and ask to be let off at Patihani (if that doesn't ring a bell, ask for *Safari Narayani*). From here, it's a pleasant fifteen-minute stroll south on a dirt road towards Ghatgain and the river. Express buses run to Jagatpur from Kathmandu (1 daily) and Pokhara (2 daily), and local buses trundle from Narayangadh roughly every hour until 3pm; the journey takes one hour from Narayangadh.

Once at Ghatgain, most locals will be able to point you in the right direction for any of the three competing budget **lodges** (❶), which are close together in the heart of the village, making the most of the stunning river view. They can't provide hot water or elaborate tourist meals, and none of them have got phones, but you can expect clean rooms, decent *daal bhaat*, and the offer of a guide. *Ghumtee Riviera Lodge* is just a row of brick-and-mud bungalows, set in shady grounds, while *Riverview Lodge* consists of two lovely little cottages facing each other across a garden, one end of which is open to the river. *Sunset View Lodge* is one simple longhouse; while there's no garden to speak of, you've got the whole river to look at, and it's run by a very friendly family. Far, far at the other end of the scale, the package-only *Safari Narayani Lodge* (☎056/ 22131 or 01/522871; ❾) is like a mirage. A flashy, riviera-style complex built around a large swimming pool, it's affiliated to the *Narayani Safari Hotel* in Narayangadh.

Meghauli

Some 19km west of Ghatgain, **MEGHAULI** has all the ingredients to become a serious competitor to Sauraha. Bhimle, the area of park just across the Rapti River here, boasts superb rhino and tiger habitat, and it's also universally hailed as the best birdwatching site in Chitwan, while the countryside and traditional Tharu and Baahun villages surrounding Meghauli make for great outside-the-park exploring. And to top it all off, for several days in early December Meghauli's airstrip hosts one of Nepal's most absurdly enjoyable events, the **Elephant Polo Championship**, which is definitely worth adjusting your schedule to see – the action is surprisingly fast-paced and sporting.

Few independent travellers make it here, however, as it's a two-day trek from Sauraha, or about two hours by local **bus** from Narayangadh (roughly every half-hour). Buses stop at the newest, easternmost end of the village, known as Parsadhap Bazaar, at the end of the scruffy gravelled road from Narayangadh. There is also one daily express bus from Kathmandu. Unless you're staying at the *Tiger Tops* luxury lodge, just inside the park, or you're or able to charter your own plane, you won't be using the **airstrip**, which lies about 1.5km south of the bus stop. Another 2km beyond that is the Rapti river crossing, where dugouts will ferry you across for a small fee. The Bhimle guard post, where you have to show your park permit or pay an entrance fee, is 3km into the park.

On the main street of Parsadhap bazaar, right where the bus turns around, *Quality Lodge* (☎056/25940; ❶) is as yet little more than two ultrabasic mud-hut **rooms** in a back yard, but the owner has plans. Much more attractive are the rustic, stilted huts of *Chital Lodge* (no phone; ❸), set in a mixture of farmland and light forest around 1km south and east of the airstrip. You'll have to ask someone in the bazaar to take you there, but once there you'll have no problems: the owner is a keen bird expert who speaks good English and can arrange just about anything his counterparts in Sauraha can – elephant and jeep rides, guided walks, and onward bus or plane tickets. *Rhino Resort* (☎056/24134, ✉rhino@unlimit.com; ❽ including activities) is an ugly hotel in the same area that has nothing in common with the resorts inside the park except its price.

Luxury lodges and tented camps

The **luxury lodges** and **tented camps** that are inside Chitwan National Park are among the most expensive lodgings in Nepal. The owners pay the government massive fees to stake out exclusive concession areas, with the result that you really feel like you've got the park all to yourself. Some are lavish lodges with permanent facilities, others are more remote tented camps – camping in the softest sense, with fluffy mattresses, solar-heated showers and fully stocked bars – and some are both. The prices quoted below, which are per person based on double occupancy, include all activities and meals (taxes are extra), but most resorts offer various other packages, perhaps with transport included, or as part of a wider tour. **Book ahead** for these places, either through an agent or by calling directly – they all have professional websites that give a reasonable idea of what to expect. They'll arrange your travel there and back by private vehicle, plane or raft, which costs extra unless otherwise stated below.

Chitwan Jungle Lodge ☎01/228458, ⓦwww .chitwanjunglelodge.com. The biggest operator in the park, with 32 decent if not remarkable rooms. $170 per person for two-night, three-day package including transport from Kathmandu by car.

Gaida Wildlife Camp ☎01/434520, ⓦwww .visitnepal.com/gaida. Lodge situated uncomfortably close to Sauraha, though it's acknowledged to have the best rhino habitat. $135 per person per night; $110 per person per night for the jungle camp 8km south at the base of the hills.

Island Jungle Resort ☎01/220162, ⓦwww .visitnepal.com/islandresort. Often overcrowded lodge and tented camp on an island in the middle of the Narayani River. Excellent for wildlife. $200 for two nights at the lodge, $180 at the tented camp.

Machan Wildlife Resort ☎01/225001, ⓦwww .nepalinformation.com/machan. Well-designed

lodge with a natural swimming pool. $225 for two nights.

Temple Tiger Wildlife Camp ☎01/221585, ⓦwww.catmando.com/temple-tiger. Lodge and tented camp at the west end of the park. One of the best for wildlife sightings. $200 per night.

Tharu Village ☎01/411225, ⓦwww.tigermountain .com. A relative of *Tiger Tops*, where cultural activities outside the park are as much a part of the mix as wildlife inside the park. $377 for three nights.

Tiger Tops ☎01/411225, ⓦwww.tigermountain .com. The first, and still the most fashionable, with an excellent location for wildlife and renowned service. Most guests consider it well worth the premium prices. Perched on stilts, the lodge is pure jungle Gothic. $892 for two nights in the lodge and one in the tented camp; $733 for two in the camp and one in the lodge.

Royal Chitwan National Park

Whether the **ROYAL CHITWAN NATIONAL PARK** has been blessed or cursed by its own riches is an open question, and the coexistence of the valley's people and wildlife has rarely been easy or harmonious, even before the creation of the national park. In the era of the trigger-happy maharajas, the relationship was at least simple: when Jang Bahadur Rana overthrew the Shah dynasty in 1846, one of his first actions was to make Chitwan a private hunting preserve for rulers and visiting dignitaries. The following century saw some truly hideous **hunts** – King George V, during an eleven-day shoot in 1911, killed 39 tigers and 18 rhinos. In those days the technique, if you could call it that, was to send *shikari* (trackers) into the forest to locate a tiger and set out a buffalo calf as bait. The sahibs were then alerted, loaded onto elephants and, joined by other huntsmen, the whole party of as many as 600 elephants and riders would approach the spot from all directions. As the circle closed, helpers would spread white sheets between the advancing elephants to keep the tiger from breaking through. High up in their *howdahs*, the sahibs could get off shots at point-blank range.

Still, the Ranas' patronage afforded Chitwan a certain degree of protection. So did malaria. That all changed in the early 1950s, when the Ranas were thrown out, the monarchy was restored, and the new government launched its **malaria-control programme**. Settlers poured in and **poaching** went unpoliced – rhinos, whose horns were (and still are) valued for Chinese medicine

Park people

A familiar Sauraha scene for many years has been the stream of bicycle-toting locals crossing the Rapti at dusk, wading or being ferried across the river before disappearing into the trees of the national park on the far side. Picturesque evening ritual it may be, but it's one that is coming to an end.

In the late 1990s, over 20,000 people lived within the park boundaries, most of them in **Padampur**, the area immediately opposite Sauraha. Inevitably, villagers were forced to compete with the park's animal population for forest resources; the ever-increasing numbers of wild animals, on the other hand, would regularly raid farmers' crops, causing widespread damage and even deaths. The situation became increasingly unsustainable, and the government finally decided to **relocate** Padampur's villagers from the park itself to a degraded forest area, to the northeast of the national park, which extends from Bis Hajaar Tal towards the hills of the Mahabharat Lekh. While this programme leaves Chitwan itself free of human settlement (in accordance with the increasingly discredited "wilderness" model of national park conservation), it is likely to accelerate the destruction of a vital wildlife "corridor", one of the few that still connects the plains and the hills.

Many villagers are delighted to be relieved of the threat to their crops and lives posed by wild animals, and the compensation seems reasonably fair, though inevitably, there have been allegations of corruption. However, there are worrying complications. Foremost is the very fact that people are being forced to leave their homes to make way for animals and the tourists that come to see them. A great deal of knowledge, and the cultural beliefs that go with it, stands to be lost in the move as well – the local Tharu people are renowned for their use and knowledge of wild plants. But the most pressing issue for the villagers themselves is that there is, as yet, no adequate source of **water** in the relocation area. Ten thousand people have already left Padampur, and the rest are due to be moved before 2004.

and Yemeni knife handles, were especially hard-hit. By 1960, the human population of the valley had trebled to 100,000, and the number of rhinos had plummeted from 1000 to 200. With the Asian one-horned rhino on the verge of extinction, Nepal emerged as an unlikely hero in one of conservation's finest hours. In 1962, Chitwan was set aside as a **rhino sanctuary** (it became Nepal's first national park in 1973) and, despite the endless hype about tigers, rhinos are Chitwan's biggest attraction and its greatest triumph.

Chitwan now boasts around 550 **rhinos** – over a quarter of the world species total – and numbers are growing healthily. Poaching isn't nearly the problem here that it is in India, no doubt thanks to the deployment of an entire army battalion in the park, although killings do still occur, especially along the park's southern border. Around 100 **tigers** inhabit Chitwan, including a large number of cubs, which is encouraging news in the light of dwindling tiger populations almost everywhere else in South Asia. Chitwan also supports at least 400 **gaur** (Indian bison), found mainly in the drier upland areas, and provides a part-time home to as many as 45 wild **elephants** that roam between here and India. Altogether, 56 mammalian species are found in the park, including sloth bear, leopard, langur and four kinds of deer. Chitwan is also Nepal's most important sanctuary for **birds**, with more than 500 species recorded, and there are also two types of **crocodile** and over 150 types of **butterflies**. (For more detail on Tarai wildlife, see "Natural history" in Contexts.)

But Chitwan's seesaw battle for survival continues. While its forest ecosystem is healthy for the time being, **pollution** from upstream industries is endangering the rivers flowing into it: gangetic dolphins have now disappeared from the Narayani, and gharial crocodiles are only hanging on thanks to human

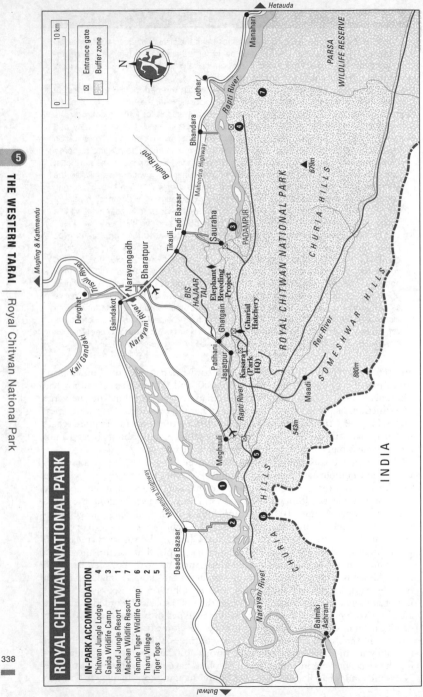

ROYAL CHITWAN NATIONAL PARK

IN-PARK ACCOMMODATION

Chitwan Jungle Lodge	4
Gaida Wildlife Camp	3
Island Jungle Resort	1
Machan Wildlife Resort	7
Temple Tiger Wildlife Camp	6
Tharu Village	2
Tiger Tops	5

Entrance gate
Buffer zone

0   10 km

N

PARSA
WILDLIFE RESERVE

Hetauda

Manahari

Lothar

Rapti River

Bhandara

679m

CHURIA HILLS

Mahendra Highway

Tadi Bazaar

Saraha

PADAMPUR

ROYAL CHITWAN NATIONAL PARK

Tikauli

Bharatpur

Narayangadh

BIS
HAJAAR
TAL

Elephant
Breeding
Project

Ghatgain

Gharial
Hatchery

Reu River

SOMESHWAR HILLS

Devghat

Gaindakot

Patihani

Jagatpur

Kasara
(Park
HQ)

Maadi

880m

Kali Gandaki

Narayani River

Rapti River

543m

CHURIA

INDIA

Meghauli

Mahendra Highway

HILLS

Daada Bazaar

Narayani River

CHURIA
HILLS

Balmiki
Ashram

Buriti Rapti

Trisuli River

▲ Mugling & Kathmandu

▲ Butwal

intervention (see p.345). The government is relocating the communities that still exist within the park (see p.337), but with more than 300,000 people now inhabiting the Chitwan Valley, human **population** growth represents an even graver danger in the long term. **Tourism** has undoubtedly helped make animals and trees worth more alive than dead, but only to those few in the tourist industry – for everyone else, it's another potential cause for resentment, since while the government is telling them to stay out of the park, it is actually *encouraging* foreigners to enter.

The key to safeguarding Chitwan, everyone agrees, is to win the support of local people, and there's some indication that this is beginning to happen. The much-touted open season on **thatch–gathering** in the park each January was an early attempt to offer some compensation to those inconvenienced by the park. The 1995 **Buffer Zone Act** gave financial support to communities living in the 750 square kilometres around the park, with half of park entrance fees allocated for local use: thirty percent of it in community development work and 25 percent in compensation for damage caused by wild animals. It sounds great, but there's never enough money available: the price for someone killed by a tiger or rhino is around $350, and it's less than half that for serious injury; there's no money available at all in compensation for crop damage.

The **King Mahendra Trust for Nature Conservation** (KMTNC; Ⓦ www .kmtnc.org.np), funded by the World Wildlife Fund and other international agencies, was set up in 1982 to carry out research on tiger populations. From 1989, however, the Trust became active in general community development efforts such as building schools, health posts, water taps and appropriate technology facilities (biogas plants that produce electricity from animal dung look set to be a great success), as well as in conservation education and training for guides and lodge-owners. The KMTNC has also been instrumental in helping set up **community forests** (see p.346), which now cover around 4000 hectares of land surrounding the park. Eight of the fourteen forests in eastern Chitwan are now earning from ecotourism, and the prospect of collecting hefty entrance fees is turning local people into zealous guardians of the environment. Such measures stand to give locals a real stake in the park's continued protection; without them, even an army battalion won't be enough.

When to visit

The fact that Chitwan is the easiest to visit of all Nepal's national parks also makes it by far the most popular, although how busy it actually gets is heavily influenced by the **season**. The months of October and November are relatively cool (though still pleasantly warm) but the most popular activities can get booked up, the tall grass makes sightings much rarer, and there's something depressing about your main confrontation with wildlife being another trained elephant topped by tourists. Tourist numbers tail off in the winter months of December and January, but after the grass is cut (usually in late Jan), visitors flock in to take advantage of the easy sightings, particularly in March. From April onwards, the park gets almost unbearably hot – particularly in the steamy monsoon months of July, August and September – but at least you'll have the place to yourself.

Park practicalities

There are no formal **park entrances** to Chitwan, given that the boundary is formed by the river. In **Sauraha**, where almost all visitors are based, daily park **entry permits** (Rs500) are purchased at the ranger's office (daily 6–9am &

Staying alive in the jungle

Lodge owners and guides often play down the risks associated with tracking wildlife, so as not to scare off business. In fact, **safety** is a serious issue in Chitwan, and a year doesn't go by without one or two fatalities in the park; those killed are usually locals during the January thatch-gathering, or guides protecting their clients. There are no emergency medical facilities in or near the park – the closest hospital is in Bharatpur, a minimum two-hour evacuation when you add up all the stages, which means if there's major bleeding the patient is essentially out of luck.

The greatest danger comes from **rhinos**, who have poor eyesight, a keen sense of smell and a tendency to charge at anything they perceive to be a threat. If a rhino is about to charge it will lower its head and take a step back; if it does, try to run in a zigzag path and throw off a piece of clothing (the rhino will stop to smell it), or hide behind – better yet, climb – the nearest big tree. **Sloth bears** can also be dangerous if surprised. Fortunately, there is little danger to visitors from **tigers** (the same isn't always true for locals – see p.370). If a bear or tiger charges, climb a *small* tree – so they can't climb it after you. Don't get anywhere near a mother with young ones of any of these species.

The best safety tip is not to try and sneak into the jungle without a **guide**, but even a guide can't guarantee invulnerability. Most guides are young and gung-ho, and in their eagerness to please will sometimes encourage tourists to venture too close to animals. And no matter how competent, a guide can't know where all the animals are, nor can he, in an emergency, assist more than one person at a time. For this reason most reputable guides will limit **group size** to four clients – it's in your interest to support them in doing so.

1.30–4pm) to the left of the visitor centre. The permit queue can be slow around opening time, so get there early, or have someone from your lodge wait for you (a surcharge may be payable). Once you've got your permit, your guide will then take you across the river and into the national park by canoe or, in low water, by wading. From **alternative bases** such as Ghatgain or Meghauli, it's even simpler: there's no ranger's office so you can't buy your permit in advance; once across the river your guide will help you buy one from one of the army checkposts on the other side.

Wherever they're bought, permits are valid for one day only, but allow you access to **community forest** areas the following day as well. These lie **outside the national park** proper, but as they form part of the raft of activities offered in Sauraha, they're described below.

Elephant rides should be booked a day in advance at the same office; in busy periods you may even need to pay for someone from your lodge to queue overnight. Ask to see the ticket before setting off, as guides sometimes try to sneak their clients into the park with invalid tickets, or take them to forested areas outside the park where a permit isn't necessary.

Chitwan **maps**, sold all over Sauraha, are helpful if you're planning to do any nonstandard explorations in the park or unguided excursions outside it: Mappa/Karto Atelier's map is expensive (Rs650) but it's the best.

Guides

Guided activities such as jungle walks, elephant rides, canoe trips and jeep rides vie for your attention once you've arrived in the vicinity of the park. In fact, for safety reasons (see box above), visitors are not allowed to enter the park on foot without a certified **guide**. For the most part, Sauraha's guides are keen and personable, and some of them are among Nepal's finest. Most are well versed in what tourists want to know, while the best are more than capable of explaining the park's animals, birds, butterflies, trees, plants and indeed its entire ecosystem in competent English. Their knowledge of species (especially birds) can be encyclopedic.

Guides are **certified** by the King Mahendra Trust as "senior", "junior" or "assistant", and should be able to show their credentials. However, certification level isn't a very good indicator of **experience**, because it only takes a year or so to reach senior status – the question you need to ask prospective guides is how many *years* they've been guiding in Chitwan. Unfortunately, leading tourists through a jungle full of two-ton horned animals is a hazardous occupation, and anyone with any sense gets out of it as soon as they can, so it may be hard to find someone with more than three or four years' experience. Note that less experienced guides are also apt to speak less English, so it's harder for them to impart what information they do know, and there's more risk of miscommunication in a dangerous situation. (If your guide yells *look*, that means "hide" in Nepali!)

To **find a guide**, ask other travellers if they've found someone they can recommend. Every lodge has its own in-house guides, or you could hire one through United Jungle Guide Service (☏056/80039), a syndicate of freelancers who've joined forces and purport to maintain high standards; other services are just one-man outfits. The Bird Education Society (☏056/80113, ✉hlc@mos.com.np), with an office near Sauraha's main Restaurant Chowk can put you in touch with excellent, committed guides but, obviously enough, they tend to specialize in birds. Freelance guides tend to have more experience, but there are some excellent in-house guides. Another possible reason to go with one of your lodge's guides is that it will probably be easier to put together a group of four, which lowers the per-person cost. Guide **fees** depend on the activity and, to some extent, on the experience of the guide, and are detailed in the relevant sections below.

Activities inside the park

Promises of "safari adventure" in Chitwan can be misleading. While the park's **wildlife** is astoundingly concentrated, remember that the dense vegetation doesn't allow the easy sightings you get in the savannas of Africa (especially in autumn, when the grass is high). Many guides assume that everyone wants to see only tigers and rhinos, but there are any number of birds and other animals to spot which the typical safari package may not cover, not to mention the many different ways to simply experience the luxuriant, teeming jungle: **elephant rides**, **jeep tours**, **canoe trips** and just plain **walks** each give a different slant.

The following **activities** are most commonly done inside Chitwan National Park; bear in mind that you'll need to add the cost of an entry permit to the prices quoted. All activities can, and in most cases should, be arranged through your lodge, or via a guide service in Sauraha. For certain popular activities it's essential to book the night before, or even earlier during the cut-throat months of October, November and March. Most activities are half-price for children under ten.

Jungle and bird walks

Walking is the best way to observe the park's prolific **birdlife**. The Chitwan region is an important stopover spot for migratory species in December and March, as well as being home to many year-round residents – look for parakeets, Indian rollers, paradise flycatchers, kingfishers, hornbills, cranes and literally hundreds of others. The Bird Education Society in Sauraha is an excellent

△ Royal Chitwan National Park

source of local information and knowledgeable guides, and sells a checklist that's indispensable for any serious birder.

Walking allows you to appreciate the smaller attractions of the jungle at your own pace: orchids, strangler figs, towering termite mounds, tiger scratchings or rhino droppings piled up like cannonballs. Experienced jungle-walkers say they get their best animal sightings on foot, although that usually doesn't apply when they've got four flat-footed neophytes in tow. Throw away that shopping list of animals; you have to be content with what's on offer. You are virtually guaranteed to see a **rhino** (probably several), and deer and monkeys are easy to spot, but tiger sightings are rare – maybe one or two a week.

The best **season** for walking is spring, when the grass is shorter, though at other times of year you can compensate by spending more time in the *sal* forest and riverine habitats. No matter when you go, bring lots of water. The **cost** for a morning's walk is Rs250–500 per person (depending on the guide's level of experience and the number of clients), and Rs400–800 for a full day. An all-day walk doesn't necessarily increase your chances of seeing game – most of the rhinos hang out close to Sauraha – but it gets you further into the park where you aren't running into other parties every two minutes. In cool weather some guides lead all-day walks in the Churia Hills, where you may see gaur (Indian bison) as well as deer, monkeys and a huge number of bird species.

Elephant rides

In terms of cost per hour, a jeep's a better deal, but how often do you get to **ride an elephant**? The pachyderm's stately gait takes you back to a time, as recently as the early 1950s, when this was the way foreign delegations entered Nepal. The *phanit* (driver) sits astride the animal's neck, giving it commands with his toes and periodically walloping its huge skull, and attentively fending branches out of passengers' way. An elephant is the safest way to get around in the grasslands – especially in summer and autumn, when the grass towers 8m high – and it's the best way to observe **rhinos** and possibly wild boar or sloth bear without scaring them off, since the elephant's scent masks their own.

The National Park keeps half a dozen rideable animals – the other sixty-odd are on patrol duty – and sends them out on one-hour-plus trips in shifts in the early morning and late afternoon. The **cost** is a steep Rs1000 per hour, not including the Rs100-odd fee for your lodge to arrange the trip for you. You can often sign yourself up at the ranger's office at 6am for one of that day's rides, but if you do this you're apt to get second-class treatment at the boarding platform. In really busy times, the only way to find a mount is to get your lodge to send someone to queue overnight. "**Private**" elephants make trips into the community forests, usually Kumroj (see p.346), and are booked through lodges or guides. Note that elephants don't work on major holidays, such as the eighth and ninth days of Dasain, and Lakshmi Puja.

Canoe trips

Floating down either of the Sauraha area's two rivers in a dugout **canoe** gives you your best shot at seeing **mugger crocodiles** (which, unlike the pointier-snouted gharials, prefer such marshy areas), and is also a relaxing way to watch birds and look for occasional wildlife on the shore. It's best done in winter, when the water is cool and the muggers sun themselves on the gravel banks; ruddy shelducks may be seen in profusion at this time, too. In hot weather, the outing is less rewarding, though you'll be assured of plenty of birds.

The standard itinerary is to depart from near the Baghmara Community Forest and float down the **Budhi Rapti** (Old Rapti) River for about half an hour to the Elephant Breeding Project (see p.347), then walk or jeep back to your lodging. The trip isn't actually within the park itself, but a park permit is required. The time spent on the water is brief, and if you're not in the first couple of canoes that morning or afternoon you may not see much. The canoe ride **costs** about Rs250 per person, plus the usual rate for a guided walk, jeep or ox-cart ride back.

Somewhat longer trips on the main **Rapti River** are more worthwhile, though there's a tendency to pack too many people into one boat, which isn't the most peaceful way to see the park. Trips cost upwards of Rs500, depending on the length of the route. When such trips are permitted, you can return either through the park along a heavily used trail (the animals know better than to hang out there) or outside the park via the Elephant Breeding Centre.

Jungle treks

To get well clear of the Sauraha crowds you need to walk for two or more days, overnighting en route outside the park – think of it as a **jungle trek**. Staying with the trekking analogy, there's one "teahouse" route in the park, plus any number of other possibilities for those willing to stay in private homes. Which **area** you head for depends on your interest – discuss it with the guide. The Churia Hills are best for birds, while the teahouse route is excellent for animals. There's a fair chance of seeing bears in the Maadi Valley.

The teahouse route follows the forest road from **Sauraha to Kasara** and on **to Meghauli**, or vice versa. It takes two days of roughly equal length, or you could just do one half or the other. The Sauraha–Kasara leg is more commonly trekked, and is also the route taken by jeep tours out of Sauraha. There are of course no teahouses inside the park, but you can spend nights at Meghauli and Ghatgain (see pp.334 and 335). It's also possible to carry on trekking for a further two days (you could also start from Meghauli), overnighting at **Maadi**, in a beautiful valley just inside the park's southern boundary and then returning to Sauraha. This permits you to get to less-visited parts of the park's interior, such as Tamar Tal, which is excellent for birdwatching. You can return to Sauraha by local buses or arrange to have a jeep take you back. Go with a guide who's done this trek before – most haven't. The **cost** of doing a jungle trek is simply the guide's daily rate (Rs400–800), plus his food and lodging.

Jungle trek itineraries are limited by the fact that **camping** is currently not allowed inside the park, though this policy could change (ask at guide services). In the meantime, the next-best thing to camping in the park is to spend a night in an observation tower in the Baghmara or Kumroj community forests (see p.346).

Jeep rides

Hiring a **jeep** for a half-day gives you the chance to get deep into the jungle, but it is relatively disruptive, and will set you back around Rs2500 for a four-seater. If you can't get a group together, sign up for a half-day **jeep tour** (Rs700). The park only allows four or five jeeps in at a time, but as long as you book early enough your lodge will get you a seat on whichever vehicle is going. The **best months** are from February to April, after the grass has been cut and the new shoots attract the deer. Note that after the monsoon (until Dec), jeeps can't cross the river; during that time shorter, lamer, cheaper trips may be run outside the park.

For big game, you're limited to what you can see through the dusty wake of a Russian army-surplus vehicle in the midmorning or afternoon, which pretty much means **deer**. The standard jeep tour includes a stop at **Lami Tal** ("Long

Lake"), which should be a prime spot for watching **birds** and **mugger crocodiles**, but things get pretty sleepy in the heat of the day. The tour continues to the gharial crocodile breeding project and Kasara Durbar.

Kasara and the gharial crocodile breeding project

Chitwan National Park's headquarters lie at **Kasara**, about 15km west of Sauraha. Jeep tours occasionally pass through, taking in the crocodile breeding project, but it's not somewhere you'd go out of your way to visit. Hourly buses run from Narayangadh to Jagatpur, on the opposite bank of the river, from where you can cross the water in a small dugout canoe ferry (or, once it's complete, via the huge and vastly expensive new bridge being built to serve Maadi's tiny community of key voters). There are no facilities other than a couple of simple lodges in Jagatpur, however, and you'd do far better to base yourself in Ghatgain, just upstream.

Overlooking a small army base, **Kasara Durbar** was constructed in 1939 as a royal hunting lodge, and now serves as the park's administrative headquarters. The meagre **museum** inside is closed to visitors, but someone might let you in if you're determined to see the collection of skulls and school project-like displays. Baby rhinos, orphaned by the work of poachers, can often be seen roaming freely and begging for food near here pending relocation.

A well-used signposted track leads about 300m west from Kasara Durbar through light forest to the **gharial crocodile breeding project**, which is Kasara's only real attraction. The longest of the world's crocodiles – adults can grow to more than 7m from nose to tail – the **gharial** is an awesome fishing machine. Its slender, broom-like snout, which bristles with a fine mesh of teeth, snaps shut on its prey like a spring-loaded trap. Unfortunately for the gharial, its eggs are regarded as a delicacy, and males are hunted for their bulb-like snouts which are believed to have medicinal powers.

In the mid-1970s, the world suddenly realized there were only 1300 gharials left, and Chitwan's project was set up in 1977 to incubate eggs under controlled conditions, thus upping the survival rate – only one percent in the wild – to as high as 75 percent. The majority of hatchlings are released into the wild after three years, when they reach 1.2m in length; more than 500 have been released so far into the Narayani, Koshi, Karnali and Babai rivers. Having been given this head start, however, the hatchlings must then survive a growing list of dangers, which now include not only hunters but also untreated effluents from upstream industries (Narayangadh's Bhrikuti Paper Mill and Gorkha Brewery are named as the main culprits) and a scarcity of food caused by the lack of fish ladders on a dam downstream in India. Recent counts indicate that captive-raised gharials now outnumber wild ones on the Narayani, which suggests that without constant artificial augmentation of their numbers they would soon become extinct. A few more-conventional-looking mugger crocodiles can also be seen at the breeding centre.

Activities outside the park

Large patches of jungle still exist outside the park in Chitwan's heavily populated buffer zone, albeit in a less pristine state. The areas designated as **community forests** were originally conceived to reduce the need for residents of this critical strip to go into the park to gather wood, thatch and other resources, but they're now nearly as rich in flora and fauna as Chitwan itself. Two forests, Baghmara and Kumroj, on the outskirts of Sauraha offer alternatives to entering the park itself, and the **elephant rides**, particularly, are often no less rewarding. Trips on these "private elephants" are a useful option for travellers on a budget, too, as the cost of park permits and activities quickly adds up.

Though it's not yet protected as a community forest proper, the **Bis Hajaar Tal** wetland area is nevertheless one of the best areas for **birdwatching** inside the park or out of it. There are plenty of animals as well, but it's one of the few areas of jungle that can be visited independently with relative safety – though as always you'll probably get more out of it in the company of a good guide.

The community forests

Closest to Sauraha, **Baghmara Community Forest** is the more popular of the two in the Chitwan region, and a good place to see rhinos and birds; you can also combine your visit with a trip to Bis Hajaar Tal, which it borders, or the Elephant Breeding Project, just to the south. Its main entrance is 1km west of Sauraha, at the end of the road past *Royal Wildlife Camp*. **Kumroj Community Forest** (also written Kumrose), 2km east of Sauraha, is further away from most lodges and you'd probably only visit on an elephant ride, though the route from Sauraha is partially forested. To get there on foot, follow the road past *Nature Safari Camp*, then make your first right and keep heading east (don't take the first right-hand fork, which leads to *Gaida Wildlife Camp*).

Elephant rides into the community forests can be reserved a day in advance by your lodge or by any Sauraha agent, and cost only Rs600 for two hours, though bear in mind that there's a fair bit of road plodding before you get into the trees. The chance of seeing rhino and deer is at least as good as in the areas of the park that government elephants reach, but other wildlife is usually more scarce. During the January thatch-gathering, however, animals in the national park may be disturbed and flee to these outlying forests.

These community forests don't yet seem to have settled on a permanent **fee structure**, but in any case your lodge or agent will handle any necessary permits. At the time of writing, park entry permit were valid the following morning for entry into the community forest, while separate permits could be purchased at the respective park gates: Rs300 for entry on an elephant and Rs150 for entry on foot.

Both Baghmara and Kumroj have concrete *machaan* (observation towers) where you can **spend the night** – good for nocturnal viewing if the moon is out. Guides will charge around Rs750 for overnight trips. As in the park, a guide is required to enter either of the community forests on foot.

Bis Hajaar Tal

Far larger than either community forest, the **Bis Hajaar Tal** ("Twenty-Thousand Lakes") area is Nepal's second-biggest natural wetland, and provides an important corridor for animals migrating between the Tarai and hills. The name refers to a maze of marshy oxbow lakes, many of them already filled in, well-hidden among mature *sal* trees. The area teems with birds, including storks, kingfishers, eagles and the huge Lesser Adjutant. The forest starts just west of Baghmara and the Elephant Breeding Project and reaches its marshy climax about 5km northwest of there. To explore this area, have a guide lead you in on foot from the breeding project, and allow a full day.

Without a guide, you'd be wise to take the long way round to avoid getting lost: cycle to Tadi Bazaar, follow the main highway 3km west to a signposted turning on the left (the village here is called Tikauli), then go southwest on a gravel road beside a canal for about 2km until you begin to see the lakes. The road initially passes through a thin strip of community forest, at the entrance

Asian elephants

In Nepal and throughout southern Asia, **elephants** have been used as ceremonial transportation and beasts of burden for thousands of years, earning them a cherished place in the culture – witness the popularity of elephant-headed Ganesh, the darling of the Hindu pantheon. Thanks to this symbiosis with man, Asian elephants (unlike their African cousins) survive mainly as a domesticated species, even as their wild habitat has all but vanished.

With brains four times the size of humans', elephants are reckoned to be as **intelligent** as dolphins; recent research suggests they may communicate subsonically. What we see as a herd is in fact a complex social structure, consisting of bonded pairs and a fluid hierarchy. In the wild, **herds** typically consist of fifteen to thirty females and one old bull, and are usually led by a senior female; other bulls live singly or in bachelor herds. Though they appear docile, elephants have strongly individual personalities and moods. They can learn dozens of commands, but they won't obey just anyone – as any handler will tell you, you can't make an elephant do what it doesn't want to do. That they submit to such apparently cruel head-thumping by drivers seems to have more to do with thick skulls than obedience.

Asian elephants are smaller than those of the African species, but their statistics are still formidable. A bull can grow up to 3m high and weigh four tons, although larger individuals are known to exist. An average day's intake is 200 litres of water and 225kg of fodder – and if you think that's impressive, wait till you see it come back out again. All that eating wears down teeth fast, which is why an average elephant goes through six sets in its lifetime, each one more durable than the last. The trunk is controlled by an estimated 40,000 muscles, enabling its owner to eat, drink, cuddle and even manipulate simple tools (such as a stick for scratching). Though up to 2.5cm thick, an elephant's skin is still very sensitive, and it will often take mud or dust baths to protect against insects. Life expectancy is about 75 years and, much the same as with humans, an elephant's working life can be expected to run from its mid-teens to its mid-fifties; training begins at about age five.

to which you pay a small access fee (Rs20 on foot, Rs40 on a bike), and then continues along the canal for another 8km or so to Gita Nagar, on the Bharatpur–Jagatpur road. The government has yet to establish a clear policy on whether or not to allow tourists into Bis Hajaar Tal, and if so how much they should pay. Until it does, you can enter for free, but expect this to change – get an update from your guesthouse.

The hattisar (elephant stables) and Elephant Breeding Project

The majority of Chitwan's elephant workforce is housed at the government **hattisar** (elephant stables), on the northwestern edge of Sauraha. The best time to visit is mid-afternoon, when the elephants are sure to be around for feeding time. In hot weather they're taken down to the river for a bath at midday – immensely photogenic.

Sauraha lodges offer jeep tours out to the **Elephant Breeding Project** (Rs15 at busy periods), 4km west of the village, where baby elephants are the main attraction. Until the mid-1970s, Nepal's Parks Department commonly bought its elephants from India, where they were captured in the wild and trained in captivity. As the wild population shrank this procedure became increasingly unaffordable, so the government began breeding and training its own elephants, first at the old *hattisar* and then, in 1988, establishing this separate facility, where elephants can mate in peace and mothers and babies can receive special attention. At any given time the project is home to a couple of breeding bulls and ten to fifteen cows, and usually a couple of calves. The young elephants need to spend as much time as possible with their mothers to become socialized into elephant society, so it's best to arrive here in early morning or late afternoon – in the middle of the day they're usually off on educational trips to the river and the jungle.

You can visit the project independently either on foot or bicycle, though you have to cross the Budhi Rapti just before you get there; it's fordable for most of the year, and a boatman will ferry you across in high water. You're better off coming with a guide, though, who'll be able to explain the goings-on and then take you on to Bis Hajaar Tal (see p.346).

Narayangadh and around

It's hard to travel far in Nepal without at least passing through **NARAYAN-GADH**: the construction of the Mugling–Narayangadh highway has made it the gateway to the Tarai and the busiest crossroads in the country. What was once a far-flung intersection is now a kilometre-long strip of diesel and *daal bhaat*, and a hotbed of prostitution. Its sister city, **BHARATPUR**, continues to the east without a visible break, though as the headquarters of Chitwan District, Bharatpur is tangibly more upmarket, boasting a large regional college, a couple of breweries and an airstrip. Unflattering as all that may sound, you may have occasion to pause in the area, and the side trip to the sacred confluence of **Devghat**, 5km upstream of Narayangadh, makes for a refreshingly cultural outing from Chitwan.

Buses serving the northward Mugling Highway (to and from Pokhara, Gorkha and Devghat) have their own bus park at the north end of Narayangadh. All other express buses serving the Mahendra Highway stop at the fast-food parade just east of Pulchowk (the intersection of the Mugling and Mahendra highways). There are two additional bus parks for local services: buses and minibuses to Tadi Bazaar (for Sauraha) and eastern Chitwan District start from Sahid Chowk, about 500m east of Pulchowk; minibuses to Meghauli and Jagatpur start from just north of Sahid Chowk – walk north for 50m, take the first right down a small lane, and it's on the left after 200m. Frequent flights for Kathmandu (4–5 daily; $63 on RNAC) leave from Bharatpur's **airstrip**, just south of the Mahendra Highway, and can be booked at any travel agent or airline office.

Rikshas should take you anywhere within Narayangadh and Bharatpur for Rs15 or less.

Devghat

DEVGHAT (or Deoghat), 5km northwest of Narayangadh, is a lot of people's idea of a great place to die. An astonishingly tranquil spot, it stands where the wooded hills meet the shimmering plains, and the Trisuli and the Kali Gandaki **rivers** merge to form the Narayani, one of the major tributaries of the Ganga (Ganges). Some say Sita, the heroine of the *Ramayan*, died here. The ashes of King Mahendra, the present king's father, were sprinkled at this sacred *tribeni* (a confluence of three rivers: wherever two rivers meet, a third, spiritual one is believed to join them), and scores of *sunyasan*, those who have renounced the world, patiently live out their last days here hoping to achieve an equally auspicious death and rebirth. Many have retired to Devghat to avoid being a burden to their children, to escape ungrateful offspring, or because they have no children to look after them in their old age and to perform the necessary rites when they die. *Pujari* (priests) also practise here – their professional signs are the only advertising you'll see – and often take in young candidates for the priesthood as resident students.

Riding roughshod over local objections, the government hopes to build a hydroelectric project just downstream of the confluence, partly to supply increased demand in Chitwan district. Quite apart from the disturbance of large-scale construction works, some allege that the project will cause the sacred spot to be flooded by the pondage spreading upstream. Fortunately, perhaps, it's unlikely that funds will be found, but it might be worth asking locally before planning a visit.

Buses shuttle every couple of hours between Narayangadh and Devghat, taking about half an hour, but it's quite pleasant to **walk**. Head north from the Pokhara bus park along the main highway to Mugling and after 1km turn left on a paved road under an arch – Devghat is at the end of the road, about 5km through forest. Either way, you come to the Trisuli and cross it by a dramatic suspension footbridge, which was immortalized in the classic Nepali film *Kanchhi*, when the heartbroken lover attempted suicide from it. From the far side of the bridge, bear left up and into the village. You can also cross the river further downstream by **dugout canoe** – for the return trip, the ferryman, if he thinks he can be spared from his duties, might even consent to take you all the way back to Narayangadh for a suitable fee.

Dozens of small shrines lie dotted around the village, but you come here more for the atmosphere than the sights. Vaishnavas (followers of Vishnu) congregate at Devghat's largest and newest temple, the central *shikra*-style **Harihar Mandir**, founded in 1998 by the famed guru Shaktya Prakash Ananda of Haridwar. Shaivas (followers of Shiva) dominate the area overlooking the confluence at the western edge of the village. To get to the confluence, turn left at a prominent *chautaara* at the top of the path leading through the village: **Galeshwar Ashram**, on your right as you walk down the steps, and **Aghori Ashram**, further downhill on the right, are named after two recently deceased holy men. A follower of the outrageous Aghori tradition (see p.191), the one-armed Aghori Baba, who was often referred to as the "Crazy Baba", claimed to have cut off his own arm after being instructed to do so in a dream. Various paths lead upstream of the confluence, eventually arriving at **Sita Gupha**, a sacred cave that is closed except on Makar Sankranti, and **Chakrabarti Mandir**, a shady temple area housing a famous *shaligram* that locals say is growing.

A huge **pilgrimage** is held at Devghat on Makar Sankranti (Jan 14 or 15), while Shiva Raatri, falling on the new moon of February–March, brings many Indian devotees. At other times, sadhus and pilgrims do *puja* at the point where the rivers meet – cremations are also held here – and old-timers meditate outside their huts in the sun. Be sensitive to the residents, and don't disturb them or touch anything that might be holy: many are orthodox Baahuns and your touch would be polluting.

The last bus back to Narayangadh leaves at 6pm. If you get stuck, a couple of teahouses near the Trisuli bridge on the Devghat side can provide really barebones **lodging**, but frankly, Devghat is the sort of place that visitors should leave in peace after the sun goes down.

Practicalities

Most **accommodation** in Narayangadh is fairly crummy, and usually seedy to boot. For something more salubrious, head for one of the resort-style hotels around the Bharatpur airstrip, or across the bridge to one of a couple of river-side guesthouses on the more peaceful west bank of the Narayani. **Food**, plentiful but not wildly exciting, can be found all around Pulchowk. Standing out slightly from the greasy spoons and whisky shacks is *Royal Rest House*'s restaurant, while the dining room of *Safari Narayani Hotel* does superb, and not much more expensive, meals.

Accommodation

Island Jungle Resort Bharatpur ☎056/20730. Set back from the highway and quite leafy, with a swimming pool. **⑤**

Quality Guest House Pulchowk, Narayangadh ☎056/20939. In the maelstrom of town, but a cut above the others, with solar-heated hot water. **②**

Royal Rest House Pulchowk, Narayangadh ☎056/22898. The largest of several inns here, cavernous and noisy but with good food. All rooms have attached bath and some have a/c. **④–⑤**

Safari Narayani Hotel Bharatpur ☎056/25514. Pleasantly shaded grounds with a pool and a good restaurant. **⑦**

Satanchuli Inn Behind the Pokhara bus park, Narayangadh ☎056/21151. The best-situated budget option, especially for visiting Devghat. Bare but clean and large rooms, some with a river view. **②**

Uncle's Lodge West of Narayani bridge, Narayangadh ☎056/22502. A friendly throwback to gentler times, with a delightful garden and river-front location. **②**

Lumbini Tarai

Hordes of travellers hurry through this ancient part of the Tarai, west of Chitwan; few take the time to look around. It's best known, unfairly, for **Sonauli**, the main tourist border crossing between Nepal and India. Yet only 20km away is one of Nepal's premier destinations, **Lumbini**: birthplace of the Buddha and the site of ruins going back almost three thousand years.

Two highways – the Siddhartha and the Mahendra – connect the region with Pokhara and the rest of the Tarai, and buses between Sonauli and Kathmandu are frequent. The journey to Lumbini takes a little extra effort, but is well worth it. As in most other parts of the Tarai, accommodation and food are readily available here but usually very simple.

Butwal to Sonauli

Westwards from Narayangadh, the Mahendra Highway runs across a washboard of cultivated fields, briefly climbs over a jungle-cloaked spur of the Churia Hills, and passes long stretches of heavily used but seemingly healthy forest. It's a relatively painless 110km to Butwal.

Butwal

Crouching uninvitingly at the point where the Tinau river spills out onto the plains, **BUTWAL** is an ugly modern town of convenience. It's the hub of the Lumbini administrative zone: north lies Pokhara; south is Sonauli and the

Indian border; and to the west, the Mahendra Highway barrels along towards Nepalganj and Nepal's western border.

Placed at the start of an important trade route to Tibet as well as the pilgrim trail to Muktinath, the **tax post** at Butwal was for centuries a tidy little earner for Palpa (Tansen) and then Kathmandu. Much later, it came to be a staging post for Nepal's most lucrative export: Gurkha soldiers, bound for the recruiting office at Gorakhpur in India. In the early nineteenth century, Nepal and the East India Company fell into a dispute over the territory around Butwal, and the murder of some British police here touched off a two-year **war with Britain**. Nepal scored several improbable early victories here and elsewhere but, outnumbered four to one, was eventually forced to surrender. Under the terms of the resulting treaty, the Tarai territories from Butwal west had to be ceded to the British (Nepal struck a deal to get the disputed land around Butwal back the same year). Any reminders of the past are, however, conspicuously absent in modern Butwal.

Many **buses** originate or terminate at this busy crossroads – see p.377 for routes and frequencies. Express services are now based at the brand new bus park, to the south of town on the main Sonauli road (the Siddhartha Highway), but some buses still stop off at "Traphik Chowk", a busy crossroads and bazaar area 500m north on the same highway. Local buses use the old bus park in the town proper, four blocks to the west of Traphik Chowk.

Practicalities

Butwal has its share of ghastly highway-side dives, but there are a number of fairly professional **hotels** within easy riksha-range of the bus park. The noisy Traphik Chowk is overlooked by a number of reasonable places, among which the *Hotel Kandara* (℡071/40175; ❷–❺) has a garden and a good range of rooms, from basic budget boxes to air-conditioned suites. For a quieter and more inspiring setting, head two blocks west into the bazaar, where *Santosh Guest House* (no phone; ❶) is dingy and down-at-heel, but friendly and characterful in its way. Another couple of blocks further west, just south of the old, local bus park, *Hotel Sindoor* (℡071/40189, ✉hsindoor@mail.com.np; ❺) is a bit out of the way, but is well-established and much the most peaceful in town; the standard rooms are a bit shabby for the price, but the deluxe suites live up to their billing. The hotels overlooking the new bus park are just too noisy to be worthwhile, but the small, friendly *Hotel Sahara* (℡071/45612; ❸–❺), 100m north, is set just far enough back off the main Siddhartha Highway, and has clean, light rooms, some with a/c.

The more expensive hotels are your best bet for Indian and Westernish **food**, while a few *bhojanalaya* around Traphik Chowk serve decent Nepali fare. A couple of communications shops near Traphik Chowk provide inexpensive **internet** access.

Bhairawa (Siddhartha Nagar)

Half an hour south by bus, **BHAIRAWA** (officially, the name has been changed to **SIDDHARTHA NAGAR**, but it's not catching on) is a virtual rerun of Butwal, if slightly less frenetic. Its bazaar supports a sizeable minority of Muslim traders and, like so many border towns, exists primarily to peddle imported goods to acquisitive Indians. Its only recommendation is that it's better than Sonauli.

For **orientation** purposes, think of Bhairawa's three main streets forming an upright triangle: the eastern side is the Siddhartha Highway (which continues north to Butwal and south to the Indian border), Bank Road runs along the south, and Narayanpath along the west. *Hotel Yeti* stands on a roundabout at the southeastern apex of the triangle and is a handy landmark; rikshas and shared jeeps bound for Sonauli wait here. The road to Lumbini breaks west from the highway about 1km north of the *Hotel Yeti*, just north of the triangle's northern apex.

Practicalities

As in many Tarai cities, Bhairawa's **accommodation** is all either cheap in a very Nepali way or upscale in a more Indian style; there's not much middle ground. *Hotel Yeti's* dining room does competent Indian and Chinese **meals**, and *Pashupati Restaurant*, opposite *Hotel Yeti*, is good for South Indian vegetarian meals and snacks.

Accommodation

City Guest House Bank Rd ☎071/23481. Standard cold-water lodge in a lively but noisy part of the bazaar. The nearby *Hotel Sayapatri* is equivalent. ❶

Hotel Everest Bank Rd ☎071/20317, ✉htl_evst @mail.com.np. Pricey for what you get, but it is probably the cleanest and most comfortable of the cluster along Bank Rd, and has a reasonably good restaurant. ❹

Hotel Lumbini Pagoda On the border highway, 500m south of Bank Rd ☎071/21837. Just barely screened from the new Siddhartha Bus Park by its

small garden, but the air-cooled rooms are pleasant enough, and it's convenient for a quick getaway. ❹

Hotel Pawan Main Rd, just south of Bank Rd ☎071/23680. International-type hotel with most of the trimmings. ❽

Hotel Shantanu On the border highway, 500m north of Bank Rd ☎071/21545. Spacious and well-kept, with some air-conditioned rooms. ❻

Hotel Yeti Corner of the border highway and Bank Rd ☎071/20551. Central and very professional; the staff have long experience helping travellers get to Lumbini or at least out of Bhairawa. ❻

Moving on

The new **bus park**, for all express services, lies 500m south of *Hotel Yeti* on the main Siddhartha Highway, but some local buses still drop off and pick up in town, at the main crossroads by *Hotel Yeti*. The ticket offices are in the middle of the bus park, and while there shouldn't be a problem getting a seat, it's worth booking as early as possible to get a comfortable one near the front. Note that the last day-buses to Kathmandu and Pokhara set off at 11.30am, so try and arrive early from India to be able to enjoy the views on the way. All the afternoon buses, no matter what time they leave (hourly between 4.30–8pm for Kathmandu, or between 4.30–7.30pm for Pokhara) are night-bus services and arrive the following morning.

Cars and **jeeps** can be rented by the day (Rs1500 plus fuel) or for the journey to Lumbini (Rs300 one way) or Tilaurakot (about Rs1200 return) – arrange through the better hotels or any travel agent around the main intersection near *Hotel Yeti*. You might be able to rent a **bike** or **motorcycle** informally through your guesthouse.

Travel agents can also book internal **flights** from Bhairawa to Kathmandu (6 daily; $79). The airstrip is 10km north of town, but be aware that there are plans to transform it into an international terminal, which would disrupt flights. That said, the plans (never mind the planes) seem unlikely to take off.

Sonauli (Belahiya) and the border

The little border scrum of **SONAULI** (Soo-*no*-li; technically the Nepali side is known as **BELAHIYA**) is an unflattering introduction to Nepal if you're just arriving, and a rude send-off if you're leaving. It's by far the most popular border crossing between Nepal and India, however, and while it's not quite as awful as Raxaul/Birganj (see p.385), there's no need to linger: all the main tourist facilities and transport connections are found in Bhairawa, 4km north.

Indian currency is readily accepted in Sonauli, and sometimes in Bhairawa, but not beyond. Nepal-Rastra **bank** has a foreign-exchange counter that's open much the same hours as the border, and registered **moneychangers** in Sonauli keep long hours; rates are the same as elsewhere in Nepal. If changing Nepali into Indian rupees, make sure the moneychanger hasn't offloaded torn notes on you, which are hard to pass in India. **Food** won't be a problem: roadside shacks serve up decent Nepali rice and noodle dishes, and Indian-style snacks.

The border

The **border** is officially open round the clock, but Nepalese immigration officers are likely to be in their beds after 9 or 10pm. Nepalese visas are available on the border for US dollars but Indian visas have to be obtained in advance through an embassy (see p.179). Figure on half an hour to get through Nepalese and Indian border formalities, unless you're crossing with a vehicle; appalling traffic jams on the Nepalese side mean this can take hours. Remember that Nepal time is fifteen minutes ahead of India.

If you're **entering Nepal**, make straight for Bhairawa (see p.351), the starting point for all buses elsewhere in Nepal. Local buses, microbuses and jeeps make the ten-minute journey almost continuously (Rs5 in either currency); many jeeps continue through to Butwal (Rs17). See the Bhairawa section for more advice on onward travel – and note that there are no air-conditioned tourist buses through to Kathmandu, whatever agents in Gorakhpur may say. A smart alternative is to continue on past Bhairawa to nearby Lumbini (see below): Sonauli's one-man-and-a-desk "travel agencies" can arrange jeeps to Lumbini (Rs300 one way) or other destinations. Note that if you're coming from Varanasi you should set off as early as possible if you want to carry on into Nepal the same day.

Leaving Nepal is a simple enough matter of getting off whatever transport brought you here from Bhairawa and walking across the border. Tourist buses and sardine-can jeeps (which leave for Gorakhpur as soon as they're very full), depart from just south of Indian immigration – an easy 200-metre walk from the Nepalese side, so offers of riksha rides aren't to be taken seriously. The tourist buses connect Sonauli with Gorakhpur (6 daily; 3hr) and Varanasi (1 daily; 10hr). Indian government buses depart from a point nearly 1km south of the border, and provide services to Gorakhpur (hourly; 3hr), Varanasi (every 2hr; 12hr) and, for masochists, Delhi (6 daily; 24hr). From Gorakhpur you can make broad-gauge **train** connections throughout India, but be wary of rip-offs – Nepalis are wont to nickname it Chorpur, or "thief-town".

Lumbini

After I am no more, Ananda! Men of belief will visit with faithful curiosity and devotion to the four places – where I was born ... attained enlightenment ... gave the first sermons ... and passed into Nirvana.

The Buddha (c.543–463 BC)

For the world's one billion Buddhists, **LUMBINI**, 22km west of Bhairawa, is where it all began. **The Buddha's birthplace** is arguably the single most important historical site in the country – not only the source of one of the world's great religions but also the centre of Nepal's most significant **archeo-logical finds**, dating from the third century BC. With only modest ruins but powerful associations, it's the kind of place you could whizz round in two hours or rest in for days, soaking up the peaceful atmosphere of the wooded park and its scattering of monasteries, founded by countries from all over the Buddhist world.

The Buddha has long been a prophet without much honour in his own country, however, and the area around Lumbini is now predominantly Muslim. The main local **festival** is a Hindu one, commemorating the Buddha as the ninth incarnation of Vishnu – it's held on the full moon of the Nepali month of Baisaakh (April–May). Celebrations of **Buddha Jayanti** (the Buddha's birthday) are comparatively meagre because, as the local monks will tell you with visible disgust, Buddhists from the high country think Lumbini is too hot in May.

Pilgrims used to stick to the more-developed Indian sites of Bodh Gaya, Sarnath and Kushinagar, but in the 1970s, the government, with the backing of the United Nations, authorized a hugely ambitious **master plan** for a five-square-kilometre **religious park** consisting of monasteries, cultural facilities, gardens, fountains and a tourist village. After a very slow start, the plan is finally starting to take shape under the direction of (or perhaps in spite of) the Lumbini Development Trust. Roads enter the master-plan area from several directions, with the **main entrance gate** at the southeastern edge. A road leads straight from there to the **Sacred Garden**, which contains all the arche-ological treasures associated with the Buddha's birth. To the north of the Sacred Garden, two "**monastic zones**" are beginning to be filled by an international array of temples, overlooked by the grand Shanti Stupa, or Peace Pagoda. Alongside, a miniature wetland reserve has been established for the endangered sarus crane, and 600,000 trees have been planted throughout the site, attracting many birds and animals.

Of course there is ample cause for scepticism, not least the nakedly commer-cial aspirations of the Nepalese government – transforming the airport at Bhairawa into an international terminal has even been mooted – yet if the remaining plans come off, Lumbini could grow to be quite a cosmopolitan religious site. Japanese tour groups have begun to add Lumbini to their whirl-wind tours of the Buddhist holy places.

Like many places in Nepal, Lumbini is much more enjoyable in early morning and late afternoon, when it's cool and peaceful. If you only see it in the heat of the day, with tour groups and school parties trooping around and the sounds of construction activity emanating from the temples, you'll probably be disap-pointed. For this reason it's highly recommended to stay overnight. A number of expensive resort **hotels**, aimed at tour groups, have sprung up in and around the site, while local lodges in the adjacent villages of Buddha Nagar and Pararia provide a budget alternative.

Getting there

If you're travelling between Kathmandu and India, it's easy enough to stop in Lumbini along the way: the single night-bus from Kathmandu arrives at Lumbini's park gate at 6am, while the single day-bus arrives at dusk; neither take any longer than the buses direct to Sonauli and the border. Coming from anywhere other than Kathmandu, first go to Bhairawa or Sonauli, where you can pick up a **jeep**, either directly on the street or through any travel agent. The fare should be Rs300 one way, and about Rs400 for a return trip with an hour or two's waiting time. As long as you're hiring a vehicle, consider having

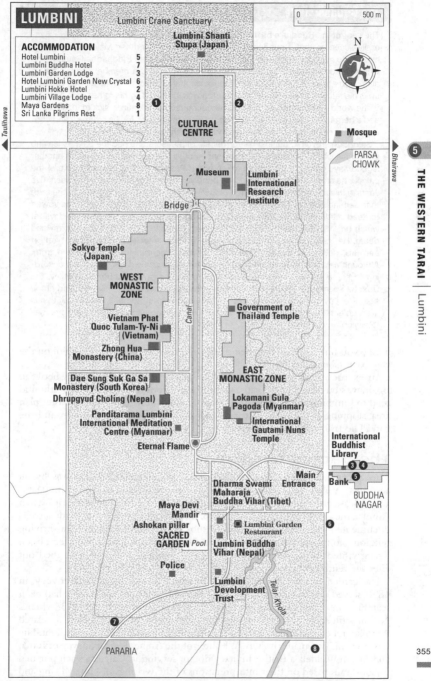

LUMBINI

Lumbini Crane Sanctuary

Lumbini Shanti Stupa (Japan)

0   500 m

N

ACCOMMODATION

Hotel Lumbini	5
Lumbini Buddha Hotel	7
Lumbini Garden Lodge	3
Hotel Lumbini Garden New Crystal	6
Lumbini Hokke Hotel	2
Lumbini Village Lodge	4
Maya Gardens	8
Sri Lanka Pilgrims Rest	1

①   **②**

CULTURAL CENTRE

Mosque

Taulihawa

Bhairawa

PARSA CHOWK

Museum

Lumbini International Research Institute

Bridge

Sokyo Temple (Japan)

WEST MONASTIC ZONE

Canal

Government of Thailand Temple

Vietnam Phat Quoc Tulam-Ty-Ni (Vietnam)

Zhong Hua Monastery (China)

EAST MONASTIC ZONE

Dae Sung Suk Ga Sa Monastery (South Korea)

Dhrupgyud Choling (Nepal)

Panditarama Lumbini International Meditation Centre (Myanmar)

Eternal Flame

Lokamani Gula Pagoda (Myanmar)

International Gautami Nuns Temple

International Buddhist Library

③ **④**

Main Entrance

Bank   **⑤**

BUDDHA NAGAR

Dharma Swami Maharaja Buddha Vihar (Tibet)

Maya Devi Mandir

◻ **Lumbini Garden Restaurant**

Ashokan pillar

SACRED GARDEN   *Pool*

Lumbini Buddha Vihar (Nepal)

⑥

Police

Lumbini Development Trust

Telar Khola

⑦

PARARIA

⑧

▼ *Indian Border*

The Buddha: a life

The year of the Buddha's **birth** is disputed – it was probably 543 BC – but it's generally accepted that it happened at **Lumbini** while his mother, Maya Devi, was on her way to her maternal home for the delivery. He was born Siddhartha Gautam ("he who has accomplished his aim"), the son of a king and a member of the Shakya clan, who ruled the central Tarai from their capital at Tilaurakot (see p.360). Brought up in his father's palace, Prince Siddhartha was sheltered by his father from the evils of the world, until, at the age of 29, he encountered an old man, a sick man, a corpse and a hermit: old age, sickness and death were the end of life, he realized, and contemplation seemed the only way to understand the nature of suffering.

Siddhartha revolted against his former life of pleasure and fled the palace, leaving behind his wife, child and faithful servant – not to mention his horse, which another legend says promptly died of a broken heart. Passing through the east gate of the palace, he shaved his head and donned the yellow robe of an ascetic. He spent five years in this role before concluding that self-denial brought him no closer to the truth than self-indulgence. Under the famous *bodhi* tree of Bodh Gaya in India, he vowed to keep meditating until he attained **enlightenment**. This he did after 49 days, at which time Siddhartha became the Buddha, released from the cycle of birth and death. He made his way to Sarnath (near Varanasi in India) and preached his **first sermon**, setting in motion, Buddhists believe, *dharma*, the wheel of the truth. Although he's said to have returned to Kapilvastu to convert his family, and according to some stories he even put in an appearance in the Kathmandu Valley, the Buddha spent most of the rest of his life preaching in northern India. He **died** at the age of eighty in Kushinagar, about 100km southeast of Lumbini, saying "all things are subject to decay. Strive earnestly." For a fuller account of Buddhism, see "Religion" in Contexts.

it take you first to Tilaurakot (see p.360) and then drop you in Lumbini on the way back (about Rs1200).

An excruciatingly slow local **minibus** (every 30min; 1hr) shuttles between Bhairawa's bus station (you can also pick it up from the start of the westbound road to Lumbini), and Pararia, the village immediately south of the master plan area, stopping at the main east gate and Buddha Nagar on its way round the park. The last bus back is at 5pm.

The Sacred Garden

The **Sacred Garden**, where the Buddha was reputedly born, was by all accounts a well-tended grove in his day. It was consecrated soon after his death, and at least one monastery was attached to it by the third century BC when Ashoka, the great North Indian emperor and Buddhist evangelist, made a well-documented pilgrimage to the spot. Ashoka's patronage established a thriving religious community, but by the time the intrepid Chinese traveller Hiuen Tsang visited in the seventh century it was limping, and must have died out after the tenth century.

The garden was lost for at least six hundred years, and its **rediscovery**, in 1896, solved one of the last great mysteries of the Orient. Europeans had been searching in earnest for the site since 1830, but it wasn't until 1893, when a Nepali officer on a hunting expedition claimed to have found a related Ashokan relic some miles to the west, that the first solid clue came to light. The race was on. Two main rivals, A.A. Führer of the Archeological Survey of India, and Austin Waddell, a British military doctor serving in Calcutta, each pursued various trails based on their interpretations of the writings of Hiuen Tsang and other early pilgrims to Lumbini. In the end, the site was found more by chance than by science. In 1896, Führer's Nepali escort, General Khadga Shamsher Jung Bahadur Rana, suggested they rendezvous in Pararia before proceeding to the intended dig site. While awaiting Führer's arrival, the general was led by locals to an ancient pillar near the village and had his peons begin excavating it. The pillar was already known to at least one British official in the area, who had investigated its visible inscriptions and dismissed them as "mediaeval scribblings", but no one had ever bothered to dig below the surface. When Führer saw the much older inscription revealed by General Rana's excavations, he immediately recognized the pillar as the one described by the early travellers, and claimed credit for the find in his reports. Although he was later stripped of his credentials for his falsifications, he continues to be known as the discoverer of Lumbini.

The Maya Devi Mandir and sculpture

Centrepiece of the Sacred Garden, the **Maya Devi Mandir** contains brickwork dating back to 300 BC, making it the oldest known structure in Nepal. Unfortunately, a major restoration project has reduced it to a pile of bricks that's barely visible under another layer of bricks, piled on to protect the original ones. The whole thing is cordoned off under an ugly tin roof, spoiling the harmony of the entire garden. The plan is to put everything back together again with portions of each layer left exposed to illustrate the original structure's 800-year architectural evolution, but this probably won't happen for years.

Excavations done in the course of the restoration confirmed earlier speculation that the known Gupta-period (fourth to sixth centuries AD) temple sat atop foundations from the earlier Kushana and Maurya periods. In fact, the lowest foundation seems to indicate a **pre-stupa structure** of a kind that existed at the time of the Buddha, suggesting that the site was venerated well before Ashoka's visit and adding further weight to Lumbini's claim as the Buddha's birthplace. Near the lowest level, archeologists also found a reddish-brown, 70cm-long stone that some believe is the "**marker stone**" that Ashoka is reputed to have placed at the precise location of the Buddha's birth.

The excavation and restoration of the Maya Devi Mandir has been something of a botched chapter in the annals of archeology. The project, launched in 1990, was originally conceived as a simple "renovation", which was supposed to mean trimming back a large **pipal tree** whose roots had been interfering with the temple for many years. But with little public consultation, the Japan Buddhist Federation, the organization leading the effort, unilaterally launched a full-scale excavation and cut down the tree, which had been regarded by many as a living link with the Buddha's day.

The temple derives its name from Maya Devi, the Buddha's mother, for until its restoration it housed a famous bas-relief **sculpture** depicting her and the newborn Buddha in the Mathura style (fourth or fifth century AD). The sculpture is currently housed in a small building nearby, though there are plans to restore it to the temple site, sheltered under a golden roof. So worn are the sculpture's features, due to the flaky quality of the sedimentary stone used to make it, that archeologists at first dismissed it as Hindu because locals were worshipping the image as the wish-fulfilling goddess Rumindei (believed to be a corruption of "Lumbini Devi"). A recent replica reconstructs the tableau: Maya Devi grasping a branch of the flowering *saal* tree for support, a tiny Buddha standing fully formed at her feet, and (ecumenical, this) the Hindu gods Indra and Brahma looking on. The sculpture illustrates an elaborate

Buddhist nativity story, according to which the baby Buddha leapt out of the womb, took seven steps and proclaimed his world-saving destiny.

The Ashokan pillar and other remains

West of the temple, the **Ashokan pillar** is the oldest monument in Nepal. It's not much to look at – it resembles a smokestack – but the inscription (also Nepal's oldest), recording Ashoka's visit in 249 BC, is the best available evidence that the Buddha was born here. Split by lightning sometime before the seventh century, its two halves are held together by metal bands. Pillars were a sort of trademark of Ashoka, serving the dual purpose of spreading the faith and marking the boundaries of his empire: this one announces that the king granted Lumbini tax-free status in honour of the Buddha's birth. The carved capital to this pillar, which early pilgrims such as Hiuen Tsang describe as being in the shape of a horse, has never been found; the weathered stone lying on the ground beside the pillar is the lotus- or bell-shaped "bracket" upon which it would have rested.

The square, cement-lined **pool** just south of the Ashokan pillar is supposed to be where Maya Devi bathed before giving birth to the Buddha. Heavily restored **brick foundations** of buildings and stupas around the site, dating from the second century BC to the tenth century AD, chart the rise and fall of Lumbini's early monastic community. The two mounds north and south of the garden – unhappily crowned by an irrelevant brick pillar and four giant plastic water butts – aren't ancient, they're archeological debris removed during amateur excavations in the 1930s led by Field Marshal Kesar Shamsher Rana.

The Tibetan and Nepali monasteries

Two active monasteries face the Sacred Garden and are open to the public; neither is tremendously old, and like all buildings not sanctioned by the master plan they're slated for eventual demolition (it's looking increasingly unlikely that anyone will enforce this, though). The **Dharma Swami Maharaja Buddha Vihar**, a Tibetan monastery established by the well-known lama Chogye Trichen Rinpoche and financed by the king of Mustang, displays a typical array of prematurely aged frescoes and gilded Buddhas and *bodhisattva* in glass cabinets. It provides a winter residence for up to fifty monks from Chogye Trichen's monastery in Boudha, who can be heard chanting in the early morning and mid-afternoon; only a skeleton crew stays on during the hot months.

The Theravada **Lumbini Buddha Vihar**, or "Nepali monastery", offers less to look at, but its solitary gold-robed monk, the Venerable Vimalananda, speaks good English and is interesting to talk to. Built by the government of Nepal, the monastery has the feel of something designed by an international committee, with an eclectic mix of Newar woodwork, Burmese and Thai images and Tibetan-style paintings. You can stay and eat in the monastery's guest wing for a small donation.

Around the master plan area

A walk northwards from the Sacred Garden, pleasant for its own sake in the cool of an evening, hits the highlights of the slowly unfurling master plan. An elevated path passes through what's supposed to be a reflecting pool encircling the Sacred Garden, and beyond burns an **eternal flame**, a symbolic remembrance of the "Light of Asia".

From here you can follow the kilometre-long central canal past the East

(Theravada) and West (Mahayana) **Monastic Zones**, where 41 plots have been set aside for temples and monasteries representing each of Buddhism's major sects and national styles of worship. At least half a dozen have already been built, some of them quite impressive – the Burmese (Myanmar) **Lokamani Gula Pagoda**, done in the style of Rangoon's famous Shwedagon temple, and the Chinese **Zong Hua Monastery**, a sort of mini-Forbidden City featuring a big Buddha statue, are highlights. There seems to be more than a bit of religious one-upmanship going on here, and the area may someday turn into a Buddhist Disneyland, but it's still interesting to see so many different manifestations of Buddhism assembled in one place.

The canal ends at what is being billed as Lumbini's **Cultural Centre**, which at the time of writing was decidedly lacking in culture, or for that matter, any sign of life at all. The tubular buildings of the Japanese-built **Lumbini International Research Institute** and an aimless, half-empty **museum** (Mon & Wed–Sun 10am–5pm, Fri closes at 3pm; free) are in place, while the planned restaurants and shops remain stubbornly on paper. If you can find one – try asking at the research institute – it's well worth hooking up with one of the Lumbini Development Trust's archeologists, who sometimes freelance as guides.

North of the Cultural Centre, the white-and-gold **Lumbini Shanti Stupa** soars 41m over the parkland. The impressive monument was finally completed in November 2001 by Nippozan Myohoji, an endearing Japanese Buddhist organization that's also responsible for the so-called Peace Pagoda in London's Battersea Park, as well as seventy other stupas round the world. Beyond, the **Lumbini Crane Sanctuary** is one of the last refuges of the beautiful sarus crane, the world's tallest flying bird, and one of its most endangered. About thirty of Nepal's 200–300 sarus cranes reside here, along with storks, egrets and other arboreal birds. The Lumbini master plan area is itself something of a bird sanctuary, thanks to its wetlands and forests, with 165 species recorded.

Practicalities

Lumbini's **accommodation** is spread thinly over a wide area. The pleasant village of Buddha Nagar (also known as Mahilwar), strung along a side road near the main eastern gate, offers a cluster of simple guesthouses, while a number of luxury hotels have recently opened both inside and outside the park. To really get close to the spirit of the area, stay in one of the **monasteries**: the Nepali (Theravada), Korean and Tibetan monasteries shelter pilgrims informally for a modest donation but are sorely lacking in things like bedding. You may be invited to join the monks (or nuns) for meals.

The only sources of **food** around the Sacred Garden area are *Lumbini Garden Restaurant*, which charges rather a lot for unexceptional tourist and Indian dishes, and a grass-shack eatery in the Nepali monastery compound, which serves much simpler, cheaper fare. Nepal-Bank of Ceylon, located in Buddha Nagar, on the corner of the main road, has **foreign exchange** facilities.

Accommodation

Hotel Lumbini Buddha Nagar ☎071/80142. Clean and well kept, with a restful atmosphere. All rooms are en suite. ❸

Lumbini Buddha Hotel South of the Sacred Garden ☎071/80114, ✉lumbinibh@mail.com.np. Lovely, peaceful location in a shady grove not too far from the Sacred Garden. Rooms have fans and

attached baths with hot water, and there are also a few dorm beds (Rs400). The small restaurant has a short, simple tourist menu. ❻

Lumbini Garden Lodge Buddha Nagar ☎071/80146. Plain but pleasant rooms with shared bath. Posters to brighten things up, and a small garden. ❷

Tilaurakot and around

The ruins of **TILAURAKOT**, 24km west of Lumbini, are believed to be the remains of ancient **Kapilvastu**, seat of the ancient Shakya kingdom and the childhood home of Prince Siddhartha Gautam. Tilaurakot gets far fewer visitors than Lumbini, yet its ruins are at least as interesting, and its history arguably even more so. Shaded by mango, *kusum* and *karma* trees, they have a serenity that Lumbini has begun to lose.

Admission to the **excavation** site is free, and the lonely guards will probably be happy to give you a tour around the grounds (donation expected). Among the visible remains are a couple of stupa bases, thick fortress walls and four gates. Looking out across the ruins from the **eastern gate** could hardly be a better place for a moment's meditation, as it's said to be from here that the Buddha walked out on nearly thirty years of princely life to begin his search for enlightenment. It's doubtful that this is literally the ruins of the palace of King Suddhodana, the Buddha's father, for the style of bricks used aren't thought to have been developed until the third century BC, but it may well have been built on top of it; assuming the earlier structure was made of wood, no trace of it would remain. Indian archeologists argue that Piprahwa, just south of the border, is the true site, but excavations at Tilaurakot in 2000 uncovered potsherds and terracotta beads contemporaneous with Buddha's lifetime, helping to corroborate the Nepalese claim.

A small **museum** (Mon & Wed–Sun 10am–5pm, Fri closes 3pm; Rs15), opposite the start of the side road to the Tilaurakot site, displays some of the three thousand coins found in the area (including one bearing the Shakya name), together with Lumbini and Kapilvastu pottery spanning three distinct periods and a thousand years. Even older pottery discovered in caves near Jomosom, high in the Himalaya, is for some reason also displayed here.

Other archeological sites

Tilaurakot is only one of several archeological sites dating to the time of the Buddha scattered in the countryside surrounding Taulihawa. Some Buddhists make a pilgrimage circuit of the whole lot, but this is only practical in a vehicle rented in Bhairawa (driven by someone who knows the way to all the sites). **Niglihawa**, 10km northeast of Taulihawa, is the location of a broken Ashokan pillar associated with one of the mythical Buddhas of a previous age. **Sagarhawa**, 5km further to the northwest, contains an ancient water tank identified as the site of a notorious Shakya massacre. The Ashokan pillar and brick stupa at **Gotihawa**, 6km south of Taulihawa, commemorate another previous Buddha, while the *pokhari* at **Kudan**, 2km southwest of Taulihawa, is said to be where the Buddha returned after his enlightenment to preach the *dharma* to his father and young son.

Practicalities

The easiest way to get to Tilaurakot is by **jeep** from Sonauli or Bhairawa (Rs1200 or so return, depending on waiting time), which enables you to hit Lumbini en route. Don't get locked into a rushed half-day tour of Lumbini and Tilaurakot, though – negotiate plenty of waiting time, and consider staying over at Lumbini on the way back. Getting there by public transport, you're stuck with the irregular **minibuses** (roughly hourly; 1hr) which make their way from Bhairawa to **Taulihawa**, 22km beyond Lumbini on the same road; you can flag these down at Lumbini's Parsa Chowk, but don't expect to get a seat. From the centre of Taulihawa, rikshas are usually available to take you the last 3km along the main (paved) northbound road to an obvious intersection where the museum is on the left and a paved road on the right leads 400m to the site. If you've got a bicycle you could pedal on the paved road from Lumbini to Tilaurakot in less than two hours.

Basic **food** is available at Taulihawa. If you get stuck, you can **stay** at *New Siddhartha Guest House* (❶) or a couple of other Nepali inns a short distance north of the town centre along the road to Tilaurakot.

The Far West

Until recently, the sheer misery of travelling the Mahendra Highway was enough to deter all but the most dedicated from entering Nepal's remote **far west**. Now, with the highway completed, this once-neglected quarter of the country is opening its doors to travellers. It's still a hell of a haul to get here from Kathmandu, but Delhi is just twelve hours by bus from the far western border crossing, and the smooth, fast road between the two passes two of the richest wildlife parks in Nepal, **Bardia National Park** and **Sukla Phanta Wildlife Reserve**. The partly Muslim city of **Nepalganj** is the largest city in the west, and the hub for all flights to remoter airstrips. The Mahendra Highway makes good time to Nepalganj, 250km west of Butwal, crossing the Duduwa Hills (350m ascent) and following the green and pleasant valley of the Rapti River (no relation to the river of the same name in Chitwan). North of here lies Dang, home of the white-clad Dangaura Tharus and fine cycling country. The last 40km to Kohalpur, the turning for Nepalganj and Birendra Nagar, passes through the Kusum–Ilaka forest, which is being eyed as a potential extension area of Bardia National Park.

Nepalganj

Industrial and transport hub of the far west – for what little industry and transport there is in the far west – **NEPALGANJ** is, more interestingly, Nepal's

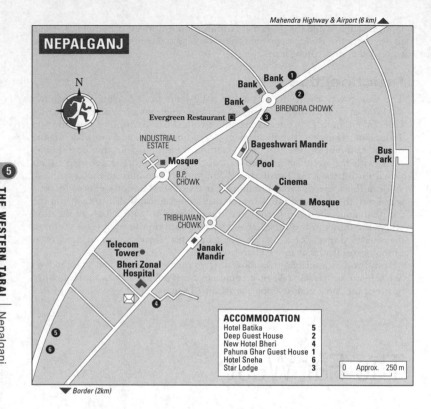

N

Bank
Bank 1
Bank 2
BIRENDRA CHOWK
Evergreen Restaurant 3

INDUSTRIAL
ESTATE
Mosque
B.P.
CHOWK

Bageshwari Mandir
Pool

Bus
Park

Cinema

Mosque

TRIBHUWAN
CHOWK

Telecom
Tower
Bheri Zonal
Hospital

Janaki
Mandir

4

5

6

ACCOMMODATION

Hotel Batika	5
Deep Guest House	2
New Hotel Bheri	4
Pahuna Ghar Guest House	1
Hotel Sneha	6
Star Lodge	3

0   Approx.   250 m

▼ Border (2km)

most Muslim city. The presence of Muslims in the Tarai is hardly surprising, of course, since the border with India, where Muslims comprise a significant minority, was only determined in the nineteenth century. Until just prior to the 1814–16 war with the British, this part of the Tarai belonged to the Nawab of Oudh, one of India's biggest landowners; after Nepal's defeat it was ceded to the East India Company and only returned to Nepal as a goodwill gesture for services rendered during the Indian Mutiny of 1857. A fair few Muslims fled to Nepalganj during the revolt – Lucknow, where the most violent incidents occurred, is due south of here – and others filtered in during the Rana years, seeing chances for cross-border trade. The resulting permanent Muslim community is self-contained, but maintains business and family links with India. Indeed, the entire city feels overwhelmingly Indian, with its cheap neo-Mughal architecture and frenetically mundane bazaar.

In the heart of the sprawl is **Tribhuwan Chowk**, the lively but dilapidated intersection of the city's two main shopping thoroughfares, south of which the Indian-style Janaki Mandir that sits in the middle of the road like a toll booth. The **Muslim quarter** lies northeast of Tribhuwan Chowk – picturesque is probably too strong a word, but it's worth a wander if you've never been to India. The mosques in this area are disappointingly modern, though, and at any rate out-of-bounds to nonbelievers. Hindu worship and trade is centred around the nondescript but active **Bageshwari Mandir**; behind the temple is a large pool with a jaunty statue of Mahadev (Shiva) in the middle – marvellously kitsch. Shrines across the lane from the Bageshwari entrance are to Shiva and Bhairab.

The **bus park** has been inconveniently banished to the extreme northeast end of the city, and it might be a good idea to buy an onward ticket when you arrive to avoid the extra trip later on. You can change money at a number of **banks** on the main road either side of Birendra Chowk.

Accommodation

Hardly anybody sets out to see Nepalganj, but a few people heading further west end up spending an unintended night here. If you're flying to any of the far-western airstrips there'll be a change in Nepalganj and, all too often, some problem or other with the onward flight.

Hotel Batika South of the centre ☎081/21360. Professional, well-run place with decent rooms, some with a/c. Attractive grounds, with a small, intermittently operational pool. ⑤

Deep Guest House Near Birendra Chowk ☎081/20818. Insulated by a row of shops from the worst of the street noise. Relatively smart for the price, with some decent "deluxe", air-conditioned rooms as well as plainer ones with fans. ②–④

New Hotel Bheri Near Bheri Zonal Hospital ☎081/20213, ⑨21618. Homely, restful hotel in a quiet, clean location, arranged around a small shady garden. Has some air-conditioned rooms. ⑤

Pahuna Ghar Guest House Near Birendra Chowk ☎081/22358. Fairly clean and businesslike, but the location on the noisy main road is ugly. ①

Hotel Sneha South of the centre ☎081/20487, ⑧hotel@sneha.wlink.com.np. Has a whiff of the Raj: secluded grounds and a classy feel. Musty but well-fitted out rooms, with and without a/c. ⑥

Star Lodge Near Birendra Chowk ☎081/22257. One of the friendlier and better-swept hotels in the bazaar, but it's still fairly dark and dank. ①

Eating

Nepalganj's busiest **eating** area is around Birendra Chowk, where scores of *dhaba* keep curries simmering in pots, cafeteria-style – just ask them to lift lids to see what's on the go. In this area and around Tribhuwan Chowk you'll also find many places serving basic *daal bhaat* as well as a few sweet-shops. In the evenings, vendors in the bazaar dish up curd and *raabri*, a local speciality made from sweetened cream flavoured with cardamom and saffron. For anything more formal you're best off trying the *Evergreen Restaurant*, 200m south of Birendra Chowk, or eating in your hotel: *New Punjabi* hotel's restaurant looks unenticing, but the Indian-style food is good; for Western food, try the *Sneha* or *Batika* hotels.

Moving on

Westbound **bus** services are reasonably frequent, and depart from the main road north of the bus park. Only a handful of buses head east, and they nearly all travel at night because of the distances involved. See p.377 for a rundown of express routes, and consider flying. **Motorcycles** can also be rented for about Rs400 per day.

Two local buses leave at around 12.30 and 2.30pm for Thakurdwara and Bardia National Park, but they take an interminable four hours. Renting a ratty, old, canvas-sided jeep with room for three or four passengers plus luggage will cut the journey time by almost half, and should cost no more than Rs2500 for the trip to Bardia, including fuel, though you'll likely be quoted more. Vehicles can be usually arranged through any of the better hotels or directly from where they wait on the main road southwest of B.P. Chowk. Best of all, arrange for a jeep from any Bardia lodge to meet you at Nepalganj airport.

Nepalganj is the hub for all **flights** in Nepal's western region, including those to trekking regions such as Jumla, Simikot, Bajhang or Dolpo. Travel details (p.377) lists flight info, but be aware that at the time of writing, Maoist activity had recently caused many routes to close temporarily. Almost every private airline flies the Kathmandu–Nepalganj route at least daily, and RNAC (☎081/20239) serves the mountain airstrips. During the winter trekking season, private airlines often run **charter** services to the mountain airstrips over and above the scheduled flights listed. RNAC also flies weekly to the far western border towns of Mahendra Nagar and Dhangadhi, but at the time of writing these flights went via mountain airstrips and were unreliable. All the airlines have offices around Birendra Chowk or B.P. Chowk, but there's no need to go to them – have your hotel make the booking. The **airport** is 6km north of town and is reachable by shared tempo or riksha.

The **border crossing** of Jamunaha, 5km south of Birendra Chowk, is open to tourists; get there by cycle riksha. There's nothing at the border besides immigration and customs offices. Buses connect Rupaidia, the town on the Indian side of the border, with Lucknow (7hr).

Bardia National Park and Thakurdwara

With Chitwan becoming increasingly mass-market, **BARDIA NATIONAL PARK**, northwest of Nepalganj and the largest area of undisturbed wilderness left in the Tarai, beckons as an unspoiled alternative. Budget lodging is available, but there's nothing like the commercialism of Chitwan. Indeed, if this description oversells the comparisons, it's because Bardia has everything Chitwan has except the crowds: in 1999, 78,000 people visited Chitwan, while just 3,300 visited Bardia. As the word gets out about Bardia, transport connections are getting easier and facilities more comfortable, but the park's distance from Kathmandu will shield it from the masses for many years to come. At the time of writing, Bardia was one of many areas with a significant **Maoist** presence (see p.498). As everywhere, this is unlikely to affect visitors other than in

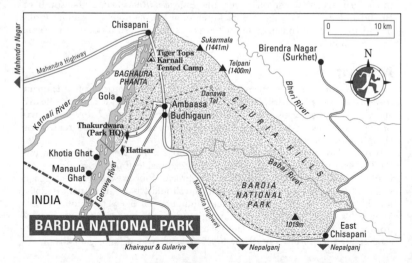

the shape of police roadblocks, which may increase journey times, and a scarcity of alcohol. However, you may just meet the odd curious communist asking a few questions.

In 2001, the government announced a huge eastward **extension of Bardia** that will increase the park's area by half as much again to nearly 1500 square kilometres, but it'll be some years before this affects visitors. At present, virtually all of Bardia's lodgings are within walking distance of the park headquarters at **Thakurdwara**, 12km off the highway in a game-rich corner of the park near the Geruwa River.

Ecologically, Bardia spans an even greater range of habitats than Chitwan, from thick riverine forest and *sal* stands to *phanta* (isolated pockets of savanna) and dry upland slopes. The **Geruwa**, a branch of the awesome **Karnali River**, forms the park's western boundary and major watering hole, and the density of wildlife and birds along this western edge is as great as anywhere in Asia. The **Babai River** drains the core area to the east of Thakurdwara, forming a sanctuary-like *dun* valley teeming with game, but it is out of bounds to visitors.

Like Chitwan, Bardia is widely hailed as a conservation success story. **Rhinos**, hunted to extinction here in the early twentieth century, were reintroduced in the mid-1980s and now number at least fifty. Many were quickly lost to poaching, but they have been progressively replaced by 48 others, all translocated from Chitwan at vast expense; there are about enough for most visitors to see one. Bardia is also home to around seventy **tigers**, but you'll be lucky to get a sighting – it's said that a tiger is a hundred times more likely to see you than you are to see it. Because of the park's remoteness, and minimal human disturbance, tiger experts regard it as the most promising place in Nepal in which to maintain a viable breeding population. For the same reasons, the park has also become an important sanctuary for migratory **wild elephants** of western Nepal and adjacent portions of India, and around thirty animals spend at least part of the year here. One of them, a docile tusker known to locals as Raja Gaj, stands 11 feet 3 inches (3.4m) at the shoulder and is believed to be the biggest Asian elephant alive.

The Geruwa is one of the few places anywhere where you may be able to get a peep at rare **gangetic dolphins**; a half dozen or so still survive in the river's deep channels, and some are thought to migrate from the Indian side during the monsoon. You can also fish for huge **mahseer**. By 1989, the mugger and gharial **crocodile** populations in the river were reduced to less than a dozen of each species, but a successful project to release juveniles raised from hatchlings means they can now be easily spotted in winter. Five species of **deer** – spotted, sambar, hog, barking and swamp – can be seen in abundance, along with **langurs** and **wild pig**. **Nilgai** ("blue bull"), bovine-looking members of the antelope family, roam the drier upland areas, while a few dozen graceful, corkscrew-horned **blackbuck** (featured on the back of Nepal's ten-rupee note) are just about surviving in an unprotected grassland area south of the park. More elusive are sloth bear, leopard and other nocturnal creatures, as well as the endangered hispid hare, which survives in Bardia's grasslands. The park is also home to nearly 400 bird species, three of which – the Bengal florican, the lesser florican and the sarus crane – are endangered. The commonest sight of all around Bardia are **termite mounds**, looking like sand-coloured volcanoes, which reach their greatest height – up to 2.5m – in the *sal* forest here.

Thakurdwara

A sleepy collection of Tharu farming settlements, **THAKURDWARA** is archetypal Tarai. The main centre is a kind of village green where local buses stop, encircled by a small bazaar known locally as the "mandir" because of its temple. Most visitors never need stray this far from the park headquarters, however, which lie about 1km north of the bazaar at the centre of a straggle of roads sparsely dotted with local homes and mud guesthouses. There are no other tourist facilities, and precious few even for locals – farmhouses and guesthouses alike use lanterns after dark.

The small mandir near the bus stop serves as the focus of activities for a modest *mela* (religious fair) held on the first day of the month of Magh (mid-Jan). A few other park-related points of interest are scattered in and around the leafy headquarters compound, but most of the action is inside the park. In short, it's a lot like Sauraha was in the good old days: quiet, remote and adventurous.

Tourism will inevitably change Thakurdwara, but conservationists are already taking steps to ensure it doesn't repeat Sauraha's mistakes, and the King Mahendra Trust (see box on p.370) is working on ways to help local people literally make money from the park.

Getting there

From Kathmandu, the quickest and easiest way to get to Thakurdwara and Bardia is to **fly** to Nepalganj and travel the rest of the way by jeep (2hr 30min). This is standard procedure for the more expensive package tours of Bardia, but you can do the same thing independently. Even if you don't want to spend the money on the flight, consider renting a **jeep** in Nepalganj or Mahendra Nagar. Besides making for a more comfortable journey and greater flexibility, the vehicle will enable you to explore the park more fully (see "Jeep rides", p.371).

The next-quickest, but by no means easiest, way to get to Bardia **from Kathmandu or Pokhara** is to take a night bus bound for Dhangadhi or Mahendra Nagar, getting off at Ambaasa, the tea-shack turning for Thakurdwara. This is a hell of a way to come – aside from the usual miseries of night travel, it's hard not to fret about missing the stop in the dark, despite the reliability of the ticket-boys, since night buses pass Ambaasa between 3 and 6am.

If you have the time, it's far more relaxing to take a **day bus**, and overnight in Lumbini (see p.353) on the way. Day buses from Butwal, Nepalganj, Dhangadhi and Mahendra Nagar pass Ambaasa on their way to other destinations, and direct local services to Thakurdwara originate in Nepalganj. Night buses heading eastwards from Mahendra Nagar or Dhangadhi should also get you to Ambaasa before dark. Guesthouse jeeps don't normally wait at Ambaasa in the afternoon, but you can call ahead to request a ride.

Guesthouse jeeps do wait at Ambaasa specifically for the arrival of prospective pre-dawn guests, ready to ferry them the final 12km to Thakurdwara. You'll get a free ride if you stay in their guesthouse for a couple of nights, otherwise it's a rather steep Rs500 flat fee. If you feel more comfortable booking ahead, ring one of the guesthouses directly or arrange it through a travel agent in Kathmandu or Pokhara. If you pay the first night in advance at an aligned travel agent, most places will guarantee a jeep is waiting for you, and will even pick you up from Nepalganj. At present there's no phone service at Ambaasa but lines are expected to be installed within the near future; until they are, you can call from Budhigaun, 5km east of Ambaasa, and wait to be picked up there. A requested jeep ride is "free" if you stay at the guesthouse that's providing it, though as usual this will translate into a higher room price. Alternatively, catch one of the local buses to Thakurdwara; they pass through Budhigaun at around 4 and 7pm. The Thakurdwara bus stop is a long walk from most lodgings, though, and if it's after dark you'll probably have no choice but to let yourself

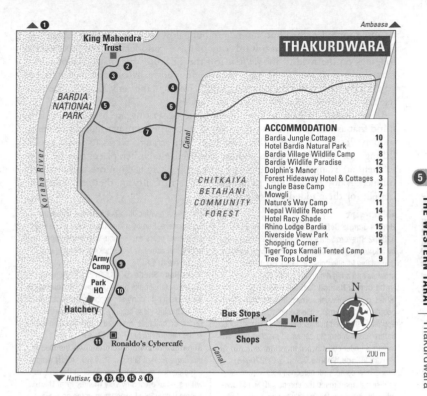

THAKURDWARA

BARDIA
NATIONAL
PARK

Koraba River

Canal

King Mahendra
Trust

CHITKAIYA
BETAHANI
COMMUNITY
FOREST

Army
Camp

Park
HQ

Hatchery

Ronaldo's Cybercafé

Bus Stops

Shops

Mandir

N

0   200 m

ACCOMMODATION

Bardia Jungle Cottage	10
Hotel Bardia Natural Park	4
Bardia Village Wildlife Camp	8
Bardia Wildlife Paradise	12
Dolphin's Manor	13
Forest Hideaway Hotel & Cottages	3
Jungle Base Camp	2
Mowgli	7
Nature's Way Camp	11
Nepal Wildlife Resort	14
Hotel Racy Shade	6
Rhino Lodge Bardia	15
Riverside View Park	16
Shopping Corner	5
Tiger Tops Karnali Tented Camp	1
Tree Tops Lodge	9

▼ Hattisar, ⑫, ⑬, ⑭, ⑮ & ⑯

be guided by a guesthouse tout. A stream crossing between Ambaasa and Thakurdwara may be impassable during and immediately after heavy rain, but if so, your guesthouse will get you across somehow if they know you're coming.

All of the information above may become `redundant if plans to tarmac the road to Ambaasa come to fruition, in which case tourist buses are likely to ply the route direct from Kathmandu and Pokhara.

Finally, without a doubt the most enjoyable way to get to Bardia is by **raft** down the Karnali River (see p.466). Most commercial trips on the Karnali include the option of finishing up with two or more nights at a Bardia lodge.

Accommodation

If you're picking up a jeep in Ambaasa, you may not have too much choice about where you spend your first night or two. Don't worry: most **lodges** are very similar, and they're all acceptable. Pioneered in (and steadily disappearing from) Sauraha, the formula is simple: mud-and-thatch huts arranged around a garden, with a simple dining pavilion serving *daal bhaat* and approximations of Western dishes. A few places have more hotel-like concrete bungalows, which have as many drawbacks – like being ugly, damp and airless – as advantages, and some have solar-heated water. Atmosphere comes mainly from a lodge's guests, or the lack of them; you'll quickly get a feel for who's staying where. Most **budget lodges** offer a choice of huts with attached bathrooms for a standard Rs350, or with a shared toilet/shower block for Rs250. A couple of the local places will go below this price, but they're not supposed to. You may pay a little more for a detached hut, a concrete bungalow or an established reputation. Tour agents may push you towards one of three considerably more **expensive** lodgings on the road to the *hattisar* (off the Thakurdwara map), any of which may also rent rooms by the night to anyone who really can't stand thatch, but you'll have to negotiate your own price. *Tiger Tops*, the only lodge in the park itself, is well worth it if you've got the money.

All the lodges in Thakurdwara at the time of writing are listed, but bear in mind that as visitor numbers are so small, places here are particularly prone to sudden closure. All except the most basic can arrange access to jeeps, cycles, fishing rods, guides, elephants and the like. Well-established places may be more efficient at arranging activities, but they're also likely to be more commercially minded. Many lodges offer **packages**, but as in Chitwan, these provide little benefit for their added cost (see p.328).

Budget

Bardia Jungle Cottage ☎084/29714 or 01/428552. Thakurdwara's original budget lodge, run by a knowledgeable former assistant park warden. Unbeatable location near the Park HQ, lovely grounds and a big dining area. ❷–❹

Hotel Bardia Natural Park ☎084/29722, ✉nat_park@npj.wlink.com.np. Run by local Tharu people, this is a small collection of fairly well-appointed thatched huts, some with smart attached bathrooms. A mosquito-screened *machan* (watchtower) is under construction in the grounds. ❷–❸

Bardia Village Wildlife Camp ☎01/370818. Brand-new camp, with detached huts spread generously far apart round the compound. The knowledgeable owner caters mostly to tour groups. ❸

Bardia Wildlife Paradise ☎084/29715. On the road to the *hattisar*, 1km south of Park HQ. A small place, somewhat lacking in shade and rather far from the action, though it's close to the river. ❷

Forest Hideaway Hotel & Cottages ☎084/29716, ✉hideaway@forest.wlink.com.np. Long-established lodge with excellent leafy grounds and rooms with or without shared bathroom. Management is somewhat brusque, but staff are friendly and it's usually full of travellers. Price includes breakfast, but even so it's relatively expensive. ❸–❹

Jungle Base Camp ☎061/31691, ⌨www.geocities.com/junglebasecamp. Small, friendly and well-run lodge with a few quirky touches, like a thatched dining terrace accessed across a tiny moat by two baby bridges. There's a choice of adjoining rooms with shared bathrooms, or a couple of mud cottages with attached bathrooms and attractive extras such as floor cushions. ❷

Mowgli (no phone). A few rustic, Tharu-owned huts with a bucket for a shower; you'd never know it was a guesthouse if you weren't told. ❶

Nature's Way Camp (no phone). On the road to the *hattisar*, 200m south of Park HQ. Tiny family

place with few facilities but a unique and warm atmosphere. Run by a legendary local guide with seventeen years experience, who discourages un-ecological activities like smoking, drinking and eating meat. ❷

Hotel Racy Shade ☎084/29722, ✉shreepd @yahoo.com. Funky place popular with long-term travellers for its party atmosphere. Perhaps this is why it's a little less smartly kept than others. Detached cottages are more expensive than rooms in the semi-detached huts. ❷–❸

Riverside View Park (no phone). On the road to the *hattisar*, 1km south of Park HQ. Utterly simple – the garden still wasn't complete at the time of writing – but owned by very friendly local Tharu people with a lot of experience in the park. ❷

Shopping Corner (no phone). Two small rooms in a lean-to against a family home beside the village shop. Utterly basic, but the owners are friendly and the sons have guiding experience. ❶

Tree Tops Lodge (no phone). Run by a friendly family, but the brick and concrete bungalows are rather less jungly than most. ❷

Midrange and expensive

Dolphin's Manor ☎01/420308. On the road to the *hattisar*, 1km south of the Park HQ. Unenticing deluxe tents or lifeless stone bungalows. Meals are eaten in a huge banquet hall that's completely out of keeping with local architecture. ❺

Nepal Wildlife Resort ☎01/258492, ⌨http://bardia.hoops.livedoor.com. On the road to the *hattisar*, 500m south of Park HQ. Brand new, rather smart semi-detached concrete bungalows. One of the new generation of expensive tour-group resorts, with reasonable facilities but little atmosphere. ❺

Rhino Lodge Bardia ☎084/29720 or ☎01/418400, ⌨www.nepal-safari.com. Just short of the *hattisar*, 3km south of Park HQ. Nicely decorated, carpeted rooms in locally-styled concrete

chalets. Good facilities, but with a buttoned-up, package-tour feel. ⑤
Tiger Tops Karnali Tented Camp ☎01/411225 or 084/29565, ⓦ www.tigermountain.com. Inside the park, overlooking the Geruwa River, this offers a good, old-fashioned luxury safari experience, with the full range of activities led by experienced guides. Two nights at the tented camp and a third at the affiliated *Karnali Lodge*, just outside the park, costs $585, not including flights. ⑨

Other practicalities

There are no **restaurants** in Thakurdwara, but there are a couple of snack stalls in the bazaar, and another at *Ronaldo's Cybercafé*, near the park headquarters. Most people eat at their own lodge, or drop in at a neighbouring place if it's looking lively. Guesthouses can **change money** informally, but only cash. A few local people, supported by the King Mahendra Trust, make and sell **handicrafts** out of their homes. **International calls** can be made from any guesthouse with a phone, from shops in the bazaar, and from *Ronaldo's*, which also has **internet** connection. Charges are relatively expensive for both. There's a local **health post** and pharmacy near the bus stop, and the nearest hospital is in Nepalganj.

Moving on

The simplest and quickest way to move on from Thakurdwara is to have your guesthouse make your travel arrangements for you. All charge Rs500 for a jeep to Ambaasa (you could split the cost with other travellers), where you can pick up buses heading east and west. Guesthouses can also book seats on **night buses** to Kathmandu and Pokhara, which pass through Ambaasa in the afternoon. They charge a hefty Rs100 or so commission on top of the cost of the bus ticket, but it's well worth paying for a guaranteed seat, and almost impossible to do it yourself.

Making your own way is slower: catch one of the morning **local buses** to Nepalganj (4hr), which leave the bazaar (Thakurdwara) at around 8 and 10am. If you're heading to Pokhara and Kathmandu, take the earlier bus, which gets you in to Nepalganj in plenty of time to book a confirmed seat on a **night bus**, all of which leave Nepalganj in the afternoon. Otherwise, get off at Kohalpur, the turnoff 13km north of Nepalganj, where you can book seats on the day express buses bound for Butwal and destinations east. You should also be able to book a night bus at Kohalpur, but there's less to do while you wait. Heading west, get off at Ambaasa and flag down any bus that's going. You should be able to get to Mahendra Nagar before dark, though you may end up having to change buses at Chisapani or Atariya (the turning for Dhangadhi). Your lodge may also be able to book **plane** tickets out of Nepalganj.

Activities in and around the park

Bardia's menu of activities is similar to Chitwan's; you'll find lengthier descriptions of walks and elephant rides in that section. All **access to the park** is via the main headquarters entrance, crossing the Koraha River from there. Park **entry permits** cost the standard Rs500 per day, you can buy them from the **ticket office** inside the headquarters compound, or have your guesthouse do it for you. The same goes for elephant-ride tickets and vehicle and fishing permits.

While you're at the HQ, stop by the park's reptile **hatchery**, a small, zoo-like facility where gharial and mugger crocodiles are raised from eggs before being released into local waters, and the **Tharu Museum** (daily 10am–4pm; Rs50), which gives a basic introduction to local culture.

Bardia in the balance

Nepal's wildlife parks never sit easily with the inhabitants of nearby villages, who not only are barred from their former woodcutting areas but also must cope with marauding animals. In the case of **Bardia National Park**, the potential for resentment is especially high, because the government has actually reintroduced rhinos to the area, giving local farmers a headache they thought they'd gotten rid of. It's estimated that half the crops in fields adjoining Bardia are damaged by wildlife (primarily rhinos and elephants), and every year sees at least one search for a tiger that has become too old and unfit to hunt, and turned man-eater. A dozen or so locals are killed each year – four people were killed by a single tiger in the spring of 2001 alone, one of them a motorcyclist who was dragged from his bike as he rode along the main east–west (Mahendra) highway, where it passes through the park.

As in Chitwan (see p.336), Bardia's long-term viability depends as much on human factors as ecological ones, and recent initiatives have reflected this. The UNDP-sponsored "**Parks and People Project**", which worked on community development in the "buffer zones" adjoining the park, came to an end in December 2001, but the **King Mahendra Trust for Nature Conservation** will continue many of its initiatives, and between thirty and fifty percent of the National Park's income is spent in the buffer zones. Current projects are aimed at income-generation activities by locals, encouraging efforts to start up hotels, and providing training in guiding, lodge-management and cooking for tourists. Despite such efforts, though, very few local Tharu people work directly in Bardia's tourist trade.

People-centred activities have to be balanced with the needs of wildlife. **Chitkya Community Forest**, along the eastern border of the park, is being managed to allow it to regenerate naturally, providing a source of firewood and increased habitat for animals in the park. Elsewhere, the problem is rather that bushes and trees encroach on the vital grassland needed by deer and tigers, and locals are given controlled access to collect wood.

The largest new project looks set to prioritize the needs of animals over humans. The **Terai Arc Landscape** programme, sponsored by WWF, aims to create "wildlife corridors" linking eleven national parks, including Sukla Phanta, Bardia and Chitwan in Nepal, and Dudhwa and Corbett National Parks in India. Such corridors reflect natural migration patterns, and are seen as vital for maintaining viable breeding populations. In 1994, for example, a large herd of wild elephants migrated from India's Dudhwa National Park to Nepal's Sukla Phanta Wildlife Reserve, and from there along the Churia Hills to Bardia. Less than ten years later, however, deforestation and population growth are closing off this route, and the animals risk being marooned in separate national parks. Wildlife corridors are seen as the only way for animal populations to be able to exchange genes without the aid of trucks and tranquillizer guns.

Walks

Although rhino danger is somewhat lower here than in Chitwan, it would still be extremely foolish to enter the park on foot without a **guide**. Hire one informally though your lodge, or ask who's available at the park office. **Prices** depend on levels of experience, and you'll only find that out by asking around; expect to pay Rs300–400 per person for a half-day, or Rs500–600 for a full day. Although Bardia guides generally speak less English and are less well trained than those at Chitwan, they know the territory and can keep you out of harm's way. See p.340 for jungle safety tips.

As in Chitwan, tall grass restricts visibility and makes jungle walks more dangerous and less satisfying before the thatch is cut in mid-January. Most walks entail wading through some streams, so bring sandals as well as walking shoes. Your guide will be able to suggest routes tailored to your interests. Most walks inside the park take a northerly bearing from Thakurdwara, roughly paralleling the Geruwa River through mixed grassland and jungle. Some of the best rhino habitat, as well as areas favoured by wild elephants, are found in the riverine corridor between Thakurdwara and **Gola**. Tigers, bears, boars, nilgai and (in the river) dolphins may be sighted, and you're assured of seeing deer, monkeys and all manner of birds. The track to **Baghaura Phanta**, about 7km northeast of Thakurdwara, is a prime birdwatching route.

To watch Bardia's hardest-working employees enjoying some down-time, visit the government **hattisar** (elephant stable), outside the park about forty-minutes' walk south of the HQ. Although it's not set up as a breeding centre, this *hattisar* usually has a baby elephant or two in residence, thanks to the nocturnal visits of wild bulls. Remaining outside the park, the road continues southwards along the river past **Manaula Ghat** and **Khotia Ghat**, two of the best places to look for dolphins.

Camping isn't allowed inside the park (except at *Tiger Tops*), which limits the scope for longer hikes. However, guides have developed a two-day trek from Ambaasa to **Danawa Tal** and then up to **Telpani** (1400m), a high point along the crest of the ridge that forms the park's northern boundary, where you can camp out and then return via Chisapani the next day. The route is mostly through *sal* forest – monkeys and deer are the most visible inhabitants, though there's some possibility of seeing rhinos or elephants at Danawa Tal; the view of the Surkhet valley from Telpani is great. This walk is best done in the winter months. Another possibility for a nocturnal experience is to arrange with a guide to sleep out in a **machan** (tower) in Chitka Community Forest; bring a mosquito net.

Elephant rides

You can arrange **elephant rides** yourself at the HQ ticket office, or have your guesthouse do it for you. The **charge** is Rs1000 per person per hour, for up to three hours – longer rides take you deeper into the park and provide more chances to see animals. Rides must be **reserved** the day before, but it may be advisable to book a day or two in advance if there are many other tourists in the village, as only nine rideable elephants are kept here, and not all of them may be on duty on any given day. Departures are in the early morning and late afternoon from a platform at the far end of the HQ compound. The usual route heads west and north from the HQ into mixed jungle and grassland, where you could see (in approximate order of likelihood) deer, langurs, boar, rhino, bears and tigers.

Jeep rides

A **jeep** might or might not increase your chances of surprising game, but it will certainly enable you to penetrate remoter parts of the park where the animals aren't as wary of humans. Inevitably, however, vehicles disturb much of the wildlife you've come to see. Most lodges have their own jeeps, and **prices** begin at Rs2000 for small jeep for a half-day, so it's well worth getting a group together; alternatively, most lodge-owners can book you on a jeep that's already organized – either way, you'll end up paying Rs1000 per person. If you've brought your own hired jeep to Bardia, you'll need to obtain a special permit from Park HQ to enter the park with it (Rs1000 per day).

Most trips are confined to the network of tracks in the park's western sector, which takes you through *sal* forest and the grasslands of **Baghaura Phanta** (where there's a view tower) and gives access to pristine stretches of river and rich wildlife habitat. Given more time you could continue north to Chisapani to look for gharials and dolphins. Note, however, that vehicles can't cross the Koraha River to access this area until mid- or late November. From Ambaasa, you can follow a track eastwards to **Danawa Tal**, a wetland at the base of the foothills where rhinos and elephants are sometimes spotted. The road continues from there into the idyllic Babai valley, where most of Bardia's elephants live, but entrance to this area is currently restricted.

Nepal's only herd of blackbuck antelope congregates around a big *phanta* well south of the park at **Khairapur**, 32km from Thakurdwara by road and most easily reached by vehicle. From Thakurdwara, drive north to Ambaasa, then 3km south along the Mahendra Highway to Budhigaun, and then take the road south from there; look for the herd on your left as you approach Gulariya. Blackbuck were actually thought to be extinct until three were sighted here in 1973; careful management brought their number up to 100–150 by the mid-1980s. Bids to create a separate wildlife reserve here have so far come to nothing, however, and numbers are dropping once more: in 2001 the herd was estimated at just 55 heads.

River trips
Once on the River Geruwa, you've got just as good a chance of seeing dolphins, muggers, monkeys and birds as you would on foot, and you may even be lucky enough to glimpse an elephant or tiger. A couple of lodges have **rafts**, and others will book you on one of them if places are available: for Rs2000 per person you can do a one-day float from Chisapani to the *hattisar*, just before Gola Ghat, a one-hour walk from the ghat takes you to a water-hole where rhino have been regularly seen.

Another option offered by some lodges is a half-day **dugout canoe** ride, costing Rs400–500 per person for a two-person boat and Rs600 for a four-seater. Book at least a day in advance.

Fishing
The Karnali/Geruwa is renowned for its **mahseer**, a sporting fish related to carp that can weigh up to 40kg. If you catch one, release it: the *mahseer* population is declining due to pollution, dams, barriers and a general lack of headwaters protection. The Babai is superb for *mahseer* and *goonch*, another huge fish. Be alert for crocodiles.

Fishing is allowed everywhere on the Karnali and Geruwa rivers (you can fish as part of a raft trip), but on the Babai, it's restricted to the waters below the dam (the Mahendra Highway crossing). You'll need a **fishing permit**, which costs Rs300 per day and can be obtained from the ticket office at Park HQ. *Bardia Jungle Cottage* rents fishing gear, but if you're at all interested in angling you'll want to bring your own – and strong tackle.

Bike rides and Tharu villages
Some guesthouses in Thakurdwara rent **bicycles** (for around Rs50 per day), which opens up a host of possibilities for exploring the surrounding countryside. Two dirt roads head south from Thakurdwara and take you through numerous traditional Tharu villages. The one past the *hattisar* and on along the riverbank to Khotia Ghat (see p.371) gets far more tourist traffic. Cycling north along the road to Ambaasa is also a possibility, but not advisable alone, due to the presence of wild animals. Given more time and a packed lunch, you could conceivably cycle to Chisapani or some of the other spots normally only reached by jeep. It might be worth joining a guided "village walk" to learn more about local Tharu culture, if you can get past the human-zoo aspect of it.

West of the Karnali River

The "far west" of Nepal, beyond the **Karnali River**, is a foreign land for most Nepalis – a remote, underdeveloped region which has long been neglected by the Kathmandu government. In fact, Delhi is closer than the Nepalese capital by bus and, until the completion of the Karnali bridge in the mid-1990s, the region was literally cut off altogether in the monsoon, the Karnali effectively forming Nepal's western border.

The westernmost section of the Mahendra Highway was finally completed in 2000, after a twitchy Indian government had insisted on replacing the Chinese who were originally contracted to do the job. Twenty-two major bridges carry just 215km of asphalt, but at last the road finally lives up to its alternative name of the East–West Highway; it's likely to bring new trade and industry to the region, and to become a major route for travellers between Nepal and India. The little-visited **Sukla Phanta Wildlife Reserve**, which lies just outside the relatively laid-back border town of **Mahendra Nagar**, makes for an excellent stopover.

Mahendra Nagar

The Mahendra Highway ends at **MAHENDRA NAGAR**, a border town with a good deal of spark thanks to day-tripping shoppers from India. Its bustle is only a border aberration, however, for the outlying region is one of the more traditional parts of the Tarai. Rana Tharu sharecroppers work the fields, maintaining an apparently happy symbiosis with their old-money landlords, and their villages, scattered along dirt tracks north of the Mahendra Highway, still consist of traditional communal longhouses.

Mahendra Nagar is laid out in an unusually logical grid south of the highway, with the **bus park** at the northwestern end. Walk south from the bus park for 500m and you come to a roundabout: to the left (east) is Main Road, the street with the bazaar, and to the right (west) is the road to the **airstrip** (3.5km) and Sukla Phanta Wildlife Reserve (see overleaf). RNAC has discontinued its week-

---

The Karnali

The Mahendra Highway emerges from Bardia National Park to vault the mighty **Karnali River**, surging out of a gap in the rugged foothills, on what is reputed to be the longest single-tower **suspension bridge** in the world. The exotic design of this World Bank-funded structure appears to have been dictated mainly by the foreign contractors' need for a showcase project, but it's an impressive sight as you rush along the smooth new tarmac. Look out for gharial crocodiles basking on the rocks as you pass over.

An even bigger showcase project may be in the pipeline for the Karnali: the construction of a mammoth **dam** upstream of the bridge. The 10.8-gigawatt **Karnali-Chisapani Project** would be one of the largest hydroelectric installations in the world, costing as much as US$8 billion. The fashion is moving away from such megaprojects, however, and the new apple of the government's eye is a partnership project with a French charity to build a simple **tunnel** across the neck of a major bend on the Upper Karnali. At 2.2km long, with a drop of 140m, the tunnel would generate 300 megawatts at a cost of less than half a billion, and what's more, the developers promise to spend US$200 million on local development projects. The project would also give some impetus towards completing the long-overdue road from Surkhet to Jumla. See p.537 for more on hydroelectric projects in Nepal.

ly flights from Mahendra Nagar to Kathmandu via Bajhang, but may in time resume them.

Mahendra Nagar's two best **hotels** are both well-accustomed to travellers and can rent out jeeps for visiting Sukla Phanta. *Hotel New Anand* (☎099/21693; ❹–❺) is tucked 20m down a lane leading south off Main Road, just opposite the piazza-like bazaar; it has a good range of rooms (the best ones with hot running water and a/c), a good in-house restaurant and internet connection. *Hotel Sweet Dream* (☎099/22313; ❷–❹) sits out on the highway east of the bus park and has large but bare rooms, some with fans and attached bathrooms, though you'll have to exchange the noise of the bazaar for the noise of the highway. Inexpensive and fairly decent rooms can be found at *Royal Guest House* (☎099/21906; ❷), opposite the bus park, and *Hotel Anand* (☎099/21678; ❷), on Main Road, just round the corner from *New Anand*.

Several *dhaba*, concentrated mainly along the first lane leading off the bazaar, do a fair range of Nepali and Indian **food**. Rastriya Banijya Bank, 250m south of the bazaar on the third lane, can **change** Indian rupees and US dollars, but other currencies may be beyond its abilities (Mon–Thurs & Sun 7–9am & 10am–2pm, Fri 7–9am & 10am–noon). Indian currency is readily accepted and unofficially exchanged everywhere in Mahendra Nagar.

The border

The **border** begins 6km west of Mahendra Nagar, reached by shared tempo or (slower) cycle riksha, *tonga* or bus. A rough road traverses the one-kilometre no-man's land between the Nepalese and Indian immigration posts. From Indian immigration you can catch a cycle riksha (Rs15 IC per person) across the wide Mahakali River along the top of a huge flood-control/irrigation barrage and then a further 4km to Banbaasa, the first Indian town. The road across the barrage is only one lane wide, which is why the border is open to vehicles only at certain times in each direction, and why there are always lines of traffic waiting to cross; for pedestrians and cyclists it's open from 6am to 7pm.

Banbaasa is relatively friendly for a border town, but accommodation is poor, and since crossing the border is fairly time-consuming, you'll want to make an early start from Mahendra Nagar to avoid being stuck there. Buses connect Banbaasa to Bareli (the nearest broad-gauge rail station; 2hr 30min), Almora (6hr), Naini Tal (7hr), Haridwar (9hr) and Delhi (10hr). Narrow-gauge trains from Banbaasa are slow and infrequent, so you're better off taking a bus.

If you're **entering Nepal**, visas are available at the border for US dollars cash. Refer to p.377 for onward bus information. The travel agent's booth next to immigration can book through-tickets, including jeep transport, to Bardia National Park – though this means you'll be committed to at least one night's stay in whichever lodge they sell to you. There are direct night buses and a single marathon day bus from Mahendra Nagar through to Kathmandu, but unless you're on urgent business you'd do better to make the journey in stages: Sukla Phanta Wildlife Reserve, Bardia National Park and Lumbini all make worthwhile stopovers.

Sukla Phanta Wildlife Reserve

The great swaths of natural grassland (*phanta*) in Nepal's extreme southwest could almost be mistaken, albeit on a smaller scale, for the savannas of East Africa. **SUKLA PHANTA WILDLIFE RESERVE**, south of Mahendra Nagar, is dotted with them, and touring the reserve is, for once, really like being on safari. Sukla Phanta is home to the world's largest population of

swamp deer – sightings of 1000 at a time are common – as well as a good concentration of **tigers**. It's also astonishingly rich in **birds**, with 470 species having been counted here, one of the highest concentrations in Nepal. Rare species include the Bengal florican, the giant hornbill and a lone pair of sarus cranes.

Several four-wheel-drive tracks crisscross the reserve, making itineraries flexible, but first stop is bound to be the **Sukla Phanta** at the southwestern end, a rippling sea of grass that turns silvery-white in October (*sukila* means white in the local Tharu dialect). You're guaranteed **swamp deer** here, and in quantity – make for the view tower in the middle and scan for them with binoculars. As *barasingha* ("twelve-pointer"), the swamp deer was one of Kipling's beloved *Jungle Book* animals – "that big deer which is like our red deer, but stronger" – and common throughout the plains and hills. Today it's an endangered species, finding safety in numbers in the *phanta* and particularly the boggy parts where seasonal fires don't burn off the grasses. The species' high density in Sukla Phanta assures plenty of prey for the reserve's 32 **tigers**, who seem to be surviving despite sharing their territory – deviant behaviour by tiger standards. The riparian area along the Chaundhar River from **Singpur** northwards supports the reserve's greatest concentration of tigers. You'll be lucky to see Sukla Phanta's solitary **rhino**, who tends to roam in the southern

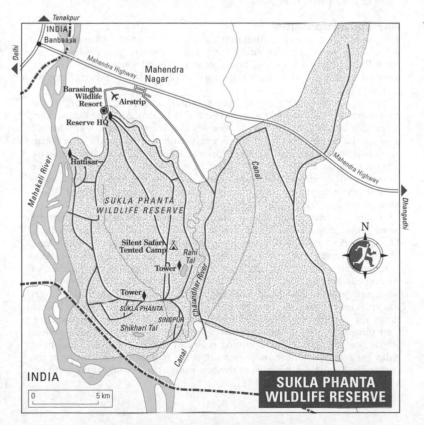

phanta area, though she is likely to be joined by others translocated from Chitwan in the future.

Having seen your obligatory *phanta*, make a beeline for **Rani Tal** (Queen's Lake), near the centre of the reserve. Surrounded by riotous, screeching forest, the lake – a lagoon, really – is like a prehistoric time capsule, with trees leaning out over the shore, deer wading shoulder-deep around the edges and crocodiles occasionally peering out of the water-hyacinth-choked depths. In the early morning, the **birdlife** is amazing, a dazzling display of cranes, cormorants, eagles and scores of others. You can watch all the comings and goings from a tower by the western shore. Nearby is an overgrown **brick circle**, 1500m in circumference, which locals say was the fort of Singpal, an ancient Tharu king (Rani Tal is said to have been his queen's favourite spot).

Though you'd think they'd be hard to miss, chances are Sukla Phanta's **elephant herd** will give you the slip – they now seem to spend most of their time in Bardia National Park and India's Corbett National Park. The dominant male of this herd, dubbed Thula Hatti ("Big Elephant"), was killed in 1993 by a home-made mine, planted either by poachers or by a farmer trying to protect his crops. Before his demise, Thula Hatti was believed to be the world's biggest Asian elephant, and was even featured in a BBC documentary. Other elephant herds live in the forested Churia Hills, in the "tail" of the reserve that extends north of the Mahendra Highway.

Park practicalities

The Sukla Phanta Reserve **entrance** is 5km southwest of Mahendra Nagar, not far from the airstrip. The **entry fee** is Rs500 per day (plus a vehicle entry fee of Rs2000), and the opening hours are from around 8am to sunset. The best **time to visit** is after the *phanta* is burned back in mid-November; after April it's too tall to see anything.

For many years, staying at the luxury **tented camp** in the heart of the reserve was the only feasible way to visit Sukla Phanta. A family outfit, *Silent Safari* (☏099/21912 or 01/520523, ⓦwww.silentsafari.com), runs customized trips in the reserve for about $145 per person per night. It's a one-man operation, and a trip with Colonel Hikmat Bisht – former hunter, military attaché, patrician landowner and self-styled man of the forest – is one of the most delightfully idiosyncratic experiences in Nepal. His tented camp is comfortable and unpretentious, and well-situated deep in the *sal* forest – real Mowgli country, dripping with bohemia ("Tarzan") vines.

Another good way to visit the reserve is to **rent a vehicle** from one of the better hotels in Mahendra Nagar (about Rs1500 a day, plus fuel and permits). The only alternative to *Silent Safari* is to **stay** at *Barasingha Wildlife Resort* (☏099/21892; ❷) a rather ill-made copy of Bardia's attractive thatched-cottage camps, situated right beside the park gate and headquarters. At the time of writing (just after opening), it offered few options to really get into the reserve, but it can provide a **guide** of sorts (Rs500) and a bicycle, which should get you to Rani Tal, though you'd be hard-pressed to make the game-rich areas along the Chaundhar River, which lie about 25km from the entrance. **Camping** is allowed at certain restricted spots and would make an excellent way to see the park if you're willing to spend two days walking. **Elephant rides** are available, but the starting point, at the *hattisar* 8km southwest of the reserve headquarters, is miles from the best game area so you're unlikely to see much.

Travel details

Day buses

Bhairawa to: Birganj (4 daily; 8hr); Butwal (every 15min; 1hr); Janakpur (1 daily; 10hr); Kathmandu (15 daily; 8hr); Lumbini (every 30min; 1hr); Taulihawa for Tilaurakot (hourly; 1hr).

Butwal to: Bartun for Tansen (every 15min; 2hr); Bhairawa (every 15min; 1hr); Birganj (3 daily; 7hr); Dhangadhi (1 daily; 9hr); Janakpur (2 daily; 9hr); Kathmandu* (8 daily; 7hr); Mahendra Nagar (2 daily; 11hr); Nepalganj (5 daily; 6hr); Pokhara* (16 daily; 7hr); Sonauli (every 10min; 10min).

Lumbini to: Bhairawa (every 30min; 1hr); Kathmandu (1 daily; 10hr).

Mahendra Nagar to: Butwal (2 daily; 11hr); Dhangadhi (every 30min; 1hr); Kathmandu (1 daily; 13hr); Nepalganj (5 daily; 5hr).

Narayangadh to: Bandipur (1 daily; 5hr); Devghat (8 daily; 30min); Gorkha (14 daily; 2hr 30min); Jagatpur (hourly; 1hr); Kathmandu (12 daily; 5hr); Meghauli (every 30min; 1hr); Pokhara (every 30min; 4hr).

Nepalganj to: Dhangadhi (7 daily; 6hr); Kathmandu (3 daily; 12hr); Mahendra Nagar (5 daily; 5hr).

Tadi Bazaar for Sauraha: Kathmandu (5 daily; 6hr); Narayangadh (every 20min; 45min).

* Tourist bus service also available

Night buses

Bhairawa to: Biratnagar (1 daily; 13hr); Birganj (1 daily; 10hr); Janakpur (1 daily; 12hr); Kathmandu (10 daily; 8hr).

Butwal to: Birganj (3 daily; 10hr); Janakpur (3 daily; 12hr); Kathmandu (14 daily; 12hr); Mahendra Nagar (2 daily; 12hr); Nepalganj (5 daily; 8hr); Pokhara (4 daily; 10hr).

Lumbini to: Kathmandu (1 daily; 12hr).

Mahendra Nagar to: Biratnagar (1 daily; 22hr); Birganj (1 daily; 16hr); Butwal (2 daily; 11hr); Kathmandu (4 daily; 17hr); Pokhara (2 daily; 16hr).

Narayangadh to: Kakharbitta (2 daily; 12hr).

Nepalganj to: Kathmandu (4 daily; 15hr); Pokhara (3 daily; 14hr).

Flights

Note that services are subject to cancellation and change.

Kathmandu to: Bhairawa (8 daily); Bharatpur (4–5 daily); Dhangadhi (1 weekly); Mahendra Nagar via Nepalganj (1 weekly); Meghauli (1 daily); Nepalganj (4–9 weekly).

Nepalganj to: Bajhang/Chainpur (1 weekly); Bajura (4 weekly); Birendra Nagar/Surkhet (1 weekly); Chaurjhari/Jajarkot (2–4 weekly); Dhangadhi via Bajura (2 weekly); Dolpo/Dunai (4 weekly); Jumla (3 weekly); Kathmandu (4–9 weekly); Mahendra Nagar via Bajhang (1 weekly); Rukum (1 weekly); Sanfebagar (2 weekly); Simikot (1 weekly).

6

The Eastern Tarai and hills

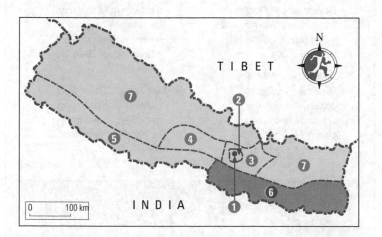

Highlights

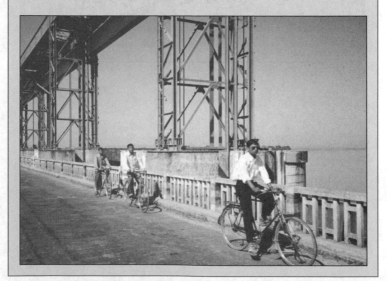

6

The Eastern Tarai and hills

T he **eastern Tarai** – the southern flatlands east of Chitwan – is lusher and more tropical than the west, but also more populous and industrial. It's also, if anything, more Indian. Although the foothills are usually within sight, the main east–west highway sticks to the plains, where the way of life is essentially identical to that of Bihar and West Bengal just across the border; in many parts of this region, Nepali is the second or even third language, after Maithili, Bhojpuri or other North Indian dialects.

Most travellers only flit through here on their way to the border crossings of **Birganj** (for Patna) and **Kakarbhitta** (for Darjeeling), and outside these places you won't find a speck of tourist hype. The cities are admittedly awful, but with one outstanding exception: **Janakpur**, a pilgrimage centre that's immensely famous among Hindus but seldom visited by Westerners, and which provides all the exoticism of India without the attendant hassles. Although large tracts of jungle are less common east of Chitwan, birdwatchers can check out **Koshi Tappu Wildlife Reserve**, straddling the alluvial plain of the mighty Sapt Koshi River.

The few visitors that get to the **eastern hills** tend to be trekkers bound for the Everest or Kanchenjunga massifs, which rear up like goalposts on the northern horizon, or rafters running the Sun Koshi. Most other potential visitors are put off by the prospect of a twenty-odd-hour bus trip from Kathmandu, but the journey is far more enticing if you're entering Nepal from the east anyway. By turns riotously forested and fastidiously terraced, the hills are great for day-hiking. Just two all-weather roads serve the area, one climbing to the lovely Newar town of **Dhankuta** and rowdier **Hile**, and the other crawling up the steep green slopes to **Ilam**, Nepal's tea-growing capital.

Buses make good time through the eastern Tarai on the Mahendra Highway, and the Dhulikhel–Sindhuli Highway, if it's ever completed, will make getting to the east even easier. However, most of the places described in this chapter are located on side roads, thus requiring various degrees of extra toil to get to. Also, **tourist facilities** in this region are minimal, adding to the difficulty (or adventure) of travelling here. You won't find much Western cuisine, but the Indian and Nepali food is wonderful. If you're cycling, many of the small bazaars en route can provide basic food and, at a pinch, lodging. A phenomenon specific to eastern Nepal is the **haat bazaar**, or weekly market, and it's worth trying to coincide with one or two of these pan-cultural extravaganzas.

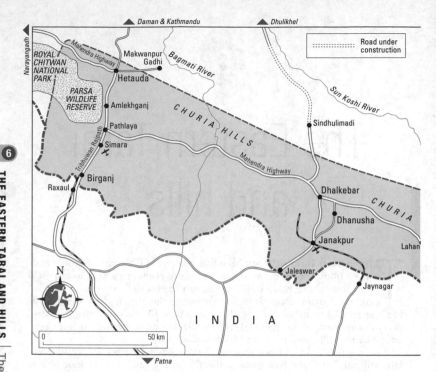

The Eastern Tarai

For travellers coming by road from other parts of Nepal, **Hetauda** is the gateway to the eastern Tarai. The **Tribhuwan Rajpath** enters the town from the north and continues south to the Indian border at Birganj. Coming from the west, it's an easy two-hour bus ride from Narayangadh (Chitwan) to Hetauda along the **Mahendra Highway**, which hugs the hills as it follows the attractive *dun* (inner Tarai valley) of the Rapti River. East of Hetauda, the highway barrels along the plains all the way to Nepal's easternmost border, at Kakarbhitta, and is well-served by buses serving the three big cities of the eastern Tarai: Birganj, Nepal's unappealing trade capital, Biratnagar, a main industrial centre that holds no interest for the visitor, and **Janakpur**, the holiest of Tarai towns.

The Rajpath: Hetauda to Birganj

There is something peculiarly sinister and ominous about the jungle of the Tarai. You have that feeling that danger in one form or another lurks around every corner ... Over everything a strange, oppressive silence broods ... A big gray ape chatters at us maliciously from his perch on an overhanging rock. A leopard, camouflaged almost to invisibility by his spotted hide, steals on stealthy feet across the road.

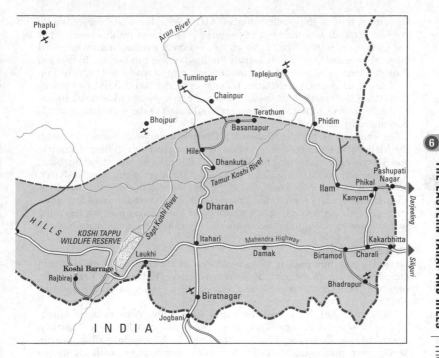

> There is a sudden crash of underbrush behind the jungle wall – an elephant or a tiger perhaps.
>
> E. Alexander Powell, *The Last Home of Mystery* (1929)

For centuries the only developed corridor through the Tarai, the gentler southern section of the **Tribhuwan Rajpath** was, before air travel, every foreigner's introduction to Nepal. A narrow-gauge railway used to run from Raxaul, the last Indian station, as far as Amlekhganj; dignitaries were transported from there by elephant over the first band of hills to Hetauda before being carried the rest of the way to Kathmandu by donkey or sedan chair. Those few who made the journey during Nepal's isolation years before 1951, such as our Mr Powell, did so only by invitation of the prime minister or king. The construction of the Rajpath in the 1950s eliminated the need for elephants and sedan chairs, but the railway wasn't decommissioned until the 1970s.

If you're arriving from India, the Rajpath makes an exhilarating introduction to Nepal, particularly if coupled with an overnight stay in Daman, from where there's a superb Himalayan panorama. The dramatic northern section of the Tribhuwan Rajpath, including Daman, is covered in Chapter Three.

Hetauda

Clumped around the junction of the Mahendra Highway and the Rajpath, **HETAUDA** is still a staging-post on the India–Kathmandu route, but whatever romance it may once have had has long-gone today. It's a restless, transient place, where Indian trucks rumble through with fuel and bulk goods bound for Kathmandu, and buses stop at all hours. Prostitution is common, helping make the city a link in the transmission of AIDS from India to Nepal. Among Nepalis, Hetauda is probably most famous for its cement plant, whose output has built many of the Tarai's factories and concrete bazaars, and its industrial estate, responsible for much of Nepal's prodigious beer production. In fairness, though, Hetauda isn't all industry and ugliness, and its roads are brightened up by lines of deep-green *ashok* trees. Tributaries of the Rapti River run peacefully along the town's southern and western edges (bearing Hetauda's industrial effluents to Chitwan, unfortunately), and much of the surrounding area is dominated by *sal* forest.

The centre of Hetauda is **Mahendra Chowk**, a four-way intersection with the Mahendra Highway coming in from the west, the Rajpath from the north, and the two of them merging for some 30km along the highway heading south. The intersection's eastern spoke is gravelled only as far as the Bagmati River, 25km away, but an earthen road continues from there all the way to Chapagaun, Tika Bhairab in the Kathmandu Valley. Road conditions are variable: private jeeps can only get through in dry weather and must have a pass, but this route would make an adventurous excursion on a motorcycle or mountain bike.

Practicalities

Hetauda's busy **bus park** is 150m southwest of Mahendra Chowk; the main entrance to it is from the north. If you're trying to get to Daman or Kathmandu, only five buses serve this route and four of them overnight on the way (see p.409).

Cyclists will probably **spend the night** here, as there are no other worthwhile places to stay between Daman and the border or Chitwan. Fortunately, *Motel Avocado & Orchid Resort* (☎057/20235, ✉avocado@wlink.com.np; ❸–❻) more than compensates for Hetauda's shortcomings, with a range of rooms from budget cells to smart suites with attached bath. Located in a quiet, shady compound 500m north of Mahendra Chowk, the grounds include an orchid garden and a small grove of avocado trees planted by displaced Californians when this was the USAID guesthouse. Running a distant second is *Lidolun* (☎057/20937; ❹), south of Mahendra Chowk opposite Standard Chartered bank; it has a good range of well-kept rooms, some with a/c. There are several cheaper choices north of Mahendra Chowk (such as *Neelam Lodge*; ❶) or west of it (*Hetauda Rest House*; ❶). North is quieter.

Food outside the guesthouses is unexceptional, but you'll find a number of tea stalls and *sekuwa* vendors near *Neelam Lodge*.

South to Birganj

Heading south over the low **Churia Hills**, the Rajpath, merged with the Mahendra Highway here, enters a strange landscape of stunted trees, wide gravel washes and steeply eroded pinnacles. These hills are the newest wrinkle in the Himalayan chain, heaved up as the thirty-million-year-long collision between the Indian and Asian continental plates ripples southwards – less than half a million years old, they're so young that the surface sediments haven't yet been eroded to expose bedrock.

Leaving the hills once and for all, the road passes **Amlekhganj**, the former rail terminus (now Nepal's main fuel depot), and 4km further on, the entrance to **Parsa Wildlife Reserve**. An annexe of Chitwan National Park, providing secondary habitat for many of its sub-adult tigers, the reserve isn't developed for tourism.

The Mahendra Highway branches off east at **Pathlaya**, 3km south of the Parsa entrance, while **Simara**, another 3km south, heralds a dreary succession of factories and fields that continues all the way to Birganj. For obscure reasons of national security, Nepal passed a law in the mid-1980s requiring that all new factories must be built at least 10km from the Indian border, which is causing the major border cities to flare northwards. Simara has an **airstrip**, with at least five daily flights to Kathmandu ($61); a taxi to or from Birganj will cost Rs500.

Birganj and the border

BIRGANJ isn't one of the best places to spend time in Nepal, but it sure beats Raxaul, its evil twin across the border. (Where Birganj had the good sense to build a highway bypass and out-of-town bus park, making the commercial core reasonably liveable, Raxaul has done nothing of the kind and is all but paralyzed.) Birganj has exploded in the last ten years on the back of cross-border trade with India, its population having almost tripled since 1991. The construction of a $29m Inland Container Depot, or "dry port", connected by broad-gauge railway line to Raxaul and ultimately Calcutta, should keep Birganj's accelerator pedal pressed firmly to the floor – assuming the Indian government doesn't hold Nepal to ransom over access to its rail network.

Unless you have business interests, or you're bizarrely curious to see the only railway left in Nepal, there's no conceivable reason to come here except to

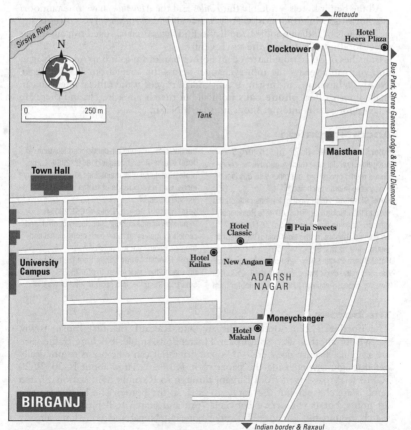

cross the border to or from Varanasi, Calcutta or other points in northeast India. Even then, you're more likely to use Sonauli (see p.352) because of its better connections within Nepal, although if you're visiting Nepal as part of a bigger tour of the subcontinent then travelling this route could save some backtracking. **Buses** connect Birganj with Kathmandu, Pokhara and a few major Tarai cities (see p.409). The new bus park is located almost 1km east of the clock-tower, beyond the bypass (and off our map). Rikshas and shared tongas (horse carts) provide transport from there.

If you're stranded in Birganj, you could probably kill a few hours in the old-ish market area around **Maisthan**, a mother-goddess temple just off the main drag. Beyond that, though, the city has little to offer: **Adarsh Nagar** is a fairly humdrum market area that's unlikely to appeal to anyone except Indian con-sumers, and the new west side of town is devoid of interest.

Practicalities

Cross-border commerce means that there's quite a lot of comfortable **lodging** in Birganj, but it's pricey for what you get. Hotels and guesthouses are grouped mainly in Adarsh Nagar and along the road going out to the bus park. All things considered, Adarsh Nagar, with it's concentration of facilities, has more going for, it.

All the better hotels – notably the *Kailas* and the *Makalu* – have fine tandoori **restaurants**, while the nearby *Puja Sweets* and *New Angan* serve up tempting assortments of Indian goodies. You'll also find *sekuwa*, *momo*, fried fish and other street food in stalls around the town centre.

Branches of Standard Chartered and other **banks** are found in Adarsh Nagar, and you can also use the moneychanger across the street from *Hotel Makalu*. Nearly all businesses in Birganj accept Indian rupees at the official rate. You can make international **phone calls** from all but the cheapest hotels, and there are a few phone-cum-internet shops in Adarsh Nagar.

Accommodation

Hotel Classic , Adarsh Nagar ☎051/24070. The budget feel renders the most-expensive air-condi-tioned rooms overpriced, but otherwise this is a reasonable midrange choice. ❸ –❺
Hotel Diamond 200m west of the bus park on the road to the clock tower ☎051/27465. Reasonably new, so standing out from most of its cheaper, grottier neighbours for the time being. Well-kept if unattractive rooms. ❸
Hotel Heera Plaza 500m west of the bus park on the road to the clock tower ☎051/23988, ⓕ23916. Swanky expense-account kind of place not far from

the bus park, offering air-conditioned isolation. ❺
Hotel Kailas Adarsh Nagar ☎051/22384. Large, professional and well maintained, if slightly anony-mous, with a wide range of rooms in addition to the standards. ❷
Hotel Makalu Adarsh Nagar, ☎051/23054, ⓔhmakalu@mos.com.np. Absolutely central, and somehow managing to be both professional and friendly. Rooms are top notch. ❺
Shree Ganesh Lodge 200m from the bus park on the road to the clock tower ☎051/26685. Clean and smart for the price, in a spartan kind of way. ❷

The border

The **border** is 2km south of Birganj, and **Raxaul**, the first Indian town, sprawls for another 2km south of it. Horrendous, smoke-belching traffic jams are a regular occurrence here – if you're driving it can take hours to physically get through, leaving aside the paperwork. Rikshas charge about Rs30 (Rs20 IC) to ferry passengers from Birganj through to Raxaul's train station. Shared tempos are cheaper, but they only go as far as the border. The border is open 24 hours, but if you arrive between 7pm and 5am you'll probably have to search around for someone. If you're entering Nepal and you don't already have a visa, make sure you have the correct change in cash (US dollars). Indian visas are not available at the border.

Raxaul is the terminus of a metre-gauge rail line and has daily direct train service to Calcutta (24hr), departing in mid-morning; for other destinations, change at Patna (5hr). Buses also depart for Patna several times a day.

East to Kakarbhitta

Resuming its eastward journey at Pathlaya, the **Mahendra Highway** cuts through extensive forest alternating with farmland. Timber and sugar are important exports of this area. Sugar cane, which is harvested in winter with the help of Indian migrant labourers, is processed by numerous small factories and a couple of big ones visible from the road. After 55km the highway crosses the **Bagmati River**, its volume here about ten times bigger (and cleaner, thanks to dilution) than in the Kathmandu Valley. This section of the Mahendra Highway was originally constructed with Soviet assistance, which explains the monumental road signs and bus shelters.

East of the turn off for Janakpur (see next page) at Dhalkebar, the highway enters more-settled country, and things become increasingly Indian. For a long stretch after the nondescript market town of Lahan, there's very little to remind you that you're in Nepal.

The landscape changes markedly at the **Sapt Koshi**, Nepal's biggest river. Crossing the **Koshi Barrage** – not a dam, but a network of dykes and flood-control gates – you can look in amazement at the immense body of water that squeezes through here before fanning out again into the shimmering haze of India. Keep an eye out for the gangetic dolphins (see box on p.397), which can sometimes be seen fishing and playing in the outflow. The open stretches of sand and water just upstream of the barrage make the **Koshi Tappu Wildlife Reserve** a mecca for bird enthusiasts. Reaching the far side, the highway bends north and runs parallel to a disused railway. Until the tracks were severed in a 1988 earthquake, it was used to haul rubble to build up the seven- to ten-metre embankments that keep the Sapt Koshi in check during the monsoon.

The landscape is particularly flat and featureless east of the Sapt Koshi to **Itahari**, a major junction town and the turning for Biratnagar, Nepal's second-biggest city and its beleaguered industrial capital. A huge chariot festival marks Krishna's birthday in the middle of the month of Bhadau (late Aug/early Sept), but there's no other reason to come here, except perhaps to change planes for one of the flights on into the eastern hills. Even if you're changing buses, it's better to do so at Itahari, which is also the junction for Dharan (see p.401).

For its final and smoothest leg, to the border at **Kakarbhitta**, the Mahendra Highway traverses the more-picturesque districts of Morang and Jhapa. Once renowned for its virulent malaria, **Morang**'s forest has now been almost entirely cleared and the land homesteaded by immigrants from the hills; the half-timbered houses are the work of transplanted Limbus. **Jhapa**, further east, has had a somewhat longer history of settlement, and is known for tea cultivation: its shaded plantations are a reminder that Darjeeling is barely 50km away as the crow flies, and Ilam (see p.406), Nepal's prize tea-growing region, sits in the hills just north of here. Though the roadside bazaars are monotonously similar in this area, the countryside is idyllic: banana trees and thatched-roof houses on stilts (one strategy for dealing with heavy monsoon rains) give it a classically Asian look.

Janakpur and around

JANAKPUR, 165km east of Birganj, is indisputably the Tarai's most fascinating city. Also known as **Janakpurdham** (*dham* denoting a sacred place), it's a holy site of the first order, and its central temple, the ornate Janaki Mandir, is an obligatory stop on the Hindu pilgrimage circuit. Although Indian in every respect except politically, the city is, by Indian standards, small and manageable: motorized traffic is all but banned from the centre, tourist hustle is largely absent and the poverty isn't oppressive. The surrounding countryside is delightful, and Janakpur's short, rickety **railway** – the only passenger railway still operating in Nepal – makes for an unusual way to experience it.

Hindu mythology identifies Janakpur as the capital of the ancient kingdom of **Mithila**, which controlled a large part of northern India between the tenth and third centuries BC. The city features prominently in the *Ramayan*, for it was in Janakpur that **Ram** – the god Vishnu in mortal form – wed **Sita**, daughter of the Mithila King Janak. Recounting the divine couple's later separation and heroic reunion, the *Ramayan* holds Ram and Sita up as models of the virtuous husband and chaste wife; in Janakpur, where the two command almost

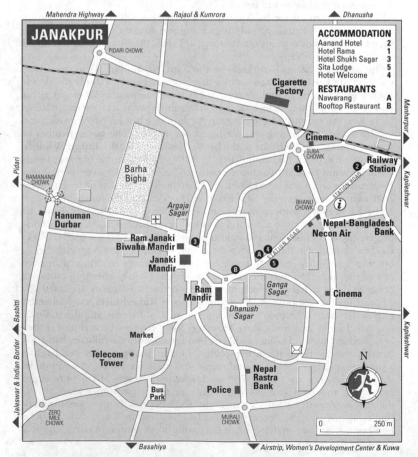

cult status, the chant of "Sita Ram, Sita Ram" is repeated like a Hindu Hail Mary, and sadhus commonly wear the tuning-fork-shaped *tika* of Vishnu. Mithila came under the control of the Mauryan empire around the third century BC, then languished for two millennia until Guru Ramananda, the seventeenth-century founder of the sect of Sita that dominates Janakpur, revived the city as a major religious centre.

Despite the absence of ancient monuments to confirm its mythic past – no building is much more than a century old – Janakpur remains a strangely attractive city. Religious fervour seems to lend an aura to everything; the skyline leaves a lasting impression of palm trees and the onion domes and pyramid roofs of local shrines. Most of these distinctively shaped buildings are associated with **kuti** – self-contained pilgrimage centres and hostels for sadhus – some five hundred of which are scattered throughout the Janakpur area. The city's other distinguishing feature is its dozens of **sacred ponds** (*sagar* or *sar*), which here take the place of river ghats for ritual bathing and *dhobi*-ing. Clearly man-made, the roughly rectangular tanks might, as locals claim, go back to Ram's day, although it's more likely that they've been dredged over the centuries by wealthy merit-seekers.

Janakpur is a long haul from Kathmandu – ten or more hours by **bus** – and only four-odd services ply the route during the daytime. The rest are night buses. If and when it is completed, the new Dhulikhel–Sindhuli Highway is expected to bring the travel time down to eight or nine hours, making Janakpur a lot more accessible. In the meantime, your only other options are to break the journey in Hetauda or Birganj (the latter is better for getting a seat on to Janakpur) or fly. Necon Air **flies** daily from Kathmandu ($60).

Arrival and information

Janakpur lies 25km south of the Mahendra Highway. It's a small city arranged in a classic concentric fashion, with a few main roads extending outwards from a compact core. **Station Road**, which runs from near the **Ram Mandir** northeastwards to the train station, is the nearest thing to a commercial thoroughfare, and it also happens to contain virtually all of Janakpur's lodgings and restaurants. Another important road heads northwestwards past the main **Janaki Mandir** to **Ramanand Chowk**, which is turning into something of a main entrance to the city. The main **bus park** is an easy riksha ride southwest of the centre. The **airstrip**, 2km further to the south, is a longer, more tedious ride.

Staff at the **tourist office** (Mon–Thurs & Sun 10am–4pm, Fri 10am–3pm) don't speak much English, but then the vast majority of the people they deal with speak Hindi, Maithili or Nepali. Nevertheless, the office may be useful for learning about upcoming festivals. It's on Station Road, 50m east of Bhanu Chowk (named after Bhanu Bhakta Acharya, a much-loved Nepali poet, whose statue graces the intersection), on the first floor.

Accommodation

Janakpur's few **lodgings** are aimed more at Indian pilgrims than Western visitors, and are all of the crummy, concrete variety. Bus and truck noise isn't a problem, for once, but the kuti around the Janaki Mandir manage to create a hell of a racket over their loudspeakers. While the scarcity of accommodation normally doesn't present a problem, you need to **book** well ahead during the big festival times.

Aanand Hotel Station Rd ☎041/23395, ℉20196. A perpetually half-completed building with the rudiments of a garden seating area. Smarter rooms with hot water are more expensive. ❷–❸

Hotel Rama Near Suba Chowk ☎041/20059. The quietest, most formal and cleanest option in town, though it's rather far from the sights. More expensive upstairs rooms are quite spacious and have hot water and a/c. ❸–❺

Hotel Shukh Sagar ☎041/20488. Great (but noisy) location overlooking the Janaki Mandir. Reasonably clean, with a good sweet shop/vegetarian restaurant downstairs. ❷

Sita Lodge (no phone). Cheap and dingy. A few comparable places with or without English signs can be found nearby. ❶

Hotel Welcome ☎041/20646, ℱ20922. Staff here have lots of experience in dealing with foreigners. Wide range of rooms, from poky boxes to spartan air-conditioned suites. ❷–❻

The City

Central Janakpur is remarkably car-free, thanks partly to a prohibition on commercial traffic entering the core but also to a general dearth of private vehicles. It's a joy to get around here – just watch out for all the cyclists. Though the city is easy enough to navigate on foot, **rikshas** wait in efficient ranks all over town and are supposed to stick to a fixed-price structure; whether they do or not, you'll rarely pay more than Rs10. You may be able to rent a **bicycle** informally through your hotel.

The Janaki Mandir

A palatial confection of a building in the Mughal style, the **Janaki Mandir** (pronounced *Jaa*-nuh-kee) is supposed to mark the spot where a golden image of Sita was discovered in 1657 and, presumably, where the virtuous princess actually lived. The present plaster and marble structure, erected in 1911 by an Indian queen, is already looking a little mouldy. Its outer building encloses a courtyard and inner sanctum, where at least twice a day (generally 8am and 4pm) priests draw back a curtain to reveal an intricate silver shrine and perform various rituals for attending worshippers; non-Hindus are allowed to watch, and the priests even seem willing to bestow blessings on unbelievers. It's an enchanting place at night and early in the morning, when the devout gather in lamplit huddles and murmur haunting hymns. The temple is also a traditional place for boys to undergo the ritual of *chhewar* (the first shaving of the

---

Janakpur's festivals

At any time of year, Janakpur's atmosphere is charged with an intense devotional zeal. New shrines are forever being inaugurated and idols installed, while kuti loudspeakers broadcast religious discourses and the mesmerizing drone of *bhajan*. Pilgrimage is a year-round industry, marked by several highlights in the **festival** calendar:

Parikrama As many as 100,000 people join the annual one-day circumambulation of the city on the day of the February–March full moon, many performing prostrations along the entire eight-kilometre route. The pilgrimage coincides with the festival of Holi, when coloured water is thrown everywhere and on everyone.

Ram Navami Ram's birthday, celebrated on the ninth day after the March–April full moon, attracts thousands of sadhus, who receive free room and board at the city's temples.

Chhath Women bathe in Janakpur's ponds and line them with elaborate offerings to the sun god Surya at dawn on the third day of Tihaar (Diwali). Women in the villages surrounding Janakpur paint murals on the walls of their houses.

Biwaha Panchami The culmination of this five-day event – Janakpur's most important festival – is a re-enactment of Ram and Sita's wedding at the Janaki Mandir, which draws hundreds of thousands of pilgrims on the fifth day after the new moon of November–December.

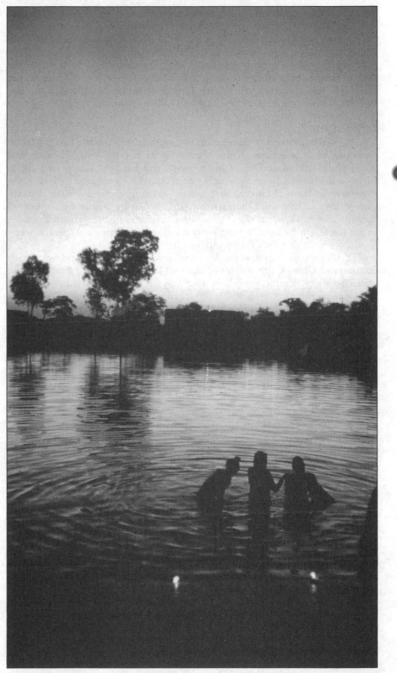

391

△ Janakpur

head), and male dancers in drag (*natuwa* in Nepali), who are often hired to perform at the ceremony, may sometimes be seen here.

Climb the stairs to the roof of the outer building for a view of the central courtyard and the dense, brick-laned Muslim village butting right up against the temple's rear wall: one of Janakpur's most extraordinary aspects is the way rural life can be seen almost in the heart of the city. North of the temple, the modern, Nepali pagoda-style **Ram Janaki Biwaha Mandap** (Ram Sita Wedding Pavilion) houses a turgid tableau of the celebrated event.

Other sights

The city's oldest, closest quarter lies to the south and east of the Janaki Mandir – making your way through this area, with its sweet shops, puja stalls and quick-photo studios, you begin to appreciate that Janakpur is as geared up for Indian tourists as Kathmandu is for Western ones. The main landmark here, the pagoda-style **Ram Mandir**, isn't wildly exciting except during festivals. Immediately to the east, **Dhanush Sagar** and **Ganga Sagar** are considered the holiest of Janakpur's ponds. The sight of Hindus performing ritual ablutions in the fog at sunrise here is profoundly moving, and during festivals the scene is on a par with Varanasi's famed ghats in India.

Walk westwards from the Janaki Mandir to the highway and you reach **Ramanand Chowk**, the nucleus of many of Janakpur's *kuti* and a major sadhu gathering place during festivals. A four-way arch bearing a statue of Guru Ramananda, the saint responsible for Janakpur's modern fame, is gradually being constructed over the intersection that bears his name. Two well-known establishments, Ramanand Ashram and Ratnasagar Kuti – the latter, rising grandly in the midst of farmland, looking uncannily like a Russian Orthodox church – are located west of here but, like most *kuti*, they are closed to non-Hindus, whose presence would necessitate all sorts of ritual cleansing.

If by this time you're tiring of the serious side of Hinduism, head to **Hanuman Durbar**, a small *kuti* 150m south of Ramanand Chowk on the west side, which until 1998 was home to the world's biggest (well, fattest) rhesus monkey. Priests still proudly display photos of the late great monkey, and they are optimistically fattening up another one as his replacement.

Around Janakpur

Janakpur's holy traditionalism extends into the surrounding countryside, which is inhabited by Hindu castes and members of the Tharu and Danuwar ethnic groups, and features some of the most meticulously kept farmland you'll see anywhere. You can ride the narrow-gauge **railway** east or west and, during the cooler winter months, great bike rides can be made along several roads radiating out from the city.

The Janakpur Women's Development Center

Hindu women of the deeply conservative villages around Janakpur are rarely spared from their household duties, and, once married, are expected to remain veiled and silent before all males but their husbands. Fortunately, their rich tradition of folk art (see box opposite) offers them an escape from this isolated existence. The nonprofit **Janakpur Women's Development Center** (mid-Feb to mid-Nov Mon–Thurs & Sun 10am–5pm; mid-Nov to mid-Feb 10am–4pm; free), 3km south of town, provides a space for women from nearby villages to develop personally and artistically. Founded in 1989, with assistance from several international aid organizations, the artists' cooperative helps its fifty-odd members turn their skills into income – and the fact that some have

Maithili painting

For three thousand years, Hindu women of the region once known as Mithila have maintained an unbroken tradition of **painting**, using techniques and ritual motifs passed down from mother to daughter. The colourful, almost psychedelic images can be viewed as fertility charms, meditation aids or a form of storytelling, but on a deeper level they represent, in the words of one critic, "the manifestation of a collective mind, embodying millennia of traditional knowledge".

From an early age Brahman girls practise drawing complex symbols derived from Hindu myths and folk tales, which over the course of generations have been reduced to *mandala*-like abstractions. By the time she is in her teens, a girl will be presenting simple paintings to her arranged fiancé, perhaps using them to wrap gifts; the courtship culminates with the painting of a **kohbar**, an elaborate fresco on the wall of the bride's bedroom, where the newlyweds will spend their first four nights. Depicting a stylized stalk of bamboo surrounded by lotus leaves (symbols of male and female sexuality), the *kohbar* is a powerful celebration of life, creation and everything. Other motifs include footprints and fishes (both representing Vishnu), parrots (symbolic of a happy union), Krishna cavorting with his milkmaids, and Surabhi, "the Cow of Plenty, who inflames the desire of those who milk her". Perhaps the most striking aspect of the *kohbar* is that, almost by definition, it's ephemeral: even the most amazing mural will be washed off within a week or two. Painting is seen as a form of prayer or meditation; once completed, the work has achieved its end.

Women of all castes create simpler **wall decorations** during the autumn festival of Tihaar (Diwali). In the weeks leading up to the festival they apply a new coat of mud mixed with dung and rice chaff to their houses and add relief designs. Just before Lakshmi Puja, the climactic third day of Tihaar, many paint images of peacocks, pregnant elephants and other symbols of prosperity to attract a visit from the goddess of wealth. Until Nepali New Year celebrations in April, when the decorations are covered over with a new layer of mud, they're easily viewable in villages around Janakpur.

Paintings **on paper**, which traditionally play only a minor part in the culture, have grown to become the most celebrated form of Maithili art – or Madhubani art, as it's known in India, where a community-development project began turning it into a marketable commodity in the 1960s. More recently, the Janakpur Women's Development Center (see opposite) has helped do the same in Nepal, making Maithili paintings a staple of Kathmandu tourist gift shops. When working on paper, the artist first outlines the intended design in black, then adds a border and embellishes every remaining space with fantastic detail, and finally illuminates it with brilliant, poster-paint colours. Many artists concentrate on traditional religious motifs, but a growing number are depicting people – mainly women and children in domestic scenes, always shown in characteristic doe-eyed profile.

gone on to start their own companies is a sure sign of the project's success. But more importantly, the centre empowers women through training in literacy and business skills, and support sessions in which they can share their feelings and discuss their roles in family and society.

Initially specializing in Maithili paper art, the centre has since branched into other media and now has separate buildings for sewing, screen-printing, ceramics and painting. Visitors are welcome to tour the beautiful, mango-shaded facility, and to meet the artists and learn about their work and traditions. A **gift shop** sells crafts made on the premises, as well as the JWDC's own booklet, *Master Artists of Janakpur*, a sensitive treatment not only of Maithili art but also of the women who make it here.

The centre is a fifteen-minute riksha (Rs50) or bike ride from Janakpur. Head south towards the airport and make a left turn about 1km after Murali Chowk (look for the big painted arch and signs). Bear right after about 200m, passing through the well-kept village of **Kuwa**. Set in a walled compound, the centre is on the right after about 500m. If in doubt, ask for Nari Bikas Kendra, or just have a riksha wallah take you – they all know the way.

The Janakpur Railway

If you've already had dealings with Indian trains, Janakpur's **narrow-gauge railway** will be less of a thrill, but it's still an excellent way to get out into the country. On a misty winter's morning, the ride past sleepy villages and minor temples is nothing short of magical. Built in the 1940s to transport timber to India from the now-depleted forest west of Janakpur, the railway these days operates primarily as a passenger service. It was under threat of closure at the time of writing, so check locally.

Janakpur station, at the top of Station Road, is the terminus for two separate lines, each about 30km long: one eastbound to **Jaynagar**, just over the border in India, and the other westbound to **Bijalpura**. Departure times vary seasonally, and are subject to frequent disruptions, but in general the Jaynagar service runs three times a day (departing at around 7am, noon and 3pm and returning to Janakpur at around noon, 2pm and 6pm) and takes two to three hours one way. The Bijalpura service runs only once a day, departing Janakpur in the late afternoon and returning the next morning. That makes the Jaynagar line the more feasible for a day-trip: you could ride all the way to Khajuri (last stop before the border) and then catch the train as it passes through on the way back, or get off somewhere earlier and walk or cycle around that area until the train returns.

The **fare** to Jaynagar is Rs18 in second class or Rs35 in first, the latter being far from luxurious but perhaps a shade less crowded. Arrive early for a seat; on the way back you'll probably end up riding on the roof.

Other villages

Dozens of villages dot the land around Janakpur at regular intervals, each with its own mango grove and a sagar or two. Subsistence farming – livestock, grains, vegetables and fish – is virtually the only occupation here: you'll rarely see even the smallest shop.

From Kuwa and the Janakpur Women's Development Center, a road heads east to Lohana and then **south** to Bahuarwa, Devdiha and, about 10km from Janakpur, larger and more prosperous **Nagarain**. There are two other ways to get between Janakpur and Nagarain, so you can make a loop – the better (less travelled) of the two is the road heading south from the bus park, which passes through Basahiya, Donauli and Bishnupur, and eventually wends its way eastwards to Nagarain via Phulgama (this entails a stream crossing). The third way to Nagarain is simply the main road south past Kuwa and the airport. This rather shadeless road, which is served by infrequent, claptrap buses, continues to the Indian border, 3km beyond Nagarain.

Westwards from Ramanand Chowk, you can follow a dirt lane through the huts of Pidari, over the train tracks and through some nice shady groves, and finally to **Khurta**, a substantial community with grain mills and a Friday-afternoon market. A separate track heads west from near "Zero Mile" to Basbitti and Bhramarpura.

North from Suba Chowk, the road to Dhanusha has been rendered a bit less interesting by being upgraded, but you can make a couple of nice detours where it bypasses the villages of Bhenga and Thumana. **Dhanusha** (Dhanushadham), 18km from Janakpur, is an important pilgrimage site. According to the *Ramayan*, it was here that King Janak staged an Arthurian contest for the hand of his daughter, Sita, declaring that the successful suitor would have to prove himself by lifting an impossibly heavy bow. After all others had given up, Ram picked up the bow with ease, and broke it in two for good measure. Villagers can point you to a walled compound encircling a volcanic rock that's said to be a piece of the bow.

There are also several picturesque villages on either side of the main road that connects Janakpur to the Mahendra Highway. Loveliest is **Kumrora**, on the right about 4km north of Pidari Chowk, a tidy Brahman settlement of one- and two-storey houses and particularly expressive wall murals. To avoid the worst of the roadside grunge around Pidari Chowk, take a back way just to the east, via Rajaul, which joins the main road halfway.

Practicalities

If you enjoy Indian **food**, you'll eat like a rajah in Janakpur. *Hotel Welcome*'s and *Hotel Rama*'s restaurants all do beautiful veg and non-veg meals, while various places around the Janaki Mandir offer pure vegetarian food. For Nepali fare, the line of places around the corner from *Hotel Welcome*, on Station Road, is just the ticket; ask for the *Nawarang* (its sign is in Nepali only). For Indian sweets or *chiura dahi* (beaten rice and curd), take your pick from a host of *mithai pasal* near the Janaki and Ram temples. To sample the local brew, ask for *sophi* or *dudhiya*, fennel- and aniseed-flavoured spirits that are just about drinkable when mixed with soft drinks. Western dishes can be had at the *Rooftop Restaurant*, on Station Road.

Nepal Rastra **bank**, at the southern end of town, exchanges some foreign currencies. Nepal Bangladesh Bank, at Bhanu Chowk, can change cash but not travellers' cheques. Many shops along Station Road offer international and trunk **telephone** services, and a couple of them have **email**. Janakpur has a **hospital**, but hope you never need it; pharmacies and private doctors' practices can be found along the street in front of the hospital.

Moving on

For **bus** frequencies and travel times from Janakpur, see p.409. Note that Sajha tickets are purchased at Ramanand Chowk, not at the bus park, and the Sajha bus to Kathmandu originates there (another Sajha service, originating in Jaleswar, also stops there). Tickets for night buses to Kathmandu are also sold from desks along Station Road near the *Aanand Hotel*, but go to the bus park for a better seat assignment. Necon Air, just off Bhanu Chowk (☎041/21900), flies daily from Janakpur to Kathmandu ($60).

There is a small-time **border crossing** about 20km east of town at Jaleswar, and another at Jaynagar, but neither of these is officially open to foreigners.

Koshi Tappu Wildlife Reserve

Straddling a floodplain of shifting grassland and sandbanks north of the Koshi Barrage, **Koshi Tappu Wildlife Reserve** is the smallest and most low-key of the Tarai's parks. There's no great appeal to most travellers – there are no tigers or rhinos, nor even any jungle – but **birdwatchers** can have a field-day here. Koshi Tappu is one of the subcontinent's most important wetlands, and thanks to its location just downstream from one of the few breaches in the Himalayan barrier, it's an internationally important residing, staging and wintering area for waterfowl and waders.

Some 465 **bird** species, many of them endangered, have been counted here. Flocks of up to 50,000 ducks used to be seen in winter and spring, though numbers have been lower in recent years. Most of Nepal's egrets, storks, ibises, terns and gulls are represented, as are at least five globally threatened species, including the black-necked stork, red-necked falcon, swamp frankolin and the utterly impressive lesser adjutant (there have been no recent sightings of the even more astounding greater adjutant). November and December are the optimum months to see winter migrants, and mid-February to early April are best for the late migratory species.

The reserve was established to protect one of the subcontinent's last surviving herds of **wild buffalo** (*arnaa*), believed to number 150–170 animals. However, wildlife experts are concerned about the number of domestic buffalo getting into the reserve and mating with the wild ones. None of the **gharial crocodiles** released here from the Chitwan hatchery have survived, but there are **mugger** crocodiles and many species of **turtle** and **fish** – the delicious, catfish-like *jalkapoor* is a favourite of royalty. **Gangetic dolphins** can sometimes be seen playing in the water above or below the barrage. Also inhabiting the reserve are blue bull (*nilgai*), wild boar, langur and spotted deer (*chital*).

With no rhinos or large carnivores, Koshi Tappu is comparatively safe for entering **on foot**, but take a guide and local advice: wild elephants have been known to maraud in this area. Rides on **elephants** (Rs1000 per hour) and trips in **canoes** (from Rs2500) can also be arranged through *Koshi Tappu Village Rest House*), or at the reserve headquarters. Two rivers join at the reserve: the Trijuga generally hugs the western embankment, while the Sapt Koshi usually forms two main channels, along the east side and down the middle, and tends

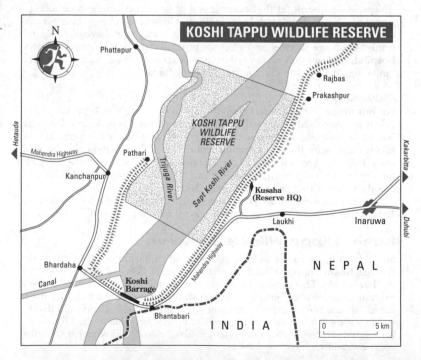

Nepal's river dolphins

Nepal's *susu*, or **gangetic dolphins**, belong to one of only four species of freshwater dolphins in the world, and like their cousins in the Amazon, Yangtse and Indus, they are highly **endangered**. A small, isolated population survives in the far west of Nepal, downstream of the Chisapani gorge in the Karnali River, but few people can make a rough guess as to how many dolphins actually live there, and fewer still have seen them.

Nepal's other main group of dolphins, however, cavorts openly in the outflow of the Koshi Barrage, less than a dozen kilometres from Koshi Tappu Wildlife Reserve, and within a few hundred metres of the country's busiest highway. Their blind snouts (they use echo-location) and muddy brown backs arch smoothly out of the turbulent water before vanishing again – a sight too sudden and quick for photography, but it'll make you catch your breath. You can't be sure of even such a brief glimpse, however, as the dolphins periodically disappear south across the Indian border, and there's no guarantee that they will survive to return – they're **threatened** by nets, deliberate poisoning, destruction of their habitat and, most seriously of all, by river pollution. A possible refuge for the dolphins is the Koshi Tappu Wildlife Reserve, but the huge Koshi Barrage makes it inaccessible to them during all but the wettest months of the year.

Locals may be able to advise you where best to **spot dolphins**, as many are openly fond of their susu, recognizing its importance as an indicator of the river's health. A legend recounts that the ancient king Bhagirath prayed to Shiva to bring a great river to his kingdom. After a thousand years, the god finally consented to grant the king's wish, and he fashioned a river from his flowing dreadlocks, naming it Bhagirathi (the queen of the Ganges). Shiva decided that the river needed a husband, and created the dolphin to be the messenger king who would spread the news of the river's creation. The legend concludes: "without a husband, there is no wife; without the messenger king, who will bring the message of the river?"

to shift from one to the other every couple of monsoons. Between these three channels lie a number of semi-permanent islands of scrub and grassland that are the main stomping ground for blue bull. (*Tappu* means "island" in Nepali, which is an accurate description of this floodplain in the wet summer months.) Birds and buffalo are best viewed along the Sapt Koshi, but given the way the rivers change course it's impossible to give specific advice on where to look. It may be necessary to cross one or more channels to reach the current hot area, which can be done only on a canoe trip. Stalking the wild cousins of common water buffalo is sometimes hard to take seriously, especially when they moo. Yet these are big animals with very big horns – those of a mature bull can measure over two metres from tip to tip – and while they normally run away at the first scent of humans, you have to make sure not to threaten them or block their escape route.

Park practicalities

The reserve is marked by a yellow sign beside the Mahendra Highway, about 12km east of the Koshi Barrage – or, if you're coming from the other direction, 3km west of Laukhi. From here an access road leads 3km north to the **reserve headquarters** (generally known as the warden ophis). An **entry permit** costs Rs500 per day.

Most of the 500 or so foreigners who visit Koshi Tappu come on fairly expensive **package tours**, flying in and out of Biratnagar and staying in one of two small tented camps. *Koshi Camp* (℡01/247078, ⊛http://ecoclub.com /koshicamp; $125 per person per night), is located just outside the northeastern corner of the reserve, near the village of Prakashpur, and is reached via a separate road. *Aqua Birds Unlimited Camp* (☎01/256310, 𝕎www.aquabirds.com .np; $198 per person for a two-night, three-day package), is just a few minutes' walk from the reserve headquarters. Both camps provide accommodation in deluxe twin-bedded tents with solar hot-water showers, serve decent food and have experienced guides. All meals, activities and transportation to and from Biratnagar are included in the price.

A single **lodge**, *Koshi Tappu Village Rest House* (☎025/21488; ❻), stands in the heart of the village adjoining the reserve headquarters. It's an overpriced but attractive, local-style thatch-and-mud cottage with fans and electricity, and the two owners know the reserve well – though they're perhaps not as strong on birds as the guides at the deluxe places. The price includes meals, but activities are extra. It's also possible to **camp** at the headquarters (Rs300 per night).

Kakarbhitta and the border

Once-sleepy **KAKARBHITTA** has recently graduated from lowly village status and is now officially entitled **Mechinagar**, the municipal capital of Nepal's easternmost district. With an ever-growing population – over 40,000 at the last count – and increased cross-border activity, there's plenty of hustle and noise, but most (if not all) of it is unthreatening, and since it's mainly a gateway for people, not goods, Kakarbhitta still feels like a back-door entry point. Most of those using it are Indians, hopping over from Darjeeling for some quick shopping, or heading to Biratnagar for business; the presence of over 100,000 Bhutanese refugees in camps west of here (see box opposite) probably contributes to the flow as well.

As with most border towns, you won't want to stay in Kakarbhitta any longer than necessary, but if you have some time on your hands you could take a stroll in any direction into the surrounding countryside, though it's not advisable to go alone. The pleasantly green Satighata tea estate is just ten-minutes' walk south of town, and a Buddhist monastery run by Tamangs can be visited on the way. A walk along the banks of the Mechi River, just east of town, is nice at sunset or sunrise.

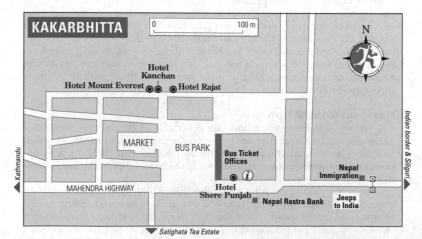

Lhotshampas: Nepal's other refugees

Every visitor to Nepal knows about its Tibetan refugees. But few have heard of its **Bhutanese refugees**, who far outnumber Tibetans in Nepal and are much worse off. Some 100,000 ethnic Nepalis, forcibly expelled from Bhutan in 1991–92, are effectively interned in eastern Nepal, pawns in an obscure political stalemate.

Members of Nepali hill groups, notably Rais and Limbus, began migrating into Bhutan in significant numbers as long ago as the mid-nineteenth century, eventually accounting for at least a third of Bhutan's population and earning the designation **Lhotshampas** (southerners), after the southern hill areas where they came to predominate. Right up to the early 1980s, multicultural government policies encouraged their integration with Bhutan's ruling **Drukpas**. However, during the mid-1980s, the continued influx of ethnic Nepalis and a rise in Nepali militancy in neighbouring Darjeeling and Sikkim gave rise to a wave of Drukpa nationalism. The Drukpas, believing their language and unique culture to be under threat, were quick to make scapegoats of the Lhotshampas – who, not coincidentally, controlled lands that were emerging as the economic powerhouse of Bhutan.

In 1986, King Singye Wangchuk instituted the **Drig Lam Namzha** code of cultural correctness, which among other things required all residents of Bhutan to wear traditional heavy wool garments that were neither natural nor practical for the southerners. In 1988, after a national **census** was taken, the government began a process of systematic discrimination against anyone who couldn't provide written proof of residency in Bhutan in 1958, and rescinded citizenship status for "anti-nationals", a group defined to include any opponents of the ruling regime. A campaign of ethnic cleansing gathered momentum, culminating in 1991 when "illegal" families were forced to sign **"voluntary migration forms"** and evicted from their lands with little or no compensation. "Anti-nationals" (and their families) were harassed, imprisoned, tortured and raped.

The refugees fled initially to India, but receiving little encouragement there, most continued on to their ethnic homeland, Nepal. As their numbers swelled, the Nepalese government, wanting to keep the problem out of sight, established **refugee camps** at Timai (just east of Kakarbhitta) and Goldhap (south of Birtamod), Pathari (southeast of Itahari) and, biggest by far, Beldangi I, II and II (north of Damak). Since then, a number of international and Nepali NGOs have built housing, schools, health posts and other essential facilities in the camps under the direction of the UN High Commission on Refugees (UNHCR). Conditions are fairly liveable, but residents are desperately poor, dependent on aid or scarce (and illegal) labouring work. Some 20,000 children have now been born in the camps – without citizenship, without prospects and without any legal rights.

The crisis shows no signs of being resolved anytime soon, despite endless rounds of talks. Nepal, with its constant changes of government, has lacked a clear negotiating position and has failed to take its case to the international community. Bhutan's position remains basically unchanged: it continues to insist that it expelled only a small number of illegal immigrants, and that the vast majority of those who left did so of their own free will. It is no more inclined to accept "foreign" or "dissident" elements than it was ten years ago, especially given their claims for compensation, and will only talk of accepting a small number of "verified" refugees. India, ignoring the international convention of free transit, has closed its borders to refugees attempting to return of their own accord. Other countries have taken weak or noncommittal positions, partly because they have a hard time believing that picturesque little Bhutan could do any wrong. The refugees themselves are desperate to return to their homes and lands, even under the threat of further persecution, and observers all agree that **repatriation** is the only permanent solution. Preparing for a long haul, aid agencies have shifted their focus from relief work to **income-generation projects** that will give the refugees some economic independence.

Practicalities

All of Kakarbhitta's **accommodation** is within spitting distance of the bus park, so it's easy to shop around – you can judge these books by their covers. Two better places that have stood the test of time are the excellent *Hotel Rajat* (☎023/62033; ❶–❺), and the slightly less expensive *Hotel Kanchan* (☎023/ 62015; ❶–❺), side by side at the north end of the bus park. The *Rajat* is run by very professional Newars from Kathmandu, and has internet connection, a good restaurant and a small garden/parking area; the *Kanchan* is more ordinary, but the owners are friendly. Both have common-bath and air-conditioned options as well as midrange, fan-cooled rooms. The *Shere Punjab* (☎023/ 62477; ❸–❺) is uncomfortably in the thick of things, but the more expensive rooms, some with a/c, are clean, well-furnished and shielded from the worst of the bus-park noise. At the bottom end, *Hotel Mount Everest* (☎023/62026; ❶) is cheap and not too dire.

Most guesthouses have their own **restaurants**, among which *Hotel Rajat*'s is probably the best. Moneychangers and lodges will swap Nepalese and Indian rupees at the market rate, but to change hard currency you'll have to use the **bank** (Nepal Rastra, the pink building on the south side of the highway sign-posted only in Nepali; daily 7am–6pm), which may be reluctant to change larger sums. International and long-distance **phone calls** are possible from the better guesthouses and various ISD shops.

Bus tickets for travel within Nepal can easily be purchased from the desks lining the east side of the bus park; there's a bewildering number of them, but anyone will point you towards the right one. Night buses to Kathmandu and Pokhara leave Kakarbhitta in staggered intervals between 3pm and 5.30pm, but book at least a couple of hours ahead to be sure of a good seat. Dharan and Janakpur make good intermediate destinations from here on the safer day buses (see p.409). Travel agents around the bus park can book **flights** to Kathmandu from Bhadrapur ($109) or Biratnagar ($50). Bhadrapur is much closer, but hard to get to (rent a jeep for around Rs300), and its airstrip can accommodate only very small planes; Biratnagar is three hours away by bus, but has more-frequent and reliable flights.

Just up from *Hotel Shere Punjab*, the **tourist office** (Mon–Thurs & Sun 10am–5pm, Fri 10am–2pm) may be able to provide some impartial advice on onward travel. The manager of *Hotel Rajat* is also a useful source of information.

The border

The wide Mechi River forms **the border**, about 500m east of town. Formalities are pleasantly relaxed, even with a vehicle. Nepalese immigration is open 24 hours a day, though it may be hard to find anyone after dark. Obtaining a Nepalese visa is expedited by having the correct cash in US dollars – if you have anything else they'll make you go to the bank (after hours you'll have to hope that travel agents can sell you enough dollars).

If you're **entering India** here, chances are you're heading for Darjeeling, Sikkim or Calcutta. For any of these destinations, you'll probably be best off taking one of the host of shared jeeps that are clustered just opposite Nepalese immigration. Most of these shuttle **to Siliguri** (IC Rs30 per person), where the toy train to Darjeeling and bus services to Gangtok and Kalimpong all originate. It's easy to continue by bus or riksha from Siliguri to the main, broad-gauge railway station at New Jalpaiguri ("NJP"), 4km away, but you can pay the jeep driver an extra Rs40 IC or so to continue straight through. At New Jalpaiguri you can pick up train services to Calcutta and Delhi, or make your way to the **Bagdogra** airport, with flights to Calcutta and Delhi, and helicopters to Darjeeling and Gangtok. Other jeeps run all the way from Kakarbhitta to Darjeeling (Rs100 per person; 4 hr), Gantok (Rs130 IC) and Kalimpong (Rs80 IC).

It's also possible to take a riksha or walk the 2km to the first Indian settlement, Raniganj, and take a local bus from there to Siliguri, but that's a lot of extra work to save a few rupees.

The eastern hills

Two main roads link the Tarai with the hills east of the Sapt Koshi – the **Dhankuta road**, leaving the Mahendra Highway at Itahari, and the **Ilam road**, beginning at Charali. **Bus** services are more fickle on these than along the Mahendra Highway, but this is made up for by the availability of **shared Land Rovers**, which are faster than buses and don't cost much more. This section describes short hikes in the area; treks are covered in Chapter Seven, or you could easily create your own by following the porters' routes that head out from the roadheads into the hills.

The Dhankuta road

Call it development, or call it colonialism by another name, but the big donor nations have staked out distinct spheres of influence in Nepal. Despite the closure of the Gurkha Camp at **Dharan**, the bustling gateway to the eastern hills, almost half of the British Army's Gurkha recruits still come from the area, and the old ties are strongly felt. Britain's twenty-year aid programme, based in the airy ridge-top bazaar of **Dhankuta**, has now been handed over to His Majesty's Government, but agriculture, forestry, health and cottage industries are still in operation. The biggest and most obvious British undertaking, however, is the **road** to Dharan, Dhankuta, Hile and beyond. Constructed with £50 million of British taxpayers' money, it remains the flag-bearer for the "Green Roads" programme, which aims to connect Nepal's district capitals to the existing highway network and, thereby, to the rest of the world.

The Dhankuta road is also one of the few routes into the *pahaad* (the "Middle Hills") that doesn't involve strenuous walking. While there are few grand monuments or temples, this region is a bastion of traditional Nepali hill culture. The bazaar towns of **Hile** and **Basantapur**, in particular, give a powerful taste of what lies beyond the point where the tarmac runs out.

Dharan and around

From the Mahendra Highway, the Dhankuta road winds languidly through forest as it ascends the Bhabar, the sloping alluvial zone between the Tarai and the foothills. **DHARAN**, 16km north of the highway, sits a slightly cooler 300m above the plain.

Dharan hit world headlines in 1988 when a powerful **earthquake** killed 700 people and flattened most of the town. Disaster struck a second time at the end of 1989 when the **British Army**, foreseeing forces reductions, pulled out of Dharan and handed its Gurkha Camp back to HMG. The withdrawal dealt a blow to would-be recruits here, who must now travel all the way to Pokhara to compete for even fewer places in the regiments (for more on the Gurkhas, see p.274). Fortunately, Dharan has bounced back smartly. Earthquake-damaged areas have now been almost entirely rebuilt, the city's western half has actually grown into quite a neat little enclave of retired Gurkhas' bungalows, and the former Gurkha Camp has been reincarnated as a fancy medical institute.

However, Dharan's **bazaar**, which runs the length of the main street between Chatta and Bhanu chowks, remains as earthily Nepali as ever. For many people throughout the eastern hills this is still the proverbial Bright Lights, where they come to sell oranges by the sackload and spend their profits on pots and pans, radios, watches, clothing, haircuts and bottles of Urvashi from well-stocked spirits stalls. In the area northeast of the central Bhanu Chowk, you'll see hill women investing the family fortune in gold ornaments – the age-old safe haven – and shops selling silver coins to be strung into necklaces. If you happen to be in the market for a cauldron, check out the brass-workers' quarter further east.

A Rs25 riksha or tempo ride west of the bus park, the **British Gurkha Camp** (as it's sometimes still called) is now officially the home of the **B.P. Koirala Health Science Institute**, which runs an extensive medical teach-

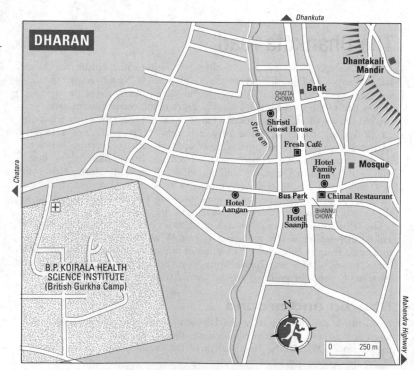

ing facility; rolling in Indian aid, it's throwing up new buildings all over the place. You can wander freely around the peaceful grounds – it's like a university campus during summer break – and visit the decaying golf course in the southeastern portion.

An easy path leads up to the modest **Dantakali Mandir**, on a low ridge just east of the bazaar, and continues on to two other temples, Buddhasubbha and Bindyabasini. **Chatara**, 15km west of Dharan, is the finishing point for rafting trips on the Sun Koshi. Walk an hour north of Chatara and you'll reach the sacred confluence of **Barahakshetra**, site of a temple to Vishnu incarnated as a boar (Barahi) and an annual pilgrimage on the day of the full moon of October–November.

Practicalities

Accommodation in Dharan is generally poor, and made worse by bus-park noise. Two reasonably quiet places are *Hotel Aangan* (☎025/20640; ❸) and *Shristi Guest House* (☎025/20569; ❷). *Aangan* has the better facilities, with clean, decently furnished rooms, geyser hot water and TVs in the more expensive rooms; *Shristi* has a more cheerful feel in its en-suite and air-conditioned rooms. *Hotel Saanjh* (☎025/22010; ❹) is similar to *Aangan*, but smaller and noisier. Of several lodges around the bus park, *Hotel Family Inn* (☎025/20848; ❷) is the cleanest and quietest, but that's not saying much.

Several **restaurants** do quite tasty Nepali, Indian and even Continental dishes – pizza has somehow made it all the way to Dharan. The restaurants at the *Aangan* and *Saanjh* hotels are worth trying, as is the upstairs, cabin-style *Chimal Restaurant*, overlooking the jeep park. *Fresh Café*, further up the bazaar, is Nepal's answer to a fast-food joint, with burgers, "momo meals", pizzas and *dosas*. Other, more local-oriented *bhojanalaya* just west of Chatta Chowk serve *daal bhaat*, *sekuwa* and *sokuti*.

Moving on

Buses run from Dharan to Biratnagar and Kakarbhitta at least every half-hour during the day, less frequently to Birganj (see p.409 for route details). To reach other Tarai destinations, change at Itahari or Biratnagar. If you want to go straight to Kathmandu, you'll have to book ahead on one of the few day buses, which leave very early, or the night buses that leave mid-afternoon. Buses to Dhankuta and points north depart from the eastern side of Bhannu Chowk and are basically local and chronically overcrowded; it can be a real ordeal getting a seat, but shared **jeeps** (Land Rovers) are faster, more comfortable and only slightly more expensive.

Dhankuta and around

From Dharan the road switchbacks abruptly over a 1420-metre saddle at Bhedetar, with dramatic views and some competent roadside restaurants, then descends to cross the Tamur Koshi at Mulghat (280m) before climbing once again to **DHANKUTA**, stretched out on a ridge at 1150m. Though you'd never guess it by looking at it, Dhankuta is now the administrative headquarters for eastern Nepal. There are of course bigger, more developed cities in the eastern Tarai, but Nepal is, after all, a hill country run by hill people, and so the job of administering the region naturally falls to a hill town.

Dhankuta is a small, easy-going, predominantly Newar town, with pedestrian-only streets, shady *chautaara* and a friendly, well-to-do feel. Steps lead up from the bus park to the main **bazaar**, which climbs north along the ridge. The lower half of the bazaar, up to the police station, is paved and reasonably active; the upper half is quieter but also picturesque, lined with whitewashed, tiled and carved Newar townhouses. The outlying area is populated by Rais, Magars and Hindu castes, who make Dhankuta's **haat bazaar**, on Thursday, a tremendously vivid affair. The **Dhankuta Museum** (mid-Feb to mid-Nov Mon, Wed–Fri & Sun 10am–5pm; mid-Nov to mid-Feb same days 10am–4pm; Rs5), located near the top of the bazaar, displays ethnic and archeological artefacts of eastern Nepal. To get to it, walk up the flagstoned bazaar to the four-way intersection of Bhim Narayan Chowk, marked by a statue, then follow the road to the right around and down for 250m – the museum is a whitewashed building above the road on the left, signposted only in Nepali.

Although you can't see the Himalaya from here, the area makes fine **walking** country, and you're bound to run into chatty aid workers or ex-Gurkhas on the trail. In **Santang**, a Rai village about 45 minutes southeast of town, women can be seen embroidering beautiful shawls and weaving *dhaka*, which is as much a speciality of the eastern hills as it is in the west (see p.318). You can walk to Hile in about two hours by taking short cuts off the main road: stick to the ridge and within sight of the electric power line.

Practicalities

Dhankuta's most salubrious **place to stay**, the *DFID Nepal Guest House* (℡026/20259; ❹), only has five rooms and is used by British government officials, so phone ahead. Located 200m south of the bus park, it features a garden, solar hot water, well-furnished rooms, a sitting room and stodgy Western fare. Cheapies in the bazaar are cold-water, trekking-standard outfits with minimal command of English, but pleasantly traditional wooden interiors. *Hotel Parichaya* (❶), near the police station, is friendly and clean, as is the nearby *Hotel Sunrise* (❶). Plenty of eateries in the bazaar do *daal bhaat*, *pakauda* and the like, and one or two can rustle up *momo*, *thukpa* and curries.

Hile and beyond

Most buses to Dhankuta continue as far as **HILE** (*Hee*-lay), 15km beyond Dhankuta and 750m higher up along the same ridge. If you're here to start (or finish) a trek to Everest or Makalu – and you'd be crazy to come all this way and not trek – Hile might seem anticlimactic. Yet this spirited little settlement is one of the most important staging areas in eastern Nepal, and would merit a stay even if it weren't a trailhead.

Poised over the vast, hazy Arun Valley, Hile's bazaar strip straggles up the often fog-bound ridge, drawing a transient swirl of ethnic peoples who walk in from miles around to trade: Tamangs and Sherpas from the west, Newar and Indian traders from the south, and Rais from their heartland of the roadless hillsides all around. The most visible minority, however, are Bhotiyas (see p.508) from the northern highlands, who run a number of simple wooden lodges. Undoubtedly one of the most exotic things you can do in Nepal is sit in a flickering Bhotiya kitchen sipping hot millet beer from an authentic **tongba**: unique to the eastern hills, these miniature wooden steins with brass hoops and fitted tops look like they were designed for Genghis Khan.

Other than drink a tongba, or maybe visit a couple of one-room *gompas*, the only thing to do in Hile is browse the bazaar. What you see are the only goods that will make it further into the hills: plastic containers, readymade clothes, metal pots, salt, ballpoint pens and packet-noodles. Porters gather in Hile by the dozens, and the trail to Tumlingtar, three days up the Arun Valley, is like a *doko* highway. Hile's **haat bazaar**, on Thursday, is lively, but not as big as Dhankuta's.

Magnificent **views** (even by trekking standards) can be had just a half-hour's hike from Hile – as long as you're up early enough to beat the clouds. Walk to the north end of the bazaar and bear right at the fork up a dirt lane (left leads into the jeep park); after 100m a set of steps leads up to join the Hattikharka trail, which contours around the hill. The panorama spreads out before you like a trekking map: to the northwest, the Makalu Himal floats above the awesome canyon of the Arun (though Everest is hidden behind the crest, you can see its characteristic plume); the ridges of the Milke Daada zigzag to the north; and part of the Kanchenjunga massif pokes up in the northeast.

Encouraged by a recently liberalized market, some landowners in this area have begun to cultivate tea, which is already big business to the east of here in Ilam (see p.406). You can visit the **Guranse tea estate**, whose main entrance is just down the road from the bazaar.

Practicalities

Hile's **lodges** are pretty savvy about catering to foreigners, though innkeepers don't speak much English. Of the half-dozen Bhotiya places in the bazaar (all ❶), *Hotel Gajur* is perhaps the most atmospheric, and its kitchen is legendary for *momo*, *sokuti* and tongba. In addition to the guesthouses, many stalls at either end of the bazaar do Nepali/Tibetan **food** such as *momo*, *sokuti* and chow mein. The Rastriya Banijya **bank**, opposite the small *gompa* at the southern end of the bazaar, can change cash and travellers' cheques.

Moving on

When it's time to **move on**, you can get a night bus direct to Kathmandu if you're in a hurry, but it's a brutal eighteen-hour ride. If possible, break the journey into two or more days, with stops in Janakpur and/or Chitwan. Buses leave Hile every half-hour for Dharan (last bus down is at 5.30pm), from where you can pick up onward connections.

Turning round and going home isn't obligatory, however, as dirt roads penetrate further and further into the hills each year. From the northern end of the bazaar, **jeeps** and the occasional battered bus bump and rev their way down a seasonal dirt road which now reaches the **Arun river**, passing the agricultural research station at Pakhribas en route. At the river, the road reverts to a foot trail that breaks north towards Tumlingtar, and west towards Bhojpur (famous for its *khukuri* knives).

Most buses from Dhankuta rumble north and east on another dirt road as far as **Basantapur**, a dank, almost Elizabethan bazaar that lies a dusty 21km – nearly three hours by bus – from Hile. You get tremendous views of the Makalu massif for much of the way, and Kanchenjunga pops into view near the end. The hills above Basantapur are a delight for walking: mixed pasture and dense mossy forest, rhododendrons, orchids and jasmine, and plenty of friendly villages. As long as the road isn't blocked by snow or landslides, or impassably wet, you can pick up a shared jeep from Basantapur to **Tehratum**, a four-hour ride to the east, from where the road is eventually going to be extended through to Phidim, Taplejung and Ilam. Another road, rougher still, continues north from Basantapur towards the beautiful Newar towns of **Chainpur** and **Tumlingtar**, halfway to the Tibetan border.

None of these roads see more than a handful of foreigners every year. If you really want to explore the eastern hills, however, leave them behind and go on foot.

The Ilam road

Like the Dhankuta road, the **Ilam road** keeps getting longer: originally engineered by the Koreans to connect the tea estates of Kanyam and Ilam with the
Tarai, it now goes all the way to Taplejung, the most common starting point
for Kanchenjunga treks (however, nobody in their right mind would go to
Taplejung by road when they can fly). The road is paved and in excellent shape
as far as Ilam, but it's extremely steep and entails a couple of monster ascents
totalling 2300m elevation gain.

A few express **buses** to Ilam come through from Dharan and points further
west, but a more frequent, crowded service begins from Birtamod, located on
the Mahendra Highway 8km west of the actual start of the road at Charali. The
78km journey takes about four hours by bus; shared **jeeps**, also departing from
Birtamod, are somewhat faster and more comfortable. Be sure to catch the bus
or jeep in Birtamod, as you won't get a seat if you try to board in Charali.

After traversing lush lowlands, the road begins a laborious 1600m ascent to
Kanyam and its undulating monoculture of tea. At Phikal, a few kilometres further on, a paved side road leads steeply up for 10km to **Pashupati Nagar**, a
small bazaar at 2200m just below the ridge that separates Nepal and India here.
Some diplomatic kerfuffle has so far prevented this border crossing from being
opened to all foreigners, but it's very popular with Nepalis and Indians, since
it's only 35km by sealed road from there to Darjeeling. Shared jeeps wait at the
turnoff at Phikal, from where the road descends 1200m in a series of tight
switchbacks to cross the Mai Khola before climbing another 700m to Ilam
(1200m).

Ilam and around

To Nepalis, **ILAM** (Ee-lam) means tea: cool and moist for much of the year,
the hills of Ilam district (like those of Darjeeling, just across the border) are
perfect for it. Ilam town, headquarters of the district, sits right on the edge of
a tea estate, which gives it almost a wine-country atmosphere. Unfortunately,
the bazaar itself is rather shoddy, though it contains some nice old wooden
buildings, and there are no mountain views from anywhere very close by. It's
unlikely that you'd travel all this way just for some tea, though there are plenty
of **hikes** and some good **birdwatching** in the area.

Settled by Newars, Rais and Marwaris (a business-minded Indian group with
interests in tea), Ilam was eastern Nepal's main centre of commerce at one
time. While hill towns like Ilam have lost much of their trading importance to
the Tarai in recent years, the Thursday *haat bazaar* here still draws shoppers from
a wide radius, and of course tea cultivation provides an anchor for the local
economy.

A single tourist **hotel**, *Green View Guest House* (☎027/20616; ❸) has clean,
large and well-furnished rooms with windows looking out over the tea gardens, and geyser hot water. *Danfe Guest House* (☎027/20045; ❷), just down the
road, is a classic bare-bones trekking inn, but with a superb location in among
the tea bushes. Various noisy, smelly and avoidable lodges overlook the bus park.

Simple **meals** are available at loads of eateries along the main drag – *daal
bhaat* is generally very good in Ilam. Two places that can be recommended are
Changwa Hotel, about midway along the bazaar, and *Kanchanjhangha Restaurant*,
a tiny, welcoming wooden shack near the top end.

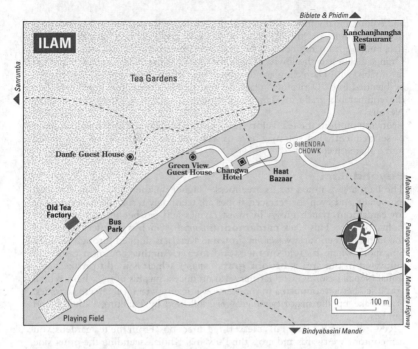

Map labels:
Biblete & Phidim
Kanchanjhangha Restaurant
ILAM
Sanrumba
Tea Gardens
Danfe Guest House
BIRENDRA CHOWK
Green View Guest House
Changwa Hotel
Haat Bazaar
Maibeni
Old Tea Factory
Bus Park
N
Paltangemor & Mahendra Highway
Playing Field
0 100 m
Bindyabasini Mandir

The tea gardens and factory

Ilam's **tea gardens** carpet the ridge above town and tumble down its steep far side; between April and November you can watch the pluckers at work, and at other times it's just a relaxing place to be. Nepal's first tea estate, it was established in 1864 by a relative of the prime minister after a visit to Darjeeling, where tea cultivation was just becoming big business. Marwaris, who had already cornered the cardamom trade here, soon assumed control of the plantation on a contract basis, an arrangement that lasted until the 1960s when the government nationalized this and six other hill estates under the direction of the Nepal Tea Development Corporation (NTDC). In 1999, however, the government granted a fifty-year lease on all seven estates to an Indian company. The impact of new, hard-nosed efficiencies is already being felt: the 140-year-old tea factory in Ilam town has been closed and workers have lost their pensions, but production is increasing after years of hopeless lassitude.

Gazing at the undulating lines of tea bush may be pleasant enough, but to actually try the product – Nepali tea, even in Ilam, is made with low-grade tea dust from Tarai plantations, along with lots of milk and sugar – and see how it's made, you'll need to return back down the main road as far as Paltangemor (1hr 30min by jeep). The Kanyam **tea factory** here, built using British aid money in 1985, is the largest in the district. Staff are not quite used to visitors yet, so you may need to ask around for the manager, but once inside you're likely to be welcomed with a short (free) **tour** and a cup of tea.

The process begins with the plucked leaves being loaded into "withering chutes" upstairs, where fans remove about half their moisture content. They're then transferred to big rolling machines to break the cell walls and release their juices, and placed on fermentation beds to bring out their characteristic flavour and colour. Finally, most of the remaining moisture is removed in a wood-fired drying machine, and the leaves are sorted into grades, which basically refer to size, ranging from the coveted SFTGFOP (Super Fine Tippy Golden Flower Orange Pekoe) to the lowly PD (Pekoe Dust). Ilam's premium tea compares favourably with Darjeeling's, and indeed most of it is exported to Germany to be blended into "Darjeeling" teas. The best Ilam tea here costs much less than the comparable grade in Darjeeling, though it's still too expensive for most Nepalis.

Moving on from the tea factory, transport up to Ilam and down to Birtamod passes frequently, but you may have to stand on a local **bus**, or wedge yourself into a shared jeep.

Beyond Ilam

The Ilam area is noted for its greenness – higher up, the jungle is profuse and exuberant, and even the terraced slopes are teemingly fertile. Keep an eye out for cardamom, which grows in moist ravines and has become an important cash-crop here. This black **cardamom** (*sukumel*), which is an inferior form of the tropical green variety (*elaichi*) grown in Kerala, is shipped through India to Singapore where it's sold on the world market. Another common cash crop cultivated in this area is **broom grass** (*amliso*), which is used to make traditional Nepali besoms. Local farmers also produce a surplus of milk here, which you'll see being transported in canisters on horseback to local cheese factories. Rais make up the majority of villagers, followed by Baahuns, Chhetris and Limbus.

Rewarding **walks** set off in at least three directions. From the tea gardens, you can contour westwards and cross the Puwamai Khola, ascending the other side to Sanrumba, site of a Tuesday market (there are supposed to be views of Kanchenjunga from further along this ridge). A trail heading east from Ilam descends to cross the Mai Khola, where the annual Beni Mela attracts thousands of Hindus on the first day of Magh (Jan 14 or 15), and continues on to Naya Bazaar. A sacred pond atop a wooded ridge north of Ilam, Mai Pokhri can be reached by walking or hitching along the road towards Phidim and making a right at Biblete, 2km from the bazaar, from where it's another two-hours' ascent, passing through rhododendron and magnolia forest; a shorter trip could be made by riding a shared jeep one-way. If you're looking for a quick leg-stretch, check out the small but attractively situated Bindyabasini Mandir, about 1km down the main road from the bus park.

The **Mai Valley**, which Ilam overlooks, is renowned for its **birds**: the dense, wet habitat and abundant undergrowth provide cover for some 450 species. However, the valley spans a large range of elevations, so to see anywhere near that number of species you have to move around a lot, and you'll need a guide brought from Kathmandu, Chitwan or Koshi Tappu. Lowland species such as drongos, bulbuls and flycatchers (as well as the more exotic Asian fairy bluebird, blue-eared barbet and pale-headed woodpecker) are best observed in the Sukarni forest southwest of Ilam, below the Soktim tea estate. Temperate birds (tits, finches, warblers, barwings, minlas and many others) inhabit the oak-rhododendron forest of the upper Mai Valley to the northeast of Ilam, from Mabu up to Sandakpur on the Indian border, at elevations of 2000m to 3000m.

Sandakpur itself is well known in India for its sunset and sunrise views, taking in – on a clear day – the mountains from Kanchenjunga to Everest, and views of the plains and hills as far as Darjeeling. From Biblete, jeeps can be hired to follow a dirt road north (passing Mai Pokhri on the way) until it peters out at Maimajhuwa. From here, a trail climbs the Goruwala Daada, taking around four hours up to the viewpoint. A proposed cable-car link hasn't yet developed beyond the wistful dreaming stage, but there's a lodge on the Nepalese side of the border – and numerous guesthouses just across the way, on the Indian side. A local guide would be useful if you don't know any Nepali – ask at *Green View Guest House* in Ilam.

Buses ply the road north of Ilam to **Phidim** and **Taplejung** – most people heading this far into the mountains will, rightly enough, be trekking.

Travel details

Day buses

Biratnagar to: Birganj (6 daily; 6hr); Dhankuta (4 daily; 4hr); Dharan (every 15min; 1hr 30min); Janakpur (4 daily; 6hr); Kakarbhitta (every 20min; 3hr); Kathmandu (1 daily; 10hr).
Birganj to: Bhairawa (4 daily; 8hr); Biratnagar (6 daily; 6hr); Butwal for Sonauli (4 daily; 6hr); Dharan (3 daily; 8hr); Gorkha (2 daily; 7hr); Janakpur (every 20min; 4hr); Kakarbhitta (1 daily; 8hr); Kathmandu (8 daily; 8hr); Pokhara (5 daily; 8hr).
Dhankuta to: Basantapur (every 30min; 3hr); Biratnagar (4 daily; 3hr); Dharan (every 30min; 3hr); Hile (every 30min; 30min).
Dharan to: Basantapur (every 30min; 6hr); Biratnagar (every 15min; 1hr 30min); Birganj (3 daily; 8hr); Dhankuta (every 30min; 3hr); Hile (every 30min; 3hr 30min); Ilam (1 daily; 6hr); Janakpur (1 daily; 6hr); Kakarbhitta (every 15min; 3hr).
Hile to: Basantapur (every 30min; 2hr 30min); Dhankuta (every 30min; 30min); Dharan (every 30min; 3hr 30min); Kakarbhitta (3 daily; 5hr).
Ilam to: Birtamod (every 30min; 3hr); Dharan (1 daily; 6hr); Phidim (3 daily; 4hr).
Janakpur to: Bhairawa (2 daily; 9hr); Biratnagar (4 daily; 6hr); Birganj (every 20min; 4hr); Butwal (2 daily; 9hr); Dharan (1 daily; 6hr); Kakarbhitta (7 daily; 7hr); Kathmandu (4 daily; 11hr).
Kakarbhitta to: Biratnagar (every 20min; 3hr); Birganj (1 daily; 8hr); Birtamod (every 10min; 30min); Dharan (every 15min; 3hr); Hile (3 daily; 5hr); Janakpur (7 daily; 7hr); Kathmandu (3 daily; 14hr); Pokhara (1 daily; 15hr).

Night buses

Biratnagar to: Bhairawa (1 daily; 14hr); Birganj (2 daily; 10hr); Kathmandu (8 daily; 14hr).
Birganj to: Bhairawa (1 daily; 10hr); Biratnagar (3 daily; 9hr); Butwal for Sonauli (3 daily; 10hr); Kakarbhitta (2 daily; 13hr); Kathmandu (12 daily; 12hr); Mahendra Nagar (1 daily; 16hr); Pokhara (3 daily; 10hr).
Dhankuta to: Kathmandu (1 daily; 17hr).
Dharan to: Kathmandu (10 daily; 15hr).
Hile to: Kathmandu (1 daily; 18hr).
Ilam to: Kathmandu (2 daily; 20hr).
Janakpur to: Bhairawa (1 daily; 12hr); Butwal (3 daily; 12hr); Kakarbhitta (4 daily; 11hr); Kathmandu (18 daily; 11hr); Nepalganj (2 daily; 14hr); Pokhara (1 daily; 16hr).
Kakarbhitta to: Bhairawa (1 daily; 14hr); Birganj (2 daily; 13hr); Janakpur (4 daily; 11hr); Kathmandu (13 daily; 15hr); Narayangadh (2 daily; 12hr); Nepalganj (1 daily; 19hr).

Flights

Biratnagar to: Bhojpur (1–3 weekly); Kathmandu (10–15 daily); Lamidanda (2–4 weekly); Phaplu (2 weekly); Taplejung (2–5 weekly); Tumlingtar (daily).
Kathmandu to: Bhadrapur (5 daily); Janakpur (1 daily); Lamidanda (4 daily); Lukla (4–14 daily); Phaplu (4 daily); Ramechhap (1–3 weekly); Rumjatar (1–3 daily); Simara (5–10 daily); Tumlingtar (2 daily).

Trekking

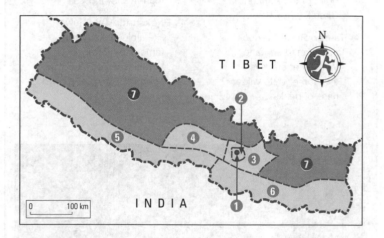

CHAPTER 7

Highlights

✳ **Teahouses** Caravanserais of the Himalaya, with colourful proprietors, multicultural clienteles and improbable cuisines. **See p.431**

✳ **The Thorung La** Crossing this 5415-metre pass is the exhilarating high point of the Annapurna Circuit. **See p.438**

✳ **Tsergo Ri** An overlook above the Langtang Valley that surveys an awesome white wilderness of peaks. **See p.442**

✳ **Kala Pattar** The classic viewpoint of Everest and its neighbours, reached after at least a week's ascent. **See p.448**

✳ **Pangpema** Base camp for the north face of Kanchenjunga – you can't get more remote than this. **See p.451**

✳ **Phoksundo Tal** A jewel-like alpine lake made famous by Peter Mattheissen's *The Snow Leopard*. **See p.453**

7

Trekking

R earing up over the subcontinent like an immense, whitecapped tidal wave, the **Himalaya** (Hee-*maal*-ah-yah) are, to many travellers' minds, the whole reason for visiting Nepal. Containing eight of the world's ten highest peaks – including, of course, Everest – Nepal's 800-kilometre link in the Himalayan chain literally overshadows all other attractions. More than just majestic scenery, though, the "Abode of Snow" is also the home of Sherpas, yaks, yetis (?) and snow leopards, and has always exerted a powerful spiritual pull. In Hindu mythology, the mountains are where gods meditate and make sacrifices, while the Sherpas hold certain peaks to be the very embodiment of deities; mountaineers are often hardly less mystical.

You can **trek** just about anywhere in Nepal – the country's trail network is far more extensive than its roads – but most trekkers stick to just a few well-established routes where teahouses and other amenities make it easy to go without carrying a lot of gear and without knowing Nepali. These **teahouse routes** are popular because they're true classics in one way or another, offering close-up views of the very tallest peaks, especially dramatic scenery or ethnic diversity. However, with popularity has come commercialization and a loss

---

Warning: maobaadis and khaobaadis

As this book goes to press, there have been no attacks against foreign trekkers by Nepal's **Maoist** rebels (see p.498). The most popular trekking areas – Annapurna, Everest (above Lukla) and Langtang/Helambu – are at this time still considered virtually risk-free, and the areas east of Everest and from Rara Lake westwards are probably safe too. However, there have been violent clashes uncomfortably close to some of the other, less developed trekking areas, such as Solu, Dolpo, Ganesh Himal and Rolwaling, while a large section of undeveloped midwestern Nepal is under armed Maoist control and therefore completely off-limits.

Extortion is perhaps a greater threat than physical violence. A few trekking parties passing through Maoist fringe areas have been stopped by *maobaadis* (Maoists) and forced to contribute monetarily to the cause (the trekkers were given receipts for their "donations"). And emboldened by the general decline in law and order in the hills due to the insurgency, some **local bandits** have taken to posing as Maoists and mugging passers-by, earning themselves the nickname *khaobaadis* (literally, "eatists").

You're strongly urged to **check official travel warnings** (see p.21) before leaving your home country, and, upon arrival in Kathmandu, to consult with the Kathmandu Environmental Education Project (see p.423) on the current safety of areas where you plan to trek. And please **don't trek alone**.

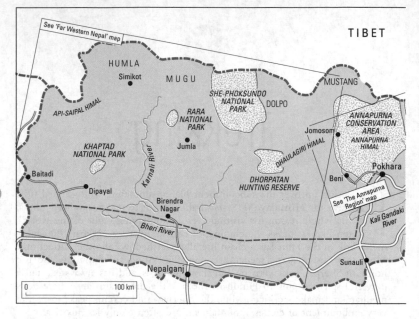

of much of what once made these treks special. For those who put a high priority on getting away from it all, there are many other less-developed routes.

Trekking needn't be expensive nor agonizingly difficult. On teahouse treks you can eat and sleep for less money than you'd spend in Kathmandu. Trails are often steep, to be sure, but you walk at your own pace, and no standard trek goes higher than about 5500m (the *starting* elevation for most climbing expeditions). That said, trekking is not for everybody – it's demanding, sometimes uncomfortable, and it does involve an element of risk. It's not really worth doing unless you feel able to devote several days or more to it.

This chapter is organized to help you decide if you want to trek, and if so, how and where you might like to do it. The first section covers things you need to know about trekking in general, and the second gives overviews of the most popular, and a few of the more notable out-of-the-way, treks. It is *not*, however, intended to take the place of a trekking guidebook; we detail some good ones in Contexts, p.566.

Seasonal considerations

Where you go trekking and how you do it will depend to a great extent on the time of year. **Autumn** (Oct–Nov) is normally dry, stable and very clear, although bear in mind that bad weather can strike in any season: some of the worst landslide and avalanche disasters have been triggered by freak autumn storms. Temperatures are usually moderate during this period, though, making it a good time for any trek. It can be cold at night higher up, but not as cold as it gets later on in the year, and the daytime temperatures are pleasantly cool for walking. At low elevations it may still be quite hot during the day. Autumn is the most popular season for trekking, though, so all standard routes – especially Annapurna and Everest – will be maxed, porters will charge top dollar, and flights will be tight. Don't expect solitude.

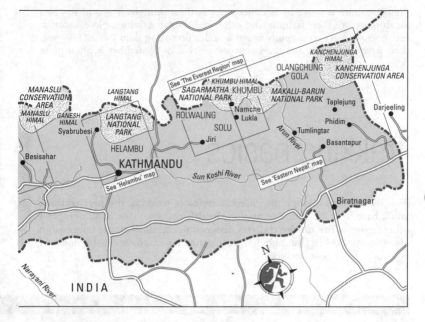

Winter (Dec–Jan) is for the most part dry and settled, albeit colder. When precipitation does fall, the snow line drops to 2500m and sometimes lower. Passes over 4000m may be uncrossable due to snow and ice, and some settlements described in trekking guidebooks may be uninhabited. High-altitude treks, such as Everest, require good gear and experience in cold-weather conditions, as temperatures at 5000m can drop below minus 20°C and heavy snow can fall. Below 2000m, temperatures can be quite spring-like, though valleys are often filled with fog or haze. The teahouses that remain open are much quieter than in the autumn, and proprietors have more time to chat.

Temperatures and the snow line rise steadily during **spring** (Feb–April), while the likelihood of precipitation increases. The warmer weather also brings more trekkers, though not as many as in autumn. The main factor that keeps the numbers down is a disappointing haze that creeps up in elevation during this period. By April, you probably won't get good views until you reach 4000m or so. The most colourful rhododendrons bloom in April, between 2000m and 3000m.

It gets that much hotter, hazier and unsettled in May and early June. The warming Asian landmass has begun drawing air up from the south, ushering in the **pre-monsoon** – a season of erratic weather and increasingly frequent afternoon storms. The trails and teahouses again begin to empty out. This is a time for going high, but be prepared for rain, especially in traditionally wet areas such as Annapurna and eastern Nepal.

Few foreigners trek during the **monsoon** (mid-June to late Sept), because of the rain, mud, leeches, travel difficulties and general lack of mountain views. (The leeches along the mid-elevation trails are not for the squeamish!) However, treks in the Himalayan rain shadow and in Nepal's far west are sheltered from the brunt of the monsoon. Even in wet areas, mornings are often clear, and wildflowers and butterflies can be seen in abundance. Authentic

Nepali culture is more in evidence, too, as the summer off-season is when locals return to their farming and other traditional activities. Note also that the monsoon isn't consistently rainy: it builds up to a peak in July and August, then tapers off again, and the last week or two of September is often quite dry.

Trekking basics

This section runs through the different **styles** of trekking, the **preparations** you'll have to make before setting off, **health** matters to be mindful of, and other factors of **life on the trail**. It's designed to complement the information given in standard trekking guides, with particular emphasis on the nuts and bolts of independent trekking.

Trekking with children

The potential problems when considering whether to go **trekking with children** are obvious: will they walk? Will he/she let a porter carry them in a *doko*? What if they get sick? What if the weather is bad?

All of the above notwithstanding, you may well find that if you do decide to take the plunge, trekking with kids is one of the best things you ever do; and if you team up with someone else who's trekking with children, so much the better. Kids can have endless adventures together, and parents can relax knowing that their charges have each other for company. Trekking can be an unforgettable experience for children, with something to delight them around every corner: chickens, goats, jingling donkey trains; frogs, bugs and other creepy crawlies; waterfalls and caves, temples and prayer wheels, leaves and sticks and *shaligrams* for the finding. All that plus being the centre of attention everywhere they go. You should have realistic expectations, though, and the tips below will help you get the best out of trekking with small children.

Routes Stick to easy ones; it's not advisable to take a young child above 3500m due to the risks of AMS. The standard teahouse routes generally offer more comforts and easier access to emergency services, although with the help of a good agency, it's not out of the question to take children off the beaten track.

Pace Trekking speed will depend on the age and sportiness of your youngest child. Play it safe and plan on very modest days, stopping by mid-afternoon and allowing the occasional rest day.

Weather School vacations don't coincide with the best trekking seasons; however, trekking can be a highly educational experience, so it may well be worth going for the better weather, even if it means taking kids out of school.

Health and safety Trekking carries most of the same hazards as a weekend camping trip at home, requiring the same precautions and packing. The extra concern is tummy bugs: teach kids to drink only boiled or purified water, keep hands and foreign objects out of mouths, and wash hands frequently (sanitary wipes come in handy). Establish clear ground rules about not wandering off, not running, not ven-

Trekking independently

Trekking independently – making all your own arrangements instead of going through a trekking company, carrying your own pack and staying in teahouses – saves money and gives you a more individualized experience, but is more limiting than an organized trek. Most budget travellers choose this way simply because it's cheaper.

The **cost** of lodging is negligible, and there's very little else to spend your money on besides a porter or guide (if you choose to hire one) and **food**. Even in the Annapurna and Everest regions, where trekker menus may tempt you to order relatively expensive items, the average tab for three meals a day is unlikely to go over Rs600 ($8). Along other standard routes you'll probably find you spend Rs400–500 ($5–7) a day, and off the beaten track it may actually be impossible to spend more than Rs300 ($4) a day. These guidelines don't take into account such nonessentials as beer, soft drinks and chocolate, which rise in price as you ascend further from the nearest road (a single beer can sell for $5 in some remote locations). Hiring a porter to carry your stuff will add considerably to your daily cost (see overleaf).

Doing it yourself gives you more **control** over many aspects of the trek: you can go at your own pace, stop when and where you like, choose your travelling companions and take rest days or side-trips as you please. The downside is

turing close to dropoffs, and staying well clear of animals. Bathroom arrangements in the more primitive trekking inns may put children off, so you may want to avoid trekking with a child who isn't potty trained – partly because of the diaper dimension, partly because of the extra risks and hassles a child that young would pose.

Food and drink Some kids love *daal bhaat* – they can eat it with their fingers – but many turn up their noses. Fortunately, it's never a problem to get familiar Western dishes on the teahouse routes.

Lodging Kids usually love the novelty of each new teahouse, and get doted on continuously. If you're trekking with an agency, you'll probably camp in tents with plenty of home comforts.

Transportation Getting to the trailhead by bus or taxi is fine for grownups, but for children, a couple of hours on winding mountain roads is a recipe for car-sickness. If possible, rent a more comfortable vehicle, or fly.

Porters You'll almost certainly want a porter for each child. Almost all porters are great playmates/babysitters, despite the language barrier, and they can carry the child for all or part of the trek in a *doko* that's been customized to let the legs dangle out the back; agencies usually have deluxe versions on hand, but any *doko* can be modified on the spot. Naturally, you'll want to be very careful about the porter you hire to carry your child along precarious trails; make sure he or she is agile, conscientious and sober, and treat him or her well. It's worth paying porters more than the standard daily wage, buying them shoes, and making sure they know you'll tip them well at the end.

What to bring You'll need the same range of clothes for your child as for yourself, only more and warmer. Bring just a few unflashy games or toys that have a lot of play value per ounce. You'll kick yourself if you don't bring a video camera, or at least a still camera; a handheld tape recorder is also useful, both for recording and for playing story tapes. You won't need as many story books as you might think, as bedtime comes early.

that you have to spend two or three days lining up bus or plane tickets, renting equipment, buying supplies and perhaps tracking down a porter or guide. A more serious drawback is that you're effectively confined to a few mass-market **teahouse routes**; trekking to remote areas is difficult unless you speak Nepali or you're prepared to deal with considerable porter logistics. Moreover, some of the most alluring areas are restricted to organized groups.

Life on the trail is described later, but suffice it to say that an independent trek is likely to be less comfortable than one arranged through an agency. Lodges can be noisy and lacking in privacy, while the food is often fairly uninteresting. The active teahouse **social scene** goes some way to compensating for this, however – even if you start out alone, you'll quickly meet up with potential trekking companions.

By not being part of a group, you're better placed to learn from Nepali ways rather than forcing local people to adapt to yours. Equally important, a high proportion of the money you spend goes directly to the local economy (whereas most of the money paid to trekking agencies goes no further than Kathmandu, and often finds its way overseas). However, as an independent trekker you must guard against contributing to **deforestation**. If you or your porters or guides stay in teahouses and order meals cooked over wood fires, you encourage innkeepers to cut down more trees. Fortunately, kerosene is replacing wood in the most popular areas. See the box on p.430 for tips on minimizing your environmental impact.

Hiring porters and guides

Porters are an important part of the Himalayan economy, and there's no shame in hiring one. With a porter taking most of your gear, you only have to carry a small pack containing the things you need during the day; this can be a great relief at high elevations, and it's all but essential when trekking off established routes, where tents, food and cooking equipment have to be brought in. As porters rarely speak much English, you might want to pay more for a **guide** who does. In the Annapurna area many guides are willing to carry gear as well, but this isn't always the case: ask. Guides are only strictly necessary on esoteric routes, but any trek will be enlivened by the company and local knowledge of a good guide, who may well take you on unusual side trips to visit the homes of family and friends. Employing a guide or porter will also tend to earn you more respect in the eyes of local people. But it's also true that a guide may cramp your style by steering you to certain inns, and may actually restrict your contact with local people by conducting all negotiations on your behalf.

Hiring a porter or guide is simple enough: just ask at your guesthouse, or try a reputable trekking agency or equipment-rental shop. Hiring someone off the street is riskier, but it will save you money and the guide/porter will end up better-off too. Another strategy is simply to wait till you get to the trailhead or airstrip: there are usually porters and guides waiting for work at the starting points of the popular treks, and they usually know the area better than someone hired in Kathmandu. If you start out without help and change your mind later, you may be able to hire a porter at one of the major trailside towns, such as Namche and Manang. The hiring process is informal and not always reputable, so shop around and interview more than one candidate if necessary. Take the time to talk a while, maybe over tea or a meal, to get a feel for whether you'll get along. A guide who's actually from the area you plan to trek in is vastly preferable to one who's not, because he or she will have family and friends along the way and will be respected by the local people.

The typical daily **wage** for a porter is about Rs400 ($5) a day, and for a guide upwards of Rs750 ($10). If you hire the porter through an agency or other middleman, rather than directly, you'll be charged 50–100 percent more. Be clear whether or not the agreed amount includes food – it shouldn't – and don't pay too much of it up front (fifty percent is pretty standard). Don't over-negotiate: Rs100 a day is trivial to you, but can make a huge difference to your porter. Expect also to give your guide or porter a **tip** equivalent to about one day's extra pay for each week worked, assuming the work was well done. It's also nice to make a gift of any spare gear or clothing at the end of the trek.

The **responsibilities** of employing a porter or guide cannot be overstated. Several porters die needlessly each year, typically because their sahib (pronounced "sahb") thought they were superhuman and didn't mind sleeping outside in a blizzard. You *must* make sure your employees are adequately clothed for the journey – on high-altitude treks, this will mean buying or renting them good shoes, a parka, sunglasses, mittens and a sleeping bag. Establish beforehand if something is a loan. If they get sick, it's up to you to look after them, and since most porters hired in Kathmandu and Pokhara are clueless about altitude-related problems, it's your responsibility to educate them. You should also obtain insurance for your guide/porter, if she or he doesn't already have it – KEEP can advise on this.

If you've never trekked before, don't try to organize a trek off the teahouse routes. Finding a guide familiar with a particular area will be hard, and transporting him with a crew of porters and supplies to the trailhead a major (and expensive) logistical exercise. Getting a trekking agency to do it might not cost much more.

Organized trekking

Organized treks are for people who haven't got the time or inclination to make their own arrangements, or who want to tackle ambitious routes that can't be done independently. They **cost** from $20 to $150 a day, depending on the standard of service, size of the group, remoteness of the route, and whether you book the trip in your home country or in Kathmandu. The price should always include a guide, porters, food and shelter, although cheap outfits often charge extra for things like national park fees and transport, and may cut other corners as well. The cheaper the price, the more wary you need to be.

A trek is hard work however you do it, but a good company will help you

Trekking companies in Nepal speak the green lingo as fluently as anyone, but in many cases their walk doesn't match their talk. Here are some specific **questions** to put to them to find out what they're actually doing to minimize their impact on the environment. You may not find a company able to answer every question satisfactorily, but the exercise should help establish which outfits are genuinely concerned.

• Do they carry enough kerosene to cook all meals for all members of the party, including porters?

• What equipment do they provide to porters – tents, proper clothing, shoes, UV sunglasses?

• Do they separate trash and carry out all non-burnable/non-biodegradable waste?

• How many of their staff have attended the Kathmandu Environmental Education Project's annual Ecotrek workshop on responsible trekking? (Attendees will be able to show a certificate.)

• Do staff have wilderness first-aid training?

along with a few **creature comforts**: you can expect appetizing food, "bed tea" and hot "washing water" on cold mornings, camp chairs and a latrine tent with toilet paper. Depending on the size of your party, a guide, *sirdar* (guide foreman) or "Western trek leader" (native-English-speaking guide) will be able to answer questions and cope with problems. Trekking groups usually sleep in **tents**, which, while quieter than teahouses, may be colder and are certainly more cramped. The daily routine of eating as a group can get monotonous, and gives you **less contact** with local people. There's something to be said for safety in numbers, but trekking with a group imposes a somewhat **inflexible itinerary** on you, and if you don't like the people in your group, you're stuck.

In theory, organized treks are more **environmentally sound**, at least in the national parks and conservation areas, where trekkers' meals are supposed to be cooked with kerosene. Sometimes, however, cooks use wood so they can sell the kerosene at the end of the trek – and, worse still, for each trekker eating a kerosene-cooked meal, there may be two or three porters and other staff cooking their *bhaat* over a wood fire.

But the main advantage of organized trekking is it enables you to get **off the beaten track**: there's little point in using an agency to do a teahouse trek. The more crowded and commercialized the teahouse routes become, the more rewarding it is to get away from them. A number of companies now offer "wilderness" treks, which forsake the traditional village-to-village valley routes for obscure trails along uninhabited ridgelines. Shop around and you'll also find special-interest treks based around Tibetan Buddhism, shamanism, birdwatching, rhododendron-viewing, medicine and even trail construction or trash cleanup. Many companies also run trips that combine trekking with rafting, cycling and wildlife-viewing.

Budget operators

Small **budget operators** in Kathmandu and Pokhara, charging $15–25 a day, are notoriously hard to recommend: most are fly-by-night setups offering mainly customized treks – they're rarely competent to handle anything beyond the mass-market routes. Many represent themselves to be trekking operators when in fact they're merely agents, taking a commission and providing very little service for it. A few of the more established budget companies run scheduled treks, but again, usually only to the most popular areas. In this category,

A few bad apples

This is an advisory notice for women contemplating trekking alone with a male guide: reports in the past few years suggest that a number of guides, including a few owners of seemingly reputable agencies, make a practice of **sexually harassing or assaulting their female clients**. The vast majority of Nepali guides are good as gold, but women should be aware that there are a few bad apples. The best way to avoid them is to follow the recommendations of people you trust, insist on meeting the guide before hiring, bring along a trekking partner, and nip any unwanted advances in the bud with a frank "I don't want to sleep with you". You might also consider hiring a female guide – see p.302.

names change often and standards can quickly rise and fall. A good place to start your search would be KEEP's list of member trekking agencies and its trekker logbooks.

Bigger operators

Kathmandu's **big operators** mainly package treks on behalf of overseas agencies, but they may allow "walk-ins" to join at a reduced price, and some offer cheaper treks specifically for the local market (typically priced at $30–60 a day). For specifics on agencies in Kathmandu, see p.168. Request brochures to make sure your schedule coincides with theirs; for customized treks to exotic areas, make contact several months in advance, or be prepared to wait up to a week in Kathmandu while arrangements are being made.

Overseas agencies

Booking through an **overseas agency** lets you arrange everything before you leave home, but expect to pay £50–100/US$80–160 per day. Some agencies have their own Nepali subsidiaries in Kathmandu, others use independent outfitters like those listed on p.168. Overseas agencies will look after all your arrangements up till the time you leave your home country, and will also play a part in maintaining quality-control in Nepal. Some may allow you to join up in Kathmandu at a reduced price. See pp.13, 16 and 17 for names and addresses.

Trekking peaks and mountaineering

His Majesty's Government has designated eighteen lesser summits, ranging in elevation from 5587m to 6654m, as **trekking peaks**. These peaks offer a compromise between a standard trek and a full-on mountaineering expedition, ranging in difficulty from moderately steep glacier walks to technical, multi-day rock and ice climbs. You need to be especially fit and able to cope with very cold and potentially stormy conditions; previous climbing experience is preferable for the easier peaks, and essential for the harder ones.

Climbing a trekking peak takes more time than most standard treks – three to four weeks is typical – and **costs** at least $20 per day if done independently, quite a bit more if you go with an agency. Contributing to the cost are the trekking peak **permit** ($350 and up, depending on size of party), the salaries of a Nepal Mountaineering Association-certified *sirdar* and at least a few porters, plus transportation and equipment for both trekkers and staff. Some peaks are located in restricted areas, for which an additional permit fee is payable. The *sirdar* can help with logistics and advise on what extra equipment to bring or obtain in Kathmandu. It will take several days to a week to organize a trekking peak expedition from scratch in Kathmandu.

Another couple of hundred higher peaks are open only to **expeditions**, which must comply with additional regulations and pay higher fees (from $1500 up to $70,000 in the case of Everest Southeast Ridge). Further **information** on trekking and expedition peaks is available from the Nepal Mountaineering Association (℡01/434525, ⊛www.nma.com.np).

Equator Expeditions, Thamel Northwest (℡01/415782, ℮equator@mos .com.np), runs a **mountaineering school** for beginners in the Everest region. Sessions, held in April and October–November, cost $1800 for three weeks or $2000 for four weeks (inclusive of accommodation in Kathmandu). A cheaper option is to trek to the Everest region independently and join up with Equator for a six-day course on Lobuje East. At $700 a person, this actually works out cheaper than organizing the climb of this trekking peak yourself, plus you get instruction. This course is held only a couple of times a year, so check with Equator for dates.

Preparations

Arranging a trek is like anything else in Nepal: complications arise, things inevitably take longer than planned, but it's unquestionably worth it in the end. Obviously, trekking independently involves more preparation than joining an organized group. The remainder of this chapter is geared specifically to independent trekkers, although most of the information will apply to groups as well.

Permits and other formalities

Trekking permits are now no longer required for most areas, including all the standard routes in the Annapurna, Everest and Langtang/Helambu/ Gosainkund areas. This is a welcome improvement to a system which previously obliged would-be trekkers to spend hours queuing for paperwork, and which supported a large contingent of dubious brokers and corrupt officials. (There is some talk of reintroducing a modest trekking fee for all areas, but this time specifically to fund a network of police checkposts to increase trekker security.) A permit is still required for treks that pass through the so-called **restricted areas** of Kanchenjunga, Olangchung Gola, Rolwaling, Manaslu, Upper Mustang, Dolpo, Mugu, Humla and Api-Saipal. Permits for these must be obtained by or through a registered agency, and for some a government liaison officer (basically a chaperone whose job is to make sure you stick to your stated route) is required.

If your trek goes through any of the national parks or conservation areas, you'll have to purchase a separate **entry ticket** (Rs1000 or Rs2000 for most areas). In most cases the fee is simply collected at the entry point, but for Annapurna treks you must purchase your ticket in advance in Kathmandu or Pokhara. Children under ten receive free admission.

Before setting off on any trek, **register with your embassy** in Kathmandu, as this will speed things up should you need rescuing. You can have KEEP or the Himalayan Rescue Association forward the details to your embassy. It's also advisable to be **insured** for trekking – note that travel-insurance companies may add a surcharge to their rates to cover "hazardous sports" such as trekking.

Information, maps and books

The best sources of current trekking **information** are the Kathmandu Environmental Education Project, Himalayan Rescue Association and Himalayan Explorers Connection, all with offices in Kathmandu (see p.96). HRA also maintains two rescue and information posts in the Annapurna and Everest regions, while KEEP has a satellite visitors' centre in the Helambu region and is planning to open another in Pokhara. These are nonprofit organizations that rely on membership dues and donations to do their work. All have libraries of trekking-related books, logbooks full of comments from returning trekkers (invaluable for tips on routes and trekking agencies), staff who can advise on trail conditions and equipment, and notice boards for finding trekking partners and used equipment. KEEP also sells books, water-purification tablets, anti-leech oil and other trekking-related items. KEEP doesn't take a position on independent versus agency trekking, but encourages trekkers to use their clout as consumers to effect changes in the trekking industry; exhibits in the office give a primer on trekkers' impact on the environment and culture. HRA provides information on altitude sickness, health and weather, while HEC offers a range of services for its members, including homestay and volunteer programmes, equipment loans for porters, communications and luggage storage.

Nepal's trekking regions are fairly well **mapped**, although the rule, as always, is you get what you pay for. The best map for a particular trek will vary from year to year, as companies leapfrog past each other with new editions. The locally produced Himalayan Map House/Nepa, Mandala and Shangri-la series include colour maps of the most popular routes; generally these work fine if you stick to the main trails, although they can't really be relied upon for off-trail route-finding. The pricier Geo-Buch ("Schneider") maps of the Everest and Langtang/Helambu areas have much more reliable contours and topo details, though they're way out of date for villages. All of these are available in the bigger tourist bookshops. For more obscure treks that aren't well depicted by the standard series, try the HMG/FINNIDA maps, produced by His

Trekking information on the web

🕸 **www.everestnews.com** Expedition reports, climber profiles and extensive info on Everest and other major peaks.

🕸 **www.gorp.com/gorp/location/asia/nepal.htm** Articles on outdoor activities in Nepal.

🕸 **www.hec.org** The Himalayan Explorers Connection's website features trip reports, a newsletter, information on volunteer opportunities and other useful stuff.

🕸 **www.high-altitude-medicine.com/** Excellent info on AMS and high-altitude health, with links.

🕸 **www.keepnepal.org** Tips on environmentally sensitive trekking from the Kathmandu Environmental Education Project.

🕸 **www.nma.com.np** The Nepal Mountaineering Association's website: information on trekking and expedition peaks (not often updated) and official application forms for permits.

🕸 **www.project-himalaya.com** Excellent introductory advice, trail reports, "e-guides" to obscure routes, and updates to the Trailblazer trekking guides (by the authors).

🕸 **www.trekinfo.com** A mix of useful info and links to trekking companies, plus a good message board.

Majesty's Government in co-operation with the Finnish aid agency – they're superb and not too expensive, though they're not designed specifically for trekking. These maps are only patchily available in tourist bookshops, but the full series is sold at Maps of Nepal, west of *Everest Hotel* in Kathmandu.

The trekking **guidebooks** and general books on the Himalaya listed in Contexts (p.566) can easily be bought in Kathmandu or Pokhara. All-Nepal guidebooks, such as Stephen Bezruchka's *Trekking in Nepal: A Traveler's Guide* and Stan Armington's *Trekking in the Nepal Himalaya*, give a broad perspective that's useful when doing initial research, but on the trail you might prefer to carry one of the slimmer, trek-specific guides such as those in the Trailblazer series.

What to bring

Having the right **equipment** on a trek is obviously important, though when you see how little porters get by with, you'll realize that high-tech gear isn't essential. Bring what you need to be comfortable, but keep weight to a minimum. The equipment list below is intended mainly for independent trekkers staying in teahouses. If you're planning to camp, you'll need quite a few more things, and if you're trekking with an agency you won't need so much.

Equipment checklist

Almost all the items listed below can be purchased in Nepal. Those marked (*) can be rented. But if you want to be absolutely sure of having it, bring it with you.

Essentials
Backpack* – one with an internal frame and hip belt is best
Sleeping bag*
Medical kit – see p.427
Water bottle
Iodine and/or **water-purification system** – see p.27
Toiletries
Towel
Flashlight (torch), plus spare batteries and bulb
Pocket-knife
Matches
Sunglasses – a good UV-protective pair, ideally with side shields if you expect to be in snow
Sunscreen, **lip balm** – at altitude you'll need SPF30+, or zinc oxide
Map and **guidebook**

Footwear
Hiking boots* – leather or Gore-Tex boots are best if wet or snowy conditions are expected
Trainers – okay for most low-elevation trails, handy for evenings
Flipflops or **sport sandals** – may be useful for evenings at low elevations

Clothes
Shirts/T-shirts
Trousers – baggy (to leave room for thermal underwear) and with plenty of pockets; separate lightweight pair for warm days
Skirt/dress – mid-calf length is best
Shorts – not recommended on off-the-beaten-track routes.
Sweat pants – can be worn over shorts in the morning; also good for evenings
Socks – several thin cotton/blend and thick woollen pairs
Underwear – thermal underwear is essential for high-altitude or winter treks

By **renting** bulky or specialized items in Nepal, you'll avoid having to lug them around during the rest of your travels. Kathmandu has dozens of rental shops, and Pokhara a somewhat more limited selection; if you're trekking in the Everest region, you can rent high-altitude gear in Namche. However, you might have trouble finding good gear during the busy autumn trekking season. You'll be expected to leave a deposit of money or an international air ticket. Inspect sleeping bags and parkas carefully for fleas (or worse) – if there's time before setting off, have them cleaned – and make sure zippers are in working order. You can also **buy** equipment quite cheaply (see p.166). If you buy or rent boots, obviously make sure they fit properly, and break them in before hitting the trail.

Clothes must be lightweight and versatile, especially on long treks where conditions vary from subtropical to arctic (many first-time trekkers underestimate the potential for extremes in temperature). What you bring will depend on the trek and time of year, but in most cases you should be prepared for sun, rain, snow and very chilly mornings; dress in layers for maximum flexibility. As explained in "Cultural hints" (Basics, p.75), Nepalis have innately conservative attitudes about dress: in warm weather, women should wear calf-length dresses or skirts and a top that covers the shoulders; men should wear a shirt and long

Sun hat – helpful at both low and high elevations
Wool sweater or **fleece jacket**
Bandana – to use as a handkerchief, sweatband or scarf
Parka* – preferably filled with down or lightweight fibre
Warm hat – one that covers the ears is best
Mittens/gloves
Rain shell/poncho – breathable waterproof material (such as Gore-Tex) is best

High-altitude gear (optional)
Gaiters* – worth having for passes where snow is likely
Gloves – thermal liners and waterproof outer shell
Down pants* and **booties** – welcome luxuries on cold evenings
Telescoping hiking poles* – may be useful for keeping your balance in snow or for descents
Ice axe* – may be needed for icy passes in winter
Crampons* – ditto

Other useful items
Day pack
Foam mat* – optional for teahouse treks on the main routes
Camera, film, spare batteries
Toilet paper – see "Conservation Tips", p.430
Wet wipes – for high-altitude washing
Whistle – for emergencies
Sewing kit
Stuff sacks – handy for separating things in your pack and for creating a pillow when filled with clothes
Plastic bags – a big one to cover your pack in the rain, small sealable ones for many uses
Candles
Emergency snack food – biscuits and chocolate can be bought along the way on teahouse routes
Entertainment – book, cards, musical instrument, hacky-sack, juggling balls, etc
Journal

pants (shorts traditionally indicate low status, though this is less of an issue nowadays along the popular trekking routes). Both sexes should wear at least a swimsuit when bathing.

For **footwear**, running shoes will suffice for most trekking situations, and serve as a good backup for evenings. However, you'll regret it if you run into mud or snow and only have trainers. Hiking boots, by providing better traction, ankle support and protection, will take you through a greater range of the sort of conditions you're likely to encounter. Leather boots are heavier than synthetic ones, but, being sturdier and more easily waterproofed, are recommended for treks at high elevations or during the winter or monsoon. Bring plenty of socks, because you'll be changing them often.

A **sleeping bag** is strongly recommended. Most teahouses will furnish quilts or blankets on demand, but you don't know who used the bedding last or what surprises might lurk therein. A three-season bag is adequate for mid-elevation treks; above 4000m, or in winter, you'll need a four-season bag and possibly a liner.

Bringing **camera** equipment involves a trade-off between weight and performance – a pocket-size point-and-shoot model might be a good compromise. An SLR body with long and short zoom lenses will produce better results, especially with a tripod and polarizing filters, but it's heavy and obtrusive. You'll find more general tips on photography in Basics.

Health and emergencies

Guidebook writers tend to go overboard about the **health** hazards of trekking, particularly altitude sickness. Don't be put off – the vast majority of trekkers never experience anything worse than a mild headache. That said, health is of paramount concern when doing any strenuous physical activity, and all the more so when trekking, which may take you a week or more from the nearest medical facilities. Stomach troubles can spoil a trek, while injuries or altitude sickness, if untreated, could prove fatal. It's best to err on the side of caution.

Children, seniors and people with disabilities have all trekked successfully, but a minimum **fitness** level is required. Needless to say, the better prepared you are physically, the more you'll enjoy the trek. Don't allow yourself to be talked into biting off more than you can chew – choose a trek that's appropriate to your abilities, or you'll have no fun and could conceivably get into trouble. If you're in any doubt about your ability to cope with strenuous walking, see your doctor. It's also worth seeking advice if you have any allergies, especially to antibiotics.

Stomach troubles

The risk of **stomach troubles** is particularly high while trekking, and water is the usual culprit: you need to drink lots of fluids on the trail. Innkeepers normally boil water and tea, but not always for long enough, and at high altitudes the boiling point of water is so low that a longer boiling time is necessary. All running water should be assumed to be contaminated – wherever you go, there will be people, or at least animals, upstream.

Treating water is not only the best line of defence against illness, it also reduces your reliance on boiled or bottled water. For more on treatment methods, see p.27.

See p.28 for tips on treating stomach upsets.

First-aid checklist

This is a minimum first-aid kit – trekking guidebooks usually give much longer lists. Most of the items can be purchased in Nepal for much less then they cost back home. See p.28 for tips on self-diagnosis.

For injuries
Plasters/Band-Aids – large and small sizes
Gauze pads
Sterile dressing
Surgical tape
Moleskin or **"Second Skin"** – synthetic adhesive padding for blisters
Elastic support bandages – for knee strains, ankle sprains
Antiseptic cream – for scrapes, blisters, insect bites
Tweezers
Scissors
Thermometer – one that also reads low temperatures, in case of hypothermia

For illnesses
Aspirin or other pain reliever
Cold medicine
Throat lozenges – sore throats are common at high elevations
Diarrhoea tablets
Oral rehydration formula – to replace fluids lost due to diarrhoea
Allergy tablets – if you need them (especially in spring)
Tinidazole – an anti-protozoan, for giardia
Antibiotics – Ciprofloxacin, Norfloxacin or Cephalosporin for intestinal bacteria, Erythromycin for throat/bronchial infections. Other drugs may also be used – consult a doctor or trekking guidebook
Diamox – for treatment of mild AMS symptoms (see below)

Minor injuries

Most minor injuries occur while walking downhill; **knee strains** are common, especially among trekkers carrying their own packs. If you know your knees are weak, bind them up with crepe (ace) bandages as a preventive measure, or hire a porter. Good, supportive boots reduce the risk of **ankle sprains** or twists, but the best prevention is just to pay careful attention to where you put your feet: don't try to admire the scenery and walk at the same time. A walking stick or hiking pole(s) can help.

It's hard to avoid getting **blisters**, but make sure your boots are well broken-in, and always wear two pairs of socks, changing them regularly (especially if they get wet). Apply protective padding (eg moleskin) to hotspots as soon as they develop, making sure to clean and cover blisters so they can heal as quickly as possible.

Acute mountain sickness

Barraged by medical advice and horror stories, trekkers all too often develop altitude paranoia. The fact is that just about everyone who treks over 4000m experiences some mild symptoms of **acute mountain sickness (AMS)**, but serious cases are very rare, and the simple cure – descent – almost always brings immediate recovery.

At high elevations there is not only less oxygen but also lower atmospheric pressure. This combination can produce a variety of unpredictable effects on the body: it can cause the brain to swell, fill the lungs with fluid, or suppress appetite and cause muscle tissue to waste away. The syndrome varies from one person to the next, and strikes without regard for fitness – in fact, young people seem to be more susceptible, possibly because they're more hung up about admitting they feel rotten.

Prevention

Most people are capable of acclimatizing to quite high elevations, but the process takes time and must be done in stages. The golden rule is **don't go too high too fast**. Above 3000m, the daily net elevation gain should be no more than 500m; take mandatory acclimatization days at around 3500m and 4500m – more if you're feeling unwell – and try to spend these days day-hiking higher. These are only guidelines, and you'll have to regulate your ascent according to how you feel. Trekkers who fly directly to high airstrips have to be especially careful to acclimatize.

Drink plenty of **liquids** at altitude, since the air is incredibly dry. The usual adage is that unless you pee clear, you're not drinking enough. Keeping warm, eating well, getting plenty of sleep and avoiding alcohol will also help reduce the chances of developing AMS.

Acetazolamide (better known under the brand name **Diamox**) has been shown to improve respiration at altitude, which can accelerate acclimatization. Some doctors recommend a preventive dose (125mg twice a day) for people trekking at high elevations, though note that the Himalayan Rescue Association does not endorse the preventive use of Diamox for trekkers. Diamox is a diuretic, so it's all the more important to keep hydrated while taking it; some people also experience minor side effects such as numbness and tingling sensations.

Symptoms

AMS usually gives plenty of warning before it becomes life-threatening. Mild **symptoms** include headaches, dizziness, insomnia, nausea, loss of appetite, shortness of breath and swelling of the hands and feet; one or two of these shouldn't be cause for panic, but they're a sign that your body hasn't yet adjusted to the elevation. You shouldn't ascend further until you start feeling better, or, if you do keep going, you should be prepared to beat a hasty retreat if the condition gets worse. Serious symptoms (persistent vomiting, delirium, loss of co-ordination, bubbly breathing and bloody sputum, rapid heart rate or breathlessness at rest, blueness of face and lips) can develop within hours, and if ignored can result in death.

Cure

The only effective cure for advanced AMS is **descent**. Anyone showing serious symptoms should be taken downhill immediately, regardless of the time of day or night – hire a porter or pack animal to carry the sufferer if necessary. Recovery is usually dramatic, often after a descent of only a few hundred vertical metres.

Diamox may be taken to relieve mild AMS symptoms, although it has to be stressed that it does nothing to treat the underlying cause of AMS. For further advice on AMS, visit the Himalayan Rescue Association's aid posts at Manang (on the Annapurna Circuit) and Pheriche (on the Everest trek).

Other dangers

Other altitude-related dangers such as hypothermia and frostbite are encountered less often by trekkers, but can pose real threats on high, exposed passes or in bad weather.

The symptoms of **hypothermia** are similar to those of AMS: slurred speech, fatigue, irrational behaviour and loss of co-ordination. Low body temperature is the surest sign. The treatment, in a word, is heat. Get the victim out of the cold, put him or her in a good sleeping bag (with another person, if necessary) and ply with warm food and drink.

Frostbite appears initially as small white patches on exposed skin, caused by local freezing. The skin will feel cold and numb. To treat, apply warmth (*not* snow!). Avoid getting frostbite a second time, as this can lead to permanent damage.

Common-sense **precautions** bear repeating: wear or carry adequate clothing; keep dry; cover exposed extremities in severe weather; eat lots and carry emergency snacks; and make for shelter if conditions get bad.

Avalanches can be a serious hazard in certain areas such as the Annapurna Sanctuary and the Thorung La. If you don't know how to recognize avalanche zones or gauge avalanche danger, ask for a crash course at one of the HRA posts.

Snowblindness shouldn't be a worry as long as you're equipped with a good pair of sunglasses. On snowy surfaces you'll need proper glacier glasses with side shields.

Emergencies

Ninety-nine percent of the time, trekking in Nepal is a piece of cake and it's hard to imagine something going wrong. But while few trekkers ever have to deal with **emergencies** – illness, AMS, storms, missteps, landslides and avalanches are the main causes – they can happen to anyone.

Bezruchka's *Trekking in Nepal* gives full advice on **emergency procedures** and a rundown of hospitals, aid posts, airstrips and radio transmitters found near the main trekking routes. In non-urgent cases, your best bet is to be carried by porter or pack animal to the nearest **airstrip** or **health post**, although bear in mind that medical facilities outside Kathmandu and a few other major cities are very rudimentary. Where the situation is more serious, send word to the nearest village with a phone or radio transmitter to request a **helicopter rescue**. A typical rescue costs upwards of $1200, and they won't come for you until they're satisfied you'll be able to pay; being registered with your embassy will speed the process of contacting relatives who can vouch for you.

Trekking life

A trek, it's often said, is not a wilderness experience. Unlike most other mountain ranges, the Himalaya are comparatively well settled, farmed and grazed – much of their beauty, in fact, is man-made – and the trails support a steady stream of local traffic. If you're trekking independently, you'll probably be sleeping and eating in teahouses and making equal contact with locals and other foreigners. You'll need a good deal of **adaptability** to different living situations, but the payback comes in cultural insights, unforgettable **encounters**, and, of course, **breathtaking scenery**. Nepal does have a lot of unsettled backcountry, of course, and it's possible to experience it if you're willing to camp and carry your own supplies; this is easier to do with the aid of a trekking agency.

Getting there

The trailhead is typically reached at the end of a long, bumpy bus ride (or a short, bumpy flight), and **getting there** is an integral part of the experience. This is also a big factor in deciding where to trek, as the going and returning can eat up two days (or more) and, in the case of treks reached by air, can represent a significant expense.

Specific advice on bus, taxi and plane options is given where relevant in the trekking-area descriptions later in the chapter. Thanks to the deregulation of the domestic airline industry, getting a seat on a plane in or out of mountain airstrips isn't nearly the hassle it was a few years ago, but bad weather can halt flights for days, so don't lock yourself into having to catch a flight on a particular day. Helicopter services are officially allowed to carry only charter groups. In a pinch you may be able to talk your way onto a chopper heading back to Kathmandu empty, but it will probably cost more than going by plane. See Basics for general information on bus and air travel.

Trails

Trekking in the Himalaya is no stroll in the park. If you're not an experienced outdoors person, prepare yourself for serious, strenuous **walking**. Most trekkers take it in easy stages, from one glass of *chiya* to the next – there's no race to the top. It's best to set off early each morning to make the most of the clear weather, as clouds usually roll in around midday. Pad your schedule for

---

Conservation tips

The main environmental problem in the Himalaya is **deforestation**, and trekking puts an additional strain on local wood supplies: it's been estimated that one trekker consumes, directly and indirectly, between five and ten times more wood per day than a Nepali. In addition, trekkers leave **litter**, strain local **sanitation systems** and contribute to water **pollution**. The following are suggestions on how to minimize your impact on the fragile Himalayan environment.

• Where the choice exists, eat at teahouses that cook with kerosene, electricity or propane instead of wood.

• Bring plenty of warm clothes so you (and your porter) are less reliant on wood fires to keep warm.

• Try to time your meals and co-ordinate your orders with other trekkers; cooking food in big batches is a more efficient use of fuel.

• If trekking with an agency, see that all meals are cooked with kerosene or propane, and complain if they aren't.

• Decline offers of hot showers except in inns where the water is heated by electricity, solar panels or fuel-efficient "back boilers".

• Treat your own drinking water rather than relying on bottled or boiled water. Plastic water bottles can't be recycled in Nepal and pose a serious litter problem in trekking areas. Water sterilized by boiling uses precious wood or other fuel.

• Use latrines wherever possible. Where there's no facility, go well away from water sources, bury your faeces and burn your toilet paper. Better yet, don't use toilet paper at all – use water, as Nepalis do.

• Use phosphate-free soap and shampoo, and don't rinse directly in streams.

• Deposit litter in designated rubbish bins, where they exist. Elsewhere, carry all non-burnable litter back out – that includes tins, plastic bottles and especially batteries.

rest days, weather and contingencies, and make time for at least one unusual side trip – that's when things get really interesting.

Trails are often steep and rough, and river crossings sometimes precarious. You may occasionally **get lost**, but not for long: stopping to chat and ask directions is part of the fun, and a good opportunity to learn some Nepali. Don't **trek alone**, or at least stay within sight of other people and spend nights in the company of others, as they can help you if you get hurt and can detect signs of AMS or hypothermia. Nepalis think all lone travellers are a bit odd, so you might find it worthwhile teaming up with others just to avoid the constant question, *Eklai?* ("Alone?"). Be sure to read "Cultural hints" in Basics; again, *don't* give pens or rupees to children, whether they ask or not – if you do, every trekker that comes after you will be hounded for handouts.

Teahouses

Teahouses along the major trekking routes are efficient little operations, with English signs, menus and usually an English-speaking proprietor. Although they cater exclusively to trekkers and their porters, most of these tourist inns still follow the Nepali tradition of providing practically free lodging (usually Rs50 or less per room, except at high elevation) so long as you eat your meals there. Private rooms are available along the popular routes, but elsewhere it may be necessary to take dormitory accommodation. The beds will normally have some sort of padding, but a foam mat may come in handy, and a sleeping bag is recommended. Many places have wood stoves or kerosene heaters, and a growing number have electricity.

You'll find fewer comforts on **less-trekked trails**, where lodgings are likely to be private kitchens and meals are eaten by the fire amid eye-watering smoke, and you may have to sleep on the floor. Such places rarely advertise themselves, but once you've spent a little time off the beaten track you'll start realizing that almost every trailside house with an open front is potential shelter.

Recommending specific trekking lodgings is beyond the scope of this chapter. At any rate, they come and go so quickly that your best advice will be from trekkers coming the other way.

Food and drink

Trekking cuisine is a world unto itself. Although teahouses' plastic-coated cardboard menus promise tempting international delicacies, items often turn out to be permanently *paindaina* (unavailable), and you'll notice that the "spring roll" wrappings, "enchilada" tortillas, "pizza" crusts and "pancakes" all bear more than a passing resemblance to chapatis. But at any rate, eggs, porridge, custard and even apple pie are all reassuringly familiar, and goodies like chocolate and muesli are available on the main trails.

However, many trekkers order "Western" food simply because it's there, not because it's good, and indeed it costs much more than **local food**. In highland areas you'll be able to eat such Tibetan dishes as *momo, thukpa* and *riki kur*, and instead of porridge you might be served *tsampa* (see "Eating and drinking" in Basics). At lower elevations, *daal bhaat*, chow mein, packet noodles and seasonal vegetables are the standard offerings. A further advantage of eating local fare is that it's almost always quicker: there are usually unlimited quantities of *daal bhaat* steaming away on the back burner, whereas foreign food has to be made specially. On less-travelled routes, where *daal bhaat*, *dhedo* and potatoes are often the only food available, you'll have to force yourself to eat large amounts to get enough calories and protein (you might also want to bring vitamin tablets).

When **ordering**, bear in mind that the cook can only make one or two things at a time, and there may be many others ahead of you: simplify the process by co-ordinating your order with other trekkers. Most innkeepers expect dinner orders to be placed several hours in advance, and there's usually a dog-eared notepad floating around on which you're meant to keep a tally of everything you've eaten. Eating dinner at a teahouse other than the one where you're staying is very much frowned upon. Pay when you leave, and be sure to bring plenty of small money on the trek, since innkeepers often have trouble making change.

Tea and hot lemon are traditionally the main **drinks** on the trail. Bottled soft drinks, water and even beer are common along the popular routes, but the price of each bottle rises by Rs15–25 for each extra day it has to be portered from the nearest road. Don't miss trying *chhang*, *raksi* and *tongba* – again, see Basics for fuller explanations of these alcoholic specialities.

Sanitation

Washing and toilet facilities, where they exist, range from primitive to modern. Off the established routes or at higher elevations, you'll have to bathe and do laundry under makeshift outdoor taps in freezing cold water (which explains why hot springs are such major attractions). Most teahouses in the Annapurna and Everest regions have solar or electric-heated showers. Others will offer washing water that has been heated on a wood fire, but this is an environmentally dubious practice. Most teahouses provide outdoor latrines (*chaarpi*), and a few even have indoor flush toilets, but don't be surprised if you're pointed to a half-covered privy hanging over a stream, or simply to a paddock.

The treks

Nepal's mountains can be divided into five regions, the first three being most suitable for first-time independent trekkers. On a limited budget and schedule, you'll probably be restricted to the **Annapurna** and **Helambu–Langtang** regions, north of Pokhara and Kathmandu respectively. Given more time, you'll be able to tackle **Everest** or some of the longer Annapurna routes independently. If you've trekked before, or are particularly adventurous, you might consider trekking independently in some of the other, less-trafficked routes in **eastern** and **far western Nepal**. With enough money, you can employ a trekking agency to take you just about anywhere.

The Thamelization of the most popular routes has already been mentioned. Along with the crowds and commercialization also eventually come overhead electric wires, roads, vehicles, concrete buildings and other modern trappings – all of which local people generally welcome, but which detract from the experience most trekkers are after. Given the steady march of progress, the appearance and pleasantness of trekking routes is continually changing, and guidebook writeups

Teahouse treks at a glance

This list omits treks that require agency or extensive porter support.

Trek	Days*	Best Months	Elevation (m)	Difficulty	Comments
Helambu	3–10	Oct–April	800–3600	Moderate	Easy access, uncrowded, varied; only modest views.
Pokhara–Trisuli	3–10	Nov–March	400–1450	Easy	Pleasant hill walk, snow-free in winter; basic teahouses; some Maoist risk.
Gosainkund	4–7	Oct–Dec, Feb–May	1950–4380	Strenuous	Sacred lakes; usually combined with Langtang or Helambu.
Poon Hill	4–6	Oct–April	1100–3200	Moderate	Easy access, excellent views; very commercial.
Siklis	4–7	Oct–April	1100–2200	Moderate	Easy access; uncrowded village trek.
Rara	6–8	Oct–Nov, April–June	2400–3500	Moderate	Fly in; must be prepared to camp; pristine lake and forest.
Lower Kali Gandaki	7–9	Nov–April	900–3200	Moderate	Longer version of Poon Hill, returning a less commercial way.
Langtang	7–12	Oct–May	1700–3750	Moderate	Beautiful alpine valley close to Kathmandu.
Annapurna Sanctuary	8–12	Oct–Dec, Feb–April	1100–4130	Moderate to strenuous	Spectacular scenery, easy access; acclimatization necessary.
Jomosom/Muktinath	10–14 (5–7)	Oct–April	1100–3800	Moderate (Easy)	Spectacular, varied; very commercial. (For the shorter, easy variation, fly to Jomosom and walk down.)
Everest (Lukla fly-in)	14–18	Oct–Nov, March–May	2800–5550	Strenuous	Superb scenery; flights can be a problem; acclimatization necessary.
Annapurna Circuit	16–21	Oct–Nov, March–April	450–5380	Strenuous	Incredible diversity and scenery; high pass requires care and acclimatization.
Everest (Jiri walk-in)	26+	Oct–Nov, March–April	1500–5550	Very strenuous	Wonderful mix of hill and high-elevation walking, but with a lot of up-and-down; can save time by flying one way.
Everest (Eastern route)	28+	Nov, March	300–5550	Very strenuous	Similar, but with an even greater net vertical gain.

* Not including transport to and from the trailhead.

and word-of-mouth reputations don't always keep up. Fortunately, it cuts both ways: some long-established treks lose their appeal over time, while other fantastic routes that were previously inaccessible or unteahouseable open up. Keep an ear out for the Next Great Trek.

The sections below give overviews of the areas and describe the major trekking possibilities within them, but for step-by-step route descriptions you'll need a full-blown trekking guidebook (see "Books" in Contexts). The box on the previous page summarizes the major teahouse treks.

North of Pokhara: Annapurna

Nearly sixty percent of all trekkers walk in the **Annapurna** region north of Pokhara. The popularity is well deserved, since nowhere else do you get such a rich feast of spectacular scenery and varied hill culture. Compared to most other regions, **logistics** are simple: treks all start or finish close to Pokhara, and transportation to trailheads is well developed; with great views just two days up the trail, short treks are particularly feasible. Pokhara is a very relaxing place to end a trek, and if it's also your starting point then you'll be able to store excess luggage and rent equipment here as well.

That said, the popular treks in the Annapurna region have become highly **commercialized** and culturally rather tame – this is the Costa del Trekking.

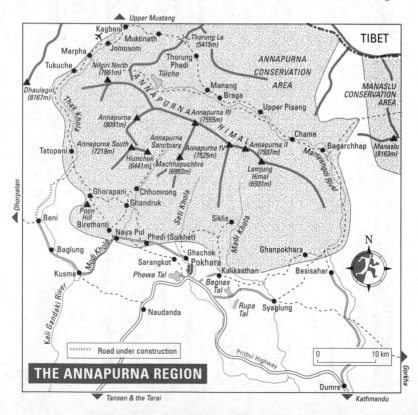

THE ANNAPURNA REGION

Road under construction

0   10 km

If you're looking to get away from it all, go elsewhere. Also note that there are frequent reports of **theft** and sometimes even violence against trekkers in this region, so don't trek alone, keep your things in sight at all times and always lock your door when you leave your room.

The **Annapurna Himal** faces Pokhara like an enormous sofa, 40km across and numbering nine peaks over 7000m, with Annapurna I above all at 8091m. It's an area of stunning diversity, ranging from the sodden bamboo forests of the southern slopes (Lumle, northwest of Pokhara, is the wettest village in Nepal) to windswept desert (Jomosom, in the northern rain shadow, is the driest).

The *himal* and adjacent hill areas are protected within the **Annapurna Conservation Area Project (ACAP)**, for which you have to pay a Rs2000 **entry fee**. You must purchase your entry ticket in advance at ACAP offices at Lakeside in Pokhara or Tridevi Marg in Kathmandu, or you'll have to pay double at the ACAP entry checkpost. The money goes to a good cause. A quasi-park administered by a non-governmental trust, ACAP has won high praise for its holistic approach to tourism management. Its twofold aims are to protect the area's natural and cultural heritage, while at the same time ensuring sustainable economic and social benefit for local people. To take the pressure off local forests, the project has set up kerosene depots and installed microhydro-electric generators to provide alternative fuels, and has supported the creation of tree nurseries and reforestation efforts. Lodge owners benefit from small-business training and low-interest loans, enabling them to invest in things like solar water heaters and efficient stoves, while rubbish pits, latrines, health posts and a telephone service have been established with ACAP entry fees.

The Jomosom trek

The **JOMOSOM TREK** is an acknowledged classic: an ideal sampler of Himalayan scenery and culture, and, not surprisingly, the most developed stretch of trail in Nepal. **Food and lodging** are of a relatively high standard: most lodges have electricity and hot showers, and some look like they've been imported wholesale from Thamel. All have English menus and outdo each other with the Westernness of their cuisine.

The full Jomosom trek – round-trip from trailhead to Muktinath – takes ten to fourteen days, but most people cut trail time roughly in half and minimize backtracking by **flying** from Pokhara to Jomosom ($55), or vice versa. Flying in and walking out to Beni makes for an instant hit of high mountains and an easy downhill trek. The most popular trailhead, Naya Pul, is reached by **taxi** or **bus** from Pokhara; it's also possible to start from Lakeside, Phedi (Suikhet) or Beni (see p.302 for transport advice). The first half of the trek, which can be done on its own as a loop, is described first.

To Poon Hill

If you haven't time to do the full Jomosom trek, you can get a taster of it by turning the first half into a circuit of four to six days. The route ambles through steep, lush hill country, taking in some lovely Gurung villages and, weather permitting, rewarding you with outstanding views of the Annapurnas and Machhapuchhre. The **trails** are wide and well maintained, though steep in places. The highest point reached is 3200m, which shouldn't present any altitude problems, but it's high enough that you'll need **warm clothes** at night. Rain gear is also advisable.

Poon Hill, a day and a half northwest of Naya Pul and 2000m higher, is literally the high point of this instant-gratification route: watching the mountains at sunrise from here is probably the single most done thing in the trekking universe. (There's no need to set your alarm in **Ghorapani**, the village below Poon Hill, as you'll be awakened at 4am by the daily stampede of sunrise seekers.) If clouds block your view, as they often do, it's well worth hanging on for an extra day. You can vary the return trip by heading east through magnificent stands of giant rhododendrons dripping with orchids to the pretty Gurung town of **Ghandruk**, headquarters of the ACAP, with a visitor centre and museum. From Ghandruk, trails head up to the Annapurna Sanctuary and down to Naya Pul and Phedi (Suikhet).

The Thak Khola

North of Poon Hill, the trail drops into the valley of the **Thak Khola** (also known as the Kali Gandaki) and the fun really begins: as you follow the course of the world's deepest gorge – the 8000-metre hulks of Dhaulagiri and Annapurna tower on either side – the scenery changes by the mile. The valley is also famous for its ethnic diversity, Thakalis being the dominant group. Make way for their jingling donkey trains, which feature so prominently in this area.

The walking actually gets easier after Poon Hill (and by this time you should be in better shape), and the trail stays below 3000m until the last day's climb to Muktinath at 3800m. There's essentially only one route through the Thak Khola, so unless you carry on up over the Thorung La (described in "The Annapurna Circuit", opposite) or fly back from Jomosom, some **backtracking** is unavoidable; but by the same token, you can walk as far as you like and head back when you need to.

The towns of the Thak Khola are worthy destinations in their own right. **Tatopani** is renowned for its Western food, videos (cringe) and **hot springs** (*taato paani* means "hot water"). Further up, the trail passes through thick, monkey-infested forest to **Tukuche**, the main Thakali trading centre until Jomosom took over, and **Marpha**, a tidy, stone-clad village surrounded by apple and apricot orchards. **Day-hikes** and overnight trips up from the valley floor are the best way to appreciate the incredible dimensions of the Thak Khola and the peaks around it: little-trekked trails lead to North Annapurna Base Camp, the Dhaulagiri Icefall and Dhampus Pass. If you like beachcombing, you'll enjoy hunting for *shaligram* fossils (see p.321) along the river here, though it's illegal to keep them. Above Tukuche, the vegetation dies out as you begin to enter the Himalayan rain shadow, and a savage, sand-blasting wind from the south makes it unpleasant to trek after midday. **Jomosom**, though it gives its name to the trek, is no place to linger unless you've got business at the airstrip – far more romantic is the fortress town of **Kagbeni**, only a couple of hours further on, with its medieval buildings and terracotta Buddhist figures. Geographically speaking, you're on the edge of the Tibetan plateau here, with the main Himalaya chain looming magnificently to the south.

Finally, it's a 1000-metre climb up a side valley – out of the wind, thankfully – to poplar-lined **Muktinath**, one of the most important religious sites in the Nepal Himalaya. The *Mahabharat* mentions Muktinath as the source of mystic *shaligrams*; a priest will show you around the Newar-style temple and its wall of 108 water spouts, while further down the trail you'll find a Buddhist shrine that shelters two miraculous perpetual flames. Yartung, a madly exotic **festival** of horse-riding, is held at Muktinath around the full moon of August–September.

The lower Kali Gandaki

On the return journey, if you don't feel like slogging back up the endless stairs to Ghorapani, you can keep following the Kali Gandaki River south to the roadhead, a low-key **valley walk** with occasionally impressive views. Since there's little up-and-down, it's possible to make good time. This route sees far fewer trekkers than the main Jomosom trail, so **accommodation** and **food** are cheaper but more rudimentary. At this low elevation the weather is balmy in winter, but in spring and early autumn the heat can be unpleasant. The trail passes through cultivated land and villages, where Magars and Gurungs are the dominant **ethnic groups**, as well as through a few Newar bazaars.

The Pokhara–Baglung Highway is being extended northwards, bound eventually for Jomosom, but progress is slow. At the time of writing the end of the road was about 15km north of Beni, with regular buses to Pokhara departing from Beni.

The Annapurna Sanctuary

The aptly named **ANNAPURNA SANCTUARY** is the most intensely scenic short trek in Nepal. From Ghandruk on the Jomosom route, the trail bears north-northeast into the very heart of the Annapurna range: following the short, steep Modi Khola, it soon leaves all permanent settlements behind, climbs through dense bamboo jungle and finally, rising above the vegetation line, makes for a narrow notch between the sheer lower flanks of Machhapuchhre and Hiunchuli. Once past this sanctuary "gate", it stumbles across moraines to a cluster of huts (often still called "Machhapuchhre Base Camp") and, further on, to the so-called **Annapurna Base Camp**, both of which get very crowded in season. Wherever you stand in the sanctuary, the 360-degree views are unspeakably beautiful, and although clouds roll in early, the curtain often parts at sunset to reveal radiant, molten peaks. The altitude is 4100m: dress for snow.

The sanctuary can be treated as a side trip from the Jomosom trek, adding five to seven days, or an eight- to twelve-day round trip from Pokhara, accessed from Naya Pul or Phedi (Suikhet). The actual distance covered isn't great, but **altitude, weather** and **trail conditions** all tend to slow you down – the trail gains more than 2000m from Ghandruk to the sanctuary, so unless you're already well acclimatized you'd be wise to spread the climb over four days. Frequent precipitation makes the trail extremely slippery at the best of times, and in winter it can be impassable due to snow or avalanche danger.

The Annapurna Circuit

The **ANNAPURNA CIRCUIT** is a challenging but rewarding three-week trek with excellent views, plenty of cultural contact and the greatest net vertical gain of all the popular routes. Starting in subtropical paddy at about 500m, the trail ascends steadily to the 5415m Thorung La (Thorung Pass) before returning along the previously described Jomosom route. A minimum of sixteen days is required, but a few extra days should be set aside for digressions, acclimatization and other contingencies. The trek is strenuous, and you'll need boots, gloves and very warm clothes for the pass, and a good four-season sleeping bag for a night spent above 4400m.

Although the eastern half of the circuit is less developed for trekkers than the Jomosom side, **food and lodging** are always available, and somewhat cheaper. The full circuit is best done between mid-October and mid-December – crossing the Thorung La is iffy to impossible from late December till March, while the lower parts of the trek are uncomfortably warm from April onwards. Snow can block the pass at any time of year, so be prepared to wait it out or go back down the way you came.

Nearly everyone goes around the circuit anticlockwise, the only reason being that the Thorung La makes a longer climb from the Jomosom side, requiring an extra acclimatization day above Muktinath. The upshot of this is that if you go anticlockwise you'll be in step with the same people for the entire trek, whereas if you go clockwise you'll be constantly passing people coming the other way. The current **starting point** is Besisahar, but it's gradually moving northwards as the trail is replaced by road; Besisahar is reachable by direct public bus from Kathmandu or (probably better) by tourist bus to Dumre on the Prithvi Highway and then by jeep from there. If you're coming from Pokhara, you can avoid Dumre and instead follow the Pokhara–Trisuli trek (see below) to Besisahar in two days.

The circuit follows the Marsyangdi Valley north and then west all the way to the pass. The first few days are a long preamble through terraced farmland and frequent villages, with only fleeting views to whet your appetite, but then, in the course of two days, the valley constricts and the trail climbs steeply, leaving the paddy behind and passing through successive climatic zones: temperate forest, coniferous forest, alpine meadows and finally the arid steppes of the rain shadow. The walk from Chame to **Manang** – especially along the high route via Upper Pisang – is spectacular and shouldn't be rushed. The sight of the huge, glacier-dolloped Annapurnas towering almost 5000m above the valley will stay with you forever. Manang's architecture, like that of all the older villages here, is strongly Tibetan; *gompa* at Manang and **Braga** are well worth visiting. Manang also has an airstrip (charters only) and a Himalayan Rescue Association post, where staff give daily talks on AMS. If you're going for the **Thorung La**, the next night will probably be spent at Thorung Phedi or the even higher "Thorung High Camp", grotty places where you'll be woken up at 3am by trekkers who've been told (wrongly) that they have to clear the pass by 8am. The climb up the pass, and the knee-killing 1600-metre descent down the other side to **Muktinath**, is a tough but exhilarating day. The remainder of the circuit follows the Jomosom trek (see p.435).

An alternate route leaves the main trail near Manang and ascends to **Tilicho**, an extraordinary high-altitude lake, crossing three passes over 5000m before descending rapidly to Jomosom. This is a hard, three-day slog. Two teahouses operate sporadically, but be prepared to camp.

Other Annapurna treks

Aside from the fact that they're in the same general area, the following treks have little in common with the Coca-Cola routes described above. You'll typically find only Nepali food and lodging along these trails, and except for the Pokhara–Trisuli and Siklis routes, you'll need to be equipped to camp or be willing to stay in people's homes. If you're not trekking with an agency (obligatory for Upper Mustang and Around Manaslu), you'll probably want to go with a guide.

Pokhara–Trisuli

A main thoroughfare before the completion of the Prithvi Highway, the old **POKHARA–TRISULI** trail now sees little porter traffic, and even fewer trekkers. A gentle, low-altitude trek, it wanders through typical hill country and dozens of laid-back ethnic villages, with Annapurna, Manaslu and Ganesh Himal popping up often enough to keep things ticking over scenically. This is the only serious trek that's guaranteed to be snow-free all year, making it a good choice for winter (it's uncomfortably hot for trekking at other times of year). However, it passes through areas of recent Maoist activity, so get current advice before going.

The trek can be done in six days, but allow eight or ten; many trekkers start or finish at Gorkha, the midway point, for an easy outing of four to five days. There are any number of ways to get started from Pokhara, but to bypass a lot of road-walking, take a taxi to Begnas Tal and take any trail heading east and north towards Besisahar on the Annapurna Circuit – try to go by way of **Ghanpokhara**, a lovely Gurung village – finally reaching **Gorkha** (off the Annapurna Region map) in a minimum of three days (more like five via Ghanpokhara). From there it's another four days or so of undulating between subtropical valleys and scenic ridges to Trisuli, which is linked by road with Kathmandu.

The Siklis trek

An alternative to other short treks in the region, the **SIKLIS TREK** probes an uncrowded corner of the Annapurna Conservation Area under the shadows of Lamjung Himal and Annapurnas II and IV. The main teahouse itinerary takes about a week, starting at Begnas Tal and heading north to the Madi Khola, then following the river's west bank up to well-preserved **Siklis** (1980m), Nepal's biggest Gurung village. After backtracking a bit you strike westwards over the thickly forested ridge that separates the Madi and Seti drainages and then descend via Ghachok, another Gurung settlement, to reach the Pokhara–Baglung Highway. Many other variations are possible. As part of an effort to develop this into a model eco-trekking route, ACAP has funded the construction of a small museum and cultural facility in Siklis.

The Royal trek

Although this is the shortest, easiest and lowest trek described in this chapter, it's rarely attempted by independent trekkers because of the lack of teahouse accommodation en route. On the other hand, it's fairly popular with groups and families. It's been known as the **ROYAL TREK** ever since Prince Charles took a rally-the-troops swing along it in 1980 to visit the villages of Gurkha recruits. Taking just three or four days, it starts (or ends) at the Bijalpur Khola, just east of Pokhara Bazaar. From there it heads westwards, ascending a ridge to Kalikasthan (another possible starting point, reached by rough road from Pokhara), and follows the ridgeline eastwards past Thulakot and Begnaskot (good views) to Syaglung, then bends back westwards to Begnas Tal via Sundari Daada. The route goes no higher than 1420m, making it doable during winter.

Upper Mustang

UPPER MUSTANG, the high-desert headwaters of the Thak Khola, was closed to foreigners until 1992, and still retains much of its medieval Tibetan culture. Permits to trek there are expensive – $700 for the first ten days, $70 per day thereafter – and are issued only to agency-organized groups, which keeps visitor numbers in check. Unfortunately a road is under construction through the area, so see it before it's ruined.

The restricted area officially begins at Kagbeni, and groups usually fly in and out of Jomosom, just a half-day's walk to the south. The trip takes a minimum of ten days, following the Thak Khola north to two walled cities (one, Lo Monthang, is the seat of Mustang's nominal king) before doubling back on the same trail.

It takes about three weeks to trek **AROUND MANASLU**, a challenging circuit east of the Annapurna area that ventures into the extremely remote Manaslu Conservation Area and over a 5200-metre pass. This trek is restricted to organized groups, and requires a special trekking permit ($75 per week; $90 in Sept–Nov). Maoist activity may make it impossible to do the full circuit.

The trek usually starts in Gorkha (off the Annapurna Region map), first heading east and then north up the valley of the Budhi Gandaki, and finally rounding behind Manaslu (8163m) over the Larkya La (5213m). From there it's two days down to Bagarchhap on the Marsyangi River. The rest of the trek follows the Annapurna Circuit in reverse down to Besisahar.

North of Kathmandu: Helambu, Langtang and Gosainkund

Trekking **north of Kathmandu** is curiously underrated and relatively uncrowded. The most accessible of all the trekking regions, it's well suited to one- or two-week itineraries, which is handy if you're trying to cram a trek into a short stay in Nepal or you don't want to stray far from Kathmandu. What it lacks in superlatives – there are no 8000-metre peaks in the vicinity (unless you count Shisha Pangma, across the border in Tibet) – it makes up for in base-to-peak rises that are as dramatic as anywhere. Langtang, in particular, delivers more amazing views in a short time than any other walk-in trek in Nepal, with the possible exception of the Annapurna Sanctuary.

Two distinct basins and an intervening *lek* (ridge) lend their names to the major treks here; each stands on its own, but given enough time and good weather you can mix-and-match them. **Helambu** is closest to Kathmandu, comprising the rugged north–south valleys and ridges that lie just beyond the northeast rim of the Kathmandu Valley. North of Helambu, running east–west and tantalizingly close to the Tibet border, lies the high, alpine **Langtang Valley**, which in its upper reaches burrows spectacularly between the Langtang and Jugal Himals. **Gosainkund** comprises a chain of sacred lakes nestled in a rugged intermediate range northwest of Helambu. One practical inconvenience is that the connections between these three treks aren't reliable – winter snow may block the passes between Helambu and the other two – and done on their own, the Langtang and Gosainkund treks require you to retrace your steps for much of the return journey.

Food and lodging here are less luxurious than in the Annapurna and Everest regions, but never a problem on the main trails. All these routes take you into **Langtang National Park**, for which there's an Rs1000 entry fee.

Helambu

HELAMBU (or Helmu) is great for short treks: access from Kathmandu is easy, and an extensive trail network enables you to tailor a circuit to your schedule. The area spans a wide elevation range – there's a lot of up-and-down – but the highest point reached is only 2700–3200m (depending on route), so acclimatization is rarely a problem. Winter treks are particularly feasible. The peaks of Langtang Himal are often visible, but the views aren't as close-up as in other areas. Helambu was once considered a hidden, sacred domain, and its misty ridges and fertile valleys are still comparatively isolated; relatively few

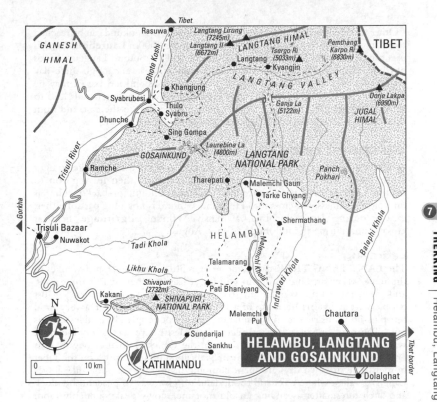

people trek here, and with so many trails to choose from, those that do tend to spread themselves out. Helambu's Bhotiyas call themselves **Sherpa**, although they're only distant cousins of the Solu-Khumbu stock: their ancestors probably migrated from Kyirong, the area just north of the Kodari border crossing. Tamangs are also numerous, while the valley bottoms are farmed mainly by Hindu castes.

Sundarijal, a taxi or local bus ride from Kathmandu, is the most common **starting point**, but alternative trailheads include Sankhu, Kakani, Nagarkot and Malemchi Pul. However you go, first impressions are somewhat dispiriting – the Kathmandu Valley approaches are heavily populated, and the route from Malemchi Pul involves a rather tedious local bus ride from Panchkhal on the Arniko Highway – but things quickly improve as you get up onto the ridges. Entering the region from the Kathmandu Valley takes you through the new and not especially dramatic **Shivapuri National Park** (so designated, one suspects, simply to squeeze another Rs1000 entry fee out of foreigners).

Most trekkers make a loop around two main ridges on either side of the Malemchi Khola, staying high and avoiding the construction work on a big water-diversion project going on in the valley, and taking in the villages of **Malemchi Gaun**, **Tarke Ghyang** and **Shermathang**. The walk between the second two is especially rewarding, passing picturesque monasteries and contouring through forests of oak, rhododendron and *lokta*, whose bark is used to make traditional paper. Countless other trails strike west and east to villages that see few trekkers.

Other variations on Helambu are more challenging. Gosainkund can be reached by a long, rugged day's walk from Tharepati, via the 4600m **Laurebina La**; this pass can be tricky in winter due to ice and snow. The route to Langtang heads north from Tarke Ghyang over the 5122m **Ganja La**, a very tough three-day traverse for which you'll need a tent, food, crampons and ice axe (it may be impassable between Dec and March). From Tarke Ghyang, lesser trails lead to **Panch Pokhri** (3800m), a set of lakes two or three days to the east, and from there you could continue east or south to the Arniko Highway.

Langtang and Gosainkund

In contrast with Helambu, the Langtang and Gosainkund treks make straight for specific destinations, gaining elevation quickly and then leaving you to explore at your own pace. To return, a certain amount of backtracking is unavoidable, unless you cross into Helambu. Culture is not a big part of either, except during Janai Purnima, a massive Hindu **pilgrimage** held at Gosainkund during the full moon of July–August.

Langtang

The **LANGTANG TREK** can be done in as little as a week, but day-hikes in the upper valley are sure to detain you for at least another two or three days, and given more time you'll want to add Gosainkund to the itinerary. Most people start at **Syabrubesi**, site of a Tibetan resettlement project, a very local ten-plus-hour bus ride from Kathmandu; watch your bag and valuables on this bus. (The road to Syabrubesi, a spectacularly destructive feat of engineering, was built to reach a lead and zinc mine in the Ganesh Himal. A new road is now planned to be built by China from Syabrubesi up to Rasuwa on the Tibet border.) The first two days are spent climbing briskly up the gorge-like lower Langtang valley, where oaks and rhododendron give way to peaceful hemlock and larch forest; after ascending an old moraine, snowy peaks suddenly loom ahead and the gorge opens into a U-shaped glacial valley. Springtime is excellent for flowers here, and in autumn the berberis bushes turn a deep rust colour.

Two Bhotiya villages occupy the upper valley: **Langtang** (3300m), the bigger of the two, makes a good place to spend an extra night and acclimatize, while **Kyangjin** (3750m) boasts a small *gompa*, a cheese "factory" (fabulous yogurt) and an attractive chalet-lodge. Lodges here can fill up early in high season, since there aren't that many places to stay, and all trekkers must pass through these villages both going and returning. The **Langtang Glacier** is a full day's walk further up the valley. You'll want to spend at least a couple of nights in the upper valley to explore the glaciers and ascend **Tsergo Ri** (5033m), from which you can view an awesome white wilderness of peaks.

You can **return** by crossing into Helambu over the Ganja La (see above), but most people go back down the valley, varying the trip by going via Khangjung, high up on the grassy northern side. The trail to Gosainkund branches off at Thulo Syabru.

Gosainkund

GOSAINKUND can be trekked on its own in as little as four days, but because of the rapid ascent to high elevation – 4380m – it's best done after acclimatizing in Langtang or Helambu. Combined with either of these, it adds three or four days; a grand tour of all three areas takes sixteen or more days.

From either Dhunche (served by buses from Kathmandu; see p.264) or Thulo Syabru (on the Langtang trek), trails ascend steeply through mossy rhododendron forest to the monastery and cheese factory of **Sing Gompa** at 3250m.

The climb from Dhunche is particularly brutal. Above Sing Gompa, the trail ascends through tall fir stands before emerging above the tree line for increasingly panoramic views of the high peaks (Laurebinayak is a beautiful place to stop) and finally entering the barren upper reaches of the Trisuli River, where glacial moraines and rockslides have left a string of some half-dozen **lakes** (*kund*). Several lodges sit by the shore of **Gosainkund**, the most sacred of the lakes and renowned among Nepali Hindus. A famous legend recounts how Shiva, having saved the world by drinking a dangerous poison, struck this mountainside with his *trisul* to create the lake and cool his burning throat. In good weather you can climb a nearby summit (5144m) for superb views.

Everest (Solu-Khumbu)

Everest – or to give it its proper Nepali name, **Sagarmatha** ("Brow of the Ocean"), or its even more proper Sherpa name, **Chomolungma** ("Mother Goddess of the World") – is more a pilgrimage than a trek. As with all pilgrimages, it is a tough personal challenge with a clear goal at the end. Lasting images, however, are of the revelations along the way: remote monasteries, irrepressible Sherpas, and peaks with almost human moods and personalities. Prior experience isn't necessary, but treks in this region require extra effort.

The Everest region is the main trekking destination east of Kathmandu, and in terms of popularity it runs second to Annapurna. It divides into two distinct areas. The lower, greener and more populous country to the south is known as **Solu**: if you're not flying in, you'll probably begin at Jiri and spend the first week of your trek walking eastwards across Solu's deep canyons and tall ridges. **Khumbu**, wedged between Solu and the Tibetan border, comprises the spectacular, harsh landscape of Everest and the surrounding peaks and glaciated valleys.

The challenge of **getting there** puts many people off. The choice is between **flying** into Lukla, at 2800m on the doorstep of Khumbu ($83 from Kathmandu), and taking the **bus** to Jiri in Solu (which adds 5–7 days' walking each way). In an ideal world, you would walk in from Jiri to get acclimatized and fly out of Lukla to avoid backtracking, but it seldom works out that way, as high-season flights may be booked up by organized trekking parties or grounded due to bad weather. Largely for this reason, more than half the people who trek Everest go with a group.

The walking in Solu is very strenuous, while in Khumbu, **altitude** is the overriding factor: to get a good look at Everest, you'll have to spend at least four nights above 4000m and at least one at around 5000m. There is a risk of developing acute mountain sickness (AMS) and you must know the signs. Not only is this the highest of the standard treks, it's also the **coldest**, so you'll need a good sleeping bag, several layers of warm clothes, and sturdy boots that will keep out mud and snow. A great help on this front are the rental shops of Namche, in Khumbu, where you can stock up on high-altitude gear and return it on the way back down. Because of weather, the **trekking "window"** is especially short in Khumbu – early October to mid-November, and late March to late April – and this, in turn, creates a seasonal stampede on the trails and at the Lukla airstrip. Winter isn't out of the question, but it's just that much colder.

While Everest isn't as heavily trekked as Annapurna, its high-altitude **environment** is even more fragile. Khumbu, with only four thousand inhabitants, receives about ten thousand trekkers a year (plus probably twice as many

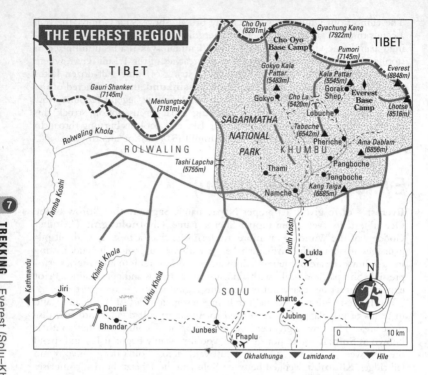

porters). Locals spend three times longer collecting firewood than they did a decade ago, and the demand for wood is now estimated to be three times the regeneration capacity of the area. Even some trek leaders privately admit that the best thing for Khumbu would be to give it a rest from trekking for a few years. Most of Khumbu is protected within **Sagarmatha National Park**, which is helping to preserve the remaining forest, but it can't be said often enough: have as little to do with wood-burning as possible.

The popular trails through Solu-Khumbu are all equipped with **teahouses**. The main Jiri–Lukla–Namche–Base Camp route is very straightforward, but a **guide** is advisable if you're planning to do anything unusual. Solu-Khumbu is the easiest area in Nepal to hire a **woman porter** – a Sherpani – although few speak enough English to serve as guides.

Solu: the Jiri walk-in

The **JIRI WALK-IN** follows the historical route that all Everest mountaineers and trekkers had to take before it was possible to fly to Lukla. It's still fairly popular, mostly as a budget approach to Everest but also as a trek in its own right, and innkeepers along the trail are reasonably accustomed to serving Westerners (another approach is described later in the "Eastern Nepal" section). There has been some Maoist activity in this area, though, so inquire about safety before going.

The starting point is Jiri (see p.261), a gruelling ten- to twelve-hour **bus** ride from Kathmandu; enquire about an express bus service, which is supposed to be starting up. The Kathmandu–Jiri bus route is notorious for theft, so keep your things with you inside. The Jiri road is now being extended, and it may soon be possible to travel by jeep to Deorali, cutting the first day and a half off the trek. It's also possible to **fly** to Phaplu, four days east of Jiri, though it's not much cheaper ($77) than flying all the way to Lukla, three days further on.

Everest

In 1841, while taking routine measurements from the plains, members of the Survey of India logged a previously unnoted summit which they labelled simply Peak XV. Fifteen years later, computations revealed it to be the world's highest mountain, and the British subsequently named it after **Sir George Everest**, head of the Survey of India from 1823 to 1843. The mountain's **elevation** was believed to be 8848m for many years, until more-accurate GPS measurements in 1999 established a new (still unofficial) height of 8850m (29,035ft).

Politically off-limits until the early twentieth century, the climb to the summit was first attempted from the Tibetan side in 1922 by a British party that included **George Mallory**, who coined the famous "because it is there" phrase. Two years later, Mallory and Andrew Irvine reached at least 8500m – without oxygen – before disappearing into a cloud; a 1999 search found Mallory's body, but failed to establish whether the two had reached the summit before their deaths. Several more attempts were made until World War II suspended activities, and climbs were further hampered by the Chinese invasion of Tibet in 1950, which closed the northern approach to mountaineers.

With the opening of Nepal in 1951, however, attention turned to southern approaches, and a race between the Swiss and the British was on. The mountain was finally scaled, using a route via the South Col, by New Zealander **Edmund Hillary** and Sherpa **Tenzing Norgay** in a British-led expedition in 1953. Throughout the next two decades, increasingly big expeditions put men – and women, starting with **Junko Tabei** of Japan in 1975 – on the top by various routes. In the mid-1970s the trend shifted from large-scale assaults to small, quick "alpine-style" ascents. Dominating the field for more than a decade, **Reinhold Messner** was one of two climbers to reach the summit without oxygen in 1978, and in 1980 he made the first successful solo ascent of Everest.

Other records continue to fall. In 1988, New Zealander **Lydia Bradey** became the first woman to tackle Everest without oxygen. In 1999, **Babu Chhiri Sherpa** set the record for longest time spent on top of the summit (21 hours), and in 2000 achieved the fastest ascent from Base Camp (16 hours, 56 minutes). Tragically, Babu Chhiri died in a fall on Everest in 2001, while attempting the summit for a record-tying eleventh time. That record remains, at least for the time being, with **Appa Sherpa**. Slovenian Davo Karnicar completed the first uninterrupted **ski descent** from summit to base camp in 2000. The following year, Marco Siffredi of France and Stefan Gatt of Germany **snowboarded** the mountain (Siffredi made it all the way to base camp), and husband and wife Bertrand and Claire Bernier Roche of France flew a tandem **paraglider** off the summit, taking eight minutes to return to base camp. The **oldest** summiteer is Sherman Bull (aged 64), and the **youngest** Temba Tsheri Sherpa (16). They both reached the top in 2001, along with the **first blind climber**, Erik Weihenmayer.

One record that can only be broken is the number of people who have reached the summit. At the time of writing, more than 1400 climbers had successfully ascended Everest, and with "commercial" Everest expeditions opening up the mountain to less experienced climbers (who pay as much as $65,000 for a place) the number is rising rapidly. So, too, is Everest's **death toll**. At the time of writing, nearly 170 people had died on the mountain (eight of them in the much-publicized guided-climb fiasco chronicled in Jon Krakauer's *Into Thin Air*; see "Books" in Contexts). Historically, three out of every hundred climbers ascending above Base Camp have perished.

Cutting across the lay of the land, the trail bobs between valleys as low as 1500m and passes as high as 3500m: the ups and downs can be disheartening, but the fitness and acclimatization gained here pay off later on. A few glimpses of peaks – notably Gauri Shankar (7145m) – urge you along during the first five or six days, although Solu's lasting images are of tumbling gorges, rhododendron forests and terraced fields hewn out of steep hillsides. Solu has benefited from several projects funded by **Edmund Hillary's Himalayan Trust**; groups of children may accompany you on their way to one of the "Hillary" schools in the area.

The route passes through some important Sherpa villages, notably **Bhandar** and **Junbesi**, the latter with an active monastery and a "village tourism" programme. Most trekkers are understandably impatient to get up to Everest or back to Kathmandu, but side trips to the cheese "factory" at **Thodung** and **Thubten Chholing Gompa** north of Junbesi are fascinating. From **Jubing**, a Rai village five days in, the trail finally bends north towards Everest, following the valley of the Dudh Koshi. Two days later, it sidesteps Lukla and joins the well-trodden route to Khumbu.

The bulk of traffic through Solu consists of porters humping in gear for trekking groups and expeditions flying into Lukla, and this is reflected in the no-frills **food and lodging** available.

Khumbu: the Everest trek

The trail north from Lukla is the trunk route of the **EVEREST TREK**: everyone walks it at least once, and all but a few backtrack along it as well. Most trekkers follow it to the end at Kala Pattar (the classic viewpoint of Everest) and Everest Base Camp, both about eight days northeast of Lukla; quite a few combine this with a trip to the beautiful Gokyo Lakes, about the same distance north of Lukla.

Khumbu **lodges** are heavily geared for trekkers, and you should have no trouble getting a bunk and a good meal along the busier trails. Prices aren't unreasonable, considering the distance supplies have to be carried, but they do rise steadily as you go up. An additional expense is the Rs1000 entry fee for **Sagarmatha National Park**.

Lukla to Everest Base Camp and Kala Pattar

From **Lukla**, the trail meanders north along the Dudh Koshi before bounding up to **Namche** (3450m), where Khumbu and the serious scenery start. Nestled handsomely in a horseshoe bowl, the Sherpa "capital" has done very well out of mountaineering and trekking over the years. Besides trekking equipment, Namche's shops sell absolutely anything a trekker could desire, albeit all at inflated prices – film, maps, batteries, Mars bars from around the world, a dozen styles of Swiss Army knife. There's also a bank, a post office, a bakery, a place calling itself "the world's highest bar", and even internet access. Try to make your trip coincide with the pan-cultural **Saturday market**, or visit the national park **visitors' centre**, perched on the ridge east of town, which contains an informative museum. **Thami**, a beautiful few hours' walk west of Namche, makes an excellent side trip.

Beyond Namche, the trail veers northeast into a tributary valley and climbs to **Tengboche**, surrounded by protected juniper forest and commanding a show-stealing view of everybody's favourite peak, Ama Dablam (6828m). Tengboche's much-photographed monastery was rebuilt in the early 1990s, after the earlier one burned down when its newly installed electrical wiring

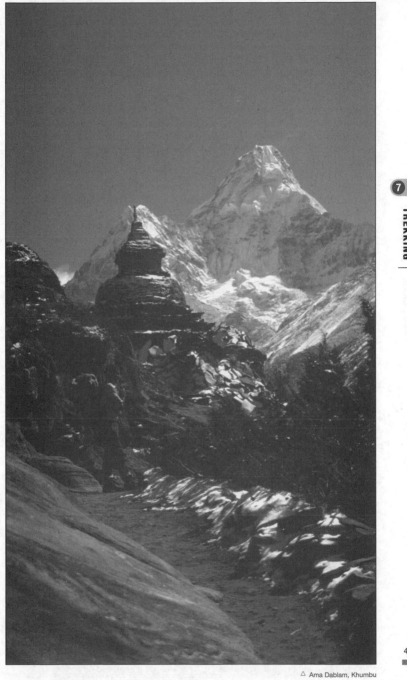

△ Ama Dablam, Khumbu

malfunctioned (is there a lesson in this?). Mani Rimdu (see p.58), the Sherpa dance-drama festival, is held here on the full moon of November–December. The trail continues to **Pangboche**, containing Khumbu's oldest *gompa*, where for a donation the lama will show you some yeti relics, and on to **Pheriche** (4250m), site of a Himalayan Rescue Association post (AMS talks are held every afternoon during the trekking season). From here up, settlements are strictly seasonal, and their stone enclosures and slate-roofed huts are reminiscent of Scottish crofts.

From Pheriche the route bends north again, ascending the moraine of the Khumbu Glacier and passing a series of monuments to Sherpas killed on Everest, to reach **Lobuche** (4930m). Another day's march along the glacier's lateral moraine brings you to **Gorak Shep** (5180m), the last huddle of teahouses – and a cold, probably sleepless night. The payoff comes when you climb up the grassy mound of **Kala Pattar** (5545m): the extra height provides an unbelievable panorama, not only of **Everest** (8848m) but also of its neighbours Lhotse (Nepal's third-highest peak, at 8516m) and Nuptse (7861m), as well as the sugarloaf of Pumori (7165m). A separate day-trip can be made across the amazing Khumbu Glacier to **Everest Base Camp**. In spring you may encounter a half-dozen or more expedition parties here, constantly ferrying supplies up the dangerous Khumbu Icefall to higher camps; the climbers may be happy to have well-wishers, but if they seem wary of trekkers you can't blame them.

Gokyo Lakes

The scenery is every bit as good at **Gokyo Lakes**, in the next valley to the west, and other trekkers are noticeably fewer. If you're equipped to cross a snowy pass and are good at route-finding, you can be there in two days from Gorak Shep, crossing the strenuous **Cho La** (5420m) west of Lobuche. Otherwise, you'll have to backtrack almost to Namche, and then follow the Dudh Koshi north for two days to Gokyo, set beside the immense Ngozumba

The yeti

The **yeti** ("man of the rocky places") has been a staple of Sherpa and Tibetan folklore for centuries, but stories of hairy, ape-like creatures roaming the snowy heights first came to the attention of the outside world during the early days of British rule in India. Explorers in Tibet reported seeing mysterious moving figures and large, unidentified footprints in the snow – captivated by the reports, an imaginative Fleet Street hack coined the term "abominable snowman" – but it wasn't until 1951, during the first British Everest expedition from the Nepal side, that climber Eric Shipton took clear **photographs** of yeti tracks. Since then, several highly publicized **yeti-hunts**, including one led by Sir Edmund Hillary in 1960, have brought back a wealth of circumstantial evidence but not one authenticated sighting.

Sceptics dismiss the yeti as a straightforward **myth**, of course, arguing that the hairy creatures in question are more likely bears, and that the oversized footprints could be any animal's tracks, melted and enlarged by the sun. Meanwhile, relics kept at the *gompa* of Pangboche and Khumjung have failed to provide scientific proof of the yeti's existence. The "skulls" have been examined by experts and deemed to be made of serow (Himalayan wild goat) skins, while the skeletal hand at Pangboche is presumed to be human. Yet yaks continue to be mauled, and Sherpas insist the yeti isn't a hoax. Perhaps the most significant aspect of the yeti is humans' reaction to it: we want it to exist, like the Loch Ness Monster – some secret part of the world that mankind hasn't yet discovered and explained – yet in our endless curiosity we want to find and dissect it. Thankfully, it has eluded us so far.

Glacier (the biggest in Nepal). Several brilliant-blue lakes, dammed up by the glacier's lateral moraine, dot the west side of the valley above and below Gokyo. The high point of Gokyo is an overlook called, again, **Kala Pattar**, surveying a clutter of blue teeth – Cho Oyu, Everest and Lhotse are just the ones over 8000m – and the long grey tongue of the Ngozumba Glacier. You can also scramble north beside the glacier as far as Cho Oyu Base Camp.

Eastern Nepal

Treks in **eastern Nepal** are hampered by a fundamental problem of access: Hile, the principal trailhead, is an eighteen-hour **bus** ride from Kathmandu. **Flights** are worth looking into, as they're good value for money here – the one from Kathmandu to Tumlingtar costs only $65. The east is relatively well-off, so in the settled areas **food** and **lodging** is easy to come by, but it's seldom geared for trekkers.

Ethnically, eastern Nepal is even more diverse than the Annapurna region: Rais and Limbus are dominant in the hills (Gurungs and Magars are found in smaller numbers), while Sherpas, Tamangs and other Bhotiyas inhabit the high country, and Hindu castes the valleys. Makalu, Kanchenjunga and other big peaks provide stunning **views** from most high points. Flora and fauna are also of great interest to specialists, especially the **butterflies** and other insects of the upper Arun Valley, and the **rhododendrons** of the Milke Daada.

The Everest eastern route

While still not nearly as developed as the Jiri walk-in, the **EASTERN ROUTE** to or from Everest is becoming more popular, and facilities along it are expanding yearly. It's usually treated as an "escape route" from Everest by

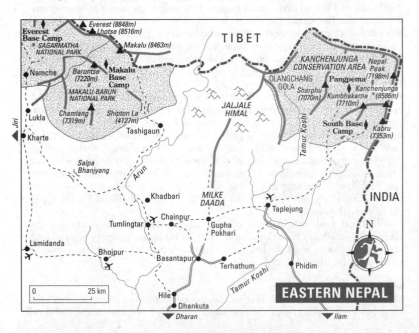

trekkers who want to avoid the long backtrack to Jiri; there's no reason why the itinerary can't be done in reverse, except perhaps that it's better to gain some confidence on the more developed Everest trails before tackling this less-trekked region. Another factor to consider is the **season**: try to do the lower section of the trek when it's cooler.

From the Everest region, the **route** leaves the Jiri walk-in at **Kharte**, about a day south of Lukla, and heads southeastwards to reach Tumlingtar five to seven days later. Part of this stretch traverses the Makalu-Barun Conservation Area (see below), and an entrance fee may be required. The first half of the trek passes through tangled hills inhabited mainly by Rais; after reaching a high point at the lush Salpa Bhanjyang pass (3350m), it descends steadily to the deep, hot and predominantly Hindu Arun Valley. **Tumlingtar** is a busy bazaar overlooking the Arun River; there are one or two flights a day from there to Kathmandu ($65). If you're returning to Kathmandu by bus, carry on to Hile (see p.404), two days south and 1400m higher. The route is equipped with **tea-houses** and a guide isn't needed, but don't expect English signs or fancy food. You'd be wise to bring a few provisions just in case.

For more adventure, you could carry on walking from Tumlingtar **to Basantapur** (see p.405) by way of **Chainpur**, a tidy village renowned for its brassware, or even further **to Taplejung** (daily flights to Kathmandu; $137) via the Milke Daada (see below Another route aims roughly due south from Lukla **to Lamidanda** (daily flights to Kathmandu; $66). If you can't get on a flight there, trails continue south to the Tarai or east to Hile via Bhojpur, Nepal's most famous *khukuri*-making centre.

Other treks in eastern Nepal

Many hill treks north of Hile and Ilam are feasible without supplies. Bhojpur, Chainpur and Khadbari, quintessential Newar hill towns within two or three days' walk of Hile, all make great targets. This is fine country for adventurous trekkers who like exploring places that aren't written up in guidebooks, and this book isn't going to spoil that pleasure by writing about them.

However, here are three more-conventional treks which, though they would be difficult to do independently, are finding their way into agency brochures.

The Milke Daada

A long north–south ridge famed for its rhododendrons, the **MILKE DAADA** can be linked up with a visit to Chainpur for a seven- to ten-day trek that combines spectacular flora with one of Nepal's best bazaars. The route goes no higher than 3500m, but takes in plenty of mountain views. From Basantapur (p.405) the route heads north, initially following the main porter trail to Taplejung and then continuing north through the lush cloudforest of the Milke Daada. Various trails to **Chainpur** branch off to the west; from there you can continue to the airstrip at Tumlingtar ($65 to Kathmandu) or return to Hile. Alternatively, you could head east from Gupha Pokhari to Taplejung ($137 to Kathmandu).

Basic **food and lodging** can be found along most of this route, but the absence of teahouses north of Gupha Pokhari limits an independent trekker's ability to explore the Milke Daada. Groups with porter support can continue north into the Jaljale Himal.

Makalu Base Camp

MAKALU BASE CAMP, reached by a two- to three-week trek from Hile up the Arun Valley and over the Shipton La (4127m), requires a tent and food for most of the way. Much of this trek passes through the wild and remote **Makalu–Barun National Park** (Rs1000 entry fee) and the contiguous **Makalu–Barun Conservation Area**. Established in 1992, the park is intended to stem the growing human pressure around the base-camp area and preserve what is regarded as one of the most biologically diverse areas in the Himalaya. The conservation area, which forms a protective buffer zone in the inhabited area south and east of the park, is supposed to be modelled on the Annapurna Conservation Area Project and operate on similar principles of involving locals in conservation. There's really only one route to the base camp, so you're obliged to retrace your steps most of the way back.

Kanchenjunga

The most incredible trek in this part of Nepal is to the foot of **KANCHEN-JUNGA**, the third-highest peak in the world at 8586m. Kanchenjunga is an expensive trek because it's officially restricted to agency-organized groups and, given its remote location in the extreme northeastern corner of the country, it generally involves flying into **Taplejung** ($137 from Kathmandu). Unofficially, it may be possible to do this trek independently, but you'd still have to have an agency arrange your permit ($10 per week). There's also a Rs1000 fee to enter the newly established **Kanchenjunga Conservation Area**. To save money and take in some pretty hill country, you could walk to Taplejung from Basantapur (see p.405) in three days, but you'd still have to have a couple of porters toting your supplies for the upper elevations. The route forks a few days northeast of Taplejung, one trail going to the so-called North Base Camp at **Pangpema**, the other to the South Base Camp and the Yalung Glacier. You'll need at least two weeks – four to do it all justice.

Far western Nepal

West of Dhaulagiri, the Himalaya subside somewhat and retreat north into Tibet, while the foothill zone broadens, the climate becomes drier and the people poorer. The northern third of the region, left in the rain shadow of the Himalaya, receives little monsoon moisture – in every way but politically, this highland strip is part of Tibet. Jagged Himalayan grandeur isn't so much in evidence, but there's a wildness and a vastness here, and the feeling of isolation is thrilling. The **far west** is the deep end of trekking in Nepal, and the treks here are well off the beaten track: they're a chore to get to, they require a lot of preparation and, with the exception of Rara Lake, you'll find that very few Westerners have gone before you. All that might appeal if you're an experienced trekker looking for new challenges, but if you're a first-timer without agency support, forget it. Furthermore, Nepal's **Maoists** are most active in the far west, so get the latest advice before even thinking of trekking in this area.

Logistics make or break a trek in the far west. Given the distances involved, you'll probably want to **fly** to the starting point, but the only airline providing scheduled (non-charter) service to the far western airstrips is RNAC, which is renowned for dysfunctional service and the inability to confirm bookings for the return flight in advance. **Food and lodging** are in uncomfortably short supply, so you'll need to bring a tent, cooking utensils and at least some provisions. You should be prepared to carry it all yourself, because **porters** here are a fickle lot and often can't be spared from their farmwork. **Guides** familiar with the area are also scarce, so you shouldn't venture out without a reasonable command of Nepali. If you go on an **organized trek** you may not be entirely

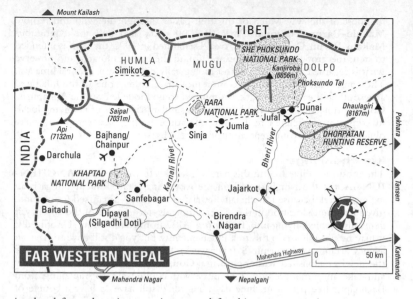

Map labels:
- Mount Kailash
- TIBET
- HUMLA
- Simikot
- MUGU
- SHE PHOKSUNDO NATIONAL PARK
- Kanjiroba (6656m)
- DOLPO
- Phoksundo Tal
- Saipal (7031m)
- RARA NATIONAL PARK
- Dunai
- Jufal
- Dhaulagiri (8167m)
- Api (7132m)
- Bajhang/Chainpur
- Sinja
- Jumla
- Darchula
- DHORPATAN HUNTING RESERVE
- Karnali River
- Bheri River
- KHAPTAD NATIONAL PARK
- Jajarkot
- Baitadi
- Sanfebagar
- Dipayal (Silgadhi Doti)
- Birendra Nagar
- INDIA
- FAR WESTERN NEPAL
- Mahendra Highway
- 0   50 km
- N
- Mahendra Nagar
- Nepalganj
- Pokhara
- Tansen
- Kathmandu

insulated from these inconveniences, and for this reason agencies may try to steer you towards more easterly destinations.

As roads gradually penetrate into the far west, trekking might become easier. In the meantime, the three treks described below are the most realistic possibilities.

Rara National Park

RARA NATIONAL PARK is the best known of the far western trekking areas, but has fallen somewhat into disuse in recent years. The usual itinerary is a loop that starts and ends at Jumla, 150km north of Nepalganj, and takes about eight days. The country is a sea of choppy, mostly forested mountains, offering only glimpses of Himalayan peaks, but the highlight is Nepal's largest lake, surrounded by a wilderness area of meadows, forest and abundant wildlife.

To get to the trailhead you first have to **fly** to Nepalganj ($99 from Kathmandu) and then from there to Jumla ($57); flights are supposed to be daily in season, but are often cancelled. The alternative is to walk in from Birendra Nagar (Surkhet), which adds a week each way. **Food** can be bought in Jumla, but beyond the bazaar it's often unavailable at any price. There are **lodges** in Jumla and a bunkhouse at the lake; in between, there are a few teahouses where you might be able to stay, but camping is more pleasant and certainly more reliable. The **park fee** is Rs1000.

Technical difficulties aside, Rara makes a fair compromise between the popular treks and the really obscure ones, and in a way combines the best of both worlds: like the popular treks, Rara is given detailed route descriptions in the trekking books, so you can do it without an organized group or even a guide, yet it's remote enough to ensure that you'll see few – if any – other foreigners. Starting at Jumla (2400m), the route crosses two 3500-metre ridges before reaching pristine **Rara Lake** at 3000m. The park is one of the best places in Nepal to see mountain **wildlife**, including Himalayan black bear, tahr, goral, musk deer and the rare red (lesser) panda. Autumn and spring are the **best seasons**, and Rara is particularly worth considering in May and June, when the weather elsewhere is getting too hot or unpredictable. A day and a half south of the lake is **Sinja**, where the ruins of the capital of the twelfth- to fourteenth-century Khasa dynasty (see "The historical framework" in Contexts) can be viewed across the river.

Dolpo and She-Phoksundo National Park

DOLPO (sometimes written Dolpa) is an enormous, isolated district northwest of Dhaulagiri and bordering Tibet, the western half of which has been set aside as **SHE-PHOKSUNDO NATIONAL PARK**, Nepal's biggest. The park protects an awe-inspiring region of deep valleys, unclimbed peaks, remote monasteries and rare fauna. The **best time to go** is September, with May–June and October–November close behind.

Dolpo was the setting of Peter Matthiessen's *The Snow Leopard* (see "Books" in Contexts), and until recently the book was as close as most foreigners were allowed to get to it. It's now open to trekking, but only by organized groups. Unofficially, it might be possible to arrange a trekking permit for **Southern (Lower) Dolpo** through an agency and do everything else independently. The permit costs $10 per week, and a trek there will take a week to ten days. There are some teahouses in Lower Dolpo, but it's a food-deficit area so you'll need to bring several days' worth of provisions. Guides and porters can be hired near the airstrip. The agency-trekking requirement for **Northern (Upper) Dolpo** is strictly enforced, and the permit is much more expensive: $700 for the first ten days, $70 per day thereafter.

There's no safe alternative to **flying** into Dolpo these days, because approaches from the south pass through Maoist strongholds. Most people fly in and out of Jufal, the airstrip for Dolpo District ($77 from Nepalganj); flying into or out of Jumla, about five-days' walk further west, is also possible ($57 from Nepalganj). From Jufal the route heads east to Dunai and then north, entering the park after about a day (Rs1000 **entry fee**) and reaching the village of Ringmo and the stunningly blue **Phoksundo Tal** after another two days. There are plenty of day-hiking opportunities around the lake. Beyond lies Northern Dolpo.

Humla and treks to Tibet

Tucked away in the extreme northwestern corner of Nepal, **HUMLA** is high, dry and strongly Tibetan. Snowcapped peaks hem the district in on three sides and shut out most outside influences, including the monsoon. It's open only to organized groups, and the permit costs $90 for the first week, $15 per day thereafter (treks into Tibet carry additional fees of at least $500). This area is prone to food shortages and in recent years has experienced serious spring and early-summer famines, so it's essential to bring all the food you'll need – and then some.

RNAC **flies** from Nepalganj to **Simikot** (Humla's district headquarters) most days of the week in season ($88). The most popular trek from there heads west along the Humla Karnali River to the **Tibet** border, about five-days' walking, from where a jeep will take you to **Lake Manasarowar** and the starting point for the three-day-plus circumambulation of sacred **Mount Kailas**. (The Humla Karnali trail is in the process of being turned into a road, which will soon make it possible to drive the entire way from Simikot to Manasarowar. Those who prefer to walk will still be able to take a more northerly route to the border.) Staying in Nepal, the likeliest itinerary is a seven- to nine-day walk to Jumla, stopping at Rara Lake along the way. The trail involves a good deal of up-and-down, but goes no higher than 3600m. In May–June, which is the **best time** to go, the wildflowers are out of this world.

Travel details

Buses

Kathmandu to: Basantapur (no direct buses, change at Dharan or Hile); Besisahar (5 daily; 8hr); Dhunche (3 daily; 8hr); Gorkha (5 daily; 6hr); Hile (2 daily; 18hr); Jiri (5 daily; 10+hr); Malemchi Pul (no direct buses, take any bus up the Arniko Highway and change at Panchkal; 5hr); Pokhara (12 daily; 8hr); Sundarijal (20 daily; 1hr); Syabrubesi (1 daily; 10hr); Taplejung (no direct buses, take a Kakarbhitta bus and change at Birtamod).

Pokhara to: Baglung (22 daily; 3hr), Begnas Tal (every 20min; 45min); Besisahar (no direct buses, take any eastbound bus and change at Dumre; 5hr); Gorkha (2 daily; 5hr); Naya Pul (10 daily; 2hr); Phedi/Surkhet (10 daily; 1hr).

Flights

Biratnagar to: Bhojpur (1–2 daily); Lamidanda (2–3 weekly); Taplejung (3–5 weekl); Tumlingtar (2 daily).

Kathmandu to: Biratnagar (10–12 daily); Lamidanda (1–2 daily); Lukla (up to 14 daily) Nepalganj (6–8 daily); Phaplu (2–5 daily); Pokhara (18–28 daily); Tumlingtar (1–2 daily). For flights to other western airstrips, change at Nepalganj. For flights to other eastern airstrips, change at Biratnagar.

Nepalganj to: Jufal/Dunai (2–7 weekly); Jumla (2–7 weekly); Simikot (2–7 weekly).

Pokhara to: Jomosom (5–7 daily).

Rafting and kayaking

CHAPTER 8

Highlights

* **Kayak school** How cool is it to be able to say you learned to kayak in the Himalayas? See p.460

* **The Seti** A tame, picturesque, easily accessible river, warmed by geothermal springs. See p.463

* **The Bhote Koshi** A short adrenaline rush on the steepest and hardest of Nepal's raftable rivers. See p.463

* **The Marsyangdi** A magnificent, continuously technical stretch of river, soon to be dammed. See p.464

* **The Sun Koshi** The perfect introduction to rafting in Nepal: eight varied days through remote hill country. See p.465

* **The Tamur** Six days of challenging whitewater in the far east, with an optional trek in. See p.466

8

Rafting and kayaking

I n recent years, **rafting** and **kayaking** have really boomed in Nepal, with many visitors coming to the country specifically for river-running. The reason? Big mountains mean big, exciting, scenic rivers. Nepal has some of the best whitewater on earth – a few of the longer trips are world classics, offering the experience of a lifetime – and rafting in Nepal is incredible value for money when compared to other countries. So if you ever thought you might like to try rafting or kayaking, then this might be the place to do it.

A river trip is a wonderful way to experience Nepal. You actually see more of the traditional countryside while rafting than you do on one of the apple-pie treks, and in fact some of the remoter trips entail mini-treks through little-visited areas just to get to the put-in point. Then there's the sheer escapism of life on the river: camping on white-sand beaches, campfires under the stars, warm water (most rivers in Nepal are at lower, semitropical elevations), jungle-clad slopes, wildlife and birds (bring your binoculars), and the tranquillity of being away from towns and roads. And of course there are the thrills, laughter and companionship that come from shooting rapids. It's also worth mention-ing that almost all rivers in Nepal are clean, and there are almost no nasty bit-ing insects on the beaches (mosquitoes are very rare).

When to go

Time of year makes an enormous difference to water volumes: flows during the height of the monsoon (July and Aug) are ten or more times greater than in February and March. The major rivers are off-limits to all but experts during the monsoon, and if you're a beginner you probably won't want to try rafting until mid-October, when things have calmed down.

The water is more manageably exciting in late October to November, which is the peak rafting season, and becomes mellower (but colder) from December through to April or May, when snowmelt begins to add to flows again. Winter isn't as chilly as you might think, since most raftable river sections are below 500m elevation, but it's a slow time for tourism generally in Nepal, so many river operators don't run trips then. March and April are the best months for long, warm days and excellent birdwatching.

However, different rivers are at their best at different times of the year – for example, the Sun Koshi is actually quite good starting in late September – so which river you go on will depend to a large extent on when you're in Nepal. Also note that a given trip will take less time in high water than when the water is running more slowly.

Information, books and maps

You'll be able to get most or all of your questions answered by your rafting company, assuming you're going on an organized trip. For independent information, though, get hold of a copy of the **guidebook** *White Water Nepal*, by Peter Knowles (see "Books" in Contexts), which provides comprehensive river descriptions and advice on logistics, equipment and everything else. For basic information, updates and links to operators, visit Ⓦwww.raftnepal.org. The Nepal River Conservation Trust's website (Ⓦwww.nepalrivers.org) provides some information of a more environmental bent.

It's always nice to know where you are, even if you're being guided. *White Water Nepal* gives small-scale but quite useful **maps** of all the raftable rivers. Himalayan Map House publishes rafting maps for the more popular rivers (such as the Sun Koshi and Trisuli), showing rapids, put-in points and so on. For other areas, trekking maps can at least keep you oriented.

Rafting operators and agents

A fairly sophisticated river-running industry exists in Nepal, with dozens of Nepali and Western-run **rafting operators** offering both scheduled and customized trips. Unless you're an experienced kayaker (see p.460) or are on some sort of a self-organized expedition, you'll go with one of these companies. The standards of most operators are high and exceed international guidelines, but as with most things in life, you get what you pay for, and Nepal has its share of rip-off artists. Trip prices and quality vary enormously, so if you buy the cheapest trip from a budget operator you may have a thoroughly miserable and dangerous experience.

A few of the more reputable Nepal-based operators are listed in the Kathmandu and Pokhara sections (pp.169 and 303). These deal with bookings from overseas, but they'll also take walk-in clients, and if you can muster up a few friends you can arrange your own customized departure. Booking with an agency in your own country (see the lists on pp.13, 16 and 17) is more expensive, of course, but it guarantees arrangements ahead of time: in high season the best trips are fully booked months in advance.

Some of the cut-price outfits in Kathmandu and Pokhara aren't bad, but making recommendations would be misleading – companies come and go, and standards rise and fall from one season to the next. Shop around, and press operators hard on the criteria given below. Only use a company belonging to the Nepal Association of Rafting Agents, a trade body that sets safety standards, requires its members to employ only trained and licensed guides, and handles complaints.

Many places advertising rafting trips are merely **agents**, who usually don't know what they're talking about and who will add their own commission (low or high) to the operator's price, so you're strongly advised to **book directly with the rafting operator**. Another reason for dealing directly with the operator is that you can find out who else is booked on the trip, which might well influence your enjoyment.

Costs

Trips booked in Nepal **cost** $15 to $75 a day, depending on the river, number of people in the party, and standard of service. For trips on the Trisuli and Kali Gandaki (the most popular rafting rivers), upmarket companies typically charge $30–40 a day to a walk-in customer, which should include transport to and from the river by private bus and good, hygienic meals. Budget outfits offer these trips for around $20 a day, but at that price you can expect to travel by local bus and be served pretty unappetizing food; anyone charging less than $20 is likely to make you buy your own bus tickets and meals. Other more remote rivers cost $10–20 a day extra. These prices assume full rafts, which hold up to seven paying passengers each.

When reckoning cost per day, bear in mind that a "three-day" trip is rarely three days of solid rafting: you may be travelling to the river most of day one, with just an hour spent on the river that afternoon, rafting for maybe four hours on day two, and then travelling back on your last day.

Be sure to check that your travel **insurance** policy covers your proposed activity. If you're going to be away from main roads then helicopter rescue may be needed, and no helicopter will take off without cash in hand or the assurance of repayment by an insurance company. Leave a copy of your travel policy with the operator, highlighting the telephone number they should contact in case of an emergency.

Note that government **rafting permits** are no longer required.

Equipment

Most companies use **paddle rafts**, in which everyone paddles and the guide steers from the rear – lots of group participation and fun. On less exciting oar trips, the guide does all the work, giving the clients the chance to sit back and enjoy the scenery.

Your rafting company will advise on what to **bring**, but you'll definitely need a swimsuit, sunglasses, plenty of suntan lotion, rubber-soled shoes or sport sandals, a change of clothes and shoes for camp, a towel, a head torch/flashlight and spare batteries. Cotton T-shirts and shorts are standard river wear, but if the weather is likely to be cold and/or wet, bring thermal tops and trousers, since cotton provides no warmth when wet; the better companies furnish wetsuits, thermal tops and paddling jackets. Tents, foam mattresses and waterproof bags are normally supplied, but you need to bring your own sleeping bag (rentable in Kathmandu or Pokhara). Some companies provide special waterproof boxes or barrels for cameras, but a better idea may be to buy a disposable waterproof camera (sold in Kathmandu).

Safety and the environment

By and large, rafting is a reasonably safe activity with a much better accident rate than, say, mountain-biking or skiing (or, for that matter, trekking). However, **safety** is a perennial worry because there are few government controls on Nepal's low-end operators. In recent years there have been a couple of fatalities of Western clients – the first in two decades, mind you – and it's probably no coincidence that these involved low-budget operators.

Make sure the company supplies lifejackets, helmets and a full first-aid kit, and satisfy yourself that the rafts are in good running order and that there will be a safety demonstration before entering the river. There must be a minimum of **two rafts**, in case one capsizes. In high-water conditions or on more difficult rivers, the rafts should be self-bailing and there should be **safety kayakers** to rescue "swimmers". (A few companies provide safety kayaks on all trips as a matter of course.) Most important of all, **guides** must be trained, certified, have experience guiding on the stretch of river in question, and speak adequate English (there should be an opportunity to meet guides before departure).

Some river trips may be unsafe due to **Maoist activity** (see p.413). Check official travel warnings (see p.21) before leaving your home country, and when you get to Kathmandu ask about the current safety of rafting rivers with local information sources such as the Nepal Tourism Board, the Kathmandu Environmental Education Project (see pp.95 & 96), or with rafting companies.

Rafters have the same responsibilities to **the environment** as trekkers, particularly regarding firewood, sanitation and litter – see the tips on p.430.

Kayaking and other river sports

Nepal has taken off as one of the world's leading destinations for recreational **kayaking**, and is now recognized as the best country for whitewater multi-day trips. The old myths of Nepal's rivers being only for macho expeditions have now largely been exploded, and the message has got out that they're easily accessible and suitable for all abilities, including beginners.

Most visiting kayakers start by booking on a rafting trip for a warm-up – often on the Sun Koshi or Kali Gandaki rivers. If you book on as a kayaker, the rafting company will normally provide you free use of a kayak as part of the deal, or give you a discount of around $10 a day if you have your own boat. If you're thinking of **bringing your own kayak**, talk to others who've visited Nepal recently and search for up-to-date advice through the internet, as some have ended up paying high excess-baggage charges on the way back. There's a wide selection of modern kayaks available for **rent** at around $15 a day in both Kathmandu and Pokhara – the latter has become quite a thriving centre for kayakers, with an excellent rental outlet (Ganesh Shop). It's worth bringing all your own kayaking gear with you, but this also is available for rent if necessary.

Kayak schools are a recent development in Nepal, as travellers – often people who've got a taste for it through a rafting trip – have begun to realize that this is a perfect place to learn to kayak. Most clinics operating out of Pokhara start with a half-day introduction on Phewa Tal and then proceed to the nearby Seti River for another four-days' practice and paddling with rafting support. The Seti is warmed by geothermal springs, making it a very pleasant place to practice rolling. Other kayak schools operate out of the riverside resorts on the Bhote Koshi and upper Sun Khoshi rivers, not far from Kathmandu. Typical price for a five-day course is around $300, which includes tuition, gear, food, transport, raft support and camping – that's great value.

Yet another conveyance for enjoying Nepal's whitewater is the **hydrospeed**, a sort of boogie board for swimming down rivers. Pokhara's Ganesh Shop rents out hydrospeeds with wetsuits and helmets for $15 a day. It also rents out inflatable canoes (known as **"duckies"**) and **catarafts** for those planning a do-it-yourself trip.

The rivers

Your choice of **where to raft** will be largely dictated by what the rafting companies are running when you're in Nepal. But within that context, consider what you're after in a river trip – thrills, scenery, culture, relaxation – as well as how much time and money you're willing to invest.

Note that the building of new roads and dams is putting the status of Nepal's rafting rivers in a state of flux. A number of proposed or planned hydroelectric dams and diversions – an important part of the country's development strategy – may eventually shorten or eliminate some popular rafting trips, and put more pressure on the remaining ones. But on the other hand, roads – which are supposedly being extended to every district headquarters as part of another strategic policy, and are sometimes also built to access new dams – can open up previously unrunnable river sections by creating new put-in and take-out points.

The descriptions that follow are given roughly in order of most to least popular/accessible.

The Trisuli

Perhaps seventy percent of all raft trips are done on the **Trisuli**, west of Kathmandu, and this is an obvious choice if your time is limited and you're looking for a short introduction to rafting at the cheapest possible price. Most itineraries are two or three days. The Trisuli has some rapids of medium difficulty (Class 3+) and good scenery, though it's hardly wilderness – the main road to Kathmandu follows it the entire way, and campsites can be noisy. In October and November you'll have to share the river with many other parties and perhaps compete for beaches. Some operators have their own fixed campsites or lodges which can work really well, ranging from private, green, semi-luxurious safari-style resorts to windblown village beaches complete with begging kids and scavenging dogs. Check out the camps and lodges carefully, especially with regard to how close a camp is to the noisy highway.

When booking, ask where the put-in point is: anything starting at Kuringhat or Mugling will mainly be a relaxing float. The best whitewater section is upstream of Mugling, from Charaundi to Kuringhat, and this can be done as a full-on half-day trip (perhaps as a break in the journey from Kathmandu to Pokhara).

The Trisuli lies en route between Pokhara, Kathmandu and Chitwan National Park, so it makes sense to incorporate your raft trip into your travel schedule to cut down on time in buses. Your rafting company will normally be able to help you plan the logistics and look after your luggage. However, raft-

RAFTING RIVERS OF NEPAL

N

TIBET

Karnali

Kali Gandaki

Marsyangdi

Pokhara

Trisuli

Bhote Koshi

Arun

Tamur

Bheri

Seti

KATHMANDU

Nepalganj

Narayani

Narayanghat

Sun Koshi

Biratnagar

Sapt Koshi

0   150 km

INDIA

Below is a summary of the international classification system of rafting river difficulty.

Class 1 Easy. Moving water with occasional small rapids. Few or no obstacles.

Class 2 Moderate. Small rapids with regular waves. Some manoeuvring required but easy to navigate.

Class 3 Difficult. Rapids with irregular waves and hazards that need avoiding. More difficult manoeuvring required but routes are normally obvious. Scouting from the shore is occasionally necessary.

Class 4 Very difficult. Large rapids that require careful manoeuvring. Dangerous hazards. Scouting from the shore is often necessary and rescue is usually difficult. Kayakers should be able to roll. Turbulent water and large irregular waves may flip rafts. In the event of a mishap, there is significant risk of loss, damage and/or injury.

Class 5 Extremely difficult. Long and very violent rapids with severe hazards. Continuous, powerful, confused water makes route-finding difficult, and scouting from the shore is essential. Precise manoeuvring is critical and for kayakers rolling ability needs to be 100 percent. Rescue is very difficult or impossible, and in the event of a mishap there is a significant hazard to life.

Class 6 Nearly impossible. Difficulties of Class 5 carried to the extreme of navigability. Might possibly (but not probably) be run by a team of experts at the right water level, in the right conditions, with all possible safety precautions, but still with considerable hazard to life.

ing all the way to Chitwan isn't allowed, so you'll have to travel from Narayanghat to the park by vehicle.

The upper Kali Gandaki

The **upper Kali Gandaki** is Nepal's second most popular rafting river and provides an exciting three- or four-day itinerary out of Pokhara. Serious whitewater (Class 4) starts soon after the put-in point near Baglung and continues for the whole trip to the take-out at the new dam at the confluence with the Andi Khola. This section of water is away from roads and civilization, and offers excellent upriver views of the Annapurnas and Dhaulagiri. However, it's a popular stretch of river, and camping beaches are limited in number, well used, and may be squalid. There have been quite a few accidents on this river, so choose your operator carefully.

The Kali Gandaki is probably at its best for rafting at low and medium flows: mid-October to mid-December and March to April. It's a good idea to think about adding this raft trip onto the end of a trek in the Annapurna region. Consider flying to Jomosom, trekking down the Kali Gandaki to Baglung, and then continuing down the river on a rafting trip – a journey from the highest mountains on earth to the jungle lowlands.

The Seti

Another river easily reached from Pokhara, the **Seti** offers a gentler alternative to the upper Kali Gandaki. It's a fairly tame (Class 3-) but very picturesque river, taking two or three days to float from Damauli to near Narayanghat. This is a better choice than a similar trip starting on the Trisuli, as it takes you away from the road and has a fine green jungle corridor and beautiful white-sand beaches for camping. It's a popular choice for birdwatching groups, who often schedule it into their itinerary from Pokhara to Chitwan. The water tempera-

Nepal's rivers at a glance

River	Class	Volume	Total days	River days	Scenery/wildlife rating	Overall rating	Elevation (start/finish)
Trisuli	2/3+	Big	1–4	1–4	★	★★	330m/170m
Upper Kali Gandaki	4-	Med	4	3	★★	★★	750m/500m
Marsyangdi	4+	Med	6	4	★★★	★★	850m/370m
Sun Koshi	4-	Huge	10	8	★★	★★★	625m/105m
Upper Sun Koshi	3	Med	2	1	★	★★	730m/650m
Bhote Koshi	4+	Med	2	1–2	★★	★★★	1020m/760m
Seti	3-	Small	3	2	★★	★★	345m/190m
Lower Kali Gandaki	2	Med	5	4	★★	★★	370m/170m
Karnali	4	Huge	10	8	★★★	★★★	560m/195m
Tamur	4	Med	11	6	★★	★★★	635m/105m
Bheri	3+	Med	8–10	6–8	★★★	★★	770m/195m
Arun	4-	Big	4	3	★★	★	290m/115m

Relative volumes are given because the actual flows vary so enormously according to season.

Total days = days from Kathmandu or Pokhara and back.

The overall rating is a somewhat subjective score of the river as a rafting trip, taking into account whitewater, scenery, logistics and cost:

★★★ = highly recommended

★★ = recommended

★ = specialist interest

△ Rafting the Trisuli River

ture is incredibly warm, making it a popular choice for winter trips and for kayak clinics.

The Bhote Koshi

The **Bhote Koshi**, which runs alongside the Arniko Highway to the Tibetan border northeast of Kathmandu, is probably the steepest and hardest commercial rafting river in Nepal. In low water it's like a pinball machine (and you're the ball); in medium flows it's more like being flushed down the U-bend of a toilet. A few companies specialize in this deviant experience, offering it as a one- or two-day trip out of Kathmandu (it's only a three-hour drive) using road support and empty rafts. If you have previous rafting experience or are just looking for an adrenaline rush, then this is the one for you. It's a cold river, so you'll want to run it in the window between high water and winter – November, March and April are normally the best months. The Bhote Koshi is best booked as a two-day trip, staying the night at one of the comfortable riverside resort camps (see box on opposite).

The Marsyangdi

Recently opened to commercial rafting, the **Marsyangdi** is a magnificent blue whitewater river with a spectacular mountain backdrop. Kayakers rave about it. It's a full-on, continuously technical river, like a large nonstop slalom, needing self-bailing rafts and shore support. Companies normally run it as a four-day

The Bhote Koshi resorts

In the last few years, several companies have bought land on the banks of the Bhote Koshi and upper Sun Koshi and built fixed safari-style **riverside camps**, with luxuriant gardens, flush toilets, showers, hammocks, restaurants and bar areas. Only two- to three-hours' drive from Kathmandu, these mini-resorts make great activity destinations if you want to escape from the fleshpots of Kathmandu for a night or two. Each has its own mix of activities: all offer rafting, but there is also canyoning, kayaking, trekking, rock-climbing, bungy-jumping, and mountain-biking. They also regularly host adventure events such as mountain-bike races and the Nepal International Kayak Rodeo (held annually in Nov). If you just want to stay and hang out at the camp, then typical daily rates are around $25 for food, accommodation and transport to and from Kathmandu. Many overseas rafting and kayak groups now go straight from the Kathmandu airport to one of these riverside camps, rather than spending a night in a Kathmandu hotel. Note that all these places are covered in more detail in Chapter Three, p.257.

Sukute Beach Adventure Resort (owned by Equator Expeditions) is closest to Kathmandu, at the end of the whitewater section of the upper Sun Koshi – this is a great sunny location for a kayak school, and is also used as a start point for eight-day Sun Koshi trips. **Bhote Koshi Riverside** (owned by Ultimate Rivers) is at the end of the Bhote Koshi run in a sunny location with a superb garden and bar area. **Borderland Resort** (associated with Ultimate Descents), the first camp to be built, has a well-developed garden and is conveniently located at the start of the Bhote Koshi run. Closest to the Tibetan border, **The Last Resort** (associated with Ultimate Rivers) is perhaps most famous as the site of Ultimate Bungy, reputed to be the world's longest commercial bungy jump.

trip from near Khudi (along the Annapurna Circuit trek) down to the Kathmandu–Pokhara highway, and many combine this with a scenic three-day trek from Begnas Tal (near Pokhara) to Khudi. The river is particularly beautiful in November, when levels are reasonably low and the mountain views are usually clear. Work has started on a new dam at Phaliya Sanghu, which will ruin the Marsyangdi for rafting and kayaking – so run it while you can.

The Sun Koshi

Widely acknowledged as one of the ten best rafting trips in the world, the **Sun Koshi** is the most popular of several longer floats in Nepal, and logistics are fairly easy, making it one of the cheapest in terms of cost per day. It's an eight-day run beginning at Dolalghat, three hours east of Kathmandu, and ending at Chatara, near Dharan in the eastern Tarai. If you're planning to go on from Nepal to Darjeeling, this raft trip cuts out most of the twenty-hour bus ride to the eastern border.

Relatively few companies do scheduled trips on the Sun Koshi, so you're less likely to see other parties, and the camping on beautiful white-sand beaches is great. The river traverses a remote part of the country, flowing through a varied landscape of jungle-clad canyons, arid, open valleys and sparse settlements. Unlike most rivers, which start out rough and get tamer as they descend, this one starts gently, affording a chance to build up experience and confidence prior to a steady diet of increasingly exciting whitewater (Class 3–4). This makes it an especially good choice for those doing their first river trip. It's at its best for rafting at medium to high flows – from mid-September to late October and in May and early June. Note that a new main highway is being built alongside the top 40km of the Sun Koshi; once complete (and no one knows when this will be), it'll allow shorter six-day trips on the river and will also probably halve the return time from the take-out.

Upper Sun Koshi (Lower Bhote Koshi)

Only two-hours' drive from Kathmandu, the **upper Sun Koshi** (the section above Dolalghat, often mistakenly called the lower Bhote Koshi) makes an easier alternative to the Bhote Koshi, especially at higher water levels. There are two different sections: the top one is a fun Class 3 whitewater run, the lower a mellow, scenic, flat-water float. The river is clean and blue with green valley sides, and the nearby highway is relatively quiet, so this stretch of river is an ideal choice for a half-day rafting trip close to Kathmandu, and makes a welcome escape from the city if you stay overnight at one of the resort camps on the riverside. This is a another popular river for kayak schools.

The Karnali

Nepal's biggest and longest river, the **Karnali** provides perhaps the finest trip of its kind in the world. Way out in the remote far west, it requires a long bus ride to Birendra Nagar (many groups fly to Nepalganj) and then about three-hours' rough bus ride to the river. Most rafting trips last eight days, with challenging, big-water rapids, superb canyons, pristine wilderness and plentiful wildlife. The biggest rapids (Class 4) come in the first couple of days, with the river gradually mellowing after that. You can raft the Karnali right into Bardia National Park, where wild elephants, tigers, crocodiles and rhinos may sometimes be seen from the river. Pulling into a luxury safari camp and being met with a tray of cold beers makes a magnificent climax to this long river trip; many parties take the opportunity to spend a few extra days watching wildlife in Bardia.

The Karnali is best run at low to medium levels – it's a particularly good choice in March and April, though the nature of the channel makes it lively at all times outside of high water. There are plentiful driftwood supplies for campfires, so this makes it a popular choice for overseas kayak groups around Christmas. It's also renowned as Nepal's premier fishing river, with giant *mahseer* (a freshwater perch) and catfish.

The Tamur

Only recently opened to rafting, the **Tamur** offers six days of fabulous and challenging whitewater in a remote and scenic valley in eastern Nepal, coupled with a highly scenic trek. The river is at its best in medium flows – it would be a nightmare at high levels – with the optimum time (after a normal monsoon) being the end of October to early November. Note that the final day of the trip from Mulghat (where a highway crosses the river) can be added as an exciting extra day to a Sun Koshi trip.

The logistics of getting to the put-in point are a bit involved, starting with a twenty-hour bus ride to Basantapur. However, the four-day walk in from there, along a high ridge with wide panoramas of Kanchenjunga and the Everest peaks, is often described as one of the most beautiful treks in Nepal. It is possible to fly from Kathmandu to Taplejung ($137, with a stopover in Biratnagar), only a couple of hours' hike from the put-in point at Dobhan, but flights may be delayed by weather, so it's more reliable to fly to Biratnagar and then take a taxi or bus from there to the Basantapur trailhead.

The Bheri

The **Bheri** offers a shorter and easier alternative to the Karnali, of which it's a tributary. It's one of the most scenic rivers in Nepal, with golden cliffs, green jungle, crystal-clear green water, white-sand beaches, excellent fishing and good birdwatching, all coupled with a powerful current and sparkling rapids of moderate difficulty. Access is from the Nepalganj–Birendra Nagar road, a total of about fifteen hours of bus travel from Kathmandu (via Nepalganj). Few companies raft the Bheri at the moment, but improved roads mean that it is likely to become deservedly more popular in the future.

The lower Kali Gandaki

The **lower** section of the **Kali Gandaki**, starting from Ramdi Ghat on the Siddhartha Highway, offers a longer alternative to the Seti. It's a medium-volume and relatively easy river, with the same beautiful scenery as the Seti, and it flows through a completely unspoilt and untouristy valley of pretty villages, small gorges and jungle-backed beaches. Although the river is easily accessible, it takes longer to get to than the Seti, making it less crowded – ideal as the perfect river for a relaxed, romantic, away-from-it-all break with your partner. Like the Seti, this is probably a good choice for a do-it-yourself "duckie" trip.

The Arun

A powerful and famous river that dominates eastern Nepal, the **Arun** offers a shorter and easier alternative to the Sun Koshi, with big rapids of moderate difficulty and a fine jungle corridor. A few companies offer trips on this little-travelled river, but the necessity of flying in to Tumlingtar ($57), near the put-in point, makes it relatively expensive for such a short trip.

This chapter was updated by Peter Knowles, author of *White Water Nepal*

8

RAFTING AND KAYAKING | The rivers

Mountain-biking

CHAPTER 9

Highlights

* **Shivapuri National Park** Seldom-travelled unpaved roads threading through a forest preserve. See p.479

* **Nagarkot** Hill station with Himalayan views and virtually unlimited downhill possibilities. See p.480

* **The Arniko Highway** The road to the Tibet border, with cool stopovers and the option of rafting. See p.482

* **The Tribhuwan Rajpath** A classic monster climb and descent, now with a delightful new return route. See p.482

* **Begnas Tal** The gateway to miles of pastoral backroads east of Pokhara. See p.484

9

Mountain-biking

t's long been conventional wisdom that the best way to get around Nepal, with its huge trail network and terrible roads, is to walk. Nowadays, thanks to the increasing availability of rental mountain bikes, route information and organized tours, you'll do just as well to ride. **Mountain-biking** provides a more intimate experience of the land and its people than you'll get through the smudged windscreen of a speeding jeep or bus and, like trekking, it enables you to get to places vehicles can't – but at a much faster and more exciting pace.

A few hardy people come to Nepal specifically to tour the country – or the subcontinent – by bike. Others join organized tours in which cycling is the main event, or is an important mode of travel that links other activities such as trekking, rafting and wildlife-watching. But most who mountain-bike in Nepal do so only casually, pedalling around temples and villages on their own, or perhaps taking a more challenging guided off-road ride. It should be stressed, however, that biking in Nepal almost always means *mountain*-biking: a road bike is not recommended, even for the lowlands, because of the generally rough or at best unpredictable surfaces of the roads.

The sense of what's possible on a mountain bike in Nepal is expanding all the time. Much of the country has yet to be explored on wheels, and tour operators and bike-shop gurus are continually pioneering new off-road rides. Meanwhile, **road construction** is creating new routes and giving access to many others, making loops possible and producing an exponential increase in the biking possibilities. On the downside, however, new and upgraded roads bring more traffic, which is becoming a serious problem in certain parts of the country, particularly Kathmandu. The rapid pace of change also makes it hard for any guidebook to keep up: what's fun now might be unpleasant by the time you get there, but by the same token what's unrideable now might be fantastic. The best advice is to seek the latest information locally.

Despite Nepal's Himalayan mystique, it's not all steep: the Kathmandu Valley's slopes are generally easy, and the Tarai is just plain flat. There are rides to suit all **abilities**. The longer and more scenic routes do tend to require a high level of fitness, and there are monster ascents (and descents) for those who relish that sort of thing, but there are also plenty of relaxed village-to-village rambles and gentle downhill rides.

No special **paperwork** is required unless you plan to cycle in one of the remote restricted trekking areas, in which case you'll need a special permit, obtainable only through a trekking agency (see Chapter Seven). Biking is not permitted in most national parks and conservation areas.

Nepal's **Maoist** insurgents aren't currently active along the biking routes described in this chapter. Still, you should be aware of the potential risk, especially if you're thinking of venturing into off-the-beaten-track areas – see the warning for trekkers on p.413.

Seasonal considerations

While mountain-biking is a year-round activity in Nepal, some **seasons** are better than others. When you travel will influence where you ride.

If you have a choice, go for **October to December**, when there's little chance of rain and the visibility is as good as it gets. During this period temperatures get gradually cooler and the comfort zone shifts down in elevation. Not that it ever gets very cold at biking elevations – in fact, even in December and January the days are pleasantly cool anywhere up to about 3000m, though snow may occasionally be encountered as low as 2000m. December and January also happen to be the most comfortable months for cycling in Pokhara and the Tarai, which are hot at other times of year. The shortening days are also a factor, though, and by December you'll need to be off the roads or trails by 4.30pm or so.

From **January to March** the story is the same in reverse, with the days lengthening and growing warmer. This too is a good time for biking, as fewer tourists are around and hotels are fairly quiet, though the visibility isn't as good as in the autumn. In April, May and the first part of June, the weather just keeps getting hotter (too hot to cycle anywhere but the highest roads and trails), the air gets hazier, and afternoon showers become more common. On the plus side, you can take advantage of long daylight hours.

The monsoon (**mid-June to late Sept**) is generally not the best season for cycling, since the air is hot and damp, the mountains are usually hidden by clouds, and the trails are muddy. However, this is prime riding time in Tibet and Ladakh, which are shielded from the rains by the Himalaya.

Another seasonal consideration is the **Himalayan Mountain Bike Race Series**, usually held in November. Organized by Himalayan Mountain Bikes, one of the better-known tour operators, this three-race event runs over three consecutive weekends, with tours offered between races. The courses span a range of terrain in the Kathmandu Valley, and attract a respectable showing of international-calibre riders.

Information and maps

The bike shops in Kathmandu and Pokhara are your best sources of up-to-date **information** on trails, roads, equipment and servicing. Go easy on the questions, though, because they're in business mainly to sell tours, and won't want to divulge all their secret routes.

To date, no one has written a **guidebook** to mountain-biking in Nepal, although James Giambrione's *Kathmandu Valley Bikes & Hikes* (see "Books" in Contexts) gives excellent coverage of its more limited area. This makes it all the more important to go armed with a good **map**. The Mapple/Karto Atelier series, though not produced specifically with bikers in mind, are very accurate and cover the most popular areas. Another series produced jointly by His Majesty's Government and FINNIDA, the Finnish aid agency, covers the entire country in a detailed scale (1:25,000) and is dead accurate, but these maps are hard to find – try Maps of Nepal in Naya Baneswar, Kathmandu. Other trekking maps may prove useful for certain rides. HMG's 1:500,000 country map, which comes in three sheets, is the best road map for long-distance touring, though it's now somewhat dated. Even the most accurate maps soon go out of date in fast-changing Nepal.

Organized versus independent biking

Like trekking, mountain-biking can be done **independently** or as part of an **organized tour**. With mountain-biking, the specialized equipment involved and the difficulty of route-finding make additional cases for joining a tour, but ultimately it mainly comes down to how you prefer to travel and what you can afford.

Organized tours

There are two good reasons for joining an **organized bike tour**, the first being ease of logistics. Everything is arranged for you, saving lots of pre-departure time and headaches, and maximizing the chances that all will go more or less according to plan. The itinerary will be well planned, avoiding the dead ends and unwanted overnight stops that often come with a self-organized trip. Good bikes and all the necessary gear will be provided, and guides will take care of bike maintenance and on-the-spot repairs as well as ensuring that the bikes are safe at night. On longer tours, a "sag wagon" will tote heavy gear, provide emergency backup, and whisk you past the busier or less interesting stretches of road to ensure that you spend as much time as possible hitting the highlights. Basically, the operator does everything but pedal the bike for you – and if you don't want to pedal very much, they'll even drive you to the top of a hill and let you cycle down.

Second, if you're into single-track riding, your guide will show you trails you'd never find on your own. And, like trekking guides, biking guides can interpret the culture and answer any questions.

Of course, joining a tour is quite a bit more expensive than doing it yourself. A one-day trip will typically cost $20–25, while longer excursions work out to $45 or more per day because of the extra expenses of vehicle support and accommodation (the standard of the latter has a big effect on price). The lists on pp.13 and 16 includes some overseas companies that offer mountain-bike tours. However, almost all tours booked through these companies are organized by a few **operators** in Kathmandu (see p.169), and you can save money by booking directly with them. These companies usually require a minimum of four people for vehicle-supported tours, but can organize shorter customized trips for just two people. Contact operators in advance to see if they've got any trips already scheduled for the time you're planning to be in Nepal.

Cycling independently

Cycling independently, you can do just about everything a tour group can do, and more cheaply and flexibly, but it takes a certain pioneering spirit and a greater tolerance for discomfort. It's up to you to rent or bring your own equipment and to arrange food and (on overnight trips) accommodation; if starting from Kathmandu, you'll need to organize transport out of the city or else put up with some ugly traffic in the early stages. You'll probably make some mistakes when creating your own itinerary and finding your own way, which might mean spending more time than you'd intended on certain stretches, getting lost, or making a wrong turn and having to backtrack (or carry, if you're riding trails), On the plus side, you'll have more direct contact with local people than you would with a group, especially if you make an unplanned detour.

Day-trips in the Kathmandu and Pokhara valleys are the easiest ones to do on your own, since you can rent bikes in both cities. Though you probably won't find the obscure trails that a tour company would take you on, you'll no doubt stumble upon others and have adventures of your own making. Bear in mind, however, that if you're riding long-distance without vehicle support, you'll have to tote your own gear and will probably find yourself spending many nights in very primitive lodges where little English is spoken and foreigners are considered the evening's entertainment. This will be par for the course if you're on a long tour of the subcontinent, though, and in fact you'll probably find the going much easier in Nepal than in India: the roads, for the most part, are less busy, and there's less staring, hassling and risk of theft.

Equipment

The main dilemma facing the independent cyclist is what, if any, **equipment** to bring to Nepal. Since good (and not-so-good) bikes can be rented here, you'll probably be better off not bringing a bike from home unless you plan to do a lot of riding. However, certain clothing and accessories are worth taking with you, especially if you think you'll make use of them while doing other activities such as trekking or rafting.

Renting or buying a bike in Nepal

Rental bikes fall into two categories in Nepal. Those of the first type – cheap **Indian-made bikes**, available from streetside vendors for Rs150–200 per day – really only qualify under the loosest definition of the term "mountain bike". Superficially, they look the part – some even have full suspension – but they're heavy and uncomfortable to ride, their components are incredibly flimsy, little attention is paid to maintenance, and they rarely come with a helmet. You wouldn't want to take one of these bikes on trails or rough roads, where a malfunction could spell disaster. They're mainly intended for around-town use, though you could probably chance taking one on easy there-and-back day-rides and perhaps on a modest overnight loop on paved or graded unpaved roads. The rule of thumb is not to ride an Indian-made bike further than you're prepared to walk back with it.

For any sort of hard or long-distance riding you'll need a **real mountain bike**, which can be rented from only a few specialist bike shops/tour operators in Kathmandu and Pokhara. These bikes are good but not top of the line – they're usually fairly new or at least reasonably well maintained, and feature decent components (though not necessarily shocks). A helmet and basic tool kit should come with the bike. The daily rate will be Rs500–1000, depending on quality and features; you'll be expected to leave a passport or something of value as security. You may also be expected to pay for damage or above-normal wear-and-tear if you've been careless. Be sure to reserve these bikes as far ahead as possible, especially during busy times, because the choice is limited.

Whichever kind of bike you rent, it's your responsibility to make sure all is to your liking before setting off. **Check** brakes and brake pads, test spoke tension (they should all be taut), ensure that tyres have sufficient tread and are properly inflated (check inflation while sitting on the bike), test the chain for tautness, and work the bike through its gears to see that the derailleurs function smoothly. And make sure the bike has a bell – you'll be using it a lot.

Since mountain bikes are currently only rentable in Kathmandu and Pokhara, and you'll have to return the bike to where you rented it, you'll probably end up just doing excursions from those places. However, there are a number of other fine mountain-biking bases around the country, so you might consider lugging a rental bike along by bus.

You may be able to **buy** a decent used bike from a departing traveller, especially toward the end of the autumn or spring seasons – check notice boards in Kathmandu or Pokhara. The only new bikes for sale in Nepal are the cheesy Indian-made ones, which cost Rs6000 and up with gears.

Bringing a bike from home

Bringing a bike from home avoids the vagaries of renting and, depending on how much time you plan to spend in the saddle, can save a significant amount of money. You may also feel safer or more comfortable on your own bike, especially if it has full suspension or other features you cherish. For any long-distance tour, especially one that involves India as well as Nepal, you'll obviously want to bring your own bike. However, don't bring a bike unless you have the time, energy and commitment to use it a lot – if not, it will just be a millstone that you have to lug everywhere and keep safe.

Airlines (both international and domestic) will accept a bicycle as baggage at no extra charge, so long as it doesn't put you over the weight or checked-item limit. No special container is needed, but you'll be expected to deflate the tyres and swivel the handlebars to be parallel with the frame. Nepalese customs will want verbal assurance that the bike will be returning with you when you leave the country, but this shouldn't be a problem and should not cost money. Domestic airlines' willingness to accept bikes as baggage is always dependent upon available luggage space, so check in early.

Clothes and other equipment

Other than a helmet and water bottle, no special gear is necessary for simple day-trips. But if you're planning a long-distance ride, especially an independent one, you'll need to give a lot of thought to what to bring.

Cycling **clothing**, shoes and gloves aren't easily obtainable in Nepal, nor is good waterproof/windproof outerwear. Note that tight-fitting Lycra clothing, while functional, is embarrassing and potentially offensive to many Nepalis, especially when worn by women. To avoid causing offence, wear a pair of comfortable shorts and a T-shirt over your body-hugging bike gear. As for warm clothes, you'll probably only need one layer, maybe two in winter at higher elevations, which can be purchased in Nepal.

A **helmet** and water bottle will come with a better rental bike. If renting a cheaper one, you may be able to buy a helmet in one of the Kathmandu department stores, and you can always make do with a mineral water bottle. Be sure to have iodine for water purification – for more specifics on this, see p.27. If you're attached to your saddle/seat or pedals, bring them along and have them fitted to your rental bike. **Panniers** and racks can be rented from the better bike shops, and camping equipment (sleeping bags, mats, tents) from trekking shops. Locally made daypacks and waist-packs are sold all over tourist areas, and you can pick up bungy cords in motorcycle accessory shops. If you

Equipment checklist

You won't need everything on this list. Items marked by (*) can be purchased in Nepal, and those marked by (**) can also be rented.

Lightweight breathable waterproof shell (eg Gore-Tex)	Energy bars and electrolyte powder
Windbreaker*	Sunscreen*
Cycling top and shorts	Sunglasses*
Modest T-shirt and shorts	Torch/flashlight*
Fleece top*	Daypack or waist-pack*
Warm hat and gloves*	Panniers**
Cycling gloves	Security cable/lock
Helmet**	Shock cords (bungy cords)*
Pollution mask*	Puncture repair kit and spare inner tube
Stiff-soled shoes suitable for biking	Pump
Water bottles* or backpack water holder (eg Camelbak)	Tool set
	Bike bell*
Iodine (tablets, crystals or solution)*	Spare parts
First-aid kit* (see p.427)	Bike lube
	Whistle for emergencies

do much riding in Kathmandu you'll do well to wear a face mask to protect against the dust and pollution – good (expensive) ones are sold in department stores, and pharmacies sell cheaper surgical masks.

A bike – especially a fancy one brought from home – can go missing at the blink of an eye, so a good **lock** and cable are essential. Only cheap ones are sold in Nepal. Lock the bike to something permanent, and bring it inside at night, or you could find yourself lonely and walking. Puncture-repair places are everywhere on the roads, but it's still advisable to come with your own **patch kit**, inner tube(s), pump and basic tool kit, especially if riding off-road. If you bring your own bike you'll of course want to bring more tools, spare parts and lube.

Repairs and service

At least two of the Kathmandu tour operators (Himalayan Mountain Bikes and Dawn Till Dusk) have **workshops** with trained bike mechanics, a full range of tools and even a stock of spare parts. These are good places to go for servicing if you've been cycling around the subcontinent for weeks or months.

Local bike **repair shops**, found in every town and crossroads, are equipped mainly to fix Indian-made models, but they can patch any sort of flat (puncture) and are often remarkably adept at figuring out mountain bikes and performing improvised repairs and mini-tuneups. Just be sure to ask the price first: a puncture repair should cost Rs10–20.

Riding conditions

A number of different mountain-biking experiences are possible in Nepal, ranging from one-day trail rides to months-long tours of the subcontinent. The country itself is incredibly varied: a ride in the hills is naturally going to be more strenuous and challenging than a ride through the flat Tarai or one confined to the undulating floor of the Kathmandu Valley. It's hard to generalize, but this section describes the various riding conditions you're likely to encounter.

Highways

You can count Nepal's long-distance **highways** on one hand. That's not good news for cyclists, because it means that all heavy-vehicle traffic converges on those few lanes and makes them more congested and polluted than one might expect. The situation on Kathmandu's city streets is downright awful (see p.94). Add the disrespect or just lack of consideration afforded to cyclists by drivers and you'd be best advised to avoid busy roads altogether. Fortunately, though, the unpleasant stretches are limited mainly to central Nepal (principally on the Kathmandu–Pokhara and Mugling–Birganj routes). Although highway cycling always entails a certain amount of dust and exhaust fumes, the traffic diminishes noticeably as you get further from Kathmandu; the eastern and particularly the far-western portions of the Mahendra Highway are delightfully rural.

Bear in mind that you don't have to pedal all the way from A to B. If you want to skip a busy section or a steep climb, or avoid backtracking, take a **bus** or a **taxi**. The latter come in especially handy in the Kathmandu Valley, where all it takes is a comparatively short lift to get past the urban blight and out into fine cycling country. And in a mountainous country like Nepal, there's a lot to be said for getting a lift to a high point and then riding down. It's usually no problem to load your bike on the roof of a bus for an extra charge of Rs40–80, depending on the distance and your negotiating skills. Lay the bike down flat and tie it down securely (bungy cords are useful for this), and make sure that other luggage isn't loaded on top of it.

Lesser roads and trails

Nepal has a surprising number of paved and unpaved secondary **roads**, most of which see very little traffic. Many other primitive, half-completed or half-washed-out roads can also be found – a good map will help you locate them. If you're adventurous, the possibilities for exploring off the beaten track, especially just beyond the rim of the Kathmandu Valley and in the Tarai, are almost unlimited.

Off-road riding in Nepal is probably not like what you're used to back home. Although there are zillions of **trails**, most aren't suitable for mountain-biking because they're too steep, stepped and heavily used by humans and animals. A few bikers have "ridden" trekking trails to Everest Base Camp and elsewhere, but have ended up carrying their bikes between fifty and eighty percent of the way (for most people, carrying even twenty percent of the way would be too tedious). The mountainous national parks and conservation areas are now officially out of bounds for cycling anyway.

There are some excellent single-track rides, but it takes a lot of exploring to find them (a good reason to go with a tour). If you do go off-road, give other people and livestock **priority** on the trail. Local people won't be expecting anything to come through at any pace faster than walking, so slow down around all signs of habitation, and signal your approach by ringing your bell or yelling "*Saikal aiyo!*" ("Cycle coming!"). It will often be necessary to dismount. Maintain a watchful eye for children, who like to grab hold of the back of bikes and run alongside, or throw stuff at your spokes. Be careful around buffalo and other livestock because it's easy to send them stampeding down a narrow trail, obliging their owners to chase after them. If you manage to kill an animal you'll be liable for its replacement value: a chicken, for example, will cost you Rs200–300, and a duck at least Rs500. Whatever happens, it'll be your fault.

Pedestrians and other hazards

Pedestrians in Nepal will frequently walk right into oncoming traffic without so much as looking left or right. There's an inherent attitude of "let others watch out for me": once the pedestrian sees an oncoming vehicle he or she has the responsibility to avoid it, so it's better not to look. This also helps explain the widespread use of horns and bells, the sounding of which sends the message, "I'm here, so don't say I didn't warn you". The result is a constant chain reaction of swerving cars, buses, tempos, motorcycles and bikes, all honking like crazy.

On a bicycle, you're near the bottom of the pecking order. Cars and buses will squeeze you off the road, motorbikes will approach you head-on, and taxis will suddenly veer around obstacles without any apparent regard for your presence. Add to this cud-chewing cows in the middle of major intersections, children blithely playing beside highways and bus drivers sharing their seats with two others. You'll quickly see there are no road rules, that police have little control, and if you hit someone you'll almost surely be asked to pay compensation, whether it was your fault or not. This is what you need to be ready for on the roads – but still, it's a lot better than taking the bus.

The single saving grace is the slow speed at which most vehicles travel in Nepal. However, fancy new cars and smooth new highway surfaces are tempting many to go faster.

Many of the same environmental do's and don'ts for trekking also apply when mountain-biking, especially if you're camping. See p.430.

Route-finding

Little English is spoken in the village areas that are best for riding, so asking directions will be a whole lot easier if you have a few basic phrases in Nepali. The most important piece of information to communicate is the name of the next destination or village on your route. Don't point when asking directions, as most people will say yes out of courtesy, even if they don't know – it's better to put your hands in your pockets and ask "Which way to?" Do this several times in a short distance to be sure you've got the right answer. Numerous trail intersections can make it difficult to provide accurate directions, and unfortunately one wrong turn may leave you carrying your bike for hours to reconnect with the right path.

Don't ask how far it is to a given destination – rather, ask how long it takes to get there. The answer will be the walking time in hours; you'll somehow have to convert that to riding time. Distances on the map bear little relation to actual difficulty, since a day's ride may entail an ascent and/or descent of 1000 or more vertical metres. The most realistic benchmark is "hours riding per day", and most people will find a six- to seven-hour day, including lunch break, to be sufficient. Plan to arrive at your destination three or four hours before dark, which provides for a balanced day and time for some sightseeing, repairs, washing and relaxing on arrival.

Routes

There are so many potential **cycling routes** in Nepal that it's hard to catalogue them systematically. The following itineraries are grouped as being out of either Kathmandu or Pokhara, since those are the only places where you can rent a decent mountain bike.

If you're planning a long-distance bike tour then you'll probably combine Nepal with India or Tibet – those routes are summarized in Basics, p.18.

Rides based in the Kathmandu Valley

Kathmandu is not the best place to be based if you're planning to do much biking around the valley. For rides toward the south, you'll make a cleaner escape from the traffic by staying in Patan. The highly rideable eastern valley and rim routes are best explored from bases like Bhaktapur, Nagarkot, Dhulikhel or Panauti. The following rides are described in the same order as the corresponding place descriptions in Chapters Two through Six. Refer to the map on p.186 unless otherwise indicated.

Shivapuri National Park

Shivapuri National Park, which protects Kathmandu Valley's northern rim, contains some superb mountain-biking possibilities; bear in mind, though, that the entry fee is expected to increase from Rs250 to Rs1000. The little-used road network begins right at the Budhanilkantha entrance, where two main routes present themselves. The dirt road to the left snakes generally westwards for at least 15km, at which point the hill resort of Kakani is only about 2km further east along the ridge by trail (some carrying is required). This ride is more enjoyable done from Kakani to Budhanilkantha. For a shorter loop starting and ending in Budhanilkantha, ride to the Tokha Hospital and then descend along a steep, sandy road.

The road to the right (east) of the main entrance contours and climbs out of the valley, passing the monastery of Nagi Gompa and reaching the watershed's easternmost point at Jhule after about 20km. From Jhule you can choose to leave the park and bike southwards to Nagarkot, or descend to the valley floor at Sankhu. Alternatively, you can stay on the park road for another 8km beyond Jhule, rounding the Shivapuri ridge and reaching Chisopani, a village on the main Helambu trekking trail, from where you can cycle to Nagarkot.

Nagarjun Ban variations

Little changed over the years, the forest preserve of **Nagarjun Ban** offers wilderness-style riding under a beautiful canopy of trees. Entering via the southern gate, you embark on a challenging eighteen-kilometre ascent on a jeep trail; the last 2km increases in gradient to reach a final elevation of 2096m. The return trip to the north gate is an additional 12km via a less established trail: it's best not to bike this solo.

A marvellous new section of trail now leads to Nagarjun's western entrance from Sitapaila, a village west of Swayambhu. Contouring high above the Mahesh Khola, this sometimes narrow single-track provides excellent riding for intermediate and above riders (not recommended for others). The road beyond Ichangu Narayan, a temple northwest of Swayambhu, links with this trail beyond the village of Baralgaun. Once in the forest preserve, keep to your left and you'll come out at the northern gate.

Another way to get to or from Nagarjun is via Tokha, a well-preserved village reached by trail from the Ring Road at Gongabu. From Tokha you can proceed in a north-northwest arc along excellent undulating dirt trails and through classic villages all the way to the southern gate of Nagarjun.

Dakshinkali and beyond
The sealed **Dakshinkali** road carries little traffic, and strings together a varied series of fascinating cultural sights (see p.214). The ride out is almost all uphill, though gradual, and of course the return offers the rewards of an excellent descent. You can explore further on dirt roads heading south from the Dakshinkali gate and west from Pharping. The latter is now a through-road that goes all the way to the Kulekhani Reservoir, with connections from there to the Tribhuwan Rajpath and the Tarai – see p.482.

The Lele Valley
The Bungamati, Chapagaun and Godavari roads provide the backbones for some easy loops through the southern valley; see p.215 for ideas. For something a bit harder and longer, head east from Chapagaun past the Bajra Barahi temple (this track eventually meets the paved Godavari road), then strike south on a smaller road that crosses a steep, forested ridge and enters the **Lele Valley**. From there, you can choose from a number of trails and small roads heading south into unspoiled and little-visited hill country. The road that fords the stream just south of Tika Bhairab passes the *Malla Alpine Resort* and ascends to an elevation of more than 2000m at Tinpani Bhanjyang before descending toward the Tarai; road conditions are variable and you may not be able to get all the way through.

The Lakuri Bhanjyang
The 30km road connecting Patan with Panauti is a superb intermediate-level ride that can be done in either direction. From Patan, ride out of town on the road past Sundhara and the Eastern Stupa. The first section to Lubhu, a brick-making and handloom centre 6km beyond the Ring Road, is busy and uninteresting, but the pavement ends a few kilometres later. Now a jeep track, the road climbs gradually at first and then commences a serious 500-metre switchback ascent through a woodcutters' area to the **Lakuri Bhanjyang**. On a clear day, the view of the valley and mountains from here is splendid. The second half of the ride is a sweet descent through the close, rural valley of the Bebar Khola and its scattered Tamang, Chhetri and finally Newar settlements to Panauti, where you can spend the night. From there you can link up with Dhulikhel-area rides (see p.482).

From the Lakuri Bhanjyang, additional trails venture off to the north via the *Adventure Tented Camp* and west down to Godavari and Bishanku Narayan.

Around Nagarkot
Bike up to **Nagarkot** and the options before you are almost unlimited. Rough roads and trails radiate in all directions – to Sankhu and Changu Narayan to the west, Nala and Banepa to the south, Hiuwapati and Panchkhal to the east, and Chisopani and the Helambu trails to the north. All these routes are described in more detail in the Nagarkot section starting on p.244. However, there are endless forks, many of which lead to dead-ends or really treacherous descents, so don't bike alone.

Unless you're a very strong rider, the ascent will probably be all you care to do in a day, and in any case you'll want to spend the night in Nagarkot for the views the next morning. As long as you're making it a multiday trip, you might

△Mountain-biking

consider continuing on to Dhulikhel, Namo Buddha and Panauti (if you go south); the Tibet border (going south or east); or Shivapuri (north).

Dhulikel, Namobuddha and Panauti

Dhulikel, which ideally should have been reached after several-days' biking around the eastern valley, is the traditional starting point of a very popular circuit to the Buddhist stupa of **Namobuddha** and (optionally) on to the Newar town of **Panauti**. (Actually, Panauti is perhaps the better starting point nowadays, given the increasing urbanization around Dhulikhel.) The so-called Namobuddha circuit, which offers several hours of biking and additional trails that can turn it into an all-day ride, is described in the Dhulikhel section on p.254; for a map of the area, see p.253.

The Arniko Highway and the Tibet border

Connecting Kathmandu with the **Tibet border** at Kodari, the **Arniko Highway** is an adventurous three- to five-day round-trip, depending on where you start from and where you overnight. The road gets much quieter and better for cycling after Dhulikhel – you can detour around the busy first section by cycling to Dhulikhel via Nagarkot, Nala or the Lakuri Bhanjyang and Panauti. From Dhulikhel, the Arniko Highway descends 600m and then ascends more than 800m to the border; for a map and a fuller description of the route, see p.255. Excellent overnight accommodation is available near the border at the *Borderland Resort* and the *Last Resort*, and at the *Sunkoshi Adventure Retreat* in Palanchowk, a village that's an interesting cultural side-trip and the gateway to further rides down to the Sun Koshi River and northwestwards back to the highway. You can break your ride at any of these places for a day or more of rafting or other outdoor activities (bungy jumping is the highlight at the *Last Resort*). Simpler lodging can be found in towns along the way.

If you want to cross the border on a bike, you'll have to join a tour, for the reasons explained on p.180.

The Trisuli Road

The **Trisuli Road** heads northwestwards out of the valley, skirting the hill station of Kakani before plunging nearly 1500m to Trisuli Bazaar and the subtropical valley of the Trisuli River. A description of the road and the towns along it starts on p.262.

Kakani is usually considered an overnight ride, since it has accommodation and mountain views that are best seen in the morning. From there you can connect to Shivapuri National Park: head east past the agricultural station, carry for a short distance to the park entrance (Rs250 fee, may soon rise to Rs1000), and then you'll be on a nice dirt track with some short rutted climbs; at a fork, the high trail leads to Nagi Gompa and Chisopani, while the lower one descends to Budhanilkantha and the road to Kathmandu.

Trisuli, a full day's ride from Kathmandu, also makes a good – if spartan and hot – base for two-wheeled exploits. Rural roads and tracks extend for miles in several directions: east to the historic forts of Nuwakot and beyond, south and then east up the Tadi Khola, west up the lovely Samari Khola towards Gorkha, and north up to Dhunche and Syabrubesi (trailheads for Langtang) and eventually to the mining operation at Somdang.

The Tribhuwan Rajpath

The spectacular and little-used **Tribhuwan Rajpath** racks up a total elevation gain of more than 1700m from Kathmandu to a cloudforested pass through the

Mahabharat Lek, before descending an even more dizzying 2300m to the Tarai. For a map and detailed route account, see p.265.

For a classic two-days-plus loop out of Kathmandu, make for **Daman**, a mountain viewpoint just below the pass. It's a very long day's ride up the Rajpath, taking between six and nine hours in the saddle, almost all of it climbing. Inexperienced bikers shouldn't attempt the ascent, but might consider hiring a vehicle to Daman and riding back down (bike tour companies can arrange this). Even if you're an expert you'll want to skip the first 26km, which is jammed with slow-moving trucks and slick with oil – take a taxi or bus to Naubise, where the Rajpath branches off from the main Kathmandu–Pokhara highway. After overnighting in Daman, you can return via Markhu and the Kulekhani Reservoir, following a delightful new road over to Pharping in the southern Kathmandu Valley. A much longer loop, with epic ups and downs, would be Daman–Sim Bhanjyang–Bhimphedi–Kulekhani–Pharping.

To the Tarai: Chitwan and Janakpur

From the Kathmandu Valley, the most pleasant way to get to **the Tarai** is along the Tribhuwan Rajpath, either via Naubise and Daman or Kulekhani and Bhimphedi (see above). That will bring you to Hetauda, two days from Kathmandu, where good accommodation is available.

From there, a right turn takes you westwards along the Mahendra Highway to **Chitwan National Park**, a half-day's ride. There are plenty of places to stay in Sauraha, the main tourist village outside the park, and a few off-the-beaten-track lodgings in other villages that a bike will enable you to get to. The entire area offers many flat village trails to explore by bike (for more on these, see p.332). You can return to Kathmandu, or move on to Pokhara, via Narayanghat, Mugling and the Prithvi (Kathmandu–Pokhara) Highway. The Prithvi Highway is very busy and not necessarily recommended for cycling, but is nonetheless a very beautiful road, especially between Mugling and Pokhara, and afternoon traffic in that section can be light. Interesting side-trips to Gorkha, Manakamana and Bandipur (all described in Chapter Four) are possible. Another option is just to put your bike on a bus.

Heading east out of Hetauda, the Mahendra Highway traverses the eastern Tarai to the border town of Kakarbhitta, a jumping-off point for Darjeeling. The highway is sometimes interestingly rural, sometimes rather urbanized, and always flat. You'll definitely want to spend a night or two in **Janakpur**, a holy city south of the highway and the hub of a network of lovely rural tracks.

Rides based in Pokhara

The "Pokhara Valley" section of Chapter Four (starting on p.306) gives more detail on roads and bikeable destinations in that area. Here are a few recommended itineraries.

Sarangkot and beyond

The hilltop viewpoint of **Sarangkot** makes a great focus for an intermediate-level day-trip or overnight. From the Bindyabasini temple in the bazaar, follow the road westwards for about 5km to where the pavement gives out; this is as far as most vehicles go, but on a bike you can keep going up the road, which doubles back and becomes steep and rough. It angles generally westwards for 3km until it reaches a junction: Sarangkot is another 3km along to the right, while the left-hand fork leads to Naudaada. Most people will find the 850-metre ascent to Sarangkot quite enough for one day, and will want to spend the night.

The preferred way down – but it could also be used as a longer, more gradual way up – is via Naudaada. The first 10km is an enjoyable track that contours along the south side of the ridge through forest, terraced farmland and villages, with an optional side-trip on foot up to the remains of historic Kaskikot. The track finally reaches the Naudaada on the Baglung Highway, at which point you can either return to Pokhara, an easy 32-kilometre coast, or continue deeper into the hills (the highway now reaches well beyond Beni, to a point some 70km beyond Naudaada).

Begnas and Rupa Tal

An unpaved road follows a ridge between two beautiful lakes, **Rupa Tal** and **Begnas Tal**, and then westwards nearly to Besisahar on the Annapurna Circuit trek. A network of trails is developing in this region that can offer one or several days' riding – inquire at Pokhara bike shops, and get hold of the most up-to-date map you can find. Good prospects include the trail north of Begnas Tal through Begnaskot and Kalikasthan (this is the Royal Trek), where a road leads back to Pokhara; and the unpaved road eastwards through Shyauli to Besisahar, the trailhead for the Annapurna Circuit, and thence back to Pokhara (with a side-trip to Bandipur). Accommodation is available at Begnas Tal.

The Seti River

Unpaved roads head downstream along the **Seti River**, with dramatic overlooks of the canyon and views of the mountains. The road on the south side of the canyon goes on for miles, and leads to some more-remote trails further to the southeast. The cycling is easy, though don't forget that you're going downhill and you'll eventually have to climb back up.

To the Tarai: Chitwan, Lumbini, Bardia and Sukla Phanta

The easiest route to **the Tarai** is along the Prithvi Highway to Mugling and then south from there to Narayanghadh, which is only a short hop from **Chitwan National Park** (see the previous page). It's mostly downhill and you can pedal it in a day, or take it slower and make side-trips to Bandipur, Gorkha and Manakamana. However, as noted above, this route gets heavy traffic, and cyclists are at the bottom of the pecking order.

A more adventurous and strenuous route follows the winding, scenic Siddhartha Highway southwards to Butwal. This ride requires some long stints in the saddle and several overnight stops: one will certainly be Tansen, an attractive hill town and an excellent base for day-rides, but you'll need to camp or be prepared to overnight in a house one night between Pokhara and Tansen. It's a fast downhill ride from Tansen to Butwal, and from there it's a flat and easy couple of hours to the Buddha's birthplace, **Lumbini**. Limited lodging is available in Butwal, Bhairawa and Lumbini.

If you're heading into India, you can make for the border at Sonauli, only a couple of hours south of Butwal. But again there's a more adventurous option: following the Mahendra Highway westwards through a beautiful *dun* valley and Nepal's undeveloped far west to the border crossing at Mahendra Nagar. En route you'll be able to lay over at **Bardia National Park** and/or **Sukla Phanta Wildlife Reserve**: both are less commercial alternatives to Chitwan, and give access to plenty of village cycling.

This chapter was revised and expanded for this edition with help from Peter Stewart, owner of Himalayan Mountain Bikes in Kathmandu and Pokhara.

contexts

contexts

The historical framework

For a tiny Himalayan backwater, Nepal has played a surprisingly pivotal role in Asian history. In its early days, the country reared the Buddha and hosted the great Indian emperor Ashoka; much later, its remarkable conquests led it into wars with Tibet and Britain, and during the past three decades it has come to be regarded as a vital buffer state by both India and China. Its name and recorded history go back nearly 3000 years, although it has existed as a nation for barely 200: before 1769, "Nepal" referred only to a kingdom based in the Kathmandu Valley.

Beginnings

Neolithic tools found in the Kathmandu Valley indicate that humans have inhabited parts of Nepal for tens of thousands of years – and the fact that the shrines of Swayambhu and Changu Narayan are located on hilltops suggests that ancient animists may have lived and worshipped there as much as 200,000 years ago, while the valley floor was submerged under a primordial lake. The Newar creation myth, which tells of the *bodhisattva* Manjushri releasing the waters and establishing Swayambhu, perhaps preserves a dim racial memory of that prehistoric era.

Nepal's early semi-mythological genealogies aren't borne out by any archeological evidence, but at some points they tally with other sources. The **Kirat** (or Kiranti) tribe pops up in several Hindu texts – and even in Ptolemy – although the term might well have applied to all hill people in the first millennium BC. Significantly, the Kirats were often described as a warlike people known for carrying deadly knives. By the sixth or seventh century BC, the Kirat name was used by two distinct groups, one controlling the eastern hills and the other the Kathmandu Valley: whether either or both of these groups descended from the original Kirats is disputed.

Hindus were by this time encroaching on the less malarial parts of the Tarai and founding the city-states of **Mithila** (modern Janakpur), the scene of many of the events in the *Ramayan* epic, and **Kapilvastu** (now Tilaurakot), where the Buddha spent his pre-enlightenment years during the sixth century BC. North India was unified under the **Mauryan empire** (321–184 BC), whose most famous ruler, Ashoka, was responsible for spreading Buddhism throughout the subcontinent, including parts of Nepal. Following the fall of Maurya, North India was again divided among a number of states and Hinduism began a slow but inexorable comeback in the Tarai.

Early dynasties

Nepal's history comes into sharper focus with the arrival of the **Lichhavis**, a clan claiming descent from a North Indian dynasty, who overthrew the Kirats in the second century AD and established their capital at Deopatan (modern Pashupatinath). Exploiting Nepal's position as a trading entrepôt between India and Tibet, the Lichhavis founded a strong, stable and culturally sophisticated dynasty. No buildings from the period survive, but contemporary accounts by Chinese travellers describe "multi-storeyed temples so tall one would take them for a crown of clouds" – perhaps a reference to the pagoda style that was to become a Nepali trademark. Under Lichhavi sponsorship, artisans ushered in a classical age of stone sculpture and produced Nepal's most acclaimed pieces, many of which still casually litter the Kathmandu Valley. Although Hindus, the Lichhavis endowed both Hindu and Buddhist temples – Pashupatinath and Swayambhu were built, or at least expanded, during their rule – and established a policy of religious tolerance that has been maintained to the present day.

Much of what we know about the Lichhavis comes from a handful of stone inscriptions whose authors were probably more intent on self-praise than historical accuracy. The earliest inscription, dated 464 AD and still on view at Changu Narayan, extols **Mandev** (often spelled Manadeva), the legendary builder of the Boudha stupa. The greatest of the Lichhavi line, **Amsuvarman** (605–621) is said to have composed the first Sanskrit grammar and built a splendid palace believed to have been located at present-day Naksal in Kathmandu. "Down to the reign of this monarch the gods showed themselves plainly in bodily shape," intone the Nepalese chronicles, "but after this they became invisible." By this time Nepal had become a vassal of Tibet, and Amsuvarman's daughter Bhrikuti, who was carried off by the Tibetan king, is popularly credited with introducing Buddhism to Tibet.

The Lichhavi era came to a close in 879, and the three centuries that followed are sometimes referred to as Nepal's **Dark Ages**. The "darkness" is entirely at our end: no coins and only a dozen stone inscriptions survive from the period, and no foreign accounts throw light on what was happening in the region. The Nepalese chronicles record a long list of **Thakuri kings**, the title being probably a Hindu honorific and not that of an hereditary dynasty; these kings may well have been puppets installed by one or more of the powers controlling the Tarai at the time. Nonetheless, learning and the arts continued to thrive, and from the eleventh century onwards the valley became an important centre of tantric studies (see "Religion", p.488).

The Khas and Mallas

While the Thakuris were ruling central Nepal, yet another Hindu clan, the **Khas**, were migrating up from the plains and carving out a small fiefdom in western Tibet. In the early twelfth century a Khas king, Nagaraja, moved his capital down to Sinja in the Karnali basin and established a powerful dynasty, which at its height controlled a broad sector of the Himalaya from Kashmir to present-day Pokhara. The history of the Khas is little understood, though, for they left few written records and only minor ruins at Sinja (now Hatsinja) and Dullu, south of Jumla. However, linguists believe Sinjali may have been one of the key languages out of which Nepali developed.

Nepal entered a new and much better documented period of its history when the Thakuri king of Bhaktapur, Arideva, took the title **Malla**, probably in the year 1200. Malla was, in fact, a popular form of royal address in India at the time – the Khas kings also called themselves Mallas – but the name has come to be associated with at least three separate dynasties, lasting more than five centuries, that presided over the renaissance of Nepali culture during which most of the temples and palaces still on display in the Kathmandu Valley were built.

The early Malla era was marked by great instability: the Khas mounted several raids on the valley, although they were never able to gain a ruling foothold, and in 1349 Muslims swept up from Bengal and pillaged both Hindu and Buddhist holy sites in a brief spree of destruction and violence. Despite these disruptions, trade flourished, many of the valley's smaller cities were founded, and Arniko, the great Nepali architect, was dispatched to the Ming court to instruct the Chinese in the art of building pagodas. **Jayasthiti Malla** (1354–95) inaugurated a period of strong central rule from Bhaktapur, but his most lasting contribution was to dragoon his Buddhist subjects into the Hindu hierarchy by dividing them into 64 occupational **castes** – a system which remained enshrined in Nepali law until 1964. Malla power reached its zenith under **Yaksha Malla** (1428–82), who extended his domain westwards to Gorkha and eastwards as far as present-day Biratnagar. Upon his death, the kingdom was divided among three sons, and for nearly three centuries the independent city states of Kathmandu, Patan and Bhaktapur (and occasionally others) feuded over lucrative trade arrangements with Tibet. Judging by the opulent palaces built during this period, there must have been enough to go around, and the intense rivalry seems to have been good for both art and business.

The Khas kings didn't fare so well, and by the late fourteenth century their empire had fragmented into a collection of petty provinces. The Muslim conquest of North India during the early part of the century figured indirectly in Khas's downfall: a steady stream of princes from Rajasthan, which had borne the brunt of the invasion, limped into the Khas hills in search of consolation prizes, and rapidly wheedled their way into positions of power. Those who took the reins of the Khas provinces came to be known as the **Baaisi Rajya** (Twenty-two Kingdoms), while others who subjugated Magar and Gurung states further east became the **Chaubisi** (Twenty-four).

Unification

For three centuries the Chaubisi and Baaisi confederacies were able to maintain an uneasy status quo, forming numerous defensive alliances to ensure that no one state could gain control over the rest. Divided, they were small, weak and culturally backward. **Gorkha**, the most easterly territory, was no different from the rest, except that it was that much closer to the Kathmandu Valley and that much more jealous of the Mallas' wealth. Under the inspired, obsessive leadership of **Prithvi Narayan Shah** (1722–75), Gorkha launched a campaign that was to take 27 years to conquer the valley, and as long again to unite all of modern Nepal.

At the time of Prithvi Narayan's rise to the throne, in 1743, rivalry between the three Malla kings had reached an all-time high. Still, Gorkha wasn't nearly strong enough to invade Nepal outright; Prithvi Narayan first captured Nuwakot, a day's march northwest of Kathmandu, and from there directed a ruthless twenty-year **war of attrition**. By 1764 he was able to enforce a total blockade, starving the valley and at the same time replenishing Gorkha's coffers with Tibetan trade. Kirtipur was targeted for the first major battle, and surrendered after a six-month siege. Answering a plea from the Kathmandu king, Jaya Prakash Malla, the East India Company sent in 2400 soldiers against the Gorkhalis, who proceeded to cut them to shreds; only 800 returned. On the eve of Indra Jaatra in 1768, Jaya Prakash, by now rumoured to be insane, let down the city's defences and **Kathmandu fell** to the Gorkhalis without a fight. They took Patan two days later, and Bhaktapur the following year, and by 1774 had marched eastwards all the way to Sikkim.

Suspicious of Britain's growing influence in India, Prithvi Narayan adopted a closed-door policy that was to remain in force until the 1950s. Missionaries were thrown out forthwith: "First the Bible, then the trading station, then the cannon", he warned. The bloody **battle for succession** that followed Prithvi Narayan's death set the pattern for Nepali politics well into the twentieth century. Yet when they weren't stabbing each other in the back, his successors managed to subdue Gorkha's old Chaubisi and Baaisi rivals in the west, so that by 1790 Nepal stretched far beyond its present eastern and western borders. Lured on by promises of land grants – every hillman's dream – the Nepali army became a seemingly unstoppable fighting machine, with Kashmir in its sights.

Westward progress was interrupted, however, by a brief but chastening **war with Tibet**. Troubles had been brewing for some time over trade relations, and the Tibetans were growing alarmed by Nepal's encroachments on their ally, Sikkim. In 1788 and again in 1791, Nepal invaded, plundered a few monasteries and exacted tribute from Tibet, but in 1792 the Tibetans launched a counter-attack, penetrating as far as Nuwakot and forcing Nepal to accept harsh terms.

Nepal's further adventures in the west brought it into increasing **conflict with Britain**'s East India Company, which by now controlled India, and open hostilities broke out in 1814 when Nepal annexed the Butwal sector of the Tarai. For the British, the dispute provided a perfect pretext to "open up" Nepal, which had been so tantalizingly closed to them, and thus to muscle in on trade with Tibet. Britain attacked with a force of 50,000 men against Nepal's 12,000, expecting an easy victory; in the event it took two years and heavy losses before Nepal was finally brought to heel. The **Treaty of Segauli** forced Nepal to accept its present eastern and western boundaries and surrender much of the Tarai, and worst of all, to admit an official British "resident" in Kathmandu. Yet so impressed were the British by "our valiant opponent" – as a plaque at an Indian battle site still proclaims – that they began recruiting Nepalis into the Indian Army before the treaty had even been signed. These companies formed the basis for the famed **Gurkha regiments** (see p.274). Britain restored Nepal's Tarai lands in return for its help in quelling the Indian Mutiny of 1857.

The Rana years

The Kathmandu court was practically paralysed by intrigue and assassinations during the first half of the nineteenth century, culminating in the ghastly **Kot massacre** of 1846, in which more than fifty courtiers were butchered in a courtyard off Kathmandu's Durbar Square. In the ensuing upheaval, the shrewd young general who had instigated the massacre, **Jang Bahadur**, seized power, took the title **Rana** and proclaimed himself prime minister for life, an office which he later made hereditary by establishing a complicated roll of succession. (Though the "Rana" title has generally been equated with that of a prime minister, technically it conferred a grade of kingship. The holder's full title was Shri Tin Maharaja – short for Shri Shri Shri Maharaja; "Shri" being an honorific prefix. The king's was, and still is, Shri Paanch – Five Shri – Maharajdhiraj).

For the next century, the kings of Nepal were nothing more than puppets, while Ranas ruled like shoguns and packed the court with their ever-increasing offspring. Authoritarian and blatantly exploitive, they built grandiose palaces while putting virtually no money into public works, suppressed education for fear it would awaken opposition, and remained firmly isolationist to avoid losing control to the British. (Ironically, an impoverished Nepal suited Britain, since it assured a steady supply of willing Gurkha cannon fodder.) Only a handful of foreign dignitaries were allowed to enter – usually only as far as Chitwan – and even the British resident wasn't allowed to venture beyond the Kathmandu Valley. To survey Nepal and Tibet, Britain had to send in Indian spies disguised as Buddhist monks.

Yet Jang Bahadur knew the value of staying on good terms with the British Raj, now at its zenith; in 1850 he broke with tradition and travelled to England, where he met Queen Victoria and by all accounts cut a dashing figure. He returned with several Western affectations, including a fondness for Neoclassical architecture and epaulettes; soon after, to his credit, he abolished the practice of *sati*.

Other Ranas continued in the same vein. **Chandra Shamsher Rana**, who came to power in 1901 by deposing his brother, is best known for building the thousand-roomed Singha Durbar and (belatedly) abolishing slavery. He also made some feeble attempts at modernization, including the construction of Nepal's first college, railway, hydroelectric plant and paved roads. By 1940, underground resistance against the regime was developing, and **Juddha Shamsher Rana** had four plotters executed; after the fall of the Ranas these men were declared martyrs and a monument south of Kathmandu's Tudikhel was erected in their honour.

The monarchy restored

The Ranas' anachronistic regime wasn't able to survive long after World War II, from which over 200,000 soldiers returned with dangerous ideas of freedom and justice. In 1947 the British quit India, and with them went the Ranas' chief support. The new Indian government mistrusted the Ranas, and became genuinely worried about Nepal's weakness as a buffer state after the Communist takeover of China in 1949. Seeking stability, India signed a far-reaching "**peace and friendship**" **treaty** with Nepal in 1950 which, despite the upheavals that were to follow, remains the basis for all relations between the two countries.

Later the same year the strategic balance shifted again as a result of the Chinese invasion of Tibet, and the **Nepali Congress Party**, recently formed in Calcutta, called for an armed struggle against the Ranas. Within a month, King Tribhuwan had requested asylum at the Indian embassy and was smuggled away to Delhi; the next morning, the Nepali Congress Party launched simultaneous assaults on Birganj and Biratnagar. Sporadic fighting continued for two months until the Ranas, internationally discredited, reluctantly agreed to enter into negotiations. Brokered by India, the so-called **Delhi Compromise** arranged for Ranas and the Congress Party to share power under the king's rule, with Nepalis given the right to vote in the parliamentary-style democracy.

The compromise was short-lived. **Tribhuwan**, a previously retiring figure, emerged as a "hero of the revolution" and an adroit politician, and before the end of 1951 he had dismissed the Rana prime minister. This was an end to the Rana regime, but not Rana influence: by an agreement that has never been made public, the Shah royal family continues to appoint Ranas to most key military posts, and the families are inseparably tied by marriage. In his four years as king, however, Tribhuwan neither consolidated his power nor delivered the elections he promised. Unaccountable to the voters, the party bosses who controlled the interim government weren't much of an improvement over the Ranas.

Panchaayat politics

Crowned in 1955, **King Mahendra** lost no time in offsetting the parties' power by developing his own grassroots network of village leaders, forcing the parties to do likewise. They demanded elections; the king stalled, but finally agreed to a vote in 1959. Amazingly, the Nepali Congress Party won eighty percent of the seats, and under Prime Minister **B.P. Koirala** began bypassing palace control and creating a party machine very much like India's. Mahendra was none too pleased with this **"experiment with democracy"**, as it came to be called – the following year he sacked the cabinet, banned political parties and threw the leaders in jail. For the rest of his reign he relied on heavy police measures to quell dissent.

In place of democracy, Mahendra offered the **"partyless" panchaayat system**, a uniquely Nepali form of government that grew out of the king's old-boy village network. Village councils (*panchaayat*) were established to look after local affairs; these were to send one representative on to a district council, which in turn elected members to a national assembly. The king chose the prime minister and cabinet and appointed one-fifth of the national assembly, which served as a rubber stamp for his policies. "Partylessness" meant, of course, one party – the king's. The *panchaayat* system conveniently preserved an illusion of democracy while silencing opposition and ensuring loyalty to the king: in other words, it was a new and improved version of absolute monarchy. Corruption was the same as before, only now more decentralized, as every village *panchaayat* wallah had a tiny piece of the pie.

India was unhappy with the changes, but Mahendra, unlike his father, didn't owe his crown to India, and sought wider international support. He threw open Nepal's doors to **foreign aid**, which endeared him to the major powers, enriched the state's coffers and swelled the bureaucracy (see "Development dilemmas", p.530). After the 1962 Sino-Indian border war, Mahendra was able to exploit Nepal's buffer position with particular skill, alternately playing off the two powers against each other to obtain economic and military aid; for example, no sooner had India completed the Tribhuwan Rajpath, Nepal's first highway from the plains to Kathmandu, then Mahendra persuaded the Chinese to extend the road to Tibet, much to India's horror. The **"China card"** became an important unofficial strand of foreign policy, but ultimately it was to help bring about the downfall of the *panchaayat* system.

King Birendra assumed power after Mahendra's death in 1972, although for astrological reasons wasn't actually crowned until 1975. Educated at Eton and Harvard, the young king set out as an enlightened reformer, taking steps to curb the bureaucracy and cronyism that had flourished under his father. Reacting to Mahendra's laissez-faire policies on tourism – which had become Nepal's major industry – he cracked down on the growing hippie population by tightening visa restrictions. In 1975, in what was to be the shrewdest and most popular move of his career, the new king proposed designating Nepal a **Zone of Peace**, a Swiss-style neutrality pledge that would at first glance appear to be completely unassailable. India, however, has consistently opposed the measure as a violation of the 1950 "peace and friendship" treaty, which provides for mutual defence, while cynics like to point out the irony of Nepal – home of the Gurkhas, the world's most formidable mercenary soldiers – declaring itself a peace zone.

Birendra's domestic reforms soon ran out of steam, and discontent grew over corruption and the slow pace of development. Widespread uprisings broke out in 1979, forcing the king to promise a national **referendum** in which voters could choose between the *panchaayat* system and multiparty democracy. Democracy lost by a margin of 55 to 45 – many say the vote was rigged – and the *panchaayat* system was retained.

During the 1980s Birendra proved himself to be an earnest but weak leader, easily manipulated by advisers and the queen; forever chaperoned by minders with walkie-talkies, he simply fell out of touch with the people. Despite token tinkerings with the system, the gravy train got more crowded throughout the decade, and insiders, sensing that the regime's days were numbered, tried to grab all they could in the time remaining. In 1988 the king's brother, Dhirendra, was forced to relinquish his title as prince, ostensibly because he'd married a foreigner but ultimately to distance the family from wide-ranging corruption charges against him. Political opponents were imprisoned, while freedom of speech and the press was curtailed. Diplomats insist Birendra was uninvolved with any shady dealings, but he would have had to be incredibly naive not to have known what was going on in his name.

Democracy restored

The chickens started coming home to roost in 1989, when India, outraged by (among other things) Nepal's purchase of anti-aircraft guns from China, retaliated with a crippling **trade embargo**. The government rode out the immediate crisis until the Indian elections eight months later, when a more conciliatory government eased the embargo. But after eight months of hardship, inflation and police action, Nepalis were fed up, and India could no longer be cast as the villain.

The previous year had witnessed China's failed pro-democracy movement at Tiananmen Square and the spectacularly successful revolutions in Eastern Europe: Nepalis were enormously stirred by these examples. Seeing their chance, the banned opposition parties united in the so-called **Movement to Restore Democracy**, demanding an end to the *panchaayat* system and the creation of a constitutional monarchy. They called for a national day of protest on February 18, 1990 – a date already designated by the government, with unintended irony, as Democracy Day. Hundreds of opposition members were duly placed under house arrest, and the planned revolt got off to a shaky start. Yet Faagun 7 (the Nepali date of Democracy Day) marked the true launch of the **Jana Andolan** ("People's Movement"), which in subsequent weeks gathered strength.

On April 3, protesters overran Patan, and three days later an estimated 200,000 people marched up Kathmandu's Durbar Marg towards the Royal

Palace. The army fired into the crowd, **killing** at least 45 people, and an ominous shoot-on-sight curfew was imposed. Finally moved to action by the massacre, the king dissolved his cabinet, legalized political parties and invited the opposition to form an interim government. The *panchaayat* system was dead.

After a few hiccups, the changeover to democracy proceeded in an orderly, if leisurely, fashion. By November 1990 the interim government had ratified a **new constitution** guaranteeing free speech, human rights and a constitutional monarchy. Under its provisions, the king "reigns but does not rule": he remains the commander-in-chief of the armed forces, but cannot make any executive decisions without consulting the prime minister and cabinet. The old Rastriya Panchaayat was replaced by a Parliament consisting of a directly elected House of Representatives and a smaller National Assembly. The Zone of Peace policy was quietly dropped.

After a suitable interval to allow the news of democracy to percolate into the remoter regions, Nepal's first free **elections** in more than thirty years were held in May 1991. The Nepali Congress Party, which had paid its dues in exile for three decades and could claim much of the credit for bringing down the *panchaayat* system, won a narrow majority. But while the rest of the world was backpedalling from communism as fast as it could, Nepal's several Communist parties put in a strong showing, maintaining their traditional strongholds in the east and, incredibly, sweeping the comfortable Kathmandu Valley. The National Democratic Party, largely packed with former *panchaayat*-wallahs, went down in a ball of flames. It was a clear referendum against the old guard, but a less than enthusiastic vote of confidence for the Congress Party.

Congress, communism and breakdown

Any government inheriting such immense challenges with so slender a mandate was probably doomed to disappoint, and the first **Nepali Congress** government's honeymoon was short-lived. Unemployment, Indianization and political infighting produced widespread disillusion, forcing Prime Minister Girija Prasad Koirala, brother of the late B.P. Koirala, to step down in 1994. The ensuing election produced a hung parliament, with the **Communist Party of Nepal–United Marxist-Leninist (CPN-UML)**, the largest of several Communist parties, stepping forward to form a minority government. Among supporters, Asia's first democratically elected Communist government kindled much idealism, but lacking a parliamentary majority could only pursue a modest programme of reform.

The Communists' leadership came to an abrupt end after only nine months, when the Supreme Court nullified the earlier election results and reinstated the previous parliament. This controversial decision was to have a crippling effect on the functioning of the Nepalese state, and in the ensuing five years, five governments attempted to cobble together coalitions in every combination: centre-right, left-right and centre-left. The resulting **political instability** took its toll on Nepal's already lagging development. Preoccupied by short-term concerns and petty crises, successive governments were in no position to take decisive action or follow through on earlier plans. Nepalis looked on helplessly as their unaccountable leaders engaged in unseemly squabbles, forged

Machiavellian alliances and lined their pockets at the public's expense. **Corruption** and cronyism became institutionalized – political parties relied on kickbacks to support themselves and created elaborate systems of patronage, while constant political infighting meant that any accusation of wrongdoing could be dismissed as party-political. Frequent changes of government gave politicians a further incentive to grab it while they could.

All this caused Nepalis to lose faith in their new democracy, and provided fertile ground for the seeds of what would become an all-out revolutionary movement. Convinced by the failure of the 1994–95 Communist government that change wasn't possible by working within the system, members of the **Nepal Communist Party (Maoist)** went underground and in February 1996 declared a "**People's War**" from their base in the midwestern hills (see box on p.498). The Congress government of the time, led by Sher Bahadur Deuba, paid little heed. It was a miscalculation that Deuba, and the country, would later regret.

Prospects for healing Nepal's political malaise seemed to brighten with the announcement of parliamentary elections in 1999. Fed up with do-nothing minority and coalition governments, the voters gave the Nepali Congress a majority on the understanding that there would be no passing the buck this time. Once again hopes were dashed. The party itself was soon riven by infighting, as its two septuagenarian strongmen, **Krishna Prasad Bhattarai** and **Girija Prasad Koirala**, took turns undermining each other's leadership and fending off younger successors. Koirala, who succeeded Bhattarai as prime minister after less than a year, vowed to control corruption, improve governance and solve the Maoist problem. He did none of these things, and instead solidified his reputation as a power-hungry manipulator. Indeed, he himself was hounded by accusations of corruption involving kickbacks on the lease of a Royal Nepal aircraft, and presided over a legislative session in which literally no action was taken.

Meanwhile, the **Maoist insurgency** grew in strength. By early 2001, the rebels controlled nearly a quarter of the country and had established their own governments in several midwestern districts. Their cadres were becoming better trained and armed, and their raids more damaging. On the fifth anniversary of the People's War, Maoist leader Pushpa Kamal Dahal – better known by his nom de guerre **Prachanda** ("the Fierce") – issued three preconditions for peace: a new constitution, an interim government with seats for Maoists, and the abolition of the monarchy.

With the government still fighting the insurgency with ordinary police officers, who were ill-equipped for guerrilla warfare, Prime Minister Koirala came under increasing criticism for failing to ensure peace and security. Though Koirala made noises about deploying the army, he, like all Nepali politicians, knew that the army owed its allegiance to the king – and to ask the king to deploy troops would tip the balance of power back toward the palace. He had mooted an **Integrated Security and Development Package**, a "hearts and minds" offensive that would use army troops to defend disputed territory and at the same time to build roads and oversee other development projects, but the military brass had declined; he had pushed for the creation of a paramilitary **Armed Police Force** with broad powers to combat the rebels, but couldn't get it through parliament. When the Maoists launched their deadliest attacks so far in April 2001, killing seventy policemen, he finally got the go-ahead on both the above initiatives – but then something happened that no one on earth could have foreseen.

Tragedy and emergency

On the evening of June 1, 2001, King Birendra, Queen Aishwara and seven other members of the royal family were **massacred** in the Royal Palace, plunging Nepal into its deepest crisis yet. Eyewitnesses said Crown Prince **Dipendra** killed his family and then apparently turned the gun on himself (see box on. Dipendra survived on a life-support machine for almost two days, posing a dilemma for the palace that would only exacerbate an already explosive situation.

The **rules of succession** clearly indicated that the crown prince was next in line for the throne, with no exception made for extraordinary circumstances such as regicide. Protocol further dictated that the king's death could not be announced until his successor was named, and that, once named, the new king

The mystery of the royal massacre

It's hard to convey the complexity of emotions felt by Nepalis after the **royal massacre** of June 1, 2001. Compared to, say, the Kennedy assassination, this was an even more profound national trauma. The chief victim was not an elected official but rather a monarch who had ruled for thirty years, and whose family was inextricably linked with the birth of the nation. Nepal's king had always been a symbol of national unity – a ruler who held dozens of ethnic groups and castes together in peaceful coexistence – and as the elected government went from bad to worse, Nepalis increasingly viewed the monarchy as the country's one pillar of stability and moral certainty. Many literally regarded the king as a reincarnation of the god Vishnu; to all, he was a supreme father figure, a powerful archetypal role in a traditional Hindu society.

Most monstrous of all, the alleged killer was the king's own son. In a culture where parents still command the highest respect from their children, and where murder is rare, such a crime is almost unheard of. The massacre of nearly an entire family was unprecedented; that it occurred within the royal family was beyond comprehension. Nepalis felt grief at their loss, anger toward whoever was responsible, and shame at the egregious breaking of taboos. But above all they felt **disbelief**: it seemed impossible to make sense of what had occurred, either logically or emotionally.

For many Nepalis, a kind of closure came with the release of the so-called **High Level Committee Report**, just two weeks after the tragedy, which clearly implicated the crown prince as the shooter. Based on the testimony of survivors and palace employees, the report described how, prior to the fateful family gathering, Dipendra drank whisky and ordered his aide de camp to bring him his customary hashish cigarette laced with "another unnamed black substance"; shortly after, he became unsteady on his feet and had to be helped back to his room, where he was later seen lying on the floor and heard retching. A few minutes later, he emerged in camouflage fatigues with an automatic weapon in each hand and opened fire in the billiard room where the royal family was assembled, targeting the king first and then others. After spraying the room with bullets three separate times, he retreated to the garden where he apparently shot his mother, who had fled, and finally himself.

But the hastily produced report was riddled with **unexplained gaps** and unanswered – indeed unasked – questions. Why was the first response of the royal aides de camp on duty that night to call a doctor, rather than to overpower the attacker, and why did it take them ten minutes to do that? What was the mysterious "black substance" rolled into Dipendra's cigarette? Why were no post-mortems performed on the victims? Why did Dipendra, who was right-handed, shoot himself behind the left ear? Why did a soldier throw the weapon lying next to Dipendra's body into a pond?

was automatically above reproach. It wasn't until the afternoon following the massacre that Radio Nepal broke the official silence by announcing simply that Birendra was dead and his son Dipendra had succeeded him as king; and that, since the new king was "mentally and physically unfit to carry out his responsibilities", Gyanendra – the dead king's younger brother – was to serve as regent. The public had to learn of the true scale of the tragedy, and of Dipendra's alleged role in it, from foreign media; this de facto **news blackout** smacked of a cover-up, heightening anxiety and fuelling widespread rumours. When the bodies of the dead royals were solemnly taken to Pashupatinath to be cremated that evening, within 24 hours of death in accordance with Hindu tradition, many citizens lined the route in silent vigil, but others chanted aggressive pro-monarchy slogans and some even stoned the prime minister's car.

Suspicions only intensified the next morning, when Gyanendra, constrained by protocol, issued a cryptic statement that the victims of the massacre had been killed by "a sudden discharge of an automatic weapon". Later that day,

The report didn't begin to address the question of motive: that was left to palace-watchers and media commentators, who speculated that Dipendra was driven to the act out of rage at not being allowed to marry his sweetheart **Devyani Rana**. The queen had adamantly opposed the match, and according to some reports had threatened to make Dipendra's younger brother Nirajan crown prince if it happened. Add to that Dipendra's lethal temper, his fetish for weapons (he volunteered as a weapons tester for the Royal Nepal Army), his private anguish at having reached thirty and still not being king and his frustration at being given little responsibility in the meantime; mix all this with an ill-advised cocktail of alcohol and drugs, and – observers concluded – you had a recipe for a violent psychotic outburst.

If the majority of Nepalis accepted this version of events, it was still too much to swallow for many, and the report's shortcomings only gave new life to various **conspiracy theories** that had circulated since the massacre. Far-fetched as these theories were, they were arguably no more so than the idea that the heir to the throne of Nepal would kill his entire family over his choice of bride. The most popular ones centred on the suspicion that it was no accident that Gyanendra, alone among the immediate family, was absent from the palace that evening, and that his son Paras, who was present, escaped unhurt. It was tempting to believe that Gyanendra had somehow engineered the massacre to catapult himself and his son up to the top of the line of succession. Others connected the killings with the Maoists, whose interests would be served by discrediting the monarchy. The Maoists in turn claimed it had been a plot co-ordinated by the American CIA and its Indian counterpart. Whoever did it, some said, killed Dipendra and replaced him with a stand-in wearing a lifelike mask (which would account why Dipendra reportedly neither spoke nor showed any expression during the rampage). Others held Dipendra was a patsy, drugged and given weapons and a go-get-'em by the real perpetrators and then bumped off after he'd done the deed.

The truth, whatever it is, will probably never be known. The case is well and truly closed now, for the royal palace is immune from investigation, and most of the evidence has been destroyed or compromised. Outwardly, Nepalis have ended their mourning and resolved to move on: whether Dipendra did it or not, they realize, either way the implications are unthinkable, and beyond the power of ordinary people to alter; there's nothing to be gained by sticking one's head above the parapet over it. But serious damage has been done, both to the national psyche and to the institution of the monarchy, which will not quickly heal.

when Dipendra's death and **Gyanendra's ascension** were announced, emotions boiled over and **riots** broke out. Despite the imposition of an official curfew, hundreds of protesters, many of them with their heads shaved as a mark of mourning, denounced Gyanendra and his son Paras, demanded an investigation, and attempted (unsuccessfully) to block the funeral procession of Dipendra's body, fearing that vital forensic evidence would be destroyed. Maoists reportedly streamed into the capital to stoke the demonstrations. The following day the government declared a shoot-on-sight curfew; two people were killed and forty wounded in clashes.

Gyanendra quickly moved to avert further bloodshed by ordering an official investigation into the massacre. (Wisely, he sidestepped the question of whether he would name **Paras** – who was almost universally hated for his unchecked criminal behaviour – as crown prince; he waited until the happier days of Dasain, several months later, to make that announcement.) Outward displays of anger dissipated, as people looked to the new king to lead them out of the crisis. Gyanendra's reputation as a shrewd businessman and a take-charge leader went before him, as did the expectation that he would take a harder line against the Maoists and a more pragmatic approach to relations with India and China. Many took comfort in the knowledge that he had actually served as king once before: in 1950, the infant Gyanendra occupied the throne for three months during the

Anatomy of a revolution

Since 1996, Nepal's **Maoist insurgency** has grown from an obscure conflict into the country's most urgent political priority. Thousands have died and tens of thousands have been displaced; vast sums have been diverted from development to the military; the economy has been devastated; and basic freedoms have been curtailed.

The rebels' stated aim is to replace the country's constitutional monarchy with a **people's republic**, transferring power from the "reactionary ruling classes" to the "oppressed masses". This is to be achieved by means of a violent revolution, because according to the Maoists' analysis, Nepal's "semi-feudal, semi-colonial" system cannot be fixed from within. Exactly what their "People's Republic of Nepal" would look like is hard to say, but the district-level "people's governments" they've set up in their occupied territory probably give some indication. In many respects they're doing more for their people than the official government ever did – redistributing land, launching grassroots development projects and conducting programmes to empower women and minorities – as well as continuing to operate schools, courts, health posts and other institutions. On the other hand, they offer no democratic process, commandeer residents' property and labour, intimidate dissidents and kill political enemies; effectively, their policies proceed from the barrel of a gun. How the Maoists would manage the economy is anybody's guess, considering that so far they've financed their operations mainly by robbing banks and demanding protection money.

The Maoists' revolutionary **strategy** is based on Mao's original blueprint, adapted for Nepali soil and incorporating lessons learned from Peru's Shining Path and other (failed) Maoist movements. Nepal, like Mao's China, is overwhelmingly rural, so the revolution is to be carried out by peasants rather than urban proletarians. The primary task has therefore been to consolidate power in the **countryside** – something the Maoists have proved remarkably successful at. Starting with a foothold in the midwestern hills, the ragtag army has gradually expanded its territory by picking off police stations and district offices one at a time, and is now able to engage government forces along an expanding frontline while launching diversionary attacks in many other parts of the country. Despite sustaining heavy losses, the Maoist fighting force is now estimated to number 5000 to 10,000 cadres armed with increasingly exile of his grandfather, Tribhuwan, in India. Others, however, darkly pointed to a legend in which the saint Gorakhnath warned the founder of modern Nepal, Prithvi Narayan Shah, that his dynasty would last only ten generations after him. If you count Dipendra's two-day reign, Gyanendra is the eleventh successor to Prithvi Narayan: for the doomsayers that's evidently close enough.

The country didn't have the luxury of grieving for long in any case. The royal massacre gave the Maoists a golden opportunity to tap into anti-monarchist feelings, and they stepped up their offensive with renewed attacks on government positions in the countryside and even some minor bombings in the hitherto safe Kathmandu Valley. Within six weeks, they had provoked a fresh crisis by holding several dozen police officers hostage in the western district of Rolpa. Koirala secured the new king's permission to send army troops to the rescue, but it was his last act. Within days, he was brought down by a no-confidence motion and was replaced by **Sher Bahadur Deuba**, during whose previous administration the Maoists had declared their People's War. Keenly wanting to make up for his earlier mistake, Deuba immediately negotiated a **ceasefire** and persuaded the Maoists to enter **peace talks**. The country breathed a sigh of relief.

It was a measure of the contempt in which the mainstream parties were held that, up to this point, the Maoists had enjoyed a good deal of sympathy among

sophisticated weapons captured during earlier battles. Less successful has been a secondary strategy to foment mass uprisings in **urban areas**, where the Maoists have sympathizers but few hardcore followers.

The question of whether the Maoists will succeed remains open. Militarily, they've come a long way, and have basically outfought the Nepalese police, but it's hard to imagine them ever defeating the much more formidable Nepalese army, which is already receiving material support from India and has been promised $20 million in "anti-terrorism" aid from the United States. Nor is it clear that the rebels could ever achieve a critical mass of civilian support, especially in the cities, where the "reactionary ruling classes" have the greatest motivation to oppose them.

The final **outcome** will depend largely on what the Maoists are prepared to settle for. At times their leadership has indicated a willingness to negotiate, only to withdraw and redouble the offensive. Some observers believe these about-faces are deliberate ploys to give the rebel forces time to regroup for the next escalation; others say they're the result of hotheaded cadres sabotaging any compromise. Either way, the effect is that the Maoists seem determined to see their revolution through to the bitter end. Caught up in the parallel universe of their ideology, hundreds of miles from the nearest reality check, they're convinced of the dialectical inevitability of victory.

The People's War is essentially a symptom of poverty, unemployment and bad governance – it's a desperate struggle by desperate people. The tragedy is that it was so avoidable. In the early years of the insurgency, the government could have removed the resentment that fuelled it simply by channelling a fair share of development assistance to the impoverished rural areas where eighty percent of Nepalis live. Instead, Kathmandu responded with heavy-handed security operations, leading to a cycle of violence and reprisals that played right into the Maoists' hands. Now it's far too late for easy solutions: the sides are entrenched, the hatreds deep, the demands seemingly irreconcilable. Since neither the government nor the Maoists appear capable of achieving outright victory, they may well maintain a crippling standoff for years. But since neither side can really afford to do so, there is hope that – sooner rather than later – they'll be forced to return to the negotiating table.

common people and even intellectuals. Their passive support evaporated rapidly in the summer of 2001, when it began to appear that the rebels were negotiating in bad faith: reports of continued intimidation and extortion suggested they were merely playing for time, while isolated incidents of rape and temple-desecration belied the Maoists' supposed integrity. These suspicions were confirmed in November, when the Maoists abruptly withdrew from the peace talks and, two days later, launched **co-ordinated attacks** on several locations, killing more than 200 soldiers and civilians. It was the highest death toll since the insurgency began, and the first time that the rebels attacked army positions. Hardest hit was Salleri, not far from the Everest region; a few weeks later the rebels bombed the Lukla airstrip, used by Everest trekkers.

Government reaction was swift. The king declared a **state of emergency** – suspending civil liberties such as freedom of the press and freedom of assembly, and giving the government broad powers to arrest suspects and impose curfews – and authorized the mobilization of Nepal's 50,000-strong **army** against the Maoists. Taking its cue from America's war on terrorism, the government officially declared the Communist Party of Nepal (Maoist) a **terrorist organization** and warned that any found helping them would be prosecuted as terrorists. In the first few months of the emergency, the government imprisoned 5000 people, including more than 100 journalists, under this provision; human-rights activists accused HMG of using it as a smokescreen for detaining, torturing and killing political opponents as well as suspected Maoists. Less publicized was the shelving of the Integrated Security and Development Package in all but one district, signalling that the government was now pinning its hopes on a military solution to the Maoist problem.

As this book went to press, the emergency was still in force, and due to press censorship it was impossible to determine whether the government's anti-Maoist offensive was achieving its aims. There were regular reports of successful "search and destroy" operations by the security forces, but no clear sign that the Maoists were weakening. The spring of 2002 actually saw an escalation in the scale and deadliness of their attacks, with major battles fought in the western districts of Achham and Dang, as well as a growing campaign of destruction of dams, telecommunications facilities and other infrastructure. In six years of what was beginning to look like civil war, more than 3000 people had died, the economy was in tatters, portions of the countryside had been depopulated as villagers fled the fighting, and ordinary Nepalis, weary of life under emergency restrictions, held little hope for the future.

The ethnic landscape

For at least 5000 years, what is now Nepal has straddled the boundary line between two of the world's major ethnic families. To the north, fenced off by the Himalaya, live the Mongoloid peoples of central and eastern Asia; to the south, historically held at bay by the malarial Tarai, are the Indo-Aryans of the Indian Subcontinent. The mountains and jungles on either side have acted as semi-permeable barriers to human migration, allowing determined people into the rugged country within but then isolating them to evolve their own unique cultures. Over the course of millennia, successive waves of immigrants have produced a complex human geography.

Despite its tiny proportions, Nepal is as culturally diverse as Europe, with something like fifty ethnic/linguistic groups represented within its borders. Several of these groups have their own traditional homelands where they're the majority, although in recent times the ethnic map has been greatly blurred by internal migration. Cultural and religious practices remain fairly distinct, though, and intermarriage is still uncommon outside of the anonymous cities. Considering their differences, Nepal's ethnic and caste groups exhibit an amazing level of mutual tolerance.

The Hindu castes

The majority of Nepalis are relative newcomers, descendants of Hindus who fled the Muslim conquest of northern India, or of their converts. They're generically referred to as the **Hindu castes**, since they imported the caste system from India and continue to abide by it, or as **Parbatiyas** ("Hill-dwellers"), since they dominate the middle hills and valleys. In India, Hindus are divided into four primary castes (see p.513), but nearly all the early Hindu migrants to Nepal were of the two highest orders, Brahmans and Kshatriyas (called **Baahuns** and **Chhetris** in Nepal), who had the most to lose from the advance of Islam. These are sometimes called the "twice-born" castes, because males are symbolically "reborn" through an initiation rite at the age of thirteen and thereafter wear a sacred thread (*janai*) sash-like over one shoulder next to the skin, which must be changed annually during the festival of Janai Purnima. Though initially only a small minority themselves, the refugee Hindus' high birth and sense of entitlement gave the ambition necessary to subjugate the rest, and in the process to provide the country with much of its cultural framework, including its *lingua franca*, Nepali.

Baahuns

Although **Baahuns** (Brahmans) belong to the highest, priestly caste, they're not necessarily the wealthiest members of society, nor are they all priests. However, they have a significant edge in Nepali society. Baahuns' priestly duties historically required that they be able to read and write, and this, combined with their symbiotic links with the ruling caste, has long given them privileged access to government jobs in the cities and towns. The vast majority of politicians and civil servants are Baahuns — even half the Maoists' leaders belong to the caste — and many others are teachers, lawyers and other professionals whose

Multiple identities: caste, ethnicity and class

Nepal's confusing **social divisions** can be simplified by thinking of the population as two halves, one of which divides itself according to caste, as in India, and the other according to ethnic group. Nepalis, however, make more fine-grained distinctions, and to complicate matters, members of one group may take a different view of their own status than others do.

The terms Nepalis use to make these distinctions express concepts that are somewhat alien to outsiders. The broadest is **jaat**, which in its general sense means class or category; when applied to people, it signifies any kind of social division or grouping, whether based on ethnicity, caste or hereditary occupation. The related word **janajaati** refers collectively to Nepal's **ethnic minority groups**, as distinct from the Baahun-Chhetri majority who make up the rest of the population.

Varna, an ancient Sanskrit word still used in Nepal and India, translates as "**caste**" in the classical Hindu sense. The **caste system** divides people by profession, separates them in matters of marriage and contact, and ranks them hierarchically. The hierarchy is effectively defined by rules regarding ritual pollution, which dictate who may accept food, water and physical contact from whom. Society places major hurdles in the way of intercaste marriages, as the couple are likely to be cut off from their families (a serious punishment in a country where connections are everything) and cold-shouldered by others, and the higher-born of the two will have to accept the other's lower caste. A person's professional opportunities are also constrained by these rules: a low-caste person would have difficulty running a shop, for example, since higher castes would refuse to enter it. Although Nepal's *janajaati* exist for the most part outside the classical caste system, they were officially assigned places – relatively low ones – in the nineteenth century, and even today are often referred to as "castes".

A **thar** – usually defined as a **clan** – is a subset of an ethnic group or caste. Members of a *thar* have a common surname, which may or may not indicate common lineage. In some ethnic groups, *thars* are like subcastes, with one's surname indicating the family's hereditary occupation and position in the social hierarchy. In these *thars*, caste-like rules may also apply: for example, members may be prohibited from marrying outside the group (on the other hand, small *thars*, in which members are all closely related, may require marriage outside the group).

Less systematically, people may be categorized by **barga** – "**class**" in the socioeconomic sense of degree of wealth, status and education. Thanks to greater social mobility in modern times, socioeconomic class is now not so heavily determined by caste or other aspects of birth, so a Nepali belonging to what is still sometimes called the "backward classes" may in fact also be a member of the upper class. Some families manage to escape the stigma of their caste entirely by moving (usually to a city) and changing their surname, although it takes more than one generation to pull this off.

Thus every Nepali has multiple identities – that is, belongs to multiple *jaats* – based on ethnicity or mother tongue, caste, clan and status. Depending on the situation, they will classify themselves or others according to any of these divisions.

work requires connections and inside knowledge of the system. Priests, who generally follow their fathers into the vocation, administer rites for fixed fees. Some make a full-time living out of it, others officiate part-time alongside other work.

In the countryside, most Baahuns are farmers, and tend to live in well-spaced two-storey houses that are easily distinguishable from the more clustered hamlets of other groups. Rural Baahuns are often as not as poor as their low-caste neighbours, but they have a reputation for moneylending and for subjecting their borrowers to crippling interest rates and swift foreclosures.

Orthodox Baahuns observe a range of rules to maintain the purity of their caste – certain foods (such as onions and hens' eggs) and alcohol are prohibited – and won't eat with lower castes or permit them to enter the house. Extra restrictions are placed on women, who, for example, have to keep strict seclusion during menstruation and for ten days after childbirth, when they're considered polluted.

Chhetris

The majority of Parbatiyas are **Chhetris**, who correspond to Indian Kshatriyas, the caste of warriors and kings. While Baahuns usually claim pure bloodlines and exhibit the classic Aryan features of their caste, Chhetris are a more racially mixed lot and may easily be mistaken for members of other ethnic groups.

Most Chhetris are descended from the **Khas**, an early wave of Hindu refugees from the Muslim conquest who settled in the far western hills, and over time abandoned their orthodox religious practices. When later Hindus arrived from India with an eye to colonizing Nepal's hills, they allowed Khas and other tribals who converted to Hinduism to become honorary Chhetris (in the early days, Baahuns were willing to bend the rules to gain allies), while the offspring of Baahun and Khas marriages were assigned to a new subcaste, the Khatri Chhetri, whose members nowadays go by the abbreviated surname KC. Those whose Khas ancestors didn't convert or intermarry are now called **Matwaali Chhetris** – "alcohol-drinking" Chhetris – but because they follow a form of shamanism and don't wear the *janai*, some anthropologists consider them a separate ethnic group. Chhetris of pure Kshatriya blood – notably the aristocratic **Thakuri** subcaste of the far west, who are related to the royal family – can be as twitchy about caste regulations as Baahuns, but most are more relaxed.

Being of high caste, Chhetris can move relatively easily in society, and they're favoured for commissions in the military and, to a lesser extent, jobs in other branches of government and industry. Significantly, it was a Chhetri who unified Nepal and gave the country its abiding martial character, and the old warrior-caste mentality remains a key in understanding the politics of modern Nepal, for Chhetris occupy the palace and command the army to this day.

Dalits

A significant number of Sudras – members of the lowest, "untouchable" caste – have also immigrated to Nepal's hills over the centuries. These so-called **Dalits** ("Oppressed") suffer severe disadvantages in Nepali society. Although untouchability was officially abolished in 1963, and the caste system was never as rigidly observed in Nepal as in India, caste discrimination is not as yet a punishable offence. To orthodox Hindus, Dalits carry the threat of ritual pollution, and in many parts of the country they're not allowed to enter temples or even shops and tea stalls. It's no statistical accident that Dalits are less educated, poorer and suffer higher mortality rates than the national average, or that there is only one Dalit MP.

Dalits are sometimes collectively called the **occupational castes**, as they fall into several occupation-based *thars*, such as the Sarki (leather-workers), Kami (blacksmiths), Damai (tailors/musicians) and Kumal (potters). While the importance of the work performed by these castes traditionally helped offset their lowly status, nowadays their wares are increasingly being marginalized by mass-produced items. Typically landless and uneducated, many are turning to tenant farming, portering and day-labouring to make ends meet.

Ethnic groups of the hills

Nepal's **hills** are home to a number of ethnic groups that have maintained their distinct cultural identities despite inroads by Hindu castes. They are generally short, stocky, swarthy people who exhibit Mongoloid features and speak Tibeto-Burman dialects – signs that their ancestors probably migrated from what is now Tibet or southwestern China. The women traditionally wear half-length blouses, print skirts, headscarves, heavy gold jewellery and *pote malla* (multiple strands of glass beads); many men have abandoned the elfish *daura suruwal* (homespun cotton shirt and jodhpur-like pants) of old, but few would be caught without a *topi* (Nepali cap) on his head or a *khukuri* (machete) in his waistband.

The traditional religious practices of the hill ethnic groups often have an animist (nature-worshipping) basis, overlaid by shamanistic and ancestor-worshipping practices, and with various admixtures of either Hinduism or Tibetan Buddhism, according to the group. Compared to their Hindu neighbours, they're more flexible in their social dealings, allowing women quite a bit of freedom, tolerating elopement and divorce, and happily eating meat and drinking alcohol.

Hardy, self-sufficient peasant farmers, the men of these tribes have long supplemented family income by working as soldiers or labourers, often leaving home for months or years at a time. Gurungs, Magars, Rais and Limbus form the backbone of the Gurkha regiments (see p.274), and also account for a fair proportion of the Nepalese army.

Gurungs and Magars

Leavened with nothing but the water of God
Comes from Rumjatar the flour of millet pounded,
Gurungs have mastered the knowledge of God
And Brahmans are left astounded.

Jnandil (c.1821–83)

Although **Gurungs** are a common sight around Pokhara, where many have invested their Gurkha pensions in guesthouses and retirement homes, their homeland remains the middle elevations, from Gorkha to the southern slopes of the Annapurna Himal (with a smaller concentration in the eastern hills). The majority of Gurungs who don't serve in the military keep sheep for their wool, driving them to pastures high on the flanks of the Himalaya, and raise wheat, maize, millet and potatoes. Gurungs were once active trans-Himalayan traders, but the Chinese occupation of Tibet ended that, while other traditional pursuits such as hunting and honey-gathering are being encroached upon by overpopulation.

A unique Gurung institution is the **rodi**, a kind of fraternity or sorority for adolescent boys or girls, in which members maintain their own *rodi ghar* (clubhouse) and hold chaperoned social events with other *rodis*. Designed to help boys and girls mix and ease them into adulthood, the *rodi* is giving way to more modern forms of courtship. The Gurung form of shamanism is coming under pressure, too, as Hinduism advances from the south and Buddhism trickles down with Tibetan settlers from the north. Gurungs employ shamans to propitiate ghosts, reclaim possessed souls from the underworld, and guide dead souls to the land of their ancestors – rituals that contain clear echoes of "classic"

Siberian shamanism and are believed to resemble those of pre-Buddhist Tibet. (For an excellent introduction to Gurung shamanism, visit Pokhara's Tamu Kohibo Museum – see p.298.)

A somewhat less cohesive group, **Magars** are scattered throughout the lower elevations of the western hills and in some parts of the east. A network of Magar kingdoms once controlled the entire region, but the arrival of Hindus in the fifteenth century brought swift political decline and steady cultural assimilation. After centuries of coexistence with Hindu castes, most Magars employ Baahun priests and worship Hindu gods just like their Chhetri neighbours, differing only in that they're not allowed to wear the sacred thread of the "twice-born" castes. Similarly, with farming practices, housing and dress, Magars are an adaptable lot and not easily distinguished from surrounding groups. Even the Magar language varies from place to place, consisting of at least three mutually unintelligible dialects (nowadays most Magars speak Nepali as their first language). Despite the lack of unifying traits, however, group identity is still strong, and will probably remain so as long as Magars keep marrying only within the clan.

Tamangs

Tamangs dominate Nepal's central hills between about 1500m and 2500m and constitute, numerically, the country's largest ethnic minority: about one in every five Nepalis is a Tamang. The tribe is thought to have originated in Tibet and migrated south in prehistoric times, which accounts for their Mongoloid features but leaves the significance of their name (which means "horse trader" in Tibetan) unexplained. Tamangs follow a form of Buddhism virtually indistinguishable from Lamaism – religious texts are even written in Tibetan script – but most also worship clan deities, employ *jhankri* (shamans) and observe major Hindu festivals.

Despite their numbers, Tamangs are one of Nepal's most **exploited** peoples, and have been ever since the Gorkhali conquest of the late eighteenth century. Geography has been the Tamangs' downfall. The new rulers of Nepal, requiring land to grant to their victorious soldiers, arbitrarily appropriated much of the vast Tamang homeland surrounding the Kathmandu Valley. Displaced from their lands, Tamangs became tenant farmers or bonded labourers for their new masters, or freelanced as porters or woodcutters. Many drifted down to the Kathmandu Valley, to fetch and carry for the new aristocracy. The Tamangs carried out these menial functions so efficiently that the government came to view them as a strategic asset and prohibited them from serving in the Gurkha regiments. More recently, Tamangs are being deprived of another source of income – woodcutting – due to deforestation and the closing off of the Shivapuri Watershed.

Lacking land and opportunities, the Tamangs remain at the bottom rung of the economic ladder. They are the porters, the riksha wallahs, the cart-pullers of Kathmandu. Tamangs comprise an estimated 75 percent of the carpet industry's workforce, and create many of the *thangka* and other "Tibetan" crafts sold in Nepal – for contract wages, of course. Boys are lured to the capital to work as *kanchha* (tea boys), and girls are prime targets for brokers in the Indian flesh trade, while surveys show a disproportionate number of prison inmates in Nepal are Tamangs. A silent underclass in their own homeland, Tamangs often compare themselves to another displaced group, the Tibetans – only nowadays even the Tibetans are the Tamangs' bosses.

Rais and Limbus

The original inhabitants of the eastern hills were the Kirats, a warlike tribe mentioned in the *Mahabharat* who may well have been the same Kirats who ruled the Kathmandu Valley in semi-mythological times. If it ever existed as a single entity, the Kirat nation fragmented long ago into several tribes, the most important two now being referred to as **Rais** and **Limbus**. In fact, Rai is an honorific title meaning "chief" that was given by Prithvi Narayan Shah to the Kirati headmen as part of the process of bringing them within the Nepalese state. The earlier name for the Rais was the Khambu, or people of Khambuwan (Middle Kirat), just as the more eastern-dwelling Limbus are the people of Limbuwan (or Far Kirat). Rais and Limbus, however, divide themselves into numerous *thars*.

There's an old saying that there are as many Rai languages as there are Rais. Despite official statistics, which claim far fewer, there may be as many as thirty Rai languages – not just dialects – most of which are mutually unintelligible; this in a population of around half a million. This linguistic evidence suggests that terms such as "Khambu" and "Limbu", just as much as "Rai", are useful catch-alls imposed by outsiders. The orally transmitted myths and legends of the Rais and Limbus differ from clan to clan, but largely agree that each clan is descended from one of ten (or more, or less) "brothers" who took different routes as they migrated to Kirat, and who settled down in different areas.

Like the Magars and Gurungs of the west, members of these dauntless hill groups make up a significant portion of the Gurkha regiments. They follow their own forms of nature- and ancestor-worship, combined with ingredients of shamanism, but increasingly also embrace Hindu practices, and sometimes elements of Buddhism as well. In the past few years, some have joined the ranks of a Kirat revivalist sect founded by the late Guru Phalgunanda, which incorporates many orthodox Hindu practices – including abstinence from meat and tobacco. Such behaviour is somewhat alien to traditional Kirati culture, which seems to have set great store by the ritual raising – and sometimes, still, sacrifice – of pigs and other animals, and even greater store by the liberal and occasionally ritual drinking of home-brewed beer and distilled *raksi*. Unusually, Rais and Limbus bury their dead (cremation is the usual practice throughout the subcontinent), and Limbus erect distinctive rectangular, whitewashed monuments over graves: four tiers high for a male, three for a female.

Rais, who have a reputation as a staunchly independent people, traditionally occupy the middle-elevation hills between the Dudh Kosi and the Arun River, while Limbuwan, as the Limbu homeland is sometimes still called, is further east, centred around the lower slopes of the Tamur Koshi Valley. Together they had the hills virtually to themselves until the late eighteenth century, when the Gorkhali army's annexation of the region set off a spate of migrations. Baahuns and Chhetris began infiltrating the Arun basin, and Newars took over the trading crossroads; at about the same time, Sherpas and Tamangs were steadily elbowing the Rais out of Solu and, more recently, Magars and Gurungs have hopped across from their traditional homelands in the west. Little wonder, then, that when the Rais and Limbus were recruited by the British in the nineteenth century to pluck tea in Darjeeling, they too headed east.

Other hill groups

A small but economically powerful clan, **Thakalis** are the ingenious traders, innkeepers and pony-handlers of the Thak Khola in the Annapurna region. Their entrepreneurial flair goes back at least to the mid-nineteenth century, when the government awarded them a regional monopoly in the salt trade. When Nepal opened to the outside world, many branched out into more exotic forms of commerce, such as importing electronics from Singapore and Hong Kong, while others set up efficient inns in the western hills. Similarly, the **Manangis** (or Manang-ba) of the upper Marsyangdi, the next valley to the east of the Thak Khola, built early trading privileges into a reputation for international smuggling and other shady activities. Women have traditionally run most of the trekking lodges in both of these valleys, while their well-travelled husbands spent most of their time away on business. In recent years, the relaxation of import restrictions and currency controls has deprived these groups of their special status, and many traders have returned to their home villages. Both groups could arguably be classified as Bhotiyas (see p.508), but their languages are more akin to Gurung than to Tibetan; Manangis are Buddhists, while Thakalis' religion blends Buddhism with Hinduism and shamanism.

Jirels, who occupy the area around Jiri, at the gateway to the Everest region, may be the offspring of long-ago intermarriage between Magars and Sherpas: they bear a physical resemblance to both, and show strong Sherpa traits in their social and religious customs and in their solid, whitewashed stone houses. Similar, but without the Sherpa influence, are the **Sunwars** of the nearby valleys east of Jiri.

A disadvantaged group that may soon disappear, **Chepangs** live in small pockets in the southernmost hills of central Nepal. Two generations ago they were secretive hunter-gatherers, only occasionally leaving their forest home to sell wood to Kathmandu furniture makers. They have since shifted to farming but, exploited through debt by Baahuns and others, many have lost their land and work as labourers. Their traditional religion is primarily animistic-shamanic, with elements of ancestor worship.

The Kathmandu Valley: Newars

The **Newars** are a special case. Their stronghold is a valley – the Kathmandu Valley – which, while geographically located within Nepal's hill region, has its own distinct climate and history; Newars themselves are careful to distinguish themselves from other hill peoples. And although they're an ethnic minority in 0 pivotal Kathmandu Valley has enabled them to exert a cultural influence far beyond their numbers. An outsider could easily make the mistake of thinking that Newar culture *is* Nepali culture.

Many anthropologists believe that the root stock of the Newars is the Kirats, a clan who legendarily ruled the Kathmandu Valley between the seventh century BC and the second century AD. However, Newar culture has been in the making for millennia, as waves of immigrants, overlords, traders and usurpers have mingled in the melting pot of the valley. These arrivals contributed new customs, beliefs and skills to the overall stew, but they weren't completely assimilated – rather, they found their own niches in society, maintaining internal social structures and traditions and fulfilling unique spiritual and professional roles. In time, these *thars* (clans) were formally organized into a Newar caste system that mirrored that of the Baahun-Chhetris and, still later, became nested within it. Thus Newar society is a microcosm of Nepali society, with many shared cultural traits and a common language (Newari), but also with an enormous amount of diversity among its members.

Newar religion is so complex that it must be described separately elsewhere (see p.518); suffice it to say here that individual Newars may identify themselves as either Hindu or Buddhist, depending on their *thar's* historical origin, but this makes little difference to their fundamental doctrines or practices. Kinship roles are extremely important to Newars, and are reinforced by elaborate life-cycle rituals and annual feasts; likewise, each *thar* has its role to play in festivals and other public events. A uniquely Newar social invention is the *Os* of temples and fountains, organizes festivals and, indirectly, ensures the transmission of Newar culture from one generation to the next. *Guthi* have been on the decline since the 1960s, however, when land reform deprived them of much of their income from holdings around the valley.

With so great an emphasis placed on social relationships, it's little wonder that Newars like to live so close together. Unlike other hill peoples, they're urbanites at heart. Their cities are masterpieces of density, with tall tenements pressing against narrow alleys and shopfronts opening directly onto streets. In the past couple of centuries, Newar traders have colonized lucrative crossroads and re-created their bustling bazaars throughout Nepal. Even Newar farmers build their villages in compact, urban nuclei (partly to conserve fertile farmland of the valley).

Centuries of domination by foreign rulers have, if anything, only accentuated the uniqueness of Newar art and architecture. For 1500 years the Newars have sustained an almost continuous artistic flowering in stone, wood, metal and brick. They're believed to have invented the pagoda, and it was a Newar architect, Arniko, who led a Nepali delegation in the thirteenth century to introduce the technique to the Chinese. The pagoda style of stacked, strut-supported roofs finds unique expression in Nepali (read Newar) temples, and is echoed in the overhanging eaves of Newar houses.

Newars are easily recognized. Traditionally they carry heavy loads in baskets suspended at either end of a shoulder pole (*nol*), in contrast with other Nepali hill people who carry things on their backs supported by a tumpline from the forehead. As for clothing, you can usually tell a Newar woman by the fanned pleats at the front of her sari; men have mostly abandoned traditional dress, but some still wear the customary *daura suruwal* and waistcoat.

Highland ethnic groups

People of Tibetan ethnicity have at various times spilled across the Himalaya and settled all the high valleys of Nepal. Cut off from their origins and from each other by harsh terrain, they have developed their own local group identities. These include (from west to east) the **Humlis** of Humla, the **Dolpo-pa** of Dolpo, the **Lo-pa** of Lo (better known as Mustang), the **Larke** of the upper Budhi Gandaki valley, the **Lhomi** of the upper Arun, and the **Olangchung** of the upper Tamur. (Missing from this list are the Sherpas of the Everest region, who are discussed separately opposite.) Nepalis call these peoples by the collective term **Bhotiya**, but this has derogatory connotations, conveying the sense of "unwashed hicks from the sticks who can't speak Nepali properly". Highlanders have been trying to get away from the Bhotiya label ever since it was applied to them in an 1854 government edict, intended to find places for all minority groups in the Hindu caste system, which placed them in the lowly category of "enslavable alcohol-drinkers" because they ate yak meat (which Hindus regarded as being almost as bad as eating beef).

In most ways, members of the highland groups are indistinguishable from Tibetans. Except in certain areas in the far west, where some have been influenced by Hinduism, they are exclusively Buddhist, and their *chorten* (stupa-like cremation monuments), *mani* walls (consisting of slates inscribed with the mantra *Om mani padme hum*), *gompa* (monasteries) and prayer flags (*lung ta*: literally, "wind horse") are the most memorable man-made features of the Himalaya. Farmers, herders and trans-Himalayan traders, they always settle higher and further north than other ethnic groups. The climate there is harsh, and life is a constant struggle to eke out a living by growing barley, buckwheat and potatoes, and herding yaks and yak hybrids. Their villages vary in appearance: those in the west are strongly Tibetan, with houses stacked up slopes so that the flat roof of one serves as the grain-drying terrace of the next, while in the east houses are more likely to be detached and have sloping, shingle roofs. Like Tibetans, they like their tea flavoured with salt and yak butter, and married women wear trademark rainbow aprons (*pangden*) and wraparound dresses (*chuba*).

Unencumbered by caste, highlanders are noticeably less tradition-bound than Hindus, and women are better off for it: they play a nearly equal role in household affairs, speak their minds openly, are able to tease and mingle with men publicly, and can divorce without stigma. (That said, highland peoples still tend to consider a female birth to be the result of bad karma, and during death rites lamas customarily urge the deceased to be reincarnated as a male.)

Sherpas

Nepal's most famous ethnic group, the **Sherpas** probably migrated to Solu-Khumbu four or five centuries ago from eastern Tibet; their name means "People from the East". They were originally nomads, driving their yaks to pasture in Tibet and wintering in Nepal, until change came from an unlikely quarter: the introduction of the potato in the 1830s is believed to have been the catalyst that caused Sherpas to settle in villages, and the extra wealth brought by this simple innovation financed the building of most of the monasteries visible today.

Sherpas maintain the highest permanent settlements in the world – up to 4700m – which accounts for their legendary hardiness at altitude. Their mountaineering talents were discovered as early as 1907, and by the 1920s hundreds of Sherpas were signing on as porters with expeditions to Everest and other Himalayan peaks – from the Tibet side, ironically, as Nepal was closed to foreigners at the time. When mountaineering expeditions were finally allowed into Nepal in 1949, Sherpas took over the lion's share of the portering work, and four years later Tenzing Norgay reached the top of Everest, clinching Sherpas' worldwide fame. The break couldn't have come at a better time, for trans-Himalayan trade, once an important source of income, was cut short by the Chinese occupation of Tibet in 1959. Since then, Sherpas have deftly diversified into tourism, starting their own trekking and mountaineering agencies, opening lodges and selling souvenirs. Conveniently, the trekking season doesn't conflict with summer farming duties.

Sherpas are devout Buddhists, and most villages of note support a *gompa* and a few monks (or nuns). But there are a few animist elements as well: they revere Khumbila, a sacred peak just north of Namche, as a sort of tribal totem, and regard fire as a deity (it's disrespectful to throw rubbish into a Sherpa hearth). Sherpas eat meat, of course, but in deference to the *dharma* they draw the line at slaughtering it – they hire people of other groups to do that.

Tarai groups

Until recently, the **Tarai** was sparsely populated. A few areas – notably Kapil-vastu (Lumbini) and Mithila (Janakpur) – were cleared of jungle and settled by Hindu castes in ancient times; the rest was the domain of the forest-dwelling groups described below.

But Nepalis and North Indians have long viewed the Tarai as the last fron-tier. People have been chipping away at the forest from both sides for centuries, and since the early twentieth century – when, as a preliminary step to abolish-ing slavery, the Nepali government encouraged slaves to homestead in the Tarai – it's been seen as a place where a settler can clear the land and start a new life. In the 1950s, the government's malaria-control programme accelerated the process, and the Tarai has now been largely cleared, tamed and transformed by several million gung-ho immigrants from the hills and India.

Tharus

Two mysteries surround Nepal's second-biggest ethnic minority, the Tarai-dwelling **Tharus**: where they came from, and how they came to be resistant to malaria. Some anthropologists speculate that the tribe migrated from India's eastern hills, filtering across the Tarai over the course of millennia. This would account for their Mongoloid features and Hindu-animist beliefs, but it doesn't fully explain the radically different dialects, dress and customs of different Tharu groups. Isolated by malarial jungle for thousands of years, bands of migrants certainly could have developed their own cultures – but why, given such linguistic and cultural evolution, would the name "Tharu" survive with such consistency? Confusing the issue are the Rana Tharus of the far west, who claim to be descended from high-caste Rajput women who were sent north by their husbands during the Muslim invasions and, when the men never returned for them, married their servants. (There's some circumstantial evidence to support this, as Rana Tharu women are given extraordinary auton-omy in marriage and household affairs.)

As to the matter of malaria resistance, red blood cells seem to play a role – the fact that Tharus are prone to sickle-cell anaemia might be significant – but very little research has been done. At least as significant, Tharus boost their nat-ural resistance with a few common-sense precautions, such as building houses with tiny windows to keep smoke in and mosquitoes (and ghosts) out.

As hunter-gatherers, Tharus are skilled at fishing, snaring pigs and other small animals, and using plants for myriad medicinal and practical purposes. Modern times have forced them to become farmers and livestock raisers, clearing patches in the forest and warding off wild animals from flimsy watchtowers called *machaan*. Their whirling stick dance evokes their uneasy but respectful rela-tionship with the spirits of the forest, as do the raised animal emblems that dec-orate their doorways. Fishing remains an important activity – given the Tarai's high water table, it's easy enough to scoop out a pond and stock it – and you're likely to see fisherwomen wielding hand-held nets between crossed poles, or carrying their catch home in wicker boxes.

Tharu houses are made of mud and dung plastered over wood-and-reed frames, giving them a distinctive ribbed effect. Traditionally, western Tharus built communal longhouses, big enough for a half a dozen families or more and partitioned by huge vial-shaped grain urns, but most have now moved up to detached models. While clothing varies tremendously by area, Tharu women often wear thick silver bracelets above the elbow; tattooing of the forearms and lower legs is common among older women but is falling out of fashion with the younger generation.

The Tharus have fared poorly during the recent land rush. They've been easily swindled or bought out by incomers, and most now are reduced to sharecropping. Traditional culture is still strong in the far west, particularly among the Dangauria and Rana groups, but in other areas it's been all but drowned by a tide of hill, Indian and Western tendencies. Like indigenous peoples the world over, their traditional skills and knowledge of their environment seem to count for little these days.

Other Tarai groups

Several other localized aboriginal groups still inhabit the Tarai and live in similar fashion to the Tharus. The two most likely to be encountered are the **Danuwars**, who are widely distributed in the eastern Tarai, and the **Majhis**, who live in riverside settlements between the Bagmati and the Sun Koshi. Both groups traditionally rely more on fishing than hunting or farming; Majhis, additionally, are ferrymen, plying the rivers of the Tarai (and the lower hills) in dugout canoes.

As mentioned, a small proportion of the Tarai's **Hindu caste** families can claim residency going back to ancient times, but most are first- or second-generation immigrants from India. They maintain close cultural, social and economic ties with their homeland: they speak the languages prevalent in the adjacent parts of India (Hindi, Bhojpuri, Maithili and Bengali, from west to east), hold generally conservative views on religion, caste-consciousness and the role of women, and look across the border for trade and marriage prospects. Unlike the Hindu castes of the hills, those in the Tarai span the full range of castes found in India, from Brahmans down to Sudras.

In addition, a significant number of Muslims – called **Musalmans** in Nepal – inhabit the western Tarai, especially around Nepalganj, where they're in the majority. Although theirs is primarily a religious, rather than an ethnic, identity, Musalmans are quite different culturally from Nepalis and other Indians. For one thing, their monotheism sets them entirely apart from every other group in the region. In addition, they have their own language (Urdu), clothing styles and customs (including the institution of purdah for women). Most are farmers, tailors or shopkeepers; those who specialize in selling bangles and in "teasing" cotton quilts may often be seen in Kathmandu and other hill towns.

Religion: Hinduism, Buddhism and Shamanism

To say that religion is an important part of Nepali life is a considerable under-statement: it *is* life. In the Nepali world view, just about every act has spiritual implications; the gods are assumed to have a hand in every success or mis-fortune and must be appeased continuously. Belief and ritual form the basis of the whole social order, governing the way husbands relate to wives, par-ents to children and even the king to his subjects.

Three religious strands intertwine in Nepal: **Hinduism**, **Buddhism** and **shamanism**. In theory, these faiths are philosophically incompatible, but Nepalis, being an exceptionally tolerant lot, tend to overlook the differences. As practised by the masses, each employs superstition and rites of passage to get followers through the present life, and codes of behaviour to prepare them for the next; Hindu priests, Buddhist lamas and tribal shamans play similar roles in their respective communities. Indeed, it's really only outside observers who bother to distinguish between the religions and dwell on their outward differ-ences – most Nepalis find such distinctions needlessly academic.

Hinduism is the state religion of Nepal, and the government claims that ninety percent of the population is Hindu. However, there are social advantages to professing Hinduism in Nepal, and official statistics don't reflect the extent to which many Nepalis blithely combine Hinduism with Buddhist or shamanistic beliefs. In general, Hinduism prevails at the lower elevations and Buddhism in the Himalaya, while shamanism is strongest among the ethnic minorities of the hills.

Hinduism

Hinduism doesn't conform to Western notions of what a religion should be, and indeed the word "religion" is totally inadequate to describe it. Hindus call it *dharma*, a much more sweeping term that conveys faith, duty, a way of life and the entire social order. Having no common church or institution, its many sects and cults preach different dogmas and emphasize different scriptures. On social matters, Hinduism can be tragically rigid – witness the caste system – and when it comes to rituals, rather petty. Yet it's a highly individualistic sys-tem, offering worshippers an almost limitless choice of deities and admitting many paths to enlightenment. By absorbing and neutralizing opposing doc-trines, rather than condemning them as heresies, it has flourished longer than any other major religion.

Hinduism has been evolving since approximately 1600 BC, when **Aryan** invaders swept down from central Asia and subjugated the native Dravidian peoples of the Indus and Ganges plains. They brought with them a pantheon of nature gods and goddesses, some of whom are still in circulation: Indra (sky and rain) is popular in Kathmandu, while Surya (sun), Agni (fire), Vayu (wind) and Yama (death) retain bit parts in contemporary mythology. These so-called

Vedic gods were first immortalized in the **Vedas** ("Books of Wisdom"), which were probably written between the twelfth and eighth centuries BC, and it was during this period that most of the principles now identified with Hinduism were thrashed out.

To make sure they stayed on top of the conquered Dravidians, the Aryans banned intermarriage and codified the apartheid-like **caste system**; *varna*, the Sanskrit word for caste, means "colour", and to this day members of the higher castes generally have lighter skin. Initially, four castes were established: Brahmans (priests), Kshatriyas (warriors and rulers), Vaisyas (traders and farmers) and Sudras (artisans and menials); over time, the lower two divisions spawned innumerable occupational subcastes. The *Rig Veda*, Hinduism's oldest text, put a divine seal of approval on the arrangement by proclaiming that Brahmans had issued from the head and mouth of the supreme creator, Kshatriyas from his chest and arms, Vaishyas from his thighs and Sudras from his feet.

Entrusted with the brain work, Brahmans (Baahuns in Nepal) proceeded to exploit their position by inventing preposterously complex rituals and sacrifices, and making themselves the indispensable guardians of these mysteries (cow-worship probably dates from this period). Despite this stagnation, the philosophical foundations of Hinduism were laid during the late Vedic period and recorded in a series of discourses known as the **Upanishads**. Ever since, Hinduism has run along two radically different tracks: the Brahmans' hocus-pocus popular religion, with its comic-book deities and bloody sacrifices, and the profound, intuitive insights of gurus and *rishis* (teachers).

The essence of Hinduism, unchanged since the *Upanishads* were written, is that the soul (*atman*) of each living thing is like a lost fragment of the universal soul – **brahman**, the ultimate reality – while everything in the physical universe is mere illusion (*maya*). To reunite with *brahman*, the individual soul must

Aum

"AUM" is a word that represents to our ears that sound of the energy of the universe of which all things are manifestations. You start in the back of the mouth, "ahh," then "oo," you fill the mouth, and "mm" closes the mouth. When you pronounce this properly, all vowel sounds are included in the pronunciation. AUM. Consonants are here regarded simply as interruptions of the essential vowel sound.

All words are thus fragments of AUM, just as all images are fragments of the Form of forms. AUM is a symbolic sound that puts you in touch with that resounding being that is the universe. If you heard some of the recordings of Tibetan monks chanting AUM, you would know what the word means, all right. That's the AUM of being in the world. To be in touch with that and to get the sense of that is the peak experience of all.

A-U-M. The birth, the coming into being, and the dissolution that cycles back. AUM is called the "four-element syllable". A-U-M – and what is the fourth element? The silence out of which AUM arises, and back into which it goes, and which underlies it. My life is the A-U-M, but there is a silence underlying it, too. That is what we would call the immortal. This is the mortal and that's the immortal, and there wouldn't be the mortal if there weren't the immortal. One must discriminate between the mortal aspect and the immortal aspect of one's own existence ... that's why it is a peak experience to break past all that, every now and then, and to realize, "Oh ... ah ..."

From *The Power of Myth*, by Joseph Campbell, reproduced with permission of Doubleday.

go through a **cycle of rebirths** (*samsara*), ideally moving up the scale with each reincarnation. Determining the soul's progress is its **karma** – its accumulated "just desserts" – which is reckoned by the degree to which the soul conformed to **dharma**, or correct Hindu behaviour, in its previous lives. Thus a low-caste Hindu must accept his or her lot to atone for past sins, and follow *dharma* in the hopes of achieving a higher rebirth. The theoretical goal of every Hindu is to cast off all illusion, achieve release (*moksha*) from the cycle of rebirths, and dissolve into *brahman*.

Hinduism has assembled a vast and rich body of mythology over the past three millennia, largely in an effort to personalize *brahman* for the masses. Early on, a few of the Vedic gods were renamed, relieved of their old nature associations and given personalities to illustrate divine attributes. The concept of the **Hindu "trinity"** – Brahma the creator, Vishnu the preserver and Shiva the destroyer – was developed, and the process of god-creation was speeded by the invention of numerous **avatar**, or manifestations of gods. Hinduism's best-loved epics, the *Mahabharata* (pronounced *Mahabharat* in Nepal) and the *Ramayana* (*Ramayan*), portray two of Vishnu's *avatar*, Krishna and Ram, as models of human conduct. (Although as often as not Hindu gods, like their Greek counterparts, are made out to be vain and foolish.)

The explosion of deities has given rise to a succession of **devotional cults** over the centuries, the most important of which nowadays are Vaishnava (followers of Vishnu), Shaiva (Shiva) and Mahadevi (the mother goddess); the last often goes by the name Shakti, a tantric term explained on p.517. Brahma is rarely iconographically depicted and consequently not widely worshipped.

The Hindu pantheon

Hinduism is often alleged to have 33 million **gods**, which may be simply a way of saying that there are more of them than anyone chooses to count. Many of the most popular Nepalese gods, or at least their particular forms, are found only within Nepal itself, and the legends surrounding them may be closely intertwined with earlier animist or nature-worshipping traditions. Gods such as Pashupati – Lord of the Animals, a form of Shiva associated with a wooded hill outside of Kathmandu – clearly predate the arrival of Hinduism to Nepal, but were later given places in the Hindu pantheon by priests determined to bring the local animists into their fold. Even today, the process of "Hinduization" continues, with many of the ancestral spirits and nature gods of the Nepali hill peoples being given Hindu names and places in the Hindu pantheon, their worship adapted to fit more conventional Hindu rituals. When pressed, Nepalis often refer to their local deities as aspects of Mahadev (Shiva), Vishnu or one of the other well-known, mainstream gods, either out of respect for foreigners' potential bewilderment or out of a widespread notion that they all boil down to one supreme god in the end – a paradox that isn't that hard to sustain if you've been trained that everything in this world is illusion anyway.

The most important Hindu gods, described below, can easily be identified by certain trademark implements, postures and "vehicles" (animal carriers). As for gods' multiple arms and heads, these aren't meant to be taken literally – they symbolize the deity's "universal" (omnipotent) form – while severed heads and trampled corpses signify ignorance and evil.

Vishnu

Vishnu (often known as **Narayan** in Nepal) is the face of dignity and equanimity, typically shown standing erect holding a wheel (*chakra*), mace (*gada*), lotus (*padma*) and conch (*sankha*) in his four hands, or, as at Budhanilkantha, reclining on a serpent's coil. A statue of **Garuda** (**Garud** in Nepal), Vishnu's bird-man vehicle, is always close by. Vishnu is also sometimes depicted in one or more of his ten incarnations (*das avatar*), which follow an evolutionary progression from fish, turtle and boar to the man-lion **Narasimha**, a dwarf, an axe-wielding Brahman and the legendary heroes **Ram** and **Krishna**.

Ram is associated with **Hanuman**, his loyal monkey-king ally in the *Ramayan*, while Krishna is commonly seen on posters and calendars as a chubby blue baby, flute-player or charioteer. Interestingly, Vishnu's ninth *avatar* is the Buddha – this was a sixth-century attempt by Vaishnavas to bring Buddhists into their fold – and the tenth is Kalki, a messiah figure invented in the twelfth century when Hindus were being persecuted at the hands of Muslim invaders.

Vishnu's consort is **Lakshmi**, the goddess of wealth, to whom lamps are lit during the festival of Tihaar. Like Vishnu, she assumed mortal form in two great Hindu myths, playing opposite Ram as the chaste princess Sita, and opposite Krishna as the passionate Radha.

Shiva

Shiva's incarnations are countless, ranging from the hideous Bhairab, who alone is said to take 64 different forms, to the benign Pashupati ("Lord of the Animals") and Nataraj ("King of the Dance"). To many devotees he is simply **Mahadev**: Great God. The earliest and still the most widespread icon of Shiva is the **linga**, a phallic stone fertility symbol often housed in a boxy stone *shivalaya* ("Shiva home"). (The phallic aspect of the *linga* is perhaps overplayed by non-Hindus. Gandhi wrote: "It has remained for our Western visitors to acquaint us with the obscenity of many practices which we have hitherto innocently indulged in. It was in a missionary book that I first learned that the Shiva *linga* had any obscene significance at all.") Shiva temples can be identified by the presence of a *trisul* (trident) and the bull **Nandi**, Shiva's mount, who is himself something of a fertility symbol.

Many sadhus worship Shiva the *yogin* (one who practises yoga), the Hindu ascetic supreme, who is often depicted sitting in meditative repose on a Himalayan mountaintop, perhaps holding a chilam of *ganja*. Pashupatinath is the national shrine to Shiva as **Pashupati**, and is patronized by Pashupata, Kaplika and other Shaiva sects, who take it to be Shiva's winter home. Another popular image of Shiva is as the loving husband with his consort, Parbati: the two can be seen leaning from an upper window of a temple in Kathmandu's Durbar Square. Nearby stand two famous statues of **Bhairab**, the tantric (see p.517) interpretation of Shiva in his role as destroyer: according to Hindu philosophy, everything – not only evil – must be destroyed in its turn to make way for new things.

Mahadevi

The mother goddess is similarly worshipped in many forms, both peaceful and wrathful, and many of these are reckoned to be the consorts of corresponding Shiva forms. As **Kali** ("Black") she is the female counterpart of Bhairab, wearing a necklace of skulls and sticking out her tongue with bloodthirsty intent; as **Durga** she is the demon-slayer honoured in the great Dasain festival. In Nepal she is widely worshipped as **Bhagwati**, the embodiment of female creative power. In all these forms, the mother goddess is appeased by sacrifices of uncastrated male animals. On a more peaceful level, she is also **Parbati** ("Hill", daughter of Himalaya), Gauri ("Golden") or just **Mahadevi** ("Great Goddess").

Ganesh and others

Several legends tell how **Ganesh**, Shiva and Parbati's son, came to have an elephant's head: one states that Shiva accidentally chopped the boy's head off, and owing to an unexplained restriction on the god's restorative powers, was forced to replace it with that of the first creature he saw. The god of wisdom and remover of obstacles, Ganesh must be worshipped first to ensure offerings to other gods will be effective, which is why a Ganesh shrine or stone will invariably be found near other temples. Underscoring Hinduism's great sense of the mystical absurd, Ganesh's vehicle is a rat.

Of the other classical Hindu deities, only **Annapurna**, the goddess of grain and abundance (her name means "Full of Grain"), and **Saraswati**, the goddess of learning and culture, receive much attention in Nepal. Saraswati is normally depicted holding a *vina*, a musical instrument something like a sitar.

Buddhism

The Buddha was born Siddhartha Gautama in what is now Nepal (see p.356) in the fifth or sixth century BC, and his teachings were in many ways a protest against the ritualism to which popular Hinduism had by then been reduced. The Buddha rejected the Hindu caste system and the belief in a creator God, while adapting its doctrines of reincarnation and *karma*, along with many yogic practices. The result was a nontheistic, pragmatic philosophy that placed a greater emphasis on the active pursuit of enlightenment.

Whereas the Hindu ideal is to reunite with the Creator, the Buddhist goal is **nirvana**, a state of being where wisdom and compassion have completely uprooted the "three poisons" of greed, hatred and delusion. The essence of the Buddha's teaching is encapsulated in the **four noble truths**: existence is suffering; suffering is caused by desire; the taming of desire ends suffering; and desire can be tamed by following the **eightfold path**, a set of deceptively simple guidelines for achieving *dharma*. He called the whole prescription the **Middle Way** because it avoided the extremes of sensual indulgence and asceticism, both of which were popularly believed to lead to enlightenment if pursued with sufficient vigour (and the Buddha had tried them both pretty vigorously before rejecting them).

As it developed, Buddhism became a full-time monastic pursuit for many followers. But for most lay people, the lonely quest for enlightenment was too hardcore and impersonal; to restore emotional elements that had been lost in the monastic movement, Buddhism evolved a populist strand known as **Mahayana** ("Great Vehicle"). Reintroducing elements of worship and prayer, Mahayana Buddhism developed its own pantheon of *bodhisattva* – enlightened intermediaries, something akin to Catholic saints, who have forgone *nirvana* until all humanity has been saved. Many of these were a repackaging of older Hindu deities, who were now given new names and roles as protectors of the *dharma*.

Followers of the original teachings called their school **Theravada** ("Way of the Elders"), but to Mahayana Buddhists it came to be known, somewhat disparagingly, as **Hinayana** ("Lesser Vehicle"). This tradition remains active in Sri Lanka and much of Southeast Asia. It was the Mahayana doctrine that came to Nepal, around the fifth century, and also spread to China, Korea and Japan, adapting differently to each. Buddhism in India was dealt a death blow in the seventh century by Muslim invasions, which destroyed the great monastic universities and the thousands of monks who lived in them; what was left of Buddhism was effectively absorbed into the ocean of Hinduism.

Tantra and Vajrayana

Even as Buddhism was on the wane in India, a new religious movement was developing in Bengal and Bihar that would give a radically new bent to both Buddhism and Hinduism. **Tantra** erupted like the punk rock of religion, proclaiming that *everything* in life can be used to reach enlightenment. The five things normally shunned in orthodox Hinduism and Buddhism as poisons – meat, fish, parched grains, alcohol and sex – are embraced on the tantric path. Sex, in particular, is regarded as the central metaphor for spiritual enlightenment, and it is this inversion of the sacred and profane that has given *tantra* its undeserved risqué reputation: the fact is that sexual tantric practices are employed only in very special circumstances. *Tantra* abounds in esoteric imagery, *mantra* (verbal formulas) and *mandala* (diagrams used to aid meditation), which together make up a sort of mystic code intended only for initiates.

According to **Hindu tantra**, the female principle (**shakti**) possesses the creative energy which is capable of activating the male force. The gods are powerless until joined with their female counterparts – in tantric art, Bhairab is often shown locked in a fierce sexual embrace – and in many of her guises the mother goddess has become Shakti, one half of a tantric union of sexual opposites. The human psyche, too, is held to consist of male and female forces that must be harnessed: followers of Hindu *tantra* are trained to visualize the body's female energy rising like a snake from the level of the sexual organs, ascending the seven psychic centres (*chakra*) of the spinal column to reach the male principle at the top of the head, resulting in realization.

Buddhist tantra, known as **Vajrayana** ("Thunderbolt Way"), reverses the symbolism of these two forces and makes the male principle of "skill in means" or compassion the active force, and the female principle of "wisdom" passive. In tantric rituals, these forces are symbolized by the hand-held "lightning-bolt sceptre" (*vajra*; *dorje* in Tibetan), which represents the male principle, and the bell (*ghanti*), representing the female. Expanding on Mahayana's all-male pantheon, Vajrayana introduces female counterparts to the main Buddha figures and some of the *bodhisattva*, and sometimes depicts them in sexual positions.

Lamaism (Tibetan Buddhism)

Vajrayana Buddhism found its greatest expression in Tibet, which it reached (by way of Nepal) in the eighth century. At the time, Tibet was under the sway of a native shamanic religion known as **Bon**; Vajrayana eventually overcame Bon, but only by taking on board many of its symbols and rituals, thus creating the spectacularly distinct branch of Buddhism that outsiders call **Lamaism**. (Unrepentant Bon priests were banished to the Himalayan periphery, and even today vestiges of the Bon tradition may be encountered while trekking in Nepal: for example, a follower of Bon will circle a religious monument anticlockwise, the opposite direction to a Buddhist.)

Lamaism turned Bon's demons into fierce guardian deities (*dharmapala*) – these can usually be seen flanking monastery (*gompa*) entrances – and incorporated elements of Bon magic into its meditational practices. Since blood sacrifices were out of the question, they were adapted into "vegetarian" offerings in the form of conical dough cakes called *torma*. The *Bardo Thödol* ("Tibetan Book of the Dead") is basically a shamanic guide to the after-death experience that probably owes much to Bon.

While its underlying principles aren't very different from those of Mahayana Buddhism, Lamaism has a tendency to express them in incredibly esoteric symbolism. The **Wheel of Life**, often depicted in *thangka* and frescoes at monastery entrances, is an intricate exposition of the different levels of rebirth and the limitations of the unenlightened state. The **stupa** (*chorten* in Tibetan), an ancient abstract representation of the Buddha, is developed into a complex statement of Buddhist cosmology, and Buddhahood is refracted into five aspects, symbolized by the five transcendent or *dhyani* (meditating) Buddhas, which can be seen in niches surrounding the Swayambhu stupa. **Prayer wheels**, usually bearing the mantra *Om mani padme hum* ("Hail to the jewel in the lotus"), are Tibetan innovations that aid meditative concentration, and **prayer flags** also bear mantra and wishes for compassion which are meant to be picked up and spread by the wind.

An important feature of Tibetan Buddhism are its **bodhisattva**, which are often mistaken for deities. Held to be emanations of the *dhyani* Buddhas, they are used in meditation and rituals to help develop the qualities they symbolize, and also serve as objects of devotion. The most popular figures are **Avalokiteshwara** (**Chenrezig** in Tibetan), a white male figure with four arms (or, sometimes, a thousand), who represents compassion; **Tara**, a white or green female figure, also representing compassion; and **Manjushri**, an orange-yellow male youth gracefully holding a sword above his head, who represents wisdom. Though these figures are peaceful and benign, there are also wrathful ones with bulging eyes, often wearing human skins and drinking blood, who symbolize the energy and potency of the enlightened state and the sublimation of our crudest energies.

From the beginning, Tibetan Buddhism placed great emphasis on close contact with a **lama**, or spiritual guide, who can steer the student through the complex meditations and rituals. Teachings were passed on orally from lama to disciple, so the divergence of various sects over the centuries has had more to do with different lineages than with major doctrinal differences. The leader of each sect, and indeed of each monastery, is venerated as the reincarnation (*tulku*) of his or her predecessor, and is expected to carry on the same spiritual tradition. Of the **four main sects**, the oldest is the Nyingma-pa ("Red Hats"), founded in the eighth century by Guru Padma Sambhava, who, if all the stories told about him were true, meditated in every cave in Nepal. The Sakya-pa broke away in the eleventh century, tracing their line from the second-century Indian philosopher Nagarjun. The Kagyu-pa order emerged in the eleventh and twelfth centuries, inspired by the Tibetan mystic Marpa and his enlightened disciple Milarepa, who also meditated his way around Nepal. The Gelug-pa ("Yellow Hats") sect, led by the Dalai Lama, is the only one that takes a significantly different theological line. Born out of a fifteenth-century reform movement to purge Lamaism of its questionable religious practices, it places greater emphasis on study and intellectual debate.

The Newar synthesis

Ask a Newar whether he's Hindu or Buddhist, the saying goes, and he'll answer "yes": after fifteen centuries of continuous exposure to both faiths, the Newars of the Kathmandu Valley have concocted a unique synthesis of the two. To religious scholars, the Newar religion is as exciting as a biologist's missing link, for some believe that it provides a picture of the way Mahayana and Vajrayana Buddhism functioned historically in India.

Until the eighteenth century, most Newars held fast to the original monastic form of tantric Buddhism – as the *bahal* of Kathmandu and Patan still bear witness – while their rulers pursued the Hindu tantric path. However, the Kathmandu Valley has become progressively "**Hinduized**" since the unification of Nepal: the monasteries have largely disappeared, their monks have married, and the title of Vajracharya (Buddhist priest) has become a hereditary subcaste like that of the Baahun (Brahman) priests. Although the acceptance of caste and the decline of monasticism have shifted the balance in favour of Hinduism, at the popular level the synthesis remains as well bonded as ever.

When Newars refer to themselves as **Buddha margi** (Buddhist) or **Shiva margi** (Hindu), they often do so only to indicate that they employ a Vajracharya or Baahun priest. Even this doesn't always hold true, though, as many *jyapu* (farmers) call themselves "Hindu" and attend Hindu festivals, yet still use Vajracharyas. Newar religion is less concerned with theology than it is with the performance of day-to-day rituals to keep the individual on the right side of deities and other supernatural forces.

Newars observe a large range of rituals, from the individual to the collective and from the private to the public. **Puja**, common to almost all Nepalis as well as Newars, is any act of worship or propitiation offered to avoid a deity's displeasure or obtain its blessing. A personal ritual, *puja* may be done before a shrine in the home, an open-air statue or sacred spot, or a temple deity. An integral part of most Newar worship is the *"puja* of five offerings", consisting of flowers (usually marigolds), incense, light (in the form of butter lamps), *abhir* (coloured powder) and various kinds of purified food (usually rice, dairy products or sweets).

A typical Newar will undergo five or more **rites of passage** (*samskars*) in his or her life: the rice-feeding ceremony, when the baby is given its first solid food; the pre-pubescent tonsure ceremony for boys, in which the head is shaved (except for a small tuft at the back); the pre-pubescent *ihi* ceremony for girls, in which they are symbolically married to the god Narayan to ensure (it's said) they can never be widowed; *kyeta puja*, the male initiation rite, marking a boy's fully fledged membership in the community; *barha*, a purification rite observed by girls around the time of the first menstruation; marriage, which traditionally is solemnized by the serving of a platter containing 84 different kinds of food; three old-age *samskars*, held at 77 years, seven months and seven days, 83 years, four months and four days, and 99 years, nine months and nine days; and the one nobody can escape, death and cremation.

Most of these rites of passage are accompanied by elaborate **purification ceremonies** and family feasts, the details of which vary by *thar* (clan or subcaste). Similar ceremonies and feasts are held at private gatherings of patrilineal groups during the Newars' many **festivals** (see p.55) and during **digu puja**, the annual reunion based around the worship of the clan deity (*digu dyo*).

Newar **priests**, like those of other ethnic groups, officiate at the more important rites and festivals, and may also give private consultations for wealthier patrons at times of illness or important decisions. Temple priests preside over the act of **darshan** (audience with a deity), providing consecrated water for the devotee to wash him or herself and to bathe the deity, leading the *puja* and the symbolic offering of food to the deity, and bestowing on the devotee a **tika**, a mark on the forehead made with coloured powder, yogurt and rice. The *tika*, along with the consecrated food offering (called **prasad**), confer the deity's blessing and protection.

Animal sacrifice is an important part of Hindu Newar religious practice (see p.215). Newar priests don't perform sacrifices, but they do preside over the rituals that precede them. This brings up one of the rare differences between Hindu and Buddhist Newars: while Hindu Newars are enthusiastic sacrificers – they call the bloody ninth day of the Dasain festival *Syako Tyako* (roughly, "the more you kill, the more you gain") – Buddhists seldom participate.

Many other members of Newar society function in spiritual capacities, either as full-time parapriests or in bit parts during rites of passage and festivals. Members of the Vajracharya subcaste, **Gubhajus** are tantric healers who employ *vajrayana* techniques and accoutrements to cure ailments caused by malevolent spirits. **Baidyas** play a similar role but draw from a more diverse range of Hindu, Buddhist and shamanic techniques including *jhar-phuk* ("sweeping" away bad influences and "blowing" on healing mantras), *puja*, amulets and ayurvedic medicines. **Jyotish** – astrologers – specialize in helping clients deal with planetary influences and their corresponding deities (see box below).

A visit to the astrologer

His name is Joshi – in Newar society, all members of the astrologer subcaste are called Joshi – and to get to his office I have to duck through a low doorway off a courtyard in the old part of Patan and feel my way up two flights of wooden steps in the dark, climbing towards a glimmer of light and the sounds of low murmuring. At the landing I take off my shoes and enter the sanctum. Joshi-ji doesn't even look up. He's sitting cross-legged on the floor behind a low desk, glasses perched on the end of his nose, scowling over a sheaf of papers and, except for his Nepali-style clothes, looking exactly the way I'd always pictured Professor Godbole in *A Passage to India*. Shelves of books and scrolls are heaped behind him, and over in one corner a small shrine is illuminated by a low-watt bulb and a smouldering stick of incense. An older couple is seated in front of Joshi-ji's desk, nervously asking a question of the great man; he pushes his glasses up on his forehead, scribbles something, then pulls himself up to answer in melodic, nasal tones. I settle down on the floor next to two other waiting couples and together we keep a respectful silence.

To Newars, the **astrologer** is a counsellor, confessor, general practitioner and guide through the maze of life. With the priest and the doctor, he acts as mediator between the self and the universe (which are one); and since astrology is but one branch of Hindu knowledge, his prognostications on important occasions are considered as important as a priest's blessings, and he is often called upon to provide a second opinion on a doctor's diagnosis. He knows most of his clients from birth. For new parents, the astrologer will prepare complex planetary charts based on the baby's precise time and place of **birth**, together with a lengthy interpretation detailing personality traits, health hazards, vocational aptitude, characteristics of the ideal marriage partner, and a general assessment of the newborn's prospects. When a **marriage** is contemplated, he will study the horoscopes of the prospective couple to make sure the match is suitable, and if so, he'll perform further calculations to determine the most auspicious wedding date. During an **illness**, he may prescribe a protective amulet, gemstone or herbal remedy corresponding to the planets influencing the patient. He may also be consulted on the advisability of a business decision or a major purchase.

While Western astrology is well suited to an independent, egocentric culture, **Hindu astrology** is much more at ease with the insignificance of the individual in the midst of the vast cosmos. And unlike the Western system, which is regarded more as a tool for personal fulfilment, the Hindu tradition emphasizes external events and how – and when – to deal with them. The **horoscope** represents a snapshot of the subject's *karma*: at the precise moment of reincarnation, the planets display the tally,

The Newar pantheon

All the Hindu and Buddhist deities already discussed are fair game for Newars, along with a few additional characters of local invention. Some deities specialize in curing diseases, others bring good harvests – as far as Newars are concerned, it doesn't matter whether they're Hindu or Buddhist so long as they do the job.

Perhaps the most widely worshipped of the Newars' deities is **Ajima**, the grandmother goddess, who is both feared as a bringer of disease and misfortune and revered as a protectress against the same. There are innumerable Ajimas, each associated with a particular locality. In many cases, goddesses worshipped as Durga, Bhagwati or Kali are also regarded by Newars as Ajimas; these include the **Ashta Matrika**, the eight mother goddesses, whose temples in and around Kathmandu are considered especially powerful. Similar are the

and although it's misleading to speak in terms of planetary "influences", the *karma* that they reveal strongly implies the future course of one's life. The astrologer's role, then, is to suggest the best way to play the hand one was dealt.

The Hindu method of generating horoscopes follows the same essential principles as in the Western tradition, although technical differences between the two will produce somewhat different results. Hindu astrology recognizes the same twelve **signs of the zodiac**, albeit under different (Sanskrit) names, and assigns many of the same attributes to the planets and houses. The basic **birth chart** indicates the **sun sign** (the sign corresponding to the sun's position at the time of birth), the ascendant or "rising" sign (the sign rising above the eastern horizon at the time of birth) and the positions of the moon and the five planets known to the ancients, plus a couple of other non-Western points of reference. The positions of all of these are also noted in relation to the twelve **houses**, each of which governs key aspects of the subject's life (health, relationships and so on). The chief technical difference between Western and Hindu horoscopy is in how they line up the signs of the zodiac with respect to the earth. Western astrologers use the **tropical zodiac**, in which Aries is always assumed to start on the spring equinox (March 21, give or take a day), even though a wobble in the earth's axis causes the actual constellations to drift out of sync by 30° (one sign) every 2150 years – that's why it's now Pisces that the sun enters on March 21, and within the next century or two, astrologically speaking, we will officially enter the age of Aquarius. Hindu astrologers, on the other hand, go by the **sidereal zodiac**, which takes all its measurements from the *actual* positions of the constellations. (Technically speaking, this is a pretty profound difference, but since the Western and Hindu methods of interpretation are different, it all comes out in the wash.) If you have a horoscope done in Nepal, you'll probably be presented with a beautifully calligraphed scroll detailing all these measurements in chart and tabular form, using both tropical and sidereal measurements.

If charting a horoscope is largely a matter of mathematical donkey work, **interpretation** is an intuitive art requiring great eloquence and finesse. The astrologer can draw on numerous texts describing every conceivable conjunction of planets, and the positive and negative effects of every planet on every house; but at the end of the day, the usefulness of the reading must come down to the astrologer's own skill and experience. As I found on my visit to Joshi-ji, the specifics aren't everything. The astrologer isn't peddling facts; he's offering insight, hope, reassurance and a dash of theatre.

David Reed

tantric **Bajra Yoginis** (or Vajra Joginis), who command their own cults centred at four temples around the Kathmandu Valley. Local manifestations of Ajima are represented by clusters of round stones (*pith*) located at intersections and other strategic places around Newar cities and towns. Chwasa Ajima, the Ajima of the crossroads, has the power to absorb death pollution, which is why Newars traditionally deposited possessions of deceased persons at certain crossroads locations. In rural areas, the term **Mai** is often used interchangeably with Ajima to refer to a local nature or mother goddess. **Nag** (snake deities), who control the rains and are responsible for earthquakes, may be similarly indicated by modest roadside markers, and are offered *puja* during the monsoon festival of Nag Panchami.

Machhendranath, honoured as a rainmaker *par excellence*, typifies the layering of religious motifs that so frequently takes place among the Newars. To be accurate, only Hindus call the god Machhendranath; Buddhist Newars know him as **Karunamaya** or by any of a number of local names. He is commonly associated with Avalokiteshwara, the *bodhisattva* of compassion, who is invoked by the mantra *Om mani padme hum*. Depending on his incarnation (he is said to have 108), he may be depicted as having anything up to a thousand arms and eleven heads. While it's unclear how Avalokiteshwara came to be associated with the historical figures of Machhendranath and Gorakhnath – who are considered saints by Hindus – it was certainly in part the result of a conscious attempt by Hindu rulers to establish religious and social bonds by grafting two Hindu saints on to a local Buddhist cult.

Kumari, the "Living Goddess", is another often-cited example of Newar syncretism (religious fusing): although acknowledged to be an incarnation of the Hindu goddess Durga, she is picked from a Buddhist-caste family. **Bhimsen**, a mortal hero in the Hindu *Mahabharat*, who is rarely worshipped in India, has somehow been elevated to be the patron deity of Newar shopkeepers, both Hindu and Buddhist.

Manjushri, the *bodhisattva* of wisdom, has been pinched from the Buddhist pantheon to play the lead part in the Kathmandu Valley's creation myth (although he is often confused with Saraswati, the Hindu goddess of knowledge). He is always depicted with a sword, with which he cuts away ignorance and attachment, and sometimes also with a book, bow, bell and *vajra*. Likewise **Tara**, the embodiment of the female principle in Vajrayana Buddhism, assumes special meaning for Newars, who consider her the deification of an eighth-century Nepali princess.

Other supernatural forces

The traditional Newar worldview doesn't make a sharp distinction between the physical and spiritual worlds. Even in an age of cable TV and modern medicine, many Newars – like Nepalis in general – still attribute their ill health or other troubles to a variety of supernatural causes. According to some psychologists, these beliefs are an understandable coping mechanism against the many hardships of life in Nepal, and a safe way to displace repressed tensions and jealousies stemming from living in very close quarters and under rigid social strictures.

Newars have a rich lore of **demons**, **ghosts** and **spirits** who meddle in human affairs and, like deities, must be propitiated to safeguard passage through their respective domains. Demons are sometimes thought to be the wrathful or perverted manifestations of deities, or more often as supernatural ogres, vampires and the like. Some demons, such as the *lakhe*, are regarded somewhat fondly, or, like the *betal*, can also serve as temple protectors. *Bhut pret* – restless ghosts – are thought to be the spirits of people who died an accidental or violent death and were not administered the proper funeral rites. Other evil spirits take the form of poltergeist-like dwarves, furry balls, or temptresses with their feet pointing backwards; the design of traditional Newar windows is intended to prevent such spirits from entering the house. Since spirits are believed to attack mainly at night and are repelled by light, the fear of them has abated somewhat since electrification.

All too often, Newars blame their troubles on **witches** (*bokshi*), who are believed to be able to cast "black" tantric spells by giving the evil eye or reciting mantras over their victims' food. Evidence of bewitchment is often seen in bruises called "*bokshi* bites". "Witches" are usually neighbours, in-laws or other people known to their alleged victims. Although laws prohibit false accusations of witchcraft, this doesn't protect many people (particularly elderly women) from suffering unspoken fear and resentment for their alleged dark arts.

A final category of supernatural forces is negative **planetary influences** (*graha dosa*), caused by the displeasure of the deity associated with the offending planet.

Shamanism

Shamanism is followed in diverse ways throughout the world by peoples that have been overlooked by the great institutional religions. Variously described as medicine men, witch doctors or oracles, shamans perform mystical rituals to mediate between the physical and spiritual realms on behalf of their flock.

Shamanism, which is thought to have originated in Siberia or Mongolia, is a vital element in the traditional culture of most of Nepal's native ethnic groups. It may even be one of the most ancient strands of religious life in the Himalayan region, though it would be futile to try to separate it from animist or nature-worshipping practices, which are themselves thoroughly intertwined with Himalayan forms of Hinduism and Buddhism. The picture is further confused by the fact that many of Nepal's ethnic groups have adopted at least outward forms of Hinduism or Buddhism.

Whatever its origins, it's certain that shamanism is still widely practised in the eastern and western hills, and even in Kathmandu, where the shaman's double-headed drum can sometimes be heard beating behind closed doors. How widely it's practised isn't known, however, as shamans perform most of their rituals in private homes, often at night, and have a tendency to guard their esoteric knowledge jealously, wrapping it up in archaic, poetic language that veers between the mystical and the mystifying. Shamanism's associations with "primitive" culture have led many more-urbane Nepalis to publicly shun or ridicule it in favour of more "modern" beliefs such as orthodox Hinduism – even if they will privately call on a shaman to exorcise a new house or deal with a case of toothache. There are signs of new confidence, however, with a Gurung shamanic cultural centre and training school in Pokhara (see p.298), and a government project to use shamans to conduct health awareness campaigns in rural areas.

In Nepali, the generic terms for shaman are **jhankri** and **dhami**, but these are the words of a language foreign to shamanic traditions. Most ethnic groups clearly distinguish in their languages and practices between the true shaman, whose duties, rituals and powers are concerned with the spiritual world, and other types of tribal priest, whose concerns may be with seasonal rituals, rites of passage or tribal myth, and whose roles have been more easily absorbed by mainstream Hinduism and Buddhism. For all the many local variations, a *jhankri* – usually carrying a double-sided drum and often wearing a headdress of peacock feathers – is always unmistakable. And even across ethnic and religious divides, *jhankris* may come together on high hilltops or at lakes deep in the mountains for *melas*, or religious fairs.

The *jhankri* may be "called", or born, or both, and his (almost never her) main job is to maintain spiritual and physical balance, and to restore it when it has been upset. As a healer, he may examine the entrails of animals for signs, gather medicinal plants from the forest, perform sacrifices, exorcise demons, chant magical incantations to invoke helper deities, or conduct any number of other rituals. As an oracle, he may fall into a trance and act as a mouthpiece of the gods, advising, admonishing and consoling listeners. As the spiritual sentry of his community, he must ward off ghosts, evil spirits and angry ancestors – sometimes by superior strength, often by trickery. All this, plus his duties as funeral director, dispenser of amulets, teller of myths and consecrator of holy ground and so on, puts the *jhankri* at the very heart of religious and social life in the hills. Little wonder that Hinduism and Buddhism have been so shaped in Nepal by shamanistic traditions, producing unique forms of these great religions that, like the shaman, seek to touch the spiritual world.

Music and dance

There are as many different styles of Nepali music and dance as there are ethnic groups. These traditional arts are rarely performed outside Nepal, which means that you'll be in a position to appreciate some wonderfully rare sounds and sights as you travel around the country. Meanwhile, a new wave of non traditional Nepali music is beginning to break into the world-music charts, and as a traveller in Nepal you'll be able to sample the full range and pick up the latest releases.

Classical and religious

Little attempt has been made to chart the history of Nepali music. However, one of the earliest influences surely must have been **Indian classical music**, which goes back to a time when there was no distinction between India and Nepal, and to a region that extended well beyond the present borders of India. Classical music of the north Indian style flourished at the courts of the Malla kings and reached its zenith in Nepal under the Rana prime ministers, who patronized Indian musicians in their court to the exclusion of Nepali folk performers. Though it was always primarily an aristocratic genre, there is still a lively classical music network in Kathmandu, with tourist culture-shows supplementing public performances (and private recitals – for example, bimonthly at the royal palace).

Newar Buddhist priests still sing esoteric **tantric hymns** which, when accompanied by **mystical dances** and hand postures, are believed to have immense occult power. The secrets of these are closely guarded by initiated priests, but a rare public performance is held on Buddha Jayanti, when five *vajracharya* costumed as the Pancha Buddha dance at Swayambhu.

The contemporary layman's form of sacred music is **bhajan** – devotional hymn-singing, usually performed in front of temples and in rest houses. *Bhajan* groups gather on auspicious evenings to chant praises to Ram, Krishna or other Hindu deities; during festivals they may carry on through the night, and round-the-clock vigils are sometimes sponsored by wealthy patrons. Like a musical *puja*, the haunting verses are repeated over and over to the mesmeric beat of the tabla and the drone of the harmonium.

Sherpas and other highlanders have their own ritualistic music rooted in **Tibetan Buddhist** traditions. Rhythm is more important than melody in this crashing, banging music, which is the exclusive preserve of monks. There's a hierarchy of instruments in the lamaist orchestra, from the *ghanti* (bell), *sankha* (conch shell) and *jhyaamta* (small cymbals), through the *bugcham* (large cymbals), *kangling* (small trumpet, made from a human thigh bone) and *dhyangro* (bass drum), to the *gyaling* (jewel-encrusted shawm, or oboe) and *radung* (a ten-foot-long telescopic trumpet, which looks like a Swiss alpenhorn and produces a sound like a subsonic fart). The human voice forms a separate instrument in the mix, as monks recite prayers in deep, dirge-like chanting.

Folk

For Nepalis where electricity and videos haven't yet reached, **folk music** (*git lok*) and dancing is still just about the only form of entertainment available. On holidays and festival days, the men of a village or neighbourhood will typically gather in a circle for an evening session of singing and socializing; as a rule only the men perform on these occasions, while the women look on.

The musical backing always consists of a **maadal** (horizontally held two-sided drum), and often also includes other drums, harmonium and *murali* (bamboo piccolo) or *bansuri* (flute). After some preliminary tapping on the *maadal*, a member of the group will strike up a familiar verse, and all join in on the chorus; the first singer runs through as many verses as he can remember, at which point someone else takes over, often making up comical verses to suit the occasion. Members of the group dance to the music one at a time, each entertaining onlookers with his interpretation of the song in swirling body movements, facial expressions and hand gestures.

Young men and women of the hill tribes also sing improvised, flirtatious call-and-response duets known as **dohori**; the woman may even take the lead in these, forcing the man to come up with rejoinders to her jesting verses. They also sing and dance together (though again, not at the same time) at **rodi ghar**, the Nepali equivalent of a sock hop. Originally a Gurung institution, *rodi* has been embraced by many other hill groups as an informal, musical means of courtship. In addition, women also sing in the fields to ease the burden of manual work – especially during *ropai* (rice transplanting), which has its own traditional songs.

Folk musical traditions vary among Nepal's many ethnic groups, but the true sound of Nepal may be said to be the soft and melodic – but rhythmically complex – music of the hills. Of several hill styles, **jhyaure**, the *maadal*-based music of the western hills, has emerged as the most popular. **Selo**, the musical style of the Tamangs that's performed to the accompaniment of the *damphu* (a one-sided, flat, round drum), has also been adopted by other ethnic communities. The music of the **Jyapu** (Newar farmers) has a lively rhythm, provided by the *dhime* (big two-sided drum) and a host of other drums, percussion instruments and woodwinds, though the singing has a nasal quality that's hard for outsiders to appreciate.

Although folk music is, by definition, a pursuit of amateurs, two traditional castes of professional musicians exist in Nepal. Wandering minstrels, known as **gaaine** or **gandarbha**, have always served as an important unifying force in the hills, relaying not only news but also songs and musical styles from village to village. Accompanying themselves on *sarangi* (four-stringed fiddles), *gaaine* once thrived under patronage from local chieftains, whose deeds were the main topics of their songs. They're on the decline nowadays, but a few still ply their trade in the villages north of Pokhara, in the far west, and in Kirtipur in the Kathmandu Valley (these are not to be confused with the hack *sarangi* sellers of Thamel and Lakeside). Their repertoire includes sacred songs in praise of Hindu deities, bittersweet ballads of toil and triumph, great moments in Nepali history and political commentary and even government propaganda.

Much more numerous are the **damai**, members of the tailor caste, who for generations have served as wedding musicians (see below), and may also be employed at shrines to play during daily offerings and blood sacrifices. The tai-

lor-musician combination isn't as strange as it might sound: Nepalis traditionally used to have just one set of clothes made each year, for the autumn Dasain
festival, so tailors needed an occupation to tide them over during the winter
and spring. Handily, that's the wedding season, when musicians are much in
demand.

Weddings and festivals

Until recently, no wedding could be complete without **paanchai baajaa** (five
instruments), a traditional Nepali ensemble of *sahanai* (shawm), *damaha* (large
kettledrum), *narsinga* (C-shaped horn), *jhyaali* (cymbals) and *dholaki* (two-sided
drum). Despite the name, bands ideally number nine members – eleven is the
legal maximum, set to keep wedding costs down. "They got married without
paanchai baajaa" is still a euphemism for living together. However, town and
city folk nowadays prefer the more modern sound of **band baajaa**, in which
the musicians trade their traditional instruments for Western brass horns and
clarinets, and their ceremonial dress for fanciful, military-style uniforms.

Raucous and jubilant, *paanchai* or *band baajaa* is considered an auspicious
accompaniment to processions, Hindu rituals and life-cycle rites. During a
wedding, the band accompanies the groom to the home of the bride, plays
during the wedding ceremony, and again during the return procession. Apart
from performing popular folk songs and film favourites, the musicians have a
traditional repertoire of numbers for specific occasions – for example, the
"bride-requesting tune", in which the shawm player mimics the bride's wail-
ing as she departs from her family home, and the music of the rice-transplant-
ing season, which imitates the body rhythm of the workers.

Festivals bring their own interwoven forms of music and dance, especially
in the Kathmandu Valley. The Newars of the valley are renowned for their spectacular **masked dances**, in which the dancers enter a trance-like state to
become the embodiments of the gods they portray, gesturing and gyrating
behind elaborately painted papier-mâché masks. Best known of these are
Bhaktapur's Nawa Durga dancers and their supporting musicians: their vigor-
ous dance-drama, held on the tenth day of Dasain, recounts the victory of the
goddess Durga over a buffalo demon. In Kathmandu, several different troupes
perform during Indra Jaatra.

Virtuoso **drummers**, the Jyapus (Newar farmers) of the valley provide the
rolling beat for processions on festival days: generally they beat enormous
cylindrical drums (*dhime baajaa*) in groups with two sizes of cymbal. At some
shrines, in addition to a singing group, there is a complement of nine drums
(*nawa daaphaa*), which are played in sequence during festivals with various
accompanying instruments. Another type of popular processional band, *bansuri
baajaa*, combines flutes and barrel drums.

Tibetans and other highlanders have their own form of dance-drama, **cham**.
Tengboche hosts the most famous of such performances, Mani Rimdu, on the
day after the full moon of October–November (another performance is held
at Thami in May), when monks wearing masks and costumes represent various
good and bad guys in the story of Buddhism's victory over the ancient Bon
religion in Tibet. Monasteries at Boudha and Swayambhu also present *cham*
dances around Losar (Tibetan New Year).

Modern music

Pre-1951, Nepal had no radio and no recording industry, and those few artists who travelled to Calcutta to record their songs on 78rpm were known only to a handful of aristocrats with record-players. The dawn of modern Nepali music came in 1952, the year after the fall of the Ranas, when **Radio Nepal** was established; only a year later, Dharma Raj Thapa made recording history, selling 3000 copies of a novelty song about the conquest of Everest by Hillary and Tenzing Norgay.

A home-grown **recording industry** took root under King Mahendra (1955–72), himself something of a patron of the arts, and with it came Nepal's first wave of **recording stars**. Still the best loved of these, though he died in 1991, is Narayan Gopal, whose songs are praised for their poignant *sukha-dukha* (happiness-sadness); the late Aruna Lama is also remembered for her renditions of sad and sentimental numbers. Kumar Basnet remains popular for his folk songs, while Meera Rana is still in her prime, belting out classical, folk and even pop tunes. Several of Nepal's foremost composers also came out of this era, including Amber Gurung, Nati Kazi and the late Gopal Yonjan.

More recently, the growth of the Nepali **film industry** has opened up new horizons for composers and singers; television, introduced in the mid-1980s, has provided a further boost. These have in turn contributed to the establishment of new recording studios and cassette- and CD-reproduction concerns. That said, cinema and TV have also done their share of harm. By copying third-rate Indian productions, Nepali films have mainly enlarged the market for lowest-common-denominator music, turning audiences and musicians away from traditional styles and opening the floodgates to slick, Indian-produced *masaala* ("spicy": a little of this, a little of that).

Other recent developments have cut both ways, too. Tourist culture-shows have inevitably led to the commercialization of Nepali culture and music, yet they've also helped preserve folk arts by providing a source of income for musicians and dancers. **Ghazal**, another Indian import (see p.159), has done nothing for Nepali music, but it too pays the rent for Nepali musicians. Even Radio Nepal gives with one hand and takes away with the other, by providing an important outlet for musicians but at the same time blurring regional differences.

A few Nepali groups have recently achieved crossover success with East-meets-West **fusion music**, employing traditional instruments in non-traditional arrangements and recording to high production standards. The flute-sitar-tabla trio Sur Sudha has defined this sound: members Prem Rana (flute), Bijaya Vaidya (sitar) and Surendra Shrestha (tabla) are the closest thing Nepal has to international stars, and have done much to advance Nepali music by establishing a musical institute and producing albums by other artists.

Pop music is of course a growing proposition with young urban Nepalis. Locally produced material has made huge strides with the showing of videos on Nepal TV and, especially, Nepal Channel.

Gopal Yonjan, the original author of this essay, was one of Nepal's most beloved musicians. Like Narayan Gopal, with whom he is often compared, Yonjan wrote and performed songs that touched Nepalis deeply, though they were unknown to non-Nepali-speakers. He was also a source of great pride and inspiration for members of his Tamang ethnic group, who suffer considerable racial discrimination in Nepal. He died in 1997.

Discography

Folk/Classical

Prem Avatari *Flute Recital*. Classical ragas (musical movements).

Kumar Basnet *The Best of Kumar Basnet*. A collection of old and new tunes from the reigning king of Nepali folk.

Gandharba *Gandharbas and Their Melodies*. Non-clichéd folk songs played in lively style on traditional instruments.

Prabin Gurung and others *Simsime*. Dulcet instrumental arrangements of folk standards.

Vijaya Kumar Sunam *Traditional Folk Tunes of Nepal*. Instrumental renditions of Nepali standards, often with unconventional instruments.

Tarabir Tuladhar *Sitar Recital*. Classical ragas.

Various artists (produced by Sur Sudha) *The Himalayan Lores*. Excellent compilation of classic recordings of favourite Nepali folk songs by the original artists.

Various artists (produced by Sur Sudha) *Nepal My Nepal*. Instrumental renditions of folk standards featuring solo *saranghi*.

Various artists (produced by Sur Sudha) *Royal Maestros of Nepal*. Vintage recordings of classical ragas by four legendary Nepali musicians.

Modern/Popular

Ranjit Gazmer *Chino* and *Lahuray*. Nepali film music.

Narayan Gopal *Blue Notes: Modern Songs by Narayan Gopal*. Compilation of folk and *ghazal* hits by the late number one vocalist.

Amber Gurung *Kahiry Lahar Kahiry Tarang*. Good lyrics and music, although Gurung is a better composer than singer.

Prakash Gurung *Jhooma*. Nepali film music.

Prem Raj Mahat & Rekha Shaha *Simsimi Panima*. Nepali pop rooted in the folk tradition, by a male–female duo.

Nepathya *Minpachasma* and *Resham*. The best albums to date by a band that pioneered the *lok-pop* (folk-pop) genre.

Gopal Yonjan *Kanchi* and *Sindoor*. Nepali film music.

Instrumental fusion

Chautari Band with Pancha Lama *Jharana*. A slick Nepali–Japanese collaboration, mellifluously combining Lama's *bansuri* (wooden flute) and other Nepali and Western instruments.

Moment *Music for Relaxation*. The addition of violin to the standard tabla and flute ensemble lends accessibility to this fusion music based on classical ragas. (Tarang, Heart Sutra and Inside Nepal – groups that feature most of the same musicians – make very similar music.)

Sur Sudha *Festivals of Nepal*, *Images of Nepal*, *Melodies of Nepal* and others. Nepal's musical ambassadors adapt traditional tunes to create a distinctive instrumental sound featuring airy, birdlike flute backed by sitar and tabla.

Homnath Upadhya *Prastar Improvisation III: Towards the Peace*. East–West fusion music on traditional Nepali and Indian instruments.

Vajra *Relaxation Music of Nepal*. More Sur Sudha-inspired music, featuring flute and water bowls.

Development dilemmas

Nepali schoolchildren are frequently asked to write essays on "What I Would Do if I Were King". There are, of course, no right answers. Nepal is sloshing with foreign experts, all clamouring to offer their suggestions – and money – yet despite the efforts of the past five decades the country remains impoverished. Some say Nepal's underlying problems, and the inefficacy of foreign aid, will keep it forever backward, while others point to tangible improvements that have been made in areas such as child mortality and literacy. Still others claim that Nepal's problems have been overstated by the government (to ensure continued aid) and development agencies (to justify their payrolls).

"**Development**" is a word like "progress": it means different things to different people, and all too often is assumed uncritically to be a desirable end in itself. Throughout the world – not only in Nepal – no one has yet worked out whether development is in fact a Good Thing, and if so what form it should take. But after spending time in the field, many aid workers conclude

This is How a Nation Pretends to Survive

This is Machhapuchhre, Your Excellency!
And that's Annapurna.
And, beyond that are
The ranges of Dhaulagiri.
You can see them with your naked eyes.
I don't think you'll need any binocular, sir.
We want to open a three-star hotel, Your Excellency!
Will you give us some loan?

Your Excellency!
This is Koshi, that's Gandaki
And, that one, yes, that blue one, is Karnali.
You might have read in some newspapers
That rivers in Nepal are on sale.
But that's not true, sir.
In fact, we have named our zones
In the name of these rivers.
It's our plan to generate electricity from them.
Will you give us some loan?

This is Kathmandu Valley, Your Excellency!
I mean country's capital,
Which contains three cities –
Kathmandu, Lalitpur and Bhaktapur.
Please mind the smell!
You may use your handkerchief, if you like.
It's true we have not been able to build
Either the sewer or public lavatories.
But in the next five-year plan
We are definitely going to introduce
"Keep the City Clean" programme.
Will you give us some loan, Your Excellency!

Min Bahadur Bista

that Nepalis – who lead rich and elegantly simple lives, nearly self-sufficient and unencumbered by many modern problems – have more to teach the "developed" (some would say *over*developed) world than it has to teach them.

Pragmatists usually argue that development is going to come anyway, and communities should at least be given a fair choice as to what kind of development they want, rather than being forced to choose between development and nondevelopment. But while no one advocates withholding aid or denying Nepalis' aspirations to certain material improvements, many in the development world reckon that Nepali schoolchildren are probably better able to solve their own problems than foreign experts, and that Nepalis ought to be the ones who decide what is appropriate development for Nepal.

Most people agree that Nepal's overarching problem – "challenge", in development parlance – is **poverty**. With a per-capita income of just $220, it's one of the world's poorest nations; more than forty percent of Nepalis live below a minimally set poverty line. This bleak situation can be traced to a number of factors: steep terrain, which makes farming inefficient and communications difficult; landlocked borders; few natural resources; a rigid social structure that entrenches the rich against the poor; ineffective central government; and a comparatively late start (the Nepalese government did essentially nothing for its people before 1951). Unable to do anything about these causes, most development organizations have devoted themselves to alleviating symptoms.

All too often, foreigners (and Nepalis too) have tended to think of development as a matter of identifying, measuring and solving a series of problems in isolation. But the problems of a developing country like Nepal are highly **interconnected**, and "solving" one often only succeeds in shifting it to another area. For example, better health and sanitation are obvious requirements, but providing them increases the rate of population growth, at least in the short term. Curbing population is no simple task, for it is rooted in poverty and the low status of women. In the meantime, agriculture has to be improved to feed the growing population, deforestation reversed to stop the fuelwood crisis, and industry developed to provide jobs. Irrigation projects, roads, hydroelectric diversions are needed … you get the idea. Even if you resolve that development should be left to Nepalis, better education will be required to get the ball rolling, and that means not so much building schools as addressing the poverty that keeps children from attending classes.

The following sections only scratch the surface of complex issues. Many simplifications have been made. Some issues are unique to Nepal, but many – if not most – are common to the entire "developing" world. The vast majority of people in the "developed" world are dangerously ignorant of the terrible pressures building in the poorer nations; travelling in Nepal offers a chance to witness the inequities first-hand and grapple with some of the dilemmas, which cannot help but make you re-examine your own lifestyle.

Population

Rapid **population growth** has consequences that are felt in every other area. Nepal's population, 24 million at the time of writing, is growing at an annual rate of 2.27 percent, which means that each year there are about 540,000 more Nepalis than the last. Those extra people place a corresponding extra burden on already inadequate health care, education and other services. They add to the already unsatisfiable demand for water, electricity and roads. And they

Everyone loves to give **aid** to Nepal. The country receives $300–400 million annually in direct grants and concessionary loans (not counting the value of technical assistance), making it one of the world's leading aid recipients on a per-capita basis.

Foreign development projects in Nepal fall roughly into three categories. **Bilateral** (and multilateral) aid – that is, money given or lent by foreign governments directly to Nepal – has financed most of the infrastructure (roads, dams, airports), as well as many ongoing social programmes. Many smaller projects are carried out by hundreds of international **non-governmental organizations (NGOs)**; some of these are well known, such as Oxfam, CARE and Save the Children, while others are just one person doing fieldwork and raising sponsorship money in his or her home country. Voluntary NGOs, such as Britain's Voluntary Service Overseas (VSO) and the US Peace Corps, generally don't run their own projects, but instead slot volunteers into existing government programmes. Finally, **international lending bodies** like the World Bank and Asian Development Bank act as brokers to arrange loans for big projects with commercial potential – usually irrigation and hydroelectric schemes.

Many of these organizations do excellent work; almost all are motivated by the best possible intentions. However, money cannot automatically solve Nepal's problems, as some of the biggest projects have learned to their cost. By paying their imported experts ten or twenty times more than Nepalis to do the same job, the big bilateral missions can cause resentment or, worse, encourage Nepalis to gather round the aid trough instead of doing useful work. And to the extent that they import experts and materials, they undermine Nepalis' ability to do things for themselves, fostering a crippling **aid dependency** that now permeates almost every level of society. In 1983, foreign aid made up forty percent of Nepal's development budget; since the early 1990s it has ranged between sixty and seventy percent. Some wags joke that the country can't *afford* to develop, lest it jeopardize development funding.

So why is everybody clamouring to give aid to Nepal? For bilateral donors, foreign aid is a handy way of buying **political influence**. China and India are forever one-upping each other with offers to Nepal, which they regard as a crucial buffer state; and while Nepal is of less strategic interest to the main Western powers, they're happy to throw some small change Nepal's way just to ensure a compliant regime.

Aid is also a means of stimulating the donor country's own domestic economy: for example, more than half of British aid to Nepal is paid directly to British **contractors**. Thus the emphasis of aid is usually on Western-style techno-fixes and economic growth, rather than appropriate technology and self-sufficiency. Encouraging farmers to, say, irrigate and buy fertilizers to grow cash crops may raise their income, but not necessarily their quality of life. It will, however, give Western banks a capital project to finance, Western contractors an irrigation system to build, Western chemical companies a new market for fertilizers, and Western consumer-goods companies new consumers. Meanwhile, Nepalese cash crops will be exported out of the area, even as Nepalis suffer malnutrition.

Even when foreign governments and agencies try to step back and let Nepalis do their own thing, their charity may still have a corrupting influence. The latest fashionable philosophy is that the best way to get things done is to finance **local NGOs**, which, it's assumed, have a better handle on local problems and solutions than foreign experts. Sounds great in theory, but what's the result? An explosion in local NGOs for every conceivable cause, all sounding just as right-on as could be: "small-scale" this, "women's development" that, "environmental" whatever. There is little co-ordination between them, resulting in inefficient competition for resources and overlapping functions – and since only a quarter of these organizations are registered with the government, there is little scrutiny of their activities: many aren't doing much besides writing grant proposals, and the only development they're assisting is that of their director's bank balance.

require the country's economy to somehow create enough new jobs to keep the additional breadwinners employed.

But **population control** isn't just a matter of passing out condoms. In Nepal, as in many other countries, children are relied on to do many time-consuming chores – fetching water, gathering fuel, tending animals – and are also considered an investment for old age, since there's only a token state pension to draw on. Moreover, Nepalis tend to have large families because they can't be sure all their children will survive. Hindus, especially, keep trying until they've produced at least one son, who alone can perform the prescribed rites (*shradha*) for his parents after they've died.

While it's not the place of aid workers to contradict Hindu beliefs, population-control efforts can have little impact unless the **status of women** (see p.541) is raised, which to a great extent is a matter of providing them with paid employment opportunities. Earning income doesn't merely empower women; it makes it more expensive for them to have children, since to do so means stopping work. Education can also play an important part in bringing down birth rates – but the education must be targeted not only at women, who already know they're repressed, but also at men, who do the repressing. Many "women's programmes" have failed because they've assumed that women only need to be provided with the awareness and skills to improve their situation; in fact they can do little if their husbands still hold the power.

The other reasons for high fertility could be removed by lowering the current high levels of poverty and child mortality, and by providing ready sources of fuel and water to reduce the need for extra hands. It's often said that "development is the best contraceptive", and indeed, there is a close correlation between rising standards of living and declining birth rates. Unfortunately, in most countries this so-called **demographic transition** involves a period of rapid population growth until the birth rate settles down to match the lower death rate. Some East Asian countries have seen their birth rates fall more or less simultaneously with their economies' rise, but Nepal is not, alas, in the same economic league.

Indeed, 2001 census figures show Nepal has failed to reduce its population growth rate over the past decade. The population has a biological momentum that is unlikely to be checked in the present generation, simply because of the number of girls already born and approaching child-bearing age. Meanwhile, the government's **family planning** efforts are still woefully inadequate: only fifteen percent of Nepalis practise any form of contraception at all. The remoteness of villages makes it all the more difficult to get the message out.

If Nepal's population doubles or triples, where will all the extra people live? As it happens, this is not a brand-new situation, for some parts of the middle hills have probably been overpopulated for a century or more. **Emigration** – to Kathmandu, the Tarai, India and, more recently, overseas – has always regulated the people pressure. Even so, it's estimated that the country's urban population will double in the next decade, and most of this increase will be taken up by the Kathmandu Valley and a half-dozen Tarai cities.

Health

Nepal's **health** indicators are nearly all bad, but are showing encouraging signs of improvement. Average **life expectancy** is now 58 – up from a bare 43 in 1975 – though studies indicate that members of economically disadvantaged groups can still expect to live 15 years less than the average. Moreover, Nepal is the only country in the world where men live longer than women. Females are the last in the family to eat and are expected to work harder. And childbirth is still a very real hazard for Nepali women: due to poor prenatal care and unsterile conditions during delivery, the odds of a given birth resulting in the death of the mother are 1 in 200 – which is especially scary when you consider that the average Nepali woman has 4.6 children.

More than half of Nepali children are **malnourished**, sixteen percent of them seriously. As a result, **child mortality** is distressingly high. That means that, on average, one out of every ten Nepali children will die before he or she reaches the age of five. The chances of survival are better in places like Kathmandu, but conversely, they're even worse in remote areas. Still, this is an improvement over 1960, when the figure was almost one in three. The introduction of cheap oral rehydration packets, together with immunization programmes, are largely responsible for saving these lives.

Poor sanitation, unsafe water and crowded, smoky conditions contribute to Nepal's high rates of disease – up to eighty percent of the population are estimated to be suffering from **parasitic infections** at any given time. **Tuberculosis** is on the decline, thanks to a World Health Organization initiative, but is still a major killer: each year about 8000 Nepalis die of the disease, and 40,000 new cases of active TB are reported, a quarter of them of the "multiple-drug resistant" strain, which is virtually untreatable. The incidence of **leprosy** is also coming down, now standing at between 8000 and 15,000 cases, but on a per-capita basis this remains one of the highest rates in the world. More positively, mosquito spraying in the Tarai has reduced **malaria** cases to about 25,000 annually (compared with two million a year during the 1950s), although even this is on the way back up.

While Nepal avoided the **AIDS** epidemic for many years, it now appears to be heading up the steep side of the bell curve: an estimated 65,000 Nepalis are now infected with HIV. Women employed in the sex industry and men driving long-distance trucks or performing seasonal work away from home have been the main agents in transmitting the disease from India, while poor blood screening, medical reuse of needles and ignorance of the proper use of condoms all threaten to aid its spread. Worst hit by the disease are intravenous drug users, of whom there are an estimated 30,000 in Nepal, half of them in the Kathmandu Valley.

Improved public **sanitation** is gradually being introduced, and is seen as the surest way to combat a number of debilitating diseases. However, there is a long way to go: only twenty percent of Nepalis have access to toilet facilities of any sort (including outhouses), and in the booming Tarai cities, covered sewers are barely keeping pace with growth. Communal taps and wells have been built in many villages to provide **drinking water**, yet only 48 percent of Nepalis have access to safe water.

Alcohol and **tobacco consumption** are also significant public-health problems in Nepal. There are no statistics on alcoholism, but it's believed that more than half of adult Nepalis smoke. The government has a vested interest in ignoring these problems because it owns the country's biggest cigarette company, and (like all governments) it obtains substantial tax revenue from the sale of tobacco and alcohol – and of course politicians and bureaucrats receive big kickbacks in return for awarding lucrative business licences in these industries. However, under pressure from Maoist-affiliated women's groups, the government agreed in 2001 to restrict the hitherto unfettered advertising of alcohol and to raise the legal drinking age to 24.

The Ministry of Health is one of the biggest and most bloated branches of His Majesty's Government. Most of its budget pays for salaries and seminars in Kathmandu, while **hospitals** and **health posts** in the regions remain poorly funded. Many parochial hospitals lack even a single resident doctor, since the vast majority of qualified physicians prefer to practise in the Kathmandu Valley, where they can make much more money in private practice. For most Nepalis, health care means a clinic that's a day or more's walk (or piggyback ride) down the trail and where the only person on staff may be a health assistant with ayurvedic training.

Agriculture

Many experts believe that **agriculture** must receive the main thrust of development efforts in Nepal. With about eighty percent of Nepalis still making their living from the land, they say, it's unrealistic to look for miracles elsewhere. Others contend that the country is over-reliant on agriculture and should try to diversify away from it.

Nepal's farmland is already among the most intensely cultivated in the world. A mere twenty percent of the land area is arable; clearing new land for cultivation only adds to deforestation, so it's preferable to find ways of increasing the productivity per hectare. Yields are currently very low even by regional standards – for example, rice and wheat yields are less than half of those in China – but of course that means there's plenty of room for improvement. Various methods have been tried in Nepal, as in other countries. Agriculture experiment stations have achieved some success in showcasing **high-yielding seeds** and animal breeds. **Pesticides** and chemical **fertilizers** are now widely used in the Kathmandu Valley and Tarai, though nationwide the use of these inputs is still relatively low (one-fifteenth that of China's). Moreover, they're often misused, due to poorly thought-out subsidy programmes and a lack of information: for example, many farmers apply urea (nitrogen), which is heavily subsidized, but not phosphorous and potash, which aren't, with the result that yields actually decrease. And in the Kathmandu Valley, where produce used to be organic by default, it is now often laced with unhealthy levels of agricultural chemicals.

Since Nepal experiences huge seasonal fluctuations in rainfall, **irrigation** is another high priority for improving productivity. Only fifteen percent of Nepal's arable land is currently irrigated, limiting productivity and also the effectiveness of improved seeds and chemical fertilizers. Small-scale community projects are being built with generally good results, but the big canal systems underwritten by the government and foreign funders are often inefficient and poorly maintained, and tend to benefit only the bigger landholdings. It's been estimated that a big government-built system costs at least eight times more per hectare than a community-built one.

Tractors and other **mechanized equipment** don't do much for the yield per hectare, but they do improve the yield per *farmer*. Aided by agricultural loans, an increasing number of Tarai farmers are investing in machinery; in most parts of the hills, though, smaller landholdings and stair-stepped terraces make mechanized farming impractical.

One reason landholdings are small is because they've been subdivided among the sons of each new generation. Many farms have simply become too small to feed a family – which is why so many Nepalis are now undernourished. Land also tends to become concentrated in the hands of a few who are adept at legal manoeuvring, such as moneylenders, who seize it through foreclosure. The government tried to redress the inequities in land ownership through **land reform** in the 1960s, but the rules weren't very well enforced. In 2001 the Deuba government proposed a radical new land-reform package, but it was bogged down by competing political interests and stalled by the Maoist emergency.

Despite a 1964 law prohibiting landlords from charging tenant farmers annual rents of more than fifteen percent of their crop, many farmers are locked in a hopeless cycle of debt and victimized by unscrupulous lenders. **Credit** is therefore a pressing need. Various government programmes extend credit to poor farmers to tide them over lean months, with variable success, but the official Agriculture Development Bank, which was created to make loans for simple improvements, has unfortunately grown so bureaucratic that only wealthier farmers can avail themselves of it. Microcredit loan programmes (see p.542) look more promising.

Because of the above, food production is not keeping pace with population growth. Nepal, a country that was agriculturally self-sufficient until the 1970s, now imports some of its rice. Though this is a blow to national pride, it's probably indicative of a necessary transition in which Nepali farmers with access to roads are moving away from growing staples – which they can't do as cheaply as Indian farmers – in favour of **cash crops** that they can raise more competitively. For this reason, the government has identified road extension as another agricultural priority. But while, on a national level, Nepal need not grow as much food as it eats, localized **food deficits** are a serious problem: in the remote northwestern districts of Humla and Mugu, where the climate doesn't permit enough food to be grown to meet the local demand, and where people can't afford to buy much from elsewhere, famines and emergency food airlifts are a regular spring occurrence.

Deforestation

In the Nepal hills, population, agriculture and environmental damage combine in a worrying vicious cycle: the need for more food leads to more intensive use of the land, which degrades the environment and lowers productivity, which further increases pressure on the land. An expanding population needs not only more **firewood**, but also more **fodder** for animals, which provide manure to maintain soil fertility. Overuse of firewood and fodder contributes to **deforestation**, as does any expansion of farmland. Removing soil-anchoring trees also causes **erosion** and landslides, which not only reduce the productivity of the land but also send silt down to the Bay of Bengal, contributing to disastrous **floods** in Bangladesh.

Or so goes the theory. In practice, there are counterbalancing forces: for example, the further people have to walk to find firewood or fodder, the more likely they are to emigrate, taking pressure off the area's resources. No one has a clear idea of the rate of forest loss in Nepal – studies give wildly differing estimates, and some indicate net forest cover is now actually increasing thanks to reforestation efforts. The most that can be said is that the situation is definitely bad in some areas, but not so bad, or even quite hopeful, in others. Experts still don't know to what extent deforestation contributes to erosion, but most agree that its effects are secondary to the natural erosion processes caused by the sloughing and shifting of very young mountains.

Even the government now admits it got it wrong in the 1950s, when it **nationalized the forests** to protect them. Before that, the forests had been competently managed by local communities; but when the trees were taken away from them, locals felt they had no stake in their preservation, and because government enforcement was weak they easily plundered them. Since the 1980s HMG's policy of **community forestry** has given local forests back to the people, recognizing that villagers are in fact very ecologically minded and will manage their forests responsibly and sustainably so long as they don't fear renationalization. This faith in local people has been richly vindicated, and all the evidence suggests that the policy has halted or reversed deforestation in most areas.

Deforestation is viewed differently **in the Tarai**, where the trees have been felled as a matter of policy to make way for settlers and to earn money for the government through state-sanctioned timber sales. Although the vast majority of the Tarai's magnificent native forest has gone in the past four decades, the rate of logging has almost come to a standstill in recent years – ironically, because of the collapse of the government-owned timber corporation. Meanwhile, Nepal has won praise abroad for setting aside large chunks of what remains as **national parks** and wildlife reserves. However, the government can expect mounting resistance from its own people, who question why such valuable land should be set aside for tourists and crop-destroying animals (see p.370).

While community forestry has helped safeguard the supply of trees, appropriate-technology initiatives have sought to reduce the demand for them. Several groups have worked hard to introduce "**smokeless**" **chulo** (stoves), which burn wood more efficiently and reduce unhealthy kitchen smoke. Yet even this simple innovation illustrates the dilemmas of tampering with traditional ways: Nepalis complain that the new stoves aren't as easy to regulate and don't emit enough light, while the lack of smoke allows insects to infest their thatched roofs. That's one reason why many Nepali households are converting from thatch to corrugated metal. **Electric appliances**, such as rice cookers and microwaves, can save even more wood by eliminating the need for many fires altogether. However, the up-front cost of these appliances is too high for the average peasant family, most of whom don't have electricity anyway. Furthermore, there are downsides to electricity use.

Electricity

Many see **electricity** – specifically hydroelectricity – as Nepal's greatest natural resource and a vital engine for development. The country's steep, mountain-fed rivers are estimated to have hydroelectric potential to the tune of 83 million megawatts – enough to power the British Isles. Unfortunately, due to the cost of getting materials and technical experts into the rugged backcountry, this potential is rather expensive to harness. Ironically for a country so richly endowed, only fifteen percent of Nepalis have access to electricity.

Rural electrification is slowly increasing that proportion, though, and that, along with urbanites' growing use of electrical appliances, is driving up electricity demand by about ten percent a year. Most economic planners see this as a healthy trend, and regard a growing supply of electricity as essential for stimulating domestic industry and creating employment. It can also encourage local economic development, reduce fuel-wood use, and benefit women and children by freeing up time otherwise spent gathering wood. But electricity is of no use to people who can't afford it, and it can only play a limited role in offsetting deforestation: as far as most rural Nepalis are concerned, wood is free, whereas electricity costs rupees – and electric appliances cost dollars. Also, paradoxically, electrification can actually add to the pressure on forests, because electric lights encourage people to stay up later at night and burn more wood to keep warm.

For many years Nepal relied on international donors and lending bodies to finance the handful of **large-scale hydroelectric** projects that provide most of its electricity. Since the mid-1990s, when these showcase megaprojects started falling out of favour with the development powers-that-be, the country has pursued a strategy of licensing private-sector companies to build mostly small- to medium-sized diversions. This approach has significant advantages over the old one: somebody else is paying the cost and bearing the risk; the government can usually negotiate in advance a good rate for the electricity to be produced by the project; and there's less potential for corruption, since the funding doesn't pass through government ministries. That said, some of these projects are still very big and disruptive to the environment, not to mention unpopular with another sector of the economy, the rafting industry. For their part, foreign companies have eagerly queued up for the privilege of exploiting

The end of the road

Gazing down from the hill, over terraces of paddy fields, we could see the first truck making its hesitant journey up the spiralling new dust road. Local people ran down the main street of the bazaar to meet the first iron monster to complete the ascent.

For them it was the excitement of seeing a machine that moved along the ground. For me it was the feeling that here, at last, was a link with the outside world. There was the weekly plane to Kathmandu, of course. But with only eighteen seats – and $30 a seat at that – it was hardly significant to most people.

Excitement about the road lasted quite a while. Then people became less frightened and awe-struck, and the verges were no longer dotted with rapt, admiring observers. Those who could afford the fare became seasoned travellers and were no longer to be seen vomiting out of the windows as the truck lurched along. In fact it became an accepted part of daily life – rather like the plane, it came and went, affecting few people.

But down by the airstrip, a shantytown of temporary shacks sprang up overnight with the coming of the road. Here was where all the goodies that came by truck from India were to be found: plastic snakes that wriggled, gilt hair-slides, iron buckets, saucepans and – best of all – fresh fruit and vegetables.

For us foreigners, and the paid office workers, accustomed to going for weeks with nothing but potatoes and rice in the shops, it seemed like paradise. Every day more and more apples, oranges, onions, cabbages and tomatoes would make their way up the hill. There was even a rumour that ten bottles of Coca-Cola had been sighted in the bazaar.

One morning, as I was eyeing a big plastic bucket full of huge Indian tomatoes in a local shop, a woman pulled my arm. "Don't you want to buy mine?" she asked. And there, in her *doko*, were a few handfuls of the small green local tomatoes.

Just a fortnight earlier I would have followed her eagerly, begging to be allowed to buy some. Now the shopkeeper laughed at her: who would want to buy little sour green tomatoes when there were big sweet red ones to be had?

For women like her, trudging in for miles from one of the surrounding villages to sell her few vegetables, there was no longer a market. The influential bazaar shop-

Nepal's hydropower, with a view to **exporting** surplus output to India at a profit. Unfortunately, their ardour has cooled quite a bit lately due to the Maoist insurgency, and many proposed projects will probably be postponed until the political situation is more stable.

For many years Nepal's electricity supply has fallen well short of demand, and the national electricity authority has had to resort to frequent **load-shedding** (scheduled power cuts) during the spring, when the rivers and reservoirs feeding the hydroelectric turbines are at their lowest. New hydro projects that have been brought on line in the past few years, including the $450-million Kali Gandaki "A", are supposed to put an end to load-shedding, at least for the next few years. Not that there won't still be electricity shortages during the dry months, but the hope is that Nepal will be able to cover them through seasonal power swaps with India. However, experts warn that Nepal won't really have year-round electricity security until it builds a high-dam project, which – unlike most of its other "run-of-river" diversions – would store water behind a reservoir to even out the seasonal fluctuations.

Microhydro projects can't deliver the kind of power industry needs, but they are appropriate technology for mountain villages too remote to be economically connected to the grid. Scores of these have been installed (both with foreign and private Nepalese funding) to supply electricity for a few hundred households each.

keepers negotiated deals with the Indian traders with their truckloads of vegetables. The new road meant new money for the shopkeepers – but less for the poor, whose livelihood was undermined and who had no way of buying the wonderful new merchandise.

There were other casualties, too. Gaggles of poor women, who had made a living out of carrying people's baggage from the airstrip to the bazaar, were once a common sight, haggling in angry, spirited voices over the price of their services. But with the coming of the new road, people simply boarded one of the trucks – baggage and all. Ragged and downtrodden at the best of times, these women were reduced to silently and gratefully accepting any rate people were prepared to pay for their help.

I began to wonder about the road. But I needn't have worried. Soon the monsoon rains arrived and the swelling river took charge of things. Within days the bridge was completely washed away, leaving several trucks stranded on the wrong side of the river, never to return to India.

The original truck continued to creak up and down the winding road between the airstrip and the bazaar, its fuel being hoisted across the river by rope-pulley, but became so overcrowded that one day it broke down halfway up the hill. As the road had been almost completely washed away by the rain, it was simply left there in the middle of the road.

When the monsoon ended, the truck was overgrown with creepers and made a very pleasant home for a local family.

By then the grand new road was little more than a memory. The women porters went back to climbing regularly up and down the hill; the shantytown vanished as quickly as it had appeared; and everyone went back to eating rice and potatoes as before.

Last I heard, a foreign-aid agency had decided to rebuild the road, with a proper bridge this time: in the interests of development.

Anna Robinson-Pant

Anna Robinson-Pant worked for three years as a VSO volunteer in Doti District, in the far western hills. Reproduced by permission of New Internationalist Publications ⓦ www.newint.org.

Nepal is also a good candidate for **solar power**. The introduction of locally manufactured solar water-heaters is helping to take some of the pressure off the electric grid and the forests. Though photovoltaics are relatively expensive for so poor a country, so too is the cost of extending the grid ($60,000 per kilometre), which means that in remote areas without hydroelectric potential it can actually work out cheaper to install solar cells. **Biogas** – gaseous fuel produced by the fermentation of organic material such as manure and agricultural waste – is also proving to be cost-effective; the Dutch government has subsidized the establishment of local small-scale plants throughout Nepal.

Roads

Roads, like big hydroelectric and irrigation projects, don't come out well in straight cost-benefit analyses in Nepal, nor do they promote equitable development. The wealthy – bus owners, truckers, merchants, building contractors – benefit from road-building, while porters and shopkeepers along the former walking route lose out. Nevertheless, roads form an important part of Nepal's development strategy because it's virtually impossible to deliver services, administer projects, maintain order or even collect taxes in areas not served by roads. Moreover, roads improve people's productivity, make it possible for farmers to sell their crops for cash, and generally stimulate the economy.

The government has long had the goal of extending roads to each of its 75 district headquarters; all the easy ones are done, and 14 districts remain. Each year many new roads are boldly etched into hillsides, only to be washed away in the next monsoon (see box on p.538). Foreign donors subsidize much of the road-building programme – India and China have vied to build most of Nepal's main highways over the years – but they rarely fund maintenance costs, so as the road network grows it becomes more potholed.

In most parts of Nepal, where roads aren't practical, appropriate technology is called for. **Footbridges** put villages within easier reach of jobs and health facilities, and enable them to get their produce to local markets more efficiently, making them perhaps the most useful and popular type of public-works project. Where footbridges are deemed too expensive, an innovative alternative is the *tar pul* – "wire bridge" – a human-powered gondola that travels along a set of wires suspended over a river.

Education

Nepal's education system has come a long way in a short time. Before 1951 there were few government **schools**, and they were open only to the children of elites – now there are primary schools within walking distance of most villages, and legions of private ones in the cities and towns. However, the government schools are chronically underfunded, especially in rural areas, with poorly trained teachers, huge classes and few materials (or even furniture). Any family that can afford to do so sends its children to private school. This has produced a two-track educational system that is widening the gap between the haves and the have-nots.

Indeed, the poorest families derive very little benefit from the system at all. The trouble is that "free" public education is actually quite expensive for families who depend on their children for labour, and thus many students are forced to drop out very early. According to one estimate, only sixty percent of boys – and just forty percent of girls – finish primary school. **Literacy** is still only 52 percent – up from 40 percent a decade ago, true, but the gulf between males (66 percent) and females (38 percent) who can read remains wide.

Nepal's proportion of qualified **teachers** is very low: only 46 percent are trained, and few of them are trained well – a recent scandal concerned the revelation that a large number of supposedly qualified teachers held falsified teaching certificates. Many aid programmes have therefore focused on teacher training. Low pay is another problem, sapping teachers' motivation and contributing to an estimated fifty-percent *teacher* absentee rate. Observers believe education could be a powerful catalyst for change in Nepal, but many complain that the current curriculum is geared for churning out bureaucrats and should be made more vocational and relevant to a peasant population. Others charge that the system is too politicized and centralized, and is incapable of improving itself.

Those who do finish high school and go on to one of Nepal's **colleges** or **universities** often find that there's no work for them when they graduate – a common problem in most countries, but all the more acute in Nepal, whose nonagricultural sectors are particularly poorly developed. A further cultural complication is the prevalent attitude towards education in Nepal: equated with high status, it is all too often pursued merely to avoid physical labour, which carries low status. This, ironically, has the effect of removing many of Nepal's most highly trained people from the productive workforce. Frustrated by a lack of opportunities or just plain bored, the educated youth of the cities make up a growing class of angry young men given to revolutionary talk and *goonda* antics.

Women

Outside the relative sophistication of Kathmandu, Hindu **women** are a long way from liberation. In remote rural areas, they're considered their husband's or father's chattel, given or taken in marriage for the price of, say, a buffalo. Discrimination against orthodox Baahun women in the name of religion is especially harsh: during menstruation and for ten days after giving birth, for example, their touch is considered as polluting as that of an untouchable. Buddhist women are treated much more equally, and wealthy urban Hindu women may easily flout conventions, but even these women don't enjoy true power-sharing. Indeed, when it comes to gender roles, wealthy urbanites can be as traditional as any villager: the popularity of foetal ultrasound testing services in Kathmandu and the Tarai suggests that many couples are seeking to eliminate unwanted females.

Nepalese law explicitly withholds many **legal and political rights** from women. A female may not inherit property unless she's still unmarried at age 35 – and if she subsequently marries, she has to give her inheritance back. As a widow, she has no right to a share of the family property. A man may divorce his wife (or, in practice, take a second wife) if she fails to produce a son; needless to say, it doesn't work the other way around. A controversial amendment to the Civil Code that would eliminate some of these discriminatory provisions was passed in Parliament in 2002, and at the time of writing was awaiting royal assent.

Several development problems already touched on – gender inequities in health care and education, and the failure of population-control efforts – arise directly from the low status of women in Nepal. One study found that 73 percent of Nepali women suffer from **domestic violence**. Although **child marriage** has been outlawed, women are still married off very young – 34 percent are wed by the age of fifteen, 66 percent before they're eighteen. Only with the 2002 Civil Code amendment has **abortion** been made legal; prior to that, it was treated as homicide in nearly all circumstances – even in cases of rape or incest, and women whose babies were stillborn ran the risk of being charged with murder as well. It's hoped that that the new law will reduce the number of unsafe backstreet abortions, which are believed to be the cause of up to half of all maternal mortality in Nepal.

Most tragic of all is the **trafficking** of Nepali girls for Indian brothels. It's estimated that each year, between 5000 and 10,000 Nepali girls and women – twenty percent of them under the age of sixteen – are sold into **sexual slavery** in India, where patrons prize them for their beauty and supposed lack of inhibitions. To poor Hindu families in Nepal, daughters are often regarded as burdens, costing money to be married off and then becoming another family's asset; when a broker comes offering, say, Rs15,000 for a pubescent daughter, many readily agree. This horrific trade is still most pronounced in the central hills, where it has historical roots (Tamang girls of that region were forced to serve as concubines in the courts of the Kathmandu rulers for generations), but the traffickers are said to be expanding into other areas. A prostitute may eventually buy her freedom, but ordinarily she won't be released until she's been "damaged" – which these days means she has AIDS (see p.534). Prostitution is also on the rise in Kathmandu and other Nepali cities.

So far, the government has shown little inclination to confront this national disgrace. Concerned NGOs have been left to set up homes for former prostitutes, who would otherwise be shunned by family and friends if they returned to their villages. Others are working to address the underlying causes of the problem – not only poverty in general, but specifically women's low education and earning power. If women are educated and enabled to earn money, they won't be seen as a drag on family finances and are less likely to be sold off. Two very successful efforts, the Bangladesh-based Grameen Bank and the Nepalese government's Production Credit for Rural Women programme, have targeted women's development by making **microcredit loans** to small, self-organizing groups of women and supporting the borrowers with literacy, family-planning and other training.

Children and other disadvantaged groups

Nepal has signed all the international accords on the rights of **children**, but has yet to follow up on its commitments with meaningful laws or enforcement. As already mentioned, however much their parents love them, children in poor families are counted as an economic resource from an early age. **Child labour** has always been essential in agriculture, and in the past it was common for children to work as unpaid servants for village landowners simply so there would be one less mouth to feed. Despite a 1992 law barring employment of anyone of fourteen or under, children are increasingly being relied on to earn wages as porters, domestic servants and labourers in the carpet, brick and construction industries. According to the charity Child Workers in Nepal, 2.6 million Nepali children – sixty percent of the population aged between six and fourteen – are engaged in labour. Of those, one million are performing the "worst forms of child labour" – menial or hazardous work – and sixty percent are girls. Not only are these youngsters often forced to work long hours in unhealthy conditions, and are frequently abused, they are deprived of their childhood – the right to play, be loved and be educated.

While many children are forced into the sex trade (see opposite), thousands of others working in domestic service are at high risk of **sexual abuse**. In recent years there have been highly publicized cases of foreign paedophiles preying on street children, the men getting off lightly because Nepalese law does not specifically criminalize sexual abuse of boys. (For more information on street children, see p.120.) Nor has the government yet made good on promises to set up a juvenile justice system and to allow legal representation for minors.

The **elderly** in Nepal are traditionally looked after by their sons, but economic development – which brings increased mobility and beguiling new possibilities – is breaking down such traditions. Moreover, Nepal's demographic transition will require an adjustment, as it has in other countries, as there are fewer young people to support more old people. All of this means there will be a need for more care facilities for the elderly and a meaningful national pension (currently, a meagre Rs100 per month is doled out to widows over 60 and men over 75).

Dalits – Nepal's "untouchables" (see p.503) – are still held back by poverty, lack of education and flagrant discrimination in the villages. Recently, the government has begun making noises about "uplifting" Dalits, announcing its intention to make caste discrimination punishable and forming a national commission to investigate the problems of Dalits. It's too soon to say whether this will result in concrete action; certainly very little money has as yet been forthcoming.

The government did act dramatically in 2000 to free the **kamaiyas** (bonded labourers), victims of a system of indentured servitude prevalent in the mid- and far west. Unfortunately, it failed to accompany the liberation with any policy on land redistribution or job training, with the result that most *kamaiyas* found themselves suddenly homeless and jobless.

Industry and trade

Nepal needs to create jobs – agriculture simply cannot absorb all of the country's growing workforce. Official **unemployment** stands at around five percent, but some 47 percent of Nepalis are listed as underemployed. Moreover, a developing nation like Nepal has to produce things, not only for domestic consumption but also for export, so that it can earn foreign exchange to pay for the imported technology and materials it needs for development. All of this means boosting **industry**, which in Nepal's case accounts for a relatively low proportion of gross domestic product.

Nepal has three religions, goes the old saying: Hinduism, Buddhism and **tourism**. The latter is Nepal's top foreign-exchange earner, and many see it as the country's most promising economic engine. But while the industry directly employs 200,000 people, and indirectly gives work to many more in related industries, the jobs tend to be menial and seasonal, and are very vulnerable to economic downturns: the drop in tourist arrivals due to political instability since 2001 has hit the industry very hard. Moreover, the economic benefits of tourism are highly localized, and an estimated sixty percent of the foreign exchange earned from it goes right back out of the country to pay for imported materials. True, the industry can claim some credit for shaping HMG's mostly progressive environmental record – but it's an open question as to whether the revenue earned really offsets the ecological and cultural costs. The fruits of tourism, so arbitrarily awarded, have turned legions of Nepalis into panhandlers, in much the same way that aid has done to politicians and institutions.

There are various strategies for exploiting **tourism as a development tool**. The one employed by nearby Bhutan is to admit only a small number of very high-paying tourists, thus maximizing revenue while minimizing impacts. Another approach, exemplified by independent trekking, is to encourage tourists to disperse and spend as much of their money as possible at the local level. Unfortunately, Nepal has so far failed to pursue any clear strategy, tending to go for quantity rather than quality, and to allow visitors to cram themselves into a few overused areas, which only degrades the tourist experience and undermines the industry's long-term viability. This commodity approach to tourism seems particularly short-sighted in Nepal's case, given its unique assets (after all, there is only one Mount Everest).

Other countries in the region have used their low wages and high unemployment to attract the sweatshops and assembly plants of Western brand-name companies. Without a seaport, Nepal can't even do that. Despite its disadvantage, though, it achieved surprising success in the 1990s with three exports that have since, sadly, declined. **Carpet manufacture**, which in 1994 employed 300,000 people and was poised to overtake tourism in annual revenue, has seen its volume fall by more than fifty percent due to quality-control problems, bad PR over child labour, saturation of the market and, most recently, fear on the part of international buyers that Maoist-inspired labour unions will disrupt production. Readymade **garments** and **pashmina** (cashmere) items have seen similar rises and falls, for many of the same reasons.

In many other industries, Nepal finds itself in a classic Third World bind. It can't profitably produce things like vehicles and computers because its domestic market is so small (and poor), and importing even modest amounts of these items quickly runs up a nasty trade deficit. The government has therefore put much of its energy into stimulating the production of run-of-the-mill goods for domestic consumption. In development economics, this is known as **import substitution**: for a country short on foreign exchange, a penny saved is a penny earned. Alcoholic beverages, washing powder, paper, cement and shoes have all seen dramatic increases in output.

Many of these factories have been set up as licensed **monopolies**, which give the government more control over the pace of development, but tend to concentrate wealth in the hands of a few Kathmandu fat-cats. (In most sectors the law requires that all businesses have a majority Nepali ownership, which makes for some very well-off silent partners.) A few dozen industries are still run as state-owned enterprises, most of which are slated for eventual **privatization**. However, this process is proceeding very slowly, as the government is loathe to give them up: the party in power traditionally uses state enterprises as employment agencies for its supporters, and siphons off much of their revenues for its own use.

The presence of **India** as Nepal's neighbour to the south inevitably complicates matters. Nepal's main trading partner, India levies high import duties to protect its own industries, thus benefiting Nepali border traders (who can sell imported goods for less than their Indian competitors), but crippling Nepali exporters (whose goods become uncompetitive with duty added on). The balance of power is so disproportionate that India can always present Nepal with take-it-or-leave-it **terms of trade**. Thus a Kodak plant that could have brought in much-needed foreign exchange was forced to close after only two years of operation when India reneged on an agreement and hiked import duties on Kodak film. Similarly, India recently imposed a "luxury tax" on Nepali tea leaves, making them uncompetitive with Indian tea and pulling the rug out from under the Nepali growers' market. And even if import duties weren't a factor, **economies of scale** make it nearly impossible for Nepali companies to compete in India; more and more are finding they can't even compete with Indian companies in their own market.

Economic policy

Development workers advocate all sorts of wonderful-sounding ways to bring Nepal out of poverty. Economists ask: how do we pay for it? Hard work and good ideas will amount to nothing unless they're accompanied by sound **economic policy**.

Alas, Nepal's leaders have paid little attention to economics since the restoration of democracy. Their tendency to accept whatever foreign aid is offered, without analysing how or whether it fits into the country's long-term plans, has distorted economic signals and wasted much time in the race to achieve real development. Constant political upheavals have played havoc with planning, and have made virtually all decisions subservient to short-term political calculations. These factors, along with the high costs and risks of doing business in Nepal (corruption, inflation, exchange-rate fluctuations), have in turn frightened off foreign investment.

At $1200, Nepal's per-capita gross domestic product (GDP) is the lowest in Asia. Economists estimate that if Nepal is to make significant progress in alleviating poverty, it will have to achieve long-term **economic growth** of at least six percent annually. The country achieved that target for a few years in the late 1990s, but since the escalation of the Maoist conflict the annual growth rate has plunged to about three percent – only just keeping ahead of population growth. Furthermore, most of the growth has been confined to a few urban areas, and with inflation eroding people's purchasing power, the average Nepali has experienced a steadily declining standard of living.

Most other economic indicators are heading south too. The **budget deficit** is widening, as military expenditure rises (to fight the Maoists) and revenues decline (as political turmoil dampens economic activity and investment). **Foreign debt** is steadily increasing, as an increasing proportion of foreign aid comes in the form of loans; interest on the debt now consumes a third of the national budget. The **banking** sector, which should be financing economic recovery, is in a shambles: the two biggest state-owned banks have been found to be insolvent (their portfolios weighted down by sweetheart loans to political supporters) and their management has been handed over to foreign firms. Even in the best of times, the banks operate like a cartel, keeping wealth in the hands of the elite and making it difficult for average Nepalis to finance good business ideas. (The national bank has recently moved to liberalize monetary policy, which it's hoped will shake up this old-boys' club and encourage more investment.)

One policy pursued fairly consistently by recent governments is **economic liberalization**, which has meant reducing restrictions and tariffs on imports, making the currency fully convertible, and allowing for easier licensing of businesses. These actions have helped open the door to a flood of foreign goods and capital, resulting in a dramatic increase in wealth and economic activity in the Kathmandu Valley and to a lesser extent in the urban centres of the Tarai. However, it should be noted that such policies are designed by and for those who already have the capital, and they offer little benefit to Nepal's subsistence farmers and labourers. Wealth is slow to trickle down in a country like Nepal.

Lazily addicted to foreign aid, the government made almost no effort to support itself through **taxation** for many years. Under pressure from international donors and lending institutions, HMG finally began to increase its collection of income tax and to institute a ten percent value-added tax (VAT) on the sale of most goods and services in the late 1990s. However, any attempt to collect taxes in Nepal is hindered by poor record-keeping, limited technology and tax collectors' high susceptibility to bribery.

Chronically short of funds, the government is unable to operate its infrastructure efficiently, makes short-sighted decisions, and has little left over to invest in improvements. Indeed, fiscal inefficiency is such that the government can't even utilize much of the foreign aid being offered to it.

Kathmandu Valley problems

Solutions often create their own problems. For five decades, people have been trying to get Nepal to develop – now that it has, in the **Kathmandu Valley**, many are nervously fumbling for the "off" switch.

Kathmandu appears to be following in the footsteps of other Asian capitals like Delhi and Bangkok, albeit on a smaller scale. Overpopulation is driving a growing **rural exodus**; new roads and bus services pull the landless poor away from their villages, while jobs in the tourism and manufacturing industries push them towards the Kathmandu Valley. Many immigrants land jobs and begin the difficult process of finding a place for themselves in the **big city**, and a few even find their fortune there. But there's no safety net for those who don't. They may end up squatting in the most primitive conditions imaginable – in unhealthy shacks on waste ground, in empty buildings, in the streets – and scrounging a living from the rubbish heaps or prostitution.

While poverty is a perennial problem in the valley, it's prosperity that's creating the brand-new headaches, starting with **traffic** and **pollution**. Industrial workers get to their factories by tempo or bus, while the more affluent drive their own motorbikes or cars. Goods must be moved by truck, and tourists take taxis. The result is ever-growing gridlock and an increasing smog problem from a fleet of vehicles that is doubling every six to eight years. Those who can afford to are moving out to the suburbs, and their commuting only worsens the problem. Vehicle emissions are blamed for an alarming increase in respiratory problems, which occur at twelve times the national average in Kathmandu. Health experts warn that children are particularly vulnerable to asthma, allergies and lead-related developmental problems caused by the appalling air quality. As discussed in the box on p.94, the causes of this environmental catastrophe are largely political, and require political will to solve. On the positive side, the dramatic success of electric-powered Safaa ("clean") tempos is providing a highly visible reminder that there are cleaner alternatives.

Meanwhile, sheer numbers of people are taxing the valley's other infrastructure. In Kathmandu, demand for **drinking water** exceeds the supply by 20 to 100 percent (depending on season), with the result that residents in many neighbourhoods have pressure only on alternate mornings or evenings – most pump what water they can get up to rooftop storage tanks, and supplement it with deliveries by tanker. Leaks in underground pipes account for most of the shortfall, but of the water that is delivered, much of it is monopolized by wasteful tourist hotels and restaurants. Nobody seems to be talking about fixing the leaks or improving efficiency of the water supply; instead, the government has put all its eggs into a $500-million basket called the **Malemchi project**, which will pipe water from the Helambu area northeast of the valley rim through a 27-kilometre tunnel. Malemchi will double the valley's drinking water supply, starting in 2007; by 2013, demand will have again outstripped supply and another diversion will be necessary.

Not only is water scarce in the valley, it's also highly contaminated. A 1998 study deemed fifty percent of the capital's tap water to be "unsatisfactory" – and that was based on samples taken in the dry season, when the water is cleanest. Most of the contamination comes from **sewage** permeating the soil and infiltrating into old, leaky pipes. Only thirty percent of the valley's sewage is properly treated before being discharged: municipal treatment plants are old and don't operate properly, and in many areas raw waste is allowed to drain directly into rivers. Meanwhile, many industries – notably carpet-washing factories – discharge **toxic effluents** into the rivers. Such dumping is illegal, but the Ministry of Population and the Environment doesn't have a single inspector to enforce the law. **Garbage** is another problem, not only because the valley's growing population is generating more of it, but also because its municipalities still haven't agreed on a permanent dumping site. In the meantime, much of it is being dumped in horrific landfills right beside the Bagmati River, or is burnt, adding to air pollution.

The damage that has been done to the valley's **culture** in the name of progress is less easy to quantify, but is arguably more profound. Traditional architecture is no longer valued. Members of the younger generation are drifting away from the religion of their parents. *Guthi* (charitable organizations) are in decline and have been forced to leave the upkeep of many temples to foreign preservationists. Tourism has robbed crafts of their proper use, and many performance arts of their meaning. Work outside the home has disrupted family life, and the influx of strangers has introduced social tensions and crime.

To some extent, valley residents are prepared to accept these problems as the price of progress: a little pollution or crime may seem a fair trade for improvements that keep children from dying and give people greater control over their lives. But, increasingly, Kathmanduites are worrying that they might have a "Silent Spring" in the making. What will be the effects on their children of growing up breathing air, drinking water and eating food that is not only contaminated with germs but also laced with chemicals and heavy metals? In another generation, when Nepalis are presumably more prosperous and living longer and expecting more out of life, will they be haunted by elevated levels of cancer, birth defects and allergies? And will the nation be able to afford the cost of treating all the victims of these anthropogenic diseases?

Bureaucracy, corruption and fatalism

Many aid workers identify the root cause of Nepal's slow development as "institutional problems", a euphemism that covers a multitude of sins. They speak of management bottlenecks, where **bureaucrats** hoard power to such an extent that project managers have to spend most of their time in Kathmandu queuing for signatures instead of getting things done in the field. They complain that Nepali managers are overly fond of desk jobs in the capital, regarding remote hill postings as punishment and making no secret of their disdain for the local people they're supposed to be helping. (The most coveted position in Nepal is a job that involves no work and produces a regular pay cheque.) Managers frequently leave the important work to untrained underlings, preferring instead to pass their time in seminars and "talk programmes". Slogans and planning targets are more in evidence than action, while planners tend to favour rigid, top-down approaches without consulting experts in the field. These traits aren't unique to Nepal, of course, and indeed many aid organizations are themselves centralized and top-down-oriented.

But unquestionably, Nepal's gravest institutional problem is **corruption**, which seems to plumb new depths with each short-lived government. There is little tradition of public service at the national level in Nepal, and a government job with decision-making authority has long been regarded as a licence to collect kickbacks ("commissions") from those who desire a favourable decision. Byzantine procedures are devised precisely to increase bureaucrats' chances of obtaining "speed money" from their supplicants. The opportunism is perpetuated by artificially low salaries and, no doubt, by the sight of apparently limitless piles of development loot.

Under the old *panchaayat* system, corruption was endemic but discreet; since the restoration of democracy, it has become part of the modus operandi of all parties, and extends to the very highest levels. The intense competition for power has **politicized**, and corrupted, every branch of the bureaucracy: jobs are awarded on the basis of party loyalty, not merit; the appointees are essentially ordered to skim off as much as they can for the party (plus a bit for themselves), and are given political cover to do so. With each new government comes a wave of new appointees, producing administrative upheavals. Political parties bleed state enterprises dry – Royal Nepal Airlines has been reduced to a corporate zombie by a thousand political cuts – and sanction everything up to and including kidnapping and smuggling to finance their operations. There's always a scandal in the papers, yet no politician of any stature ever seems to take a fall. Some observers have equated such systematic corruption with genocide, because the damage it's doing to Nepal's economy, and the money it's diverting from needed projects, is responsible for countless needless deaths. Over the years, foreign donors have abetted the corruption by looking the other way, not wanting to jeopardize their projects, but the situation has now become so bad, with so little aid money actually reaching its target, that some of the big donor nations have started threatening to cut off the funds.

These institutional problems are themselves only projections of Nepal's culture, elements of which seem almost designed to thwart Western-style development. One of Nepal's foremost anthropologists, Dor Bahadur Bista, argued compellingly that Nepal's greatest handicap is the **fatalism** peddled by its

Baahun (Brahman) elite. According to Bista, along with Nepalis' admirable *ke garne* ("what to do?") attitude comes an exasperating apathy, and an obstructive suspicion that development efforts are merely futile attempts to resist fate. Responsibility for actions and decisions is often passed on to higher-ups (whether a boss, an astrologer or a deity), and the relationship between present work and future goals (at least in this life) is glossed over, resulting in haphazard planning and follow-through. Moreover, Nepali society places a great emphasis on **connections** and old-boy networks (called *aafno maanche*: "one's own people"), which make it hard for members of ethnic minorities to advance, and on patronage, in which dependants are rewarded for loyalty rather than skill or innovation. Invaluable as these traits may be in a traditional village society, in a modern nation they tend to produce inept government, and foster a grovelling dependency on foreign patrons.

Prospects

The foregoing isn't intended to make it sound as if Nepal's situation is hopeless, nor that there is no way for outsiders to help. Newcomers to the field tend to be the gloomiest ones, while people with a longer perspective are able to cite many major gains. Community forestry, improvements in health, and some aspects of the hydropower programme can all be counted as successes. Recent legislation to decentralize certain government functions offers the hope of greater local control of development, and maybe even of a loosening of the dead grip of corruption.

But as this book goes to press, everything seems dependent on how the government handles the **Maoists**. The Maoist insurgency is unquestionably the consequence of past failed development policies and, unfortunately, it's also the cause of further failures: the violence has destroyed a good deal of infrastructure necessary for development, and the threat of violence has halted many projects and forced many organizations to leave the most needy areas. If any good can come out of all this, it's that Nepal's leaders might learn that they ignore development at their peril.

As a traveller, you too are playing a part in Nepal's development. With the right mixture of know-how and humility, you can be an agent of social change just by being yourself. Spent wisely, your money can bring tangible improvements to villages and families. In addition, there are plenty of good causes you may feel inclined to donate money to when you get home: with a little effort you should be able to see a few in action during your travels, and judge them by their fruits.

Natural history

The Himalaya are not only the world's tallest mountains, they're also the youngest – and still growing. Because of them, most of Tibet and parts of northern Nepal are high-altitude deserts, hidden in the Himalayan rain shadow, while many southern slopes, which bear the full brunt of the monsoon, are rainforest: nowhere in the world is there a transition of flora and fauna so abrupt as the one between the Tarai and the Himalayan crest, a distance of as little as 60km. As a result, Nepal can boast an astounding diversity of life, from rhinos to snow leopards.

Geology

The Himalaya provide graphic evidence for the **plate tectonics** (formerly known as continental drift) theory of mountain-building. According to this theory, the earth's crust is divided into a dozen or so massive plates which collide, separate and grind against each other with unimaginable force. The Himalaya are the result of the Indian subcontinental plate ramming northwards into the Asian plate – something like a car smashing into the side of a truck. It has been estimated that a 2000-kilometre cross-section of land along the collision zone has been compressed into 1000km, doubling the thickness of the crust and producing not only the Himalaya but also the vast Tibetan Plateau.

The shallow **Tethys Sea**, which once covered the entire region, was the main casualty in the process; its sedimentary deposits, now contorted and metamorphosed, can be seen at all elevations of the Himalaya. The first phase of mountain-building began around 45 million years ago, as the edge of the Asian plate, buckling under pressure from the advancing Indian plate, rose out of the sea to a height of about 2000m. Although it has since been lifted much higher, this **Tibetan Marginal Range**, which parallels the main Himalayan chain to the north, still stands as the divide between the Ganges and Tsangpo/Brahmaputra rivers. Unique among the world's major mountain ranges, the Himalaya don't form a watershed: rivers like the Kali Gandaki, Bhote Koshi (there are several by that name) and Arun cut right through the Himalaya because their courses were established by this earlier Tibetan Marginal Range.

The next major uplift occurred between 10 and 25 million years ago, when great chunks of the Asian plate were thrust southwards on top of the Indian plate, creating a low-altitude forerunner of the Himalayan range. Things appear to have remained more or less unchanged until just 600,000 years ago – practically yesterday, in geological time – when what is now the **Tibetan Plateau** was suddenly jacked up to an average elevation of 5000m, and the Tibetan Marginal Range to about 7000m. From this point on, monsoonal rains became an important erosive force on the south (Nepalese) side of the mountains, while the north, left in the rain shadow, turned into a high desert. Southward-flowing rivers, fuelled by phenomenal gradients of up to 6000m in 100km, further eroded the landscape.

Most of Nepal's present features were created at the geological last minute. Beginning around 500,000 years ago, the Tibetan rim lunged forward along numerous separate fronts to form the modern **Himalaya**. Averaging 8000m, Nepal's *himal* (massifs) show a freeze-frame of the current state of play.

But mountain-building produces downs as well as ups: around 200,000 years ago, a broad belt of foothills subsided, creating Nepal's **midland valleys**, while the southern edge of this zone curled up to form the **Mahabharat Lek** and, still further south, the **Churia Hills** (called the Siwaliks in India). These ridges rose so rapidly that they forced many southbound rivers to make lengthy east–west detours and permitted only three principal outlets to the Tarai; the Bagmati and Seti rivers were initially dammed up by the Mahabharat Lek, flooding the Kathmandu and Pokhara valleys respectively.

The Himalaya are rising still, albeit at a slower rate than previously. Periodic and severe **earthquakes** (see below) demonstrate that the earth continues to rearrange itself – one in eastern Nepal in 1988 killed 700 people – while **hot springs**, sometimes found near streams along trekking trails, are indicators of tectonic faultlines. **Erosion** is a particular problem in the Himalaya, where the mountains are continually sloughing off their skins, and landslides occur regularly during the monsoon. While **glaciers** play a part in shaping the terrain above about 5000m, the Himalaya aren't highly glaciated due to their sheer slopes (which can't support glacier-breeding snowfields) and relatively low precipitation at high elevations. On the whole, Himalayan glaciers are in a retreating phase, as they are in most parts of the world, and old moraines (piles of rubble left behind by melting glaciers) are commonly seen above 4000m.

Earthquake danger in Nepal

Nepal lies along one of the earth's great geological fault zones, where the Indian subcontinent plate joins the greater Asian plate. The collision of these two plates continues to this day at a rate of 2cm per year. Most of this compression is absorbed in the process of mountain-building, but some of it is stored as temporary tension in the earth's crust and then released in the form of **earthquakes**.

Nepal's historical record shows a pattern of infrequent but catastrophic quakes. The most recent major one, in 1988, registered a whopping 8.3 on the Richter scale and killed 700 people in the eastern part of the country; its effects would have been much worse had it struck further west. The last big one to hit Kathmandu, in 1934, was probably nearly as great in magnitude.

Earthquakes became the hot topic of conversation in Kathmandu in 2001, after an international study predicted that a "**major earthquake**", one that hits eight or more on the Richter scale, will hit Nepal "soon" – which is to say at any time within the next fifty years. Local experts contend that the less populated (and much less visited) western region is a more likely target than Kathmandu, which suffered colossal damage in 1934 – a fairly recent date in seismological terms.

If they're wrong, the consequences could be disastrous. A Japanese report predicted that if the 1934 quake hit today, as many as half of the buildings in Kathmandu would be seriously damaged, and you only have to look at the shoddy, pile-'em-high reinforced concrete constructions to have an idea of what this might mean. Unnervingly, tourist guesthouses, building ever upwards in unceasing competition for roof-top airspace, are among the main contenders for collapse. A national building code exists but has yet to be made mandatory, so essentially no attention is paid to earthquake resistance in construction, nor has the government created any emergency preparedness or disaster management system. Moreover, the Kathmandu Valley's soils are apparently of the sort that turn to soup in an earthquake, magnifying the damage.

Maybe the next big one won't be until 2050, maybe it will already have happened by the time you read this. It's not something that should stop you from going to Nepal, but it might provide yet another reason to spend most of your time outside Kathmandu.

Nepal's valleys are like vast cutaway diagrams of geological history, and trekking or rafting in them allows you to imagine the forces that have shaped the Himalaya. Igneous intrusions (usually granite) are common, but most outcrops consist of metamorphic rocks (schist, gneiss, limestone and dolomite), deposited as underwater sediments and later mashed and contorted under tremendous pressure; the wavy light-and-dark bands of the Lhotse-Nuptse Wall, in the Everest region, illustrate this. **Fossils** found in many of these layers have helped geologists date the phases of Himalayan mountain-building. The famous *shaligram* stones of Muktinath in the Annapurna region contain fossilized ammonites (spiral-shaped molluscs) dating from 150–200 million years ago. Of a much more recent origin, the bones of Peking Man and primitive stone tools have been found in the Churia Hills – proving that the Himalaya are so young that early humans were present during their creation.

Flora

Nepal's **vegetation** is largely determined by altitude and can be grouped into three main divisions. The lowlands include the Tarai, Churia Hills and valleys up to about 1000m; the midlands extend roughly from 1000m to 3000m; and the Himalaya from 3000m to the upper limit of vegetation (typically about 5000m). Conditions vary tremendously within these zones, however: south-facing slopes usually receive more moisture, but also more sun in their lower reaches, while certain areas that are less protected from the summer monsoon – notably around Pokhara – are especially wet. In general, rainfall is higher in the east, and a greater diversity of plants can be found there.

The lowlands

Most of the Tarai's remaining **lowland forest** consists of **sal**, a tall, straight tree much valued for its wood – a factor which is hastening its steady removal. *Sal* prefers well-drained soils and is most often found in pure stands along the Bhabar, the sloping alluvial plain at the base of the foothills; in the lower foothills, stunted specimens are frequently lopped for fodder. In spring, its cream-coloured flowers give off a heady jasmine scent. Other species sometimes associated with *sal* include **saj**, a large tree with crocodile-skin bark; **haldu**, used for making dugout canoes; and **bauhinia**, a strangling vine that corkscrews around its victims.

The wetter **riverine forest** supports a larger number of species, but life here is more precarious, as rivers regularly flood and change course during the monsoon. **Sisu**, related to rosewood, and **khair**, an acacia, are the first trees to colonize newly formed sandbanks. **Simal**, towering on mangrove-like buttresses, follows close behind; also known as the silk-cotton tree, it produces bulbous red flowers in February, and in May its seed pods explode with a cottony material that is used for stuffing mattresses. **Palash** – the "flame of the forest tree" – puts on an even more brilliant show of red flowers in February. All of these trees are deciduous, shedding their leaves during the dry spring. Many other species are evergreen, including **bilar**, **jamun** and **curry**, an understorey tree with thin, pointed leaves that smell just like their name.

Grasses dominate less stable wetlands. Of the fifty-plus species native to the Tarai, several routinely grow to a height of eight metres. Even experts tend to pass off any tall, dense stand as "elephant grass", because the only way to get through it is on an elephant; the most common genera are *Phragmites, Saccharum,*

Arundo and *Themeda*. Most grasses reach their greatest height just after the monsoon and flower during the dry autumn months. Locals cut **khar**, a medium-sized variety, for thatch in winter and early spring; the official thatch-gathering season in the Tarai parks (two weeks in Jan) is a colourful occasion, although the activity tends to drive wildlife into hiding. Fires are set in March and April to burn off the old growth and encourage tender new shoots, which provide food for game as well as livestock.

The middle elevations

The decline in precipitation from east to west is more marked at the **middle elevations** – so much so that the dry west shares few species in common with the moist eastern hills. Central Nepal is an overlap zone where western species tend to be found on south-facing slopes and eastern ones on the cooler northern aspects.

A common tree in dry western and central areas is **chir pine** (needles in bunches of three), which typically grows in park-like stands up to about 2000m. Various **oak** species often take over above 1500m, especially on dry ridges, and here you'll also find **ainsilo**, a cousin of the raspberry, which produces a sweet, if rather dry, golden fruit in May.

Although much of the wet midland forest has been lost to cultivation, you can see fine remnants of it above Godavari in the Kathmandu Valley and around the lakes in the Pokhara Valley. Lower elevations are dominated by a zone of **chestnut** and **chilaune**, the latter being a member of the tea family with oblong concave leaves and, in May, small white flowers. In eastern parts, several species of **laurel** form a third major component to this forest, while alder, cardamom and tree ferns grow in shady gullies.

The magical, mossy oak-rhododendron forest is still mostly intact above about 2000m, thanks to the prevalent fog that makes farming unviable at this level. **Khasru**, the predominant oak found here, has prickly leaves and is often laden with lichen, **orchids** and other epiphytes, which grow on other plants and get their nutrients directly from the air. It's estimated that more than 300 orchid varieties grow in Nepal, and although not all are showy or scented, the odds are you'll be able to find one flowering at almost any time of year. **Tree rhododendron** (*lali guraas*), Nepal's national flower, grows over 20m high and blooms with gorgeous red or pink flowers in March–April. Nearly thirty other species occur in Nepal, mainly in the east – the Milke Danda, a long ridge east of the Arun River, is the best place to view rhododendron, although impressive stands can also be seen between Ghodapani and Ghandrung in the Annapurna region. Most of Nepal's 300 species of **fern** are found in this forest type, as are many medicinal plants whose curative properties are known to ayurvedic practitioners but have yet to be studied in the West. Also occurring here are **lokta**, a small bush with fragrant white flowers in spring, whose bark is pulped to make paper, and **nettles**, whose stems are used by eastern hill-dwellers to make a hard-wearing fabric.

Holly, **magnolia** and **maple** may replace oak and rhododendron in some sites. **Dwarf bamboo**, the red panda's favourite food, grows in particularly damp places, such as northern Helambu and along the trail to the Annapurna Sanctuary. **Cannabis** thrives in disturbed sites throughout the midlands.

The Himalaya

Conifers form the dominant tree cover in the **Himalaya**. Particularly striking are the forests around Rara Lake in western Nepal, where **Himalayan spruce** and **blue pine** (needles grouped in fives) are interspersed with meadows. Elsewhere in the dry west you'll find magnificent **Himalayan cedar** (*deodar*) trees, which are protected by villagers, and a species of **cypress**. Two types of **juniper** are present in Nepal: the more common tree-sized variety grows south of the main Himalayan crest (notably around Tengboche in the Everest region), while a dwarf scrub juniper is confined to northern rain-shadow areas. Both provide incense for Buddhist rites. In wetter areas, **hemlock**, **fir** (distinguished from spruce by its upward-pointing cones) and even the deciduous **larch** may be encountered.

One of the most common (and graceful) broadleafed species is **white birch**, usually found in thickets near the tree line, especially on shaded slopes where the snow lies late. **Poplars** stick close to watercourses high up into the inner valleys – Muktinath is full of them – while **berberis**, a shrub whose leaves turn scarlet in autumn, grows widely on exposed sites. Trekking up the Langtang or Marsyangdi valleys you pass through many of these forest types in rapid succession, but the most dramatic transition of all is found in the valley of the Thak Khola (upper Kali Gandaki): the monsoon jungle below Ghasa gives way to blue pine, hemlock, rhododendron and horse chestnut; then to birch, fir and cypress around Tukche; then the **apricot** orchards of Marpha; and finally the blasted steppes of Jomosom.

Alpine vegetation predominates on the forest floor and in moist meadows above the tree line, and – apart from the dwarf rhododendron (some species of which give off a strong cinnamon scent and are locally used as incense) – many **flowers** found here will be familiar to European and North American walkers. There are too many to do justice to them here, but primula, buttercup, poppy, iris, larkspur, gentian, edelweiss, buddleia, columbine and sage are all common. Most bloom during the monsoon, but rhododendrons and primulas can be seen flowering in the spring and gentians and larkspurs in the autumn.

Mammals

Most of Nepal's rich **animal life** inhabits the Tarai and, despite dense vegetation, is most easily observed there. In the hill regions, wildlife is much harder to spot due to population pressure – along trekking trails, at least – while very few mammals live above tree line. The following overview progresses generally from Tarai to Himalayan species.

The **Asian one-horned rhino** (*gaida*) is one of five species found in Asia and Africa, all endangered. In Nepal, about 550 rhinos – a quarter of the species total – live in Chitwan, and 48 have been introduced to Bardia; they graze singly or in small groups in the marshy elephant grass, where they can remain surprisingly well hidden.

Although trained **elephants** (*hatti*) are a lingering part of Nepali culture (see p.347), their wild relatives are seen only rarely in Nepal. Since they require vast territory for their seasonal migrations, the settling of the Tarai is putting them in increasing conflict with man, and the few that survive tend to spend much of their time in India.

Koshi Tappu is the only remaining habitat in Nepal for another species better known as a domestic breed, **wild buffalo** (*arnaa*), which graze the wet grasslands in small herds. Majestic and powerful, the **gaur** (*gauri gaai*), or Indian bison, spends most of its time in the dry lower foothills, but descends to the Tarai in spring for water.

Perhaps the Tarai's most unlikely mammals, **gangetic dolphins** – one of four freshwater species in the world – are present in small numbers in the Karnali and Sapt Koshi rivers. Curious and gregarious, they tend to congregate in deep channels where they feed on fish and crustaceans, and may betray their presence with a puffing sound which they make through their blow-holes when surfacing. Dolphins are considered sacrosanct by Nepali Tharus, but are cruelly hunted in India.

The most abundant mammals of the Tarai, *chital*, or **spotted deer**, are often seen in herds around the boundary between riverine forest and grassland. **Hog deer** – so called because of their porky little bodies and head-down trot – take shelter in wet grassland, while the aptly named **barking deer**, measuring less than two feet high at the shoulder, are found throughout lowland and midland forests. **Swamp deer** gather in vast herds in Sukla Phanta, and males of the species carry impressive sets of antlers (their Nepali name, *barhasingha*, means "twelve points"). **Sambar**, heavy-set animals standing five feet at the shoulder, are more widely distributed, but elusive. Two species of antelope, the graceful, corkscrew-horned **blackbuck** and the ungainly **nilgai** (blue bull), may be seen at Bardia and Koshi Tappu respectively; the latter was once assumed to be a form of cattle, and thus spared by Hindu hunters, but no longer.

Areas of greatest deer and antelope concentrations are usually prime territory for **tiger** (*bagh*), their main predator. However, your chances of spotting one of Nepal's endangered Bengal tigers are slim: they're mainly nocturnal, never very numerous, and incredibly stealthy. In the deep shade and mottled sunlight of dense riverine forest, a tiger's orange- and black-striped coat provides almost total camouflage. A male may weigh 250kg and measure 3m from nose to tail. Tigers are solitary hunters; some have been known to consume up to twenty percent of their body weight after a kill, but they may go several days between feeds. Males and females maintain separate but overlapping territories, regularly patrolling them, marking the boundaries with scent and driving off interlopers. Some Nepalis believe tigers to be the unquiet souls of the deceased.

Leopards are equally elusive, but much more widely distributed: they may be found in any deep forest from the Tarai to the timber line. As a consequence, they account for many more maulings than tigers in Nepal, and are more feared. A smaller animal (males weigh about 45kg), they prey on monkeys, dogs and livestock. **Other cats** – such as the fishing cat, leopard cat and the splendid clouded leopard – are known to exist in the more remote lowlands and midlands, but are very rarely sighted. **Hyenas** and **wild dogs** are scavengers of the Tarai, and **jackals**, though seldom seen (they're nocturnal), produce an eerie howling that is one of the most common night sounds in the Tarai and hills.

While it isn't carnivorous, the dangerously unpredictable **sloth bear**, a Tarai species, is liable to turn on you and should be approached with extreme caution. Its powerful front claws are designed for unearthing termite nests, and its long snout for extracting the insects. The **Himalayan black bear** roams midland forests up to tree line and is, if anything, more dangerous. **Wild boars** can be seen rooting and scurrying through forest anywhere in Nepal.

Monkeys, a common sight in the Tarai and hills, come in two main varieties in Nepal. Comical **langurs** have silver fur, black faces and long, ropelike tails; you'll sometimes see them sitting on stumps like Rodin's *Thinker*. Brown **rhesus macaques** are more shy in the wild, but around temples are tame to the point of being nuisances. Many other **small mammals** may be spotted in the hills, among them porcupines, flying squirrels, foxes, civets, otters, mongooses and martens. The **red panda**, with its rust coat and bushy, ringed tail, almost resembles a tree-dwelling fox; like its Chinese relative, it's partial to bamboo, and is very occasionally glimpsed in the cloudforest of northern Helambu.

Elusive animals of the rhododendron and birch forests, **musk deer** are readily identified by their tusk-like canine teeth; males are hunted for their musk pod, which can fetch $200 an ounce on the international market. Though by no means common, **Himalayan tahr** is the most frequently observed large mammal of the high country; a goat-like animal with long, wiry fur and short horns, it browses along steep cliffs below the tree line. **Serow**, another goat relative, inhabits remote canyons and forested areas, while **goral**, sometimes likened to chamois, occurs from middle elevations up to the tree line.

The Himalaya's highest residents are **blue sheep**, who graze the barren grasslands above the tree line year-round. Normally tan, males go a slaty colour in winter, accounting for their name. Herds have been sighted around the Thorung La in the Annapurna region, but they occur in greater numbers north of Dhorpatan and in She-Phoksundo National Park. Their chief predator is the **snow leopard**, a secretive cat whose habits are still little understood.

Amphibians and reptiles

Native to the Tarai's wetlands, crocodiles are most easily seen in winter, when they sun themselves on muddy banks to warm up their cold-blooded bodies. The endangered **mugger crocodile** favours marshes and oxbow lakes, where it may lie motionless for hours on end until its prey comes within snapping distance. Muggers mainly pursue fish, but will eat just about anything they can get their jaws around – including human corpses thrown into the river by relatives unable to afford wood for a cremation. The even more endangered **gharial crocodile** lives exclusively in rivers and feeds on fish; for more on its precarious state, see p.345.

Nepal has many kinds of **snakes**, but they are rarely encountered: most hibernate in winter, even in the Tarai, and shy away from humans at other times of year. Common cobras – snake charmers' favourites – inhabit low elevations near villages; they aren't found in the Kathmandu Valley, despite their abundance in religious imagery there. Kraits and pit vipers, both highly poisonous, have been reported, as have pythons up to twenty feet long. However, the commonest species aren't poisonous and are typically less than two feet long.

Chances are you'll run into a **gecko** or two, probably clinging to a guesthouse wall. Helpful insect-eaters, these lizard-like creatures are able to climb almost any surface with the aid of suction pads on their feet. About fifty species of **fish** have been recorded in Nepal, but only *mahseer*, a sporty relative of carp that attains its greatest size in the lower Karnali River, is of much interest; most ponds are stocked with carp and catfish.

Birds

Over 800 **bird species** – one-tenth of the earth's total – have been sighted in Nepal. The country receives a high number of birds migrating between India and central Asia in spring and autumn and, because it spans so many ecosystems, provides habitats for a wide range of year-round residents. The greatest diversity of species is found in the Tarai wildlife parks, but even the Kathmandu Valley is remarkably rich in birdlife. The following is only a listing of the major categories – for the complete picture, get hold of *Birds of Nepal* (see "Books").

In the **Tarai** and lower hills, raptors (birds of prey) such as ospreys, cormorants, darters, gulls and kingfishers patrol streams and rivers for food; herons and storks can also be seen fishing, while cranes, ducks and moorhens wade in or float on the water. Many of these migratory species are particularly well 0srepresented at Koshi Tappu, which is located along the important Arun Valley corridor to Tibet. Peafowl make their meowing mating call – and peacocks occasionally deign to unfurl their plumage – while many species of woodpeckers can be heard, if not seen, high up in the *sal* canopy. Cuckoos and "brain fever" birds repeat their idiotic two- or four-note songs in an almost demented fashion. Parakeets swoop in formation; bee-eaters, swifts, drongos, swallows and rollers flit and dive for insects, while jungle fowl look like chickens as Monet might have painted them. Other oddities of the Tarai include the paradise flycatcher, with its lavish white tailfeathers and dragonfly-like flight; the lanky great adjutant stork, resembling a prehistoric reptile in flight; and the giant hornbill, whose beak supports an appendage that looks like an upturned welder's mask.

Many of the above birds are found in **the midlands** as well as the Tarai – as are mynas, egrets, crows and magpies, which tend to scavenge near areas of human habitation. Birds of prey – falcons, kestrels, harriers, eagles, kites, hawks and vultures – may also be seen at almost any elevation. Owls are common, but not much liked by Nepalis. Babblers and laughing thrushes populate the oak-rhododendron forest and are as noisy as their names suggest. Over twenty species of flycatchers are present in the Kathmandu Valley alone.

Nepal's national bird, the iridescent, multicoloured *danphe* (impeyan pheasant), can often be spotted scuttling through the undergrowth in the Everest region. *Kalij* and *monal*, two other native pheasants, also inhabit the higher hills and lower **Himalaya**. Migrating waterfowl often stop over at high-altitude lakes – ruddy shelducks are a trekking-season attraction at Gokyo – and snow pigeons, grebes, finches and choughs may all be seen at or above the tree line. Mountaineers have reported seeing choughs at up to 8200m on Everest, and migrating bar-headed geese are known to fly *over* Everest.

Invertebrates and insects

Perhaps no other creature in Nepal arouses such squeamishness as the **leech** (*jukha*). Fortunately, these segmented, caterpillar-sized annelids remain dormant underground during the trekking seasons; during the monsoon, however, they come out in force everywhere in the Tarai and hills, making any hike a bloody business. Leeches are attracted to body heat, and will inch up legs or drop from branches to reach their victims. The bite is completely painless – the bloodsucker injects a local anaesthetic and anticoagulant – and often goes unnoticed until the leech drops off of its own accord. To dislodge one, apply salt or burn it with a cigarette; don't pull it off or the wound could get infected.

Over 600 species of **butterflies** have been recorded in Nepal, with more being discovered all the time. Although the monsoon is the best time to view butterflies, many varieties can be seen before and especially just after the rains – look beside moist, sandy banks or atop ridges; Phulchoki is an excellent place to start in the Kathmandu Valley. Notable hill varieties include the intriguing orange oakleaf, whose markings enable it to vanish into forest litter, and the golden birdwing, a large, angular species with a loping wingbeat. **Moths** are even more numerous – around 5000 species are believed to exist in Nepal, including the world's largest, the giant atlas, which has a wingspan of almost a foot.

Termites are Nepal's most conspicuous social insects, constructing towering, fluted mounds up to eight feet tall in the western Tarai. Organized in colonies much the same as ants and bees, legions of termite workers and "reproductives" serve a single king and queen. The mounds function as cooling towers for the busy nest below; monuments to insect industry, they're made from tailings excavated from the colony's galleries and bonded with saliva for a wood-hard finish. **Honey bees** create huge, drooping nests in the Tarai and especially in the lush cliff country north of Pokhara. **Spiders** aren't very numerous in Nepal, although one notable species grows to be six inches across and nets birds (it's not poisonous to humans). **Fireflies**, with orange and black bodies, give off a greenish glow at dusk in the Tarai. For many travellers, however, the extent of their involvement with the insect kingdom will be in swatting **mosquitoes**: two genera are prevalent in the lowlands, one of them *Anopheles*, the infamous vector of malaria.

Books

Most of these books are a lot easier to come by in Nepal, and some will only be available there. Where the UK and US publishers are different, the UK publisher is given first; books published in other countries are indicated accordingly. Out of print (o/p) titles may still be found in Nepal, or in libraries back home. Books marked with the ☒ symbol are particularly recommended.

General

Barbara Crossette *So Close to Heaven* (Vintage). A survey of the "vanishing Buddhist kingdoms of the Himalayas", including a chapter focusing on Nepal's Tibetans, Bhotiyas and Newars.

Jeff Greenwald *Mister Raja's Neighborhood: Letters from Nepal* (John Daniel, US, o/p). The author went to Kathmandu to write the Great Asian Novel and ended up writing a series of letters – though perhaps contemplating his navel a bit too much in the process. *Shopping for Buddhas* (Lonely Planet), something of a sequel, pokes fun at the ways Westerners approach Nepalese Buddhism.

Harka Gurung *Vignettes of Nepal* (Sajha Prakashan, Nepal). This vivid travelogue, illuminated by a native's insights, is probably the best book written by a Nepali in English about his country.

☒ **Peter Matthiessen** *The Snow Leopard* (Vintage/Penguin). Matthiessen joins biologist George Schaller in a pilgrimage to Dolpo to track one of the world's most elusive cats, and comes up with characteristically Zen insights. A magnificent piece of writing, filled with beautiful descriptions of the landscape – and ever-perceptive observations of how Matthiessen's quest for the snow leopard became one of self-discovery.

Dervla Murphy *The Waiting Land* (Flamingo). A personal account of working with Pokhara's Tibetan refugees in 1965, written in the author's usual entertaining and politically on-the-ball style.

Coffee-table books

☒ **Kevin Bubriski** *Portrait of Nepal* (Chronicle Books, US). An extraordinary collection of large-format portraits that does for Nepal's indigenous peoples what E.S. Curtis's photography did for Native Americans. Bubriski has documented cultures and lifestyles that are passing within our generation: a truly important book.

☒ **Kevin Bubriski and Keith Dowman** *Power Places of the Kathmandu Valley* (Inner Traditions International, US). A collaboration by two eminently qualified authorities: rich colour photographs accompanied by well-researched text.

John Everingham and Galen Rowell *Pokhara: In the Shadow of the Annapurnas* (Book Faith India). Nice photos and informative text about Pokhara, its valley and the Annapurna region.

Jim Goodman and Thomas Kelly *Kathmandu Valley* (Book Faith India).

A collection of sumptuous photos and accompanying cultural essays.

Toni Hagen and Deepak Thapa *Nepal: The Kingdom of the Himalaya* (Himal Books, Nepal). No person alive has seen as much of Nepal as Hagen, who literally surveyed the entire country in the 1950s. His ground-breaking book, first published in 1961, has been recently updated.

Thomas Kelly and Patricia Roberts *Kathmandu: City at the Edge of the World* (Abbeville Press, US).

Stunning photography and extensive essays on culture and religion.

Eric Valli and Diane Summers *Caravans of the Himalaya* (Thames & Hudson/National Geographic). Travelogue of a journey along the Nepal–Tibet trade route, packaged for maximum armchair impact. Valli and Summers have collaborated on several other books of the same lavish ilk, notably *Hunting for Honey: Adventures with the Rajis of Nepal* (Thames & Hudson), which features amazing photos of men clinging to branches while raiding beehives.

History

Byron Farwell *The Gurkhas* (W.W. Norton). One of many books lionizing Nepal's famous Gurkha soldiers.

Percival Landon *Nepal* (Ratna Pustak Bhandar, Nepal). In two volumes, this was the most comprehensive study of the country at the time (1928) and is regarded as a classic – but having been commissioned by the Maharaja, it has a distinct political bias.

Michel Peissel *Tiger for Breakfast* (Time Books International, India). This biography of Boris Lissanevitch, the Russian émigré

who ran Kathmandu's first tourist hotel, opens a fascinating window on 1950s Nepal.

Ludwig Stiller *The Rise of the House of Gorkha* (Ratna Pustak Bhandar, Nepal). An academic but readable account of Nepal's unification and war with Britain, written by a Jesuit priest turned Nepalese citizen.

David Tomory *A Season in Heaven: True Tales from the Road to Kathmandu* (Lonely Planet). Disjointed but engrossing oral histories of the hippie trail to Kathmandu in the 1960s and 70s.

Culture and anthropology

Mary M. Anderson *The Festivals of Nepal* (Rupa, Nepal). Despite the title, this only covers the Kathmandu Valley's festivals, but it's quite readable.

Dor Bahadur Bista *Peoples of Nepal* (Ratna Pustak Bhandar, Nepal). A rather poor piece of scholarship, and now way out of date, but

still the only comprehensive overview of Nepal's ethnic groups.

Broughton Coburn *Nepali Aama: Life Lessons of a Himalayan Woman* (Anchor World Views, US). Delightful study of an earthy old Gurung woman in a village south of Pokhara. Told in her own words, and includes photos.

★ **Monica Connell** *Against a Peacock Sky* (Penguin/Viking Penguin). Beautiful, impressionistic rendering of life among the *matawaali* (alcohol-drinking) Chhetris of Jumla District, capturing the subtleties of village life in Nepal.

Loke Rajye Laxmi Devi *Nepalese Kitchen* (Lustre Press, India). Small-format booklet with a good selection of recipes, helpfully illustrated with colour photos.

★ **Hugh R. Downs** *Rhythms of a Himalayan Village* (HarperCollins, US; Book Faith India). An extraordinarily sensitive synthesis of black-and-white photos, text and quotes, describing rituals and religion in a Solu village.

James F. Fisher *Sherpas: Reflections on Change in Himalayan Nepal* (University of California, US). A before-and-after account, written by a member of Edmund Hillary's 1964 school-building team, who concludes that Sherpas are more resilient than we give them credit for.

William P. Forbes *The Glory of Nepal: A Mythological Guidebook to the Kathmandu Valley* (Pilgrims, Nepal). A lively retelling of myths from the *Nepal Mahatmya* and other medieval texts, linking them to modern-day locations.

Jim Goodman *Guide to Enjoying Nepalese Festivals* (Pilgrims, Nepal). All the arcane whys and wherefores of the Kathmandu Valley's festivals: authoritative, though not very user-friendly.

★ **Eva Kipp** *Bending Bamboo, Changing Winds: Nepali Women Tell Their Life Stories* (Book Faith India). Powerful oral histories and photographs of women from all over

Nepal, revealing not only the country's amazing cultural diversity but also the universal trials of being a Nepali woman.

Robert I. Levy and Kedar Raj Rajopadhyaya *Mesocosm: Hinduism and the Organization of a Traditional Newar City in Nepal* (University of California, US). A heavy anthropological study of Bhaktapur, but its thesis – that the city's inhabitants collectively operate a sort of well-oiled cultural and spiritual machine – is fascinating.

Stan Royal Mumford *Himalayan Dialogue: Tibetan Lamas and Gurung Shamans in Nepal* (University of Wisconsin, US). An account of myths and rituals practised in a village along the Annapurna Circuit – fascinating, once you get past the anthropological jargon.

Ram Dayal Rakesh *Folk Festivals of Mithila* (Book Faith, India). A delightful account of this Tarai region's festivals, along with related folk tales and traditional song lyrics.

Barbara J. Scot *The Violet Shyness of Their Eyes: Notes from Nepal* (Calyx Books, US). An American woman's perspective on life in the Nepali hills, striking a nice balance between observation and introspection.

Mary Slusser *Nepal Mandala: A Cultural Study of the Kathmandu Valley* (Princeton University, US). A gorgeous (but exorbitant) two-volume set, this is the definitive study of Newar culture and religion.

David L. Snellgrove *Himalayan Pilgrimage* (Shambhala, US, o/p). An insightful travelogue/anthropological account of a trip through northwestern Nepal in the 1950s.

Religion

William Buck *The Mahabharata* (Motilal Banarsidass, India). Probably the best job anyone's done of wrestling this vast epic down to a readable story in English.

P. Lal (trans) *The Ramayana of Valmiki* (Tarang, Nepal). A condensed version of the classic epic.

Barbara Stoler Miller (trans) *The Bhagavad-Gita* (Bantam, US). A poetic English rendering of Krishna's teaching.

Mattheiu Ricard *Journey to Enlightenment* (Aperture, US). A remembrance of the late Khyentse Rinpoche, with a contribution by the Dalai Lama.

K.M. Sen *Hinduism* (Viking Penguin). An accessible survey, explanatory without being too obscure.

Robert A.F. Thurman *Essential Tibetan Buddhism* (Harper San Francisco, US). A survey of basic teachings, weaving together classic texts with modern commentary. Not for beginners.

Chögyam Trungpa *The Myth of Freedom* (Shambhala, US). A useful primer on the metaphysics of Buddhist meditation, this is one of a welter of books by a master who was instrumental in packaging Buddhism for the West.

Art and architecture

Lydia Aran *The Art of Nepal* (Sahayogi, Nepal). Surprisingly good overview of Nepalese religion as well as stone, metal and wood sculpture and *thangka* paintings.

Claire Burkert *Janakpur Art: A Living Tradition* (Janakpur Women's Development Center, Nepal). As simple and understated as its subject, this slim booklet highlights the dignity of the women who create Maithili art.

Susi Dunsmore *Nepalese Textiles* (British Museum Press/University of Washington). A labour of love, this handsome, full-colour book details the patterns and techniques of all of Nepal's major ethnic groups.

Hannelore Gabriel *Jewelry of Nepal* (Thames & Hudson/Weatherhill). A thorough cataloguing of traditional highland jewellery (less coverage is given to hill and Tarai styles), with lavish illustrations.

Handicraft Association of Nepal *A Short Description of Gods, Goddesses and Ritual Objects of Buddhism and Hinduism in Nepal* (Handicraft Association of Nepal). An inexpensive booklet that may help in sorting out iconography.

Michael Hutt *Nepal: A Guide to the Art and Architecture of the Kathmandu Valley* (Shambhala, US). An in-depth discussion of iconography, design and construction, in hard cover.

Eva Rudy Jansen *The Book of Buddhas: Ritual Symbolism Used in Buddhist Statuary and Ritual Objects* (Binkey Kok, Holland; Motilal Banarsidass, India) and *The Book of Hindu Imagery: The Gods and Their Symbols* (Weiser, UK; New Age, India). Good introductory guides to the iconography of religious statuary found in Nepal.

Fiction and poetry

Laxmi Prasad Devkota *Muna Madan* (Nirala, Nepal). The most famous work by one of Nepal's best-loved poets recounts the tragic, almost Shakespearean tale of a young Newar trader who leaves his young wife to travel to Lhasa.

Michael James Hutt (ed) *Himalayan Voices: An Introduction to Modern Nepali Literature* (University of California, US; Indian Book Company, India). An excellent survey of Nepali poetry and fiction, with some commentary.

Shankar Koirala *Khairini Ghat* (Pilgrims, Nepal). A disturbing novella depicting ignorance, cowardice and cruelty in a Nepali village in the 1950s.

Kesar Lall and Tej R. Kansakar (trans) *Forbidden Fruit and Other Stories* (Ratna Pustak Bhandar, Nepal). Some of these stories, translated from the Newari, are better than others, but all shed light on Nepali culture, dealing with themes of family duty, class relationships, fate and the ever-present spectre of *dukha* (sadness).

Kim Stanley Robinson *Escape From Kathmandu* (Tor, UK). Pure potboiler, but it might be fun for the real-life *mise en scène* (action starts at the *Hotel Star* in Thamel).

Han Suyin *The Mountain is Young* (Arrow/Putnam). The first – and still only – bestseller in English set in Nepal. This 1958 East-meets-West romance is very much of its time, yet still timely, for its portrayal of "Khatmandu" shows how much has changed and, somewhat surprisingly, how much hasn't.

★ **Manjushree Thapa** *The Tutor of History* (Penguin, India). The first true literary novel written in English by a Nepali is a vivid evocation of village life, urban life, politics, social mores, alcoholism, sexism, religion and ambition in Nepal – all handled with gentle humour and compassion, and in a voice that cleverly captures the Nepali language and psyche.

★ **Samrat Upadhyay** *Arresting God in Kathmandu* (Houghton Mifflin, US). A Nepali *Dubliners*. This acclaimed collection of stories, written by a Nepali living in the US, takes on typically introspective Nepali themes – jealousy, self-doubt, desire, family tension – but with a subtlety and frankness that's quite modern. Upadhyay's forthcoming novel, *The Guru of Love*, is eagerly awaited.

Ramesh Vikal *A Leaf in a Begging Bowl* (Mandala Book Point, Nepal). Classic examples of the progressive school of Nepali literature, these short stories convey a great empathy for the common people of Nepal.

Children's books

Kanak Mani Dixit *Adventures of a Nepali Frog* and *The Leech and I* (Rato Bangala Kitab, Nepal). Fun, fanciful romps through Nepal with animal protagonists.

Eva Kipp et al *The Golden Umbrella* (Book Faith India). Read-aloud Nepali folktales. *Living in the Clouds* is a longer illustrated story of a young Sherpa girl.

Joy Stephens *Where's the Hasiya, Sanu Maya?* (Rhim-Jim Kitaab, Nepal). A bilingual story for very young ones of village life in Nepal.

Joanne Stephenson *Two Rams* (Pilgrims, Nepal). A Nepali boy meets his first Westerners. *The Decision*, for older readers, tells the story of a Gurung boy's journey to Kathmandu and back.

Natural history

Robert Fleming, Jr *The General Ecology, Flora and Fauna of Midland Nepal* (Tribhuwan University, Nepal). A simple ecology text drawing on examples mainly from the Kathmandu Valley.

★ **Richard Grimmett, Carol Inskipp and Tim Inskipp** *Birds of Nepal* (Christopher Helm/Princeton University). The authoritative guide.

★ **K.K. Gurung** *Heart of the Jungle* (David & Charles, US). The essential guide to Chitwan's flora and fauna, written by the former manager of *Tiger Tops Jungle Lodge*.

Carol Inskipp *A Popular Guide to the Birds and Mammals of the Annapurna Conservation Area* (ACAP, Nepal). A slim volume with some colour plates.

Dorothy Mierow and Tirtha Shrestha *Himalayan Flowers and Trees* (Sahayogi, Nepal). A pocket-sized guide with colour plates and some useful information at the back.

George Schaller *Stones of Silence: Journeys in the Himalaya* (Bantam, US). Written by the wildlife biologist who accompanied Peter Matthiessen on his quest for the snow leopard, this book provides a detailed view of ecosystems of the high Himalaya.

Colin Smith *Illustrated Checklist of Nepal's Butterflies* (Rohit Kumar, Nepal). Beautiful colour plates showing nearly 600 species, by the curator of the Annapurna Regional Museum.

Adrian and Jimmie Storrs *Enjoy Trees* (Book Faith, India). Beginner's guide to the more common flora of Nepal, covering flowers as well as trees, and with good sections on medicinal and religious plants.

Development and politics

Lynn Bennett *Dangerous Wives and Sacred Sisters* (Columbia University, US, o/p). Good insight into the life and position of Hindu women in Nepal.

★ **Dor Bahadur Bista** *Fatalism and Development* (Orient Longman, India). An insightful analysis of the cultural factors that stand in the way of Nepal's development, by the country's best-known anthropologist.

Jonathan Gregson *Blood Against the Snows* (Fourth Estate, UK). Carefully researched and occasionally lurid account of the royal massacre, prefaced by rather dustier diggings into the history of Nepal's monarchy.

Indra Majpuria *Nepalese Women* (M. Devi, Nepal). Though it wanders quite a bit, this forcibly gets across the hardships and problems facing women in Nepal.

★ **Neelesh Misra** *End of the Line: The Story of the Killing of the Royals in Nepal* (Penguin, India). This account of the royal massacre of 2001 is lively and illuminating, though perhaps not critical enough of the official version of events.

Charlie Pye-Smith *Travels in Nepal* (Penguin, o/p). A cross between a travelogue and a progress report on aid projects, this succeeds in giving plenty of facts and analysis without getting bogged down in institutional waffle.

David Seddon *Nepal: A State of Poverty* (Vikas, Nepal). A hard look at the issues by one of the longest-serving foreign critics of Nepal's development efforts.

Ludmilla Tüting and Kunda Dixit *Bikas-Binas, Development-Destruction* (Ratna Pustak Bhandar, Nepal). Excellent collection of articles which covers the whole gamut of dilemmas arising out of development, environmental degradation and tourism.

Health

Jim Duff and Peter Gormly *The Himalayan First Aid Manual* (World Expeditions, Nepal). Handy pocket-sized booklet, sold by the Kathmandu Environmental Education Project.

Andrew J. Pollard and David R. Murdoch *The High Altitude Medicine Handbook* (Book Faith India).

Everything you need to know for a trek; the "micro" edition contains the same text in a much more portable form.

Dr Ravi P. Thapaliya *Your Health in Nepal* (Musk, Nepal). A thorough manual on health and safety for travelling, trekking, rafting and visiting the Tarai wildlife parks.

Mountains and mountaineering

Chris Bonington and Charles Clarke *Everest: The Unclimbed Ridge* (Thunder's Mouth, US). The classic story of the bold but ill-fated first attempt of Everest's fearsome Northeast Ridge in 1982. Also look out for Bonington's retrospective, *Mountaineer: Thirty Years of Climbing on the World's Great Peaks* (Baton Wicks/Sierra Club).

★ **Maurice Herzog** *Annapurna* (Pimlico/Lyons). One of the greatest true adventure stories ever written, describing the first successful ascent of an 8000-metre peak. Herzog's dreamlike description of his altitude- and hypothermia-induced stupor on the summit, the desperate descent, and the state of his mind as he contemplated death are riveting.

★ **Jon Krakauer** *Into Thin Air* (Pan/Anchor). The best-selling first-person account of the tragedy on Everest in 1996. It's an efficient and balanced telling of a story that reads like a whodunnit and has all the elements of high tragedy: hubris, heroism, angry mountain gods, rivalry, vanity, triumph and agony. For alternative perspectives on the same events, see Anatoli Boukreev and G. Weston deWalt's *The Climb* (St Martin's/Pan), David Breashears' *High Exposure* (Canongate/Touchstone), Lene Gammelgaard's *Climbing High* (Pan/HarperCollins), Goran Kropp's *Ultimate High* (Discovery Channel, US) and Beck Weathers' *Left for Dead* (Dell, US).

Reinhold Messner *The Crystal Horizon* (Crowood/Mountaineers). Not very well written (or maybe it's the translation), but nonetheless compelling account of Messner's 1980 solo ascent of Everest. Messner's

All 14 Eight-Thousanders (Crowood Press, UK) has awesome photos and an interesting appendix of Himalayan mountaineering statistics.

H.W. Tilman *Nepal Himalaya* (Pilgrims, Nepal). A chatty account of the first mountaineering recon-naissance of Nepal in 1949–51, reprinted as part of *The Seven Mountain-Travel Books* (Diadem/The Mountaineers). Though crusty, and at times racist, Tilman was one of the century's great adventurers, and his writing remains fresh and witty.

Trekking guides

Stan Armington *Trekking in the Nepal Himalaya* (Lonely Planet). The Microsoft of trekking guides, this is for people who want to be told where to spend each night.

★ **Stephen Bezruchka** *Trekking in Nepal: A Traveler's Guide* (Cordee/The Mountaineers). The most culturally sensitive book on trekking, containing background pieces on Nepali language, culture and natural history.

Amy R. Kaplan and Michael Keller *Nepal: An Essential Handbook for Trekkers* (Mandala, Nepal). A primer on trek preparations and cultural and environmental sensitivity. Includes tips on health, porters and trekking with kids.

Wendy Brewer Lama *Trekking Gently in the Himalaya* (Sagarmatha Pollution Control Project, Nepal). An excellent, concise pamphlet on trekkers' environmental and cultural responsibilities.

★ **Jamie McGuinness** *Trekking in the Everest Region* and *Trekking in*
Langtang, Helambu and Gosainkund (Trailblazer, UK). Exhaustive and perceptive guides to all the routes in these regions.

Bill O'Connor *The Trekking Peaks of Nepal* (Crowood/Mountaineers). Describes climbing routes and trek approaches for eighteen trekking peaks.

Steve Razzetti *Trekking and Climbing in Nepal* (New Holland/Stackpole). Excellent background to many off-the-beaten-track treks and trekking-peak climbs; strong on cultural contexts, short on trail details for neophytes.

Kev Reynolds *Dolpo* and *Manaslu: A Trekker's Guide* (Book Faith India). Slim but welcome guidebooks to these areas.

Bryn Thomas *Trekking in the Annapurna Region* (Trailblazer, UK). The best guide to this popular region, though not as comprehensive as the other Trailblazer titles.

Other guidebooks

Dubby Bhagat *Peak Hour: A Handbook of the Everest Flight* (Rupa, Nepal). Chatty, first-person trave-logue of the sights seen from the standard "mountain flight".

John Burbank *Culture Shock! Nepal* (Kuperard/Graphic Arts Center). Sensitivity training for tourists, with valuable insights into social mores, religion, caste and cross-cultural relations.

James Giambrone *Kathmandu Valley Bikes & Hikes* (Langenscheidt/APA). Two dozen itineraries, accompanied by an excellent foldout route map.

Rajendra Khadka (ed) *Travelers' Tales Nepal* (Travelers' Tales Inc, US). Interesting anecdotes and musings by expats, climbers and ordinary travellers, including excerpts by Reinhold Messner and Peter Matthiessen, and the most disgusting leech story ever committed to paper.

★ **Peter Knowles** *White Water Nepal* (Rivers Publishing/Menasha Ridge Press). An indispensable companion for all rafters and kayakers, written with great wit and no nonsense; useful maps, stream profiles and hydrographs.

John Sanday *Odyssey Guide to the Kathmandu Valley* (Collins, UK). The author is the leading authority on restoration of the valley's monuments.

language

language

Nepali

asic Nepali is surprisingly easy to learn, and local people are invariably thrilled when travellers make the effort to pick up a few phrases. Knowing a little bit of the language certainly comes in handy, too, since while nearly all Nepalis who deal with tourists speak English, few people do off the beaten track.

Nepali is closely related to Hindi and other Sanskrit-based languages, so Nepali-speakers and Indians can usually catch the gist of what the other is saying. Many Nepalis in the southern Tarai speak other languages from the same family, such as Bhojpuri and Maithili, but Nepalis from the ethnic groups of the hill and mountain areas may speak one of several dozen Tibeto-Burman languages that are completely unrelated to Nepali – in fact they're further removed from it than English is. Some of these languages may only be spoken by a few thousand people within a single valley – within the Rai and Limbu ethnic groups, for example, there are as many as thirty mutually unintelligible languages and dialects.

Successive governments have reinforced the official status of Nepali, turning it from an important regional language (it's also spoken in Darjeeling and Assam) into a lingu franca and, finally, a national language. Almost everyone in Nepal now speaks Nepali; fortunately for foreigners, many of those who speak it as a second language – notably those who live along trekking routes – use a relatively simple form that's easy enough to learn and understand. Educated Nepalis, however, especially in and around Kathmandu, may employ a sophisticated version of Nepali that borrows heavily from Sanskrit, Hindi and English. For all the much-bemoaned lack of educational opportunities in Nepal, it's worth remembering that many Nepalis speak both their mother tongue and Nepali fluently, and often decent English and Hindi as well.

Nepali is written in a script known as **Devanaagari**: fortunately, there's no need for travellers to learn it since signs, bus destinations and so on are usually written in Roman script. This transliteration, though, often leads to problems of inconsistency (see box on p.23).

The most useful **phrasebooks** on the market are Lonely Planet's *Nepal Phrasebook* and Shyam P. Wagley's *Nepali Phrasebook* (Ratna Pustak Bhandar, Nepal). For a full-blown **teach-yourself book**, try *A Basic Course in Spoken Nepali*, by Tika Karki and Chij Shrestha (self-published) or David Matthews' *A Course in Nepali* (School of Oriental and African Studies, UK), both widely available in Nepal.

Pronunciation

Even when Nepali is transliterated from the Devanaagari script into the Roman alphabet using phonetic spellings, there are a number of peculiarities in pronunciation:

a as in *alone*

aa as in *father*

b sounds like a cross between "b" and "v"

e as in *bet*

i as in *police*

j as in *just*

o as in note

u as in boot

r lightly rolled; can sound like a cross between "r" and "d"

w sounds like a cross between "w" and "v"

s can sound almost like "sh"

z sounds like "dj" or "dz"

The "a" and "aa" distinction is crucial. *Maa* (in) is pronounced as it looks, with the vowel stretched out, but *ma* (I) sounds like "muh" and *mandir* (temple) like "mundeer". The accent almost always goes on the syllable with "aa" in it, or if there's no "aa", on the first syllable.

Some Nepali vowels are nasalized – to get the right effect, you have to block off your nasal passage, producing a slightly honking sound like a French "n". Nasalized vowels aren't indicated in this book, but they're something to be aware of. To hear how they should sound, listen to a Nepali say *tapaai* (you) or *yahaa* (here) – it's like saying "tapaaing" or "yahaang", but stopping just before the end.

Aspirated consonants

The combinations "ch" and "sh" are pronounced as in English, but in all other cases where an "h" follows a consonant the sound is meant to be aspirated – in other words, give it an extra puff of air. Thus *bholi* (tomorrow) sounds like b'*holi* and Thamel sounds like T'*ha*mel. Note these combinations:

chh sounds like a very breathy "ch", as in "pi*tch he*re"; almost like "tsha"

ph sometimes sounds like an "f" (as in *pho*ne) but may also be pronounced like a breathy "p" (as in ha*pha*zard)

th is pronounced as in "pu*t he*re" (as in Ka*th*mandu, not as in *th*ink)

Retroflex consonants

Finally, the sounds "d", "r" and "t" occur in two forms, dental and retroflex; to Nepali ears, English "t" falls somewhere between the two. The retroflex sound is made by rolling the tip of the tongue back towards the roof of the mouth – a classic "Indian" sound. To get the dental effect you almost need to say a "d" with the tip of the tongue right up against the teeth. An obvious example of a retroflex (and aspirated) "t" is Kathmandu, which sounds a little like a breathy "Kartmandu". Sometimes retroflexion results in a difference in meaning: *saathi* means friend, but with a retroflex "th" it means sixty.

A brief guide to speaking Nepali

Greetings and basic phrases

For advice on the nuances of some of these basic phrases, see "Cultural Hints" in Basics, p.74. Separate words for "please" and "thank you" are rarely used, though *dhanyebaad* is increasingly common in tourist areas. Politeness is indicated by your manner and by the grammatical form of the verb. If you feel like you're being rude, try just saying "thank you" in English.

Hello, Goodbye (formal) – **Namaste**
Hello (very formal) – **Namaskar**
Thank you (very formal) – **Dhanyebaad**
Yes/No (It is/isn't) – **Ho/Hoina**
Yes/No (There is/isn't) – **Chha/Chhaina**
How are things? – **Kasto chha?** or **Sanchai chha?**
It's/I'm OK, fine – **Thik chha** or **Sanchai chha**
OK!/Sure thing! (informal) – **La!**
OK!/Sure thing! (formal) – **Hos!**
What's your name (to an adult) – **Tapaaiko naam ke ho?**
  (to a child) – **Timro naam ke ho?**
My name is … – **Mero naam … ho**
My country is … – **Mero desh … ho**

I don't know – **Malaai thaahaa chhaina**
I didn't understand that – **Maile tyo bujina**
Please speak more slowly – **Bistaarai bolnus**
Please say that again – **Pheri bolnus**
I speak a little Nepali – **Ali ali Nepali aunchha**
Pardon? – **Hajur?**
No thanks – **Nai** or **Pardaina** (I don't want it)
I'm sorry, excuse me – **Maph garnus**
Let's go – **Jaun; "djam"**
It was an honour to meet you – **Hajur lai bhetera dherai khushi laagyo**
Thank you [very much] for everything – **Sapai kurako laag [dherai] dhanyabaad**
See you again – **Pheri betaunla**

Forms of address

Excuse me … – **O …**
  (more polite) – **Hajur …**
Elder brother – **Daai; Daaju** (said to men your age or older; more respectful)
Elder sister – **Didi** (women your age or older)
Younger sister – **Bahini** (women or girls younger than you)
Younger brother – **Bhaai** (men or boys younger than you)

Father – **Bua** (a man old enough to be your father)
Mother – **Aama** (women old enough to be your mother)
Grandfather – **Baje** (old men)
Grandmother – **Bajei** (old women)
Shopkeeper, Innkeeper – **Saahuji** (male)
Shopkeeper, Innkeeper – **Saahuni** (female)

Basic questions and requests

Whether you're making a statement or asking a question, the word order is the same in Nepali – to indicate that you're asking, not telling, make sure you raise your voice at the end.

Do you speak English? – **Tapaai Angreji bolnuhunchha?**
Does anyone speak English? – **Kasailaai Angreji aunchha?**
I don't speak Nepali – **Ma Nepali boldina**
Is/Isn't there [a room]? – **[Kothaa] chha/chhaina?**
Is [a meal] available? – **[Khaanaa] painchha?**
Is [smoking] okay? – **[Curot khaane] hunchha?**
Please help me – **Malaai madhat garnus**
Please give me … – **… dinus**
I'm [hungry] – **Malaai [bhok] laagyo**
I'm not [hungry] – **Malaai [bhok] laageko chhaina**
I like … [very much] – **Malaai … [dherai] manparchha**

I want/don't want – **Malaai … chaahinchha/chaaidaina**
What's [this] for? – **[Yo] ke ko laagi?**
What's the matter? – **Ke bhayo?**
What's [this] called in Nepali? – **[yas] laai Nepali maa ke bhanchha?**
What does [Choraa] mean? – **[Chora] ke bhanchha?**
Really? – **Hora?**
How – **Kasari**
What – **Ke**
When – **Kahile**
Where – **Kahaa**
Who – **Ko**
Why – **Kina**
Which – **Kun**

Negotiations

How much does this cost? – **Esko kati parchha?**

How much for a [room]? – **[Rum] ko kati parchha?**

Is there somewhere I can stay here? – **Mero laagi basne thau chha holaa?**

How many people? – **Kati jana?**

For [two] people – **[Dui] jana ko laagi**

Only one person – **Ek jana maatrai**

Can I see it? – **Herna sakchhu?**

Don't do that! (to a child) – **Teso nagara!**

Don't touch that! (to a child) – **Tyo nachalau!**

Go away! (to a child) – **Jaau!**

It's very/too expensive – **Dherai mahango bhayo**

Is there a cheaper one? – **Kunai sasto chha?**

I don't need/want it – **Malaai chaaidaina**

I don't have any change – **Masanga khudra chhaina**

Please use the meter – **Meter-maa jaanus**

Just a moment – **Ek chin** (literally, "one blink")

I'll come back – **Ma pharkinchhu**

Good job, Well done – **Kyaraamro**

Don't worry – **Chinta nagarnus**

The bill, please – **Bil dinus**

Directions

Where is the … ? – **… kahaa chha?**

Where is this [bus] going? – **Yo [bas] kahaa jaanchha?**

Which is the way/trail/road to …? – **… jaane baato kun ho?**

Which is the best way? – **Kun baato raamro chha?**

How far is it? – **Kati taadha chha?**

Where are you going? – **Tapaai kahaa jaanuhunchha?**

I'm going to … – **Ma … jaanchhu**

Where have you come from? – **Tapaai kahaabaata aaunubhaeko?** – (also means "where are you from?")

Here – **Yahaa**

There/Yonder – **Tyahaa/Utyahaa**

[To the] right – **Daayaa [tira]**

[To the] left – **Baayaa [tira]**

Straight – **Sidhaa**

North – **Uttaar**

South – **Dakshin**

East – **Purba**

West – **Pashchim**

Near/Far – **Najik/Taadha**

Time

What time is it? – **Kati bajyo?**

What time does the bus leave? – **Yo bas kati baje jaanchha?**

When does this bus arrive [in Kathmandu]? – **Yo bas kati baje [Kathmandu-maa] pugchha?**

How many hours does it take? – **Kati ghanta laagchha?**

[Two] o'clock – **[Dui] bajyo**

[Nine]-thirty – **Saadhe [nau] bajyo**

[Five] past [six] – **[Chha] bajera [paanch] minet gayo** (formal); **chha paanch** (informal)

[Ten] to [eight] – **[Aath] bajna [das] minet bakichha**

Minute – **Minet**

Hour – **Ghanta**

Day – **Din**

Day (of week) – **Bar**

Week – **Haptaa**

Month – **Mahina**

Year – **Barsaa**

Today – **Aaja**

Tomorrow – **Bholi**

Yesterday – **Hijo**

Now – **Ahile**

Later – **Pachhi**

Ago, Before – **Pahile**

Next week – **Aarko haptaa**

Last month – **Gayeko maina**

[Two] years ago – **[Dui] barsa agi**

Morning – **Bihaana**

Afternoon – **Diuso**

Evening – **Belukaa**

Night – **Raati**

Nouns

Bag, Baggage – Jholaa	Hotel/Lodge – Hotel/Laj	Room – Rum, kothaa
Bed – Khat	House – Ghar	School – Skul
Blanket, Quilt – Sirak	Husband – Srimaan	Seat – Sit
Boy – Keta	Job, Work – Kaam	Shoe – Jutta
Bus – Bas	Lamp – Batti	Shop – Pasal
Candle – Mainbatti	Mattress – Dasna, ochhan	Son – Chori
Child, Children – Ketaketi	Medicine – Ausadhi	Stomach – Pet
Clothes – Lugaa	Mistake – Galti	Success – Safalta
Daughter – Choraa	Money – Paisaa	Teahouse/Chiya pasal,
Ear – Kan	Mother – Aama	chiya dokan
Eye – Akha	Mouth – Mukh	Ticket – Tiket
Family – Pariwaar	Nose – Naak	Toilet – Chaarpi, toilet
Father – Buwa	Pain – Dukhyo	Town, Village – Gaaun
Fever – Jwaro	Paper – Kaagat	Trail/Main trail – Baato/mul
Food – Khaanaa	Person – Maanchhe	baato
Foot – Khutta	Place – Thau	Water – Paani
Friend – Saathi	Problem – Samasya	Wife – Srimati
Girl – Keti	Restaurant – Resturent,	
Hand – Haat	bhojanalaya	
Head – Taauko	Road – Baato, rod	

Adjectives and adverbs

One tricky thing about Nepali adjectives: the ones that describe feelings behave like nouns. Thus to express the notion "I'm thirsty", you have to say *Malaai thirkaa laagyo* ("To me thirst has happened").

A little – Alikati, thorai	Dirty – Phohor	Many – Dherai
A lot – Dherai	Dishonest – Bemaani	More (quantity) – Aru
After – Pachhi	Downhill – Oraallo	More (degree) – Ekdum, ajai
Again – Pheri	Dry – Sukeko	Naughty – Badmaas
All – Sabai	Early – Chaadai	Near(er) – Najik(ai)
Alone – Eklai	Easy – Sajilo	Never – Kahile paani
Already – Pahile	Empty – Khali	New – Nayaa
Always – Sadai	Enough – Prasasta	Noisy – Halla
Another – Aarko	Expensive – Mahango	Often – Kahilekahi
Bad – Kharaab, naraamro	Far – Taadhaa	Old (thing) – Purano
Beautiful – Raamro	Few – Thorai	Old (person) – Budho (male),
Best – Sabbhandaa raamro	Full (thing) – Bhari	Budhi – (female)
Better – Ajai raamro	Fun – Majaa	Only – Maatrai
Big – Thulo	Good – Raamro	Open – Khulaa
Cheap – Sasto	Happy – Khushi	Quick – Chitto
Clean – Safaa	Heavy – Garungo	Pretty, good – Ramaailo
Clever – Chalakh	Hot – Garam (person or	Right (correct) – Thik
Closed – Banda	weather)	Sad – Dukhi
Cold – Jaado (person or	Hot (liquid) – Taato	Same – Eutai
weather)	Hungry – Bhokayeko	Similar – Jastai
Cold (liquid) – Chiso	Hurt – Dhukyo	Slowly – Bistaarai
Crazy – Paagal	Late – Dhilo	Small – Saano
Dark – Adhyero	Less – Kam	Sometimes – Kahile kahi
Different – Pharak	Lost – Haraayeko	Soon – Chaadai, chittai
Difficult – Gaaro	Loud – Charko	Stolen – Choreko

Strong - **Baliyo**	Thirsty - **Tirkha**	Wet - **Bhijyo**
Stupid - **Murkha**	Tired - **Thakai**	Worse - **Khattam**
Tall - **Aglo**	Too much - **Atti**	Worst - **Sabbhandaa**
Tasty - **Mitho**	Uphill - **Ukaalo**	**naraamro**
Terrible - **Jhur**	Very - **Dherai**	Wrong - **Galti**

Verbs

The following verbs are in the infinitive form. To turn a verb into a polite command (eg, "Please sit"), just add *-s* (*Basnus*); for a request, replace the *-nu* ending with just *-u*, said through the nose, almost like "*Basun?*". For an all-purpose tense, drop the *-u* ending and replace it with *-e* (eg *jaane* can mean go, going or will go, depending on the context). The easiest way to negate any verb is to put *na-* in front of it (*nabasnus*, *najaane*).

Arrive - **Aaipugnu**	Help - **Madhat garnu**	Say, Tell - **Bhannu**
Ask - **Sodhnu**	Hurry - **Hatar garnu**	Sit - **Basnu**
Believe - **Biswas garnu**	Learn - **Siknu**	Sell - **Bechnu**
Break - **Bhaanchnu**	Leave - **Chodnu**	Sleep - **Sutnu**
Buy - **Kinnu**	Lie (speak untruthfully) -	Speak - **Bolnu**
Carry - **Boknu**	**Jhutho bolnu**	Steal - **Chornu**
Close - **Banda garnu**	Look, See - **Hernu**	Stop - **Roknu**
Come - **Aunu**	Lose - **Haraunu**	Take - **Linu**
Cook - **Pakaaunu**	Make - **Banaunu**	Think - **Bichaar garnu, sochnu**
Do - **Garnu**	Need - **Chaahinu**	Try - **Kosis garnu**
Eat - **Khaanu**	Open - **Kholnu**	Understand - **Bujnu**
Feel - **Mahasus garnu**	Put - **Raakhnu**	Use - **Prayog garnu**
Fix (attach) - **Thoknu**	Receive - **Paunu**	Wait - **Parkhinu**
Forget - **Birsinu**	Remember - **Samjhinu**	Walk - **Hidnu**
Get - **Paunu, linu**	Rent - **Bhadama linu**	Want - **Chahanu**
Give - **Dinu**	Rest - **Aaram garnu**	Wash (face, clothes) - **Dhunu**
Go - **Jaanu**	Return - **Pharkanu**	Wash (body) - **Nuhaaunu**
Hear, Listen - **Sunnu**	Run - **Daudinu**	Work - **Kaam garnu**

Other handy words

Most of the following words are what we would call prepositions. However, those marked with an asterisk (*) are actually postpositions in Nepali, meaning they come *after* the thing they're describing (eg, "with me" comes out *masanga*).

Above, Over, Up - **Maathi***	Each - **Pratyek**	Out, Outside - **Bahira***
And - **Ra**	From - **Baata***	That - **Tyo**
Because - **Kinabhane**	In, Inside - **Bhitra***	This - **Yo**
Behind - **Pachhadi***	In front of - **Agaadi***	To, Towards - **Tira***
Below, Under, Down - **Talla***	Near - **Nera***	With - **Sanga***
But - **Tara**	Or - **Ki**	Without - **Chhaina***

Numbers

Unlike the English counting system, which starts using compound numbers above 20 (twenty-one, twenty-two, etc), Nepali numbers are irregular all the way up to 100 – the following are the ones you're most likely to use. A slight

Nepali numbers

१	२	३	४	५	६	७	८	९	१०
1	2	3	4	5	6	7	8	9	10

further complication is the use of quantifying words: you have to add *wotaa* when you're counting things, *jana* when counting people. Thus "five books" is *paanch wotaa kitaab*, "three girls" is *tin jana keti*. But note these irregular quantifiers: *ek wotaa = euta*; *dui wotaa = duita*; *tin wotaa = tintaa*.

half - aada	12 - baara	50 - pachaas
1 - ek	13 - tera	60 - saathi
2 - dui	14 - chaudha	70 - sattari
3 - tin	15 - pandra	80 - asi
4 - chaar	16 - sora	90 - nabbe
5 - paanch	17 - satra	100 - ek - say
6 - chha	18 - athaara	1000 - ek hajaar
7 - saat	19 - unnais	first [time] - pahilo [palta]
8 - aath	20 - bis	second - dosro
9 - nau	25 - pachhis	third - tesro
10 - das	30 - tis	fourth - chautho
11 - eghaara	40 - chaalis	fifth - paachau

Days and months

It's unlikely you'll ever have to use these. For a list of Nepali months, which start around the middle of our months, see the festival calendar on p.55.

Sunday - Aitabar	Wednesday - Budhabar	Saturday - Sanibar
Monday - Sombar	Thursday - Bihibar	
Tuesday - Mangalbar	Friday - Sukrabar	

A glossary of food terms

Basics

The bill - Bil	Knife - Chakku	Rice (uncooked) - Chaamal
Bread - Roti	Milk - Dudh	Rice (beaten) - Chiura
Butter - Makhan	Oil - Tel	Salt - Nun
Chutney, Pickle - Achhaar	Pepper (ground) - Marich	Spoon - Chamchaa
Egg - Phul	Plate - Plet	Sugar - Chini
Food - Khaanaa	Proprietor (male) - Sahuji	Sweets, Candy - Mithaai
Fork - Kaata	(female) - Sahuni	Water - Paani
Glass - Gilaas	Rice (cooked) - Bhaat	Yogurt, Curd - Dahi

Common Nepali dishes

Daal bhaat tarkaari - Lentil soup, white rice and curried vegetables
Dahi chiura - Curd with beaten rice
Pakauda - Vegetables dipped in chickpea-flour batter, deep fried

Samosa - Pyramids of pastry filled with curried vegetables
Sekuwa - Spicy, marinated meat kebab
Taareko maachhaa - Fried fish

Common Newari dishes

Chataamari - Rice-flour pizza, usually topped with minced buff
Choyila - Buff cubes fried with spices and greens
Kachila - Paté of minced raw buff meat mixed with ginger and oil
Kwati - Soup made with sprouted beans

Momocha - Small meat-filled steamed dumplings
Pancha kol - Curry made with five vegetables
Woh - Fried lentil-flour patties served plain (mai woh) or topped with minced buff (la woh) or egg (khen woh)

Common Tibetan dishes

Momo - Steamed dumplings filled with meat and/or vegetables
Kothe - The same, fried

Thukpa - Soup containing pasta, meat and vegetables
Tsampa - Toasted barley flour

Vegetables (Tarkaari or Saabji)

Aubergine - **Bhanta**
Beans - **Simi**
Cabbage - **Banda Kobi**
Carrot - **Gaajar**
Cauliflower - **Kaauli**
Chickpeas - **Chaana**
Chili pepper - **Khursaani**

Coriander (Cilantro) - **Dhaniyaa**
Corn - **Makai**
Garlic - **Lasun**
Lentils - **Daal**
Mushroom - **Chyaau**
Onion - **Pyaaj**

Peas - **Kerau, Matar**
Potato - **Alu**
Pumpkin - **Pharsi**
Radish - **Mulaa**
Spinach, Chard, Greens - **Palungo, Saag**
Tomato - **Golbheda**

Meat (maasu)

Buffalo ("Buff") - **Raangaako maasu**

Chicken - **Kukhuraako maasu**

Goat - **Khasiko maasu**
Pork - **Bungurko maasu**

Fruit (phalphul) and nuts

Apple - **Syaau**
Asian pear - **Naaspaati**
Banana - **Keraa**
Cashew - **Kaaju**
Coconut - **Nariwal**
Date - **Chhokada**

Guava - **Ambaa**
Lemon - **Nibuwaa**
Lime - **Kagati**
Mango - **Aaph**
Orange, Mandarin - **Suntalaa**
Papaya - **Mewaa**

Peanut - **Badaam (Mampale near India)**
Pineapple - **Bhuikatahar**
Pistachio - **Pista**
Raisin - **Kismis**
Sugar cane - **Ukhu**

Spices (masaala)

Aniseed – **Sop**
Cardamom – **Sukumel, Elaaichi**
Chili – **Khursaani**
Cinnamon – **Daalchini**

Clove **Lwang**
Ginger **Aduwaa**
Saffron **Kkesari**
Turmeric **Besaar**

Some common terms

A little – **Alikati**
A lot – **Dherai**
Another – **Aarko**
Boiled [water] – **Umaaleko [paani]**
Cold – **Chiso**
Cooked – **Paakeko**
Deep-fried – **Taareko**
Delicious – **Mitho**
Enough! – **Pugchha!**

Hot – **Taato**
I'm full! – **Pugyo**
More – **Aru**
Please give me … – … **dinus**
Spicy – **Piro**
Stir-fried – **Bhuteko**
Sweet – **Guliyo**
Vegetarian – **Sahakaari**
I don't eat meat – **Ma maasu khaanna**

Some Newari phrases

Newari (Nepal Bhasa) is still the first language for many in Kathmandu Valley. It's a difficult language to learn, with many local dialects, and knowing it is no more necessary than, say, knowing Welsh in Wales, but trying out even the tiniest smidgen of it will astound and delight your innkeeper. The following phrases will get you going.

Hello – **Namaste**
Yes/No – **Jyu/Majyu**
Thank you – **Dhanyabaad/Subhay**
How are you? – **Chhitaa gaye chong?**
I am fine – **Jitaa mha(n) phu**
What's your name? – **Chigu naang chhu?**
My name is … – **Jigu naang … kha**
My country is … – **Jigu chhey … kha**
I don't understand – **Jing mathu**
Can you repeat? – **Chhaka hanna(n) dhaya dishang?**
Do you speak English? – **Chhi Englis khalhayadhiyala?**
I don't speak Newari – **Jing Newa kha(n) lhayemasa**
Please help me – **Jitaa gwali yana dishang**

Can I go in? – **Ji dune wone jyula?**
What's this called in Newari? – **Thoyatan chhu dhaigu?**
How far is it? – **Guli tappaa?**
How much does this cost? – **Thukiya guli?**
I don't want it – **Jitaa mayo**
Please give me that – **Wo chhaka biya dishang**
Begging is bad – **Phonegu jya baa(n)malaa**
A little – **Bhachaa**
Bad (Not nice) – **Ba(n)malaa**
Cheap – **Dang**
Good – **Ba(n)laa**
Hungry – **Naiya pityata**
Thirsty – **Pyaachala**
Tired – **Tyanula**

A glossary of Nepali, Newari and Tibetan terms

Abhir red powder used in Hindu worship.

Aela Newari word for distilled spirit (*raksi* in Nepali).

Agam shrine room reserved for tantric initiates.

Annapurna goddess of grain and abundance (literally, "Full of Grain"); form of Lakshmi.

Ashta Mangala the eight auspicious symbols of Buddhism.

Avalokiteshwara the *bodhisattva* of compassion (also known as Chenrezig).

Avatar bodily incarnation of a deity.

Baahun Nepali term for the Brahman (priestly) caste.

Baba holy man.

Bagh tiger.

Bahal (or **Baha**) buildings and quadrangle of a former Buddhist Newar monastery (a few are still active).

Bahil (or **Bahi**) Newari term for Buddhist monastery.

Bajra see *vajra*.

Bajra Yogini (or **Vajra Jogini**) female tantric counterpart to Bhairab.

Bakshish not a bribe, but a tip in advance; alms.

Ban forest.

Barahi (or **Varahi**) Vishnu incarnated as a boar.

Bazaar commercial area or street – not necessarily a covered market.

Beni confluence of rivers.

Betal symbol of death, often represented by a pair of skeletons flanking a temple entrance.

Betel see *paan*.

Bhaat cooked rice; food.

Bhairab terrifying tantric form of Shiva.

Bhajan hymn, hymn-singing.

Bhanjyang a pass (Nepali).

Bharat India.

Bhatti simple tavern, usually selling food as well as alcohol.

Bhimsen patron god of Newar merchants.

Bhojanalaya Nepali restaurant.

Bhot Tibet.

Bhotiya highland peoples of Tibetan ancestry (the term is often considered pejorative).

Bideshi foreigner (*gora* – "whitey" – is a slightly derogatory equivalent).

Bidi cheap rolled-leaf cigarette.

Bihar (or **Mahabihar**) Buddhist monastery (Sanskrit).

Bodhisattva in Mahayana Buddhism, one who forgoes *nirvana* until all other beings have attained enlightenment.

Brahma the Hindu creator god, one of the Hindu "trinity".

Brahman member of the Hindu priestly caste (*baahun* in Nepali); metaphysical term meaning the universal soul.

Chaarpi latrine.

Chaitya small Buddhist monument, often with images of the Buddha at the four cardinal points.

Charesh hashish.

Chautaara resting platform beside a trail with trees for shade.

Chhetri member of the Hindu ruling or warrior caste.

Chhang (or **Chhyang**) homemade beer brewed from rice or other grains.

Chilam vertical clay pipe for smoking tobacco or *ganja*.

Cholo traditional half-length woman's blouse.

Chorten another name for a *chaitya* in high mountain areas.

Chowk intersection/crossroads, square or courtyard (pronounced "choke").

Chuba Tibetan sheepskin coat; Tibetan dress.

Chulo clay stove.

Chwasa Newari word for crossroads; a place traditionally set aside for disposal of ritually unclean objects.

Daada (or **Danda**) ridge, often used to signify a range of connected hilltops.

Damaru two-sided drum.

Danphe Nepal's national bird, a pheasant with brilliant plumage.

Das Avatar the ten incarnations of Vishnu.

Daura Suruwal traditional dress of hill men: wraparound shirt and jodhpur-like trousers.

Devi see *Mahadevi.*

Dewal (also **Deval**, **Degu**) stepped temple platform; temple with prominent steps.

Dhaara communal water tap or tank.

Dhaba Indian-style fast-food restaurant.

Dhaka colourful hand-loomed material made in the Nepalese hills.

Dhami shaman; the word is often used interchangeably with *jhankri*, or even as *dhami jhankri.*

Dharma religion; correct behaviour (applies to both Hinduism and Buddhism).

Dharmsala rest house for pilgrims.

Dhoka gate.

Dhoti Indian-style loincloth.

Dhwaja see *pataka.*

Dhyani Buddhas meditating figures representing the five aspects of Buddha nature.

Doko conical cane basket carried by means of a headstrap.

Dorje Tibetan word for *vajra.*

Dun low-lying valleys just north of the Tarai (sometimes called inner Tarai, or *bhitri madesh* – "inner plains").

Durbar palace; royal court.

Durga demon-slaying goddess.

Dyochhen private "home" of a Newar deity.

Dzopkio sturdy yak-cattle crossbreed; the female is called a *dzum.*

Gaaine wandering minstrel of the western hills (*ghandarba* is now the preferred term).

Gaida (or **gainda**) rhinoceros.

Gajur brass or gold finial at the peak of a temple.

Ganesh elephant-headed god of beginnings and remover of obstacles.

Ganja cannabis, marijuana.

Garud Vishnu's man-bird carrier.

Gaun village.

Gelug-Pa one of four main Lamaist sects.

Ghama central wooden beam of a festival chariot.

Ghandarba traditional musician.

Ghanta a bell, usually rung at temples as a sort of "amen".

Ghat riverside platform for worship and cremations; any waterside locality.

Ghazal crooning, poetic, sentimental form of Indian music.

Gidda vulture; Nepali slang for Israeli.

Gompa Buddhist monastery (Tibetan).

Goonda hooligan, thug.

Gupha cave.

Gurkhas Nepali soldiers who serve in special regiments in the British and Indian armies.

Guthi Newar benevolent association that handles funeral arrangements, temple maintenance, festivals, etc.

Hanuman valiant monkey king in the *Ramayan.*

Hatti elephant.

Himal massif or mountain range with permanent snow.

Hiti Newari word for *dhaara.*

HMG His Majesty's Government.

Jaand (or **Jaar**) Nepali word for *chhang.*

Jaatra festival.

Jal holy water.

Janai sacred thread worn over left shoulder by high-caste (Baahun and Chhetri) Hindu men.

Jhankri shaman, or medicine man, of the hills.

Jyapu member of the Newar farming caste.

Kagyu-Pa one of four main Lamaist sects.

Kali the mother goddess in her most terrifying form.

Karma the soul's accumulated merit, determining its next rebirth.

Karod ten million (*crore* in India).

Kata white scarf given to lamas by visitors.

Khaobaadi one who lines his own pockets in the name of political ideology.

Khat a litter or platform on which a deity is carried during a festival.

Khola stream or river.

Khukuri curved knife carried by most Nepali hill men.

Kirtimukha common temple motif, a gargoyle-like face grappling with a snake.

Kora circumambulation or pilgrimage around a Buddhist monument.

Kot fort (pronounced "coat").

Krishna one of Vishnu's *avatar*, a hero of the *Mahabharat.*

Kumari a girl worshipped as the living incarnation of Durga.

Kund pond, water tank.

Kwapadya the public Buddha image of a *bahal* or *bahil.*

Kweri Nepali slang for foreigner.

La pass (Tibetan).

Lakh 100,000.

Lakshmi consort of Vishnu, goddess of wealth.

Lali Guraas tree rhododendron.

Lama Tibetan Buddhist priest: hence Lamaism.

Lek mountain range without permanent snow.

Lhakang interior of a *gompa*.

Linga (or **Lingam**) the phallic symbol of Shiva, commonly the centrepiece of temples and sometimes occurring in groups in the open.

Lokeshwar see *Avalokiteshwara*.

Lokta traditional Nepali paper made from the bark of an indigenous shrub.

Lungi brightly coloured wrap skirt worn by hill women.

Machaan watchtower used by Tarai farmers to ward off wild animals.

Machhendranath rain-bringing deity of the Kathmandu Valley; also known as Karunamaya or Bunga Dyo.

Mahabharat (or **Mahabharata**) Hindu epic of the battle between two families, featuring Krishna and containing the Bhagavad Gita.

Mahabharat Lek highest range of the Himalayan foothills.

Mahadev "Great God", an epithet for Shiva.

Mahadevi the mother goddess.

Mahayana nonmonastic form of Buddhism followed in Nepal, Tibet and East Asia.

Mahout elephant handler.

Mai common name for any local protector goddess.

Mandala mystical diagram, meditation tool.

Mandap pavilion.

Mandir temple.

Mani Stone slate inscribed with the mantra *Om mani padme hum*.

Mantra religious incantation.

Maobaadi Maoist.

Masaala spice; any mixture (thus *masaala* films, with their mixture of drama, singing, comedy, etc).

Masan riverside cremation platform.

Math Hindu priest's home.

Mela religious fair or gathering.

Naamlo tumpline, headstrap for carrying a *doko*.

Nadi river.

Nag snake deity or spirit, believed to have rain-bringing powers.

Nagar city.

Nak female yak.

Namaste traditional Indian greeting, now widely adopted in Nepal.

Nandi Shiva's mount, a bull.

Nanglo cane tray, used for winnowing.

Narayan common name for Vishnu.

Nath "Lord".

Nirvana in Buddhism, enlightenment and release from the cycle of rebirth.

Nyingma-Pa one of four main Lamaist sects.

Om Mani Padme Hum the mantra of Avalokiteshvara, roughly translating as "Hail to the jewel in the lotus".

Paan mildly addictive mixture of areca nut and lime paste, wrapped in a leaf and chewed, producing blood-red spit.

Padma Sambhava alias Guru Rinpoche, the eighth-century saint who brought Buddhism to Tibet.

Pahaad hill, or the area of Nepal also known as the Middle Hills; hence *pahaadi*, hill person.

Panchaayat council or assembly, the basis for Nepal's pre-democratic government.

Pandit Hindu priest.

Parbat mountain.

Parbati (or **Parvati**) Shiva's consort.

Pashmina Nepali equivalent of cashmere.

Pataasi traditional black and red-trimmed sari worn by Jyapu women around Bhaktapur.

Pataka necktie-shaped brass ornament hanging from a temple, to be used by the deity when descending to earth.

Pati open shelter erected as a public resting place.

Phanit elephant driver.

Phanta grassland surrounded by jungle.

Phedi foot (of a hill, pass, etc).

Pipal common shade tree of the fig genus; also known as *bodhi*, the tree under which Buddha attained enlightenment.

Pokhari pond, usually man-made.

Poubha Newar-style scroll painting.

Prajna wisdom (Sanskrit).

Prasad food consecrated after being offered to a deity.

Puja an act of worship.

Pujari Hindu priest or caretaker of a particular temple.

Pul bridge.

Pureth Hindu priest who makes house calls.

Rajpath, **Rajmarg** "King's Way", "King's Road".

Raksi distilled spirit.

Ram (or **Rama**) mortal *avatar* of Vishnu, hero of the *Ramayan*.

Ramayan (or **Ramayana**) popular Hindu epic in which Sita, princess of Janakpur, is abducted and eventually rescued by Ram and Hanuman.

Rath chariot used in religious processions.

Rinpoche "precious jewel": title given to revered lamas.

Rudraksha furrowed brown seeds, prized by Shaivas; it's said that the wearer of a *rudraksha* necklace must always tell the truth.

Sadhu Hindu ascetic.

Sahib honorific term given to male foreigners, pronouced "sahb"; women are called *memsahib*.

Sajha cooperative.

Sakya-Pa one of four main Lamaist sects.

Sal tall tree of the Tarai and lower hills, valued for its timber.

Sanyasin (or **Sunyasan**) Hindu who has renounced the world, usually in old age.

Sarangi Nepali four-stringed violin.

Saraswati Hindu goddess of learning and the arts.

Sati (or **Suttee**) practice of Hindu widows throwing themselves on their husbands' funeral pyres.

Sattal public rest house.

Shaiva member of the cult of Shiva (pronounced "Shaib").

Shakti in Hindu *tantra*, the female principle that empowers the male; the mother goddess in this capacity.

Shaligram fossil-bearing stones found in the Kali Gandaki River, revered by Vaishnavas.

Sherpa man from one of Nepal's highland ethnic groups, originally from the mountainous eastern district of Solu Khumbu; sometimes (incorrectly) used by foreigners to mean any Nepali guide or climber. A woman is a **Sherpani**.

Shikra (or **Shikhara**) Indian-style temple, shaped like a square bullet.

Shiva "the destroyer", one of the Hindu "trinity" – a god of many guises.

Shiva Margi a Hindu Newar.

Shivalaya one-storey Shiva shrine containing a *linga*.

Shradha Hindu death rites performed for a parent.

Shri an honorific prefix.

Sindur red mark on the parting of married women.

Sirdar Nepali trek leader.

Sita Ram's wife, princess of Janakpur, heroine of the *Ramayan*.

STOL "Short Takeoff And Landing" (read "hair-raising") landing strip.

Stupa large dome-shaped Buddhist monument, usually said to contain holy relics.

Sudra member of the lowest, menial caste of Hinduism.

Tal (or **Taal**) lake.

Tantra esoteric path to enlightenment, a major influence on Nepali Hinduism and Buddhism.

Tara Buddhist goddess; female aspect of Buddha nature.

Tashi Delek Tibetan for welcome, *namaste*.

Tempo three-wheeled scooter; also called autoriksha, tuk-tuk.

Thakuri very orthodox Chhetri subcaste.

Thangka Buddhist scroll painting.

Tika auspicious mark made of rice, *abhir* powder and curd, placed on the forehead during *puja* or festivals or before making a journey.

Tol neighbourhood.

Tola traditional unit of weight (11.5g); precious metals are sold by the *tola*, as is hashish.

Topi traditional Nepali brimless hat, either black (called *Bhadgaonle*) or multicoloured (*dhaka*).

Toran elaborate wooden carving, or metal shield, above a temple door.

Torma dough offerings made by Buddhist monks.

Trisul the trident, a symbol of Shiva.

Tudikhel parade ground.

Tulku reincarnation of a late great teacher in the Tibetan Buddhist tradition.

Upaya compassion (Sanskrit).

Vaishnava follower of the cult of Vishnu (pronounced "Baishnab").

Vaisya (or **Baisya**) Hindu caste of traders and farmers.

Vajra sceptre-like symbol of tantric power (pronounced "bajra").

Vajracharya Buddhist Newar priest.

Vajrayana "Thunderbolt Way": tantric Buddhism.

Vedas the oldest Hindu scriptures (pronounced "Bed" by Nepalis); hence Vedic gods, extolled in the *Vedas*.

Vipassana ancient and austere Buddhist meditation practice.

Vishnu "the preserver", member of the Hindu "trinity", worshipped in ten main incarnations (pronounced "Bishnu").

Yangsi reincarnated successor of a Tibetan lama.

Yoni symbol of the female genitalia, usually carved into the base of a *linga* as a reservoir for offerings.

index

and small print

Index

Map entries are in colour

K

INDEX

Twenty years of Rough Guides

In the summer of 1981, Mark Ellingham, Rough Guides' founder, knocked out the first guide on a typewriter, with a group of friends. Mark had been travelling in Greece after university, and couldn't find a guidebook that really answered his needs. There were heavyweight cultural guides on the one hand – good on museums and classical sites but not on beaches and tavernas – and on the other hand student manuals that were so caught up with how to save money that they lost sight of the country's significance beyond its role as a place for a cool vacation. None of the guides began to address Greece as a country, with its natural and human environment, its politics and its contemporary life.

Having no urgent reason to return home, Mark decided to write his own guide. It was a guide to Greece that tried to combine some erudition and insight with a thoroughly practical approach to travellers' needs. Scrupulously researched listings of places to stay, eat and drink were matched by careful attention to detail on everything from Homer to Greek music, from classical sites to national parks and from nude beaches to monasteries. Back in London, Mark and his friends got their Rough Guide accepted by a farsighted commissioning editor at the publisher Routledge and it came out in 1982.

The Rough Guide to Greece was a student scheme that became a publishing phenomenon. The immediate success of the book – shortlisted for the Thomas Cook award – spawned a series that rapidly covered dozens of countries. The Rough Guides found a ready market among backpackers and budget travellers, but soon acquired a much broader readership that included older and less impecunious visitors. Readers relished the guides' wit and inquisitiveness as much as the enthusiastic, critical approach that acknowledges everyone wants value for money – but not at any price.

Rough Guides soon began supplementing the "rougher" information – the hostel and low-budget listings – with the kind of detail that independent-minded travellers on any budget might expect. These days, the guides – distributed worldwide by the Penguin group – include recommendations spanning the range from shoestring to luxury, and cover more than 200 destinations around the globe. Our growing team of authors, many of whom come to Rough Guides initially as outstandingly good letter-writers telling us about their travels, are spread all over the world, particularly in Europe, the USA and Australia. As well as the travel guides, Rough Guides publishes a series of dictionary phrasebooks covering two dozen major languages, an acclaimed series of music guides running the gamut from Classical to World Music, a series of music CDs in association with World Music Network, and a range of reference books on topics as diverse as the Internet, Pregnancy and Unexplained Phenomena. Visit **www.roughguides.com** to see what's cooking.

Rough Guide credits

Text editors: Polly Thomas and Claire Saunders
Series editor: Mark Ellingham
Editorial: Martin Dunford, Jonathan Buckley, Kate Berens, Ann-Marie Shaw, Helena Smith, Judith Bamber, Orla Duane, Olivia Swift, Ruth Blackmore, Geoff Howard, Claire Saunders, Gavin Thomas, Alexander Mark Rogers, Polly Thomas, Joe Staines, Richard Lim, Duncan Clark, Peter Buckley, Lucy Ratcliffe, Clifton Wilkinson, Alison Murchie, Matthew Teller, Andrew Dickson, Fran Sandham (UK); Andrew Rosenberg, Stephen Timblin, Yuki Takagaki, Richard Koss, Hunter Slaton, Julie Feiner (US)
Production: Susanne Hillen, Andy Hilliard, Link Hall, Helen Prior, Julia Bovis, Michelle Draycott, Katie Pringle, Zoë Nobes, Rachel Holmes, Andy Turner, Michelle Bhatia
Cartography: Melissa Baker, Maxine Repath, Ed Wright, Katie Lloyd-Jones
Cover art direction: Louise Boulton
Picture research: Sharon Martins, Mark Thomas
Online: Kelly Cross, Anja Mutic-Blessing, Jennifer Gold, Audra Epstein, Suzanne Welles, Cree Lawson (US)
Finance: John Fisher, Gary Singh, Edward Downey, Mark Hall, Tim Bill
Marketing & Publicity: Richard Trillo, Niki Smith, David Wearn, Chloë Roberts, Demelza Dallow, Claire Southern (UK); Simon Carloss, David Wechsler, Kathleen Rushforth (US)
Administration: Tania Hummel, Julie Sanderson

Publishing information

This fifth edition published September 2002 by **Rough Guides Ltd,**
62–70 Shorts Gardens, London WC2H 9AH.
Penguin Putnam, Inc. 375 Hudson Street, NY 10014, USA.
Distributed by the Penguin Group
Penguin Books Ltd,
80 Strand, London WC2R ORL
Penguin Putnam, Inc.
375 Hudson Street, NY 10014, USA
Penguin Books Australia Ltd,
487 Maroondah Highway, PO Box 257, Ringwood, Victoria 3134, Australia
Penguin Books Canada Ltd,
10 Alcorn Avenue, Toronto, Ontario, Canada M4V 1E4
Penguin Books (NZ) Ltd,
182–190 Wairau Road, Auckland 10, New Zealand
Typeset in Bembo and Helvetica to an original design by Henry Iles.

Printed in Italy by LegoPrint S.p.A.

© David Reed 2002

632pp includes index
A catalogue record for this book is available from the British Library

ISBN 1-85828-899-1

The publishers and authors have done their best to ensure the accuracy and currency of all the information in **The Rough Guide to Nepal,** however, they can accept no responsibility for any loss, injury, or inconvenience sustained by any traveller as a result of information or advice contained in the guide.

Help us update

We've gone to a lot of effort to ensure that the fifth edition of **The Rough Guide to Nepal** is accurate and up to date. However, things change – places get "discovered", opening hours are notoriously fickle, restaurants and rooms raise prices or lower standards. If you feel we've got it wrong or left something out, we'd like to know, and if you can remember the address, the price, the time, the phone number, so much the better.

We'll credit all contributions, and send a copy of the next edition (or any other Rough Guide if you prefer) for the best letters. Everyone who writes to us and isn't already a subscriber will receive a copy of our full-colour thrice-yearly newsletter. Please mark letters: **"Rough Guide Nepal Update"** and send to: Rough Guides, 62–70 Shorts Gardens, London WC2H 9AH, or Rough Guides, 4th Floor, 345 Hudson St, New York, NY 10014. Or send an email to **mail@roughguides.com**

Have your questions answered and tell others about your trip at
www.roughguides.atinfopop.com

Acknowledgements

The editor would like to thank Clifton Wilkinson for starting the ball rolling, Claire Saunders for stepping in to help, Andy Turner for typesetting, Melissa Baker for the maps, Mark Thomas for picture research and Russell Walton for proofreading.

David Reed Thanks to Megh Ale (Adventure Centre Asia), Chris Beall, Dubby Bhagat (Everest Hotel), Hira Dhamala (Karnali Excursions), Scott Dimetrosky (Himalayan Explorers Connection), Sonam Gurung (Dawn Till Dusk Bikes), Christian Hyde, Keshav Mangal Joshi, Roopendra Joshi, Peter Knowles (White Water Nepal), Kunsang Dorje Lama (Hotel Excelsior), Mohan Mulepati (Himalaya's Guest House), Olga Murray and Ishwor Adhikari (Nepalese Youth Opportunity Foundation), Sumnima Paney (CWIN), Tony Parr (Nepal Village Resorts), Dadi Ram Sapkota, Thomas Schrom (Patan Museum), Yuyutsu R.D. Sharma (White Lotus Bookshop), Udab Shrestha (Oasis Garden Restaurant), David and Haydi Sowerwine, Peter Stewart (Himalayan Mountain Bikes), Uttar Tamata, Mostafa Vaziri.

James McConnachie Thanks to Tessa Nicholson, Gaurab Rana, Prabesh Sapkota and Richard Scholar for their friendship and support. Thanks also to Keshav Acharya (Sukla Phanta), David Allardice (The Last Resort), Ram Kumar Aryal (King Mahendra Trust for Nature Conservation), R.K. and Mugha Bantawa, Bishnu Bhatta, Colonel Hikmat Bisht (Silent Safari, Sukla Phanta), Mohan Lal Chaudhari (KMTNC, Bardia), Ramesh Chaudhari (Bird Education Society, Chitwan), Naresh T. Chhetri (Hotel Pawan, Bhairawa), Saskia Chilcott, Bed Kumar Dhakal (Royal Chitwan National Park), Harry Gibbons, Dinesh Giri (Aqua Birds Unlimited Camp, Koshi Tappu), Christian Hyde, Chris Jackson (DF!D Nepal), Marco McConnell (Jungle Base Camp, Bardia), Ganga Nepali and Ailsa Colston-Nepali (Hotel Nirvana, Pokhara), Prativa Pandey (CIWEC clinic), Anu Radha Paudel (Space Time Today), Hem and Nanda Rai, Tek Bahadur Rai, Rajendra Sakya, Dadi Ram Sapkota, B.K. Sapkota and family, B.K. Shrestha and Jeremy Southon.

Readers' letters

Thanks to all the readers who took the trouble to write in with their comments and suggestions (and apologies to anyone whose name we've misspelt or omitted):

Matt Anderson, Tiv Bluck, Lois Brooks, Peter Budge and Jane Heslington, Tim Burford, Andrew Corke, Vanessa Smith Holburn, Robert H. Jacoby, Andre Kalden, Susan Keys, Sarah Leonard, Irving Lipshaw, Anthony Mellersh, Lisa Merton and Ryan, Jon Nunney and Deborah Willott, David Patten, T.A. Phelps, Lucy Potter, Greg Price, Jeff Pyle, Amit Rosner, Jill Sazanmi, Chris Sennett, Jo Short, Stuart Silverman, Susal Stebbins, Rebecca Stonehill, Michael J. van Dam, Arlette van Stratten, "The Wandering Monkey", Christopher Westwood and family, Deborah Williams and Adrian Tempany, Orange Wong, Judy Wyld, Chris and Leesa Yeo, Jo Yuen.

Photo credits

Cover credits
Front (main image) Masked dancer at Mani Rimdu festival, Tengboche Monastery ©Robert Harding
Front (small top image) Mount Everest ©Jerry Callow
Front (small bottom image) Prayer flags ©Robert Harding
Back (top) Rice terraces ©Ffotograff
Back (lower) Boudha stupa ©David Reed

Colour intro section
Meghauli ©David Reed
Morning puja, Boudha ©David Reed
Painted Mani stone and Himalayas ©Joe Beynon/Axiom
Tarai school bus ©David Reed
Thamel ©David Reed
Kumari at Indra Jaatra ©David Reed
"Save Democracy", Kathmandu ©David Constantine/Axiom
Prayer flags at Sunset Point ©Paul Quayle/Axiom
Manidingma ©Paul Harris
Mount Everest from Kala Patthar ©Joe Beynon/Axiom
Lay of the land ©Lisa Young
Old Bhaktapur ©David Reed
Janakpur, Bhanugh Sagar ©David Reed

Things not to miss
1. View from Gokyo Peak, Everest region ©Jill Ranford/Ffotograff
2. Kathmandu market ©David Constantine/Axiom
3. Daal Bhaat ©Lisa Young
4. Bungy jump ©James McConnachie
5. Swayambhu ©David Reed
6. Boudinath Thanka School ©Paul Harris
7. Mani Rimdu festival ©Robert Harding
8. Indra Jaatra ©David Reed
9. Metal Buddhas ©James McConnachie
10. Tihaar ©Jim Holmes/Axiom
11. Rhino ©David Reed
12. Man in sunlight ©Lisa Young
13. Bhaktapur ©Paul Harris
14. Dasain ©David Reed
15. The Tarai ©David Reed
16. Trekkers' view, Ama Dablam Peak ©Joe Reynon/Axiom
17. Terraced fields ©N.C. Turner/Ffotograff
18. Momo ©James McConnachie
19. Wedding ©David Reed
20. Pashnpatinath during Shiva Raatri ©David Reed
21. Patan Durbar Square ©Lisa Young
22. Bhote Koshi rafting ©David Reed
23. Pokhara from the World Peace Pagoda ©David Reed
24. Patan Museum ©Thomas Schrom
25. Dry roasted corn and tea ©Paul Harris
26. Pashmina ©James McConnachie
27. Janaki Mandir, Janakpur ©David Reed
28. Rato Machhendranath, Patan ©David Reed
29. Mountain-biking ©Chris Caldicott/Axiom
30. Pashupatinath Mandir ©David Reed
31. Potters Square, Bhaktapur ©David Reed
32. White rhino ©Greg Balfour Evans
33. Boudha pilgrims ©David Reed

Black and white images
Swayambhu stupa spire ©David Reed (p.88)
Whitewashing Swayambhu stupa ©David Reed (p.129)
Boudha pilgrims ©David Reed (p.184)
Harvesting wheat, Bhaktapur ©Joe Beynon/Axiom (p.217)
Khware, Pananti ©James McConnachie (p.242)
Bhote Koshi Valley ©James McConnachie (p.259)
Pokhara, Phewa Tal ©David Reed (p.272)
Tansen ©David Reed (p.319)
Rhino, Chitwan National Park ©David Reed (p.324)
Elephant ride, Chitwan National Park ©David Reed (p.342)
Cycling along the Koshi Barrage ©James McConnachie (p.380)
Morning Puja, Janakpur ©James McConnachie (p.391)
Mount Everest from Kla Patthar ©Joe Beynon/Axiom (p.412)
Ama Dablam, Khumbu ©David Reed (p.447)
Kayaking on the Bhote Koshi ©David Reed (p.455)
Whitewater rafting, Sun Kosi River ©David Reed (p.456)
Whitewater rafting ©Joe Beynon/Axiom (p.464)
Mountain-bike rally ©James McConnachie (p.469)
Mountain-biking, Kathmandu Valley ©Chr Caldicott/Axiom (p.470)

stay in touch

roughnews

Rough Guides' FREE full-colour newsletter

News, travel issues, music reviews, readers' letters and the latest dispatches from authors on the road

If you would like to receive roughnews, please send us your name and address:

62-70 Shorts Gardens
London, WC2H 9AH, UK

4th Floor, 345 Hudson St,
New York NY10014, USA

newslettersubs@roughguides.co.uk

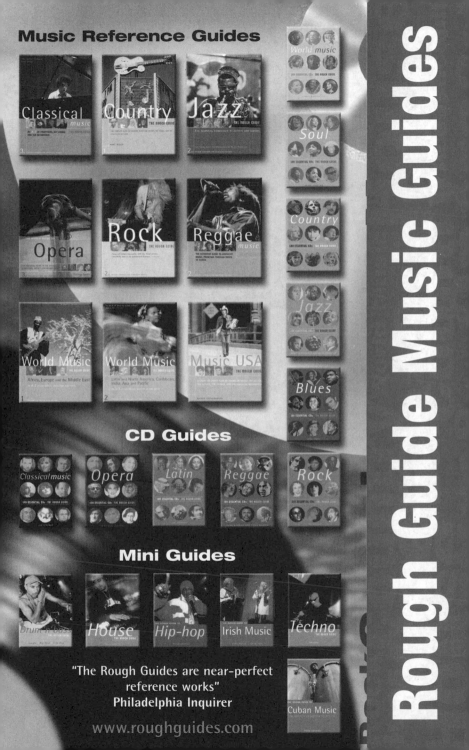

Music Reference Guides

CD Guides

Mini Guides

"The Rough Guides are near-perfect reference works"
Philadelphia Inquirer

www.roughguides.com

Rough Guide Music Guides

Rough Guides music, reference & CDs

Music

Acoustic Guitar
Blues: 100 Essential CDs
Cello
Clarinet
Classical Music
Classical Music: 100 Essential CDs
Country Music
Country: 100 Essential CDs
Cuban Music
Drum'n'bass
Drums
Electric Guitar & Bass Guitar
Flute
Hip-Hop
House
Irish Music
Jazz
Jazz: 100 Essential CDs
Keyboards & Digital Piano
Latin: 100 Essential CDs
Music USA: a Coast-To-Coast Tour
Opera
Opera: 100 Essential CDs
Piano
Reading Music
Reggae
Reggae: 100 Essential CDs
Rock
Rock: 100 Essential CDs
Saxophone
Soul: 100 Essential CDs
Techno
Trumpet & Trombone
Violin & Viola
World Music: 100 Essential CDs

World Music Vol1
World Music Vol2

Reference

Children's Books, 0–5
Children's Books, 5–11
China Chronicle
Cult Movies
Cult TV
Elvis
England Chronicle
France Chronicle
India Chronicle
The Internet
Internet Radio
James Bond
Liverpool FC
Man Utd
Money Online
Personal Computers
Pregnancy & Birth
Shopping Online
Travel Health
Travel Online
Unexplained Phenomena
Videogaming
Weather
Website Directory
Women Travel
World Cup

Music CDs

Africa
Afrocuba
Afro-Peru
Ali Hussan Kuban
The Alps
Americana
The Andes
The Appalachians
Arabesque
Asian Underground
Australian Aboriginal Music
Bellydance
Bhangra

Bluegrass
Bollywood
Boogaloo
Brazil
Cajun
Cajun and Zydeco
Calypso and Soca
Cape Verde
Central America
Classic Jazz
Congolese Soukous
Cuba
Cuban Music Story
Cuban Son
Cumbia
Delta Blues
Eastern Europe
English Roots Music
Flamenco
Franco
Gospel
Global Dance
Greece
The Gypsies
Haiti
Hawaii
The Himalayas
Hip Hop
Hungary
India
India and Pakistan
Indian Ocean
Indonesia
Irish Folk
Irish Music
Italy
Jamaica
Japan
Kenya and Tanzania
Klezmer
Louisiana
Lucky Dube
Mali and Guinea
Marrabenta Mozambique
Merengue & Bachata
Mexico
Native American Music
Nigeria and Ghana
North Africa

Nusrat Fateh Ali Khan
Okinawa
Paris Café Music
Portugal
Rai
Reggae
Salsa
Salsa Dance
Samba
Scandinavia
Scottish Folk
Scottish Music
Senegal & The Gambia
Ska
Soul Brothers
South Africa
South African Gospel
South African Jazz
Spain
Sufi Music
Tango
Thailand
Tex-Mex
Wales
West African Music
World Music Vol 1: Africa, Europe and the Middle East
World Music Vol 2: Latin & North America, Caribbean, India, Asia and Pacific
World Roots
Youssou N'Dour & Etoile de Dakar
Zimbabwe

The ideas expressed in this code were developed by and for independent travellers.

Learn About The Country You're Visiting

Start enjoying your travels before you leave by tapping into as many sources of information as you can.

The Cost Of Your Holiday

Think about where your money goes - be fair and realistic about how cheaply you travel. Try and put money into local peoples' hands; drink local beer or fruit juice rather than imported brands and stay in locally owned accommodation. Haggle with humour and not aggressively. Pay what something is worth to you and remember how wealthy you are compared to local people.

Embrace The Local Culture

Open your mind to new cultures and traditions - it will transform your experience. Think carefully about what's appropriate in terms of your clothes and the way you behave. You'll earn respect and be more readily welcomed by local people. Respect local laws and attitudes towards drugs and alcohol that vary in different countries and communities. Think about the impact you could have on them.

Exploring The World – The Travellers' Code

Being sensitive to these ideas means getting more out of your travels - and giving more back to the people you meet and the places you visit.

Minimise Your Environmental Impact

Think about what happens to your rubbish - take biodegradable products and a water filter bottle. Be sensitive to limited resources like water, fuel and electricity. Help preserve local wildlife and habitats by respecting local rules and regulations, such as sticking to footpaths and not standing on coral.

Don't Rely On Guidebooks

Use your guidebook as a starting point, not the only source of information. Talk to local people, then discover your own adventure!

Be Discreet With Photography

Don't treat people as part of the landscape, they may not want their picture taken. Ask first and respect their wishes.

We work with people the world over to promote tourism that benefits their communities, but we can only carry on our work with the support of people like you. For membership details or to find out how to make your travels work for local people and the environment, visit our website.

www.tourismconcern.org.uk

Tourism Concern
Campaigning for Ethical and Fairly Traded Touris

Image courtesy of Jamie Marshall
www.tribaleye.co.uk

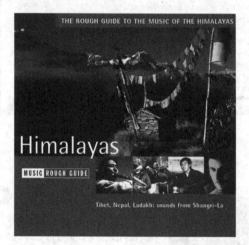

Travel Insurance

•BACKPACKERS®•

£2m Emergency Medical Expenses
Repatriation, 24 Hour Helpline
A policy designed for the
longer-term or gap year traveller.
Essential cover for up to 12 months
continuous travel.

- Worldwide Travel - *incl USA*
- Sports and Activities
- Baggage extension available.

Ages16-35	
1 Month	£22
2 Months	£41
3 Months	£59
6 Months	£109
9 Months	£155
1 Year	£189

•Annual Multi-Trip•

Europe	**£42**
Worldwide	**£58**
per year	

Cover for the frequent traveller.
The policy covers unlimited trips
up to 31 days each during a year.
17 days Winter Sports included.

•Single Trip Cover•

10 days	
Europe	**£16.50**
Worldwide	**£23.00**

Full cover for individual trips
ideal for holidays & business trips
up to 66 days. Special rates for
Families. Ski cover available.

All prices correct May 2002   Underwritten by CNA Insurance Co (Europe) Ltd.

0800 16 35 18

Full details of cover available at:
www.ticdirect.co.uk

TRAVEL INSURANCE CLUB